Best Vacation Rentals

United States and Canada

Produced by The Philip Lief Group, Inc.

Managing Editor, Richard Eastman

Edited by Constance Jones

Written and Researched by:

Julia Banks
Scott Corngold
Luz Cruz
Loren Elmaleh
Josh Eppinger
Robyn Feller
Fiona Gilsenan
Catherine Henningsen
Robert Hernandez
Robin Hohman
Mitsy Campbell Kovacs
Lisa Schwartzburg
Willy Spain
Paula Stelzner
Susan Wells
Denise Wydra

Design by Margaret Davis
Maps by Myra Klockenbrink and Charlie Williams

Best Vacation Rentals

United States and Canada

A Traveler's Guide
to Cottages, Condos,
and Castles

Prentice Hall Press
New York

The inform ation in this book is the most up-to-date available at the time of publication. However, specifics can change and we recommend that you confirm all details before making reservations. In addition, many states are currently reviewing and changing policies on the right of accommodations to refuse children as guests, and if a child-free environment is important, you should check with the establishment about its current policy.

Published by Prentice Hall Press
A division of Simon & Schuster, Inc.
15 Columbus Circle
New York, NY 10023

Produced by The Philip Lief Group, Inc.
6 West 20th Street
New York, NY 10011

ISBN 0-13-928-235-1

ISSN 1054-9773

Manufactured in the United States of America

First Edition   10 9 8 7 6 5 4 3 2 1

Contents

Introduction:
A World of Homes Away
from Home

Picture yourself on the veranda of a renovated turn-of-the-century beachhouse you've rented for the week. As you gaze out at a panoramic view of the rugged Maine coastline, thunderous waves crash against the rocks. You relax in your rocker and inhale the salt air, waiting for your friends to return from the fishing village down the road. When they do, their bicycles are laden with the makings of the evening's clambake.

Perhaps you'd rather envision a stay in a snug cabin nestled in the Colorado Rockies. A blazing fire warms the hearth while snow falls gently on the darkened forest outside. Popping a loaf of bread into the oven, you relish the memory of a perfect day on the slopes. Your children's laughter filters down from the loft above; your retriever dozes peacefully on the couch.

Or imagine instead a spring morning in an elegant apartment in the heart of San Francisco. Sunshine floods through the skylights, the Sunday paper lies scattered at your feet and Haydn wafts from the stereo. Brewing another pot of coffee, you plan an afternoon drive to Sausalito, followed by a jaunt to that special little bistro in North Beach.

Each of these vacation fantasies can come true once the secrets of the self-catered getaway are revealed. People seeking an extra element of privacy, comfort, adventure and economy on vacation have begun to discover the advantages of renting houses, cabins and apartments when they travel. Instead of settling for a cramped, nondescript room in a hotel or inn and paying for three expensive restaurant meals a day, you can enjoy the convenience and independence of homes away from home. Today, a whole world of vacation rental options—from fully staffed mansions to compact studios, from lavish resort bungalows to rustic lodges—lies open to the savvy, adventurous traveler.

Best Vacation Rentals: United States and Canada introduces you to the unique pleasures of self-sufficient travel. The properties presented in the pages that follow offer stunning locales and delightful features unavailable in traditional arrangements, creating an exciting and intimate environment seemingly designed just for you. Gardens, Jacuzzis or balconies; historic surroundings, breathtaking views or fireplaces; a taste of local color or seclusion off the beaten path—this unique option lets you choose the best setting for your next trip. The personalized touch you can get in planning a vacation of this kind allows you to indulge all of your specific needs and interests more completely than simply registering at the best local hotel.

For instance, couples can enjoy the privacy, peace and solitude offered by a romantic and secluded place of their own while senior citizens may appreciate the services, comfort and convenience of self-contained units at fully staffed resort condos. Families appreciate the extra indoor and outdoor space, savings on food and lodging and access to kitchen and laundry room facilities.

Best Vacation Rentals: United States and Canada presents a whole spectrum of self-catering accommodations. In its pages you will find vacation rental properties in every region of North America, to suit every desire and budget. This astonishing array of self-sufficient lodgings is available through several types of businesses and organizations:

- Vacation rental agencies that rent out vacation houses, apartments and condominiums owned by individuals who use them only during certain seasons.

- Hotel and resort complexes that include bungalows and apartments.

- Private owners who offer their homes for rent at certain times of year.

- Historical societies and government agencies that manage unusual properties maintained by foundations or municipalities.

This diverse combination of sources gives you access to every type of vacation rental accommodation—whether you seek a restored lighthouse, a modern townhouse or an adobe ranch—and to every vacation destination, from the most popular to the most secluded. Appendixes at the end of the book direct you to tourism boards.

Before you turn to the listings, take a moment to read "Travel Tips." It covers the nuts and bolts of self-sufficient travel and outlines exactly what to look for and what to expect when planning a self-catered vacation. As you read, you will find valuable information on selecting the appropriate type of lodging, making reservations and determining what to bring. You'll learn how to research the differences among rentals, such as frequency of housekeeping service, provision of kitchen equipment and linens and requirements for minimum stays. Specific suggestions relating to Canadian travel are featured in a special section. A short "How to Use This Guide" follows and describes how the book is organized and how to read the listings. A quick glance at these guides will help you make the most of this invaluable sourcebook, no matter which kind of getaway you choose.

Welcome to the exciting world of *Best Vacation Rentals: United States and Canada*—and have a great trip!

Travel Tips:
Making Yourself at Home

Congratulations on selecting a travel option that will make your trip more fascinating, relaxing and fun! Experienced vacation renters have found that a little preparation can go a long way toward making your vacation rental a smashing success. And with that in mind, this section shows you both what to look for and what to expect when renting a vacation home. A little research will help you get the most out of your home away from home.

What kind of vacation home is right for me?

Although many North American travelers are new to self-catering vacations—those where you make a rental home your own for the length of your stay—a dizzying array of possibilities lies open to the traveler who knows where to look. The travel-wise have been vacationing this way for decades, and the incredible abundance of vacation rentals available in every area will astound you: Secluded cabins overlooking pristine lakes; luxurious condominiums near the ski slopes— whatever your dream destination, it can be yours.

Many different sources are available. Each has distinct advantages; and all are represented in this guide.

Vacation rental agencies based in North America often represent dozens, hundreds or even thousands of rental homes and apartments, giving you an almost endless selection of properties to choose from. Many of the listings that appear in this book are handled by such agencies, most of which also offer scores more rentals than could be listed here—so when you call or write to request information on a property, inquire as well about other rentals that might be of interest. Leasing through an agency can make the job a lot easier: This arrangement ensures that your selection has met stringent quality requirements; and they handle all the financial and scheduling arrangements and any problems that may arise during your stay.

Hotel and resort complexes with bungalows or condominiums on the grounds offer less variety in lodging type but provide all of the amenities expected from a standard hotel or motel. Swimming pools, complimentary breakfasts, housekeeping/linen service and child care are only a few comforts offered in this category. And because self-catering suites or apartments in such establishments may cost no more than an ordinary hotel room, they represent a real bargain. The level of luxury often far exceeds what you might expect for the price, so resorts are guaranteed to appeal to vacationers who want to be pampered. Generally located near the action—in downtown areas or popular tourist destinations—resort condos have the added advantage of easy access to all the local attractions.

Private owners provide wonderfully personal vacation lodgings—where personal libraries, video collections, gourmet kitchens or even cars or boats are often at your disposal. And because owners may have only one property for rent, they can give undivided attention to your questions, requests and needs. Ask the owners for advice on shopping, dining, sightseeing and local activities; or have them put you in touch with neighbors you might like to meet during your stay. Private owners may not be equipped to accept your credit cards, but they'll often leave a trail of personal touches and amenities seldom found in more formal arrangements.

Historical societies and government agencies offer unique vacation rental possibilities. If you want to stay, for example, in a perfectly preserved nineteenth-century log hunting lodge or a converted landmark firehouse, these sources are for you. Maintained through private donations or public funds, such historic properties frequently rent for absurdly low rates. Many agencies are interested only in covering the cost of your stay, not in making a profit. Time spent in this truly special kind of setting could prove unforgettable, and make your vacation stay a lifelong treasured memory.

Regardless of the self-catering alternative you select, you are guaranteed to derive tremendous benefits from this kind of vacation. If you managed to locate comparable accommodations in a traditional hotel, they would likely be far more expensive. While squeezing into a good Boston hotel room for a week strains the finances of many families, a spacious two-bedroom self-catered flat—with a kitchen and maybe a fireplace or washing machine—can be quite affordable. Self-caterers save even more by eating some meals (particularly breakfasts, which are often light but expensive) at "home" instead of in restaurants.

Even when money is not an issue, the extra space and increased privacy of a house or apartment makes any vacation more pleasurable. Good-bye paper-thin walls and postage-stamp rooms! These become a thing of the past when you leave hotels behind for rentals. The freedom to whip up a midnight snack or a secret family recipe for finicky children can also be a boon to weary tourists. A place to keep your beer cold, a machine to wash your socks, or a grassy yard to nap in removes that great stress of traveling: The need to compromise on comfort.

But it's up to *you* to tap the potential of your vacation rental to the fullest. Maybe you prefer to travel with friends, and need separate bedrooms at night in addition to common areas for group activities. Perhaps your family can't live without at least two bathrooms. A private yard for your children to play in; a secluded haven miles away from the next neighbor; a wide porch to view spectacular sunsets: A vacation rental home can include any creature comforts you require while traveling. Even if no one in your party wants to be the cook, self-catering still makes sense: You'll save money while enjoying more space, greater privacy and personalized comforts not found in traditional inns or hotels.

Be sure to reserve far in advance, because the demand for these appealing properties is high among travel aficionados. Many travelers return again and again to a favorite rental, sometimes booking their time slot a year in advance. Don't worry, however, that you won't be able to find something you like: The sheer number of vacation rentals on the market almost assures a suitable property will be available wherever you're going—and whenever you're going there. But remember that the most attractive lodgings and those that represent the best value go quickly, especially in high seasons.

The various rental sources offer a wide array of vacation homes, from compact studio apartments to modern condominiums and from rustic cottages to lavish estates. When deciding among these vacation rental options, consider your traveling needs, desires and budget and make sure your lodging meets them. The location, setting, design and decor should satisfy your tastes and enhance your vacation experience. For instance: Do health problems preclude an isolated setting far from town? Would you prefer the excitement of the city? Do A-frame cabins make you feel claustrophobic? Have you always wanted to live in an elegant, antique-filled town house?

The Comforts of Home—and More

Each traveler has a unique notion of the ideal vacation lodging. (Indeed, self-catering is not for everyone.) But travelers who appreciate the advantages of renting a home away from home can expect their vacation rentals to offer certain amenities. The rentals included in this book all have kitchen facilities, living areas and at least one comfortable bed, but beyond that vary widely. As you set out to find your dream apartment or cottage from among the listings that follow, keep these few pointers in mind to help you determine how potential rentals rate.

Each listing includes information on the special features most important to travelers. Look for a mention of balconies, decks, porches or patios if you like to lounge outdoors, or of yards, gardens or extensive acreage if you long to stretch out. Imagine the perfect setting, then scour the listings for properties with water frontage, views or unusual architectural or design features. Indoors, you'll make decisions about telephones, televisions, VCRs, fireplaces, Jacuzzis, hot tubs and saunas. Many rentals come complete with barbecues, while others offer swimming pools or private beaches. Decide which items will make your vacation complete and mark the listings that meet your requirements.

Basic services are at least as important to a rental's appeal as its location is, and the listings present comprehensive information that will help you narrow your selection of possibilities. Is air conditioning important to you? Will you need a parking space? Are linens and blankets provided, and are they changed on a daily or weekly basis? Is housekeeping service included? Is it offered daily, weekly or between tenants only? Will you have the assistance of a full- or part-time maid or other staff member? Other diverse service possibilities include: Complimentary breakfast, lunch, dinner or cocktails and babysitting or other child-care services.

You can expect the kitchen to come equipped with a refrigerator, stove, cooking and eating utensils, plates and glassware (listings generally do not make specific mention of these items). Look for references to items you require in addition to the basics—such as a microwave—to help narrow your field of choices. For those who want to rent but don't plan to cook, many listings mention bars or restaurants on the premises or close by. Some rentals offer private cooks who can prepare your favorite meals without your having to lift a finger.

Having established this basic information, the listings go on to describe a colorful array of optional amenities. You'll come across everything from stereos, pianos and wet bars to security systems, valet service and meeting rooms. Some listings mention free use of bicycles, docking facilities or country-club privileges, while others make note of playgrounds, tennis courts or skiing in the area. Don't despair if your dream rental seems to be missing one key element: It might be there; we just couldn't fit it all in. If a rental sounds tempting, investigate it further by calling or writing the contact listed to learn more.

Clearly, *Best Vacation Rentals: United States and Canada* is meant to be a starting point only—the variety of amenities offered in vacation rental homes couldn't be contained in these pages. But the abundance of features that are included in these listings shows that, whatever your travel desires, self-catering can fulfill them.

Check it Out

Once you've targeted some possible properties, take the first step in planning a self-catered trip: Request brochures with photographs of those that interest you; and ask for local maps and any other available materials. If you're contacting an agency, ask for information on its rules and regulations and inquire about other properties in the area you will visit. Agencies publish extensive catalogues containing data on many more vacation rentals than *Best Vacation Rentals: United States and Canada* could accommodate, and their listings change periodically.

The agents, resorts, private owners and historical societies will provide complete details, in writing, about the properties listed in this book and let you know if anything has changed since publication. Additionally, we recommend that you speak with someone by telephone to confirm everything. As you review the material and prepare to make your final choice, be sure none of your questions are left unanswered.

Take the time to formulate a complete picture of your potential rental. If something you require is not mentioned—FAX service, for example, or a kitchen with an automatic coffee maker—ask if it is available. A kennel to make it easier to tour around without an enthusiastic Fido in tow, an on-site owner or manager to set your mind at ease, or a game room to help keep the kids busy while you sunbathe are other considerations that may apply to your individual travel situation. The athletic vacationer might ask if there's a gym on the premises, or if golf, boating, fishing, hiking or riding are available nearby.

Confirm that the property is open and available on the dates you plan to visit. Find out if your visit will fall in high season, and if the proprietor will book a reservation as far in advance as is practical to avoid disappointment. If a minimum stay is required (many vacation rentals are offered on a weekly basis), see if it applies to your off-season stay. When you are not renting an individual house, you may want to find out how many units the building, resort or restoration you've chosen encompasses. Some travelers prefer the security of large complexes; others like the intimacy of private residences.

Is the unit you want to rent the right size for your needs? Make sure it can accommodate at least the number of guests in your party and determine if the number of bedrooms included provides adequate privacy. You may wish to confirm that the beds are the size you prefer. (If you and your mate like to share a double bed, for instance, don't risk ending up with two twins.) Get a sense of the overall size of the unit, including any common areas, the kitchen and outdoor space.

Ask about any restrictions placed on guests: Are pets allowed? What about St. Bernards? Can you smoke indoors? Even if you smoke a pipe or cigar? Is the unit accessible to the handicapped? Are there steep stairs or a wheelchair ramp? Some older rentals—reached by rugged footpaths, equipped with steep stairs or built with narrow doorways—may be particularly problematic for the infirm.

Request precise rate information on the dates of your intended stay. Most rates fluctuate on a seasonal or even a weekly basis. Find out what is included in the rate quoted and what sorts of extra charges might apply. You may or may not, for instance, be charged extra for heat, for the use of certain resort facilities, for daily instead of weekly housekeeping or linen service, for extra guests or for a pet.

On the other hand, some establishments offer discounts to senior citizens, groups or guests who pay in advance. Check to see if you can take advantage of any price breaks. You may also discover tantalizing package deals, in which extra amenities or privileges are included at cut rates. Historic restorations sometimes offer packages that include the price of a unit rental plus golf or fishing privileges, tours of historic sites, cocktail parties and other bonuses.

Confirm the forms of payment accepted, and determine what kind of deposit is required to guarantee a reservation. Many properties ask for a deposit equal to one night's charge; others may request half or even all of the total rental fee up front. In some cases, the deposit may be charged by phone to a credit card, but many places will hold your reservation for seven days while they wait to receive your personal check, certified check or money order. Agencies and individuals will also often ask you to sign a rental agreement (like a short-term lease agreement) and pay a security deposit against possible harm. The deposit is refunded to you after your stay, when it is determined that there has been no damage to the property.

Finally, check to see if check-in and check-out times fit your itinerary and if you must follow any special procedures when arriving or departing.

Make sure you understand the renter's cancellation policy before putting down a deposit: You can lose the entire amount if you need to cancel and don't give enough notice. This is also a good time to find out who is responsible for assisting you if something goes wrong with your rental while you are on vacation. And read any contracts carefully before you sign. Then, once you are satisfied with the details, go ahead and make your reservation. When you do, ask for a receipt or other confirmation that your deposit has been received and your reservation finalized.

Some carefree travelers, of course, can't be tied down by reservations, or prefer to experiment with new locations once their trip is well underway. Upon arrival in some irresistibly tempting locale, adventurers can usually find self-catering accommodations through local travel information bureaus, newspaper or real estate agents. In popular tourist destinations, rentals are sometimes found simply by walking or driving around with an eye out for "vacancy" or "for rent" signs. When a charming vacant property is spied, you may be able to rent it on the spot—often for a favorable rate and no minimum stay requirement. Using this method, savvy self-caterers who don't require the security of advance planning can find wonderful lodgings at great rates. *But if you're traveling on-season, reservations are strongly recommended.*

Be Prepared

Do you need to pack any differently for a self-catered vacation than you would for a traditional one? Not really. If the unit, especially the kitchen, does not provide some item or convenience you absolutely require, think about bringing it along. Of course, if you must pack light and the missing element—a television or microwave—is not easily transportable, you might consider either doing without or renting a different property.

Those whose rentals include access to laundry facilities may choose to pack fewer clothes than usual. You may want to add a flashlight or some candles to your luggage if it will help you feel safer in a strange house. Or if you have a favorite cook's knife or corkscrew, toss it in with your toothbrush and swimsuit.

Some self-caterers pack a few non-perishable necessities—herbal tea, a pound of their favorite coffee, a special spice—if they suspect the items might be difficult to find in local stores. Others surrender entirely to their destination, savoring the adventure of shopping and eating like a local resident. Experienced international self-caterers agree it is impractical and unnecessary to carry more than the smallest food items with you.

Beyond these few minor points, making arrangements for your self-catered trip should be no different from preparing for a traditional vacation. Pack as you normally would, and get ready to have a great time!

At Home on the Road

The travel experience is distinctly different when you choose a home away from home instead of lodging in a hotel. The extra space, comfort, independence and privacy are a luxury, but those who are first-timers may wonder if it involves more work. After all, who wants to do housework on vacation? A little planning goes a long way toward making your self-catered trip carefree.

The most obvious difference between self-catered and hotel accommodations is access to a kitchen. But remember: You can make as much or as little use of it as you like. Some self-caterers prepare every meal, but others only enter the kitchen to enjoy a midnight snack in their pajamas. Whatever your preference, a few simple rules will help you minimize shopping and cooking time.

Plan your basic weekly menu before leaving home. Find out from guidebooks, your property's management or neighbors what kinds of foods and shopping facilities are available. Take into account the number of meals you are likely to eat out and design a menu based on as few ingredients as possible to avoid wasted staples and uneaten leftovers at departure time.

You'll find breakfast will be the time when you make best use of your rented kitchen, and you'll love the freedom of having your sausage and eggs in your bathrobe and slippers. So shop to make your vacation breakfasts special. Go ahead and buy the kinds of foods you normally don't indulge in.

For lunch and dinner, simple dishes requiring little advance preparation are best. Cooks who love to experiment with regional cuisines, however, have an exciting opportunity to cut loose when they travel the self-catered way—prowling the farmers' markets, fishermen's stalls and specialty shops in search of delectable local ingredients to bring home and cook up to their heart's delight.

Don't despair if you want to self-cater and can't stand the prospect of doing even minimal housework on vacation. As the listings in *Best Vacation Rentals* show, plenty of United States and Canadian vacation rentals include daily or weekly housekeeping service (this may or may not include dishwashing)—or even a full-time staff. And for those that do not include maid service during your stay, we've found that a small amount of housework on a daily basis goes a long way towards saving you from a laborious clean-up on the day of departure. It's all in choosing your dream rental and taking the time to make the simple preparations and inquiries about services necessary to insure your comfort and happiness.

Oh, Canada!

Renting a vacation home in Canada involves only slight adjustments for visitors from the United States. Small differences in currency, language and culture face all U.S. travelers in Canada; and visitors must observe customs and immigration formalities when crossing the border. We will not cover most of these points here, as you've probably found that information already in your travel guide to Canada. Certain points, however, are of particular interest to self-caterers from south of the border.

- "Apartment hotels" are an especially popular form of lodging in Canada. These consist of suites with kitchens, in a hotel setting. Prevalent in favored tourist destinations, they fill up quickly, so reserve early.

- Another self-catering option widely available in Canada are resorts with housekeeping cabins. These are geared towards outdoor sports enthusiasts and often include meal plans.

- For the most part, Canada has converted to the metric system. Bring your metric conversion table and be prepared to do a little arithmetic in the supermarket.

- An easy way to keep track of Canadian prices is to remember that Canadian currency is worth about thirty percent less than American currency. For example, a quart of milk might cost one Canadian dollar in Montreal; that's about seventy American cents.

- Canada uses the same 110 volts, 60 amps AC electricity as the United States.

- You may bring your pet across the border as long as you have obtained a veterinarian's certificate stating the animal is free of communicable diseases. Certain exotic pets, however, may be subject to quarantine.

- Canada's high season for travel is the summertime. Reserve your rental well in advance if you plan to visit during the warmer months.

- Enjoy!

How to Use This Guide

The listings in this guide appear alphabetically by state or province, city and lodging name, in that order. Listings for the United States precede those for Canada. A list of tourist boards appears at the end of the book; contact them as a valuable source of information and ideas to enhance your self-catered vacation.

Each listing contains the following information:

Rates:
Instead of quoting actual figures, prices are divided into categories. Rates change too often to be quoted exactly, but the price range provided in the listings will give you a reliable impression of the cost of a unit. More than one rate category in a listing generally reflects the difference between on-season and off-season rents. Be sure to ask specific questions about rate changes when planning your vacation to get the best possible deal. Prices are quoted per unit, not per person, and reflect conversion into American dollars. The categories are as follows:

budget	up to $75/night or $600/week
inexpensive	$76-125/night or $601-850/week
moderate	$126-175/night or $851-1,200/week
expensive	$176-250/night or $1,201-1,750/week
deluxe	$251 and up/night or $1,751 and up/week

Open:
Indicates the dates when the property is open.

Minimum Stay:
Information on the length of stay required is provided here. Minimum stay requirements may differ between the high and low tourist seasons.

Descriptive text:
This paragraph describes the highlights of the property. Outstanding features and furnishings of the unit, amenities and services available on the premises, and characteristics of the surrounding region are included. If something is not mentioned in this paragraph, do not assume it is unavailable: The description is not comprehensive and provides only an introduction to the property. For your convenience, agency listings often include a reference number for particular rentals. Use this number when you contact the agency to find out more.

Children (Yes or No):
Indicates if children are permitted.

Pets (Yes or No):
Indicates if pets are permitted. (And ask about quarantine regulations.)

Smoking (Yes or No):
Indicates if cigarette smoking is permitted. Restrictions on pipes and cigars should be confirmed with the rental proprietor.

Handicap Access (Yes or No):
Some properties, such as ground-floor units, represent themselves as partially accessible to the handicapped. Unless it has been determined, however, that the property is fully accessible, we have indicated "no" accessibility.

Payment:
Enumerates the forms of payment accepted:

C	Cash
P	Personal check
T	Travelers check
A	American Express
V	Visa
M	MasterCard
O	Other credit cards
All	All forms of payments

United States

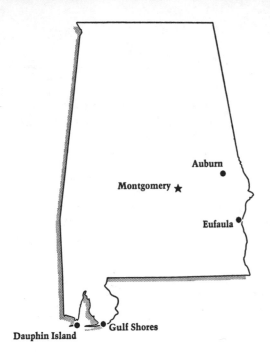

Auburn

Montgomery ★

Eufaula

Gulf Shores

Dauphin Island

Alabama

AUBURN

CHEWACLA STATE PARK *Rates: budget*
Open: year-round *Minimum Stay: two nights*
Five fully equipped rustic cabins are available on the picturesque grounds of Chewacla State Park, three miles south of Auburn. These make a pleasant and economical home base during fall football weekends, and there's plenty more to do both in the region, highlighted by the famous Tuskegee Institute National Historic Site and in the park. Constructed by the CCC in the 1930s, Chewacla offers a bounty of recreational opportunities for the whole family, including swimming, fishing and boating on a pristine 26-acre lake (fishing dinghies are supplied for free to cabin renters), tennis, playgrounds and a network of scenic hiking and bike trails, taking trekkers through the woods and mountains to such lovely vistas as the Chewacla Dam Waterfall. Contact: Chewacla State Park, P.O. Box 447, Auburn, AL 36830. Call 1-205-887-5621 or 1-800-ALA-PARK.
Children: **Y** Pets: **N** Smoking: **Y** Handicap Access: **N** Payment: **C, T, V, M, O**

DAUPHIN ISLAND

MORROW ON THE WATER   *Rates: budget-inexpensive*
Open: year-round   *Minimum Stay: three nights*

Graced with both a covered patio and sun deck, this comfortable four-bedroom house, containing a fully equipped kitchen and other completely modern amenities, enjoys a tranquil beachside position. Fort Gaines and all the other attractions and recreational facilities of Dauphin Island are nearby. When visitors want to venture further, a short drive or ferry ride brings them into Mobile, which features a truly wide variety of fascinating tourist attractions, from the World War II battleship USS *Alabama*, whose crew saw action in most of the war's major naval battles without a single casualty, to the gorgeous Bellingrath Gardens, offering one of the country's loveliest botanical displays. Contact: Boardwalk Rentals, Inc., P.O. Box 155, Dauphin Island, AL 36528. Call 1-205-861-3992.

Children: Y   Pets: N   Smoking: Y   Handicap Access: N   Payment: C, T, O

RAYNOR HOUSE   *Rates: budget*
Open: year-round   *Minimum Stay: three nights*

Situated right on the lagoon of Alabama's only barrier island, this three-bedroom house offers a complete array of modern conveniences, including a dishwasher, washer/dryer, microwave, VCR and central air and heating. The covered deck is a lovely spot for savoring the balmy gulf breezes, and the residence is superbly situated for enjoying the many recreational and cultural opportunities, as well as several important landmarks, in this prime vacation area. Steeped in history, Dauphin Island, named for the heir apparent to France's throne, was once the capital of all French Louisiana and also became a key strategic position during the Civil War. Contact: Boardwalk Rentals, Inc., P.O. Box 155, Dauphin Island, AL 36528. Call 1-205-861-3992.

Children: Y   Pets: N   Smoking: Y   Handicap Access: N   Payment: C, T, O

WILSON COTTAGE   *Rates: budget-inexpensive*
Open: year-round   *Minimum Stay: three nights*

A four-bedroom cottage sitting on the beach of Dauphin Island, this comfortable residence is in an ideal location for enjoying the climate, scenery and facilities of this delightful but often overlooked Gulf Coast resort. Civil War buffs have an extra reason for relishing this vacation spot. On the island's eastern tip, once guarding Mobile Bay, stands historic Fort Gaines, built in the 1850s and open year-round with fascinating museums and exhibits. The 1861 Union surrender of the fort to Confederate forces is re-created each January, while August brings the mammoth and colorfully detailed re-enactment of 1864's decisive Battle of Mobile Bay, when David Farragut damned the torpedoes and went full speed ahead to recapture the fort after a marathon three-week siege. Contact: Boardwalk Rentals, Inc., P.O. Box 155, Dauphin Island, AL 36528. Call 1-205-861-3992.

Children: Y   Pets: N   Smoking: Y   Handicap Access: N   Payment: C, T, O

EUFAULA

LAKEPOINT RESORT
Open: year-round

Rates: budget-inexpensive
Minimum Stay: none

Seven miles north of the charming antebellum town of Eufaula near the Alabama/Georgia border, Lakepoint State Park Resort has 29 fully equipped cabins to offer. Each two- and four-bedroom unit comes with an outdoor grill and central air and heating, and many also contain a cozy fireplace. They're all near placid Lake Eufaula, considered the "Bass Capital of the World," and with golf, tennis, a swimming pool, marina, hiking trails meandering through quiet pine forests and a quarter mile of unspoiled beach in the park area; myriad opportunities for nonfishermen are available as well. Contact: Mary Royal, Lakepoint Resort, P.O. Box 267, Eufaula, AL 36072. Call 1-205-687-8011 or 1-800-544-5253.

Children: Y Pets: N Smoking: Y Handicap Access: Y Payment: C, P, T, V, M

COMPASS POINT PENTHOUSE
Open: year-round

Rates: moderate-expensive
Minimum Stay: one week

For a luxury Gulf Shores accommodation, the Compass Point Penthouse is the top! Rising high above the water, it commands gorgeous, panoramic views of the lagoon and the gulf. This lavish residence contains four bedrooms, five and a half baths, living room, sitting room, spacious eat-in kitchen, two fireplaces, three Jacuzzi tubs and a steam shower, and it has a large deck area. The town's fine recreational and amusement facilities are all within easy reach, but there's plenty to do right at the complex, which features both an indoor and outdoor pool, a putting green and a private pier where pleasure and fishing boat excursions commence. Contact: Mayer Real Estate, P.O. Box 276, Gulf Streams, AL 36547. Call 1-205-968-7516 or 1-800-824-6331.

Children: Y Pets: N Smoking: Y Handicap Access: N Payment: C, T, P

GULF STATE PARK RESORT HOTEL
Open: year-round

Rates: budget-inexpensive
Minimum Stay: three days

The suites of Gulf State Park Resort, lying on a private stretch of sugar-white sands, provide guests with full housekeeping facilities. Enjoy a home-cooked meal in the seclusion of your elegant apartment, which offers a breathtaking sea view and contains a bedroom with two doubles or one king-sized bed, sitting room and kitchenette or savor a delicious dinner in the resort's dining room, featuring opulent seafood buffets on the weekend, the main courses supplied by local fishers. The unspoiled beach is only the beginning of the complex's lavish facilities, which also include tennis courts, an 18-hole golf course, swimming pool, picnic grounds and an 800-foot fishing pier. Contact: Reservations Clerk, Gulf State Park Resort Hotel, Box 437, Hwy. 182 East, Gulf Shores, AL 46547. Call 1-205-948-4853 or 1-800-544-4853.

Children: Y Pets: N Smoking: Y Handicap Access: Y Payment: C, P, T, V, M

HARRISON BEACH HOUSE *Rates: budget-moderate*
Open: year-round *Minimum Stay: one week*
This fetching cottage rests right on the gleaming beach of Gulf Shores, Alabama's best-known resort area. The four-bedroom residence features two decks and a balcony, each offering beautiful sea views and a handy kitchen that includes a dishwasher, microwave and washer-dryer. With many major attractions nearby, there are a number of ways to enjoy the mild weather and picturesque coastal geography: Why not go on a group horseback ride along the pristine sandy shore and through the verdant woodlands, perfumed with aromatic natural scents and covered with oaks, magnolia, pines and palmettos? Contact: Meyer Real Estate, P.O. Box 276, Gulf Streams, AL 36547. Call 1-205-968-7516 or 1-800-824-6331.
Children: Y Pets: N Smoking: Y Handicap Access: N Payment: C, T, P

NARTA BEACH HOUSE *Rates: moderate-expensive*
Open: year-round *Minimum Stay: one week*
The Narta Beach House is an attractive residence commanding sweeping views of the Gulf of Mexico. Its floor-to-ceiling windows and spacious deck give guests the maximum opportunity for enjoying the lovely scenery and soft sea breezes, while its location allows them to take advantage of the fine golf, tennis and water sports—from boating and sailing to fishing and scuba diving—that abound in the Gulf Shores area. The house contains a drawing room, extremely well-equipped kitchen and four bedrooms, with a large loft area containing an additional sleeper sofa. Contact: Meyer Real Estate, P.O. Box 276, Gulf Streams, AL 36547. Call 1-205-968-7516 or 1-800-824-6331.
Children: Y Pets: N Smoking: Y Handicap Access: N Payment: C, T, P

ONO RAINBOW *Rates: inexpensive*
Open: summer *Minimum Stay: one week*
Resting by the water on peaceful Ono Island, this quiet house offers seclusion and at the same time easy access to the attractions of Gulf Shores and Mobile Bay. The residence includes a master suite containing a sumptuous king-sized bed and two other bedrooms, as well as a pleasant sitting room and fully equipped kitchen. Steps lead down from the covered deck, which commands a scenic view of the Ole River, onto a pier featuring a double boat house. The waters in this area are particularly warm and inviting, providing fine opportunities for swimming, all kinds of boating, diving, waterskiing and a variety of other recreational diversions. Contact: Meyer Real Estate, P.O. Box 276, Gulf Streams, AL 36547. Call 1-205-968-7516 or 1-800-824-6331.
Children: Y Pets: N Smoking: Y Handicap Access: N Payment: C, T, P

RAINBOW'S END *Rates: moderate*
Open: summer *Minimum Stay: one week*
This comfortable four-bedroom beachside cottage offers a screened porch and sunny deck that both look out onto the gulf. Its fully equipped kitchen has everything needed to prepare a delicious dinner

of seafood either bought nearby right off the fishing boats or caught by the guests themselves. For an uncommon method of getting supper, join in a local tradition by taking a short drive over to the eastern shore of Mobile Bay. When word is out that the fish are running, the strange and unpredictable phenomenon the area folk call "Jubilee" occurs. For a two-hour period, masses of crab, shrimp and other marine life dazedly strand themselves along a 20-mile stretch of beach, where they can easily be grabbed—a rollicking spectacle whether you join in or just watch. Contact: Meyer Real Estate, P.O. Box 276, Gulf Streams, AL 36547. Call 1-205-968-7516 or 1-800-824-6331.

Children: Y   Pets: N   Smoking: Y   Handicap Access: N   Payment: C, T, P

SMITH BEACH HOUSE   *Rates: budget-inexpensive*
Open: year-round   *Minimum Stay: one week*

Built on two levels overlooking the gulf, this sunny beach house features three bedrooms, with additional room to accommodate up to eight, a living room, a fully equipped kitchen and a bright and spacious deck area. It's a superb vacation home for families, located right in the heart of Gulf Shores, which offers a variety of amusement facilities for children. Take them miniature golfing or to the wild and refreshing water slide park or simply hang around the clean and perfectly safe beach area that's just outside the door. Contact: Meyer Real Estate, P.O. Box 276, Gulf Streams, AL 36547. Call 1-205-968-7516 or 1-800-824-6331.

Children: Y   Pets: N   Smoking: Y   Handicap Access: N   Payment: C, T, P

SPINDRIFT   *Rates: budget-inexpensive*
Open: year-round   *Minimum Stay: one week*

Spindrift sits in a tranquil little meadow by the waters of Cotton Bayou. Cutting across the field, a private boardwalk leads from the door to a boat deck. Take a boat out on your own or join an invigorating charter cruise or angling expedition. The exceptional fishing in the area is justly celebrated in the early fall, with renowned burlfish and blue marlin tournaments as well as the exciting three-day National Shrimp Festival, drawing almost 200,000, but quieter times throughout the year offer plenty of possibilities for anyone with a rod and reel and a free afternoon. Making a comfortable home base, the three-bedroom house is well equipped with a dishwasher and washer/dryer and includes such enjoyable features as central air, a color TV and a pool table. Contact: Meyer Real Estate, P.O. Box 276, Gulf Streams, AL 36547. Call 1-205-968-7516 or 1-800-824-6331.

Children: Y   Pets: N   Smoking: Y   Handicap Access: N   Payment: C, T, P

SPYGLASS   *Rates: budget-inexpensive*
Open: year-round   *Minimum Stay: one week*

Located on West Beach, one of the best swimming areas in the Gulf Shores region, Spyglass is a homey condominium apartment building enjoying a quiet position that's also near fine shopping and seafood restaurants. The three-bedroom units provide total privacy, and each offers central air and cable television and contains a living room and a highly serviceable kitchen with a dishwasher, microwave and washer/dryer. The compound features a sparkling swimming pool, and golf and tennis are also close by. Contact: Mayer Real Estate, P.O. Box 276, Gulf Streams, AL 36547. Call 1-205-968-7516 or 1-800-824-6331.

Children: Y   Pets: N   Smoking: Y   Handicap Access: N   Payment: C, T, P

Alaska

ANCHORAGE

ANCHORAGE UPTOWN HOTEL *Rates: budget-inexpensive*
Open: year-round *Minimum Stay: none*
Actually located in the heart of the city's downtown area, the Anchorage Uptown Hotel is near superb shopping and restaurants, the Historical and Fine Arts Museum, the Performing Arts Center and Old City Hall. The hotel's comfortable one-bedroom suites each offer a living room and complete kitchen and many have a fireplace as well. Venturing out of the city, the scenic glories of Cook Inlet and Prince William Sound—still remarkably unspoiled in the wake of the oil spill—are a short drive away, while the majestic Mt. McKinley/Denali National Park can be reached by highway or the Alaskan railroad. Contact: Anchorage Uptown Hotel, 234 East 2nd Avenue, Anchorage, AK 99501. Call 1-907-279-4232.

Children: **Y** Pets: **N** Smoking: **Y** Handicap Access: **N** Payment: All

NELCHINA POINT SUITES *Rates: inexpensive-moderate*
Open: year-round *Minimum Stay: none*
Minutes from downtown Anchorage and near to jogging and bike trails, Nelchina Point is a luxury building offering self-sufficient studio, one- and two-bedroom apartments, many with a fireplace and most providing a private balcony that gives sweeping views of the city. Even though Anchorage is a modern metropolis, don't think there aren't plenty of opportunities for enjoying Alaska's wildlife and rich

historic heritage. The Alaska Zoo features an abundance of Arctic animals, while the Potter Point State Game Refuge accommodates more than 130 species of waterfowl in their natural habitat. At Eklutna, visit the St. Nicholas Orthodox Church, a remnant from the days when the state was owned by Russia, and the brightly painted Native "spirit houses," constructed by descendants of Alaska's first settlers. Contact: Mary Lou Wirum, Nelchina Point, 1601 Nelchina, Anchorage, AK 99501. Call 1-907-276-3628.

Children: Y Pets: N Smoking: Y Handicap Access: Y Payment: C, P, T, V, M

DENALI

DENALI CROW'S NEST LOG CABINS   *Rates: inexpensive-moderate*
Open: mid-May to mid-September   *Minimum Stay: none*

One mile north of the entrance to Denali National Park, home of North America's tallest peak, Mt. McKinley, the log cabins of Denali Crow's Nest offer the perfect home base for taking all the time you want to explore the natural wonders of the region. Exquisite views of the breathtaking Alaska Range, beautiful Horseshoe Lake and wild Nenana River can be savored right on the grounds; here, you can also catch the shuttle bus running through the park or book space on one of the wilderness and wildlife tours taking guests deep into untamed areas for a chance to encounter moose, caribou, dall sheep and even grizzly bears. After a day's adventure, enjoy a soak in one of the two seductive outdoor hot tubs and a hearty meal at the Overlook Bar and Grill. Contact: Carol Crofoot, Denali Crow's Nest, Mile 238.5 Parks Highway, P.O. Box 70, Denali National Park, AK 99755. Call 1-907-683-2723.

Children: Y Pets: N Smoking: Y Handicap Access: N Payment: C, P, T, V, M

FORT SEWARD

FORT SEWARD CONDOS   *Rates: budget-inexpensive*
Open: year-round   *Minimum Stay: three nights*

Located on Officer's Row, a short walk from historic Fort Seward, a restored turn-of-the-century army post, this handsome house contains fully equipped one- and two-bedroom apartments. The days of '98 are brought back to life at the Klondike Gold Rush National Historic Park in nearby Skagway. And of course the recreational and sightseeing opportunities around the region, Alaska's northern panhandle, are unsurpassed. Go on a kayaking, fishing or whale-watching expedition in the bay or take a boat or aerial tour of Glacier Bay National Park, which features no less than 16 of those magnificent bodies of ice flowing oh-so-slowly from the towering mountains into the sea. Contact: Ted or Mimi Greene, Fort Seward Condos, #3 Ft. Seward Drive, Box 75, Haines, AK 99827. Call 1-907-766-2425.

Children: Y Pets: N Smoking: Y Handicap Access: N Payment: C, P, T

HAINES

THUNDERBIRD MOTEL *Rates: budget-inexpensive*
Open: year-round *Minimum Stay: none*
The Thunderbird Motel, providing comfortable and fully equipped one- and two-bedroom units, each with a kitchenette, is in the center of Haines, a picturesque northern panhandle town nestled where lofty mountains descend into the crystal blue sea. The area offers superb fishing and an abundance of wildlife, particularly at the Chilkat Bald Eagle Preserve, home to over 3,500 of the rare birds. Also nearby runs the historic Dalton Trail—now a scenic highway—carved thousands of years ago by receding glaciers, migrating animals and the native Americans who pursued them all the way from Asia. Contact: Beatrice Spradlin, Thunderbird Motel, P.O. Box 589, Haines, AK 99755. Call 1-907-766-2131 or 1-800-327-2556.
Children: Y Pets: Y Smoking: Y Handicap Access: N Payment: C, T, V, M, A

HOMER

WOODSIDE APARTMENTS *Rates: budget-inexpensive*
Open: year-round *Minimum Stay: none*
Woodside rests under a grove of trees in the town of Homer, a charming arts and fishing community on halibut-rich Kachemak Bay, surrounded by the rugged snowcapped Kenai Mountains. The small apartment building contains six homey studio, one- and two-bedroom guest flats, each including a full kitchen; three come with a fireplace, two with a private balcony and three have particularly stunning views. The area's top attraction, Homer Spit, a long sandbar extending four and a half miles into the bay, is within easy reach, lively with eager sightseers in the summer and a colony of hundreds of eagles in the winter; it offers extraordinary year-round fishing, particularly for king salmon as large as 30 pounds. Contact: Tom or Dale Samples, Woodside Apartments, 300 Woodside Ave., Apt. #1, Homer, AK 99603. Call 1-907-235-8389.
Children: Y Pets: N Smoking: Y Handicap Access: N Payment: C, P, T

KENAI

COUNTRY APARTMENTS *Rates: budget-moderate*
Open: May 15-September 1 *Minimum Stay: none*
Within walking distance of the Kenai River, famous for its extraordinary salmon fishing, this quality apartment house provides eight self-sufficient one- and two-bedroom apartments. The residence is superbly situated for an all-encompassing visit to the breathtaking Kenai peninsula. The town itself features one of Alaska's loveliest Russian churches, and visitors also won't want to miss Kenai Fjords National Park, which offers picturesque inlets and the chance to observe sea otters, sea lions, seals and whales; the National Wildlife Range, habitat of nearly 10,000 moose; or the sublime Exit Glacier at the edge of

the immense Harding Icefield. Contact: Bev Kaiser, Country Apartments, 10819 Spur Highway, Suite 349, Kenai, AK 99611. Call 1-907-262-7881 or 1-800-365-9480.

Children: **Y** Pets: **N** Smoking: **Y** Handicap Access: **N** Payment: **C, P, T**

NOME

NANUAQ MANOR   *Rates: budget-moderate*
Open: year-round   *Minimum Stay: none*

Visitors to Nome, a vital and hardy town on the Bering Sea not far below the Arctic Circle, won't find finer housekeeping accommodations than the comfortable and well-equipped two- and three-bedroom apartments of Nanuaq Manor, each with a living room and full kitchen. A vacation to this isolated region gives the chance to experience the "real" Alaska few tourists get to see. Winter in Nome is a haunting season—cold, sure, but with an eerie beauty offering unforgettable activities such as dog-sled races, ice-fishing, cross-country skiing, snowmobiling, even ice golf. Summer, meanwhile, means perpetual light, giving visitors plenty of time to enjoy the warm-weather recreational opportunities and the boisterous festivals. Contact: Elsie K. McConnell, Nanuaq Manor, P.O. Box 905, Nome, AK 99762. Call 1-907-443-5296.

Children: **Y** Pets: **N** Smoking: **Y** Handicap Access: **N** Payment: **All**

PETERSBURG

SCANDIA HOUSE   *Rates: budget-inexpensive*
Open: year-round   *Minimum Stay: none*

Built at the turn of the century by Scandinavian immigrants in the town of Petersburg, Alaska's "Little Norway," Scandia House offers several completely modern housekeeping flats among its 24 units. There are plenty of ways to enjoy the area's natural beauty and rich cultural heritage and to observe the fishing industry that dominates the community. Three boat harbors are a short walking distance away, where vacationers can watch the fleet come in, and a local hatchery and canneries can also be visited. Those who want to do some fishing of their own can rent a skiff or charter boat and go out for salmon, halibut, shrimp, king crab and trout, while others can spend their time touring a lumber mill or exploring the majestic LeConte glacier and ice cap. Contact: Scandia House, P.O. Box 689, 110 Nordic Drive, Petersburg, AK 99833. Call 1-907-772-4281.

Children: **Y** Pets: **N** Smoking: **Y** Handicap Access: **N** Payment: **All**

THORNE BAY

MCFARLAND'S "FLOATEL"   *Rates: inexpensive-moderate*
Open: year-round   *Minimum Stay: none*

Four roomy log cabins are situated right on the beach behind this unique floating bed and breakfast lodge and sporting goods shop moored in a snug cove near the community of Thorne Bay, a 20-minute seaplane ride from Ketchikan. Each of the two-bedroom residences contains a living room and fully equipped kitchen and offers spectacular views of the bay and the surrounding forests; guests may be able to spot otter, mink, deer, black bear and a variety of ducks and other bird species right from their front door. With motor skiffs and the owner's 32-foot cruiser, the "Jeannie M," available for hire, there are a number of ways to enjoy the pristine local waters and the Floatel's Marine Adventure Tour journeys to the best fishing spots, giving guests the chance to catch their own dinner. Contact: Jim and Jeannie McFarland, P.O. Box 159, Thorne Bay, AK 99919. Call 1-907-828-3335.

Children: Y   Pets: N   Smoking: N   Handicap Access: N   Payment: C, P, T

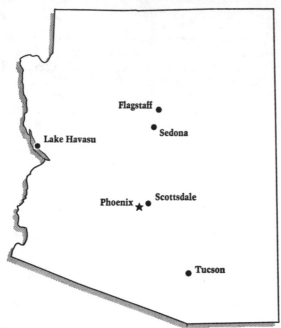

Arizona

FLAGSTAFF

FAIRFIELD FLAGSTAFF COMM. CLUB
Rates: budget-moderate
Open: year-round
Minimum Stay: none

Ride horses from the club's stables through nearby Coconino National Forest and return for a restful swim in Lake Elaine or this condominium complex's pool. The Arizona hill country is the backdrop as you sharpen your golf and tennis game on the premises before retiring to the Sunburst Lounge. The well-groomed slopes of Snowbowl, only 14 miles away, make for plentiful wintertime activity, or you can day-trip to the Grand Canyon. These tastefully decorated one- and two-bedroom units occupy a high-rise in northern Arizona. Surrounded by all the amenities of country-club living, they include kitchen, linens and maid service. Contact: Fairfield Flagstaff Comm. Club, 1900 N. Country Club Dr., Box 1208, Flagstaff, AZ 86002. Call 602-526-3232 or 800-526-1004.

Children: **Y**   Pets: **N**   Smoking: **Y**   Handicap Access: **N**   Payment: **C, T**

LAKE HAVASU

INN AT TAMARISK
Rates: budget-moderate
Open: year-round
Minimum Stay: none

An English village along the water, with unique shops beneath the reconstructed London Bridge, offers charming entertainment in this quiet desert oasis. Nearby, just a short walk from Lake Havasu beach, are the Inn at Tamarisk's comfortable one- and two-bedroom condominiums with kitchens. The area hosts many competitive events, such as the World OutBoard Classic, the International Jet Ski Race and many sailboat regattas and ski tournaments. If that's not enough excitement, partake of the scheduled free bus trips to the casinos. Contact: Inn at Tamarisk, 3101 London Bridge Road, Lake Havasu, AZ 86403. Call 602-764-3044.

Children: Y   Pets: N   Smoking: Y   Handicap Access: N   Payment: C, P, T

SCOTTSDALE

FOUNTAINS—SCOTTSDALE RANCH   *Rates: moderate-deluxe*
Open: year-round   *Minimum Stay: one month*
Amid bubbling fountains under tall palm trees on gorgeous common grounds stand these magnificent two-bedroom townhouses. Walk or bicycle to the fabulous shopping in this resort area, then return for a quick workout in the gym or maybe a dip in the pool. These townhouses include full kitchens, two and a half bathrooms, fireplaces in the living rooms, courtyard entries and lots of beautiful tile. Contact: Reva Schafer, 10619 N. Hayden Rd., Suite #100, Scottsdale AZ 85260. Call 602-483-333 or 1-800-678-0083.

Children: Y   Pets: N   Smoking: Y   Handicap Access: N   Payment: C, P, T

SCOTTSDALE CAMELBACK RESORT AND SPA   *Rates: budget*
Open: year-round   *Minimum Stay: two nights*
Nestled at the base of Camelback Mountain in a marvelous resort area lies Scottsdale Camelback Resort and Spa. These luxurious two- and three-bedroom villas are completely equipped and include daily maid service, kitchen and linens. Spend the morning soaking lazily in the pool and hot tub. The more active guests can get up a tennis game or venture two miles to the golf course. Nearby, the Grand Canyon provides excellent touring possibilities. Contact: Scottsdale Camelback Resort and Spa, 6302 E. Camelback Rd., Scottsdale, AZ 85251. Call 602-947-3300.

Children: Y   Pets: N   Smoking: Y   Handicap Access: N   Payment: C, T, V, M

SEDONA

RED ROCK RETREAT   *Rates: moderate*
Open: year-round   *Minimum Stay: none*
Surrounded by Sedona's amazingly beautiful red rock landscape, this three-bedroom, two-bathroom home is furnished completely with original artwork of the Southwest. The kitchen, dining room and living room look out on a magnificent view of the Oak Creek Country Club golf course, a Robert Trent Jones design considered one of the finest new golf courses in the country. Completely equipped with linens and cooking supplies, the house also includes a cozy rock fireplace and a golf cart. Contact: Marilyn and Ken Erickson, 979 Cart Ct., Incline Village, NV 89451. Call 702-831-6025.

Children: Y   Pets: N   Smoking: Y   Handicap Access: N   Payment: C, P, T

TUCSON

SANTA CATALINA VILLAS
Rates: budget
Open: year-round
Minimum Stay: one month
Magnificent mountain views, tranquil desert vistas, breathtaking sunsets and sparkling city lights are the backdrop for daily life at Santa Catalina Villas. Enjoy fully furnished luxury apartment living perched high above Tucson in these studios and one- or two-bedroom apartments. Each offers a private patio or balcony, complete kitchen and professionally designed interior. Dine at one of the best restaurants in Tucson and use one of the finest clubhouses in the Southwest, which offers a billiards room, exercise classes, bridge tournaments and nature hikes. Contact: Santa Catalina Villas, 7500 North Calle Sin Envidia, Tucson, AZ 85718. Call 602-742-0505.

Children: Y   Pets: Y   Smoking: Y   Handicap Access: N   Payment: C, P, T

VILLA SERENAS
Rates: budget
Open: year-round
Minimum Stay: none
Wander out your door through the peaceful, award-winning landscape of this complex, with its fountains, ponds and pools. Studios and one-bedroom condominiums decorated in contemporary furnishings and soft desert colors provide TV, phone, daily maid service and linens. Unmatched recreational facilities include a pool, spas, golf with putting greens, tennis and a nearby ski lift. Or take the kids to the Old Tucson Amusement Park, the Desert Museum, Colossal Cave or any of the many other local attractions. Contact: Villa Serenas, 8111 E. Broadway, Tucson, AZ 85710. Call 602-886-6761 or 800-345-3449.

Children: Y Pets: N Smoking: Y Handicap Access: Y Payment: C, T, A, V, M

Arkansas

ARKADELPHIA

IRON MOUNTAIN LODGE AND MARINA *Rates: inexpensive-moderate*
Open: year-round *Minimum Stay: none*
Head for the hills and these rustic log-style cottages amid the oaks at the base of Iron Mountain. Daily maid service ensures your comfort in these two-bedroom cottages, which feature fully equipped kitchens. The lodge offers boat storage, a launching ramp and a marina on De Gray Lake, from which you can undertake a variety of sporting adventures, such as fishing and water skiing. Don't miss nearby Hot Springs National Park, where 47 thermal springs deliver soothing baths in naturally therapeutic waters. Contact: Iron Mountain Lodge and Marina, 25 IP Circle, Arkadelphia, AR 71923. Call 501-246-4310.
Children: Y Pets: Y Smoking: Y Handicap Access: N Payment: C, P, T, V, M

DARDANELLE

MOUNT NEBO STATE PARK *Rates: budget*
Open: year-round *Minimum Stay: none*
Cool summer temperatures and panoramic views of Lake Dardanelle and the Arkansas River beckon visitors to Mount Nebo State Park, which rises 1,800 feet above the valleys of west central Arkansas. A favorite vacation spot since before the Civil War, the park added trails, cabins, bridges and pavilions in the 1930s, built by the Civilian Conservation Corps. Today, you'll find ten rustic and four modern cabins

available, all with fully equipped electric kitchens, air conditioning and heating for year-round comfort. This park may not be for everyone, however, as the slopes are long and steep. A park swimming pool is open throughout the summer, but parents should note there's no lifeguard on duty. Contact: Mount Nebo State Park, Route 3, Box 374, Dardanelle, AR 72834. Call 501-229-3655.

Children: Y   Pets: N   Smoking: Y   Handicap Access: N   Payment: C, P, T

EUREKA SPRINGS

BONNYBROOKE FARM   *Rates: inexpensive*
Open: February-November   *Minimum Stay: two nights*

Bonnybrooke Farm is located on 20 acres filled with blooming flowers, rock gardens and the shade of large old oak trees. Enter Wildwood Cottage through an old-fashioned French door with beveled sidelights, then enjoy inspiring views of the peaceful hillside meadows and woodlands. Decorated in shades of blue, with wooden floors and throw rugs, the cottage is quaint and peaceful. Morning Glory Cottage offers guests an opportunity to shower beneath the stars in a glass shower with full solarium front. Barn Rose offers seclusion and charm at the top of an old barn, where you'll find a glass wall overlooking the mountains and valleys below. Contact: Bonnybrooke Farm Atop Misty Mountain, Rt. 2, Box 335A, Eureka Springs, AR 72632. Call 501-253-6903.

Children: N   Pets: N   Smoking: N   Handicap Access: N   Payment: C, T, V, M

CRESCENT MOON TOWNHOUSE   *Rates: inexpensive*
Open: year-round   *Minimum Stay: two nights*

This townhouse occupies the second floor of an 1898 hand-cut limestone building, designed during Eureka Springs' early resort days. You'll find luxurious comfort in the Victorian splendor of rich antiques in polished wood and stained glass. Two charming period bedrooms and a bath with a claw-foot tub and brass shower fixtures, plus an open sitting room decorated with tasteful local crafts, help to recreate the ambiance of Victorian living. A full kitchen and color TV bring the amenities up to date, as does a hot tub on a redwood deck, the perfect place for a long soak while sipping your morning coffee. Downtown is just a short walk away, where you'll find charming shops and restaurants to explore. Contact: Nedra Forrest, Crescent Moon Townhouse, 28 Spring St., Eureka Springs, AR 72632. Call 501-253-9463.

Children: Y   Pets: N   Smoking: Y   Handicap Access: N   Payment: C, P, T, A, V, M

HOLIDAY ISLAND   *Rates: budget-moderate*
Open: year-round   *Minimum Stay: two nights*

The clean, clear waters of Table Rock Lake beckon visitors to enjoy swimming, sailing, water skiing, scuba diving and, of course, excellent fishing throughout the year. Choose from a variety of basic condominiums to luxury homes, most with a lake view, sun deck, fireplace and satellite TV. Tennis courts and two tree-lined golf courses are among the many outdoor facilities available. Explore the charm of Victorian architecture throughout Eureka Springs, or take a ride on an authentic steam railroad. A full-service marina offers anglers all the gear they'll need to catch crappie, bluegill, white bass, catfish and rainbow trout in the lake. Contact: Holiday Island Vacation Rentals, 87 Woodsdale Dr., Holiday Island, AR 72632. Call 1-800-848-4688 (in Arkansas, 501-253-7700).

Children: Y Pets: N Smoking: Y Handicap Access: N Payment: C, P, T, V, M, O

PRIMROSE PATH *Rates: budget*
Open: year-round *Minimum Stay: none*
Curl up in the bay window in this street-level townhouse and watch the Eureka Springs trolley pass by in the early morning sun. The large master bedroom features a king-sized bed with a fireplace and double French doors that open onto a private garden patio. For added luxury, you'll find a Jacuzzi for two in the bath. Located in the heart of Eureka Springs' historic district, you'll get caught up in the Victorian charm of period shops and restaurants, all nearby. Brightly colored wallpaper, stenciled floors, antique furnishings and some whimsical touches make this a charming getaway. Contact: Marcia Yearsley, Sweet Seasons Guest Cottages, 26 Spring St., Eureka Springs, AR 72632. Call 501-253-7603.

Children: Y   Pets: Y   Smoking: Y   Handicap Access: N   Payment: All

SLEEPY HOLLOW GUEST COTTAGE *Rates: budget-inexpensive*
Open: March-December *Minimum Stay: two nights*
This secluded guest house sits on the outskirts of historic downtown Eureka, where you can visit the home of temperance crusader Carrie Nation, the Hammon Museum of Bells and the Miles Musical Museum, with its grand collection of music boxes and hand organs. The house features three double bedrooms on separate floors to accommodate six people in comfort and privacy. The fully equipped kitchen comes with coffee and a variety of teas included, and a large private yard offers off-street parking. Air conditioning, heating and cable TV supplement the modern amenities. Contact: Margie Conner, Sleepy Hollow Guest Cottage, 108 Wall, Eureka Springs, AR 72632. Call 501-253-7448.

Children: Y   Pets: N   Smoking: Y   Handicap Access: N   Payment: C, P, T

THE HEARTSTONE INN AND COTTAGES *Rates: budget-inexpensive*
Open: year-round *Minimum Stay: two nights*
Honeymooners—first or second—will delight in this country cottage for two with warm knotty-pine walls and rustic rooms filled with country crafts and antiques. Country quilts warm up the queen-sized bed, and a private wooded garden complete with an old-fashioned garden swing makes the perfect romantic getaway for two. At the adjacent Heartstone Inn you can enjoy a hearty country breakfast before setting out to explore the historic Victorian village in Eureka. Contact: Iris and Bill Simantel, The Heartstone Inn and Cottages, 35 Kingshighway, Eureka Springs, AR 72632. Call 501-253-8916.

Children: Y Pets: N Smoking: Y Handicap Access: N Payment: C, P, T, A, V, M

THE LITTLE CHATEAU   *Rates: inexpensive*
Open: year-round   *Minimum Stay: none*
A charming combination of country antiques and plush frills make this cottage for eight a welcome place to get away from the bustle of modern living. Vaulted ceilings in the living room and an adorable sleeping loft enhance the nineteenth-century feeling, while a deluxe Jacuzzi for two and color TV and air conditioning bring the amenities up to date. A king-sized master bedroom features an additional bed in an alcove, and another bedroom sports an antique walnut double bed. Everyday hassles take a backseat to simple living as you explore the period shops and restaurants throughout this lovely Victorian village. Contact: Marcia Yearsley, Sweet Seasons Guest Cottages, 26 Spring St., Eureka Springs, AR 72632. Call 501-253-7603.
Children: **Y**   Pets: **Y**   Smoking: **Y**   Handicap Access: **N**   Payment: All

FAIRFIELD BAY

FAIRFIELD BAY   *Rates: budget-inexpensive*
Open: year-round   *Minimum Stay: two nights*
Nestled in the foothills of the Ozarks, Fairfield Bay offers one- and two-bedroom accommodations on Greers Ferry Lake. The units feature oversize beds, full kitchen facilities and linens. A sportsman's paradise, the area offers two championship golf courses, skiing and water sports. Visit the nearby Ozark Folk Center, a state-operated showcase for arts and crafts and area folklore or explore Blanchard Springs Caverns. White-water rafting, tennis and golf are all available nearby. Contact: Fairfield Bay, P.O. Box 3008, Fairfield Bay, AR 72088. Call 1-800-643-9790 (in Arkansas, 501-884-3333).
Children: **Y** Pets: **Y** Smoking: **Y** Handicap Access: **N** Payment: C, P, T, V, M

FORT SMITH

THOMAS QUINN GUEST HOUSE   *Rates: budget-inexpensive*
Open: year-round   *Minimum Stay: none*
The first floor of this stately brick home was built in 1863, the second floor and Corinthian columns were added in 1916 and the entire mansion was restored as a guest house in 1984. The result is a lovely fusion of old elegance and modern convenience amid reminders of Fort Smith's historic past as a frontier outpost. One- and two-bedroom suites feature private dressing rooms, a furnished kitchen with bar, bath and spacious living room. Just a mile away you'll find the courthouse where Judge Isaac C. Parker plied his harsh brand of justice so often he became known as the hanging judge of the frontier. Contact: Marty Whitfield, Thomas Quinn Guest House, 815 North B Street, Fort Smith, AR 72901. Call 501-782-0499.
Children: **Y**   Pets: **N**   Smoking: **Y**   Handicap Access: **N**   Payment: All

HIGDEN

DEVIL'S FORK RESORT AND DOCK   *Rates: budget*
Open: year-round   *Minimum Stay: none*

These two-bedroom brick cottages feature covered patios for outdoor relaxing and fish cookers to prepare the catch of the day. The use of a fishing boat, dock, ramp, slip and fishing supplies are included, and there are facilities for cleaning and freezing your prizes. Greers Ferry Lake is clean and clear and offers a swimming area with a ladder and float. If you ever tire of fishing, you'll find facilities for other sports, outdoors and indoors, or you can take a nature hike up Sugar Loaf Mountain. Contact: Devil's Fork Resort and Dock, Rt. 1, Box B, Higden, Greers Ferry, AR 72067. Call 501-825-6240.

Children: Y Pets: Y Smoking: Y Handicap Access: N Payment: C, P, T, V, M

HOT SPRINGS

BUENA VISTA RESORT   *Rates: budget-moderate*
Open: year-round   *Minimum Stay: none*

Located within Hot Springs National Park, Buena Vista Resort offers guest cottages on 10 wooded acres along the 22-mile shore of Lake Hamilton. Studio, one-, two- and three-bedroom cottages feature central heat and air conditioning for year-round comfort. You can relax on a common covered dock while your children play safely in a fenced-in yard, or leave them to explore a summer game room while you get some extra sleep. The Oaklawn Race Track offers Thoroughbred racing from February to April, and the park has many lakes and hiking trails to explore year-round. Contact: Buena Vista Resort, Route 3, Box 175, Hot Springs, AR 71913. Call 1-800-255-9030 (in Arkansas, 501-525-1321).

Children: Y Pets: Y Smoking: Y Handicap Access: N Payment: C, P, T, V, M

LAKE CATHERINE STATE PARK   *Rates: budget*
Open: year-round   *Minimum Stay: two weeks*

Set on more than 2,000 acres in the Ouachita Mountains on the shores of Lake Catherine, 17 cabins combine the natural beauty of the park with modern conveniences. All feature fully equipped kitchens, some with fireplaces, and private boat docks for exploring and fishing on the clear mountain lake. An on-site marina sells bait and rents fishing, motor- and sailboats, as well as other equipment for an exciting day on the water. The many nature trails through secluded woodlands are worth exploring by day, and there's even a nature center open in the summer, where you can learn more about the park's wildlife. Contact: Bill Saunders, Lake Catherine State Park, Rt. 19, Box 360, Hot Springs, AR 71913. Call 501-844-4176.

Children: Y Pets: Y Smoking: Y Handicap Access: N Payment: C, P, T, V, M

THE WHARF   *Rates: inexpensive-moderate*
Open: year-round   *Minimum Stay: none*

Get close to nature in these two-bedroom wood-and-stone units. Oversized whirlpool baths and glass-enclosed decks ensure the going won't get too rough. Walkways lead you through the majestic pines to Lake

Hamilton, where you can fill your days with fishing, water skiing, boating and swimming. Tennis courts are nearby, as is Thoroughbred racing at Oaklawn Race Track, open from February through April. Contact: The Wharf, 408 Long Island Drive, Hot Springs, AR 71913. Call 501-525-4604.

Children: Y Pets: Y Smoking: Y Handicap Access: N Payment: C, P, T, V, M

VILLAGE VILLAS *Rates: budget-moderate*
Open: year-round *Minimum Stay: two nights*
This resort offers five challenging golf courses—DeSoto, Balboa, Coronado, Cortez and Ponce de Leon—rated among the nation's best and all of them suitable for both amateurs and pros. Village Villas' townhouses and private homes are set among lakes and woods and feature one-, two- and three-bedroom units with large living areas and fully equipped kitchens. The Coronado Natatorium and Fitness Center provides an indoor swimming pool with sliding roof, saunas, whirpool and an exercise room overlooking Lake Coronado. Fishing opportunities abound, and from February to April you can attend the Thoroughbred racing at the Oaklawn Race Track. Contact: Village Villas, Inc., Box 5, DeSoto Center, Hot Springs Village, AR 71909. Call 1-800-643-1000 (in Arkansas, 501-922-0303).

Children: Y Pets: N Smoking: Y Handicap Access: N Payment: C, P, T, V, M, O

WEST FORK

DEVIL'S DEN STATE PARK *Rates: budget-inexpensive*
Open: year-round *Minimum Stay: none*
Thirteen rustic cabins perched along a rocky valley overlook a running stream in this pleasant state park in northwest Arkansas. The one-, two- and three-bedroom cabins are only rustic in appearance though, as they feature air conditioning and heating for year-round comfort and fully equipped kitchens for simple or elegant meal preparation. A large stone fireplace takes the chill from the night air, and the evening calm allows you to hear the wonderful sounds of wildlife throughout the park. You'll find many hiking trails and a restaurant, gift shop and supply store in the park. Some buildings date back to 1933, when the Civilian Conservation Corps worked here as part of the Works Project Administration. Contact: Jesse Cox, Devil's Den State Park, Rt. 1, Box 118, West Fork, AR 72774. Call 501-761-3325.

Children: Y Pets: N Smoking: Y Handicap Access: N Payment: C, P, T, V, M

California

CARMEL

AMES BEACH HOUSE
Open: year-round
Rates: expensive
Minimum Stay: one week

Smack dab on the beach, this two-bedroom home for four puts you that close to the Pacific and beautiful Carmel Bay. The sunny beach house features a large living room with an inviting fireplace and windows looking out onto the beach and unlimited ocean views. The dining room seats four; the kitchen includes a breakfast bar as well as a microwave and a washer/dryer. If you can tear yourself away from this spectacular spot, you may enjoy an afternoon at the nearby Tassajara Hot Springs high in the mountains of Los Padres National Forest. Sports lovers can play tennis, swim or play golf at one of the several excellent peninsula courses. Contact: The San Carlos Agency, Inc., P.O. Box 22123, 26358 Carmel Rancho Lane, Carmel, CA 93922. Call 408-624-3846.

Children: Y   Pets: N   Smoking: N   Handicap Access: N   Payment: C, P, T

CARMEL COTTAGE
Open: year-round
Rates: inexpensive
Minimum Stay: one week

This darling cottage located five blocks from the beach of Carmel Bay provides secluded accommodations for six. The fenced yard shaded with tall trees offers outdoor privacy, the perfect spot for a nap or a spell with a good book. Featuring two bedrooms, a dining area and a living room that opens right onto the cozy kitchen, the cottage tempts homebodies with a wood-burning fireplace and a color TV. This charming house provides a great spot for avid golfers, who'll find some of the country's best golf courses, including Pebble Beach, only a short drive away. Longer drives will bring you to California's historic missions and the Soledad Mission ruins. Contact: Rent A Home International, 7200 34th Avenue N.W., Seattle, WA 98117. Call 206-545-6963.

Children: Y Pets: N Smoking: N Handicap Access: N Payment: C, P, V, M

CENTRAL TOWNHOUSE   *Rates: budget-inexpensive*
Open: year-round   *Minimum Stay: one week*
You'll find this fresh and bright, newly decorated townhouse just a stroll from downtown Carmel. Accommodations for four include two bedrooms, two baths, a living room/dining area with a wood-burning fireplace, a white-tiled kitchen with a laundry area and a small deck. From here, all the pleasures and beauty of the exquisite Monterey Peninsula are yours. Great golfing, surfing and swimming, the remarkable flora and fauna of this unique location, and some of the state's best dining opportunities await you. Children of every age can spend a day or two at the Monterey Bay Aquarium and walking along the Fisherman's Wharf. And the Carmel Mission appeals to vacationers with a historical bent. Contact: PineCone Property Management, 200 Clock Tower Place, Suite D205, Carmel, CA 93923. Call 408-626-8163.

Children: Y Pets: N Smoking: N Handicap Access: N Payment: C, P, T

CIANCIARULO CONDO   *Rates: budget*
Open: year-round   *Minimum Stay: one week*
Health enthusiasts will appreciate this lovely smoke-free one-bedroom apartment right in the town of Carmel. Accommodations for four include a hide-a-bed in the beautifully appointed sunken living room, which boasts a cozy fireplace that's ideal for those cool, misty Monterey Bay nights. A separate dining room and a kitchen with a dishwasher and a disposal complete the amenities here, but you'll also find parking and laundry facilities on the premises and all of Carmel just beyond your door. Golfers flock to this peninsula for one of America's greatest concentrations of fine courses. Nature lovers can plan excursions to nearby Big Sur or the hot springs at Tassajara. And everyone will enjoy the wonderful shops and galleries for which Carmel is famous. Contact: The San Carlos Agency, Inc., P.O. Box 22123, 26358 Carmel Rancho Lane, Carmel, CA 93922. Call 408-624-3846.

Children: Y Pets: N Smoking: N Handicap Access: N Payment: C, P, T

COOK ADOBE   *Rates: moderate*
Open: year-round   *Minimum Stay: one week*
Situated only a leisurely stroll from the Carmel Bay and the Pacific Ocean, this adorable two-bedroom adobe home sleeps six in charming Carmel fashion. Beautifully appointed with vaulted ceilings, hardwood floors and Oriental area rugs, the house offers the kind of environment

that can make a vacation home more than just a place to sleep. The modern kitchen boasts a floor of Mexican tile and includes a microwave, a dishwasher, a disposal and a cozy eating area. You'll find the village of Carmel lively and stimulating, and the spectacular beauty of Big Sur is just half an hour's drive down scenic Route 1. The popular beaches below Santa Cruz are just an hour away. Contact: The San Carlos Agency, Inc., P.O. Box 22123, 26358 Carmel Rancho Lane, Carmel, CA 93922. Call 408-624-3846.

Children: Y   Pets: N   Smoking: Y   Handicap Access: N   Payment: C, P, T

ERKENBRECHER RETREAT

Rates: moderate
Open: year-round   *Minimum Stay: one week*

No vacation home could better suit a family of nature lovers than this three-bedroom house for seven. Toddlers are easily confined to the fenced yard, but the older kids will want to explore the nearby lagoon and beach, both only a short walk away. This newly refurbished house features new carpeting and hardwood floors, a living room complete with a fireplace and a dining area at the far end. You'll find a color TV in the living room and in the master bedroom. The kitchen has its own separate dining area as well as a dishwasher and microwave. Kids of every age will enjoy the County Fair in August and whale-watching at its best in February. Contact: The San Carlos Agency, Inc., P.O. Box 22123, 26358 Carmel Rancho Lane, Carmel, CA 93922. Call 408-624-3846.

Children: Y   Pets: N   Smoking: Y   Handicap Access: N   Payment: C, P, T

HILL ESTATE

Rates: deluxe
Open: year-round   *Minimum Stay: three nights*

This spacious and elegant one-of-a-kind beachfront home offers new standards of excellence in the finest of furnishings and appointments, plus an unparalleled view of the Pacific. The main level, with four bedrooms and three and a half baths, features huge living and dining rooms with windowed walls displaying the ocean to its best advantage. The gourmet kitchen is equipped with everything from fine crystal to corn-on-the-cob holders. A private guest suite on the lower level boasts a dramatic view of the coast. This home allows full appreciation of the outdoors via a private stairway to the beach. The nearby attractions of Pebble Beach, Cannery Row and the Monterey Bay Aquarium may lure you from this astounding vacation retreat. Contact: PineCone Property Management, 200 Clock Tower Place, Suite D205, Carmel, CA 93923. Call 408-626-8163.

Children: Y   Pets: N   Smoking: N   Handicap Access: N   Payment: C, P, T

KIMMEL CHARMER

Rates: moderate
Open: year-round   *Minimum Stay: one week*

You may note shades of northern California in this older Carmel charmer, a three-bedroom home made of redwood and trimmed in blue. The beautifully furnished two-story home for seven boasts fireplaces in both the living and the dining rooms. The especially gracious living room also provides a relaxing home entertainment center including a TV, a VCR and a stereo; from its French doors you can walk out onto the lovely patio. The modern kitchen features many conveniences including a washer/dryer. With this home as your vacation headquarters you can investigate the delightful town, the fairways of Pebble Beach and the natural splendors of nearby Big Sur and Pinnacles National Monument. Contact: The San Carlos Agency, Inc., P.O. Box 22123, 26358 Carmel Rancho Lane, Carmel, CA 93922. Call 408-624-3846.

Children: Y Pets: N Smoking: N Handicap Access: N Payment: C, P, T

KING OF CARMEL BEACH
Open: year-round

Rates: deluxe
Minimum Stay: one week

This modern home for six sits right on the sands of Carmel Beach—they don't come more scenic than this! You'll find the beach house down a private driveway, then you'll enter through a lovely enclosed patio. The charming foyer features whitewashed Spanish tile and leads to a living room with wall-to-wall oceanview windows. Here, surrounded by elegant but altogether comfortable furnishings, you can watch the sun play on the water or kick your feet up in front of the fireplace and watch a movie on TV. The modern kitchen includes a dishwasher, a disposal and a state-of-the-art Sub-Zero refrigerator. Ambitious cooks can bring home fresh-caught seafood from Fisherman's Wharf in nearby Monterey. Contact: The San Carlos Agency, Inc., P.O. Box 22123, 26358 Carmel Rancho Lane, Carmel, CA 93922. Call 408-624-3846.

Children: Y Pets: N Smoking: Y Handicap Access: N Payment: C, P, T

MCNEILY DUNES
Open: year-round

Rates: inexpensive
Minimum Stay: one week

Light and air will suffuse your stay at this newly built home for six situated just a few blocks from the protected sand dunes of Carmel Bay. Two stories filled with windows, French doors and vaulted ceilings include two bedrooms, a lovely living room, a dining area and a kitchen complete with a microwave, a dishwasher and a disposal. Families will especially appreciate the laundry room with a washer/dryer. You can enjoy the scenic beauty of this spot on the deck that opens off the living room or the furnished patio in the rear of the house. There could be no better place for diving into a novel or finishing a long letter. Contact: The San Carlos Agency, Inc., P.O. Box 22123, 26358 Carmel Rancho Lane, Carmel, CA 93922. Call 408-624-3846.

Children: Y Pets: N Smoking: Y Handicap Access: N Payment: C, P, T

MEYER GUEST COTTAGE
Open: year-round

Rates: budget
Minimum Stay: one week

Homebodies will appreciate the warmth and charm of this one-bedroom Carmel guest cottage. If you like privacy as well as beautiful views, so much the better, because the patio off the living/dining room reveals a beautiful span of the Pacific only a few feet from your door.

Other features of this cozy vacation home for two include a rugged stone wall, dramatic vaulted ceilings and plenty of skylights for days of endless sunshine. You can count waves or sea gulls on sunset walks along Scenic Road or challenge a companion to a game of golf at Pebble Beach. The astounding beauty of Point Lobos is just a short drive away, and when you hunger for a bit of culture, the shops, restaurants and galleries of Carmel and Monterey await you. Contact: The San Carlos Agency, Inc., P.O. Box 22123, 26358 Carmel Rancho Lane, Carmel, CA 93922. Call 408-624-3846.

Children: Y Pets: N Smoking: N Handicap Access: N Payment: C, P, T

MONTEREY TOWN HOUSE

Rates: inexpensive
Open: year-round *Minimum Stay: one week*

Centrally located just minutes from the fine shops, restaurants and art galleries of Monterey, this beautifully decorated split-level home provides vacation accommodations for four. You can leave the car in the carport and walk to the Monterey Bay Aquarium and Cannery Row, or hop in the car for a look at Pinnacles National Monument or San Simeon down the Pacific Coast Highway. At home, the living and dining rooms boast beautiful bay views as well as the comforts of a TV and a stereo. The kitchen features a microwave and a disposal as well as a laundry area with a washer/dryer. You'll sleep in elegant comfort in two master suites. Contact: PineCone Property Management, 200 Clock Tower Place, Suite D205, Carmel, CA 93923. Call 408-626-8163.

Children: Y Pets: N Smoking: N Handicap Access: N Payment: C, P, T

MORTEN'S ON THE BEACH

Rates: deluxe
Open: year-round *Minimum Stay: one week*

This elegant home for six boasts one of the best addresses in the Carmel area—Scenic Drive and 8th Avenue, right on the bay, as close to the sea as you can get. The fabulous living room features a fireplace, a wet bar, a TV, a stereo and a grand piano—as well as fantastic ocean views. Step up into the dining room, which seats six at a warm and inviting natural pine table. From the modern kitchen with a microwave and a dishwasher, you'll step through the sliding glass doors of the breakfast area out onto the lovely patio. Home after an invigorating game of tennis or a hike in the mountains near Tassajara Hot Springs, you can settle back and count gulls or clouds or waves from your windows. Contact: The San Carlos Agency, Inc., P.O. Box 22123, 26358 Carmel Rancho Lane, Carmel, CA 93922. Call 408-624-3846.

Children: Y Pets: N Smoking: Y Handicap Access: N Payment: C, P, T

TOM JOHNSON'S PLACE

Rates: inexpensive
Open: year-round *Minimum Stay: one week*

This dear cottage demonstrates the charm and color for which Carmel is renowned. Newly remodeled and pleasingly secluded, this two-story home offers a twin bedroom on the lower level. Upstairs, you'll find the inviting living room complete with a double hide-a-bed and a Franklin stove. A dining area and a kitchen featuring a microwave and a washer/dryer complete these accommodations for four. A large deck off the living room and kitchen offer incomparable Monterey Peninsula ocean views, bound to lure you from your hideaway to explore this magical place. Filled with excellent shops and galleries as well as some of the best gourmet restaurants on the West Coast, the towns around you are among the most beautiful in all California. Contact: The San Carlos Agency, Inc., P.O. Box 22123, 26358 Carmel Rancho Lane, Carmel, CA 93922. Call 408-624-3846.

Children: Y   Pets: N   Smoking: Y   Handicap Access: N   Payment: C, P, T

YANKEE POINT HOME   *Rates: moderate*
Open: year-round   *Minimum Stay: two nights*

Located in the Carmel Highlands in a choice residential area known as Yankee Point, this brand-new home offers the contemporary beauty of open beams, hardwood floors and extensive glass throughout the house. In this exclusive neighborhood, which features a private beach, towering Monterey pines and sprawling oaks, the two-story home accommodates six and offers both cable TV and laundry facilities. Climb the mountains of the nearby Coastal Range or spend a day at Tassajara Hot Springs. For a special meal, be sure to drive a few minutes south to Rocky Point Restaurant and dine above the water crashing on the rocks below. Contact: Jan Leasure, Monterey Bay Vacation Rentals, P.O. Box EA, Pacific Grove, CA 94950. Call 408-649-8216.

Children: Y Pets: N Smoking: Y Handicap Access: N Payment: C, P, T, V, M

CARMEL-BY-THE-SEA

ARTHUR'S CASTLE   *Rates: budget*
Open: year-round   *Minimum Stay: none*

Located about three blocks from downtown Carmel and nestled on a large oak-studded garden lot, this fairy-tale mini-castle offers the perfect retreat for relaxing and enjoying the gracious Carmel lifestyle. This unique home for two features a "King Arthur" stone fireplace; in the 25-foot domed living room, which also boasts French doors, wide-planked pine floors and leaded stained-glass windows. A master bedroom suite, a large dining room perfect for entertaining and a cozy kitchen with lots of built-ins complete the accommodations. With this lovely spot as a base, golfers, tennis players and lovers of clean air and beautiful scenery can savor the riches of the Monterey Peninsula. Contact: PineCone Property Management, 200 Clock Tower Place, Suite D205, Carmel, CA 93923. Call 408-626-8163.

Children: Y   Pets: N   Smoking: N   Handicap Access: N   Payment: C, P, T

HELENA

THE ELKHORN   *Rates: budget*
Open: year-round   *Minimum Stay: none*

Located in the Trinity River Canyon and surrounded by National Forest high country and rugged wilderness, this hospitality resort contains seven housekeeping cabins. All include kitchens and living areas and offer optional cleaning and laundry service. The cabins range in size from one to four bedrooms with double or queen-sized beds. The Elkhorn staff will be happy to assist in planning a fishing or hunting trip, horseback riding trek or white-water rafting experience. Explore the trails of the Trinity Alps or pan for gold in the nearby rivers, where the forty-niners sought their fortunes over a century ago. Contact: The Elkhorn, Route 299 West, P.O. Box 51, Helena, CA 96042. Call 916-623-6318.

Children: Y   Pets: Y   Smoking: Y   Handicap Access: N   Payment: C, T

LAGUNA BEACH

LAGUNA CONTEMPORARY

Rates: moderate
Open: year-round   *Minimum Stay: one week*

Located on a hillside above the charming little town of Laguna Beach, this beautiful contemporary home offers magnificent views of the Pacific Ocean. Bright and sunny with lots of windows, the house sleeps eight in four bedrooms. Its large living room features a fireplace; a dramatic terrace and an ultramodern kitchen complete the layout. In the village below, where many artists make their home, you'll find excellent shops, restaurants and galleries. Excursions throughout southern California offer such exciting destinations as Disneyland, Knott's Berry Farm and Universal Studios. The ferry to Santa Catalina Island leaves from nearby Newport Beach, and the swimming, surfing and people-watching at nearby beaches are among the best on the whole coast. Contact: Rent A Home International, 7200 34th Avenue N.W., Seattle, WA 98117. Call 206-545-6963.

Children: Y   Pets: N   Smoking: N   Handicap Access: N   Payment: C, P, V, M

LEWISTON

CEDAR STOCK CABINS

Rates: budget-inexpensive
Open: year-round   *Minimum Stay: none*

Located at the Cedar Stock Resort and Marina, these cabins offer access to the crystal-clear fishing waters of Trinity Lake, as well as the hiking and riding trails of the Trinity Alps. The cabins sleep from four to six guests, usually in double or queen-sized bedrooms, and have kitchenettes or full kitchens. Guests should bring linens with them and are invited to use the barbecue facilities. The marina rents fishing boats, canoes, jet skis, water skis and other equipment. Horseback riding, gold panning and hiking are among the activities offered in the mountains; in winter, try cross-country skiing and snowmobiling. The resort restaurant has a varied menu for the evenings you prefer not to cook at home. Contact: Cedar Stock Resort and Marina, Star Route, P.O. Box 510, Lewiston, CA 96052-9608. Call 916-286-2225.

Children: Y   Pets: Y   Smoking: Y   Handicap Access: N   Payment: C, T, V, M

CEDAR STOCK HOUSEBOATS

Rates: budget-expensive
Open: year-round   *Minimum Stay: none*

The calm waters of 20-mile-long Trinity Lake make a perfect setting for a houseboat vacation. You'll be impressed with the uncrowded serenity of this area, which has 157 miles of shoreline and quiet, tree-lined coves offering excellent fishing. The houseboats rented out by Cedar Stock Resort can sleep from six to ten guests and range from the Admiral, at 35 feet, to the deluxe 55-foot Mastercraft. The only thing you need to bring are linens—gas, life jackets, a barbecue, kitchen utensils and appliances, hot and cold water, showers and even a tape deck are all provided. The deluxe styles are equipped with a generator, air conditioning, microwave and blender, as well as 110-volt plugs for appliances. The sleeping accommodations are either bunk beds or double berths. Contact: Cedar Stock Resort and Marina, Star Route, P.O. Box 510, Lewiston, CA 96052-9608. Call 916-286-2225.

Children: Y Pets: Y Smoking: Y Handicap Access: N Payment: C, T, V, M

ESTRELLITA RESORT   *Rates: moderate-expensive*
Open: year-round   *Minimum Stay: none*

Three houseboats are available for rent here, for a unique vacation experience on Lake Trinity. After instruction, your boat is all yours, to take around the secluded coves and calm waters of this 20-mile-long lake known for its good fishing and boating opportunities. The 42-foot President sleeps eight; a 47-footer sleeps ten; the 50-foot-long vessel sleeps twelve. All houseboats come with a kitchen equipped with stove, oven, fridge, double sink and room to prepare on-board meals. Guests also enjoy hot and cold pressurized water, a cassette player and a railed outside walkway with plenty of room for lounging. You'll need to bring your own blankets and linens; a full tank of fuel will be supplied at the start of your trip. An on-board barbecue makes a perfect summer evening even better when you cook up the day's catch. Contact: Estrellita Resort, Star Route, Box 542, Lewiston, CA 96052. Call 916-286-2215.

Children: Y Pets: N Smoking: Y Handicap Access: N Payment: C, T

LAKEVIEW TERRACE CABINS   *Rates: budget*
Open: year-round   *Minimum Stay: none*

No exaggerating, this is an outdoorsman's dream: Directly in front of this cabin and RV resort shimmers Lewiston Lake, a mountain gem offering rainbow, brown and kokanee trout that you can catch from a boat or right from the shore. Trinity Lake, Lewiston's upstream neighbor, provides great waterskiing, boating and a shot at the great salmon and steelhead for which the lake is famous. The high-country angler can enjoy the nearby Trinity Alps, with its tumbling streams and granite-bound lakes. And the hunting is as great as the fishing. Come home at night to a comfortable and cozy one- to four-bedroom cabin complete with a living room, dining room and kitchen. Just outside your door, beneath the whispering pines, you'll find a barbecue and a picnic table. Contact: Herb Vanderwall, Lakeview Terrace Resort, Star Rt., Box 250, Lewiston, CA 96052. Call 916-778-3803.

Children: Y Pets: Y Smoking: Y Handicap Access: N Payment: C

STEELHEAD COTTAGES   *Rates: budget*
Open: year-round   *Minimum Stay: none*

Located at Big Flat in the heart of Trinity County, these comfortably furnished and spotlessly clean cottages with kitchenettes, satellite

TVs and VCRs afford an ideal setting for a memorable fishing holiday. Midway between Eureka and Redding, the cabins under the pines feature wonderful fishermen's pluses such as a fish smoker, a lighted fish-cleaning area and picnic tables. Of course, Trinity River fishing for salmon, steelhead and trout is right on the property. Nearby recreation offers the riches of northern California, ideal for hunting, swimming, hiking—even gold panning. And excursions to the Lake Shasta Caverns and the Hoopa Valley Indian Reservation make for a nice change of pace. Contact: Mary and Terry Auten, Steelhead Cottages, P.O. Box 570, Big Bar, CA 96010. Call 916-623-6325.

Children: YPets: Y   Smoking: Y   Handicap Access: N   Payment: C, T

TRINITY ALPS RESORT   *Rates: budget*
Open: year-round   *Minimum Stay: one week*

Since the 1920s, this resort has provided seclusion and comfort to visitors in a rustic setting in the mountains. Forty housekeeping cabins are nestled in the trees along a mile-long stretch of the Stuart Fork River, one of California's finest wild rivers. Each cabin has a sleeping veranda overlooking the rushing water, one or two bedrooms and bathrooms and a little kitchen with an icebox and stove. A general store stocks necessities and provides sporting equipment free of charge to guests; there is a dining room and large patio, where umbrella-shaded tables look out over the scenic river. Horseback riding, fishing, swimming, tennis, horseshoes and tubing are just some of the activities offered at the resort. The community center has square dancing, singalongs, movies and bingo for sociable evenings. Contact: Morgan and Nadine Langan, Trinity Alps Resort, Star Route, Box 490, Lewiston, CA 96052. Call 916-286-2205.

Children: Y   Pets: N   Smoking: Y   Handicap Access: N   Payment: C, T

MAMMOTH LAKES

ASPEN CREEK   *Rates: inexpensive-deluxe*
Open: year-round   *Minimum Stay: two nights*

The High Eastern Sierra rise dramatically behind these handsome apartments, which sleep two to eight in apartments ranging in size from one to three bedrooms. Guests at these luxury condominiums situated a short walk from chairlifts 15 and 24 share underground parking, a heated swimming pool and a sauna. Each apartment includes a full kitchen and a living room with a TV and VCR. Summer vacations take shape beautifully here with an endless assortment of activities—gondola rides to the 11,000-foot peak, mountain bike tours, fly fishing and hot-air ballooning. Tennis and waterskiing tournaments in August and the Old West Days of July are special attractions. Contact: Mammoth Properties, P.O. Box 408, Mammoth Lakes, CA 93546. Call 1-800-227-SNOW.

Children: Y   Pets: N   Smoking:Y   Handicap Access: N   Payment:C, P, T, V, M, A

SIERRA MEGEVE   *Rates: expensive-deluxe*
Open: year-round   *Minimum Stay: two nights*

Modern and convenient, these two- and three-bedroom condominium apartments provide a wonderful location for a vacation in a beautiful valley in the magnificent Eastern High Sierra. Accommodations for four to eight include a full kitchen and a living room with a TV and VCR. You'll be welcomed home from a day on the slopes—Warming Hut II and the chairlifts are right next door—by the sauna and the heated pool. If skiing is not your thing, you might prefer a rugged ride in a dog sled or a romantic sleigh ride under the stars. And if you decide you're ready for an assault on the mountain after all, the area provides excellent ski schooling for every level. Contact: Mammoth Properties, P.O. Box 408, Mammoth Lakes, CA 93546. Call 1-800-227-SNOW.

Children: Y Pets: N Smoking: Y Handicap Access: N Payment: C, P, T, V, M, A

TYROLEAN VILLAGE   *Rates: inexpensive-moderate*
Open: year-round   *Minimum Stay: two nights*

Ideal for a mixed group of snow bunnies and hot-doggers, these two- and three-bedroom units offer a perfect spot for a whirlwind vacation in the Eastern High Sierra. Equipped with kitchens, TVs and VCRs, the generously windowed rentals provide you with the basics, and Mammoth Lakes does the rest. You can park the kids at the terrific day-care facility or sign them up for ski lessons, and then you're off for a day of powder and sun. Or take the whole family snowmobiling and cross-country skiing. Mammoth's nightlife runs the gamut from cool jazz clubs to high energy rock and roll. You're bound to find the right pizza parlor or romantic firelit lounge to make your vacation complete. Contact: Mammoth Properties, P.O. Box 408, Mammoth Lakes, CA 93546. Call 1-800-227-SNOW.

Children: Y Pets: N Smoking: Y Handicap Access: N Payment: C, P, T, V, M, A

NEWPORT BEACH

BEACH HOUSE   *Rates: expensive*
Open: September 15-June 15   *Minimum Stay: none*

This spacious beachfront home offers many amenities and conveniences, but none can compare with the ground-level terrace and the upper-level balcony, both of which offer uninterrupted views of the tireless ocean and the sunset. Even from the inside of the house, the entirely windowed seaward side makes the ocean waves a part of every hour, day and night. Decorated in rattan and lacquer, the house accommodates twelve in four bedrooms and four baths. It also includes a living room with two fireplaces, cable TV, a stereo and a fabulous kitchen with a dishwasher, washer/dryer and icemaker. If you tire of the sound of the waves pounding the shore, you can wander over to the nearby golf courses and play a game. Contact: Rent A Home International, 7200 34th Avenue N.W., Seattle, WA 98117. Call 206-545-6963.

Children: Y Pets: N Smoking: N Handicap Access: N Payment: C, P, V, M

FAMILY VACATION HOUSE *Rates: expensive-deluxe*
Open: year-round *Minimum Stay: none*
Just 60 miles south of Los Angeles is where you'll find this spacious tri-level vacation home. Nestled against the ocean cliffs on a private road just steps from the white sandy beach, the house boasts many windows as well as a terrace and a balcony from which to enjoy views of the ocean and the beautiful surrounding cliffs. Accommodations for nine include a high-ceilinged living room with a handsome contemporary fireplace, four bedrooms, two and a half baths, a terrific kitchen with service for twelve and a microwave, a TV room and a laundry room. You can spend your afternoon counting waves or surfers, or exploring the desert to the east, where the elegant resort of Palm Springs displays southern California living at its most extravagant. Contact: Rent A Home International, 7200 34th Avenue N.W., Seattle, WA 98117. Call 206-545-6963.
Children: Y Pets: N Smoking: N Handicap Access: N Payment: C, P, V, M

PACIFIC GROVE

COURTNEY SEASCAPE *Rates: inexpensive*
Open: year-round *Minimum Stay: one week*
Located on the north end of the Monterey Peninsula only a short walk from Monterey Bay, this sunny two-bedroom home for seven overlooks a beautiful park as well as the Pacific Ocean. The large living room with hardwood floors and an inviting fireplace has two TVs and two VCRs, offering the perfect chance to catch up on all the movies you've missed. The kitchen features a microwave for between-tape snacks, as well as a washer/dryer. The rest of the family can investigate nearby attractions like historic and colorful Cannery Row and the Monterey Bay Aquarium. For that special kind of rest and relaxation, you can also plan excursions to the hot springs north and south of the peninsula. Contact: The San Carlos Agency, Inc., P.O. Box 22123, 26358 Carmel Rancho Lane, Carmel, CA 93922. Call 408-624-3846.
Children: Y Pets: N Smoking: N Handicap Access: N Payment: C, P, T

LOWIS CONDO *Rates: budget*
Open: year-round *Minimum Stay: one week*
Located in the lively and charming Monterey Peninsula town of Pacific Grove, this two-bedroom, two-bath condominium sleeps six. The brand-new furnishings provide comfort in the living room before the fireplace, elegance in the formal dining room. Conveniences such as a dishwasher and washer/dryer make a vacation here hassle-free, leaving more time for the thorough investigation of Monterey you desire. You can take your pick of several area golf courses, including prestigious Pebble Beach. Sunbathers and surf riders will be sure to find a beach to call their own. Famous for fine arts and crafts, the area boasts many excellent galleries and shops. Contact: The San Carlos Agency, Inc., P.O. Box 22123, 26358 Carmel Rancho Lane, Carmel, CA 93922. Call 408-624-3846.
Children: Y Pets: N Smoking: Y Handicap Access: N Payment: C, P, T

PACIFIC GROVE VICTORIAN　　　　　　　　　　*Rates: inexpensive*
Open: year-round　　　　　　　　　　　*Minimum Stay: two nights*
Half a block from the ocean and a scenic bicycling/walking trail, this restored Victorian home combines old-world charm with modern convenience. The 100-year-old house for six includes three bedrooms as well as amenities like a fireplace, cable TV and a VCR. You have the use of bicycles for rides to the aquarium or along the beautiful trail that runs from Pacific Grove to Seaside. Other nearby attractions include Fisherman's Wharf and Cannery Row. Seasonal events, like the Great Monterey Squid Festival in May and the California Wine Festival in December, abound. Contact: Jan Leasure, Monterey Bay Vacation Rentals, P.O. Box EA, Pacific Grove, CA 94950. Call 408-649-8216.
Children: Y Pets: N Smoking: Y Handicap Access: N Payment: C, P, T, V, M

PEBBLE BEACH

PEBBLE BEACH HOUSE　　　　　　　　　　　*Rates: deluxe*
Open: year-round　　　　　　　　　　　*Minimum Stay: two nights*
Look around you: Carmel Bay sparkles from dawn to dusk, with Point Lobos jutting out into the Pacific Ocean beyond. Later, a blanket of fog creeps in, settling on the ridge where this extraordinary house is perched. Watch the miraculous changes of sky and weather from one of this home's many decks—or enjoy the hot tub on the deck off the master bedroom suite. The exquisitely appointed house features huge windows, a floor-to-ceiling fireplace in the living room, a formal dining room and a family room with a wet bar. Savor breathtaking views of the ocean amid creatively landscaped seclusion. Contact: Jan Leasure, Monterey Bay Vacation Rentals, P.O. Box EA, Pacific Grove, CA 94950. Call 408-649-8216.
Children: Y Pets: N Smoking: Y Handicap Access: N Payment: C, P, T, V, M

POKKA ESTATE　　　　　　　　　　　　*Rates: expensive*
Open: year-round　　　　　　　　　　　*Minimum Stay: one week*
Golf lovers have dreamed of such things, and now they and their families can step into that dream, a gorgeous split-level home located on the second fairway of the Pebble Beach Golf Links. With ocean views from nearly every window and beautiful Oriental decorations, this three-bedroom, three-bath home offers one of the area's loveliest vacation opportunities. Accommodations for six include a living room, formal dining room, breakfast room and family room, all with floor-to-ceiling windows. The living and family rooms also feature fireplaces. From here, it's only a short walk to the beach and tennis club as well as to the very elegant Pebble Beach Lodge. Excursions to Big Sur and Tassajara Hot Springs offer a change of pace. Contact: Pine-Cone Property Management, 200 Clock Tower Place, Suite D205, Carmel, CA 93923. Call 408-626-8163.
Children: Y Pets: N Smoking: N Handicap Access: N Payment: C, P, T

PIERCY

HARTSOOK INN *Rates: deluxe*
Open: April-October *Minimum Stay: none*

Located amid 30 acres of awe-inspiring giant redwoods, this family inn offers sunbathing, swimming and fishing right in the Eel River. Take some time just to sit beneath the lacy branches of these mammoth, centuries-old trees and soak up the spiritual wonder they impart. Comfortable accommodations for two to twelve in several cottages offer unique surroundings with access to the spacious lounge and main dining room of the inn. Excursions along the scenic Pacific Coast Highway to many beautiful state parks and beaches afford dramatic ocean views. Contact: Hartsook Inn, Piercy, CA 95467. Call 707-247-3305.

Children: Y Pets: N Smoking: N Handicap Access: N Payment: C, M, O

SAN DIEGO

CAPRI BY THE SEA *Rates: budget-deluxe*
Open: year-round *Minimum Stay: three nights*

Each and every one of these one- to three-bedroom and penthouse apartments in San Diego's only oceanfront high-rise condominium offers a spectacular panoramic ocean view. Excellent building amenities include 24-hour security, a large swimming pool, a sauna, a California-style spa and roof decks with barbecues. If you're looking for a spot from which to explore the great wealth of amusements and natural beauty of the San Diego area, you really can't beat this Pacific Beach/La Jolla location. The San Diego Zoo and Balboa Park offers not only a chance to visit with some exotic friends, but also excellent regional theater, museums and guided tours. Sea World is visible from the Capri roof deck, and Mexico lies only 15 miles to the south. Contact: Capri by the Sea Rental Management, P.O. Box 99964, San Diego, CA 92109. Call 1-800-248-5262 (in California, 619-483-6110).

Children: Y Pets: N Smoking: Y Handicap Access: Y Payment: C, P, V, M

DEVON COURT *Rates: inexpensive*
Open: year-round *Minimum Stay: four nights*

Just a scant two blocks from the ocean, this two-story home in the heart of San Diego's Mission Bay district offers generous accommodations for eight. Its 1,500 square feet feature three bedrooms, three baths and kitchen amenities such as a dishwasher, washer/dryer and microwave, plus parking for two cars. Gentle sea breezes will caress you as you sit on the patio or balcony, and barbecue lovers can plan great meals of fresh Pacific Ocean fish available at nearby markets. Of course, you may want to catch your own, and San Diego is a great spot from which to go deep-sea fishing. Tamer activities in this area include visits to the San Diego Zoo in Balboa Park and golf at one of the many fine local courses. Contact: Cairncross Management, Inc., 2990 Mission Blvd., San Diego, CA 92109. Call 619-488-8312.

Children: Y Pets: N Smoking: Y Handicap Access: Y Payment: C, T

FINEST VIEW *Rates: moderate-deluxe*
Open: year-round *Minimum Stay: one week*
For a week or two in San Diego, you can have it all. This immense three-bedroom rental features three decks, including a truly huge roof deck with a barbecue and a Jacuzzi. From here you can enjoy a panorama of yachting, water sports and marine life. Beautifully furnished and architecturally inspired, this home provides the perfect spot from which to explore other indulgences, such as an afternoon at one of the area's fine health spas, a round at the gorgeous La Jolla golf course or lunch and shopping in that beautiful and elegant seaside town. Contact: San Diego Vacation Rentals, 2515 Camino del Rio S., Suite 204, San Diego, CA 92108. Call 1-800-222-8218 (in California, 619-296-1000). Ref. #26.
Children: Y Pets: N Smoking: Y Handicap Access: N Payment: C, P, T, V, M

HOLIDAY HOME *Rates: expensive*
Open: year-round *Minimum Stay: three nights*
For a holiday in the San Diego area, this handsome home situated on the Point Loma Peninsula offers an ideal spot for relaxing as well as exploring. Located only four blocks from a popular surfing beach in a quiet residential neighborhood, you'll also find Shelter Island, home of the Americas Cup, a scant five minutes away. The tastefully furnished home sleeps six and features a 75-foot deck with gorgeous ocean views. Amenities include a wet bar, a fireplace, cable TV, a washer/dryer and a microwave. Families of every size and age will enjoy a trip to nearby Sea World; the golfing at the La Jolla course just a few miles north is among the best in Southern California. Contact: Rent A Home International, 7200 34th Avenue N.W., Seattle, WA 98117. Call 206-545-6963.
Children: Y Pets: N Smoking: N Handicap Access: N Payment: C, P, V, M

INTIMATE DREAM *Rates: moderate-expensive*
Open: year-round *Minimum Stay: one week*
This lovely two-bedroom apartment stands close enough to the ocean to fill your days with spectacular views of the Pacific from your balcony and your nights with the sound of the waves to put you to sleep. The fantastic master suite has a large tub and cozy fireplace right in the bedroom. The living room boasts a fireplace too, along with a wall of sliding glass doors opening onto the balcony. A dining area and kitchen with dishwasher, microwave and washer/dryer complete these accommodations for four. When you tire of sunbathing and sunset-watching, you'll be happily located only minutes away from fishing piers, Balboa Park and the world-famous San Diego Zoo. Contact: San Diego Vacation Rentals, 2515 Camino del Rio S., Suite 204, San Diego, CA 92108. Call 1-800-222-8218 (in California, 619-296-1000). Ref. #6.
Children: Y Pets: N Smoking: Y Handicap Access: N Payment: C, P, T, V, M

LUDLOW APARTMENTS
Rates: budget-inexpensive
Open: year-round
Minimum Stay: three nights

Recently remodeled, these apartments are located on Mission Bay, right on the beach. With a choice of one or two bedrooms, as well as queen-sized fold-out couches, the apartments can comfortably house up to six guests. Each apartment contains a cable TV, linens and all dishes, and the kitchen is equipped with such extras as a toaster, a blender, a dishwasher and a garbage disposal. Maid service is provided for a worry-free vacation. The oceanfront apartments have a large second-floor balcony and a downstairs patio furnished with a shaded picnic table and chairs. Swimming, sailing, waterskiing and wind surfing are the activities of choice in sunny, warm San Diego, whose many attractions are within easy reach of these apartments. Contact: Carl Ludlow, 2445 Morena Blvd., Suite 100, San Diego, CA 92109. Call 619-488-4654.

Children: Y Pets: Y Smoking: Y Handicap Access: N Payment: C, P, T, O

MONTEREY MANOR
Rates: inexpensive-deluxe
Open: year-round
Minimum Stay: one week

With San Juan Bay just outside your door and the beautiful beaches of San Diego's Mission district only minutes away, this spacious three-bedroom townhouse provides accommodations for six and double-garage parking. The beautifully furnished and bright interior features several skylights, and the gracious dining room enjoys a mirrored wall, greatly enhancing the natural illumination. Amenities like a private furnished balcony ideal for outdoor dining and a living room fireplace make this home especially attractive. Household conveniences like a dishwasher, a microwave and a washer/dryer make this a real home away from home. Spend your days right in the Mission district or go exploring, north to San Clemente and Disneyland or south to Tijuana. Contact: San Diego Vacation Rentals, 2515 Camino del Rio S., Suite 204, San Diego, CA 92108. Call 1-800-222-8218 (in California, 619-296-1000). Ref. #11.

Children: Y Pets: N Smoking: Y Handicap Access: N Payment: C, P, T, V, M

OCEAN FRONT WALK
Rates: moderate
Open: year-round
Minimum Stay: four nights

Somehow, the address says it all—Ocean Front Walk. It seems vacationers never tire of the sea, and here its sound and smell is all around you. This two-bedroom second-floor apartment accommodates six in 1,200 square feet of modern grace and convenience. Amenities include cable TV, a barbecue, a patio, a balcony and garage parking for two cars. The Mission Bay district of San Diego provides a great point from which to immerse yourself in ocean adventures such as harbor cruises and whale-watching excursions. You can make your vacation an international one with a quick drive south to Mexico, where colorful Tijuana offers terrific shopping and bull fights. Contact: Cairncross Management, Inc., 2990 Mission Blvd., San Diego, CA 92109. Call 619-488-8312.

Children: Y Pets: N Smoking: Y Handicap Access: Y Payment: C, T

OCEANFRONT HACIENDA

Rates: moderate-deluxe
Open: year-round *Minimum Stay: one week*

You'll find this white stucco two-story home for ten in San Diego's beautiful Mission Bay district, loaded with amenities for both indoor and outdoor living. Four furnished decks—main, barbecue, hot tub and roof—offer fabulous views of the ocean. The handsomely appointed interior features a second hot tub, a firepit and a fountain, as well as gorgeous stained-glass windows. Other amenities, such as cable TV, a washer/dryer and an outdoor shower, assure you the luxurious vacation of which you've dreamed. Bicycles are available for rides around the Mission area—Sea World's just a few minutes away. Guests are bound to enjoy access to the private swim and tennis club and the fine restaurants this exquisite beach resort offers. Contact: San Diego Vacation Rentals, 2515 Camino del Rio S., Suite 204, San Diego, CA 92108. Call 1-800-222-8218 (in California, 619-296-1000). Ref. 1.

Children: Y Pets: N Smoking: Y Handicap Access: N Payment: C, P, T, V, M

ROCKAWAY

Rates: inexpensive
Open: year-round *Minimum Stay: four nights*

Situated within hearing distance of the magnificent Mission Bay beaches, you'll find this trilevel home equally convenient to both the Mission Bay Recreation Center and the Sail Boat Yacht Club. Accommodations for eight include three bedrooms and three bathrooms offering spacious relaxation. Equipped with those must-have conveniences such as a TV, a barbecue, a washer/dryer and a microwave, this house also features both a patio and a balcony. From here, you can investigate the life of this southernmost of California's beautiful cities. Days spent surfing or surf-watching or exploring the desert dotted with American Indian reservations are bound to satisfy everyone. Contact: Cairncross Management, Inc., 2990 Mission Blvd., San Diego, CA 92109. Call 619-488-8312.

Children: Y Pets: N Smoking: Y Handicap Access: Y Payment: C, T

THE BEACH COTTAGES

Rates: budget-inexpensive
Open: winter and spring *Minimum Stay: none*

Just steps from the sandy beach and ocean and within walking distance of shops, restaurants and grocery stores, the Beach Cottages consist of five one-bedroom and two two-bedroom units. The cottages are modern and decorated with cheerful bedspreads, carpets and curtains. Their modern kitchens have all the dishes and cooking supplies you'll need. Phones and color TVs have been placed in the rooms; Ping-Pong, shuffleboard and barbecues are located on the premises. Sunbathing, swimming, surfing and sailing are all popular on the oceanfront, and the many sights of San Diego are within easy reach—including Sea World, the San Diego Zoo and Old Town. Contact: The Beach Cottages, 4255 Ocean Boulevard, San Diego, CA 92109-3995. Call 619-483-7440.

Children: Y Pets: N Smoking: Y Handicap Access: N Payment: C, T, V, M, A, O

THE PENTHOUSE *Rates: moderate-deluxe*
Open: year-round *Minimum Stay: one week*

The spectacular water view from the windowed living and dining room walls of this three-bedroom unit brings you as close to the sea as you can get. Tastefully decorated and filled with those essential extras like a Jacuzzi and skylights, the house also features a fabulous deck with nonstop ocean views. Charming freestanding fireplaces enhance both the living room and the master bedroom, and decorative touches like a tiled kitchen and lush houseplants make this home more inviting still. Sports lovers may want to get tickets to a Padres game or a UCSD basketball game. Golf is at its best here, with the La Jolla and Sam Snead courses both just a short drive away. Contact: San Diego Vacation Rentals, 2515 Camino del Rio S., Suite 204, San Diego, CA 92108. Call 1-800-222-8218 (in California, 619-296-1000). Ref. #18.

Children: Y Pets: N Smoking: Y Handicap Access: N Payment: C, P, T, V, M

SAN FRANCISCO

LA GALLERIA *Rates: inexpensive-moderate*
Open: year-round *Minimum Stay: three nights*

A condominium building providing accommodations for business travelers and families, La Galleria has both one- and two-bedroom units. Tastefully decorated and situated downtown in San Francisco, the building features around-the-clock security and free parking. Each apartment's living room offers a cable TV and a comfortable couch, while the kitchen has a microwave oven and all utensils. Cleaning is done weekly. The building offers a spa with pool and sauna, plus an exercise room so you can work out or unwind after a day of climbing San Francisco's hills. There is a restaurant in the building, and a complimentary bottle of wine and goodies greet your arrival. Contact: The Hotel Alternative, 1125 E. Hillsdale Blvd., Suite 105, Foster City, CA 94404-1674. Call 415-578-1366 or 408-749-8911.

Children: Y Pets: Y Smoking: Y Handicap Access: N Payment: C, P, T, V, M, A

ST. FRANCIS PLACE *Rates: inexpensive-moderate*
Open: year-round *Minimum Stay: three nights*

One- and two-bedroom contemporary condominiums can be found here in downtown San Francisco, not far from Fisherman's Wharf, Chinatown and all the legendary sights of this well-loved city. Offering a high level of convenience, these units have a full kitchen with dishwasher, cable TV, twenty-four hour security and nearby parking. A deli market and a health club on the premises mean you needn't go far to find the creature comforts you seek. Rooms are cleaned weekly, and there are laundry facilities in the building, as well as a dry cleaner. Contact: The Hotel Alternative, 1125 E. Hillsdale Blvd., Suite 105, Foster City, CA 94404-1674. Call 415-578-1366 or 408-749-8911.

Children: Y Pets: Y Smoking: Y Handicap Access: N Payment: C, P, T, V, M, A

SANTA CLARA

LOS PADRES VILLAGE   *Rates: budget-inexpensive*
Open: year-round   *Minimum Stay: three nights*

Once a Spanish mission, Santa Clara is in the South Bay area near San Francisco. The old mission grounds, gardens and sights of the town fascinate visitors with a historical bent. Los Padres, a modern condominium complex, puts you near the San Tomas Expressway for easy access to the region's attractions. The units come complete with an excellent kitchen (including all appliances, disposal, dishwasher, iron and ironing board), living room with cable TV and free HBO and either one or two bedrooms, according to your needs. The rooms are cleaned weekly, and there is free parking as well as laundry facilities on the premises. A swimming pool, spa, tanning salon and exercise room all help make your stay more enjoyable. Contact: The Hotel Alternative, 1125 E. Hillsdale Blvd., Suite 105, Foster City, CA 94404-1674. Call 415-578-1366 or 408-749-8911.

Children: Y Pets: Y Smoking: Y Handicap Access: N Payment: C, P, T, V, M, A

SANTA CRUZ

VILLA VISTA   *Rates: expensive*
Open: year-round   *Minimum Stay: one week*

Situated right on the beach of California's dramatic coastline, this duplex home offers two separate accommodations with three bedrooms and three bathrooms each, an ideal arrangement for a large family or a group of friends. The gourmet kitchens offer food processors, trash compactors, coffee grinders—and many more appliances—as well as a separate dining area and patio. Each apartment features a wood-burning fireplace, a TV and VCR with several tapes, a stereo with a CD player and discs, and books and board games for whiling away the hours while the surf pounds outside your door. Your waterfront home affords a sweeping ocean panorama where surfers, sailboats and sunsets parade before you daily. Contact: Vacation Home Rentals Worldwide, 235 Kensington Avenue, Norwood, NJ 07648. Call 1-800-633-3284. Ref. CA105

Children: Y Pets: Y Smoking: Y Handicap Access: N Payment: C, P, T

SANTA MONICA

BEACH APARTMENT   *Rates: inexpensive*
Open: year-round   *Minimum Stay: one week*

Ideally located ten minutes from the fascinating Los Angeles neighborhoods of Beverly Hills, Venice, Pacific Palisades and Malibu, this cozy two-bedroom apartment in the very heart of Santa Monica lays all of L.A. at your feet. Situated just one block east of the bluffs above Santa Monica Bay and its beach and pier, the second-floor apartment sleeps four and includes a full kitchen and dining area. You'll find laundry facilities right in the building, plus convenient parking. A short walk takes you to the lively shopping, restaurants, movies and entertainment of one of southern California's richly historic cities. Contact: Rent A Home International, 7200 34th Avenue N.W., Seattle, WA 98117. Call 206-545-6963.

Children: Y Pets: N Smoking: N Handicap Access: N Payment: C, P, V, M

SOUTH LAKE TAHOE

EL DORADO *Rates: inexpensive*
Open: year-round *Minimum Stay: four nights*

This darling A-frame offers the particular pleasure of a vacation among the serene woods of the Eldorado National Forest. You can make this one-bedroom hideaway a lover's retreat or bring the family—the loft features one king-sized and one trundle bed. Savor the breathtaking wonder of the hot tub on the secluded outside deck, move indoors to enjoy the color cable TV, with a VCR and two free rental movies each night. Other conveniences include a microwave, a washer/dryer, a barbecue and a carport. The worldly pleasures of great casinos, shops and restaurants are all within a short drive, as are the wilds of the Sierra Nevada and some of California's best alpine skiing. Contact: M & M Property Management & Rentals, 2301 Highway #50, South Lake Tahoe, CA 95731. Call 916-542-2777 (in California, 1-800-542-2100). Ref. 1589.

Children: Y Pets: N Smoking: Y Handicap Access: Y Payment: C, P, T

FAMILY TIME *Rates: inexpensive-moderate*
Open: year-round *Minimum Stay: four nights*

Especially well suited for the vacationing family, this residence offers a smoke-free environment, an ideal home base for a holiday in the beautiful countryside surrounding Lake Tahoe. Its three bedrooms accommodate up to eight in comfort and convenience. Features such as a color cable TV, a well-equipped kitchen with microwave and a living room with a charming wood-burning fireplace ensure the kind of R & R you need. Outdoor living is enhanced by a barbecue and plenty of lawn furniture—there's even a playpen for the toddlers. Short excursions take you to many nearby state parks, and for those who like riskier fun, the casinos await. Contact: M & M Property Management & Rentals, 2301 Highway #50, South Lake Tahoe, CA 95731. Call 916-542-2777 (in California, 1-800-542-2100). Ref. 2687.

Children: Y Pets: N Smoking: N Handicap Access: Y Payment: C, P, T

HEAVENLY VICTORIAN *Rates: expensive*
Open: year-round *Minimum Stay: four nights*

All this and heaven too—that's exactly how you might feel about a vacation in this extraordinary three-bedroom Victorian. This delightfully designed residence includes tasteful furnishings and attractive features such as a Jacuzzi in each of the two baths, plus two fireplaces—one in the master suite. A washer/dryer, a fenced yard with a lovely gazebo and a garage provide the extra comfort a vacationing family enjoys. Now imagine all this only a short walk from the Heavenly Valley Tram and some of the area's finest gourmet restaurants, and your dream vacation just might take shape. Contact: M & M Property Management & Rentals, 2301 Highway #50, South Lake Tahoe, CA 95731. Call 916-542-2777 (in California, 1-800-542-2100). Ref. 3837.

Children: Y   Pets: N   Smoking: N   Handicap Access: Y   Payment: C, P, T

LAKE VIEW — *Rates: moderate*
Open: year-round — *Minimum Stay: four nights*
Virtually every room in this four-bedroom home boasts panoramic lake views. Situated very close to the great skiing at Heavenly Valley, the house offers the convenience of a color cable TV as well as a washer/dryer. Two wood-burning stoves and a wet bar make it especially comfortable and inviting. High in the mountains between Twin Bridges and Vade, you'll find an entrance to the Pacific Crest National Scenic Trail, which energetic high-country trekkers can take south to Yosemite National Park. Less ambitious vacationers might be content to go for a swim in the lake or hike to the nearest casino. Contact: M & M Property Management & Rentals, 2301 Highway #50, South Lake Tahoe, CA 95731. Call 916-542-2777 (in California, 1-800-542-2100). Ref. 4216.

Children: Y   Pets: N   Smoking: Y   Handicap Access: Y   Payment: C, P, T

MONDO TAHOE — *Rates: moderate*
Open: year-round — *Minimum Stay: four nights*
Ideally located close to skiing at Heavenly Valley, the glittering and glamorous casinos, the beach and the recreation complex, this large house provides a great vacation home for a large family or group of friends who cannot leave their beloved cat or dog at home. Accommodations for ten include three bedrooms plus a spacious sleeping loft and two baths. Features such as a color cable TV with a VCR, a wood stove, a microwave and a two-car garage endow this home with all the comforts that make a vacation genuinely restful. You're bound to enjoy the luxury of your own hot tub: What better way to wind down from a strenuous day of tennis or waterskiing in July or a weekend on the slopes in January? Contact: M & M Property Management & Rentals, 2301 Highway #50, South Lake Tahoe, CA 95731. Call 916-542-2777 (in California, 1-800-542-2100). Ref. 1184.

Children: Y   Pets: Y   Smoking: Y   Handicap Access: Y   Payment: C, P, T

PINE HAVEN — *Rates: moderate*
Open: year-round — *Minimum Stay: four nights*
Located right off Pioneer in Montgomery Estates, this remarkably spacious home for twelve backs onto the Eldorado National Forest. From its decks, you can enjoy the natural splendor of Tahoe's sky-reaching pines and a sky as lofty as the heart can conceive. Accommodations include four bedrooms, a living room with a hide-a-bed and a charming fireplace, a kitchen with a washer/dryer and a family room with a wood stove. All the worldly delights of the town of South Lake Tahoe are only a few steps away and the seemingly endless world of sporting and nature activities—boating, hiking, golf, tennis, snowshoeing, wa-

terskiing and more—are yours for the asking. Contact: M & M Property Management & Rentals, 2301 Highway #50, South Lake Tahoe, CA 95731. Call 916-542-2777 (in California, 1-800-542-2100). Ref. 2248.

Children: **Y**   Pets: **N**   Smoking: **Y**   Handicap Access: **Y**   Payment: **C, P, T**

ROMANTIQUE   *Rates: budget-inexpensive*
Open: year-round   *Minimum Stay: four nights*

The privacy of this romantic hideaway makes this charming and delightful Tahoe cabin an ideal honeymoon retreat. The discriminating couple will take special pleasure in the many features the cabin offers, including a king-sized bed, a color cable TV and a VCR. Just right for an intimate getaway, the cabin provides a fireplace as well as a wood-burning stove. Conveniences such as a washer/dryer, a microwave and a deck with a barbecue guarantee a restful stay. With this spot as your vacation headquarters, you can dip into the endless array of area activities—waterskiing, snow skiing, hiking, a game of blackjack or a spin of the roulette wheel—and retire to sweet solitude. Contact: M & M Property Management & Rentals, 2301 Highway #50, South Lake Tahoe, CA 95731. Call 916-542-2777 (in California, 1-800-542-2100). Ref. 1028.

Children: **Y**   Pets: **N**   Smoking: **Y**   Handicap Access: **Y**   Payment: **C, P, T**

SANCTUARY   *Rates: moderate*
Open: year-round   *Minimum Stay: four nights*

Bird lovers will rejoice in this sunny and spacious four-bedroom house, where the large deck overlooks a wonderful bird sanctuary. Accommodations for seven include a master suite with a Jacuzzi, three more bedrooms and a second bath, a living room and a kitchen. When you turn off the stereo or color cable TV at night, you can stretch out in front of the fireplace. Activities for every member of the family seem endless in the Tahoe area—hiking and cross-country skiing for the nature lover, shopping and fine dining for the cosmopolite, tennis, waterskiing, swimming and golf for the athlete. And it's only a short drive to the endless wonders of Yosemite National Park. Contact: M & M Property Management & Rentals, 2301 Highway #50, South Lake Tahoe, CA 95731. Call 916-542-2777 (in California, 1-800-542-2100). Ref. 1750.

Children: **Y**   Pets: **N**   Smoking: **Y**   Handicap Access: **Y**   Payment: **C, P, T**

TAHOE TREAT   *Rates: deluxe*
Open: summer   *Minimum Stay: one week*

Summer nights should always be like this—the star-studded sky a canopy overhead, the lake softening the air that caresses your face. This old Tahoe beach house offers the ultimate in vacation accommodations for six, with four bedrooms, two baths and luxury features too numerous to mention. You can enjoy the beauty and serenity of the lake from the private dock or spend your afternoons on the lovely patio with its open cabana and a brick barbecue. With Heavenly Valley and the casinos nearby, you'll not want for amusement. In fact, gaming and sports abound in this popular resort area—Squaw Valley is only a short drive away. Contact: M & M Property Management & Rentals, 2301 Highway #50, South Lake Tahoe, CA 95731. Call 916-542-2777 (in California, 1-800-542-2100). Ref. 1130.

Children: Y   Pets: N   Smoking: Y   Handicap Access: Y   Payment: C, P, T

THE LITTLE CABOOSE   *Rates: budget*
Open: year-round   *Minimum Stay: four nights*

Affectionately known as the Little Caboose, this charming little one-bedroom home offers cozy accommodations for up to four. Conveniences such as a microwave and a washer/dryer make it especially user-friendly, and the small fenced yard and handsome Swedish fireplace add grace and comfort to your stay. Surrounded by the gorgeous pines of the Tahoe forest, the house enjoys a location only a short distance from great skiing at Heavenly Valley. If you tire of the riches of California, you can plan a short excursion to nearby Reno, Nevada, where the gaming tables may suit you better. Sports enthusiasts and nature lovers can indulge their every desire for hiking, skiing, water-skiing, fishing and canoeing throughout the area. Contact: M & M Property Management & Rentals, 2301 Highway #50, South Lake Tahoe, CA 95731. Call 916-542-2777 (in California, 1-800-542-2100). Ref. 3675.

Children: Y   Pets: N   Smoking: Y   Handicap Access: Y   Payment: C, P, T

TRINIDAD

VIEW CREST LODGE   *Rates: budget*
Open: year-round   *Minimum Stay: two nights*

Uncrowded beaches, fishing harbors and breathtaking scenery highlight the stretch of northern California coastline closest to the Oregon border. View Crest, a family-run resort here, is hospitable and warm, set on a tranquil hillside with a distant view of the Pacific Ocean. Housekeeping cottages contain a full kitchen and bathroom, queen-sized bedrooms, living areas and color cable TV. Within easy reach are laundry facilities, markets and restaurants; there is a children's playground on the premises. Quiet beaches are a short drive away, and slightly further north are parks that house magnificent giant redwood groves. Thirty-five miles to the south is Eureka, a town full of restored Victorian mansions. Contact: Bill and Geri Heyne, 3415 Patricks Point Drive, Trinidad, CA 95570. Call 707-677-3393.

Children: Y Pets: N Smoking: Y Handicap Access: N Payment: C, P, T, V, M

TRINITY CENTER

BONANZA KING RESORT   *Rates: budget*
Open: year-round   *Minimum Stay: two nights*

Situated on 1,200 acres fronting Coffee Creek, these cabins sit amid meadows and pine woods, with the snow-capped Trinity Alps as a scenic backdrop. The charmingly named units—including the Kokannee, the Cedar, the Rainbow, the Ramshorn and the Sugarpine—sleep two to eight. All cabins are electrically heated and have full kitchens and bathrooms with showers; a common freezer and laundry facilities are shared by the cabins. Some of the cabins have wood stoves, with plenty of firewood supplied. The swimming hole and trout creek are perfect for wading children. Fly and bait fishing is excellent here, and on Trinity Lake visitors can rent boats and water skis. Contact: Don and Fran Lethbridge, Bonanza King Resort, Route 2, P.O. Box 4790, Trinity Center, CA 96091. Call 916-266-3305.

Children: Y   Pets: Y   Smoking: Y   Handicap Access: N   Payment: C, T

COFFEE CREEK CHALET   *Rates: budget-inexpensive*
Open: year-round   *Minimum Stay: three nights*

This chalet feels more like a private home than a vacation rental—indeed, many of the owner's personal treasures add to the decor. The loft and master bedroom have room for four, and there is an extra fold-out couch in the spacious living room. Everything is provided—linens, towels, wood for the wood-burning stove, a TV with VCR and a full kitchen. A well supplies pure water, and a country store just half a mile away stocks provisions. The chalet is surrounded by three acres of creek-front land covered with firs and cedars. The sense of solitude is remarkable, yet within a few miles there are busy marinas, good restaurants, tennis and plenty of hiking trails. The area is renowned for its fishing—Trinity Lake holds the record for smallmouth bass—and on Trinity River you can still find the hopeful panning for gold. Contact: Robert and Dee Dee Kausen, Coffee Creek Chalet, Star Route 2, P.O. Box 3969, Trinity Center, CA 96091. Call 916-266-3235.

Children: Y   Pets: N   Smoking: Y   Handicap Access: N   Payment: C, T

ENRIGHT GULCH CABINS   *Rates: budget*
Open: year-round   *Minimum Stay: three nights*

Located off the beaten path at the north end of 20-mile-long Trinity Lake, these four cabins are surrounded by cedars and pines near a babbling creek. Each cabin has a different design, but all have a kitchen, bathroom, living room and either one or two bedrooms. The largest unit encompasses 1,000 square feet and sleeps eight comfortably. All cabins are equipped with gas stoves, kitchenware, utensils and linens, and are lit and heated by electricity. Wood-burning stoves create a cozy atmosphere. Enjoy a barbecue by the stream, a visit to Trinity Lake for boating or waterskiing, a hike through the mountains or a hunting trip. Would-be gold miners can pan local rivers, while fishermen find a different bounty in the clean waters. Contact: Gary Heilig, Enright Gulch Cabins, 3500 Highway 3, Trinity Center, CA 96091. Call 916-266-3600.

Children: Y   Pets: N   Smoking: Y   Handicap Access: N   Payment: C, T

THE CEDARS LODGE ON COFFEE CREEK   *Rates: budget*
Open: year-round   *Minimum Stay: none*

Cedars Lodge assures you privacy, peace and relaxation in a wilderness area bordered by the Trinity Alps and filled with rivers, streams and lakes. The lodge for up to eight guests contains all modern amenities but lacks commercial electricity and a phone—the stove is butane and the lighting is by gas. The master bedroom contains a king-sized bed; three sleeping areas in the lofts accommodate six. Fully carpeted and heated by a big iron stove, the lodge features a fireplace perfect for snuggling up on a winter's night. This is truly a place for those who love the outdoors: A trout stream ripples past the lodge, and there are over 20 acres of grounds to explore. Hiking trips and horseback riding through the mountains can easily be arranged, as can camping treks for serious hikers. Contact: The Edmonsons, P.O. Box 2201, Avila Beach, CA 93424. Call 805-595-7756.

Children: Y   Pets: N   Smoking: Y   Handicap Access: N   Payment: C, T

WYNTOON RESORT   *Rates: budget*
Open: year-round   *Minimum Stay: two nights*

Twenty furnished cottages are offered here in a resort on the shores of Lake Trinity. Each cottage sleeps up to four, with one bedroom, a full kitchen and a bathroom. Nearby are laundry facilities, a snack bar and a complete supermarket, as well as a game room, recreation pavilion, children's playground and bicycle rental. Special events at the resort include Saturday night square dancing and Wednesday night bingo throughout the summer months. Guests can see the snow-capped peaks of the Trinity Alps in the distance; in winter the area features California's best cross-country skiing. In summer the lake is well stocked with fish, and the resort marina rents fishing and party boats. Contact: Wyntoon Resort, P.O. Box 70, Trinity Center, CA 96091. Call 916-266-3337.

Children: Y   Pets: Y   Smoking: Y   Handicap Access: N   Payment: C, T, V, M

WEAVERVILLE

COOMBS COTTAGE   *Rates: budget*
Open: year-round   *Minimum Stay: none*

A real country cottage on a historic street near downtown Weaverville, this one-bedroom accommodation is like visiting a family home. Filled with books and magazines, provided with cable TV, a fully equipped kitchen and a shady yard, Coombs Cottage makes a good base for exploring an area that is both scenic and historic. Picturesque Weaverville evokes the spirit of California's Gold Rush; visitors can try panning for gold in the Trinity River. Hikers and nature lovers can explore the mountain trails and National Forests; those who like water sports will find plenty to do at Trinity Lake, a 20-mile-long crystal-clear lake stocked with prize-winning fish. Contact: Coombs Cottage, 307 Taylor, P.O. Box 968, Weaverville, CA 96093. Call 916-623-3263.

Children: Y   Pets: Y   Smoking: Y   Handicap Access: N   Payment: C, P, T

MOTEL TRINITY   *Rates: budget-inexpensive*
Open: year-round   *Minimum Stay: none*

Located on Main Street in scenic Weaverville, this motel has kitchen units in addition to regular hotel rooms. Guests here can swim in the pool or soak in the hot tub surrounded by mountain scenery reminiscent of the European Alps. The rooms have televisions, comfortable double beds and a clean, modern setting, making this motel an ideal base from which to explore the surrounding wilderness. Visitors pan for gold in the nearby streams, fish in the rivers and boat and water ski on the lake. Fall hunting trips and all manner of winter activities make this a year-round vacation spot. In the town itself you'll find many historic sites that recall the heady days of the Gold Rush. Contact: Motel Trinity, Main Street, P.O. Box 1179, Weaverville, CA 96093. Call 916-623-2129.

Children: Y Pets: Y Smoking: Y Handicap Access: P Payment: C, T, V, M, A, O

RED HILL MOTEL *Rates: budget*
Open: year-round *Minimum Stay: none*

Nestled among towering Ponderosa pines away from the noise of the highway, this motel offers three housekeeping cottages. The units have a rustic simplicity but are modern and comfortable, with two bedrooms, a private bathroom and a kitchen. Stores and restaurants are within easy walking distance, and maid service is available. Air-conditioned in summer and electrically heated in winter, the cottages make a good base for exploring the Trinity Alps area at any time of year. Suitable for fishing or hunting trips or boating vacations, Red Hill also caters to families who come to enjoy the fresh air and children's activities by the lake. Contact: Olga Skweir, Red Hill Motel, P.O. Box 234, Weaverville, CA 96093. Call 916-623-4331.

Children: Y Pets: Y Smoking: Y Handicap Access: N Payment: C, P, T, V, M

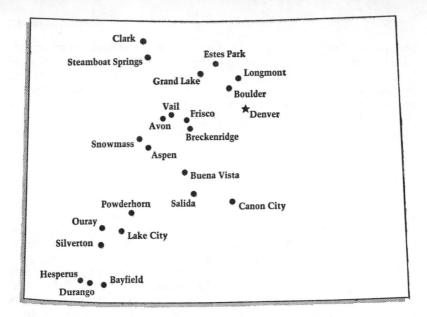

Clark
Steamboat Springs
Estes Park
Longmont
Grand Lake
Boulder
Vail
Frisco
Denver
Avon
Snowmass
Breckenridge
Aspen
Buena Vista
Powderhorn
Salida
Canon City
Ouray
Lake City
Silverton
Hesperus
Bayfield
Durango

Colorado

ASPEN

ASPEN SILVERGLO *Rates: budget-deluxe*
Open: year-round *Minimum Stay: three nights*
Located just two and a half blocks from Aspen Mountain's Silver
Queen Gondola, these studio and one- to five-bedroom apartments
with full kitchens promise warm and cozy times in front of your own
native stone fireplace. Each carefully appointed apartment has luxurious carpeting, open-beam ceilings, a living room with color cable TV
and a full kitchen. With Aspen Valley at your feet, you can choose
from a near infinity of vacation pleasures—skiing for the first-timer
and the pro, sleigh riding, dog sledding, hot-air ballooning, white-water
rafting. And the Snowmass/Aspen area offers over 100 restaurants,
from family style to fine dining. The town's shopping, galleries and
musical and theater events all make Aspen one of the richest and most
varied vacation spots. Contact: Steve Hach, Aspen Silverglo, 940 Waters Avenue, Aspen, CO 81611. Call 303-925-8450.
Children: Y Pets: N Smoking: Y Handicap Access: N Payment: C, P, T

ASPEN SQUARE *Rates: inexpensive-deluxe*
Open: year-round *Minimum Stay: one week*
With its wealth of cultural attractions, its unsurpassed skiing opportunities and the charming and warm Victorian heritage that continues
to pervade this glamorous town, Aspen is the Silver Queen of the

Rockies. And these luxury condominiums—studios, one- and two-bedroom units individually styled and appointed—provide a lovely base for enjoying all that Aspen has to offer. With niceties such as daily maid service, cable TV, fireplaces and private balconies, these homes assure you the quality holiday time you require. And of course, the heated pool, whirlpool hot tub and soothing sauna do for the body what the beautiful landscape does for the soul. Contact: Aspen Square, 617 E. Cooper, Aspen, CO 81611. Call 1-800-862-7736 or 303-925-1000.

Children: Y Pets: N Smoking: Y Handicap Access: N Payment: C, P, T, V, M, A

BOOMERANG LODGE   *Rates: inexpensive-deluxe*
Open: year-round   *Minimum Stay: none*

Designed and built by its architect/owner, this modern ski lodge blends understated contemporary design with modern convenience. Situated away from the hustle and bustle of downtown Aspen, the lodge offers a peaceful setting that is still only a short walk away from the fine shops, galleries, restaurants and nightlife of Colorado's most glamorous wintertime mecca. Studios and two- and three-bedroom apartments offer accommodations for two to six and feature full kitchens, fine modern furnishings, fireplaces and private balconies or poolside garden terraces with breathtaking views of the mountains all around. You can wind down with a sauna, daily tea and cookies, a dip in the heated swimming pool or a soak in the whirlpool. Contact: Charles Paterson, Boomerang Lodge, 500 W. Hopkins, Aspen, CO 81611. Call 1-800-992-8852 or 303-925-3416.

Children: Y Pets: N Smoking: N Handicap Access: N Payment: C, P, T, V, M, A

CSM   *Rates: deluxe*
Open: year-round   *Minimum Stay: two nights*

From its many large windows, this stately and elegant Spanish-style home for ten boasts spectacular views of Aspen Mountain, the glittering town of Aspen and the majestic surrounding mountains. Graciously appointed with the finest furnishings and wood-beamed cathedral ceilings, the house features an indoor swimming pool and a tennis court open in the summertime. Several of the bedrooms include either a sauna, a Jacuzzi or a private deck; two living rooms, a den, a kitchen and two dining areas complete the astoundingly generous accommodations. No town but Aspen could offer the natural beauty as well as the excellence in outdoor sporting opportunities, fine dining and fabulous shopping to match the standard of living provided by this home. Contact: Marsha Marriott, Coates, Reid & Waldron Property Management, 720 E. Hyman Avenue, Aspen, CO 81611. Call 1-800-222-7736.

Children: Y Pets: N Smoking: Y Handicap Access: N Payment: C, P, V, M, A

DURANT CONDOMINIUMS   *Rates: inexpensive-deluxe*
Open: year-round   *Minimum Stay: none*

Imagine this: You ski from your top-floor apartment onto Aspen Mountain, spend the day in a spray of some of the world's finest powder and come home at dusk to a panoramic view of the twinkling valley below and a crackling fire in the fireplace. Or this: You go for an early morning hike in a wildflower-filled meadow, play a couple of games of tennis, take a swim in the pool back at Durant and go out for a night on the town. With this perfect location only a block and a half from the center of town and just as close to the Aspen Mountain Gondola, these one- to three-bedroom units promise all that and more. The further conveniences of guest laundry, maid service, a Jacuzzi and color TV with HBO assure you the ease and comfort you're bound to want on your vacation in the Rockies. Contact: Reservation Dept., Condo Rental Mgmt., 747 S. Galena St., Aspen, CO 81611. Call 1-800-321-7025.

Children: Y Pets: N Smoking: Y Handicap Access: N Payment: C, P, T, A

EDGE OF AJAX #2

Rates: deluxe
Open: year-round *Minimum Stay: two nights*

This wonderfully sunny and newly decorated half-duplex offers the convenience of a downtown Aspen location, where no car is necessary. Two private decks, one with an outside Jacuzzi, face the rise of Aspen Mountain. Inside, this four-bedroom, four-bath home features the teal and terra-cotta hues of beautiful southwestern appointments; high ceilings and skylights accentuate the richness of color. Summertime Aspen pleasures are as many as the days are long—hot-air ballooning, wilderness hiking, fishing, canoeing and white-water rafting, just to name a few. And of course, the wonderful world of snow sports has its capital in Aspen. Contact: Marsha Marriott, Coates, Reid & Waldron Property Management, 720 E. Hyman Avenue, Aspen, CO 81611. Call 1-800-222-7736.

Children: Y Pets: N Smoking: Y Handicap Access: N Payment: C, P, V, M, A

LAVERY HOUSE

Rates: inexpensive-deluxe
Open: year-round *Minimum Stay: two nights*

This cozy log home located on Red Mountain boasts spectacular views of Aspen and the surrounding mountains. From the large main-level deck furnished with armchairs, a table for outdoor dining and a charcoal barbecue, the Aspen basin spreads before you wondrously. The charming interior includes a warmly paneled living room, a small kitchen, two bedrooms and a sitting room with a lichenrock fireplace. This home is perfect for those with a car who prefer to be secluded from all the activity of Aspen, but like knowing that snowmobiling, sleigh riding, ice skating and skiing as well as canoeing, fishing, white-water rafting and cultural events are all only just a few minutes' drive away. Contact: Marsha Marriott, Coates, Reid & Waldron Property Management, 720 E. Hyman Avenue, Aspen, CO 81611. Call 1-800-222-7736.

Children: Y Pets: N Smoking: Y Handicap Access: N Payment: C, P, V, M, A

LIFT ONE CONDOMINIUMS

Rates: moderate-deluxe
Open: year-round *Minimum Stay: two nights*

Located at the foot of Aspen Mountain with the Silver Queen Gondola and Lift 1A only a short walk away, these one-, two- and three-bedroom apartments make it easy for skiers to be on the slopes early for those perfect powder days. A two-block walk will land you in the midst of Aspen's many fine restaurants, galleries, shops and glimmering night life. Just down the street is Rubey Park, where you can catch a bus to Snowmass Village or anywhere within Aspen. At day's end, you'll be happy to return to your vacation home at Lift One, where each beautifully decorated apartment features a fireplace, a fully equipped kitchen, a private balcony or patio and cable TV. Guests can wind down or charge up in the swimming pool, the hot tub and the sauna. Contact: Lift One Condominiums, 131 E. Durant, Aspen, CO 81611. Call 1-800-543-8001.

Children: Y Pets: N Smoking: Y Handicap Access: N Payment: C, P, T, V, M

THE GANT   *Rates: inexpensive-deluxe*
Open: year-round   *Minimum Stay: none*
This self-contained retreat near the base of Aspen Mountain offers beautifully appointed one- to four-bedroom apartments for year-round R & R. Each apartment boasts a fireplace and a balcony with beautiful views of the surrounding mountains. In a setting of beautifully landscaped grounds, guests share resort-quality amenities, such as two heated pools with poolside patio dining, three hot tubs and five summer tennis courts with a resident pro. A famous wintertime mecca for over 100 years, Aspen has become one of America's top year-round vacation spots. Summer booms here, in daytime outdoor activities and starlit nights filled with the performances of the Aspen Music Festival, Aspen Ballet and repertory theater. Contact: Maureen Callahan, The Gant, 610 West End St., Aspen, CO 81611. Call 1-800-345-1471 or 303-925-5000.

Children: Y Pets: N Smoking: Y Handicap Access: N Payment: C, P, T, V, M, A

TIPPLE INN   *Rates: budget-deluxe*
Open: year-round   *Minimum Stay: none*
Located only 25 yards from the Aspen Mountain Gondola, here's a condominium complex for the heavy hitters. Many of these studio and two-bedroom apartments feature fireplaces as well as the amenities of color TV, a hot tub and maid service. Of course, with all the activity in Aspen, it's not likely you'll stay at home for long. Four world-class ski mountains call to both the beginner and the expert, and off the slopes there's plenty of romance in a sleigh ride. Glorious, sunny summer days are meant for tennis, golf and white-water rafting, and cool, starry summer nights are perfect for culture lovers who will thrill to the performances at the renowned Aspen Music Festival. Contact: Reservation Dept., Condo Rental Mgmt., 747 S. Galena St., Aspen, CO 81611. Call 1-800-321-7025.

Children: Y Pets: N Smoking: Y Handicap Access: N Payment: C, P, T, A

AVON

BEAVER CREEK WEST CONDOMINIUMS *Rates: inexpensive-deluxe*
Open: year-round *Minimum Stay: none*

These spacious, comfortably furnished and fully carpeted condominium apartments offer beautiful mountain living for two to six in one-, two- and three-bedroom accommodations. With accents such as a massive wood-burning fireplace (the firewood is free) and a private balcony, plus the conveniences of a washer/dryer and a color TV with HBO, an apartment here assures the finest in at-home comfort and relaxation. Guests share the indoor sauna, heated outdoor pool, two hot tubs and tennis courts. Located only minutes away from two world-class ski areas, your condo is just a couple miles west of a new ski area where the slopes are leisurely and uncrowded; there could be no better point of departure for a beautiful winter holiday. Summertime activities include horseback riding, fishing and white-water rafting. Contact: Beaver Creek West Condominiums, P.O. Box 5290, Avon, CO 81620. Call 1-800-222-4840.

Children: Y   Pets: N   Smoking: Y   Handicap Access: N   Payment: C, P

BAYFIELD

WIT'S END GUEST RANCH *Rates: moderate-deluxe*
Open: year-round *Minimum Stay: none*

Nestled in the Colorado Rockies on 276 acres, these luxury log cabins cluster in a narrow valley with peaks soaring to 14,000 feet on all sides. Among the one- to four-bedroom cabins, honeymooning couples will take special pleasure in the James B. Decker Family Cabin, which offers an additional fireplace and deck off the cozy bedroom, or the Mary Bell Moore Cabin, with a story-book bedroom in the upstairs attic. Each cabin boasts native stone fireplaces, large decks, brass beds and knotty pine interiors designed to appeal to the most discriminating tastes. A stay here features unlimited use of the resort's spas, swimming pools and tennis courts. Fishing on lakes, rivers and streams as well as a number of hunting plans are available at an extra cost. Contact: L. McCroy, Wit's End Guest Ranch, 254 C.R. 500, Bayfield, CO 81122. Call 303-884-4113.

Children: Y Pets: N Smoking: Y Handicap Access: N Payment: C, P, T, V, M, A

BOULDER

SANDY POINT INN *Rates: budget-inexpensive*
Open: year-round *Minimum Stay: none*

This modern country inn located in a quiet residential neighborhood three and a half miles northeast of Boulder offers truly spacious studio suites to vacationers, relocating families and business travelers alike. Each accommodation includes a sitting area with cable TV and a direct-dial telephone, a kitchenette with a microwave and two double beds. The owners make the central kitchen available to guests for more elaborate cooking and also provide complimentary breakfast. Nearby attractions are as varied as the Rockies, with lakes and rivers for fishing and canoeing, Rocky Mountain National Park and other protected lands for hiking and back-country exploring and a number of downhill and cross-country skiing opportunities all less than an hour away. Contact: Juanita Miller, Sandy Point Inn, 6485 Twin Lakes Road, Boulder, CO 80301. Call 1-800-322-2939 or 303-530-2939.

Children: Y Pets: Y Smoking: Y Handicap Access: Y Payment: C, P, T, V, M, A

BRECKENRIDGE

BASE NINE   *Rates: moderate-expensive*
Open: year-round   *Minimum Stay: five nights*

Whether you've come to Breckenridge to perfect your skiing techniques, sleigh ride till you drop, get your golf game down a stroke or two or get your fill of horseback riding, this feature-filled apartment for six to eight (two bedrooms, two baths) offers a gracious retreat. The full-sized kitchen includes a microwave and a washer/dryer, and the living room provides the entertainment of a stereo, a TV and a VCR. You can satisfy your insatiable hunger for beauty with the fireplace and balcony and work out the kinks in the Base Nine clubhouse, where you'll find a hot tub and a sauna. Relaxed as you're bound to be living among all these creature comforts, go the extra distance with some hot-air ballooning, white-water rafting or a return to the slope that got the best of you yesterday. Contact: Ski Country Resorts Management, Inc., 540 S. Main, P.O. Box 649, Breckenridge, CO 80424. Call 1-800-633-8388.

Children: Y Pets: N Smoking: Y Handicap Access: N Payment: C, P, T, V, M, A

CEDAR TOWNHOUSES   *Rates: expensive-deluxe*
Open: year-round   *Minimum Stay: five nights*

These gracious slopeside townhouses feature a special Southwestern interior design that centers around a warm and inviting fireplace. In the summer, you can fire up the gas grill on the patio and listen to the cool mountain stream running nearby or stroll over to the heated pool for a dip. Here, you'll enjoy all the comforts of home and then some—a private garage, several color TVs with VCRs, a component stereo system, full-sized washer/dryer and a whirlpool tub in the master bedroom. Two bedrooms sleep six people and share two and a half bathrooms. With a convenient ski-in/ski-out location near the summertime Genuine Jazz and Beethoven and Breckenridge concerts, these apartments offer the best in year-round vacation environments. Contact: Ski Country Resorts Management, Inc., 540 S. Main, P.O. Box 649, Breckenridge, CO 80424. Call 1-800-633-8388.

Children: Y Pets: N Smoking: Y Handicap Access: N Payment: C, P, T, V, M, A

INNER CIRCLE   *Rates: inexpensive-moderate*
Open: year-round   *Minimum Stay: five nights*

This newly refurbished apartment goes easy on the budget while offering the amenities hearty outdoors people require on a holiday. The one-bedroom apartment sleeps four and features a full kitchen, a balcony with a lovely view and a TV. Additional conveniences include access to a pool and on-premises laundry facilities. This address puts guests just a short walk from ski lifts, including the Quicksilver quad chair. Or you can choose between Copper Mountain, Keystone and Arapahoe Basin ski areas, all serviced by the free Summit bus system. For a little romance, keep in mind night skiing at Keystone, open till 10 P.M. Contact: Ski Country Resorts Management, Inc., 540 S. Main, P.O. Box 649, Breckenridge, CO 80424. Call 1-800-633-8388.

Children: Y Pets: N Smoking: Y Handicap Access: N Payment: C, P, T, V, M, A

PANORAMIC HOUSE   *Rates: deluxe*
Open: year-round   *Minimum Stay: five nights*

Located high above Breckenridge with breathtaking views from its three wooden decks, this sprawling and spacious home for up to 16 offers the perfect place for a family reunion or a weekend of strategic planning or corporate wind-down. The huge living area, decorated with antiques, features dark oak woodwork and skylights. Ambitious meals can be served from the two kitchens and the outdoor grill. Other amenities include a glassed-in Jacuzzi room, a game room and a washer/dryer. With the gorgeous wilderness spread out before you, you may be inspired to rise to new heights—in a hot-air balloon, on a white-water raft, on the ski trails, or simply enjoy the sights of the Rockies. Contact: Ski Country Resorts Management, Inc., 540 S. Main, P.O. Box 649, Breckenridge, CO 80424. Call 1-800-633-8388.

Children: Y Pets: N Smoking: Y Handicap Access: N Payment: C, P, T, V, M, A

PINE RIDGE CONDOMINIUMS   *Rates: budget-deluxe*
Open: year-round   *Minimum Stay: two nights*

The charming 129-year-old Victorian mining town of Breckenridge offers a perfect retreat in the heart of the Rockies any time of the year. Summer visitors delight in the gorgeous mountains for hiking and horseback riding, and snow lovers will enjoy snowmobiling, sleigh rides, ice skating and skiing so close to your vacation rental you can actually ski home at the end of the day. What better time to slip into one of this condo's two hot tubs for the best in apres-ski relaxation? Apartment accommodations include two bedrooms, two bathrooms, an optional additional sleeping loft, a gracious living room with a fireplace and a deck stocked with plenty of firewood. With the additional conveniences of a washer/dryer, a microwave and cable TV, these beautiful apartments may be your year-round ticket to the best in mountain holidays. Contact: Betty Wilson, Pine Ridge Condominiums, P.O. Box 487, 400 Four O'Clock Rd., Breckenridge, CO 80424. Call 1-800-333-8833.

Children: Y Pets: N Smoking: Y Handicap Access: N Payment: C, P, T, V, M, A

PONDEROSA LOG CABIN   *Rates: deluxe*
Open: year-round   *Minimum Stay: five nights*

Surrounded by tall, slim pine trees in beautiful woods only ten minutes outside Breckenridge, this three-level log cabin captures the romance of mountain country. The Ralph Lauren interior features fine rugs and rustic furniture in over 3,000 square feet of living that is at once both elegant and homespun in feeling. Accommodations for twelve include four bedrooms and three bathrooms and feature such lovely amenities as cozy rock fireplaces, multiple TVs and VCRs, a game room with bumper pool, an indoor hot tub and a kitchen loaded with extras like a washer/dryer. Ideal for summer family vacations, this spot offers a volleyball court and picnic grounds out back. The alpine cabin offers the perfect base for outdoor pleasures—hiking, canoeing, ice skating, sleigh riding—and the warmest, most inviting of homes to come home to. Contact: Ski Country Resorts Management, Inc., 540 S. Main, P.O. Box 649, Breckenridge, CO 80424. Call 1-800-633-8388.

Children: Y Pets: N Smoking: Y Handicap Access: N Payment: C, P, T, V, M, A

ROBIN HOOD'S RETREAT *Rates: deluxe*
Open: November 17-April 14 *Minimum Stay: three nights*

The whole world of sun and snow spreads out before you from the glass-fronted living room of this 1,800-square-foot home surrounded by pine trees. The raised two-story house sleeps up to eight in three bedrooms and also features a sunroom with a game table. Designer appointments include the cozy warmth of a wood-burning stove; conveniences such as a washer/dryer are especially desirable. You can hop in your car or truck to drive the five miles to nearby ski lifts, or explore the surrounding countryside on cross-country skis, snowmobile or snowshoes. If your plans send you to the mountains in the summer, this elegant spot is the perfect center for meadow wanderings, when the hot-air balloons compete with the birds for celestial dominance and the music and art festivals draw a crowd. Contact: Colorado High Country Rentals, Inc., 11072 North Highway 9, P.O. Box 1797, Breckenridge, CO 80424. Call 1-800-525-3882.

Children: Y   Pets: N   Smoking: Y   Handicap Access: N   Payment: C

SUNRISE RIDGE *Rates: deluxe*
Open: year-round *Minimum Stay: five nights*

Space, vistas, beauty and elegance mark these four-level townhouses overlooking the town of Breckenridge and its ski area. Each home offers gracious accommodations for up to twelve in four bedrooms and three baths, totaling 3,500 square feet of handsomely furnished and sun-drenched living. You'll enjoy the large indoor Jacuzzi, the sauna, three private wooden decks with wonderful views and two rock fireplaces. Now add the conveniences of a washer/dryer, three TVs with VCRs and a two-car garage, and see if you can make do! You'll need a car to reach the vast pleasures of the Breckenridge area, where great skiing, snowmobiling, trout fishing and stargazing are among the best the Colorado Rockies have to offer. Contact: Ski Country Resorts Management, Inc., 540 S. Main, P.O. Box 649, Breckenridge, CO 80424. Call 1-800-633-8388.

Children: Y Pets: N Smoking: Y Handicap Access: N Payment: C, P, T, V, M, A

WARRIORS REST HOUSE   *Rates: expensive-deluxe*
Open: year-round   *Minimum Stay: three nights*
Even the largest family or group can spread out in this 2,000-square-foot house situated one mile from town. Accommodations for ten include four bedrooms and two and a half baths, as well as an especially spacious living room that features a beautiful view of the surrounding countryside. You'll be sure to enjoy the special comforts of this house, such as two fireplaces, a sauna, a washer/dryer and a garage. The old mining town of Breckenridge offers not only some of the best skiing in the Rockies, but all the pleasures and conveniences of a lively resort town, where activities include tennis, swimming, helicopter skiing and sleigh riding. Contact: Colorado High Country Rentals, Inc., 11072 North Highway 9, P.O. Box 1797, Breckenridge, CO 80424. Call 1-800-525-3882.

Children: **Y**   Pets: **N**   Smoking: **Y**   Handicap Access: **N**   Payment: **C**

BUENA VISTA

MORNING STAR RETREAT   *Rates: budget*
Open: year-round   *Minimum Stay: none*
Nestled in a high mountain valley of the majestic Collegiate Peaks Range, Morning Star Retreat offers a beautiful and naturally therapeutic environment for the restoration of the body, mind and spirit. The retreat revolves around the pure geothermal mineral spas surrounded by redwood decks. A meditation tepee and sweat lodge as well as archery, basketball, horseshoes and a weight room complete the facilities. Three kitchenette units offer the perfect arrangement for a vacation of peace, serenity and beauty where special arrangements can be made for massage, acupressure and hypnotherapy treatments. Located about an hour from Aspen, you can also enjoy the snow and sun pleasures of the Rockies at their most elegant, or stay closer to home and plan your hike up one of the nearby peaks. Contact: Cathy Manning, Cottonwood Hot Springs Inn, 18999 County Road 306, Buena Vista, CO 81211. Call 719-395-6434 or 719-395-2102.

Children: **N** Pets: **Y** Smoking: **Y** Handicap Access: **N** Payment: **C,P, T, V, M, O**

CANON CITY

PARKVIEW MOTEL   *Rates: budget*
Open: year-round   *Minimum Stay: none*
At this clean and well-kept motel just west of Canon City, guests can choose a room with a kitchenette and stay at remarkably low rates for a day, a week or a month. Each room features a color TV as well as a direct-dial telephone. The surrounding area offers many wonderful excursions, including the world-famous Royal Gorge and its toll bridge, built at a breathtaking 1,053 feet above the river. In nearby Penrose, you'll find historic Indian petroglyphs, and right up scenic Route 67 is the Cripple Creek Historical Area. Skiing in the Sangre de Cristo Mountains puts Colorado's powdery slopes just a short drive

from your door. In the evening, several fine restaurants add the perfect touch to your day of business or pleasure. Contact: Joanne Edge, Parkview Motel, 231 Royal Gorge Blvd., Canon City, CO 81212. Call 719-275-0624.

Children: **Y**   Pets: **Y**   Smoking: **Y**   Handicap Access: **N**   Payment: **All**

CLARK

GLEN EDEN RESORT   *Rates: inexpensive*
Open: year-round   *Minimum Stay: two nights*

Nestled in the Elk River Valley just 18 miles north of Steamboat Springs, these one- and two-bedroom duplex homes enjoy the most serene and beautiful of natural surroundings. Warm and sunny summer days, crisp and starry summer nights—this is the season for great trout fishing right on the river or sailing on Steamboat Lake. The wintertime valley, blanketed in white, offers miles of cross-country trails, as well as unmarked powder for snowshoeing and snowmobiling. Each cozy apartment includes an efficiency kitchen, a double bathroom, a rock fireplace for year-round romance and a back porch. Guests can enjoy a swim in the heated pool, a quick game of tennis or a dip in one of the hot tubs after a day in the mountains. Contact: Rich Landon, Glen Eden Resort, P.O. Box 822, Clark, CO 80428. Call 303-879-3907.

Children: Y Pets: N Smoking: Y Handicap Access: N Payment: C, P, T, V, M, A

DENVER-LAKEWOOD

CHALET MOTEL   *Rates: budget*
Open: year-round   *Minimum Stay: none*

Conveniently located ten minutes from downtown Denver and ten minutes from the mountains, this "Mom and Pop" place offers simply furnished double rooms, several with kitchenettes and one with a fireplace. The large heated pool provides that special touch of relaxation after a morning on the slopes or an afternoon taking in the galleries and museums of Denver. The owners of these accommodations, which also feature direct-dial telephone, color TV and radio for those last-minute ski reports, speak German, Italian and French and enjoy advising guests about area facilities. Nearby, you'll find more ski areas than you can shake a ski pole at, as well as the road to 14,264-foot Mt. Evans, the highest road in the United States. Contact: Gerry Seitmann, Chalet Motel, 6051 W. Alameda Avenue, Denver-Lakewood, CO 80226-3536. Call 1-800-288-7997 or 303-237-7775.

Children: Y Pets: Y Smoking: Y Handicap Access: N Payment: C, T, V, M, A

DURANGO

EDELWEISS INN   *Rates: budget*
Open: year-round   *Minimum Stay: none*

Overlooking the scenic Animas River Valley just two miles north of historical downtown Durango, this charming inn offers simply furnished rooms with color TV and kitchenettes. The dining room of the inn offers a wonderful menu that includes braised pheasant, weiner schnitzel, hasenpfeffer and poached trout. Of course, you can catch your own trout on one of the nearby lakes, though you may prefer to spend your afternoon in quiet contemplation of the sun on the water. The area provides a wealth of other outdoor activities, such as skiing, snowmobiling and ice skating. And the whole family will enjoy a day's outing on the Durango-Silverton Narrow-Gauge Railroad. Contact: Glenn and Carol Snyder, Edelweiss Inn, 689 Animas View Drive, Durango, CO 81301. Call 303-247-5685.

Children: Y Pets: Y Smoking: Y Handicap Access: N Payment: C, T, V, M

PURGATORY VILLAGE HOTEL   *Rates: budget-expensive*
Open: year-round   *Minimum Stay: two nights*

Whether you come for the snow in winter, or the meadows, lakes and trails in summer, Purgatory in Durango offers the ultimate in Colorado mountain R & R. Purgatory Mountain boasts nine lifts, two gourmet restaurants and 62 trails on 630 acres. But chairlifts aren't just for skiing—in the summertime, you can load your mountain bike and ride to new heights, where you'll find legendary back country and incomparable panoramic vistas. You can also enjoy classical music concerts in August, and fine dining, museums and crafts shopping year-round. Each of the Purgatory Village Hotel's luxurious one-, two- and three-bedroom accommodations includes a fully equipped kitchen, a fireplace, and a balcony as well as color TV and HBO. Amenities, such as an indoor/outdoor pool, a steam room, a sauna and hot tubs, await guests returning from a day of fun and adventure. Contact: Shari Gonzales, Purgatory Village Hotel, 175 Beatrice Dr., Durango, CO 81301. Call 1-800-879-7874.

Children: Y Pets: N Smoking: Y Handicap Access: N Payment: C, P, T, V, M, A

REDWOOD LODGE   *Rates: budget*
Open: year-round   *Minimum Stay: none*

Make this your headquarters for exploring southwestern Colorado, and you'll find all of the natural beauty and rich history of this unspoiled country within a short distance from your accommodations. The lodge offers one- and two-bedroom units, many with either a full kitchen or kitchenette and all with color cable TV for a night at home. The area boasts a number of fine skiing facilities including Purgatory Mountain, about 20 miles north. Families can also enjoy an excursion to the Mesa Verde National Park, where ancient cliff dwellings recall the lives of the Anasaszi Indians. For an unusual experience, you can ride the Durango-Silverton Narrow-Gauge Railroad for a special look at this old mining territory. Contact: Karen and Bart Brown, Redwood Lodge, 763 Animas View Drive, Durango, CO 81301. Call 1-800-247-9484 or 303-247-9484.

Children: Y Pets: N Smoking: Y Handicap Access: N Payment: All

ESTES PARK

FAMILY COTTAGE   *Rates: inexpensive*
Open: May 18-October 1   *Minimum Stay: two nights*
This spacious and homey cottage for six shows off the splendor of several Rocky Mountain peaks from its large windows. A large combination deck and porch in the front and a picnic area with a charcoal barbecue enhance outdoor living just beyond your door. A large living/dining room furnished in early American decor and a kitchen complete the accommodations. As secluded as the cottage and its neighbors on this 14-acre plot of pined mountain are, the shops, grocery stores and laundromats of Estes Park are only a ten-minute ride away and several good restaurants even closer. Endless walks in the forests and meadows of the Rockies, plus golf, tennis, fishing and horseback riding, provide the kind of natural diversions you'll be looking for on a vacation in the mountains. Contact: Lee Machin, Machin's Cottages in the Pines, P.O. Box 2687, 2450 Eagle Cliff Road, Estes Park, CO 80517. Call 303-586-4276. Ref. Cottage No. 10.
Children: Y Pets: Y Smoking: Y Handicap Access: N Payment: C, P, T, V, M, A

MILES MOTEL AND COTTAGES   *Rates: budget-moderate*
Open: year-round   *Minimum Stay: none*
A half-dozen mountain peaks and an alpine golf course surround these housekeeping units and condominiums. Rocky Mountain National Park lies only a short drive away, where you'll find more natural beauty than you can imagine. The Estes Park area offers a variety of activities to suit every taste—horseback riding, swimming, country music, tennis, bowling and the many guided tours, shows and special events in the National Park. The area boasts many lakes with year-round fishing. Local residents are especially fond of the autumn, when the aspen trees of Trail Ridge Road, Fall River Road and Bear Lake turn the forests to gold. The comfortable and simply furnished apartments and cabins sleep two to ten and include color TVs and in many cases cozy fireplaces. Contact: Jan and Lee Hartland, Miles Motel and Cottages, 1250 So. St. Vrain Ave., Long's Peak Route, Estes Park, CO 80517. Call 303-586-3185.
Children: Y Pets: Y Smoking: Y Handicap: N Payment: C, P, T, V, M, A, O

MOUNTAIN VIEW COTTAGE   *Rates: inexpensive*
Open: May 18-October 1   *Minimum Stay: two nights*
The large balcony of this lovely mountain cottage for four or five offers inspiring views of Prospect, Gianttrack and Ram's Horn mountains. The large open-plan living/dining room and kitchen offers the comfort of carpeting and a fireplace, plus decorations from South America. The surrounding grounds, actually a part of Rocky Mountain National Park, offer great quiet and privacy; seated at the outdoor dining area with its own charcoal grill and picnic table, you may hear nothing louder than the birds chirping and the breeze whistling through the pines. Nearby, several stables offer horseback rides on the many scenic trails, and sports lovers will enjoy trout fishing at any one of the many

area lakes and streams. Contact: Lee Machin, Machin's Cottages in the Pines, P.O. Box 2687, 2450 Eagle Cliff Road, Estes Park, CO 80517. Call 303-586-4276. Ref. Cottage No. 11.
Children: Y Pets: Y Smoking: Y Handicap Access: N Payment: C, P, T, V, M, A

PINE GROVE COTTAGE   *Rates: budget*
Open: May 18-October 1   *Minimum Stay: two nights*
This cozy cottage for two makes an ideal honeymoon hideaway on 14 shaded acres of tall pines and rock formations right in Rocky Mountain National Park. Simply furnished with wood paneling and an open fireplace, the cottage includes a very spacious living room, a kitchen with a dining area and a bedroom with an extra-long bed. The porch offers views and scents of the surrounding pine trees, and a private picnic area features a charcoal grill, picnic table and lawn chairs. Out your back door, the stunning majesty of the Rockies awaits you, and for tamer diversions, there are a golf course, a swimming pool and tennis courts nearby. Contact: Lee Machin, Machin's Cottages in the Pines, P.O. Box 2687, 2450 Eagle Cliff Road, Estes Park, CO 80517. Call 303-586-4276. Ref. Cottage No. 8.
Children: Y Pets: Y Smoking: Y Handicap Access: N Payment: C, P, T, V, M

PONDEROSA LODGE   *Rates: budget-inexpensive*
Open: year-round   *Minimum Stay: none*
Surrounded by fragrant ponderosa pines on the Fall River, this newly rebuilt mountain lodge offers a quiet retreat where you'll find fishing and hiking virtually at your doorstep and the whole of Rocky Mountain National Park just a short drive away. "River Rooms" provide accommodations for two to six and feature color cable TV with HBO, fireplaces and sliding glass doors that open onto decks and patios along the river's edge. Two cottages sleep two to six and offer additional privacy at some distance from the lodge. The historic and colorful village of Estes Park provides for your every need—groceries, laundromat, fine dining, sporting goods. Contact: Toby Farrel, Ponderosa Lodge, 1820 Fall River Road, Estes Park, CO 80517. Call 1-800-628-0512.
Children: Y Pets: N Smoking: Y Handicap Access: N Payment: C, P, T, V, O

TRAILS WEST ON THE RIVER   *Rates: budget-inexpensive*
Open: year-round   *Minimum Stay: none*
These riverside cabins situated midway between the village of Estes Park and Rocky Mountain National Park offer serene and peaceful vacation homes for two to six people and extend a special welcome to families with small children. Children three and under stay free in portacribs available on the premises. The cabins includes decks, many with river views, as well as cozy fireplaces. Guests share an outdoor hot tub, surrounded in the summertime by a terraced garden. You can use this location to explore the wilderness of the National Park and take advantage of the many activities in the area: horse shows, rodeos, cross-country and downhill skiing, country music, theater and

square dancing, just to name a few. Contact: Lindi and David Barker, Trails West on the River, Inc., 1710 Fall River Road, Box 1631, Estes Park, CO 80517. Call 303-586-4629.

Children: Y Pets: N Smoking: Y Handicap Access: N Payment: C, P, T, V, M, A

VALHALLA RESORT   *Rates: budget-moderate*
Open: year-round   *Minimum Stay: two nights*

These warm, cozy, simply furnished individual and duplex homes enjoy a beautiful location surrounded by tall pine and aspen trees at the base of Eagle Cliff Mountain, right next door to Rocky Mountain National Park. Accommodations for two to eight in one to four bedrooms include a full kitchen, a living room (many with brick fireplace) and either a deck or a patio where a steaming cup of coffee or a barbecue for the whole family can be enjoyed. This secluded mountain retreat provides a year-round sheltered and private hot tub, heated swimming and wading pools and a nine-hole miniature golf course. The friendly owners can help you to make plans and reservations for horseback riding, rafting trips, fishing, skiing and fine dining. Contact: Ruth and Jim Tipton, Valhalla Resort, P.O. Box 1439, Estes Park, CO 80517. Call 303-586-3284.

Children: Y Pets: N Smoking: Y Handicap: N Payment: C, P, T, V, M, A, O

WILDERNESS COTTAGE   *Rates: inexpensive*
Open: May 18-October 1   *Minimum Stay: two nights*

Nestled amid the rocks and pine forest of Rocky Mountain National Park, this especially secluded mountain cottage for eight features a kitchen and a large living/dining room with panoramic picture windows. Many wildlife pictures and paintings and the added warmth of a fireplace make this a thoroughly inviting retreat. A large porch offers magnificent views of Beaver Brook Valley and Eagle Cliff as well as several Rocky Mountain peaks. Situated on a 14-acre plot that it shares with a number of other cottages, it is surrounded by beauty and serenity. An eighth of a mile from a small brook, it stands only a mile from spectacular Moraine Park, where many trails into Rocky Mountain National Park begin. Contact: Lee Machin, Machin's Cottages in the Pines, P.O. Box 2687, 2450 Eagle Cliff Road, Estes Park, CO 80517. Call 303-586-4276. Ref. Cottage No. 17.

Children: Y Pets: Y Smoking: Y Handicap Access: N Payment: C, P, T, V, M, A

FRISCO

TENMILE CREEK CONDOMINIUMS   *Rates: budget-expensive*
Open: year-round   *Minimum Stay: three nights*

Summit County is Colorado ski country, and a vacation in one of these lovely two-, three- or four-bedroom condominiums puts you only minutes away from five of the county's best ski centers. Each apartment promises a gracious stay, featuring a balcony with scenic views of the surrounding mountains, wood-burning fireplaces and color cable TV. The special touches that make your stay a real vacation include an indoor heated pool, a Jacuzzi, a sauna, laundry facilities and a large party room for that special gathering. Located just west of the Continental Divide, the village of Frisco offers the summertime pleasures of trout fishing and sailing on nearby Lake Dillon, as well as hiking and biking along the thousands of acres of unspoiled National Forest land that surround the area. Contact: Gene and Bonnie Prow, Tenmile Creek Resort, P.O. Box 543, 200 Granite Street, Frisco, CO 80443. Call 303-668-3100.

Children: Y Pets: N Smoking: Y Handicap Access: Y Payment: P, T, V, M, A

GRAND LAKE

DRIFTWOOD LODGE *Rates: budget*
Open: year-round *Minimum Stay: none*

Located ideally in the heart of Colorado's high country just three miles from the west entrance of Rocky Mountain National Park, these simply furnished one-room efficiencies and two-room suites offer the perfect base for exploring the riches of the Rockies. You can snowmobile right from the door of the lodge into the National Park or Arapaho National Forest, or enjoy the cross-country and downhill skiing just minutes away. In the summer, you'll be sure to enjoy hiking, horseback riding and trout fishing in your choice of lake or stream waters. The Driftwood's spacious grounds offer lawn games and horseshoes as well as a swimming pool and a Jacuzzi. Contact: Paul Linton, Driftwood Lodge, P.O. Box 609, Grand Lake, CO 80447. Call 303-627-3654.

Children: Y Pets: Y Smoking: Y Handicap Access: N Payment: C, T, V, M, A, O

HESPERUS

BLUE LAKE RANCH *Rates: moderate*
Open: May 1-October 15 *Minimum Stay: none*

Homesteaded in the early 1900s by Swedish immigrants, this luxurious country-style estate offers one three-bedroom cabin (with kitchen) overlooking a lake and furnished in southwestern style. Surrounding the main house you'll find the luscious gardens that supply Blue Lake Ranch's various businesses: lavender for jelly, heirloom seeds and everlasting flowers. Located only 20 minutes from Durango, the ranch offers a perfect location for exploring Mesa Verde National Park and the ancient Indian cliff dwellings there. Several of southwestern Colorado's finest ski slopes are only a short drive away, as is the thrilling Durango-Silverton Narrow-Gauge Railroad. The rainbow trout-filled lake may call out to you, or you may choose to simply relax in the hot tub or stretch out in the sun. Contact: David Alford, Blue Lake Ranch, 16919 Highway 140, Hesperus, CO 81326. Call 303-453-4537.

Children: Y Pets: N Smoking: N Handicap Access: N Payment: P, T, V

LAKE CITY

THE CRYSTAL LODGE *Rates: budget-inexpensive*
Open: June 1-Labor Day *Minimum Stay: two nights*

Located in the heart of historic Gold Rush Country in the San Juan Mountains of southwestern Colorado, the Crystal Lodge offers a fine mountain retreat where the pace is slow, the air is clean and the stars and sun are brighter than you ever remembered. Accommodations include five lodge apartments that sleep from three to four and offer the convenience of complete kitchens, and four cottages for six nestled in the trees. The lodge dining room offers the finest in old fashioned dining, featuring homemade bread and pastries as well as soups, chilis and sauces from secret recipes. Outdoor activities begin at your door with cross-country ski trails and hiking; only a stone's throw away you'll find lake and stream fishing. Contact: Harley and Caryl Rudofsky, The Crystal Lodge, P.O. Box 246, Lake City, CO 81235. Call 303-944-2201.

Children: Y   Pets: N   Smoking: N   Handicap Access: N   Payment: C, P, T

LONGMONT

BRIARWOOD INN MOTEL   *Rates: budget*
Open: year-round   *Minimum Stay: none*

Located only 26 miles from Estes Park and the seemingly endless natural beauty of Rocky Mountain National Park, these charming lodgings feature cable TV with HBO and convenient kitchenettes— and waterbeds are available at no extra charge. Guests share a luxury whirlpool spa and a gracious patio area as well as the traveler's friend, a laundromat. For an excursion along the scenic route, you can drive right through the National Park to Arapaho National Wildlife Refuge, past lakes and rivers rich with fish and even a beaver lodge or two. Daily activities in the park include guided tours, lectures and demonstrations as well as hoedowns and square dancing. Contact: Sandy Hansen, Briarwood Inn Motel, 1228 N. Main, Longmont, CO 80501. Call 303-776-6622.

Children: Y   Pets: Y   Smoking: Y   Handicap Access: Y   Payment: All

OURAY

BOX CANYON LODGE & HOT SPRINGS   *Rates: budget-inexpensive*
Open: year-round   *Minimum Stay: none*

Nestled in the San Juan Mountains of southwestern Colorado, the town of Ouray remains true to the western Colorado traditions of caring friendliness and respect for natural beauty. Secluded and serene, Box Canyon Lodge offers a number of one- and two-bedroom suites with fireplaces and kitchenettes in a setting of incomparable peace. Four large, redwood outdoor spas filled from the nearby mineral springs offer the ultimate in soothing year-round relaxation at the rear of the lodge. This country is ideal for ambling hikes through woods and verdant meadows, across land settled by the Ute Indians 700 years ago. Ouray is the site of as many as 10,000 abandoned mine shafts, tunnels and cuts from gold, silver, lead, zinc and copper mines. Contact: Barbara Uhles, Box Canyon Lodge & Hot Springs, 45 Third Avenue, Ouray, CO 81427. Call 1-800-327-5080.

Children: Y   Pets: N   Smoking: Y   Handicap: N   Payment: C, P, T, V, M, A, O

WIESBADEN HOT SPRINGS SPA & LODGINGS *Rates: budget-inexpensive*
Open: year-round *Minimum Stay: none*

The original Wiesbaden Spa, built in 1879, was known as Mother Buchanan's Bath House; today the same establishment offers the natural healing of the waters the Ute Indians considered sacred. Today's Wiesbaden offers a unique opportunity for the ultimate spa experience, in a natural vapor cave with a 110-degree soaking pool. In addition, you can enjoy the hot springs swimming pool, Universal gym equipment and several kinds of body treatments, including massage and reflexology (extra charge). A number of apartments with kitchens offer two to six people an ideal spot from which to take in the marvels of this retreat. And if all this quiet and serenity get to be too much, the area offers many attractions. Contact: Linda Wright-Minter, Wiesbaden Hot Springs Spa & Lodgings, 625 5th St., P.O. Box 349, Ouray, CO 81427. Call 303-325-4347 or 303-325-4845.

Children: Y Pets: N Smoking: N Handicap Access: N Payment: C, P, T, V, M

POWDERHORN

POWDERHORN GUEST RANCH *Rates: budget-inexpensive*
Open: June 2-September 22 *Minimum Stay: three days*

Family-owned Powderhorn Ranch, small and secluded, enjoys a wilderness setting surrounded by cattle ranches and public forest, where you'll find no noise, no pollution and no traffic. What you will find is a scattering of log cabins for two or four, many with full kitchens, each with a large front porch ideal for stretching out and trading stories with a new friend. Horseback riding, the primary activity at the ranch, opens up the grandeur and excitement of this unusual and remote country. Fishing enthusiasts can tackle rainbow, German and brook trout just steps from the doors of the cabins. And everyone can enjoy the fireworks on July 4th and the Cattlemen's Days and rodeo in nearby Gunnison. Contact: Bonnie and Jim Cook, Powderhorn Guest Ranch, County Highway 27, Powderhorn, CO 81243. Call (collect) 303-641-0220.

Children: Y Pets: N Smoking: Y Handicap Access: N Payment: C, P, T, A

SALIDA

WOODLAND MOTEL & RESIDENCE INN *Rates: budget*
Open: year-round *Minimum Stay: none*

You can bring the kids and your dog, too, to this spot north of the Sangre de Cristo Mountains, where all the spectacular richness of Colorado's high country lies before you. The friendly innkeepers here offer one- and two-bedroom apartments with kitchenettes or full kitchens as well as color TV with HBO and direct-dial telephones. For an extra indulgence, full maid service is available. From here, you can enjoy outings and day trips to the hot springs at Mt. Princeton and the Great Sand Dunes National Monument. Nearby sporting activities are plentiful and varied, including tennis, golf, bi-

cycling, white-water rafting and fishing. Contact: Steve Borbas, Woodland Motel & Residence Inn, 903 W. 1st St., Salida, CO 81201. Call 719-539-4980.
Children: Y Pets: Y Smoking: Y Handicap: N Payment: C, P, T, V, M, A, O

SILVERTON

SILVERTON BED AND BREAKFAST   *Rates: budget*
Open: year-round   *Minimum Stay: none*
Located in the landmark town of Silverton in southwestern Colorado's San Juan Mountains, these accommodations for two offer the perfect base for discovering Colorado's rich mining and railroad history. You can also enjoy excursions to Mesa Verde National Park and its fabulous mysterious cliff dwellings. Smedleys Bed and Breakfast offers spacious one-bedroom accommodations for up to four with a living room, a kitchen and color TV with HBO. Wingate House Bed & Breakfast, a fully restored Victorian "gingerbread" house built in 1886, commands an excellent view of the town and the summer arrivals of the Narrow-Gauge train. The five double rooms here share two baths, a kitchen and a living room with color TV and HBO. Breakfast at the French Bakery in downtown Silverton is included in the price of the rooms. Fritz Klinke or Loren Lew, Silverton Bed and Breakfast, 1250 Greene St., P.O. Box 2, Silverton, CO 81433. Call 303-387-5423.
Children: Y Pets: N Smoking: Y Handicap: N Payment: C, P, T, V, M, A, O

SNOWMASS

CHAMONIX-AT-WOODRUN   *Rates: expensive-deluxe*
Open: June 1-October 15; November 18-March 29   *Minimum Stay: two nights*
At slopeside Chamonix, even the name evokes the romance of the French Alps, but here you have all the modern conveniences of a luxury resort, from the exquisite appointments of your vacation apartment to the fabulous common facilities shared with other guests—an outdoor swimming pool and therapy pool. A stay at one of these two- or three-bedroom apartments offers many of the European niceties that symbolize the best in resort service, including daily maid service, complete front desk and bellman service, grocery and liquor shopping and pre-purchase of lift tickets. Each apartment features a fireplace, a washer/dryer, a whirlpool and/or a steam shower. Contact: Robyn or Jackie, Snowmass Lodging Co., 425 Wood Road, Snowmass Village, CO 81615. Call 1-800-365-0410.
Children: Y Pets: N Smoking: Y Handicap: N Payment: C, P, T, V, M, A, O

HAIGHT HOUSE   *Rates: deluxe*
Open: year-round   *Minimum Stay: two nights*
From the full-length living room windows of this charming and traditional ski chalet, you'll enjoy beautiful views of the Snowmass Valley while you're warmed by the roaring fire in the brick-hooded fireplace. Thick area rugs and warm early American-style furnishing

provide the homiest atmosphere for your vacation. Accommodations for ten include five bedrooms, three and a half baths, a kitchen and dining area and a complete family room with wood-burning stove, pool table and an outdoor Jacuzzi on the deck. With easy access to the Elk Camp slopes on Snowmass Mountain and the astoundingly rich world of the Snowmass/Aspen area beyond, you can make this wonderful home away from home the base for the most memorable summer or winter vacation. Contact: Marsha Marriott, Coates, Reid & Waldron Property Management, 720 E. Hyman Avenue, Aspen, CO 81611. Call 1-800-222-7736.

Children: Y Pets: N Smoking: Y Handicap Access: N Payment: C, P, V, M, A

WOODRUN PLACE *Rates: expensive-deluxe*
Open: June 1-October 15; November 18-March 29 *Minimum Stay: two nights*
They call it Woodrun Place, but you may call it heaven. Many of the luxury one-, two- and three-bedroom apartments in this complex feature designer decorating and include more amenities than heaven itself—kitchens with microwaves, washer/dryers, fireplaces, an abundance of natural light and saunas. Guests share the outdoor heated swimming pool and outdoor therapy pool as well as a modern exercise facility. Skiers will enjoy the special plus of a ski locker room that provides convenient ski-in/ski-out access to Fanny Hill. With one of these apartments as your vacation home, you can explore rugged back country on snowshoes or fill your lungs with the pristine purity of mountain air in alpine meadows surrounded by centuries-old evergreens. Contact: Robyn or Jackie, Snowmass Lodging Co., 425 Wood Road, Snowmass Village, CO 81615. Call 1-800-365-0410.

Children: Y Pets: N Smoking: Y Handicap: N Payment: C, P, T, V, M, A, O

SNOWMASS VILLAGE

LICHENHEARTH CONDOMINIUMS *Rates: inexpensive-deluxe*
Open: year-round *Minimum Stay: one week*
Located in a prime ski-in/ski-out setting adjacent to Lift #1 and within walking distance of the bustling and bountiful Snowmass Village Mall, these studio and one-bedroom apartments also provide the summertime plus of a heated swimming pool within the complex. Each handsomely furnished apartment features a fireplace and sliding glass doors, which open onto a private balcony. The studios, among the most spacious in Snowmass, include kitchen areas fully equipped for gourmet cooking. Holidays spent here in the Roaring Fork Valley offer many excursions within easy reach: the Silver Queen Gondola ride to the top of Aspen Mountain, wildlife expeditions at Hallam Lake Nature Preserve and hiking in the Maroon Bells Wilderness. Contact: Village Property Management, Box 5550, Snowmass Village, CO 81615. Call 1-800-525-9402.

Children: Y Pets: N Smoking: Y Handicap Access: Y Payment: C, T, V

SNOWMASS MOUNTAIN CONDOMINIUMS *Rates: inexpensive-deluxe*
Open: year-round *Minimum Stay: one week*

This beautiful complex of one-, two- and three-bedroom apartments stands on a private and quiet site with a sweeping view of the Roaring Fork Valley and the surrounding mountains. Apartments feature wood-burning fireplaces, balconies and, in top-floor units, pitched beamed ceilings. Recreational facilities include a heated swimming pool, a whirlpool, a sauna and a workout room. In winter you can walk to Ski Lift #6 or take the free shuttle bus that operates regularly throughout the day. Guests can also enjoy the use of the superb facilities of the Snowmass Club, such as an 18-hole championship golf course, 11 outdoor and two indoor tennis courts staffed by professionals, a luxurious health club complete with racquetball, squash, Nautilus and an aerobics center. Contact: Village Property Management, Box 5550, Snowmass Village, CO 81615. Call 1-800-525-9402.

Children: Y Pets: N Smoking: Y Handicap Access: Y Payment: C, T, V ST239

TERRACEHOUSE CONDOMINIUMS *Rates: moderate-deluxe*
Open: year-round *Minimum Stay: one week*

Ideally located in the heart of Snowmass and built to the contour of the mountain slope, these two-bedroom apartments boast a handsome cedar exterior surrounded by stands of beautiful aspen trees. Comfortably and contemporarily furnished, each apartment features a fireplace and a user-friendly kitchen. Nearby facilities include an Olympic-sized heated swimming pool and locker rooms, a whirlpool spa and recreation center. You can take the Snowmass free shuttle bus service to any point in the village as well as to the lifts that give access to more than 2,000 acres of magnificent skiing and a par-71 golf course. Winter and summer fun seem inexhaustible in this area. Contact: Village Property Management, Box 5550, Snowmass Village, CO 81615. Call 1-800-525-9402.

Children: Y   Pets: N   Smoking: Y   Handicap Access: Y   Payment: C, T, V

STEAMBOAT SPRINGS

BEAR CLAW CONDOMINIUMS *Rates: inexpensive-deluxe*
Open: year-round *Minimum Stay: two nights*

These one- to four-bedroom apartments for two to ten guests enjoy an ideal location for passionate skiers who cannot wait to get onto the slopes. From your door, you can ski to any of the base lifts or gondolas, with acres and acres of champagne powder glistening around you. Summertime hiking to the Continental Divide or fishing in beautiful mountain streams promises the ultimate in relaxation, a chance to get a different perspective on life. Return in the evening to lounge in the whirlpool, sauna or outdoor heated pool. Each gracious apartment features a fireplace and conveniently laid-out kitchen as well as luxurious carpeting and original artwork. Contact: Lisa M. Filkoski, Bear Claw Condominiums, 2420 Ski Trail Lane, Steamboat Springs, CO 80487. Call 1-800-232-7252 or 303-879-6100.

Children: Y Pets: N Smoking: Y Handicap Access: Y Payment: C, P, T, V, M, A

HARBOR HOTEL & CONDOMINIUMS   *Rates: inexpensive-deluxe*
Open: year-round   *Minimum Stay: none*

Located in the center of historic downtown Steamboat Springs, these simply and graciously appointed apartments for two to six offer vacationers an ideal spot from which to fully explore the area. A short walk from ice skating, day and night skiing, rodeo grounds and Howelsen Hill's ski jumping, the Harbor Condominiums offer features such as cable TV and direct-dial telephones. Guests can make unlimited use of the Harbor Spa with its two hot tubs, a steam room and sauna. Formerly a ranching community, the town of Steamboat Springs provides a huge selection of fine restaurants, fashionable shops and all the outdoor activities—skiing, horseback riding, ice skating, white-water rafting—that make the Rockies the favored vacation center for so many people. Contact: Ann Cox, Harbor Hotel & Condominiums, 703 Lincoln Avenue, P.O. Box 774109, Steamboat Springs, CO 80477. Call 1-800-543-8888.

Children: Y Pets: N Smoking: Y Handicap: N Payment: C, P, T, V, M, A, O

SKI RANCH CONDOMINIUMS   *Rates: budget-deluxe*
Open: December 20-March 31   *Minimum Stay: three nights*

Located right on the mountainside, these one- and two-bedroom (plus loft) apartments offer spectacular views of the Yampa Valley and the Village at Steamboat from their private balconies and terraces. The well-equipped kitchens include microwave ovens, and the living room boasts the charm and intimacy of a wood-burning stove. From this rustic three-story complex enjoy an easy walk to the gondola and base area, or hop on the shuttle bus that stops at your door. Here in Ski Country USA, you'll find the right slope for you amid 2,500 skiable acres, or the meadow with just the right mix of wildflowers, birds and butterflies. Contact: Martha Banning or Mark Johnson, Pine Real Estate & Management, P.O. Box 774173, 2500 Village Drive, Steamboat Springs, CO 80477. Call 1-800-235-5571.

Children: Y Pets: N Smoking: Y Handicap Access: N Payment: C, P, T, V, M

STORMWATCH CONDOMINIUM   *Rates: budget-expensive*
Open: year-round   *Minimum Stay: three nights*

This modern low-rise condominium complex stacked on a hillside offers superb views of Mt. Werner. Situated for comfort and convenience, the apartments are only a short walk or shuttle bus ride from the ski lift areas as well as the town center, where shopping and fine dining await you. You can choose from a studio, one- or two-bedroom apartment, and enjoy in every case a private balcony, a kitchen or kitchenette, a crackling fireplace and the use of an indoor hot tub. Winter adventures await you year-round here, with deep-powder skiing some of the best in the world. Summertime brings the promise of skies filled with birds, kites, and hot-air balloons, and a hot spring for every day of the week. Contact: Martha Banning or Mark Johnson, Pine Real Estate & Management, P.O. Box 774173, 2500 Village Drive, Steamboat Springs, CO 80477. Call 1-800-235-5571.

Children: Y Pets: N Smoking: Y Handicap Access: N Payment: C, P, T, V, M

VISTA VERDE GUEST & SKI TOURING RANCH   *Rates: budget-moderate*
Open: summer, winter   *Minimum Stay: three nights*

Surrounded by remarkably unspoiled national lands, this guest resort and ski touring ranch is a working cattle and horse operation. Here amid the splendor of pristine valleys and majestic elevations, you can explore country where elk, deer, bear, fox, coyote, porcupine and even the Greater Sandhill Crane roam peacefully. Activities at the ranch include guided horseback tours, invigorating day hikes to the awesome beauty of Gilpin Lake and bike tours through breathtaking back country. One- to three-bedroom log cabins, rustic and charming with hooked rugs and calico, feature wood-burning fireplaces and kitchens, although rates include plenty of home-cooked food and the warm company of a small group of guests that never exceeds 40. Contact: Frank Brophy, Vista Verde Guest & Ski Touring Ranch, Box 465, Steamboat Springs, CO 80477. Call 1-800-526-7433 or 303-879-3858.
Children: Y   Pets: N   Smoking: Y   Handicap Access: N   Payment: C, P, T

WALTON CREEK CONDOMINIUMS   *Rates: budget-deluxe*
Open: year-round   *Minimum Stay: three nights*

A warm, homey atmosphere awaits you in any one of these spacious condo apartments for four to six vacationers. This two-story low-rise building located just three-quarters of a mile from the ski slopes boasts a shuttle bus stop right in front of the door and a heated outdoor swimming pool. Each apartment features a sauna, a fireplace and a balcony or terrace overlooking the snow- and wildflower-covered fields. A washer/dryer, cable TV and a direct-dial telephone complete the conveniences. With the average winter snowfall somewhere around 27 inches and over 2,500 skiable acres in Steamboat Springs, this location will suit both the novice and the hot-dogger. When the snow melts, you'll find a wealth of adventure on mountain bikes and horseback and in kayaks, river rafts and canoes. Contact: Martha Banning or Mark Johnson, Pine Real Estate & Management, P.O. Box 774173, 2500 Village Drive, Steamboat Springs, CO 80477. Call 1-800-235-5571.
Children: Y Pets: N Smoking: Y Handicap Access: N Payment: C, P, T, V, M

YAMPA VIEW CONDOMINIUMS   *Rates: budget-deluxe*
Open: year-round   *Minimum Stay: three nights*

This contemporary three-story apartment complex built right into the side of Mt. Werner offers exquisite views of the Yampa Valley and the lively village of Steamboat Springs. Whether you come to ski the 50 miles of trails or challenge yourself on virgin snow, whether your summer passion is soaking in hot springs or hot-air ballooning, you'll find something to satisfy that special yearning in this beautiful town. Each condominium apartment features two bedrooms (some also have a sleeping loft), a living room with a gas fireplace and a private balcony. You can sweat the kinks out in your own sauna or take a dip in the communal outdoor hot tub under a star-filled sky. Then it's off to dinner at one of the area's fine restaurants and on to a performance at the theater festival. Contact: Martha Banning or Mark Johnson, Pine Real Estate & Management, P.O. Box 774173, 2500 Village Drive, Steamboat Springs, CO 80477. Call 1-800-235-5571.

Children: Y Pets: N Smoking: Y Handicap Access: N Payment: C, P, T, V, M

VAIL

LION SQUARE LODGE & CONFERENCE CENTER   *Rates: inexpensive-deluxe*
Open: year-round   *Minimum Stay: none*

Cradled in the heart of the Rockies, each of these one- and two-bedroom apartments for three to six people comes complete with a contemporary living room with fireplace, a balcony, an electric barbecue for the best in apres-ski meals, and color TV with HBO. The complex offers all the amenities of a resort—valet and laundry service, a heated swimming pool, ski storage, even a daily newspaper delivered to your door—with the privacy of a condominium suite. Nearby, you'll find some of the world's best skiing, where you can challenge yourself with the renowned powder of the back bowls or cruise down Simba to your doorstep. And summer days seem to sail by when you pass them in hot-air balloons or on scenic gondola rides. Contact: Lita Hitchcock, Lion Square Lodge & Conference Center, 660 W. Lionshead Place, Vail, CO 81657. Call 1-800-525-5788.

Children: Y Pets: N Smoking: Y Handicap Access: N Payment: C, P, T, V, M, A

WESTWIND AT VAIL   *Rates: budget-deluxe*
Open: year-round   *Minimum Stay: none*

These well-appointed and caringly furnished one- to four-bedroom condominiums offer comfort and convenience in a fabulous location only 200 feet from Vail's only gondola and within steps of the children's day facilities, the ski school, the rental shops and the free shuttle bus. Each apartment offers a cozy fireplace, a sunny private balcony with scenic views of Vail Mountain, color cable TV and a kitchen complete with a microwave. The complex's amenities include daily maid service, underground parking and ski repair. After a day on the slopes or a round of golf on one of Vail's four 18-hole PGA courses, soak out the kinks in one of two hydro-spa hot pools. Or enjoy the spacious redwood deck around the heated swimming pools, an ideal spot from which to watch the sun fade on the slopes. Contact: Paula Denissen, Westwind at Vail, 548 S. Frontage Road, Vail, CO 81657. Call 1-800-852-9378.

Children: Y Pets: N Smoking: Y Handicap Access: N Payment: C, P, T, V, M, A

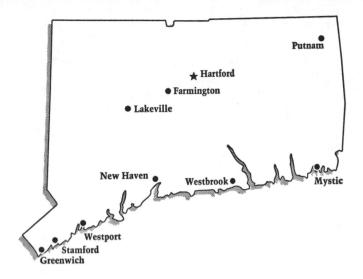

Connecticut

FARMINGTON

CENTENNIAL INN
Open: year-round

Rates: inexpensive
Minimum Stay: none

Nestled in the lovely woodlands of Farmington Valley, the Centennial Inn features elegant one- and two-bedroom units, each containing a complete eat-in kitchen and a living room with a gas-flame fireplace. Guests here receive a daily paper and complimentary continental breakfast, and may enjoy the property's private swimming pool and exercise room, take a scenic jog along one of the many trails cutting through the placid woods, or play golf at the course a half mile away. The wealthy and aristocratic town of Farmington also offers much of interest to visitors, including fine examples of colonial architecture, highlighted by the Stanley-Whitman House, an early 18th-century mansion now operating as an exquisite little museum featuring beautiful period furnishings and artifacts and handsome herb and flower gardens. Contact: Centennial Inn, 5 Spring Lane, Farmington, CT 06032. Call 1-203-677-4647 or 1-800-852-2052.

Children: Y   Pets: N   Smoking: Y   Handicap Access: N   Payment: All

LAKEVIEW

INTERLAKEN INN
Open: year-round

Rates: expensive
Minimum Stay: two nights

Eight one-bedroom townhouses, each containing a fully equipped kitchen, a living room with an inviting fireplace and a private patio or balcony, are offered at the Interlaken Inn, nestled between the Wononskopomuc and Wononpakook lakes in the beautiful Berkshire Mountains. With boats and canoes available for rent, guests keep happily busy using the inn's abundant facilities both on the lake and ashore, including a complete health and fitness center, tennis and racquetball courts, pool, sauna, and golf course. The surrounding area offers much of interest as well, from the Sharon Audubon Center to West Cornwall's lovely covered bridge, the Holley-Williams House and the Lime Rock Race Park, not to mention exceptional skiing opportunities in the winter. Contact: Interlaken Inn, Route 112, Lakeville, CT 06039. Call 1-203-435-9878 or 1-800-222-2909.

Children: **Y**   Pets: **N**   Smoking: **Y**   Handicap Access: **N**   Payment: **All**

MYSTIC

THE INN AT MYSTIC   *Rates: budget-expensive*
Open: year-round   *Minimum Stay: none*
The Inn at Mystic, set on a dramatically landscaped, 13-acre oceanfront estate, is comprised of the Colonial Inn and the Gatehouse, each offering its own brand of old-fashioned New England charm. Rooms feature patios, balconies and fireplaces; and all are equipped with a fully outfitted modern kitchen. Summer guests will enjoy the boats, canoes, fishing, and tennis facilities that are all at your doorstep— before venturing out to the local art festival and antiques and boat shows. Those who are more daring will love a cruise on a clipper ship from one of the local wharves; and the whole family will delight in the area's most famous sight—the Mystic Seaport and Museum. Contact: The Inn at Mystic, P.O. Box 216, Mystic, CT 06355. Call 203-536-9604 or 1-800-237-2415.

Children: **Y**   Pets: **N**   Smoking: **Y**   Handicap Access: **N**   Payment: **All**

STAMFORD

THE BEDFORD   *Rates: inexpensive-moderate*
Open: year-round   *Minimum Stay: none*
The Bedford places guests right in the heart of Connecticut's Fairfield County, one of America's most fashionable residential areas. The bright lights of New York City are less than an hour away, and recreational facilities on the Long Island Sound are even closer. Or simply enjoy the New England charms of Stamford, developing into a major urban center in its own right yet retaining its tranquil and distinctive small-town atmosphere. With a sunny and quiet rooftop deck, the luxurious inn offers over 40 self-contained one-bedroom units, each attractively decorated and featuring a fully equipped kitchen. Contact: The Bedford, 720 Bedford Street, Stamford, CT 06901. Call 1-203-328-2000.

Children: **Y**   Pets: **N**   Smoking: **Y**   Handicap Access: **N**   Payment: **All**

WESTBROOK

WATER'S EDGE INN AND RESORT   *Rates: moderate-expensive*
Open: year-round   *Minimum Stay: none*

Once you experience the luxurious elegance of the Water's Edge Inn and Resort, it may be hard to leave. You can enjoy your own spacious and airy villa—many of which have balconies and spectacular ocean views—and step from your front door directly onto the beach. Swim in indoor and outdoor pools; tone your muscles in the health spa; and relax afterward in a Jacuzzi. In the evening, get warm by the fireplace and dine on a gourmet meal prepared by award-winning chefs, or create your own food fantasy in a well-stocked kitchen. Golf and boating are nearby; and area theaters, museums and shops are just a short drive down the shoreline to New Haven. Contact: Water's Edge Inn and Resort, 1525 Boston Post Road, Westbrook, CT 06498. Call 203-399-5901 or 1-800-222-5901.

Children: Y   Pets: N   Handicap Access: N   Payment: C, T, A, V, M

WINDSOR

THE RESIDENCE INN   *Rates: budget-inexpensive*
Open: year-round   *Minimum Stay: none*

The Residence Inn offers a number of self-contained one- and two-bedroom housekeeping units, all tastefully appointed with full kitchen facilities and a living area and many featuring a fireplace. The town of Windsor, settled in 1639, lays claim to being the oldest town in Connecticut. A small pool, Jacuzzi and sports court are also provided for the use of guests. But visitors will want to spend plenty of time exploring this history-steeped region. Located nearby are such landmarks as the United Church of Christ, the oldest gathered congregation in North America, whose adjoining cemetary contains the tombstones of some of the country's first settlers; the Flyer House and Museum, one of Windsor's oldest structures, built in 1640; and Palisdo Green, site of the old stockade constructed during the 1637 Pequot War. Contact: The Residence Inn Hartford North, 100 Dunfey Lane, Windsor, CT 06095. Call 1-203-688-7474.

Children: Y   Pets: Y   Smoking: Y   Handicap Access: Y   Payment: All

Delaware

BETHANY BEACH

BREWER   *Rates: moderate*
Open: year-round   *Minimum Stay: one week*

Maplewood Street, where Brewer stands, abuts the Atlantic Ocean, so
renters can roll out of bed and stake a spot in the sand without losing
a second of sunshine. It's a homey, old-fashioned-looking three-story
home, with a bay window in front and enclosed porches on both sides.
Four bedrooms and two baths make it roomy enough for big families.
Its master bedroom suite has its own bath, and its kitchen was remodeled just three years ago. Big trees provide shade; half the house is
air-conditioned. Contact: Crowley Associates Realty, Inc., Rt. 1 and
Pennsylvania Avenue, Bethany Beach, DE 19930. Call 1-800-732-7433
or 1-800-242-4213 (in Delaware, 302-539-4013).

Children: **Y**   Pets: **N**   Smoking: **Y**   Handicap Access: **N**   Payment: **C, T**

HOWARD GALLIVAN   *Rates: budget-expensive*
Open: year-round   *Mimimum Stay: one week*

Back in 1903, when Bethany Beach was founded "as a haven of rest for
quiet people," the man who chose the town's name won a prime
beachfront lot for his efforts. Howard Gallivan on Oakwood Street is
that prize of a property, an easy two-block stroll to the Atlantic Ocean.
Landscaped with lots of large trees and built of wood, the house has
two wonderful front decks and a screened-in porch. It is big enough to
accommodate crowds in four bedrooms sharing three baths, and has a

big, modern kitchen. Contact Crowley Assoicates Realty, Inc., Rt. 1 and Pennsylvania Avenue, Bethany Beach, DE 19330. Call 1-800-732-7433 or 1-800-242-4213 (in Delaware, 302-539-4013).

Children: Y   Pets: N   Smoking: Y   Handicap Access: N   Payment: C, T

NEMO ASSOCIATES "AFTER DECK"   *Rates: inexpensive*
Open: year-round   *Minimum Stay: one week*

Fifth Street, where the After Deck is located, defines the northern boundary of little Bethany Beach. The property sits just three lots back from the ocean and is the end unit in a pleasant grouping of three attached homes. It features three bedrooms, one bath, a deck, big windows, air conditioning and a screened-in porch for watching the sun rise over the wide, blue-green Atlantic. Beach activities available nearby include charter boats, surf fishing, surfing on the north side of Indian River Inlet and at Fenwick Island State Park, windsurfing, ocean kayaking, crabbing and much more. Contact: Crowley Associates Realty, Inc., Rt. 1 and Pennsylvania Avenue, Bethany Beach, DE 19330. Call 1-800-732-7433 or 1-800-242-4213 (in Delaware, 302-539-4013).

Children: Y   Pets: N   Smoking: Y   Handicap Access: N   Payment: C, T

DEWEY BEACH

11 DICKINSON STREET   *Rates: moderate-expensive*
Open: year-round   *Minimum Stay: one week*

Right on an ocean block in central Dewey Beach, this luxurious duplex holds a pair of two-bedroom apartments. Both feature sun porches, air conditioning, dishwashers, washers and dryers, and they each sleep eight. The second-floor unit has one additional benefit: It rents with a third-floor deck, a perfect private tanning spot. The building is modern in style and made of wood. From it the stores, clubs and restaurants of downtown Dewey Beach are an easy walk away. Contact: Harry A. Shaud, Inc., 212 Rehoboth Avenue, Rehoboth Beach, DE 19771. Call 302-227-9451.

Children: Y   Pets: N   Smoking: Y   Handicap Access: N   Payment: C, P, T

121 HOUSTON STREET   *Rates: moderate-expensive*
Open: year-round   *Minimum Stay: season*

This Dewey Beach duplex just two short blocks from the ocean is surrounded by towering shade trees and a pleasant lawn. Both apartments feature three bedrooms (sleeping a total of six), one bath and a wonderfully large, inviting, screened-in porch. Dewey is a classic beach resort reminiscent of southern California, where almost everyone wears bathing suits and shades all day long. Shorefront diversions run the gamut from jet skiing to sailing, crabbing, windsurfing, or simply taking in the rays. Contact: Harry A. Shaud, Inc., 212 Rehoboth Avenue, Rehoboth Beach, DE 19771. Call 302-227-9451.

Children: Y   Pets: N   Smoking: Y   Handicap Access: N   Payment: C, P, T

1904 BAYARD AVENUE EXTENSION, UNITS A AND B *Rates: expensive*
Open: year-round *Minimum Stay: season*
For a little pampering and a bayside view, these two five-bedroom apartments in Dewey Beach are just what's called for. Just two blocks from the surf of the Atlantic, they sleep 10 each and sit on stilts to keep the tides, crabs, and fishing boats at bay. Built in 1988, they have building-long front decks, three and a half baths each, ample parking (which is no small thing in this bustling beach community), Jacuzzis, fireplaces, air conditioning, dishwashers and washers and dryers. Contact: Harry A. Shaud, Inc., 212 Rehoboth Avenue, Rehoboth Beach, DE 19771. Call 302-227-9451.
Children: Y   Pets: N   Smoking: Y   Handicap Access: N   Payment: C, P, T

ATLANTIC OCEANSIDE MOTEL *Rates: budget-inexpensive*
Open: May 1-November 1 *Minimum Stay: two nights*
The king-sized efficiencies at the Atlantic Oceanside lie just 100 feet from the water and are within walking distance of the shops, restaurants and clubs of Dewey Beach. Nearby, too, are opportunities for bayside crabbing, sailing, fishing and beachcombing at the beautiful Delaware Seashore State Park, just a few miles south. The Atlantic Oceanside has its own private pool, and its units, built in 1983, have been carefully soundproofed. They feature two double beds, color television, telephones, air conditioning, coffee makers, kitchenettes with microwaves, daily maid service and complimentary parking. Contact: Atlantic Oceanside Motel, 1700 Hwy. 1, Dewey Beach, DE 19971. Call 302-227-8811.
Children: Y Pets: Y Smoking: Y Handicap Access: N Payment: C, T, A, V, M

BAY VIEW INN *Rates: budget-inexpensive*
Open: May 1-September 30 *Minimum Stay: two nights*
The Bay View Inn's convenient efficiency apartments are located one block from the ocean and right next door to one of the most popular restaurants in the area, the Rusty Rudder. Dewey Beach, just south of Rehoboth, is especially popular with the young crowd, who stop in at surfside watering holes between forays on the water. The Bay View units come with two beds, kitchenettes, balconies, television, telephones, free parking and morning coffee and daily maid service. And for those who want a little variety in their surf-splashing and sunbathing, trolley service into Rehoboth is available. Contact: Bay View Inn, 1409 Hwy. 1, Dewey Beach, DE 19971. Call 302-227-4343.
Children: Y Pets: N Smoking: Y Handicap Access: Y Payment: C, T, A, V, M

THE SURF CLUB *Rates: budget-inexpensive*
Open: year-round *Minimum Stay: three nights*
Luxury, Dewey Beach style, is the keynote at the Surf Club, a motel/condominium complex where the studio apartments have all been recently remodeled. There's an ocean view from every one, along with a solarium porch, kitchenette with microwave, and tasteful, clean-lined contemporary furnishings. Little extras abound, like a swim-

ming pool, sauna, daily maid service, complimentary morning coffee and parking and cable television. The Surf Club is so close to the ocean that the sound of waves will lull you to sleep. Contact: The Surf Club, 1 Read Street, Dewey Beach, DE 19971. Call 1-800-441-8341 (in Delaware, 302-227-7059.

Children: Y Pets: N Smoking: Y Handicap Access: N Payment: C, T, A, V, M

MIDDLESEX BEACH

COX   *Rates: inexpensive-deluxe*
Open: year-round   *Minimum Stay: one week*

Middlesex Beach is an exclusive little vacation community just south of Bethany. Dune Road, where Cox is located, runs north and south between Highway 1 and the Atlantic shore. Cox is a spacious and attractive split-level house built on stilts, offering great ocean views from its long, double-level deck. It has four bedrooms, three baths, a loft, air conditioning and a screened-in porch—all just a stone's throw from the soft sand and foamy brine of the Delaware seashore. Contact: Crowley Associates Realty, Inc., Rt. 1 and Pennsylvania Avenue, Bethany Beach, DE 19330. Call 1-800-732-7433 or 1-800-242-4213 (in Delaware, 302-539-4013).

Children: Y   Pets: N   Smoking: Y   Handicap Access: N   Payment: C, T

ROSSITER   *Rates: budget-inexpensive*
Open: year-round   *Minimum Stay: one week*

Rossiter boasts its own little private beach and a lovely wooded setting near South Bethany and the winding channels of Little Assawaman Bay. Its patio is a kind of an island, situated in the middle of this contemporary house. There are three bedrooms in all, sharing two baths. Remodeled in 1987, the house offers the best of everything. From here it's a quick hop to the tidal marshes and sandy Atlantic beaches of Fenwick Island State Park. Contact: Crowley Associates Realty, Inc., Rt. 1 and Pennsylvania Avenue, Bethany Beach 19930. Call 1-800-732-7433 or 1-800-242-4213 (in Delaware, 302-539-4013).

Children: Y   Pets: N   Smoking: Y   Handicap Access: N   Payment: C, T

NEW CASTLE

THE JEFFERSON HOUSE   *Rates: budget-inexpensive*
Open: year-round   *Minimum Stay: two nights*

New Castle is one of the East Coast's prettiest little historic gems, a perfectly intact colonial village on the Delaware River, originally settled by the Swedish and Dutch over 200 years ago. A walk along its brick-paved Strand takes visitors back in time, past a Georgian mansion, tidy, slumbering rowhouses, and the Jefferson House, which holds two eminently rentable apartments. A working 19th-century fireplace keeps The Hearth toasty; it's an efficiency on the ground level, opening right onto the Strand and furnished in Victorian cherrywood. The Speak-Easy, with antique oak decor, accommodates four in a full-sized iron and brass bed and sleep sofa. Both have kitchens, but breakfasts are included. Contact: Chris Bechstein, The Jefferson House, The Strand at the Wharf, New Castle, DE 19720. Call 302-323-0999 or 302-322-8944.

Children: Y Pets: N Smoking: Y Handicap Access: N Payment: C, P, T, V, M

NORTH BETHANY

DUNDEE *Rates: moderate-deluxe*
Open: year-round *Minimum Stay: one week*
Dundee is a roomy, three-story frame house, recently built in the Ocean Ridge development north of Bethany Beach. Located at 25 Seashell Turn, it boasts six bedrooms, three baths, air conditioning, a well-equipped, modern kitchen, recreation room, building-long decks on two levels and lots of windows providing views of both the bay and the ocean. There's also a three-car garage—though beachcombers won't need cars, since the shore is just a block away. Contact: Crowley Associates Realty, Inc., Rt. 1 and Pennsylvania Avenue, Bethany Beach, DE 19930. Call 1-800-732-7433 or 1-800-242-4213 (in Delaware, 302-539-4013).

Children: Y Pets: N Smoking: Y Handicap Access: N Payment: C, T

KUHNS *Rates: inexpensive-deluxe*
Open: year-round *Minimum Stay: one week*
Situated at 9 Admiral Road in the convenient Tower Shores community north of Bethany Beach, Kuhns is a capacious five-bedroom home that sleeps a total of 12 (sharing four baths). Kuhns was completely remodeled in 1987, adding a modern kitchen and washers and dryers on both of its two floors. Its asymmetrically angled roof and huge two-level decks (which wrap around three sides of the building) combine to give it a striking facade. Central air conditioning and other amenities are included. Contact: Crowley Associates Realty, Inc., Rt. 1 and Pennsylvania Avenue, Bethany Beach, DE 19930. Call 1-800-732-7433 or 1-800-242-4213 (in Delaware, 302-539-4013).

Children: Y Pets: N Smoking: Y Handicap Access: N Payment: C, T

MALLARD LANDING *Rates: budget-expensive*
Open: year-round *Minimum Stay: one week*
Mallard Landing's North Pennsylvania Avenue location puts visitors a block away from the beach and within walking distance of downtown Bethany, where they'll find shops, restaurants and in summertime one of the region's best arts and crafts fairs. Each unit in this townhouse complex contains four bedrooms and three or three and a half baths. The modern kitchens and comfortably furnished living rooms lie on the third floor, and on the fourth floor there are lofts and private decks. Air conditioning, laundry facilities, and two parking spots are included. Contact: Crowley Associates Realty, Inc., Rt. 1 and Pennsylvania Avenue, Bethany Beach, DE 19930. Call 1-800-732-7433 or 1-800-242-4213 (in Delaware, 302-539-4013).

Children: Y Pets: N Smoking: Y Handicap Access: N Payment: C, T

REHOBOTH BEACH

11 COUNTRY CLUB DRIVE

Rates: budget-moderate
Open: year-round
Minimum Stay: one week

Ten can bed down comfortably in this Delaware seashore saltbox on the western side of town near the Rehoboth Beach Country Club. It boasts four bedrooms, two baths, a porch and outside shower, which does a good job of keeping sand out of the house. The surrounding yard is large enough for a game of Frisbee or touch football. Other amenities include air conditioning and a dishwasher. On gray days when the beach doesn't hold much allure, this vacation home makes a good starting point for trips to historic Lewes or Dover, the picture perfect colonial village of Odessa, or even further north to Delaware's Brandywine Valley, site of the DuPont estates. Contact: Harry A. Shaud, Inc., 212 Rehoboth Avenue, Rehoboth Beach, DE 19771. Call 302-227-9451.

Children: Y   Pets: N   Smoking: Y   Handicap Access: N   Payment: C, P, T

10 JERSEY

Rates: expensive
Open: year-round
Minimum Stay: two weeks

This Cape Cod-style clapboard house in Rehoboth Beach peeks from behind a picket fence south of Silver Lake, almost closer to Dewey Beach than to the Rehoboth boardwalk. Its most striking feature is a wraparound, screened-in porch on the ground level; above it is another open-air porch, fine for private sunbathing. There are four handsomely furnished bedrooms in this top-of-the-line vacation home, as well as three modern baths. Contact: Harry A. Shaud, Inc., 212 Rehoboth Avenue, Rehoboth Beach, DE 19771. Call 302-227-9451.

Children: Y   Pets: N   Smoking: Y   Handicap Access: N   Payment: C, P, T

16 PENNSYLVANIA AVENUE

Rates: budget
Open: year-round
Minimum Stay: three nights

The Pines section of rollicking, sun-loving Rehoboth Beach lies in the northern section of town, near Lake Gerar's ducks, shade trees, and peace but still close enough to the glistening sands of the seashore for action. In fact, these roomy quarters situated over a garage on Pennsylvania Avenue are within a block of the Atlantic. There's one comfortable bedroom, with tall trees brushing its window, one bath and several air-conditioning units to keep the sweat off your brow during Rehoboth's steamy summer afternoons. Contact: Harry A. Shaud, Inc., 212 Rehoboth Avenue, Rehoboth Beach, DE 19771. Call 302-227-9451.

Children: Y   Pets: N   Smoking: Y   Handicap Access: N   Payment: C, P, T

37 PENNSYLVANIA AVENUE

Rates: moderate-expensive
Open: year-round
Minimum Stay: two weeks

You can smell the salt and hear the rhythm of the waves lapping the shore from this Pennsylvania Avenue retreat just a block and a half away from Rehoboth's boardwalk area. It's nestled in the quiet Pines section of town, and with five bedrooms and two and a half baths, it's great for families. In addition to a large living room and fully equipped kitchen, there's an inviting screened-in front porch secluded by bushes and trees. Rehoboth's northern residential neighborhoods are pretty indeed, full of handsome summer cottages—some actually palatial in size—and make fine territory for bike trips. Contact: Harry A. Shaud, Inc., 212 Rehoboth Avenue, Rehoboth Beach, DE 19771. Call 302-227-9451.

Children: Y   Pets: N   Smoking: Y   Handicap Access: N   Payment: C, P, T

---

1 ROBINSON   *Rates: expensive*
Open: year-round   *Minimum Stay: one season*

Beautifully landscaped Silver Lake sits halfway between Rehoboth Bay and the Atlantic seaboard and is the center of one of the town's most peaceful, carefully maintained residential neighborhoods. This traditional clapboard home directly overlooks the lake and has been recently modernized. Current amenities include air conditioning, dishwasher and washer/dryer. One Robinson contains four bedrooms (sleeping a total of ten), three and a half baths, and both a porch and a deck. Contact: Harry A. Shaud, Inc., 212 Rehoboth Avenue, Rehoboth Beach, DE 19771. Call 302-227-9451.

Children: Y   Pets: N   Smoking: Y   Handicap Access: N   Payment: C, P, T

LAKE COMEGYS   *Rates: moderate-expensive*
Open: year-round   *Minimum Stay: two weeks*

Little Comegys Lake reflects the blue Rehoboth sky just south of larger Silver Lake. It's within walking distance of both Rehoboth and Dewey beaches, and close as well to the evocative marshlands around Head of the Bay Cove, where crabbing and fishing are good. The house has three bedrooms, two baths, two screened-in porches, a patio and splendid lake vistas. Bird-watchers will want to keep their binoculars close at hand. Other amenities include a dishwasher, air conditioning, and washer and dryer. Contact: Harry A. Shaud, Inc., 212 Rehoboth Avenue, Rehoboth Beach, DE 19771. Call 302-227-9451.

Children: Y   Pets: N   Smoking: Y   Handicap Access: N   Payment: C, P, T

SEA COLONY

SEA COLONY HIGH RISE   *Rates: budget-moderate*
Open: year-round   *Minimum Stay: one week*

Sea Colony, just south of Bethany Beach, is a sprawling, self-contained resort community with its own tennis courts, saunas and health club, indoor and outdoor swimming pools and kid's camp facilities. The eight-story high-rise sits right on the ocean; indeed, oceanfront decks make it possible to watch the sun rise over the hazy blue Atlantic. Units range in size from one to three bedrooms and come equipped with washers and dryers, air conditioning and dishwashers. The Colony is a great place to socialize with other Delaware seashore lovers. Contact: Crowley Associates Realty, Inc., Rt. 1 and Pennsylvania Avenue, Bethany Beach, DE 19930. Call 1-800-732-7433 or 1-800-242-4213 (in Delaware, 302-539-4013).

Children: Y   Pets: N   Smoking: Y   Handicap Access: N   Payment: C, T

SOUTH BETHANY

BENSON *Rates: inexpensive-expensive*
Open: year-round *Minimum Stay: one week*
The little village of South Bethany borders on Fenwick Island State Park and is crisscrossed by a picturesque web of Little Assawaman Bay inlets. Benson is a member of this inviting community, located at 8 Sea Side Drive less than a block from the beach. Numerous decks, sliding windows and an angled roofline define its facade; in the air-conditioned interior are four bedrooms and two and a half baths. The living room and kitchen are positioned on the second floor to catch the best ocean views. Included in rental are permits to facilitate parking. Contact: Crowley Associates Realty, Inc., Rt. 1 and Pennsylvania Avenue, Bethany Beach, DE 19930. Call 1-800-732-7433 or 1-800-242-4213 (in Delaware, 302-539-4013).
Children: **Y** Pets: **N** Smoking: **Y** Handicap Access: **N** Payment: **C, T**

WARD/BRULL *Rates: inexpensive-expensive*
Open: year-round *Minimum Stay: one week*
Here's another South Bethany retreat, positioned at 36 Sea Side Drive just three lots back from the ocean. Its allure is found in skylights, a wraparound L-shaped deck, comfortable furnishings and air conditioning. Ward/Brull boasts three bedrooms and two baths, with the living room and kitchen on the second floor. This property lies within walking distance of the northern reaches of Fenwick Island State Park, and it's a good base for trips to the historic Fenwick Island Lighthouse—built in 1859—and the Mason Dixon Monument. Contact: Crowley Associates Realty, Inc., Rt. 1 and Pennsylvania Avenue, Bethany Beach, DE 19930. Call 1-800-732-7433 or 1-800-242-4213 (in Delaware, 302-539-4013).
Children: **Y** Pets: **N** Smoking: **Y** Handicap Access: **N** Payment: **C, T**

Florida

AMELIA ISLAND

SUMMER BEACH　　　　　　　　　　　*Rates: budget-expensive*
Open: year-round　　　　　　　　　　*Minimum Stay: none*

The one-, two- and three-bedroom luxury condominiums of Summer Beach offer a taste of island life at its finest. Amelia Island, near the Florida/Georgia border, is not only an idyllic vacation spot, it's also steeped in history as the only U.S. location to have been under eight national flags. Guests can enjoy the area's rich cultural heritage at Fernandina, an irresistible Victorian seaport, and indulge in the vast recreational opportunities available across the island. At the complex, they'll find three swimming pools, tennis courts, a championship 18-hole golf course and horseback riding treks along a stretch of Atlantic coastline covered with a blanket of snow-white sand. Contact: Amelia Resort Management Co., Inc., 5000 Amelia Island Parkway, Amelia Island, FL 32034. Call 1-904-277-2525 or 1-800-432-3047.

Children: Y Pets: N Smoking: Y Handicap Access: N Payment: C, T, V, M

BOCA RATON

MARCO APARTMENT SUITES　　　　　　*Rates: budget-expensive*
Open: year-round　　　　　　　　　　*Minimum Stay: none*

Designed with the corporate traveler in mind, this comfortable apartment complex, one of several similar rental properties in southern Florida run by the Marco Corporation, is altogether suitable for vacationing couples and families. A full management and maintenance staff see to every need so guests are free to go about their business— whether it's business itself or simply the pursuit of Boca Raton's considerable recreational and scenic pleasures. The units range in size from one to three bedrooms and include eat-in kitchens, while the grounds offer an Olympic-sized swimming pool, tennis courts and a full gym and sauna area. Contact: Luciana Casu, Marco Corporation, Corporate Housing Division, 490 N.W. 165 Street Road, Miami, FL 33169. Call 1-800-841-8754.

Children: Y Pets: N Smoking: Y Handicap Access: N Payment: C, T, V, M, A

Cape Canaveral

ROYAL MANSIONS   *Rates: inexpensive-moderate*
Open: year-round   *Minimum Stay: none*

Designed in French Caribbean style, Royal Mansions is a waterfront residence of distinction right on the Atlantic in the fascinating Cape Canaveral region. Guests have a choice between one-bedroom apartments with either a patio or atrium or lavish two-bedroom penthouses. All come with fully equipped kitchens; the grounds feature a sparkling pool overlooking sweeping dunes and the majestic ocean. A visit to the Kennedy Space Center is a must, and there are other engrossing air and space attractions dotting the area. What's not so well known is that the entire "Space Coast" also happens to be one of the best preserved natural outposts in Florida, offering breathtaking scenery and miles of pristine beaches. Contact: Holiday Villas, 3187 W. Vine Street, Kissimmee, FL 34741. Call 1-800-344-3959.

Children: Y Pets: N Smoking: Y Handicap Access: N Payment: C, T, V, M

Destin

BREAKERS EAST   *Rates: budget-expensive*
Open: year-round   *Minimum Stay: three days*

At nearly 1,500 square feet, the apartments of Breakers East, located right outside Destin, are some of the largest two-bedroom vacation residences available in the region. Each unit faces directly toward the gulf and features a wide balcony to take full advantage of the view. This part of the state is called by many "Florida's Sandbox," but there are far more than sensational beaches offered here. The temperate subtropical climate makes the area an ideal spot for year-round outdoor pursuits of every type, and the facilities for golf, tennis, biking, swimming and a full array of other water sports are bounteous and superb. Contact: Breakers East Condominium, 1010 Highway 98 E., Destin, FL 32541. Call 1-904-837-1010 or 1-800-338-4418.

Children: Y Pets: N Smoking: Y Handicap Access: N Payment: C, T, V, M

DESTIN TOWERS   *Rates: budget-moderate*
Open: year-round   *Minimum Stay: three nights*

Destin Towers rises 16 soaring stories above the Gulf of Mexico on the Florida panhandle's beautiful Emerald Coast. Both of the bedrooms in the comfortable apartments featured here have their own bathrooms;

the units also contain a spacious living room and dining area and a very well-equipped kitchen. A cantilever balcony overlooks the pool, tennis court, clubhouse and, most spectacularly, the sugar-white sands and glistening azure waters of one of the region's top beaches. In the midst of everything Destin and the surrounding area has to offer, guests are close to golf and fishing, surfing and sailing, as well as fine dining and entertainment opportunities. Contact: Destin Towers Condominium, 1008 Highway 98 E., Destin, FL 32541. Call 1-904-837-7002 or 1-800-338-4418.

Children: Y   Pets: N   Smoking: Y   Handicap Access: N   Payment: C, T

EAST PASS TOWERS YACHT CLUB   *Rates: budget-expensive*
Open: year-round   *Minimum Stay: three nights*

Unsurpassed views of the gulf can be enjoyed in luxury from the oversized balconies of these splendid suites. Some residences boast two separate balconies, one of them perhaps a private nook off the master bedroom, but all have enough outdoor living space for dining, reclining, dancing and romancing. The interiors are similarly plush, with spacious rooms, wet bars, fireplaces, separate dressing areas and lovely decor. A heated swimming pool, a hot tub and a boat marina are at the disposal of the club's guests and the silken sands of the beach are open to all. Contact: Dale E. Peterson Realty, 321 Highway 98 E., Destin, FL 32541. Call 1-800-336-9669 (in Florida, 904-654-4747).

Children: Y   Pets: N   Smoking: Y   Handicap Access: Y   Payment: C, P, T

HOLIDAY BEACH RESORT   *Rates: budget-inexpensive*
Open: year-round   *Minimum Stay: two nights*

Located on 10 acres of beachside property running along the Gulf of Mexico, this palm-graced resort invites couples and families to enjoy its splendid amenities. The tennis courts, a game room, shuffleboard and exercise room should keep active types busy. Those who prefer just to sun and soak can enjoy either the ocean's own refreshing waters, the resort's swimming pool or the outdoor hot tub; there's even a separate wading pool for the wee ones. The attractively furnished condominiums have either one or two bedrooms and the fully equipped kitchens feature microwaves. Contact: Interval Management of America, P.O. Box 12906, Pensacola, FL 32576-2906. Call 1-800-874-0402 (in Florida, 904-433-5701).

Children: Y Pets: N Smoking: Y Handicap Access: N Payment: C, P, T, V, M

SOUTHBAY   *Rates: budget-expensive*
Open: year-round   *Minimum Stay: three nights*

With two swimming pools, a lighted tennis court, a pair of gazebos, playgrounds, shuffleboard courts and paddle boats for hire on the five-acre private lake stocked with fish, Southbay provides guests with the makings of a total holiday right where they live. The charms of Destin, a quiet little fishing village that also happens to be a premier Gulf Coast vacation spot, are also nearby for the enjoying. Southbay features two- and three-bedroom townhouse units, each with a separate dining and living room and all-electric kitchen, plus a large private patio or deck that is perhaps the best place of all to enjoy the bewitching gulf breezes. Contact: Southbay, P.O. Box 246, Destin, FL 32541. Call 1-904-837-6128 or 1-800-245-5682.

Children: Y Pets: N Smoking: Y Handicap Access: N Payment: C, T, V, M

TOPS'L BEACH AND RACQUET CLUB   *Rates: inexpensive-moderate*
Open: year-round   *Minimum Stay: three nights*

Tops'l is a self-contained resort community with everything you need to make your vacation a memorable one. After your morning run along the scenic jogging path—which skirts the Sierra Club Game Reserve—stop by the spa before heading for the glistening beach. Perhaps in the afternoon you'd like to fit in a game of golf at the course next door or have a go at tennis on one of the club's many fine courts. A pleasant evening can be had at the Heron's Roost Bar and Grill, before heading back to your holiday home. The two-bedroom residences are pleasantly furnished and feature large, open living areas and a lovely balcony. Contact: Dale E. Peterson Realty, 321 Highway 98 E., Destin, FL 32541. Call 1-800-336-9669 (in Florida, 904-654-4747).

Children: Y Pets: N Smoking: Y Handicap Access: Y Payment: C, P, T

FLAMINGO

FLAMINGO LODGE   *Rates: budget-inexpensive*
Open: year-round   *Minimum Stay: none*

The only overnight visitor accommodation located within Everglades National Park, Flamingo Lodge offers guests the ideal home base for long explorations of this fascinating untamed region—1.4 million acres of lush forests and vast prairies, rivers, marshes and mangroves coursing with exotic wildlife. Spacious, fully equipped housekeeping cottages nestled under shady palms offer renters free use of the lodge facilities, including the swimming pool and marina. There's no shortage of ways to venture into the wilderness, by land or water. Go on a tram tour or perhaps a sightseeing or charter fishing cruise, all embarking from the lodge. Bolder visitors can strike out on their own, with canoes, skiffs and even houseboats available for hire. Contact: Gene Rudolph, Flamingo Lodge, P.O. Box 428, Flamingo, FL 33030. Call 1-305-253-2241 or 1-813-695-3101.

Children: Y Pets: N Smoking: Y Handicap Access: N Payment: C, T, A, V, M

FORT LAUDERDALE

SURF & SUN APARTMENTS   *Rates: budget-moderate*
Open: year-round   *Minimum Stay: none*

Far more than a spring breaker's mecca, Fort Lauderdale is "where the condos are." And the Surf & Sun apartments, featuring studio-, one- and two-bedroom units, all with king-sized beds and complete kitchens, are splendid and affordable accommodations for singles, families or couples of all ages. The beach is only steps away, and within easy walking distance guests will find the Galleria, the town's premier shopping area. Birch Park, 180 unmarred acres of exotic flora and fauna and winding nature trails, plus a host of water sports opportunities and dozens of restaurants, bars and dance clubs are also nearby. Contact: Surf & Sun, 521 North Atlantic Blvd. (A1A), Fort Lauderdale, FL 33304. Call 1-305-564-4341 or 1-800-248-0463.

Children: Y Pets: N Smoking: Y Handicap Access: N Payment: C, T, V, M

FORT MYERS BEACH

BOATHOUSE BEACH RESORT   *Rates: inexpensive-moderate*
Open: year-round   *Minimum Stay: one week*

The Boathouse is a congenial Fort Myers Beach vacation complex with a beguiling nautical theme. Featuring brass and teak fittings, each of the fully equipped one-bedroom apartments is furnished in maritime decor, with twin bunk berths in the living area in addition to the queen-sized bed in the master suite. Individual screened porches overlook the pool area, private white beach and sparkling waters of the Gulf of Mexico. Across the street is a public 18-hole golf course, while full boating facilities, with plentiful opportunities for deep sea fishing, are also available nearby. Contact: Marquis Hotels and Resorts, 13451-27 McGregor Blvd., Fort Myers, FL 33919. Call 1-813-481-5600 or 1-800-237-8906.

Children: Y   Pets: N   Smoking: Y   Handicap Access: N   Payment: All

MARINER'S PINK SHELL BEACH RESORT   *Rates: inexpensive-expensive*
Open: year-round   *Minimum Stay: none*

This enchanting private vacation community lies on 12 tranquil acres at the tip of Estero Island, tucked between the deep fishing waters of Estero Bay and the shimmering white sands of the Gulf of Mexico. The resort features a wide array of housekeeping accommodations—one- and two-bedroom apartments and cottages with up to three bedrooms that sleep as many as ten—most offering a porch or balcony and all tastefully decorated to convey an authentic tropical ambiance. With a view of nearby Sanibel Island on the horizon, the beach, 1,500 feet long and graced with calm shallow waters, is considered one of the safest swimming areas in the entire state. There's also a large pool and a wading pool for the kids, as well as tennis courts and a private dock. Contact: Marquis Hotels and Resorts, 13451-27 McGregor Blvd., Fort Myers, FL 33919. Call 1-813-481-5600 or 1-800-237-8906.

Children: Y Pets: N Smoking: Y Handicap Access: N Payment: C, T, A, V, M

SEAWATCH ON THE BEACH   *Rates: inexpensive-expensive*
Open: year-round   *Minimum Stay: one week*

Featuring a lush tropical atrium, this modern seven-story apartment building located on engaging Estero Island has been strategically designed to provide each of its 42 units with sumptuous gulf views. The one- and two-bedroom residences contain a spacious open kitchen with counter seating, as well as a dining area. Of course, any meal can also be enjoyed, along with the scenery, on the screened terrace, a particular treat as the warm Florida sun sets over the water. A lighted tennis court, large pool and a spa are available on the grounds, and the pristine sandy beach is only steps away, while golf, sailing and superb shopping are also within easy reach. Contact: Marquis Hotels and Resorts, 13451-27 McGregor Blvd., Fort Myers, FL 33919. Call 1-813-481-5600 or 1-800-237-8906.

Children: Y   Pets: N   Smoking: Y   Handicap Access: N   Payment: All

FORT PIERCE

BINNEY DRIVE DUPLEX   *Rates: budget*
Open: year-round   *Minimum Stay: one week*

Hutchinson Island, separated from the mainland by the lovely Indian River, is a friendly, family-style community on Florida's renowned Treasure Coast. Kids of all ages will enjoy the warm sandy beaches, whether building sand castles, taking a salty plunge or strolling along the romantic boardwalk at twilight is the preferred activity. When you walk back from the beach, the green carpet of grass, leafy shade trees and pretty shrubs of this duplex will really make you feel that you're coming home. There are two nicely furnished bedrooms on each side, and the barbecue on the patio awaits your down-home cooking. Central air conditioning, cable TV and a washer and dryer are some of the modern conveniences available. Contact: Hoyt C. Murphy Realtors, South Beach, 221 South Ocean Dr., Ft. Pierce, FL 33449-3255. Call 1-800-289-4698 (in Florida, 407-461-1324).

Children: Y   Pets: Y   Smoking: Y   Handicap Access: N   Payment: C, P, T

CROSSED ANCHORS   *Rates: budget*
Open: year-round   *Minimum Stay: one week*

These handsome townhouses with their mellow wooden exteriors are found just a block away from the warm Atlantic waters. Inside are luxuriously furnished accommodations, including a sunny living room, a modern kitchen and two spacious bedrooms. There are carports to protect your auto from the elements and balconies where you can sit out and enjoy them. Once you've sampled the pleasures of life on Hutchinson Island, take a drive over the Seaway Drive Bridge, which offers splendid panoramic views of the ocean, island, river and Florida mainland. Fort Pierce, on the other side, has enough restaurants, shops and nightspots to keep you busy, or drive a bit further north to sample the big-city bustle of Orlando. Contact: Hoyt C. Murphy Realtors, South Beach, 221 South Ocean Dr., Ft. Pierce, FL 33449-3255. Call 1-800-289-4698 (in Florida, 407-461-1324).

Children: Y   Pets: N   Smoking: Y   Handicap Access: N   Payment: C, P, T

GRANADA HOUSE   *Rates: budget*
Open: year-round   *Minimum Stay: one week*

This traditional ranch house on Hutchinson Island is perfect for a family-style Floridian vacation. Spread out and make yourself at home—there are three comfy bedrooms, two bathrooms and a well-equipped kitchen in addition to the main living areas of the house. Sip a cocktail out on the patio while the kids play on the lawn and your beloved grills up a tasty seafood repast at the barbecue. There's fun for the whole family at the many public parks, lifeguarded beaches and festive boardwalks in the area. And you can easily visit Disney World without having to endure the overcrowded, plastic hotels where most tourists stay. Contact: Hoyt C. Murphy Realtors, South Beach, 221 South Ocean Dr., Ft. Pierce, FL 33449-3255. Call 1-800-289-4698 (in Florida, 407-461-1324).

Children: Y   Pets: N   Smoking: Y   Handicap Access: N   Payment: C, P, T

JACARANDA HOUSE   *Rates: budget*
Open: year-round   *Minimum Stay: one week*
Enjoying a grand location in one of the nicest neighborhoods on Hutchinson Island, this two-bedroom home is only a block away from the salt and sand of the ocean: This is a place to become the beach bum you've always secretly wanted to be. Boating, surfing, diving and swimming are all popular pursuits, as is just hanging around and looking incredibly cool. The sunny rooms are air-conditioned and comfortably furnished; cable TV and complete laundry facilities are at your disposal. There are also two carports where you can protect your wheels from the elements. Contact: Hoyt C. Murphy Realtors, South Beach, 221 South Ocean Dr., Ft. Pierce, FL 33449-3255. Call 1-800-289-4698 (in Florida, 407-461-1324).

Children: Y   Pets: N   Smoking: Y   Handicap Access: N   Payment: C, P, T

OCEAN HARBOR SOUTH   *Rates: budget*
Open: year-round   *Minimum Stay: one week*
Pool and tennis facilities are among the attractions of this modern resort complex. Of course, the excellent surfing, golf, fishing, ocean swimming and boating of Hutchinson Island are at your disposal as well. If all this sounds too gung-ho for you, there's always the perennial Florida favorite—basking in the warm sun with a tropical drink in hand. Two bedrooms and two baths are found in each unit, along with a well-equipped kitchen and nicely furnished living areas. The oceanfront location gives some rooms marvelous views of the sparkling Atlantic waters. Contact: Hoyt C. Murphy Realtors, South Beach, 221 South Ocean Dr., Ft. Pierce, FL 33449-3255. Call 1-800-289-4698 (in Florida, 407-461-1324).

Children: Y   Pets: N   Smoking: Y   Handicap Access: N   Payment: C, P, T

SEA POINTE TOWERS   *Rates: budget*
Open: year-round   *Minimum Stay: three months*
A sandy ribbon of land running along the Treasure Coast of central Florida, Hutchinson Island is a water-lover's dream. The gentle beaches offer swimming, surfing and wind surfing galore; the fishing, diving and sailing here are also superb. Even if you only want to take a pleasant stroll along the boardwalk or stand at the end of a pier and listen to the sound of the ocean, you can do that, too. The splendid situation of the Sea Pointe Towers affords views of both the Indian River and the Atlantic. The two- and three-bedroom condos are luxuriously furnished, and guests are invited to use the pool, tennis and

exercise facilities. Contact: Hoyt C. Murphy Realtors, South Beach, 221 South Ocean Dr., Ft. Pierce, FL 33449-3255. Call 1-800-289-4698 (in Florida, 407-461-1324).

Children: Y   Pets: N   Smoking: Y   Handicap Access: N   Payment: C, P, T

THE TIARA   *Rates: inexpensive*
Open: year-round   *Minimum Stay: one month*

Truly a jewel on Hutchinson Island's North Beach, the Tiara is a brand-new high-rise overlooking the blue waters of the Atlantic. The nicely furnished condominiums have either two or three bedrooms. Gentle sea breezes can be enjoyed out on the balcony, which is also a lovely spot to sip your rum punch and watch the last glimmers of twilight. There are several fine restaurants and lively nightspots in the area, and the general ambiance here is relaxed and friendly. Whether you prefer invigorating water sports or just basking in the glorious sunshine, a romantic getaway or a family get-together, this may be the holiday spot for you. Contact: Hoyt C. Murphy Realtors, South Beach, 221 South Ocean Dr., Ft. Pierce, FL 33449-3255. Call 1-800-289-4698 (in Florida, 407-461-1324).

Children: Y   Pets: N   Smoking: Y   Handicap Access: N   Payment: C, P, T

TREASURE COVE DUNES   *Rates: budget*
Open: year-round   *Minimum Stay: one week*

These luxury condominiums are tucked away on Hutchinson Island's North Beach, a lovely, unspoiled stretch of sloping sands and rolling dunes. Your two- or three-bedroom home enjoys central air conditioning and cable TV; there's a large sparkling pool outside for those who can't bear to spend a minute out of the glorious Florida sun. The complex is festively surrounded with palm trees that sway in the sultry breeze. Although in a quiet location, the condos aren't too far from the fine restaurants and tempting shops of the island and a drive across the Seaway Drive Bridge will bring you to the hustle and bustle of Fort Pierce. Contact: Hoyt C. Murphy Realtors, South Beach, 221 South Ocean Dr., Ft. Pierce, FL 33449-3255. Call 1-800-289-4698 (in Florida, 407-461-1324).

Children: Y   Pets: N   Smoking: Y   Handicap Access: N   Payment: C, P, T

FORT WALTON BEACH

SEA OATS   *Rates: budget-moderate*
Open: year-round   *Minimum Stay: four nights*

With a mild climate, warm waters and a miraculous 343 days of sun per year, Florida's Emerald Coast is a cherished haven for those from the frozen north. Sea Oats, found on lovely Okaloosa Island, enjoys a splendid location among the natural wonders and well-designed diversions of this area. Amusement parks, golf courses, restaurants, fishing piers and water sports facilities abound. The complex features lighted tennis courts and a huge swimming pool; the teen game room caters to the younger set. From the private balcony in each of the two- or three-bedroom condos, there are marvelous views of the gulf. The kitchens are fully equipped for family living, and daily maid service is available for those devoted to a truly carefree holiday. Contact: Sea Oats Resort Condominium, 1114 Santa Rosa Blvd., Ft. Walton Beach, FL 32548. Call 1-800-451-2343 (in Florida, 904-244-5200).

Children: Y Pets: N Smoking: Y Handicap Access: N Payment: C, P, T, V, M

SEASPRAY CONDOMINIUMS *Rates: budget-moderate*
Open: year-round *Minimum Stay: two nights*
Located on quiet Okaloosa Island at Fort Walton Beach, the heart of the Florida panhandle's Emerald Coast, Seaspray features 90 quality one-, two- and three-bedroom townhouse condominiums directly on the gulf and bordered to the north by Choctawhatchee Bay, the largest bay in the southeast. Each residence is built on two floors, containing a living room, dining area and fully equipped kitchen on the ground level with the bedroom(s) upstairs, and comes with either a patio or balcony looking out onto a grass courtyard and over to the gulf. A host of recreational opportunities and family amusement attractions are all within easy walking distance, while the complex itself offers a swimming pool, athletic club, lawn game area and a private beach where sailboats are available for rent. Contact: Seaspray Condominiums, 1530 Highway 98 E., Fort Walton Beach, FL 32548. Call 1-904-244-1108 or 1-800-428-2726.

Children: Y Pets: Y Smoking: Y Handicap Access: N Payment: C, T, V, M

THE BREAKERS *Rates: budget-moderate*
Open: year-round *Minimum Stay: none*
The Breakers is a seven-floor vacation center positioned on the Gulf Coast at Fort Walton Beach. From the balcony that comes with each one-, two- and three-bedroom unit, guests can savor spectacular sunrises and sunsets alike. The apartments all include king-sized beds and fully equipped kitchens, while the grounds offer tennis courts, clear freshwater pools and an exercise studio, plus a stretch of dazzling white sandy beach. For a rare water treat, rent a bright red "aquabike" available right at the complex, or stick to the old reliables like Sunfish sailboats or catamarans. Contact: Atlantic Beach Management, Inc., 381 Santa Rosa Blvd., Fort Walton Beach, FL 32548. Call 1-904-244-9127 or 1-800-888-9127.

Children: Y Pets: N Smoking: Y Handicap Access: N Payment: C, T, V, M

HOLLYWOOD

HOLLYWOOD BEACH RESORT *Rates: budget-moderate*
Open: year-round *Minimum Stay: none*
This inviting vacation complex featuring 200 studio and one-bedroom apartments, equipped with either a full kitchen or handy kitchenette, lies amid a fashionable shopping center right by the water in Hollywood. The town is one of the calmer resort areas of Florida's Atlantic coast, but is also easily accessible to the more bustling beach communities to the north and south. There's plenty to do here as well. Gamblers have three chances to get lucky: at Dania Jai Alai, the

Gulfstream Horse Track or the Hollywood Dog Track. A large free-form pool, poolside bar and kids' wading area are available for guests' enjoyment, along with a sauna and fitness center; golf, tennis, fishing and boating are also nearby. Contact: Vacation Home Rentals Worldwide, 235 Kensington Avenue, Norwood, NJ 07648. Call 1-201-767-9393 or 1-800-633-3284. Ref FL114.

Children: Y Pets: N Smoking: Y Handicap Access: N Payment: C, P, T, O

HUTCHINSON ISLAND

PLANTATION BEACH CLUB   *Rates: moderate-expensive*
Open: year-round   *Minimum Stay: one week*

A resort within a resort—offering unparalleled vacation pleasures—the Plantation Beach Club is located in the Indian River Plantation area on lovely Hutchinson Island, a serene haven just a short distance from the urban commotion of the Palm Beaches. This is an unspoiled corner of Florida's Treasure Coast, rife with opportunities to enjoy tennis, golf and boating in peace and quiet. Each elegant one- and two-bedroom housekeeping apartment at the club offers such seductive features as a home entertainment center, two TVs, a whirlpool bath and a delightful screened porch overlooking the Atlantic, while the grounds contain a pool, hot tubs, sauna and a charming picnic area. Contact: Marquis Hotels and Resorts, 13451-27 McGregor Blvd., Fort Myers, FL 33919. Call 1-813-481-5600 or 1-800-237-8906.

Children: Y   Pets: N   Smoking: Y   Handicap Access: N   Payment: All

KEY WEST

ADOBE HOUSE   *Rates: expensive*
Open: year-round   *Minimum Stay: three nights*

This festive home is decorated with Mexican flair, a reminder of the many Mexican-Americans who have settled in Key West over the years. The main house features two cheery bedrooms and one bathroom; the separate guest cottage has its own bathroom. There's a very nice swimming pool outside and of course you're not too far from the clear, shallow waters of the ocean. The Adobe House occupies a fine location in the heart of Old Town. All around you are quaint old houses; convivial nightspots; and restaurants featuring Key lime pie, conch fritters and other local delicacies. Contact: Property Management, 1213 Truman Ave., Key West, FL 33040. Call 305-296-7744.

Children: Y Pets: N Smoking: Y Handicap Access: N Payment: C, T, A, V, M

BAY VILLAS   *Rates: expensive*
Open: year-round   *Minimum Stay: one week*

Lovely views of the bay are enjoyed by every unit in this secluded condominium village. Far from the crowds, yet near to the sights and attractions of Old Town, these two-bedroom, two-bathroom condos are splendid bases for Key West holidays. Guests share the use of a lovely swimming pool and Jacuzzi, a private beach and an outdoor barbecue area. There's also boat dockage available. In addition, you'll also enjoy the conveniences usually only found at larger resorts: maid service and babysitters are available, and your hosts will be more than happy to charter a fishing or diving boat for you. Contact: Property Management, 1213 Truman Ave., Key West, FL 33040. Call 305-296-7744.

Children: **Y** Pets: **Y** Smoking: **Y** Handicap Access: **N** Payment: **C, T, A, V, M**

CASA ROMA   *Rates: deluxe*
Open: year-round   *Minimum Stay: three nights*

Once the home of Ernest Hemingway and Tennessee Williams, Key West can still inspire writers and artists with its lush tropical climate, clear waters and fragrant hibiscus blossoms. The Casa Roma is a luxurious two-bedroom house poised right on the water's edge. The interior is exquisitely furnished and pleasantly air-conditioned. Outside you'll find both a beautiful pool and a Jacuzzi overlooking the ocean. Maid service is available for those who desire total relaxation. There are also two separate guest apartments; altogether, the property can accommodate up to 10 guests. Contact: Property Management, 1213 Truman Ave., Key West, FL 33040. Call 305-296-7744.

Children: **Y** Pets: **N** Smoking: **Y** Handicap Access: **N** Payment: **C, T, A, V, M**

FRANK'S PLACE   *Rates: moderate*
Open: year-round   *Minimum Stay: three nights*

Cathedral ceilings give a delightful sense of space and openness to this charming two-bedroom home. Although it's centrally located, the house remains quite private; the deck outside is a lovely place to stretch out and catch up on your basking and lolling. After a stressful afternoon of sun worshipping, you can relax in the Jacuzzi. Along with the high ceilings, air conditioning keeps the rooms pleasantly cool; a washer and dryer are found in the house as added amenities. Sports facilities, sparkling waters and eateries galore are in the neighborhood. Contact: Property Management, 1213 Truman Ave., Key West, FL 33040. Call 305-296-7744.

Children: **Y** Pets: **N** Smoking: **Y** Handicap Access: **N** Payment: **C, T, A, V, M**

GRACIE HOUSE   *Rates: deluxe*
Open: year-round   *Minimum Stay: three nights*

A splendid pool and beautiful deck area are only part of this home's appeal. The rest is found in its magnificently restored and furnished rooms and in its fabulous location in the heart of the picturesque Old Town. All four of the spacious bedrooms are air-conditioned. The kitchen is well equipped, and a washer and dryer are at your disposal. Within walking distance of your downtown haunt are some of the most popular sights in Key West—galleries, museums, historic houses and the jolly Key West Aquarium. The cuisine at local restaurants ranges from down-home to the exotic, and you can dance until late into the night at the many lively nightspots. Contact: Property Management, 1213 Truman Ave., Key West, FL 33040. Call 305-296-7744.

Children: **Y** Pets: **N** Smoking: **Y** Handicap Access: **N** Payment: **C, T, A, V, M**

KELLY HOUSE *Rates: expensive*
Open: year-round *Minimum Stay: three nights*
Charmingly decorated with exquisite antiques, the Kelly House is a lovely holiday home for families or small groups. Guests share the use of a heated swimming pool outside, and the pleasant yard is a nice place to relax with a rum concoction after a hard day at the beach. Inside you'll find three comfy bedrooms; modern amenities include a washer and dryer. The house is pleasantly cooled by air conditioning, and maid service and babysitters are available. Key West is alive with festivities the whole year round: the year begins with the Old Island Days; April witnesses an annual Conch Republic celebration; and in October natives revel in their one-and-only Fantasy Fest. Contact: Property Management, 1213 Truman Ave., Key West, FL 33040. Call 305-296-7744.
Children: Y Pets: N Smoking: Y Handicap Access: N Payment: C, T, A, V, M

KEY WEST BEACH CLUB *Rates: expensive*
Open: year-round *Minimum Stay: one week*
Tropical luxury is yours when you stay at the Key West Beach Club. The amenities are outstanding, from the two swimming pools to the tennis courts, from the Jacuzzi tub in the master bathroom to the central air conditioning. The condominiums have either two or three bedrooms; all feature tasteful furnishings and spectacular views of the open water. Whether your ideal vacation centers on romantic walks along windswept beaches followed by an exquisite dinner in an intimate cafe or on invigorating water sports and plenty of dancing until dawn, Key West has plenty to entertain you. Contact: Property Management, 1213 Truman Ave., Key West, FL 33040. Call 305-296-7744.
Children: Y Pets: N Smoking: Y Handicap Access: N Payment: C, T, A, V, M

OCEAN KEY HOUSE *Rates: moderate-deluxe*
Open: year-round *Minimum Stay: none*
One of the finest vacation residences in legendary Key West, Ocean Key House sits on the Gulf of Mexico in the charming Old Town district. From its yacht marina there's the opportunity to partake in almost every kind of water sport—fishing charters, snorkeling, scuba and sailing trips and parasailing, to name a few—and after returning from adventures on the sea, the friendly dockside bar featuring live entertainment makes an inviting retreat. Each one- and two-bedroom apartment includes a complete kitchen, minibar and full Jacuzzi. While the lavish penthouses command the best views, every unit is treated to lovely panoramic vistas of this cosmopolitan resort. Contact: Ocean Key House, Zero Duval Street, Key West, FL 33040. Call 1-305-296-7701 or 1-800-328-9815.
Children: Y Pets: N Smoking: Y Handicap Access: N Payment: C, T, V, M

PARLEY PLACE *Rates: expensive*
Open: year-round *Minimum Stay: three nights*
With the ocean on one side and a canal on the other, this pleasant home partakes of the keys' wonderful location in several of its guises. True water connoisseurs will be pleased to know that there's a brand-new swimming pool as well. The main part of the house has two bedrooms and two bathrooms; a separate little guest bedroom has its own bathroom for a couple more vacationers. There's plenty of room to stretch out and relax here, whether in the comfortable den inside or the generous yard outdoors. Obviously, all the local water sports are well within reach, as are the intriguing shops and energetic nightlife for which the keys are known. Contact: Property Management, 1213 Truman Ave., Key West, FL 33040. Call 305-296-7744.
Children: Y Pets: N Smoking: Y Handicap Access: N Payment: C, T, A, V, M

ROYAL COTTAGE *Rates: inexpensive*
Open: year-round *Minimum Stay: three nights*
This quaint apartment is found in the heart of Old Town, which boasts not only a picturesque cluster of old clapboard houses but most of the fun and excitement of Key West's vivid social life. The pretty apartment has only one bedroom, but there's room for a couple more drowsy vacationers up in the loft. There's a nice porch out on the back where you can relax with a rum punch in hand or catch a cool breeze. Air conditioning keeps the rooms very comfortable, and a washer and dryer are at your disposal. Contact: Property Management, 1213 Truman Ave., Key West, FL 33040. Call 305-296-7744.
Children: Y Pets: N Smoking: Y Handicap Access: N Payment: C, T, A, V, M

SUMMERLAND HOUSE *Rates: expensive*
Open: year-round *Minimum Stay: one week*
Ideally situated out on the open water, this magnificent home has its own pier and boat dock. Even if you're not a nautical soul, there's no better way to enjoy the tropical sun and crystal clear water of the keys than sitting at the end of a pier and watching the boats drift by. The tranquil, very secluded grounds include a nice swimming pool, and there's also a Jacuzzi here for your relaxation pleasure. Inside you'll find three lovely bedrooms and spacious living quarters. The house has central air conditioning, and complete laundry facilities are among the amenities. Contact: Property Management, 1213 Truman Ave., Key West, FL 33040. Call 305-296-7744.
Children: Y Pets: N Smoking: Y Handicap Access: N Payment: C, T, A, V, M

WHITE HOUSE *Rates: expensive*
Open: year-round *Minimum Stay: three nights*
For a tantalizing taste of exotica—in a city known for its diversity—try the White House, with its fabulous African decor. This unique home welcomes guests with its two comfortable bedrooms, two bathrooms and festive living areas. Luxury is here as well: the indoor Jacuzzi will

help ease away the stresses and worries of the real world. Air conditioning and laundry facilities are among the other modern amenities. You're never far from the crystalline waters in Key West, nor are the fine restaurants and raucous nightspots much of a trek away. Contact: Property Management, 1213 Truman Ave., Key West, FL 33040. Call 305-296-7744.

Children: Y Pets: N Smoking: Y Handicap Access: N Payment: C, T, A, V, M

KISSIMMEE

CHELSEA SQUARE VILLAS *Rates: inexpensive-moderate*
Open: year-round *Minimum Stay: none*

Ten minutes from Disney World, Epcot and MGM Studios, this holiday villa residence makes an excellent home base, with a pool and tennis courts to enjoy at the end—or beginning—of a relentless day of fun. Two- and three-bedroom units are available, each tastefully furnished and containing a living room, dining area and fully equipped kitchen. With this central location, guests shouldn't neglect to experience the attractions of Kissimmee, offering enticing theme parks of its own as well as quieter pleasures like oak-lined streets and country roads winding through picturesque pastures. Contact: Holiday Villas, 3187 W. Vine Street, Kissimmee, FL 34741. Call 1-800-344-3959.

Children: Y Pets: Y Smoking: Y Handicap Access: N Payment: C, T, V, M

SHADOW BAY VILLAS *Rates: inexpensive-moderate*
Open: year-round *Minimum Stay: none*

The amusement parks your family has wanted to visit for years and a friendly, sunny residence with a buoyant atmosphere—what better combination? Shadow Bay, located in Kissimmee and convenient to everything Orlando has to offer, features airy two- and three-bedroom units decorated in light colors with bright tropical prints and filled with such pleasing amenities as cable TV, a VCR and a very well-equipped kitchen with a microwave. Although it may be hard—with enough exciting family attractions around to turn anyone's head—to sit still, two swimming pools and a relaxing spa are here as well for guests' enjoyment. Contact: Holiday Villas, 3187 W. Vine Street, Kissimmee, FL 34741. Call 1-800-344-3959.

Children: Y Pets: N Smoking: Y Handicap Access: N Payment: C, T, V, M

THAMES STREET VACATION VILLAGE *Rates: budget-inexpensive*
Open: year-round *Minimum Stay: three nights*

Scarcely a stone's throw from Florida's most popular attractions, each of these lovely townhouses in Kissimmee is an ideal home away from home. They are spacious and nicely furnished, with either two or three bedrooms for accommodating up to eight guests; cable TV and air conditioning are among the creature comforts you'll find here. The modern kitchens boast microwaves, dishwashers, garbage disposals and full-sized washers and dryers, which should help make your stay trouble-free. The village has its own swimming pool and lighted tennis courts, and there are several fine restaurants and lively clubs nearby. Contact: Thames Street Vacation Villas, P.O. Box 6106, Providence, RI 02940. Call 1-800-548-9417 (in Rhode Island, 401-861-0990).

Children: **Y**   Pets: **N**   Smoking: **Y**   Handicap Access: **N**   Payment: **All**

LAKE BUENA VISTA

FANTASYWORLD CLUB VILLAS   *Rates: inexpensive-expensive*
Open: year-round   *Minimum Stay: none*

Just minutes away from Walt Disney World, Universal Studios Florida, Sea World, Busch Gardens and the Kennedy Space Center, FantasyWorld is a simply fantastic base for your family's Florida vacation. Each two-bedroom townhouse enjoys daily maid service and cable TV. A screened porch is located off the separate dining and living rooms, and the kitchen is fully outfitted with a microwave, a dishwasher and a washer and dryer. You'll find plenty in the complex to amuse you, whether it's at one of the three heated pools, the seven tennis courts or the Jacuzzi; there's also a separate children's play area to keep Junior busy. Contact: FantasyWorld Club Villas, P.O. Box 22193, Lake Buena Vista, FL 32830. Call 1-800-874-8047 (in Florida, 1-800-432-7038).

Children: **Y**   Pets: **N**   Smoking: **Y**   Handicap Access: **N**   Payment: **All**

MARATHON

SEABIRD KEY   *Rates: deluxe*
Open: year-round   *Minimum Stay: one week*

How about a Florida key all to yourself? That is, except for rare species of birds and foliage (and a friendly caretaker). The only building on this private eight-acre island, a five-minute boat ride from Marathon, is a stately honey-colored house, constructed of cypress in "old Florida" style. Accommodating up to eight in luxury, the residence is elegantly furnished with nautical antiques. It contains a fully equipped kitchen with Mexican tile floors, a combination living/dining room with wraparound louvered windows that catch the ocean breezes, two bedrooms with private decks and a loft holding an additional sleeping area and a charming music room. A 17-foot Boston whaler is provided for transportation and recreation. Contact: Vacation Home Rentals Worldwide, 235 Kensington Avenue, Norwood, NJ 07648. Call 1-201-767-9393 or 1-800-633-3284. Ref FL113.

Children: **Y**   Pets: **N**   Smoking: **Y**   Handicap Access: **N**   Payment: **C, P, T, O**

MARCO ISLAND

EAGLE'S NEST BEACH RESORT   *Rates: moderate-deluxe*
Open: year-round   *Minimum Stay: one week*

Eagle's Nest Beach Resort is situated on Marco Island, one of Florida's most fashionable west-coast areas. Here, one- and two-bedroom villas are clustered around a rich palm garden containing a pool area and two spas, with tennis and racquetball courts plus a weight room and sauna also on the grounds. Overlooking the villas, a small high-rise offers additional two-bedroom apartments that command magnificent gulf views. The residences are impeccably designed to reflect a true tropical flavor, with such exquisite embellishments as terra-cotta tiling, colorful print upholstery, natural wicker furniture and graceful French doors opening onto a screened terrace. Contact: Marquis Hotels and Resorts, 13451-27 McGregor Blvd., Fort Myers, FL 33919. Call 1-813-481-5600 or 1-800-237-8906.

Children: Y   Pets: N   Smoking: Y   Handicap Access: N   Payment: All

---

SURF CLUB   *Rates: moderate-deluxe*
Open: year-round   *Minimum Stay: one week*

Lying midway along Marco Island's three and a half mile, crescent-shaped beach, the Surf Club offers posh two-bedroom condominiums that provide lavish accommodations for visitors to this dazzling Gulf Coast resort area. The units command a sweeping view either of the water or the flourishing garden area from their private balconies; all contain a living room, dining area and eat-in kitchen. After exploring the picturesque island by bike or trolley, relax by the pool or on the loggia overlooking the sun deck. If you're still up for action, how about a game of tennis or a little windsurfing? Contact: Marquis Hotels and Resorts, 13451-27 McGregor Blvd., Fort Myers, FL 33919. Call 1-813-481-5600 or 1-800-237-8906.

Children: Y   Pets: N   Smoking: Y   Handicap Access: N   Payment: All

MIAMI BEACH

RONEY PLAZA   *Rates: inexpensive-expensive*
Open: year-round   *Minimum Stay: one week*

Resting next to the sandy shores of Miami Beach, Roney Plaza is a large holiday complex offering comfortable studio, one- and two-bedroom apartments, each with a fully equipped kitchen and private balcony giving far-reaching views. The excellent facilities here include a big swimming pool and deck area terrific for either basking or socializing in the sun, plus a restaurant, bar and grocery. Downtown Miami is only a few minutes away by car, and a host of top recreational opportunities on the Atlantic are even closer. Contact: Interhome, Inc., 124 Little Falls Road, Fairfield, NJ 07004. Call 1-201-882-6864. Ref U3313/100M (studio), U3313/120-140M (1 bedroom), U3313/160M (2 bedrooms).

Children: Y Pets: N Smoking: Y Handicap Access: N Payment: C, P, T, V, M

THE ALEXANDRIA   *Rates: moderate-deluxe*
Open: year-round   *Minimum Stay: one week*

This top hotel/apartment building enjoys an ideal location right on the ocean, less than two miles from the center of Miami. Everything that visitors desire in an unforgettable Miami Beach vacation is at their command: two swimming pools, three restaurants and a bar on the grounds, a sandy stretch of beach only steps away and opportunities for tennis, yachting and shopping within easy reach. The one- and two-bedroom apartments make a luxurious home base for south Florida adventures, each offering a private balcony that commands a smashing view of the Atlantic. The complete kitchens open onto beautifully furnished living room/dining areas. Contact: Interhome, Inc., 124 Little Falls Road, Fairfield, NJ 07004. Call 1-201-882-6864. Ref. U3313/220M (1 bedroom), U3313/260M (2 bedrooms).

Children: Y Pets: N Smoking: Y Handicap Access: N Payment: C, P, T, V, M

MILTON

TOMAHAWK LANDING *Rates: budget-inexpensive*
Open: year-round *Minimum Stay: none*

For canoeing, unlike any you'll find elsewhere, try rustic Tomahawk Landing. Studio and one-bedroom cabins are available as comfortable home bases, tucked away in a pine forest or nestled by a gently flowing creek. They come with such delightful features as an outdoor grill and campfire area, some with a cozy living room fireplace or even a private swing. This is a land of pure and crystal-clear spring-fed rivers about two feet deep with soft sandy bottoms, their banks dotted with immaculate, unblemished white sandy beaches. These beguiling waterways offer matchless opportunities for tubing, kayaking, paddleboating and rafting, with special day and overnight trips available that will turn even novices into masters... and lifelong lovers of river pleasures. Contact: Adventures Unlimited Inc., Tomahawk Landing, Rt. 6, Box 283, Milton, FL 32570. Call 1-904-623-6197.

Children: Y Pets: N Smoking: Y Handicap Access: N Payment: C, T, V, M

NAVARRE BEACH

BEACHVIEW *Rates: budget-moderate*
Open: year-round *Minimum Stay: three nights*

The charming architecture and creative layout of this resort help it feel more like a cluster of holiday homes than an anonymous maze of tourist traps. The three-bedroom townhouses are set along the water's edge; fabulous views of the gulf can be enjoyed from either the patio downstairs or the spacious deck up above. The two-bedroom flats overlook the complex's swimming pool and tennis court. Cable TV is featured in all the units; some also have microwaves, washing machines and dryers—all the conveniences of home. Contact: Navarre Agency, P.O. Box 5100, Navarre, FL 32566. Call 1-800-821-8790.

Children: Y Pets: N Smoking: Y Handicap Access: N Payment: C, P, T

CHRISTIE ANN HOUSE *Rates: budget-inexpensive*
Open: year-round *Minimum Stay: three nights*

This charming bungalow stretches itself along the seashore not too far outside of town. Every room enjoys splendid views of the sea: After fixing dinner in the warm golden glow of the late afternoon sun, you can dine while gazing out at the last scarlet tendrils of sunset playing across the water. The master bedroom has an adjoining bathroom; there are two other bedrooms with double and twin beds, so the house can accommodate up to eight people. The shimmering sands creep right up to your doorstep, and the water is a stone's throw away. Contact: Navarre Agency, P.O. Box 5100, Navarre, FL 32566. Call 1-800-821-8790.

Children: Y   Pets: N   Smoking: Y   Handicap Access: N   Payment: C, P, T

LA CHATEAU HOUSE   *Rates: moderate-deluxe*
Open: year-round   *Minimum Stay: three nights*

This magnificent beach house perches on the quiet dunes above the emerald green waters of the gulf. The sprawling main floor of the house comprises a tastefully furnished living and dining area, a kitchen equipped with a microwave, a master bedroom with adjoining bath and two more sunny bedrooms. Except for the kitchen, each of these rooms opens through sliding glass doors to the fabulously large deck, an ideal place for entertaining, sipping a rum punch with friends or just watching the golden sun slip heavily into the water. Spiral stairs lead to the other level of the house, where there are two more bedrooms (La Chateau can accommodate up to 12) and another sunny balcony. A little stairway leads down to the beach. Contact: Navarre Agency, P.O. Box 5100, Navarre, FL 32566. Call 1-800-821-8790.

Children: Y   Pets: N   Smoking: Y   Handicap Access: N   Payment: C, P, T

LANGLEY'S LOOKOUT HOUSE   *Rates: budget-inexpensive*
Open: year-round   *Minimum Stay: three nights*

Navarre Beach, in addition to being a pleasant seaside resort, is also a golfer's paradise: There are 15 courses all within an hour's drive, more than enough to keep you busy every day of the week! Langley's Lookout is a pleasant holiday home perched on pilings just a bit away from the beaches. The spacious great room opens onto two pairs of cozy bedrooms, each with its own convenient bathroom. A door from the great room leads you out to the spacious deck, a fine place to enjoy supper or catch a warm breeze. Another deck is found in back, adjacent to the kitchen. Here is a chance to enjoy the indoor-outdoor lifestyle you've always dreamed of. Contact: Navarre Agency, P.O. Box 5100, Navarre, FL 32566. Call 1-800-821-8790.

Children: Y   Pets: N   Smoking: Y   Handicap Access: N   Payment: C, P, T

LOCKLIN HOUSE   *Rates: budget-moderate*
Open: year-round   *Minimum Stay: three nights*

This classic beach house perches on the water's edge not two miles outside of town. A fantastic wraparound deck graces three sides of the house, offering you a place to sit out and enjoy splendid sunrises, luxurious afternoon rays and glorious twilights. The large living and dining room upstairs overlooks the water. The kitchen is a friendly nook that's open to these sunlit areas and features a microwave. There are four bedrooms, but the three roll-away beds in the Florida room out back allow the house to accommodate up to 12 guests. Downstairs are two bedrooms, the second bathroom and another kitchen and dining area. The house is air-conditioned and features cable TV. Contact: Navarre Agency, P.O. Box 5100, Navarre, FL 32566. Call 1-800-821-8790.

Children: Y   Pets: N   Smoking: Y   Handicap Access: N   Payment: C, P, T

SANDOLLAR *Rates: budget-inexpensive*
Open: year-round *Minimum Stay: three nights*
Graced by palm trees and ornamented with zigzagging outdoor stairways, these beachside condominiums are ideal for romantic getaways. The smaller condos are cozy and convenient, with a combined living and dining room that opens onto a balcony with lovely ocean views, a kitchen equipped with a microwave and a single bedroom with another balcony of its own. The larger units have two bedrooms, each with its own adjoining bathroom. The crash of the surf will lull you to sleep at night and the soft sands of Florida's renowned Emerald Coast will invite you to sunbathe by day. Contact: Navarre Agency, P.O. Box 5100, Navarre, FL 32566. Call 1-800-821-8790.
Children: Y Pets: N Smoking: Y Handicap Access: N Payment: C, P, T

SEA HAWK II *Rates: budget*
Open: year-round *Minimum Stay: three nights*
This one-room efficiency apartment may be small, but with both a sofa bed and a trundle bed, up to four happy campers can find comfy holiday lodgings here. Besides, who needs luxurious digs when there's so much to do outside? The Gulf of Mexico and the Santa Rosa Sound ring the island with their blue-green waters, providing miles of soft, sandy beaches. Water sports facilities, interesting military museums, unique shops and all the nooks and crannies of a friendly beach resort will fill your afternoons with activity; convivial nightspots and casual restaurants will cater to your social life. When you do finally return home after a day of sun and fun, you can enjoy a bit of cable TV before getting a good night's sleep—and starting all over again tomorrow. Contact: Navarre Agency, P.O. Box 5100, Navarre, FL 32566. Call 1-800-821-8790.
Children: Y Pets: N Smoking: Y Handicap Access: N Payment: C, P, T

ORLANDO

CYPRESS CREEK GOLF TOWNHOUSES *Rates: budget*
Open: year-round *Minimum Stay: one week*
Golf, the Magic Kingdom, Epcot, Disney/MGM and Universal Studios—what more could any visitor to Orlando desire? All are within easy reach of this engaging and tranquil townhouse complex containing comfortable, fully equipped two-bedroom units, all offering a complete kitchen and washer/dryer. The golf is adjacent to the premises, which also features a large swimming pool and spa area, while the amusement parks and other top attractions, including the often overlooked historic districts and scenic wilderness areas, are a short drive away. Contact: Florida Holidays, 13100 Wayzata Blvd., Suite 150, Minneapolis, MN 55343. Call 1-612-591-0076 or 1-800-328-6262.
Children: Y Pets: N Smoking: Y Handicap Access: N Payment: C, T

VACATION VILLAS *Rates: budget-moderate*
Open: year-round *Minimum Stay: four nights*
Ideally situated between Orlando International Airport and the Disney/Epcot area, this collection of three private vacation communities provides superb family accommodations. The two- and three-bedroom units (the larger ones sleeping as many as eight) each contain such handy conveniences as a washer/dryer and a kitchen, plus every appliance needed for comfortable home living, including an automatic dishwasher and microwave oven. Apart from the world-renowned attractions located nearby, the impeccably landscaped grounds offer plenty for a delightful resort holiday, such as swimming pools, tennis courts and duck ponds; there's also a public golf course within easy reach. Contact: Vacation Villas, 6105 Granby Road, Derwood, MD 20855. Call 1-800-866-2660.
Children: Y Pets: N Smoking: Y Handicap Access: N Payment: C, P, T, V, M

VILLAGE TOWNHOMES *Rates: budget*
Open: year-round *Minimum Stay: one week*
For an affordable Orlando holiday, these quiet low-rise townhouses can't be beat. There are both one-bedroom residences sleeping four and two-bedroom units accommodating up to six, all containing full kitchens and other handy amenities; the grounds feature an inviting pool and small fishing lake. Close to the attractions for which travelers from around the world come to Orlando, it's superbly situated only 15 minutes from Disney World, Epcot and the city's other top amusement spots. Contact: Florida Holidays, 13100 Wayzata Blvd., Suite 150, Minneapolis, MN 55343. Call 1-612-591-0076 or 1-800-328-6262.
Children: Y Pets: N Smoking: Y Handicap Access: N Payment: C, T

WESTGATE VACATION VILLAGE *Rates: inexpensive*
Open: year-round *Minimum Stay: one week*
Enjoying a quiet position removed from the Orlando crowds, Westgate Vacation Village is also centrally located, less than one and a half miles from Walt Disney World. The two-bedroom apartments available here in congenial two-floor buildings contain a large living room/dining area and a well-equipped kitchen including a dishwasher, and feature either a private balcony or terrace. The grounds are fully landscaped and offer two tennis courts and a swimming pool with a Jacuzzi. A bright blue lake, where there's canoeing and other refreshing water sports, is only a short walk away. Contact: Interhome, Inc., 124 Little Falls Road, Fairfield, NJ 07004. Call 1-201-882-6864. Ref U3274/260M.
Children: Y Pets: N Smoking: Y Handicap Access: N Payment: C, T, P, V, M

PALM BEACH GARDENS

EASTPOINTE COUNTRY CLUB *Rates: budget-expensive*
Open: year-round *Minimum Stay: one month*
Centered around a championship 18-hole golf course, Eastpointe is a fashionable country club featuring a variety of fully equipped two- and

three-bedroom houses and condominium units. It's superbly situated in Palm Beach County a short drive from the spectacular Atlantic beaches. With even the smallest residences offering a private patio and 1,000 square feet of space, there's plenty of room for opulent Florida Gold Coast living. Full country-club privileges, including use of the links, tennis courts, pools and club dining room, are included in the rental price. Contact: Tom Rice, Best of Florida Realty and Development, Inc., Suite 100, 4360 Northlake Blvd., Palm Beach Gardens, FL 33410. Call 1-407-626-4600.

Children: Y   Pets: N   Smoking: Y   Handicap Access: N   Payment: C, P, T

PANAMA CITY BEACH

GULFCREST MOTEL   *Rates: budget-inexpensive*
Open: year-round   *Minimum Stay: none*

Located on Florida's "Miracle Strip," a 27-mile stretch of beach blanketed with the whitest sand you'll ever see, the Gulfcrest Motel offers housekeeping units that make a perfect home base for experiencing this premier family vacation area. Try a bit of deep sea fishing on a trolling boat or enjoy sailing, golf and tennis. Visit a whole assortment of amusement facilities, including Shipwreck Island, which features one of the world's most treacherous roller coasters, and an invigorating water theme park so vast it takes up an entire island. Efficiency studios and two-bedroom apartments, both with handy kitchenettes, are available, most featuring balconies that overlook the Gulf of Mexico. The private pool provides a change of scene if you ever tire of basking on beach. Contact: Bob and Audrey Dalton, Gulfcrest Motel, 8715 Surf Drive, Panama City Beach, FL 32408. Call 1-904-234-3328.

Children: Y Pets: N Smoking: Y Handicap Access: N Payment: C, T, V, M, A

THE COMMODORE   *Rates: budget-expensive*
Open: year-round   *Minimum Stay: two days*

Hedonism is an honorable practice at The Commodore, a large resort that caters to your holiday dreams. The white sands of the gulf lie right outside your door, positively requiring you to swim, soak, sun or just build a sand castle. The water sports facilities are impressive, whether you're interested in fishing, snorkeling or sailing. For an afternoon of natural beauty, visit St. Andrews State Park; for an evening of sophisticated dining and dancing, stop by The Treasure Ship or Captain Anderson's. The complex itself offers saunas, whirlpools, a swimming pool, a billiard room, a game room and a quiet yet not isolated location. The one-, two- and three-bedroom suites are plushly furnished and offer spectacular views from the balconies. Contact: Beach Side One Realty, P.O. Box 9360, Panama City Beach, FL 32407. Call 1-800-654-6052 (in Florida, 904-234-7099).

Children: Y Pets: N Smoking: Y Handicap Access: N Payment: C, T, A, V, M

PENSACOLA

EDEN CONDOMINIUM *Rates: budget-deluxe*
Open: year-round *Minimum Stay: three nights*
Just outside Pensacola, the City of the Five Flags, you'll find this sophisticated vacationer's paradise. Here the common resort amenities are elevated to a superior standard. The enormous tiled swimming pool is graced by three lovely waterfalls; the elegant landscaping features ponds and streams filled with Japanese goldfish. The tennis courts are lighted, the boat dock has power hook-ups and there's both a Jacuzzi and a hot tub outside. The plush apartments are individually furnished, but all enjoy balconies with fabulous views. The kitchen boasts not only a dishwasher and microwave, but also a trash compactor. The wet bar has an ice-maker, the bathtub is also a whirlpool and the color TV comes with cable. What more could you ask? Contact: Eden Condominium, 16281 Perdido Key Dr., Pensacola, FL 32507. Call 1-800-523-8141 (in Florida, 904-492-3336).
Children: Y Pets: N Smoking. Y Handicap Access: N Payment: C, P, T, V, M

PERDIDO SUN *Rates: budget-moderate*
Open: year-round *Minimum Stay: three nights*
Overlooking the emerald green waters of the Gulf of Mexico, your suite in the Perdido Sun features every popular resort amenity. Whether you've chosen a one-, two- or three-bedroom residence, the furnishings are comfy and the furnished seaside balcony enjoys stunning views. Downstairs, you can choose between swimming in the heated inside pool or in the larger pool outdoors—not to mention splashing about in the ocean. The exercise room is well equipped, and you can relax afterward in either the whirlpool spa or the sauna. Finally, water sports, tennis and an excellent golf course are all at your fingertips, as are fine restaurants and exciting nightspots. Contact: Perdido Sun, 13753 Perdido Key Dr., Pensacola, FL 32507. Call 1-800-227-2390 (in Florida, 904-492-2390).
Children: Y Pets: N Smoking: Y Handicap Access: N Payment: C, P, T, V, M

VISTA DEL MAR *Rates: budget-inexpensive*
Open: year-round *Minimum Stay: three nights*
As you might expect, the views of the sea here are breathtaking, a rich and ever-changing tapestry of pure snowy dunes, turquoise waters and white-capped waves. Nature provides the backdrop for this resort on Perdido Key—it lies along the protected national seashore—and the luxurious accommodations provide the rest. Each of the condominiums (which have either one, two or three bedrooms) boasts excellent views, lovely furnishings and a well-equipped modern kitchen. Two lighted tennis courts and a pool are found at Vista del Mar. The area is a favorite of fishers and golfers (a nearby course is home of the Pensacola Open). Water sports enthusiasts also will find plenty to do, as will

those who prefer to spend their time shopping and dining. Contact: Vista del Mar, 13-333 Johnson Beach Rd., Pensacola, FL 32507. Call 1-800-648-4529 (in Florida, 904-492-0211).

Children: **Y**   Pets: **N**   Smoking: **Y**   Handicap Access: **N**   Payment: **C, P, T**

PERDIDO KEY

COMPASS POINT   *Rates: budget*
Open: year-round   *Minimum Stay: none*

These studio apartments for four are ideal bases for enjoying the splendors of Perdido Key and the mainland beyond. Whether you're interested in the excellent angling, impressive water sports or friendly beaches of the key or even if you're adventurous enough to investigate the secrets of Pensacola—a city founded by the Spanish over four centuries ago—and check out the military museums nearby, you'll always be glad to return to your cozy home away from home. There are two balconies where you can savor the gentle breezes, and the blue waters of the gulf are just a hop, skip and a jump away. Contact: Leib and Associates Realty, 14620 Perdido Key Dr., Perdido Key, FL 32507. Call 1-800-553-1223 (in Florida, 904-492-0744).

Children: **Y**   Pets: **Y**   Smoking: **Y**   Handicap Access: **N**   Payment: **C, T, V, M**

DORY   *Rates: inexpensive*
Open: year-round   *Minimum Stay: none*

Perdido Key is one of the barrier islands stretching along the deliciously warm Gulf of Mexico. It offers visitors sugar-white sands, tropical waters and a friendly resort atmosphere still largely unspoiled by overwhelming tourist developments. A few stalwart palm trees keep watch over Dory, a pleasant little townhouse right on the gulf. Inside you'll find three comfy bedrooms and two bathrooms, along with a fireplace that completes the cozy ambiance. Sliding glass doors fill the interior with light and open onto a private balcony where you can watch the swaying shore grasses and palms underneath an endless blue sky. The house also features a garage and a Florida room. Contact: Leib and Associates Realty, 14620 Perdido Key Dr., Perdido Key, FL 32507. Call 1-800-553-1223 (in Florida, 904-492-0744).

Children: **Y**   Pets: **Y**   Smoking: **Y**   Handicap Access: **N**   Payment: **C, T, V, M**

HILL HOUSE   *Rates: inexpensive*
Open: year-round   *Minimum Stay: none*

With a private dock on the sound side of Perdido Key, this home is a wonderful holiday spot for fishers, water-skiers and boaters of all varieties. Perched on stilts, as if to catch the gentlest breeze, the house includes three sunny bedrooms and two bathrooms. There's also a spacious deck outside for enjoying all those home-cooked meals you'll supply with your daily catch. If your ideal vacation completely excludes kitchen duty, try one of the many fine restaurants in the area, whether an intimate cafe or a boisterous seafood palace. Contact: Leib and Associates Realty, 14620 Perdido Key Dr., Perdido Key, FL 32507. Call 1-800-553-1223 (in Florida, 904-492-0744).

Children: **Y**   Pets: **Y**   Smoking: **Y**   Handicap Access: **N**   Payment: **C, T, V, M**

LA MER
Rates: inexpensive
Open: year-round
Minimum Stay: none

Mediterranean stylings, arching palm trees and well-manicured grounds set the tone at La Mer. The generous rooms feature fireplaces for that extra touch of Old World charm, and the glorious balconies open directly onto the gulf. Up to six people will find comfy sleeping quarters in the larger, two-bedroom apartments; smaller suites can accommodate up to four. When you've had your daily quota of sports and shopping, sun and surf, why not spend the evening in a friendly little seafood restaurant dining with old friends and perhaps toasting some new ones? Contact: Leib and Associates Realty, 14620 Perdido Key Dr., Perdido Key, FL 32507. Call 1-800-553-1223 (in Florida, 904-492-0744).

Children: Y Pets: Y Smoking: Y Handicap Access: N Payment: C, T, V, M

LANDSEND TRIPLEX
Rates: inexpensive
Open: year-round
Minimum Stay: none

Occupying a secluded nook on the sunny shore of the gulf, this home offers all the peace and quiet you'll need for a restful vacation. Rolling sands, soft grasses and stately palms frame wonderful views of the water; the large deck and breezy gazebo are ideal for candlelight dinners or sunrise vigils. The larger unit has three bedrooms for up to eight guests; the two-bedroom part can sleep six. If all this tranquillity gets a bit too quiet, a short drive or bike ride will bring you to the fine restaurants and energetic nightlife that cluster around the larger resorts. Contact: Leib and Associates Realty, 14620 Perdido Key Dr., Perdido Key, FL 32507. Call 1-800-553-1223 (in Florida, 904-492-0744).

Children: Y Pets: Y Smoking: Y Handicap Access: N Payment: C, T, V, M

MOLOKAI VILLAS
Rates: budget
Open: year-round
Minimum Stay: none

If privacy is at the top of your holiday wish list, consider these handsome villas, each one a separate house unto itself. The mellow exteriors feature weathered clapboards and spacious decks where you can dine or recline in comfort. The houses found on the gulf side of the island have three bedrooms and share access to a lovely swimming pool. There are also boat docks available here. Two-bedroom houses for up to six are found on the other side, overlooking the sound. If you can tear yourself away from the water sports and sun worshipping long enough, try to investigate some of the historic sites in this area, which was once the haunt of Spanish explorers and treasure-hungry pirates. Contact: Leib and Associates Realty, 14620 Perdido Key Dr., Perdido Key, FL 32507. Call 1-800-553-1223 (in Florida, 904-492-0744).

Children: Y Pets: Y Smoking: Y Handicap Access: N Payment: C, T, V, M

NEW HORIZON
Rates: budget
Open: year-round
Minimum Stay: none

The silken sands of the beach are just outside your door at the New Horizon. The nicely furnished downstairs apartments have one bedroom and can accommodate up to four beach bums. The equally pleasant upstairs suites have two bedrooms and a loft and can sleep six. Large sliding glass doors fill all the apartments with the golden glow of the Florida sun; those upstairs open onto a shared balcony with a little stairway running down to the beach. The cries of shore birds will greet you in the morning, and the song of the sea will lull you to sleep. Contact: Leib and Associates Realty, 14620 Perdido Key Dr., Perdido Key, FL 32507. Call 1-800-553-1223 (in Florida, 904-492-0744).

Children: **Y** Pets: **Y** Smoking: **Y** Handicap Access: **N** Payment: **C, T, V, M**

PELICAN POINT   *Rates: inexpensive*
Open: year-round   *Minimum Stay: none*

Water sports aficionados, dedicated anglers and all those who enjoy the magnificent setting of white sands edged in crystal blue waters have long admired Perdido Key. The breezy beaches are only a heartbeat away when you stay at Pelican Point. This three-story complex offers a variety of rooms for parties of varying sizes; the largest apartment, with two bedrooms and two bathrooms, accommodates up to six people between its friendly walls. You may be tempted to spend your whole holiday basking on the beach and splashing in the water outside your door, but don't neglect to explore a handful of the secluded coves and windswept dunes of the island. Contact: Leib and Associates Realty, 14620 Perdido Key Dr., Perdido Key, FL 32507. Call 1-800-553-1223 (in Florida, 904-492-0744).

Children: **Y** Pets: **Y** Smoking: **Y** Handicap Access: **N** Payment: **C, T, V, M**

SANDY KEY   *Rates: inexpensive*
Open: year-round   *Minimum Stay: none*

This high-rise offers you all the amenities of a modern resort along with fantastic proximity to the soft white sands of the gulf. Two swimming pools, tennis courts and an exercise room are at your disposal, and you can run down to the water's edge before you can say "Perdido Key" three times fast. The three-bedroom units can accommodate eight people and the smaller apartments with two bedrooms can house up to six. All are tastefully furnished, and many feature dramatic views of the sparkling waters from their balconies. There are several pleasant restaurants in the area, and the bright lights of Pensacola are just a short drive away. Contact: Leib and Associates Realty, 14620 Perdido Key Dr., Perdido Key, FL 32507. Call 1-800-553-1223 (in Florida, 904-492-0744).

Children: **Y** Pets: **Y** Smoking: **Y** Handicap Access: **N** Payment: **C, T, V, M**

PLANTATION KEY

CHRISMARENE   *Rates: expensive-deluxe*
Open: year-round   *Minimum Stay: one week*

A secluded drive through eight lush, private acres of tall palms, tropical plants and fragrant blossoms leads to Chrismarene, located on exotic Plantation Key. Commanding stunning views of the Atlantic with nearby Tavernier Island on the horizon, this exquisite villa accommodates up to eight in its three large bedrooms. It also offers an elegant wood-paneled living room where ceiling fans whirr, a spacious glass-enclosed Florida room and a small lanai, or veranda. Guests can cook either in the lavishly equipped European-style kitchen or on the outdoor grill. Steps from the front door, there's fishing, swimming, sailing and snorkeling among intriguing coral reefs, while golf, tennis and other beaches are only a short distance away. Contact: Vacation Home Rentals Worldwide, 235 Kensington Avenue, Norwood, NJ 07648. Call 1-201-767-9393 or 1-800-633-3284. Ref FL109.

Children: Y Pets: N Smoking: Y Handicap Access: N Payment: C, P, T, O

SANIBEL ISLAND

CASA YBEL RESORT   *Rates: moderate-expensive*
Open: year-round   *Minimum Stay: none*

Built on the site of Sanibel Island's first resort, Casa Ybel maintains a gracious turn-of-the-century ambiance. Over 100 self-contained one- and two-bedroom condominiums are available, each featuring a well-equipped kitchen and sunny terrace overlooking the Gulf of Mexico. The island is one of Florida's most popular vacation areas, but Casa Ybel guests don't even have to leave the premises to enjoy every fun-filled aspect of a Sunshine State holiday. The complex includes such inviting facilities as an Olympic-sized pool with a water slide for the kids and poolside bar for the adults, six tennis courts, sailboats, bikes, beach cabanas and a full recreation staff to tend to every need. Contact: Marquis Hotels and Resorts, 13451-27 McGregor Blvd., Fort Myers, FL 33919. Call 1-813-481-5600 or 1-800-237-8906.

Children: Y Pets: N Smoking: Y Handicap Access: N Payment: C, T, A, V, M

SANIBEL COTTAGES   *Rates: moderate-deluxe*
Open: year-round   *Minimum Stay: one week*

These very private beachside villas offer "old Florida"-style architecture and decor to provide a genuine and unaffected 1920's ambiance. Bay windows with cozy window seats look out onto whitewashed terraces; the two-bedroom residences also contain huge whirlpool tubs in the master bath, as well as a fully equipped kitchen accented by elegant lacy trim. Graced with spreading grassy lawns, a charming footbridge and beguiling gazebo, the grounds are delightful to stroll around, while the tennis courts offer a chance for more active pursuits and the swimming pool, spa area, white sands and turquoise waters of the Gulf of Mexico provide blissful spots for relaxing in the warm sun. Contact: Marquis Hotels and Resorts, 13451-27 McGregor Blvd., Fort Myers, FL 33919. Call 1-813-481-5600 or 1-800-237-8906.

Children: Y Pets: N Smoking: Y Handicap Access: N Payment: C, T, A, V, M

SHELL ISLAND BEACH CLUB   *Rates: inexpensive*
Open: year-round   *Minimum Stay: one week*

On the quiet eastern end of the island, not far from the venerable Shell Island lighthouse, you'll find the friendly Beach Club, where casual relaxation has become something of an art form. The spacious two-bedroom apartments are nicely decorated with light colors and modern furnishings. Luxuriant tropical foliage graces the lovely screened terrace outside each unit. There are two very large heated swimming pools here for the pleasure of the guests, who are also invited to enjoy the delicious whirlpool and sauna. Tennis is available within the complex, a nearby marina offers boat rentals and a short drive will bring you to the public golf course. Contact: Shell Island Beach Club, 255 Periwinkle Way, Sanibel Island, FL 33957. Or call Marquis Hotels and Resorts, 1-800-237-8906.

Children: **Y**   Pets: **N**   Smoking: **Y**   Handicap Access: **N**   Payment: **All**

SONG OF THE SEA   *Rates: inexpensive-moderate*
Open: year-round   *Minimum Stay: one week*

Whitewashed walls, cheery red tiles and quaintly furnished rooms lend an air of relaxed charm to this inn on the edge of the gulf's blue waters. Creature comforts such as color cable TV, wall-to-wall carpeting and air conditioning make it a delight to the body as well as the eyes. Spacious one-bedroom apartments enjoy marvelous, unobstructed views of the gulf; the roomy studio apartments overlook the heated swimming pool and spa. Guests also enjoy the use of the tennis and golf facilities at a nearby country club. A short walk past the well-tended shrubbery and gently arching palms will bring you to the pale sands and foaming waters of the beach. Contact: Song of the Sea, 863 E. Gulf Dr., Sanibel Island, FL 33957. Call 813-472-2220. Or call Marquis Hotels and Resorts, 1-800-237-8906

Children: **Y**   Pets: **N**   Smoking: **Y**   Handicap Access: **N**   Payment: **All**

TORTUGA BEACH CLUB   *Rates: moderate-deluxe*
Open: year-round   *Minimum Stay: one week*

Sanibel Island's Tortuga Beach Club offers 42 spacious townhouse apartments contained in a small cluster of three-story buildings. Meticulously landscaped with luxuriant tropical vegetation and a scattering of vibrant flowers, the grounds feature a pool and spa area, plus four tennis courts and a congenial clubhouse. Guests may use the nearby 18-hole golf course for free. The apartments, all with two bedrooms and baths and room to sleep up to six, couldn't be more pleasantly furnished or better equipped for gracious living and elegant entertaining. Contact: Marquis Hotels and Resorts, 13451-27 McGregor Blvd., Fort Myers, FL 33919. Call 1-813-481-5600 or 1-800-237-8906.

Children: **Y** Pets: **N** Smoking: **Y** Handicap Access: **Y** Payment: **C, T, A, V, M**

ST. PETERSBURG

ISLA DEL SOL APARTMENTS   *Rates: inexpensive-moderate*
Open: year-round   *Minimum Stay: one week*

Situated on the Isla del Sol between St. Petersburg and St. Petersburg Beach in the Boca Ciega Bay, this collection of holiday apartments provides sophisticated accommodations for guests visiting the vacation hub of Florida's west coast. The island is easily reached by a toll bridge; there are gleaming sandy beaches to enjoy plus ample opportunities for golf, tennis and all water sports. The units stand next to a private swimming pool and contain a spacious combined sitting room/ dining area, a complete kitchen and two bedrooms, with either a patio or balcony looking out onto the bay or the lush countryside. Contact: Interhome, Inc., 124 Little Falls Road, Fairfield, NJ 07004. Call 1-201-882-6864. Ref U3371/160M-165M-180M.

Children: Y Pets: N Smoking: Y Handicap Access: N Payment: C, P, T, V, M

Georgia

BLAIRSVILLE

7 CREEKS HOUSEKEEPING CABINS *Rates: budget*
Open: year-round *Minimum Stay: two nights*

You'll find these cabins situated on well-tended grounds around a private lake, surrounded by the rugged mountains of north Georgia. All the cabins are nicely furnished with everything except for linens, including laundry facilities in every cabin. Most have bedrooms and an additional fold-out couch. The largest cabin, the Longview, sleeps eight; the smallest is the Ledford, which sleeps four. Most have electric heat and all have full kitchens, barbecues and TVs. Children like to watch the owner's farm animals, and the lake is kept well-stocked with bass, bream and catfish for your pleasure. Ten acres of land, a pavilion by the lake, badminton, horseshoes and an open-air chapel are all there for guests' use; within an hour's drive are several golf courses, white-water rafting sites and gold and gem panning. Contact: Marvin H. Hernden, 7 Creeks Housekeeping Cabins, Route 2, P.O. Box 2647, Blairsville, GA 30512. Call 404-745-4753.

Children: Y   Pets: Y   Smoking: Y   Handicap Access: N   Payment: C, P, T

VOGEL STATE PARK COTTAGES *Rates: budget*
Open: year-round *Minimum Stay: two nights*

High in the Chattahoochee National Forest lies one of Georgia's oldest and most popular state parks, built in the 1930s. It encompasses 36 air-conditioned cottages completely equipped with all bed linens and

kitchenware. Containing either one, two or three bedrooms, many of the cottages have porches or decks and wood-burning fireplaces. The activities at the park range from fishing or sunning on the lakeside beach to naturalist programs and miniature golf. In October the hiking trails become particularly memorable, as the foliage shimmers with a hundred brilliant hues. Park workers can tell you about the park's legendary buried gold, and the Dahlonega Gold Museum makes an interesting day trip, as do the many other state parks in the area. Contact: David Foot, Vogel State Park, Route 1, P.O. Box 1230, Highway 19/129 S., Blairsville, GA 30512. Call 404-745-2628.
Children: Y Pets: N Smoking: Y Handicap Access: N Payment: C, P, T, V, M

CHATSWORTH

FORT MOUNTAIN STATE PARK COTTAGES   *Rates: budget*
Open: year-round   *Minimum Stay: two nights*
This park is named for a mysterious and ancient rock wall stretching nearly 1,000 feet over a mountaintop. The park covers close to 2,000 acres of woods and mountains, through which 12 miles of hiking trails have been developed; for accommodation, there is a camping area and 15 rental cottages. All cottages are kept cool in summer with air-conditioning and contain either two or three bedrooms with all linens and blankets provided. There are barbecue facilities as well, and fireplaces make the cottages seem even cozier after a day spent in the fresh mountain air. Fish at a nearby lake, take your kids to the playground or go to the beach and meet new friends. Contact: Wayne Escoe, Fort Mountain State Park, Route 7, P.O. Box 7008, Chatsworth, GA 30705. Call 404-695-2621.
Children: Y Pets: N Smoking: Y Handicap Access: N Payment: C, P, T, V, M

CLARKESVILLE

LAPRADE'S RESTAURANT, CABINS & MARINA   *Rates: budget*
Open: April-December   *Minimum Stay: two nights*
Fresh mountain air and beautiful scenery characterize this resort, where traditional, hearty fare is available in a family-style restaurant. The one- to three-bedroom cabins, used by mountain fishermen for years, have been modernized with the addition of bathrooms and gas heat, and are made even more comfortable by such touches as home-sewn quilts. Guests enjoy access to Lake Burton for fishing, picnicking and swimming and are welcome to visit the marina, which rents equipment for fishing, waterskiing and boating. After a meal of hot biscuits, country sausage and fresh garden vegetables, though, you might just want to return to your front porch and sit in a rocking chair for a while. Contact: Robert Nichols, LaPrade's Restaurant, Cabins & Marina, Route 1, Highway 197 N., Clarkesville, GA 30523. Call 404-947-3312.
Children: Y Pets: N Smoking: N Handicap Access: N Payment: C, P, T

DAHLONEGA

FORREST HILLS MOUNTAIN RESORT *Rates: inexpensive-moderate*
Open: year-round *Minimum Stay: two nights*

Forrest Hills has several small lodges of two to four bedrooms and some one-bedroom cottages for guests. The cottages are romantic hideaways—no children are allowed—and they come with a canopy bed, hot tub, fireplace, color TV with VCR and a porch with a swing for "courting." The lodges also have the advantage of a full kitchen, at least two bathrooms, a living area with a fold-out couch, color TV and fireplaces. The entire grounds cover 140 acres next to a national forest area, and you are welcome to hike on the trails or stay closer to home by the swimming pool, tennis courts and game room. Riding experts at the stables will match you with the right horse; golfers can try out the Chattahoochee Country Club in Gainsville, among others. Contact: Michele Kraft, Forrest Hills Mountain Resort & Conference Center, Wesley Chapel Rd., Route 3, P.O. Box 510, Dahlonega, GA 30533. Call 404-864-6456 or 800-654-6313.

Children: Y Pets: N Smoking: Y Handicap Access: N Payment: C, T, V, M, A, O

PINE MOUNTAIN

F.D. ROOSEVELT STATE PARK *Rates: budget*
Open: year-round *Minimum Stay: two nights*

Stricken with polio in the 1920s, Roosevelt founded The Little White House in Warm Springs while seeking a place for treatment. The 10,000-acre park on Pine Mountain now contains a museum that recalls his life through memorabilia, tours and programs. The park's setting is stunning, and you can see much of it on the 23-mile Pine Mountain Trail and a separate nature trail. In the park are 21 cottages—air-conditioned in summer and heated in winter—each with either one or two bedrooms, and all with completely equipped kitchens and indoor bathrooms. Within walking distance is a swimming pool and children's playground, and there are good fishing spots and boating waters. Nearby attractions for guests include Callaway Gardens, Warm Springs Village and West Point Lake. Contact: Hal Young, F.D. Roosevelt State Park, 2970 Highway 190, P.O. Box 749, Pine Mountain, GA 31822. Call 404-663-4858.

Children: Y Pets: N Smoking: Y Handicap Access: N Payment: C, P, T, V, M

RUTLEDGE

HARD LABOR CREEK STATE PARK CABINS *Rates: budget*
Open: year-round *Minimum Stay: two nights*

The 20 heated cabins in this park each have two bedrooms completely furnished with linens, plus kitchens with all necessary cooking utensils and air-conditioning. An 18-hole golf course is situated right in the park, and there are two lakes where you can try a leisurely pedal boat ride or rent a canoe. For the horse lover, a 15-mile trail snakes through the wood; guests are welcome to hike on a further two and a half miles of trails or rent bicycles for the day. Within driving distance are some scenic and historic sites of interest, including Lake Oconee, historic Madison and Athens. Contact: Hard Labor Creek State Park, P.O. Box 247, Rutledge, GA 30663. Call 404-557-2863.

Children: Y Pets: N Smoking: Y Handicap Access: N Payment: C, P, V, M

SAUTEE

SKYRIDGE VACATION CABINS *Rates: budget-inexpensive*
Open: year-round *Minimum Stay: two nights*

Nestled in the foothills of the Appalachians, these cabins suit families, honeymooners and romantics of all descriptions—a special package known as "Country Charm Weddings" is even available. Each cedar or log cabin is surrounded by stately oaks and lush dogwoods that blaze in autumn in a fiery palette of color. The five cabins range from one to four bedrooms (plus sleeping lofts) with spacious queen and full beds, a country kitchen, a bath and a living room that features a fireplace for cozy days and nights. The cabins are heated in winter and air-conditioned in summer, and all have decks where guests can barbecue meals while admiring the white-tailed deer that fill these woods. Close by are facilities for canoeing, horseback riding, golf, tennis, white-water rafting and tubing. Contact: Skyridge Vacation Cabins, Route 1, P.O. Box 1286, Sautee, GA 30571. Call 404-878-3244.

Children: Y Pets: N Smoking: Y Handicap: N Payment: C, P, T, V, M, A, O

ST. SIMONS ISLAND

DEALVAH'S DEN *Rates: budget-inexpensive*
Open: year-round *Minimum Stay: three nights*

This pleasant clapboard house contains an upstairs apartment with two bedrooms and one bath. All linens are provided and there is a TV and phone. In the garden palm fronds flutter in the sea breeze, which bears the scent of the ocean and the smell of fresh blossoms. St. Simons Island provides plenty of recreational opportunities as well as the chance to visit historic battlefields and forts nearly 300 years old. Across the causeway on Sea Island is a long stretch of golden sand, and just three blocks from this house is another beach. Boating and fishing are popular here, as are inland sports such as golf, tennis and bicycling. Contact: Bobbie Anderson, Century 21 Island Development Co., 2481 Demere Road, Suite 101, St. Simons Island, GA 31522. Call 912-638-1023 or 800-999-1081.

Children: Y Pets: N Smoking: Y Handicap Access: N Payment: C, P, T

FRANCEY'S FANCY *Rates: budget-inexpensive*
Open: year-round *Minimum Stay: three nights*

Cathedral ceilings in the master bedroom and living room give this second-floor apartment a spacious feeling. There are two bedrooms and a combination bedroom/den as well as two full baths, providing comfortable accommodations for up to six guests. The list of extra amenities is long—linen, washing machine and dryer, microwave, phone, TV, stereo and ample closet space are provided. Visitors to this picturesque little offshore island will enjoy bike riding or exploring the coastal rivers, marshes and wooded countryside; the shorelines are dotted with sandy beaches. Among the interesting historical sites to visit are an ancient fort, a lighthouse museum and one of the Rockefellers' former holiday homes. Contact: Bobbie Anderson, Century 21 Island Development Co., 2481 Demere Road, Suite 101, St. Simons Island, GA 31522. Call 912-638-1023 or 800-999-1081.

Children: Y Pets: N Smoking: Y Handicap Access: N Payment: C, P, T

KARRAKER COTTAGE

Rates: budget-inexpensive
Open: year-round   *Minimum Stay: three nights*

A spacious sun room faces the backyard of this house, adjacent to both the master bedroom and the living/dining area. Located in the quiet residential district of Cumberland Oaks, this ground-floor unit has two bedrooms, one with en suite bathroom, a laundry room, a kitchen and a little patio to the left of the sun room. St. Simons is a popular spot for boating, fishing and swimming, and it's always a pleasure to go down to the marina and watch the yachts sail past. Among the island's historic sites is Fort Frederica National Monument, restored to its original 18th-century appearance, and the St. Simons Lighthouse, rebuilt in 1871 and now a museum. Contact: Bobbie Anderson, Century 21 Island Development Co., 2481 Demere Road, Suite 101, St. Simons Island, GA 31522. Call 912-638-1023 or 800-999-1081.

Children: Y Pets: N Smoking: Y Handicap Access: N Payment: C, P, T

KC'S COTTAGE

Rates: budget-inexpensive
Open: year-round   *Minimum Stay: three nights*

Visitors to Georgia's Golden Isles will find them steeped in history and full of recreational opportunities. This pretty cottage has shuttered windows and is surrounded by shady trees and flowering shrubbery. Inside there are two bedrooms and one bath, all completely furnished with linens, phone and TV. An outdoor hot and cold shower will rinse off the salt water from the beach just a short walk away, and an enclosed porch with a high, vaulted ceiling adorns the back of the house. St. Simons has good facilities for golf, boating, tennis, swimming and fishing. Nearby historic sites include Fort Frederica and the 25-room Rockefeller "cottage" on Sea Island. Contact: Bobbie Anderson, Century 21 Island Development Co., 2481 Demere Road, Suite 101, St. Simons Island, GA 31522. Call 912-638-1023 or 800-999-1081.

Children: Y Pets: N Smoking: Y Handicap Access: N Payment: C, P, T

LARY'S LANDING

Rates: budget-inexpensive
Open: year-round   *Minimum Stay: three nights*

Located close to the old lighthouse and museum and the golf course, this two-bedroom, two-bath condo makes a slightly exotic impression—it has its own hot tub as well as a solarium equipped with a sound system. It will be easy to relax at home—the kitchen is fully equipped and there are laundry facilities and a TV and VCR. Visitors to the Golden Isles will enjoy the scenery—tidal rivers and marshes and miles of coastline (the beach on Sea Island is nearly 10 miles long).

Historic battlefields and forts dating back nearly 300 years call to mind another era, as do the remnants of the once-magnificent plantations that were the pride of the coast. Contact: Century 21 Island Development Co., 2481 Demere Road, Suite 101, St. Simons Island, GA 31522. Call 912-638-1023 or 800-999-1081.

Children: Y   Pets: N   Smoking: Y   Handicap Access: N   Payment: C, P, T

PHYL'S PLACE   *Rates: budget*
Open: year-round   *Minimum Stay: three nights*

This luxury condo has a fireplace in the living room; a separate dining room leads to a solarium and an outdoor patio. Situated on the lower level of a two-story building, the apartment comes with all linens, laundry facilities, phone, TV and two bedrooms, one of which has an en suite bathroom and walk-in closet. Located near the golf course on Harbour Oaks Drive, guests will find that the historic sites and boating facilities on the island are within easy reach. A short trip to Sea Island will bring you to a stretch of gleaming sand and a museum that was once William Rockefeller's 25-room "cottage." Contact: Bobbie Anderson, Century 21 Island Development Co., 2481 Demere Road, Suite 101, St. Simons Island, GA 31522. Call 912-638-1023 or 800-999-1081.

Children: Y   Pets: N   Smoking: Y   Handicap Access: N   Payment: C, P, T

THE COLONEL'S QUARTERS   *Rates: budget-inexpensive*
Open: year-round   *Minimum Stay: three nights*

From the windows of this second-floor apartment a sparkling pool invites guests to take a plunge. Complete with linens, phone, TV and laundry facilities, this two-bedroom unit also boasts a solarium and vaulted ceilings that admit abundant sunlight throughout the day. A dining/living room leads to a small balcony, and there is a completely self-contained kitchen. On St. Simons, you're never far from the beach; for those who wish to make a trip, nearby Sea Island has an endless strip of gleaming sand and surf as well. Boating, tennis and bicycling are all popular pastimes, and there are several good golf courses within easy reach. Contact: Bobbie Anderson, Century 21 Island Development Co., 2481 Demere Road, Suite 101, St. Simons Island, GA 31522. Call 912-638-1023 or 800-999-1081.

Children: Y   Pets: N   Smoking: Y   Handicap Access: N   Payment: C, P, T

WINDER

FORT YARGO/WILL-A-WAY STATE PARK COTTAGES   *Rates: budget*
Open: year-round   *Minimum Stay: two nights*

An exceptional facility for the handicapped, Will-a-Way has a recreation area, a group camp that offers various programs and three cottages, which are designed to house up to six handicapped guests and their families or friends. Each of the two bedrooms in the cottages has a double and a twin bed and all linens and kitchenware are provided. The cottages are heated (and air-conditioned in summer) and have wood-burning fireplaces as well. The day-use area in Will-a-Way has an accessible nature trail, picnic area and waterfront center for boating and swimming. All guests can take advantage of the boat rental service (canoes and pedal boats), relax on the sandy lakefront beach or picnic in the shelters provided. Contact: Edwill Holcomb or Darrell Brice, Fort Yargo/Will-a-Way State Park, P.O. Box 764, Highway 81, Winder, GA 30680. Call 404-867-3489.

Children: Y Pets: Y Smoking: Y Handicap Access: Y Payment: C, P, T, V, M

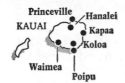

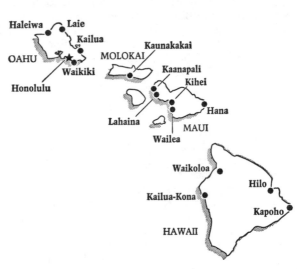

Hawaii

Hilo

DOLPHIN BAY HOTEL
Open: year-round

Rates: budget
Minimum Stay: none

Surrounded by its own lush forest and wrapped in an aura of warm hospitality, the Dolphin Bay Hotel is for those who crave the comfort, quiet and individual service one can only find in a small resort. The rooms range from studios to two-bedroom suites. Some have delightful open-air balconies, while others sport Roman-style tubs in the bathrooms; all feature well-equipped kitchenettes. Despite its quiet situation, the hotel is just a stone's throw away from the lively entertainment of Hilo, and your friendly hosts will be happy to recommend interesting historic sights and splendid natural attractions to visit during your stay. Contact: Dolphin Bay Hotel, 333 Iliahi St., Hilo, HI 96720. Call 808-935-1466.

Children: Y Pets: N Smoking: Y Handicap Access: N Payment: C, T, V, M

HAWAIIAN-TYPE HOME
Open: year-round

Rates: budget
Minimum Stay: none

Hilo is a town full of "aloha spirit," an excellent base for exploring the volcanoes of Mauna Kea and Mauna Loa, thundering Alaska Falls, a variety of historical sites and the local beaches. Perched on a cliff outside of town, overlooking Hilo Bay, is this traditional home, now open to B & B guests. The well-tended grounds encompass a swimming pool, a delightful place to sun and soak away a day or three. Your breakfast is complimentary, of course, but for lunch and dinner why not try some of the local Japanese cuisine? And there's always the island specialty—macadamia nuts—for snacks. Contact: Bed & Breakfast Honolulu, 3242 Kaohinani Dr., Honolulu, HI 96817. Call 1-800-288-4666 (in Hawaii, 808-595-7533).

Children: Y Pets: N Smoking: Y Handicap Access: N Payment: C, P, T, V, M

WAIAKEA VILLAS   *Rates: budget-moderate*
Open: year-round   *Minimum Stay: three nights*

Conveniently located in the heart of Hilo, yet surrounded by 14 acres of exotic flora and gurgling waterways, the Waiakea Villas are a perfect place to cultivate the laid-back island lifestyle you've been longing for. There's also plenty to keep active types busy in the area, from exploring Liliuokalani Gardens or Volcanoes National Park to practicing your favorite water sports off the famous black beaches of The Big Island. The nicely furnished one-bedroom suites here all come with color TV, air-conditioning and a private balcony overlooking the grounds. Contact: The Hawaiian Islands Resorts, P.O. Box 212, Honolulu, HI 96810. Call 1-800-367-7042 (in Hawaii, 808-531-7595).

Children: Y   Pets: N   Smoking: Y   Handicap Access: N   Payment: C

Kailua-Kona

ALII HALE   *Rates: moderate-expensive*
Open: year-round   *Minimum Stay: three nights*

The capacious great room in the center of the house opens through a wall of sliding glass doors to a generous lanai (veranda) where you can enjoy your meals while gazing at the ever-changing sea. Two separate bedroom suites, an airy dining room and a fully equipped kitchen round out the accommodations. Stairs from the lanai lead down to the beach, where crystalline waters alive with brilliant tropical fish and elegant corals are a delight for swimmers, snorkelers and scuba divers alike. Magic Sands Beach, just a short stroll away, is a favorite of surfers. National parks, monuments and the spectacular scenery provide abundant sightseeing possibilities; afterward, do a bit of shopping and dine in one of the fine local restaurants. Contact: Kona Vacations Resorts, P.O. Box 1071, Kailua-Kona, HI 96745. Call 1-800-367-5168 (in Hawaii, 808-329-6488).

Children: Y   Pets: N   Smoking: Y   Handicap Access: N   Payment: All

ALII VILLAS   *Rates: budget-inexpensive*
Open: year-round   *Minimum Stay: three nights*

Stately palms watch over this friendly resort just outside town, and exotic flowers fill the air with tantalizing scents. The white beach with its promise of watery fun is just outside your door, and there's also a swimming pool with a large, sunny patio for drying off or just lazing about. Polynesian playfulness characterizes comfy apartments, which all have color cable TV, full kitchens, one or two bedrooms and either stunning views of the ocean or delightful gardenside vistas.

Surfing, shell hunting, snorkeling and fishing are popular pursuits here—if you're lucky with the latter, a convenient barbecue area will help you turn supper into a private luau. Contact: Kona Vacations Resorts, P.O. Box 1071, Kailua-Kona, HI 96745. Call 1-800-367-5168 (in Hawaii, 808-329-6488).

Children: Y   Pets: N   Smoking: Y   Handicap Access: N   Payment: All

HALE KAI O'KONA   *Rates: moderate-expensive*
Open: year-round   *Minimum Stay: three nights*

Kona, the royal playground of ancient Hawaiian monarchs, awaits you with clean, white beaches and hot, sunny skies. This four-bedroom luxury townhouse will charm you with its modern rattan furnishings and the beautifully appointed master suite. From the two lanais (or verandas) that open off this house you can enjoy the daily spectacle of the fiery sun dousing itself in the warm Pacific waters. Swimming, body surfing, snorkeling and other ocean fun can be pursued at the semi-private beach outside. All the conveniences of home are present here in the microwave oven, washer/dryer and dishwasher. Contact: Kona Vacations Resorts, P.O. Box 1071, Kailua-Kona, HI 96745. Call 1-800-367-5168 (in Hawaii, 808-329-6488).

Children: Y   Pets: N   Smoking: Y   Handicap Access: N   Payment: All

KEAUHOU RESORT   *Rates: budget-inexpensive*
Open: year-round   *Minimum Stay: five nights*

A tropical garden surrounds these pleasant holiday townhouses, which themselves are clustered around a delicious swimming pool. Each one- or two-bedroom abode is beautifully furnished and boasts a modern kitchen. Vibrant bougainvillea blossoms adorn the balconies of each residence, most of which enjoy splendid views of the sea. The Keauhou-Kona Golf Course is practically at your doorstep, and the fishing grounds off Kona teem with marlin, yellowfin and ono. Swimmers, snorkelers and surfers will be delighted by these waters as well, the essence of any Hawaiian holiday. Contact: Leona Doty, Keauhou Resort, 78-7039 Kam III Rd., Kailua-Kona, HI 96740. Call 1-800-367-5286 (in Hawaii, 808-322-9122).

Children: Y   Pets: N   Smoking: Y   Handicap Access: N   Payment: C, P, T

KONA ALII   *Rates: budget-moderate*
Open: year-round   *Minimum Stay: three nights*

On the edge of town, overlooking the blue Pacific waters, is this pleasant resort with comfortable accommodations for your Hawaiian holiday. The spacious one-bedroom suites are handsomely furnished with traditional rattan furniture and boast private balconies; a sofa bed in the living room will accommodate several more guests. The thoughtful amenities include two full bathrooms, complete laundry facilities and a well-equipped kitchen with a dishwasher. The carefully tended grounds are adorned by tall palm trees and encompass one of the largest freshwater swimming pools on the coast. Some rooms overlook this festive scene, while others enjoy unobstructed panoramic views of the wide-open sea. Contact: Hawaii Resort Management, 75-5782 Kua-kini Hwy., Suite C-1, Kailua-Kona, Hawaii 96740. Call 1-800-553-5035 (in Hawaii, 808-329-9393).

Children: Y   Pets: Y   Smoking: Y   Handicap Access: N   Payment: C, P, T

KONA ISLE   *Rates: budget*
Open: year-round   *Minimum Stay: one week*

Kona, the ancient retreat of Hawaiian royalty, is renowned today for its mild coffee, soft sands and endless sunshine. The Kona Isle is an oceanfront resort with meticulously tended lawns and gardens. Some units overlook these lush plantings, while others enjoy marvelous views of the sea. The residences have one bedroom and one bathroom each and are tastefully furnished. The delightful pool is at your disposal (as are the resort's laundry facilities) and the ocean is only a few steps from your door. Not too far away are Mauna Loa and Mauna Kea, the island's twin volcanoes, with their eerie lava formations and periodic fiery outbursts. Contact: Triad Management, 75-5629-M Kua-kini Hwy., Kailua-Kona, HI 96740. Call 1-800-345-2823 (in Hawaii, 808-329-6402).

Children: Y Pets: N Smoking: Y Handicap Access: N Payment: C, T, A, V, M

KONA MAKAI   *Rates: budget-moderate*
Open: year-round   *Minimum Stay: three nights*

After a few laps in the pool or an invigorating workout in the exercise room, perhaps you'd like to relax in the Jacuzzi. Later you can prepare a bit of the daily catch out at the open barbecue area for your own private luau. Your handsome one- or two-bedroom condo just outside the village boasts tasteful decor with just a touch of Polynesian flair. Color cable TV, air-conditioning and a balcony are among the creature comforts that will help make your stay pleasant; a washer and dryer and a full kitchen are among the modern amenities that grace these homes. Contact: Kona Vacations Resorts, P.O. Box 1071, Kailua-Kona, HI 96745. Call 1-800-367-5168 (in Hawaii, 808-329-6488).

Children: Y   Pets: N   Smoking: Y   Handicap Access: N   Payment: All

KONA ONENALO   *Rates: moderate-expensive*
Open: year-round   *Minimum Stay: three nights*

Tropical serenity beside the soothing rhythm of the ocean's waves are yours at the Kona Onenalo. This secluded estate proffers 12 finely furnished Polynesian-style homes. The spacious living room, den, and two bedrooms are enhanced by the distinctive Koa wood cabinetry and creature comforts such as a wet bar. There are three bathrooms in each home and the kitchens all boast microwaves. Outside you'll find two more incarnations of this island's wonderful water in addition to the rolling surf itself: an oceanside pool and a Jacuzzi. Contact: Kona Vacations Resorts, P.O. Box 1071, Kailua-Kona, HI 96745. Call 1-800-367-5168 (in Hawaii, 808-329-6488).

Children: Y   Pets: N   Smoking: Y   Handicap Access: N   Payment: All

SEA VILLAGE   *Rates: inexpensive-moderate*
Open: year-round   *Minimum Stay: three nights*

Right on the edge of some of the world's best deep-sea fishing are the casual accommodations of Sea Village. Not only fishers, but snorkelers, divers and swimmers are delighted by these clear waters. Golf buffs don't do too badly, either, since the excellent course at Keauhou is practically next door. Those whose earthly desires culminate in sun worship can choose between the pristine beaches and the complex's own ocean-view patio, complete with a delightful pool, a Jacuzzi and a wet bar. The one- and two-bedroom suites are well designed and furnished with Polynesian flair; every residence has its own private balcony. Contact: Paradise Management, Kukui Plaza, Suite C-207, 50 S. Beretania St., Honolulu, HI 96813-2294. Call 1-800-367-5205 (in Hawaii, 808-538-7145).

Children: Y   Pets: N   Smoking: Y   Handicap Access: N   Payment: All

SLODOWN HOUSE   *Rates: deluxe*
Open: year-round   *Minimum Stay: three nights*

Has the hectic pace of modern life got you in a tizzy? What you need is a nice, long sojourn at the Slodown House, a splendid holiday abode that's sure to cure what ails you. Situated on a hillside above Kailua-Kona, this soothing house can accommodate eight world-weary visitors in its four bedrooms with three baths. There are spectacular views of the entire Kona Coast from here, a miraculous tableau of blue waters, white beaches and green hills. Near the swimming pool is a delightful little gazebo where you can enjoy the barbecue you've prepared from the daily catch. Contact: Kona Vacations Resorts, P.O. Box 1071, Kailua-Kona, HI 96745. Call 1-800-367-5168 (in Hawaii, 808-329-6488).

Children: Y   Pets: N   Smoking: Y   Handicap Access: N   Payment: All

THE KONA PRINCESS   *Rates: deluxe*
Open: year-round   *Minimum Stay: one week*

This gracious home is splendidly appointed, generously proportioned and delightfully situated—your Hawaiian dream house come true. Just a block from the soft, white sands, it enjoys panoramic views of the ocean from almost every room. Delicate palm fronds partially surround the spacious covered "lanai" (veranda), which features imported tiles and comfortable furniture. The master bedroom, one of four, is just off the soothing hydro-spa. Next to the formal dining room is the fully equipped kitchen; a dishwasher, microwave and laundry facilities are among the modern conveniences you'll find here. Contact: Rent A Home International, 7200 34th Ave. N.W., Seattle, WA 98117. Call 206-545-6963.

Children: Y Pets: N Smoking: Y Handicap Access: N Payment: C, P, V, M

WHITE SANDS VILLAGE   *Rates: inexpensive*
Open: year-round   *Minimum Stay: three days*

Well located on a crescent of white sand and framed by statuesque palm trees, this resort condominium is an ideal home away from home. The stylishly appointed living and dining areas feature mellow wooden furniture and vibrant prints. There are two bedrooms and two baths, and the convertible sofa bed in the living room can sleep a few more. You can watch the color cable TV in air-conditioned splendor or relax out on the private balcony. The complex boasts a game room, a large pool and two tennis courts, or you can try some of the snorkeling, scuba diving and surfing for which these isles are famous. Contact: Randy or Anne Kent, 115 Oakwood Place, Santa Cruz, CA 95066. Call 408-438-2489. Or contact: Triad Management, 75-5629-M Kuakini Hwy., Kailua-Kona, HI 96740. Call 1-800-345-2823 (in Hawaii, 808-329-6402).

Children: Y   Pets: N   Smoking: Y   Handicap Access: N   Payment: C, P

Kapoho

CHAMPAGNE COVE AT KAPOHO BEACH   *Rates: budget*
Open: year-round   *Minimum Stay: one week*

The striking black sands of Kapoho—legacy of the island's volcanic history—provide the ultimate in beach exotica. Whales are often seen cavorting offshore, and locals here take their water sports seriously. The house comprises two separate three-bedroom units, which can easily be opened up to one another for the pleasure of larger groups. Each floor has its own covered deck, with comfy furniture for sitting out and listening to the rolling surf. Lush tropical plantings encompass a sizable heated swimming pool, which features two shallower areas for the wee ones. Hilo is less than an hour to the north, and day trips can easily be taken to the Volcanoes National Park. Contact: Norma Godfrey, 1714 Lei Lehua St., Hilo, HI 96720. Call 808-959-4487.

Children: Y   Pets: N   Smoking: Y   Handicap Access: N   Payment: C, P, T

Waikoloa

ASTON SHORES   *Rates: expensive-deluxe*
Open: year-round   *Minimum Stay: three nights*

The tiled roofs, pale walls and bodacious arches of this complex may lead you to believe you're in a Mediterranean resort, but the luxuriant gardens and perfect weather are pure Hawaii. These deluxe condos are tastefully furnished and have either one or two bedrooms. All feature air-conditioning, washers and dryers and full kitchens with microwaves. Guests share the use of a spectacular pool and well-maintained tennis courts, and there is wonderful beach in the neighborhood. The rental includes use of a car, and not far away is the Kamuela Museum, which boasts the largest collection of artifacts from the Hawaiian monarchs. Contact: Condo Club, P.O. Box 8280, Red Bank, NJ 07701-8280. Call 1-800-272-6636.

Children: Y   Pets: N   Smoking: Y   Handicap Access: N   Payment: C

KAUAI

Aliomanu

HALE MOANA *Rates: deluxe*
Open: year-round *Minimum Stay: one week*

The polished floors, wood paneling, grass mats, classic rattan furniture and high ceilings of this gracious home create an ambience of casual elegance. Outside you'll find an enormous veranda—or "lanai," in the local tongue—where you can cool off in the shade or stretch out in the sun with a mai-tai in hand. Majestic technicolor views can be enjoyed from every room: Lush green vegetation lines the startlingly pale beach, and the water itself verges from the most delicate blue into a deep sapphire hue. There are three large bedrooms for up to nine guests, and modern creature comforts include a dishwasher and laundry facilities. Contact: Bill and Katie Payne, 9856 Sunland Blvd., Sunland, CA 91040. Call 1-800-367-5025 (in California, 818-353-9203).

Children: Y Pets: N Smoking: Y Handicap Access: N Payment: C, P

PAYNE COTTAGE *Rates: inexpensive-moderate*
Open: year-round *Minimum Stay: one week*

Only a few steps away from the excellent swimming and snorkeling of secluded Aliomanu Beach is this pleasant cottage for two to four people. The spacious great room features a high ceiling with exposed beams, handsome wood paneling and comfortable furniture that artfully blends traditional Hawaiian materials with modern styling. An arched doorway leads to a cool bedroom, and dark wooden floors run throughout. A kitchenette, a bathroom and a loft round out the accommodations; cable TV and a stereo are among the modern amenities. Contact: Bill and Katie Payne, 9856 Sunland Blvd., Sunland, CA 91040. Call 1-800-367-5025 (in California, 818-353-9203).

Children: Y Pets: N Smoking: Y Handicap Access: N Payment: C, P

Hanalei

HANALEI COLONY RESORT *Rates: inexpensive-moderate*
Open: year-round *Minimum Stay: three nights*

Reputed to be the erstwhile vacation home of Puff the Magic Dragon, Hanalei proffers a bewitching mix of open water, haunting mists and incredibly lush foliage. The warm, clear Pacific beckons to swimmers, sailors, surfers, snorkelers and water lovers of all varieties. The streams running down nearby Mount Waialeale will delight kayakers, and the trails here and at Na Pali will enthrall you with their luxuriant flora, shimmering brooks, crashing waterfalls and impressive rock formations. The Hanalei Colony Resort is a pretty condo village tucked away in a quiet cove. The combination of modern amenities such as a swimming pool, Jacuzzi and barbecues with comfy lodgings and unspoiled natural splendor could cheer even a lonely dragon. Contact: Hanalei Colony Resort, 5-7130 Kuhio Hwy., Haena, Kauai, HI 96714. Call 1-800-628-3004 (in Hawaii, 808-826-6141).

Children: Y Pets: N Smoking: Y Handicap Access: N Payment: All

Kapaa

KAPAA SANDS *Rates: budget-inexpensive*
Open: year-round *Minimum Stay: none*
Nestled between the palm trees and the open waters in a quiet cove, the Kapaa Sands offers tranquil accommodations for your sojourn on Kauai's eastern shore. Nothing but elegant palms and a carpet of green lawn lies between you and the incredibly clear waters. There's also a delightful swimming pool for those who enjoy an occasional freshwater swim. The studio and two-bedroom suites are comfortably furnished and feature generous balconies and full kitchens. Many enjoy unobstructed views of the ocean, and maid service is provided for all units. Active types may want to investigate the golf, tennis and horseback riding available in the area. Contact: Harriet Kaholokula, Kapaa Sands, 380 Papaloa Rd., Kapaa, Kauai, HI 96746. Call 1-800-222-4901 (in Hawaii, 808-822-4901).
Children: Y   Pets: N   Smoking: Y   Handicap Access: N   Payment: C, P, T

Koloa

KIAHUNA PLANTATION *Rates: moderate-deluxe*
Open: year-round *Minimum Stay: two nights*
Local regulations forbid any building on Kauai to be taller than a palm tree in order to preserve the small-town atmosphere for which the island is loved. A former sugar cane plantation, the estate is currently a landscaped garden overflowing with tropical blooms, lush fruits and exotic cacti. Each stylishly furnished one- or two-bedroom unit boasts color TV and at least one private deck or patio; daily maid service is provided and valet service is available. Activities for the kids include hula lessons, basket weaving and lagoon fishing; bigger kids will enjoy the tennis court and pool, not to mention the swimming, surfing and snorkeling down at the beach. Contact: Village Resort, 3697 Mt. Diable Blvd., Suite 150, Lafayette, CA, 94549. Call 1-800-367-7052 (in Hawaii, 808-742-6411)
Children: Y   Pets: N   Smoking: Y   Handicap Access: N   Payment: All

PRINCE KUHIO RENTALS *Rates: budget-inexpensive*
Open: year-round *Minimum Stay: one week*
The "Gold Coast" of Kauai lives up to its name, with warm, gilded beaches and a perpetual sun lighting up the deep sky—although bronze makes its appearance here, too, primarily on the hides of inveterate sun worshippers. These spacious studios and one-bedroom apartments can sleep up to four; most overlook the ocean and magnificent Prince Kuhio Park. All have color cable TV and laundry facilities are available. Across the road is a small beach well known for its excellent snorkeling; the Kukuiolona and Kiahuna Golf Courses are both nearby, and tennis can also be enjoyed in the area. Contact: Prince Kuhio Rentals, P.O. Box 1060, 5160 Lawai Rd., Koloa, Kauai, HI 96756. Call 1-800-744-1409 (in Hawaii, 808-742-1409 or 742-1670).
Children: Y   Pets: N   Smoking: Y   Handicap Access: N   Payment: C, T

Poipu

HALE HAUOLI   *Rates: deluxe*
Open: year-round   *Minimum Stay: one week*

Sitting on a generous swath of oceanfront land, this spacious home does its best to help you cultivate the peaceful, easy lifestyle of the islands. You can try your luck at fishing from the rocky shore in front of the house, or watch for the whales that winter here and the dolphins that frolic the whole year round. Kukuiula Harbor, where little boats glide in and out, is right around the corner. The main house offers guests two bedrooms, two bathrooms, a nice modern kitchen and very handsome living areas; the "pahale," or cottage, features an additional bedroom and bathroom. Wind surfing, tennis and mountain biking are popular on Kauai, the garden island, as is the gentler pursuit of shell hunting. Contact: Garden Island Rentals, 5402 Koloa Rd., P.O. Box 57, Koloa, Kauai, HI 96756. Call 1-800-247-5599 (in Hawaii, 808-742-9537).

Children: **Y**   Pets: **N**   Smoking: **Y**   Handicap Access: **N**   Payment: **C, P, T**

HALE HOKU   *Rates: inexpensive*
Open: year-round   *Minimum Stay: one week*

Starry-eyed lovers seeking a romantic hideaway on a tropical isle will be delighted with this little studio, whose name means "House of the Star." Fabulous views of the Poipu coastline can be enjoyed from these comfortable lodgings, and the beaches are just a few minutes away. For more private swimming and sunning, there's a nice pool at your disposal. Sitting out on the oceanfront lanai (veranda) with your paramour and a couple of cool tropical cocktails is a delicious way to spend an afternoon or evening. Contact: Garden Island Rentals, 5402 Koloa Rd., P.O. Box 57, Koloa, Kauai, HI 96756. Call 1-800-247-5599 (in Hawaii, 808-742-9537).

Children: **Y**   Pets: **N**   Smoking: **Y**   Handicap Access: **N**   Payment: **C, P, T**

HALE LUANA   *Rates: deluxe*
Open: year-round   *Minimum Stay: one week*

This "House of Perfect Comfort"—the meaning of its name in Hawaiian—delights all those who seek beauty and luxury in a secluded setting. Surrounded by walls of lava stone, the nicely landscaped property includes both a main house with three large bedrooms and a guest house for two more guests. In between is a generous pool surrounded by a flagstoned patio; here you can sun or swim while looking at the rolling waves of the ocean just a few feet away. In front of the house is a very shallow "keikie" beach, perfect for wading, quietly floating on a raft or just splashing about. Contact: Garden Island Rentals, 5402 Koloa Rd., P.O. Box 57, Koloa, Kauai, HI 96756. Call 1-800-247-5599 (in Hawaii, 808-742-9537).

Children: **Y**   Pets: **N**   Smoking: **Y**   Handicap Access: **N**   Payment: **C, P, T**

KA HALE KAI   *Rates: moderate*
Open: year-round   *Minimum Stay: one week*

A quaint, old-fashioned air pervades this traditional island home. The "hale," or main house, offers guests a pleasant bedroom, quiet living quarters and delightful views of the Kukuiula Small Boat Harbor from the wonderful patio. The completely separate studio, which can be rented separately or with the house, boasts a nice lawn, also overlooking the harbor. Modern conveniences in both residences include microwave ovens and color TVs. You may choose to spend your days sipping Blue Hawaiians and enjoying the scenery from this tranquil spot, or you may want to explore some of the luxuriant hillsides and secluded coves of this unspoiled island. Contact: Garden Island Rentals, 5402 Koloa Rd., P.O. Box 57, Koloa, Kauai, HI 96756. Call 1-800-247-5599 (in Hawaii, 808-742-9537).

Children: Y   Pets: N   Smoking: Y   Handicap Access: N   Payment: C, P, T

MAKAHUENA   *Rates: inexpensive*
Open: year-round   *Minimum Stay: four nights*

Right next to the lighthouse that stands guard above Keoniloa Beach, these condominiums in the desirable Poipu area offer comfortable accommodations in a splendid setting. From the lanai (veranda) and master bedroom of each two-bedroom residence you can enjoy delightful ocean views—the rosy sunrises are particularly exquisite. After a few laps in the pool or a game of tennis, you can soothe your muscles in the Jacuzzi. Golden sands and clear waters are perhaps the most important of Kauai's riches: A short stroll in one direction will bring you to Keoniloa Beach; walk the other way and you'll find yourself at Brennecke's Beach. May choosing between these two be the most difficult part of your holiday. Contact: Garden Island Rentals, 5402 Koloa Rd., P.O. Box 57, Koloa, Kauai, HI 96756. Call 1-800-247-5599 (in Hawaii, 808-742-9537).

Children: Y   Pets: N   Smoking: Y   Handicap Access: N   Payment: C, P, T

POIPU CONDOMINIUM   *Rates: budget*
Open: year-round   *Minimum Stay: none*

The master suite of this two-bedroom condo is open to guests, an unusual but highly rewarding arrangement. The cathedral ceiling and color TV in the bedroom will remind you of a posh hotel suite; the private balcony brings you face-to-face with the splendor of Hawaii. A tennis court and swimming pool are available within the complex, or you can take a short stroll to renowned Poipu Beach. Enjoying almost continual sunshine and warm weather, this area is a splendid spot to practice your tennis, golf or horseback riding; to try out some new sports such as scuba diving and wind surfing; or to just sit around and soak up the sun. Contact: Bed & Breakfast Honolulu, 3242 Kaohinani Dr., Honolulu, HI 96817. Call 1-800-288-4666 (in Hawaii, 808-595-7533).

Children: Y Pets: N Smoking: N Handicap Access: N Payment: C, P, T, V, M

POIPU PALMS   *Rates: inexpensive*
Open: year-round   *Minimum Stay: four nights*
Every afternoon in the restful bay beneath the Poipu Palms, a bevy of
turtles comes by to munch on the seaweed, or "limu," that clings to
the rocks. Watching from the observation deck as their heads pop out
of the water is a delightful way to break up a day of swimming and
sunning in this quiet retreat. The comfortable two-bedroom condos
are tastefully furnished with cheerful island motifs, and many boast
views of the sea from their covered balconies. In addition to the pool
and ocean outside your front door, golf and tennis are available in the
area. There are some colorful local markets within walking distance,
and a variety of casual and formal restaurants will cater to your gas-
tronomical pleasure. Contact: Garden Island Rentals, 5402 Koloa Rd.,
P.O. Box 57, Koloa, Kauai, HI 96756. Call 1-800-247-5599 (in Hawaii,
808-742-9537).
Children: Y Pets: N Smoking: Y Handicap Access: N Payment: C, P, T

WHALER'S COVE   *Rates: expensive-deluxe*
Open: year-round   *Minimum Stay: none*
The Whaler's Cove is found in sunny Poipu, on one of the most exquisite coves on Kauai. Whaling ships once anchored here, and now
the cove invites travelers of a different nature to enjoy its sun-drenched
sands and clear, warm waters. The elegant and spacious living room
features a wall of glass doors affording views of the sea framed by palm
trees; these open onto a partially shaded veranda, a splendid spot to
bask in the sunshine and sip a tropical drink while listening to the
sound of the surf. The accommodations also comprise a well-designed
kitchen, a dining area, a master suite with its own balcony and Jacuzzi
and another bedroom and bath. Daily maid service is provided. Contact: Whaler's Cove, 2640 Puuholo Rd., Poipu, Kauai, HI 96756. Call
1-800-367-7052 (in Hawaii, 808-742-7571).
Children: Y Pets: Y Smoking: Y Handicap Access: N Payment: C, T, A, V, M

Poipu Beach

SUNSET KAHILI   *Rates: inexpensive*
Open: year-round   *Minimum Stay: three nights*
A tasteful blend of Hawaiian and mainland furnishings grace these
one- and two-bedroom suites; all boast complete kitchens and cable
TV. From your own balcony you can watch the plumes of sea spray
rising from the mysterious Spouting Horn or enjoy the vistas of the
wide-open seas. Porpoises, whales and turtles come by regularly to
watch the tourists watching them. Other aquatic creatures—such as
surfers, swimmers and snorkelers—also consider this watery playground to be one of the best. An unbroken string of golden days will
satisfy any sun-worshipper's desires, and the sunsets here impoverish
all descriptions. Contact: Shari Abell, Sunset Kahili, 1763 Pee Rd.,
Poipu Beach, Koloa, Kauai, HI 96766. Call 1-800-367-8047, ext. 212 (in
Hawaii, 808-742-1691).
Children: Y Pets: N Smoking: Y Handicap Access: N Payment: C, P, T, V, M

Princeville

ALII KAI   *Rates: inexpensive*
Open: year-round   *Minimum Stay: three nights*

This spacious condominium is found on the lush northern shore of
Kauai, the Garden Isle. The enormous master bedroom boasts two
double beds, a dressing room and an adjoining bathroom; the other
bedroom has two twin beds. The main living areas are open, airy and
pleasantly furnished. The fireplace in the living room adds a touch of
old-world charm, and the dishwasher and laundry facilities in the
kitchen add modern convenience. There are sweeping views from the
large, wraparound deck outside. Golf, tennis, horseback riding and just
about every water sport you can think of can be enjoyed in the area and
the neighborhood boasts some very fine restaurants. Contact: Rent A
Home International, 7200 34th Ave. N.W., Seattle, WA 98117. Call
206-545-6963.

Children: Y Pets: N Smoking: Y Handicap Access: N Payment: C, P, V, M

HALE MOI   *Rates: budget-moderate*
Open: year-round   *Minimum Stay: none*

Both excellent sports facilities and utter tranquillity can be found on
Kauai, an unspoiled tropical paradise in the Hawaiian archipelago.
Snorkeling, diving, fishing, surfing and wind surfing are among the
favorite aquatic pursuits that can be enjoyed from Princeville. Other
activities include golf, tennis, and racquetball; in fact, Hale Moi overlooks a Robert Trent Jones golf course. The studio and one-bedroom
units here are nicely furnished in typical island fashion and offer fabulous views of the verdant mountains from their large windows. Contact: The Hawaiian Islands Resorts, P.O. Box 212, Honolulu, HI 96810.
Call 1-800-367-7042 (in Hawaii, 808-531-7595).

Children: Y   Pets: N   Smoking: Y   Handicap Access: N   Payment: C

PALI KE KUA   *Rates: budget-expensive*
Open: year-round   *Minimum Stay: none*

Panoramic views of the blue ocean rimmed by white beaches or of the
misty green mountains of Kauai are commanded by the Pali Ke Kua
from its clifftop situation. The one- and two-bedroom condos in this
pleasant low-rise complex are nicely decorated in the Hawaiian spirit;
the cathedral ceilings that are found in many of the living rooms create
a cool, open feeling. For your relaxation, the complex boasts a whirlpool and swimming pool in addition to the picnic pavilion shaded by
coconut and guava trees. The beach is nearby, as are abundant golf and
tennis facilities. Contact: The Hawaiian Islands Resorts, P.O. Box 212,
Honolulu, HI 96810. Call 1-800-367-7042 (in Hawaii, 808-531-7595).

Children: Y   Pets: N   Smoking: Y   Handicap Access: N   Payment: C

PU'U PO'A   *Rates: moderate-deluxe*
Open: year-round   *Minimum Stay: none*

Precipitously perched on the verdant cliffs of Princeville are these
elegant modern condominiums. Incredible ocean views are to be enjoyed from both of the splendid terraces that open out from each two-

bedroom residence, each with its own tiled bathroom and streamlined kitchen. The sparkling pool and the crystalline waters on the sugar-white beach vie for the attention of swimmers; you'll probably want to sample each of them, again and again. The Princeville Championship Golf Course should satisfy golfers and every tennis buff will relish playing on the courts of Pu'u Po'a. Contact: The Hawaiian Islands Resorts, P.O. Box 212, Honolulu, HI 96810. Call 1-800-367-7042 (in Hawaii, 808-531-7595).

Children: Y   Pets: N   Smoking: Y   Handicap Access: N   Payment: C

SEA LODGE   *Rates: budget-inexpensive*
Open: year-round   *Minimum Stay: three nights*

Kauai is the "garden isle," the most luxuriant gem in an incredibly lush tropical archipelago. Along its shoreline you'll find sandy beaches, verdant cliffs and coral reefs; the interior is filled with majestic mountains, junglelike forests and crystalline waterfalls. On a bluff overlooking the deep azure waters near Princeville are these attractive low-rise condos, ideal bases for a Kauai holiday. Sharing well-tended grounds and a delicious pool, each unit is stylishly furnished and can accommodate up to five people. There are magnificent views to be enjoyed from the open veranda, and the sound of the surf breaking will sing you to sleep. Contact: Marion or Herb Hubbard, Hestara Partnership, 25352 W. Lake Shore Dr., Barrington, IL 60010. Call 708-381-6101.

Children: Y   Pets: N   Smoking: Y   Handicap Access: N   Payment: C, P

Waimea

KOKEE LODGE   *Rates: budget*
Open: year-round   *Minimum Stay: none*

Enclosed within the bounds of the Kokee State Park are some of Hawaii's most impressive natural wonders. The Waimea Canyon's steep, rocky walls drop to a floor lushly carpeted in tropical foliage; it was dubbed "The Grand Canyon of the Pacific" by Mark Twain. Hiking trails through the dense forests lead to scenic panoramas, such as the famed Kalalau Lookout. The hunting and fishing in the clean, open air is outstanding. Enjoying the great outdoors shouldn't have to mean roughing it, a philosophy aptly incarnated in the excellent restaurant back at the lodge. The rustic cabins are well equipped with kitchenettes and wood stoves; between three and seven happy campers will find lodgings here. Contact: Kokee Lodge, P.O. Box 819, Waimea, Kauai, HI 96796. Call 808-335-6061.

Children: Y Pets: N Smoking: Y Handicap Access: N Payment: C, P, T, V, M

WAIMEA PLANTATION COTTAGES   *Rates: budget-expensive*
Open: year-round   *Minimum Stay: three nights*

Waimea is an important historic town, the site where Hawaiian kings first greeted the European explorer Captain James Cook in 1778. Today's visitors are fascinated by the traditional way of life here: Taro and sugar cane are cultivated on the hills and valleys as they have been for generations, and the "aloha spirit" of generous hospitality is alive

and well. These old plantation cottages have been completely renovated to provide comfortable accommodations with a full complement
of modern amenities. From two to nine guests will find lodgings here.
Contact: Waimea Plantation Cottages, 9600 Kaumualii Hwy. 367,
Waimea, Kauai, HI 96796. Call 1-800-992-4632 (in Hawaii, 808-338-
1625).

Children: Y Pets: N Smoking: Y Handicap Access: N Payment: C, P, T, V, M

MAUI

Hana

WAIANAPANAPA CABINS *Rates: budget*
Open: year-round *Minimum Stay: none*

Fascinating cultural monuments and intriguing natural formations are
both within reach when you stay in one of these comfy cabins operated by the state parks on the eastern coast of Maui. Whether you
explore the large cave for which the park is named, the intricate lava
formations on which it is built, the Seven Sacred Pools nearby or the
heiau (temple), you're sure to be richly rewarded with unique discov-
eries. The well-furnished cabins are equipped with kitchenettes, bathrooms, electricity and hot and cold running water; up to six people can
be accommodated. Contact: Department of Land and Natural Resources, Division of State Parks, 54 S. High St., Wiluku, Maui, HI
96793. Call 808-243-5354.

Children: Y   Pets: N   Smoking: Y   Handicap Access: N   Payment: C, P

Kaanapali

KAANAPALI ALII *Rates: moderate-deluxe*
Open: year-round *Minimum Stay: five nights*

Beautiful woodwork and colorful tiles enliven the splendid interiors of
these condominiums. In addition to the luxurious furnishings, your
holiday home features modern amenities such as air conditioning and
a microwave oven. Whether you select a two-bedroom unit or a one-
bedroom with a den, the accommodations are spacious and comfortable; every single unit offers stunning views of the sea. The complex
offers a workout gym and two pools—one for kiddies and one for the
grownups. Kaanapali is a lively resort town where you can select from
dozens of fine restaurants, enjoy the convivial nightlife of the taverns
and dance until dawn. Contact: Whalers Realty, Whalers Village, Suite
A-3, 2435 Kaanapali Parkway, Lahaina, Maui, HI 96761. Call 1-800-
367-5632 (in Hawaii, 808-661-8777).

Children: Y   Pets: N   Smoking: Y   Handicap Access: Y   Payment: All

MAUI ELDORADO RESORT *Rates: inexpensive-expensive*
Open: year-round *Minimum Stay: none*

The delightful beaches of Kaanapali, one of the most popular resorts in
the islands, are the setting for these comfy low-rise condominiums.
Each suite is tastefully appointed with modern furnishings, a blend of
Hawaiian materials and traditional design. The units range from cozy

studios to larger two-bedrooms, and all enjoy delightful balconies. The emerald swath of the Royal Kaanapali Golf Course is right outside and the Royal Lahaina Tennis Ranch is also nearby. Three tempting pools await you, or go right for the gusto and swim in the ocean's refreshing waves. The large cabana, a great place for meeting up with old friends and new, is right on the beach, only a few feet from the water. Contact: Maui Eldorado Resort, 2661 Kekaa Dr., Lahaina, HI 96761. Call 1-800-367-2967 (in Hawaii, 808-661-0021).

Children: Y   Pets: N   Smoking: Y   Handicap Access: N   Payment: All

NAPILI BAY RESORT

Rates: budget-inexpensive
Open: year-round   *Minimum Stay: five nights*

Fronds of the elegant palms graciously provide a bit of shade on the golden beaches of the Napili Bay Resort. When you're not playing in the water or soaking up a bit of the delicious sunshine, perhaps you'd enjoy some of the tennis, golf or other recreational pursuits of the area. There are also charming shops, interesting galleries and fine restaurants nearby to keep you busy. The studio apartments at the Napili Bay Resort are splendid bases for enjoying this tropical playground. Each suite features a full kitchen, a color TV, a breezy veranda—or "lanai," in the local lingo—and views of either the glorious ocean or delightful gardens. Contact: Whalers Realty, Whalers Village, Suite A-3, 2435 Kaanapali Parkway, Lahaina, Maui, HI 96761. Call 1-800-367-5632 (in Hawaii, 808-661-8777).

Children: Y   Pets: N   Smoking: Y   Handicap Access: Y   Payment: All

THE KAHANA SUNSET

Rates: moderate
Open: year-round   *Minimum Stay: five nights*

Hidden away in a secluded cove with snow-white sands, the Kahana Sunset offers all the tranquillity and privacy of your very own beach. The calm, clear waters are ideal for children and snorkelers; the latter may want to explore the reef that protects this corner of paradise. The scent of the sea mingles with exotic fragrances from the lush gardens that wend their way through the grounds. To complement these natural treasures, your hosts at the Kahana Sunset have added a wealth of modern conveniences: Each two-bedroom suite boasts a microwave oven, a washer and dryer and atmospheric ceiling fans and outside you'll find barbecue areas not too far from the swimming pool. Contact: Whalers Realty, Whalers Village, Suite A-3, 2435 Kaanapali Parkway, Lahaina, Maui, HI 96761. Call 1-800-367-5632 (in Hawaii, 808-661-8777).

Children: Y   Pets: N   Smoking: Y   Handicap Access: Y   Payment: All

Kihei

HALE KAMAOLE

Rates: budget-inexpensive
Open: year-round   *Minimum Stay: five nights*

The rolling green lawns, enigmatic palms, graceful plumeria and lavish hibiscus blooms here create a fragrant garden setting for this cluster of condominiums. Two swimming pools, a tennis court and barbecue grills add convenient creature comfort to the landscaping. Both the one-bedroom and two-bedroom condos have breezy private balconies where you can sip a mai-tai after a day in the sun and enjoy the peacefulness of twilight; most also enjoy stunning views of the sea and coastline. All are tastefully furnished in individual styles and are equipped with color TVs, washers and dryers and modern kitchens. Contact: Maui Condominium and Home Realty, P.O. Box 1840, Kihei, HI 96753. Call 1-800-822-4409 (in Hawaii, 808-879-5445).

Children: Y   Pets: N   Smoking: Y   Handicap Access: N   Payment: C, P, T

HALEAKALA SHORES RESORT

Rates: budget-inexpensive
Open: year-round   *Minimum Stay: five nights*

Just across from the silky sands and shallow waters of Kamaole Beach III, this plush condominium offers outstanding lodgings. Both the tastefully furnished living and dining room and the comfy master bedroom (with its own adjoining bath) open onto a spacious covered veranda. Another bedroom (which can also serve as a den) another bathroom and a well-equipped kitchen complete the accommodations. The large, central activity area houses a sparkling pool surrounded by lush tropical plantings, a sunny deck and a poolside veranda with barbecues for that homestyle luau. The new Wailea golf courses and the Wailea Tennis Club just five minutes away will enthrall athletic types, as will the impressive water sports activities available in the area. Contact: Maui Condominium and Home Realty, P.O. Box 1840, Kihei, HI 96753. Call 1-800-822-4409 (in Hawaii, 808-879-5445).

Children: Y   Pets: N   Smoking: Y   Handicap Access: N   Payment: C, P, T

KIHEI AKAHI

Rates: budget-inexpensive
Open: year-round   *Minimum Stay: five nights*

This wonderful resort offers the ultimate in privacy and picturesque seclusion. Gently shaded by elegantly draped palm fronds, the finely appointed rooms range from studios to two-bedroom apartments; all boast color TVs and private balconies. Piquant exotic fragrances will grace your room if you choose a garden-view condo; stunning views of the sunset are to be enjoyed from ocean-view accommodations. The complex features two pools and tennis courts. If you dream of horseback riding down windswept beaches, scuba diving in an extinct underwater volcano, wind surfing in a private cove, exploring a hidden waterfall or watching a group of humpback whales at play, all your vacation fantasies can come true on Maui. Contact: Maui Condominium and Home Realty, P.O. Box 1840, Kihei, HI 96753. Call 1-800-822-4409 (in Hawaii, 808-879-5445).

Children: Y   Pets: N   Smoking: Y   Handicap Access: N   Payment: C, P, T

LIHI KAI COTTAGES

Rates: budget
Open: year-round   *Minimum Stay: three nights*

"Lihi Kai" means "beside the sea," an apt name for this oceanfront resort. Nine lovely cottages for couples offer comfy accommodations (with full kitchens) in a garden setting. For those dedicated to a carefree holiday, maid service is available. The Wailea and Makena golf courses await golf enthusiasts, and the water sports opportunities are almost unlimited. Most of all, the golden sands, friendly smiles, and tropical gardens of papaya, coconut, guava, hibiscus and bougainvillea will all help convince you that "Maui no ka oi"—Maui is the best. Contact: Tad David Fuller, Lihi Kai Cottages, 2121 Iliili Rd., Kihei, Maui, HI 96753. Call 1-800-544-4524 (in Hawaii, 808-879-2335).

Children: Y   Pets: N   Smoking: Y   Handicap Access: N   Payment: C, T

LUANA KAI   *Rates: budget-moderate*
Open: year-round   *Minimum Stay: five nights*

With six miles of sandy beaches and acres of well-manicured lawns, regal palms and fragrant foliage, the Luana Kai is a spacious playground for the child in all of us. A practice session of putting, a friendly game of tennis or a swim in the pool can all be enjoyed on the premises; afterward, relax in the whirlpool or sauna. Or wander down to the beach and stretch out on the golden sands for a pleasant day of sun and surf. Nicely furnished accommodations await you inside, whether you've chosen a one-, two- or three-bedroom condo for your stay. They all have color TVs, washers and dryers and private balconies; most enjoy exquisite views of the ocean. Contact: The Hawaiian Islands Resorts, P.O. Box 212, Honolulu, HI 96810. Call 1-800-367-7042 (in Hawaii, 808-531-7595).

Children: Y   Pets: N   Smoking: Y   Handicap Access: N   Payment: C

MAKENA SURF   *Rates: moderate-deluxe*
Open: year-round   *Minimum Stay: five nights*

Particularly lavish accommodations await you at the Makena Surf. The apartments feature central air-conditioning, either one or two bedrooms, wet bars in the spacious living rooms, large and completely private balconies with marvelous ocean views and a full complement of modern appliances (including washers and dryers). The complex boasts both tennis courts and swimming pools, and the warm, welcoming waters of the ocean are right at your doorstep. Contact: Gloria Gros, AA Oceanfront Condominium Rentals, 2439 S. Kihei Rd., #206A, Kihei, Maui, HI 96753. Call 1-800-628-9333 (in Hawaii, 808-879-7288).

Children: N   Pets: N   Smoking: N   Handicap Access: N   Payment: C, P, T

MANA KAI MAUI CONDO   *Rates: inexpensive-moderate*
Open: year-round   *Minimum Stay: one week*

Keawakapu Beach in southern Maui is the location for this one-bedroom paradise in the sky. The views encompass not only the spectacular beach, but a lush garden overflowing with coconut palms, exotic blooms and tropical fruits. This unit features a lanai, or balcony, that stretches not only across the living room but also the bedroom. There are views of the ocean from every room, and the only sound you'll hear is the symphony of the surf. Original art and large mirrors grace the walls and the modern creature comforts include a TV, a VCR and a stereo in the living room and a dishwasher, microwave, ice crusher, coffee maker and more in the kitchen. If you desire a larger holiday home, this residence can also be rented with another studio apartment. Contact: Marilyn and Ken Erickson, 979 Cart Ct., Incline Village, NV 89451. Call 702-831-6025. Ref. A Unit.

Children: Y   Pets: N   Smoking: Y   Handicap Access: Y   Payment: C, P, T

MAUI VISTA   *Rates: budget-inexpensive*
Open: year-round   *Minimum Stay: five nights*

Just across from the golden beaches you'll find these delightful little one-bedroom apartments. Each is well equipped with a microwave oven and a washer and dryer, and on the grounds of the complex are swimming pools, tennis courts and an activity center to fill your days with fun. If you prefer, walk over to the beach to enjoy the quintessential tropical holiday, basking in the resplendent sunshine and frolicking in the clear water. There are also barbecue grills here where you can prepare your daily catch after some deep-sea fishing. Contact: Gloria Gros, AA Oceanfront Condominium Rentals, 2439 S. Kihei Rd., #206A, Kihei, Maui, HI 96753. Call 1-800-628-9333 (in Hawaii, 808-879-7288).

Children: Y   Pets: N   Smoking: Y   Handicap Access: N   Payment: C, P, T

SUGAR BEACH RESORT   *Rates: budget-expensive*
Open: year-round   *Minimum Stay: four nights*

Named for the glistening white sands beside which it stands, this resort offers all the luxury and convenience you crave. Each one- or two-bedroom suite features elegant furnishings, color TV, a modern kitchen and air-conditioned splendor. Outside you have your pick of watery amusements: the generous swimming pool, a smaller wading pool for the kiddies, a soothing Jacuzzi or the warm elixir of the Pacific itself. Other facilities on the grounds include tennis courts, a putting green, a sauna, shops, restaurants and a barbecue area for grilling up some of those mahi-mahi steaks. Contact: Condominium Rentals Hawaii, 2439 S. Kihei Rd., #205-A, Kihei, Maui, HI 96753. Call 1-800-367-5242 (in Hawaii, 808-879-2778).

Children: Y Pets: N Smoking: Y Handicap Access: N Payment: C, P, T, V, M

Koli

POLIPOLI CABIN   *Rates: budget*
Open: year-round   *Minimum Stay: none*

Polipoli Park is located on the wooded western slope of Haleakala Crater, the spectacular "House of the Sun," whose eerie landscapes and unique wildlife enchant thousands of visitors every year. Well traversed by hiking trails, the forest is a paradise for nature lovers and all those who crave a quiet retreat. The cabin sleeps up to 10 people in three bedrooms; a living and dining area and a well-equipped kitchen round out the accommodations. Contact: Department of Land and Natural Resources, Division of State Parks, 54 S. High St., Wiluku, Maui, HI 96793. Call 808-243-5354.

Children: Y   Pets: N   Smoking: Y   Handicap Access: N   Payment: C, P

Lahaina

NAPILI SHORES STUDIO CONDOMINIUM   *Rates: inexpensive*
Open: year-round   *Minimum Stay: one week*
This oceanfront studio condominium enjoys a marvelous position on quiet Napili Bay, not too far from the town of Kaanapali. Exotic gardens and rolling lawns surround the complex, which boasts two freshwater pools. The pleasantly furnished accommodations feature a large veranda. In the evening, don't miss the exquisite sight of the fiery sun sinking slowly into the sea as the neighboring island of Molokai reflects its golden light. The golf courses, tennis club and sophisticated restaurants of Kapalua are within walking distance, and the interesting old fishing village of Lahaina is a few minutes away by car. Contact: Bob Mickelson, P.O. Box 1476, Sun Valley, ID 83353. Call 208-726-9551.
Children: Y   Pets: N   Smoking: Y   Handicap Access: N   Payment: C, P, T

MOLOKAI

Kaunakakai

MOLOKAI SHORES   *Rates: budget-moderate*
Open: year-round   *Minimum Stay: none*
Virtually untouched by the tourist crowds, lovely Molokai remains a tranquil tropical paradise, an exemplar of the "aloha spirit." Within the quaint town of Kaunakakai, on several lush acres of oceanfront land, the Molokai Shores offers pleasant accommodations for your Hawaiian holiday. The furnishings of the one- and two-bedroom condos are pleasant and inviting; the views of the garden and the ocean are both exciting. Recreational facilities at the complex include a swimming pool, a velvety putting green and a picnic area complete with barbecues in addition to the generous swimming pool. And there's always the beach, the beginning and end of any tropical vacation. Contact: The Hawaiian Islands Resorts, P.O. Box 212, Honolulu, HI 96810. Call 1-800-367-7042 (in Hawaii, 808-531-7595).
Children: Y   Pets: N   Smoking: Y   Handicap Access: N   Payment: C

OAHU

Haleiwa

HALE KIMO AT SUNSET BEACH   *Rates: moderate*
Open: year-round   *Minimum Stay: one week*
Sunset Beach near Waimea Bay proffers all the swimming, surfing, snorkeling, sunning and fishing your frost-bitten northern heart could desire. Each of the two houses at Hale Kimo has three comfy bedrooms, a well-equipped kitchen and a stylishly furnished living and dining area. Perhaps the most impressive features of these houses are the marvelous wraparound porches, covered open-air living areas that are almost as large as the interior of the house itself; read, relax, sip a glass of wine or enjoy your dinner out here. Fam-

ilies will appreciate the large yard for afternoon frolics, and everyone will relish the delightful waters only a few steps away. Contact: Carolyn Wilkinson, 745 Kanaha St., Kaila, HI 96734. Call 808-261-5666.

Children: Y   Pets: N   Smoking: Y   Handicap Access: N   Payment: P, T

Honolulu

COLONY SURF MOTEL *Rates: inexpensive-deluxe*
Open: year-round *Minimum Stay: none*
This classically luxurious hotel occupies a prime location on fabulous Waikiki Beach: It's separated from the lively bustle by Kapiolani Park and an avenue of ironwood pines just a few steps from the sand. From the enormous picture windows, each one-bedroom suite enjoys unparalleled views of either the vast open seas or stately Diamond Head. The Colony Surf is also home of Michel's, an award-winning restaurant that impressively blends European opulence with the warm spirit and natural grandeur of Hawaii—"Lifestyles of the Rich and Famous" has named it the World's Most Romantic Restaurant. Contact: Colony Surf Hotel, 2895 Kalakaua Ave., Honolulu, HI 96815. Call 1-800-252-7873 (in Hawaii, 808-923-5751).

Children: Y Pets: N Smoking: Y Handicap Access: Y Payment: C, T, A, V, M

HAWAIIANA HOTEL *Rates: budget-expensive*
Open: year-round *Minimum Stay: none*
This welcoming hotel prides itself on the warmth, hospitality and courteousness of its staff. Little touches such as a sweet pineapple presented on your arrival, fresh juice daily by the pool and a newspaper at your door each morning will make you feel welcome and pampered. An oasis of calm in the bustle of the city, the Hawaiiana features fully air-conditioned rooms with complete kitchens and color TVs. Coconut leaf umbrellas provide shade near the tempting pool, and festive Hawaiian entertainment is provided several times a week. Contact: Hawaiiana Hotel, 260 Beach Walk, Honolulu, HI 96815. Call 1-800-367-5122 (in Hawaii, 808-923-3811).

Children: Y   Pets: N   Smoking: Y   Handicap Access: N   Payment: All

IMPERIAL HAWAII RESORT *Rates: inexpensive-moderate*
Open: year-round *Minimum Stay: none*
On world-famous Waikiki Beach, the Hala Suite in the Imperial Hawaii Resort puts luxurious comfort within your grasp. The master bedroom of this two-bedroom suite has its own dressing room, full bathroom and delightful balcony—a splendid way to greet the new day. There is another balcony off the spacious living room, which is fully carpeted. The open kitchen and dining area is defined by its distinctive quarry tiles. The beach awaits you below, or try some sky-high swimming at the pool and sauna on the 27th floor. Babysitting service is available for that special night on the town, and daily

maid service is included. Contact: Imperial Hawaii Resort, 205 Lewers St., Honolulu, HI 96815. Call 1-800-367-8047, ext. 225 (in Hawaii, 808-923-1827).

Children: Y Pets: N Smoking: Y Handicap Access: N Payment: C, T, A, V, M

WAIKIKI RESORT HOTEL   *Rates: inexpensive-deluxe*
Open: year-round   *Minimum Stay: none*

In the heart of town, just a few steps away from the most famous beach in the world, is this large, glittering resort with all the convenience and comfort you crave. Each air-conditioned suite comes with a color TV, a refrigerator and a private safe; some have complete kitchenettes. The view from your very own balcony will be either of the azure ocean or of the inspiring mountains. The complex has its own restaurant, which features delectable Korean delicacies and a convivial bar. The Honolulu Zoo, the Aquarium and Kapiolani Park are among the neighborhood's attractions. Contact: Ramon Kojima, Waikiki Resort Hotel, 2460 Koa Ave., Honolulu, HI 96822. Call 1-800-367-5116 (in Hawaii, 808-922-4911).

Children: Y Pets: N Smoking: Y Handicap Access: N Payment: C, T, A, V, M

Kailua

ESTATE APARTMENT   *Rates: budget*
Open: year-round   *Minimum Stay: none*

In a very secluded spot on the windward side of Oahu you'll find this private estate with its bright studio apartment for B & B guests. Your friendly host knows the island well and can help you make the most of your time here. The accommodations are cozy and comfortable (up to four guests can sleep here) and feature kitchenette facilities. Local attractions include Ulu Po Helau, the ruins of an ancient temple, and the smooth, gentle waters of Kailua and Lanikai beaches. The diverse restaurants, interesting museums and exciting nightlife of Honolulu is also well within reach. Contact: Bed & Breakfast Honolulu, 3242 Kaohinani Dr., Honolulu, HI 96817. Call 1-800-288-4666 (in Hawaii, 808-595-7533).

Children: Y Pets: N Smoking: Y Handicap Access: N Payment: C, P, T, V, M

KAULUANA   *Rates: inexpensive-deluxe*
Open: year-round   *Minimum Stay: five nights*

For a taste of the grace and style of old Hawaii, consider these accommodations on a quiet shore in Kailua. The rustic house is just a few feet from the water's edge; it enjoys absolutely stunning views of both the ocean and the mountains. Hawaiian decor is featured throughout, and up to six guests can sleep in the three bedrooms. The smaller cottage can accommodate four guests. It is set back further from the beach and boasts a large "lanai," or veranda, where you can sip a pina colada with friends or watch the brilliant hues of the sunset mellow into a gentle twilight. Contact: Dave or Ruth Lung, Kailuana, P.O. Box 841, Kailua, Oahu, HI 96734. Call 808-247-1967.

Children: Y Pets: N Smoking: Y Handicap Access: N Payment: C, P, T

Laie

HALE KEKELA BEACHFRONT PARADISE *Rates: moderate-deluxe*
Open: year-round *Minimum Stay: three nights*
Far from the concrete jungles of the big resort towns, but with all the
modern amenities you crave for a luxurious holiday, this house and
cottages may be the ideal setting for your Hawaiian vacation. The
splendidly appointed three-bedroom house features a commodious living and dining area with picture windows looking out on the grounds
and ocean. The generous lanai (veranda) is completely furnished, an
ideal spot for entertaining, dining or just relaxing. Each of the comfy
cottages can accommodate up to six. All guests enjoy use of the recreational facilities, which include Ping-Pong, volleyball, basketball
and croquet equipment, as well as children's playthings and beach
supplies. Contact: Verna Calvert, Hale Kekela B, 55-113 Kam Hwy.,
Laie, HI 96762. Call 808-293-9700.
Children: Y Pets: N Smoking: Y Handicap Access: Y Payment: C, P, T, A

VILLA LA MER *Rates: deluxe*
Open: year-round *Minimum Stay: four nights*
This elegant five-bedroom home done in the French Provincial style
is ideal for largish groups or family reunions. The living, dining and
family rooms on the first floor overlook a spectacular panorama of
sea and sand; three of the bedrooms upstairs also enjoy this view.
Two large decks and a sun deck off the second story provide plenty
of space to stretch out and enjoy the scenery. Modern conveniences
include a microwave, two refrigerators, a dishwasher and laundry facilities; an indoor barbecue, VCR and cable TV are among the other
creature comforts. Golf courses, tennis courts, elegant restaurants
and fascinating shops are just a few minutes away, and the warm
waters of the sea are waiting just outside your door. Contact: Richard Prochaska, 55-090 Naupaka St., Laie, Oahu, HI 96762. Call 808-
293-1843.
Children: Y Pets: N Smoking: Y Handicap Access: N Payment: P

WINDWARD BED & BREAKFAST *Rates: budget*
Open: year-round *Minimum Stay: none*
Overlooking stunning Laie Bay on the windward side of the island
is this spacious B & B suite. Luxurious amenities are provided
here, from the Jacuzzi on the private patio to the spectacular
ocean view from the front deck. There's swimming, snorkeling
and body surfing to be had just outside the front door, and avid shoppers only have to walk two blocks. The nearby Polynesian Cultural
Center gives you a taste of authentic Polynesian life and is well
worth a visit. Contact: Bed & Breakfast Honolulu, 3242 Kaohinani
Dr., Honolulu, HI 96817. Call 1-800-288-4666 (in Hawaii, 808-595-
7533).
Children: Y Pets: N Smoking: Y Handicap Access: N Payment: C, P, T, V, M

Waikiki

WAIKIKI LANAIS

Rates: budget-moderate

Open: year-round

Minimum Stay: none

Scarcely a heartbeat away from the center of town, this friendly resort combines considerable facilities with proximity to the varied shops, restaurants and nightspots of world-famous Waikiki. The complex itself boasts a swimming pool, a gym and a rooftop barbecue area. The one- or two-bedroom suites are nicely furnished with island motifs and, of course, they all feature airy "lanais" or balconies. In addition to the social life of Waikiki, attractions in the area include famous Waikiki Beach, Diamond Head, Kapiolani Park and the captivating Honolulu Zoo. Contact: The Hawaiian Islands Resorts, P.O. Box 212, Honolulu, HI 96810. Call 1-800-367-7042 (in Hawaii, 808-531-7595).

Children: Y   Pets: N   Smoking: Y   Handicap Access: N   Payment: C

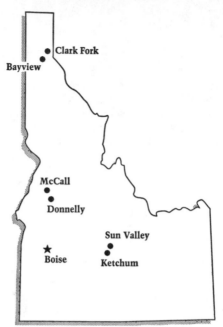

Idaho

BAYVIEW

MACDONALD'S HUDSON BAY RESORT *Rates: budget*
Open: year-round *Minimum Stay: none*

Way up in the northern tip of the state, lying among quiet evergreens by the pristine Lake Pend Oreille, Hudson Bay Resort provides comfortable, modern, fully equipped cabins. This is a land of moose, osprey and the American bald eagle, dotted with lumber mills and deep silver mines, but otherwise entirely unspoiled and an ideal vacation spot for nature lovers. The little town of Bayview, called the "floating village," is half a mile away, but boat moorings are also available right at the complex, offering skiffs and angling equipment for rent. Besides fishing, the lake provides a breathtaking locale for enjoying swimming, sailing, canoeing and waterskiing or simply savoring the sublime scenery. Contact: Gary MacDonald, MacDonald's Hudson Bay Resort, Inc., South Shore Drive, Bayview, ID 83803. Call 1-208-683-2211.

Children: Y Pets: Y Smoking: Y Handicap Access: N Payment: C, P, T, V, M

CLARK FORK

DIAMOND T GUEST RANCH *Rates: budget*
Open: May 1-December 1 *Minimum Stay: two nights*

The Diamond T Guest Ranch is an enticing rustic vacation getaway located in northern Idaho's panhandle. Eight log cabins are provided, each sleeping up to six and offering charming country furnishings and full kitchen facilities. The grounds feature a menagerie of farm animals to pet and activities to join. Guests can bring their own horses or hire a mount here for riding lessons, treks along the miles of forest trails and even campouts. Plenty of other fine recreational opportunities are available close by, including fishing in Small Lake, hiking along the Clark Fork River, boating on Lake Pend Oreille and, in the winter, superb cross-country skiing and snowmobiling. Contact: Myra Lewis, Diamond T Guest Ranch, Box 625 HCR, Clark Fork, ID 83811. Call 1-208-266-1186.

Children: Y   Pets: Y   Smoking: Y   Handicap Access: N   Payment: C, P, T

DONNELLY

LONG VALLEY MOTEL   *Rates: budget*
Open: year-round   *Minimum Stay: none*

Located in the tiny town of Donnelly in the southwestern portion of the state, the Long Valley Motel provides full housekeeping units offering peace and seclusion as well as easy access to a region of lush forests and valleys, translucent lakes and clear running streams. The residence is midway between Cascade and Payette lakes, featuring a full array of water sports activities. On the surging Payette River, visitors can brave a white-water experience they'll never forget. There's some fine skiing in the area during winter, while golf, horseback riding and even hot-air ballooning can be enjoyed in warmer weather. Contact: Kathy or David Fritschle, Long Valley Motel, P.O. Box 97, Donnelly, ID 83615.

Children: Y   Pets: Y   Smoking: Y   Handicap Access: N   Payment: C, P, V

KETCHUM

STONE HILL CONDOMINIUMS   *Rates: inexpensive-moderate*
Open: year-round   *Minimum Stay: four nights*

Overlooking Mt. Baldy and the snowy blue peaks of the Sawtooth Range in the heart of Idaho's central Rockies, Stone Hill Condominiums are nine comfortable two-bedroom townhouses a mile from the center of Ketchum. Each unit contains a fully equipped kitchen and a delightful whirlpool tub. This is a superb vacation residence for those seeking an active Idaho sports holiday, placing guests right in the hub of its most bountiful recreation area, with fishing, hiking, rafting, golf and tennis all only minutes away, as well, of course, as some of the nation's finest skiing. Contact: Stone Hill Condominiums, Valleywood Drive, Ketchum, ID 83340. Call 1-208-726-5149.

Children: Y Pets: N Smoking: Y Handicap Access: N Payment: C, P, T, V, M

McCALL

MILL PARK CONDOS   *Rates: moderate*
Open: year-round   *Minimum Stay: none*

Resting on the shores of Payette Lake in central Idaho, with a splendid view of Brundage Mountain, Mill Park Condos is a quiet little vacation retreat with only eight spacious and fully equipped three-bedroom

apartments, each offering such inviting features as a whirlpool bath, wet bar and fireplace. The complex is just outside of McCall, known as "Ski Town USA," but hardly a one-sport resort area. On the marina, one block away, excellent boating, sailing, fishing and waterskiing are available, while there's also fine rafting, hiking and golf to be found. But winter is peak season, and McCall celebrates it in style with February's annual Winter Carnival, featuring celebrated snow sculptures, and all the while the lift lines remain remarkably short. Contact: Rita Lyon, Mill Park Condominiums Brundage Mountain Co., Box 1062, McCall, ID 83638. Call 1-208-634-4151 or 1-800-888-7544.
Children: Y Pets: Y Smoking: N Handicap Access: N Payment: C, P, T, V, M

SUN VALLEY

BLUFF CONDOMINIUMS   *Rates: budget-inexpensive*
Open: year-round   *Minimum Stay: one week*
This condominium complex containing many self-contained two-bedroom units, each with a complete kitchen and terrific views, is near the chairlifts of Sun Valley. The area is best known for its unparalleled winter sports facilities, but there are pleasures here year-round, as full an assortment of recreational opportunities as any resort area in the country, plus such scenic wonders as the Sawtooth Range Recreational Area and the haunting Craters of the Moon. After sightseeing or a day on the slopes, the links, the tennis courts or the river, enjoy a refreshing swim in the complex's swimming pool or a relaxing soak in the hot tub. Contact: Bluff Condominiums, P.O. Box 186, Sun Valley, ID 83353. Call 1-208-726-0110.
Children: Y Pets: N Smoking: Y Handicap Access: N Payment: C, P, T, V, M

ELKHORN RESORT   *Rates: budget-expensive*
Open: year-round   *Minimum Stay: none*
A variety of fully equipped luxury studio to three-bedroom apartments are available at this world-class Sun Valley resort complex. Dozens of top ski runs pass right by the grounds, which offer swimming pools, spas, a health club, playground, tennis courts and a golf course, with plentiful opportunities for sleigh rides and other beguiling family activities throughout the year. Also nearby are trout streams and scenic bike trails and, for literature buffs, the intriguing Ernest Hemingway memorial, plus other pivotal haunts of the Nobel Prize-winning writer, who spent his last years in this area. Call: Elkhorn Resort, Box 6009, Sun Valley, ID 83354. Call 1-208-622-4511 or 1-800-635-9356.
Children: Y Pets: N Smoking: Y Handicap Access: N Payment: C, P, T, V, M

SAGE TERRACE   *Rates: deluxe*
Open: year-round   *Minimum Stay: one week*
For the ultimate in luxurious and ultracontemporary Sun Valley accommodations, Sage Terrace, a lavish duplex built into a hillside facing Bald Mountain, would be hard to surpass. The 3,000-square-foot residence contains three bedrooms, including a palatial master suite, and offers such glamorous custom features as stained-glass windows,

fine oak cabinetry and trim, a gourmet kitchen with two pantries, 1,500 square feet of decking and a six-foot hot tub. Set back from the main road to provide total privacy, the house commands sweeping mountain views and is ideally situated, three blocks from the Warm Springs ski lift and minutes outside the center of Sun Valley and Ketchum. Contact: Rent A Home International, Inc., 7200 34th Avenue, N.W., Seattle, WA 98117. Call 1-206-545-6824.

Children: Y Pets: N Smoking: N Handicap Access: N Payment: C, P, V, M

SUN VALLEY INN CONDOMINIUMS　　　　　*Rates: inexpensive-deluxe*
Open: year-round　　　　　　　　　　　　*Minimum Stay: none*

Part of the Sun Valley ski complex itself, site of the world's first chairlift, these fully equipped studio to four-bedroom condominiums, all clustered within easy walking distance of the lodge and village, place guests right in the center of one of the world's top resorts. Shuttle buses provide free transportation between the village and Baldy and Dollar mountains at all hours to bring the area's matchless recreational opportunities within easy reach. Condominium guests are welcome to enjoy the cozy lodge and the compound's saunas and two exhilarating outdoor glass-encased swimming pools, both open all year for a particularly refreshing coda to a day on the slopes. Contact: Sun Valley Co., Sun Valley, ID 83353. Call 1-208-622-4111 or 1-800-635-8261.

Children: Y Pets: N Smoking: Y Handicap Access: N Payment: C, P, T, V, M

WARM SPRINGS RESORT　　　　　　　*Rates: inexpensive-moderate*
Open: year-round　　　　　　　　　　　*Minimum Stay: two nights*

A short walk from the Warm Springs chairlift, this premiere resort compound is equipped with an assortment of comfortable, fully equipped holiday accommodations, from budget studios to lavish four-bedroom suites, plus many fine facilities, including a pool, sauna, hot tubs and tennis courts. Besides the extraordinary Alpine and Nordic skiing, winter in the area offers snowmobiling, ice skating, numerous indoor sports and a wild nightlife. And warm weather brings the rodeo and the chance to raft on the thundering "River of No Return," or enjoy horseback riding into the surrounding forest wilderness. Contact: Warm Springs Resort, Box 228, 119 Lloyd Drive, Sun Valley, ID 83353. Call 1-208-726-8274 or 1-800-635-4404.

Children: Y　Pets: N　Smoking: Y　Handicap Access: N　Payment: All

Illinois

CHICAGO

LENOX HOUSE SUITES *Rates: inexpensive-expensive*
Open: year-round *Minimum stay: none*

Lenox House is an elegant high-rise of 330 studio and one-bedroom full-service suites in the heart of downtown Chicago. The setting is ideal for the overnight business traveler, the vacationing family, the relocating executive—and anyone in between. Here you can enjoy the privacy of your own apartment and the optional services of a fine hotel, conveniently located only one block from the shops and restaurants of Michigan Avenue's Magnificent Mile. All units are fully and comfortably furnished, featuring a sofa bed for extra guests, a fully equipped kitchen and weekly maid service. Ask about monthly rates for extended stays. Contact: Lenox House Suites, 616 North Rush at East Ontario, Chicago, IL 60611. Call 312-337-1000 or 1-800-44-LENOX.

Children: **Y**   Pets: **N**   Smoking: **Y**   Handicap Access: **N**   Payment: **All**

GALENA

EAGLE RIDGE INN AND RESORT *Rates: budget-deluxe*
Open: year-round *Minimum stay: none*

A thick border of trees, grassy meadows and luxuriously landscaped grounds welcome you as you enter the main gates of the Eagle Ridge Inn and Resort, a year-round family vacation complex of one-, two-

and three-bedroom condominiums and townhouses, all overlooking the resort's own Lake Galena and set on 6,800 miles of hilly terrain. Warm-weather guests will enjoy two golf courses, tennis courts, fishing and water sports; while winter visitors return year after year for cross-country skiing, sleigh rides, an indoor pool and a variety of recreation programs. For the more adventurous, the surrounding area offers a treasure-trove of unusual sights, including nearby Historic Galena, the Shenandoah Riding Center and the Galena Wine Cellars. Contact: Eagle Ridge Inn and Resort, Box 777, Galena, IL 61036. Call 1-800-323-8421 or 1-800-892-22269.

Children: Y Pets: N Smoking: Y Handicap Access: N Payment: A, V, M

WHEELING

OLDE COURT INN *Rates: budget*
Open: year-round *Minimum Stay: none*

Located to the north of Chicago, minutes from O'Hare Airport, the Olde Court Inn is an excellent residence for visitors to the Windy City. Ten one- and two-bedroom units containing kitchen facilities are available, each comfortably furnished and equipped with cable TV. The four-star restaurants, lively nightclubs, thriving theaters, world-renowned museums, celebrated landmarks and historic sites of the bustling metropolis are all within easy reach, as are recreational opportunities on Lake Michigan and golfing facilities in Lake Forest. Contact: Olde Court Inn, 374 North Milwaukee Avenue, Wheeling, IL 6009. Call 1-708-537-2800.

Children: Y Pets: N Smoking: Y Handicap Access: N Payment: All

Indiana

LEESBURG

PATONA BAY RESORT   *Rates: budget*
Open: year-round   *Minimum Stay: one week*
The Patona Bay Resort, located on the west shore of Lake Tippecanoe, one of the Midwest's most beautiful bodies of water, offers 22 fully equipped beach and lakefront cottages, ranging in size from one to three bedrooms. Guests may bring their own boats, with free docking space provided at the resort, while there's also a full array of vessels, along with waterskiing and fishing equipment, available for hire. With such nearby attractions as a thriving Amish community, summer stock theaters and winter ski facilities, as well as challenging golf courses, shopping and dining, there are enough activities to keep a vacationing family busy in any season. Contact: Robert Paton, Paton Realty, R.R. 2, Box 281, Leesburg, IN 46538. Call 1-219-453-3671/70.
Children: Y Pets: N Smoking: Y Handicap Access: N Payment: C, T, V, M

LINCOLN CITY

LINCOLN STATE PARK CABINS   *Rates: budget*
Open: year-round   *Minimum Stay: one week*
Located in historic southwest Indiana, boyhood home of Abraham Lincoln, Lincoln State Park offers ten family housekeeping cabins that make superb holiday residences for the tightest budget, each equipped with kitchen facilities and accommodating up to six. The park fea-

tures a 58-acre lake stocked with game fish and offers boating facilities and a fine swimming beach. A network of hiking trails takes trekkers into unspoiled wilderness areas, through the Abraham Lincoln Boyhood National Memorial, and past other noteworthy landmarks pertaining to the early years of this famous American. Contact: Brad L. Young, Lincoln State Park, Box 216, Lincoln City, IN 47552. Call 1-812-937-4710.

Children: Y   Pets: N   Smoking: Y   Handicap Access: N   Payment: C, P, T

NORTH WEBSTER

DIXIE HAVEN
Rates: budget
Open: May-October
Minimum Stay: none

Set in the graceful, rolling hills of northeastern Indiana along the shore of Lake Webster, Dixie Haven is a choice vacation residence for families, offering a number of units that contain kitchen facilities and accommodate up to five comfortably. A wide assortment of attractions are available on the grounds and nearby to delight all ages. The lake, of course, provides a full range of water sports opportunities, including swimming, fishing, boating, and waterskiing, and within easy reach there are scenic nature trails, picnic areas, golf, tennis, and horseback riding facilities, antique shops, outdoor theaters, and a children's amusement park. Dixie Haven is also the home port of "The Dixie," a stern-wheeler boat that embarks on rollicking voyages twice daily, complete with lively music and southern-fried chicken. Contact: Dixie Haven, R.R. 1, Box 659, North Webster, IN, 46555. Call 1-219-834-2022.

Children: Y   Pets: N   Smoking: Y   Handicap Access: N   Payment: C, P

SYRACUSE

FISH AND FUN RESORT
Rates: budget-inexpensive
Open: year-round
Minimum Stay: one week

Positioned on the shores of northern Indiana's Syracuse Lake, which makes up the state's largest natural body of water, this quiet little holiday complex offers comfortable and modern housekeeping cabins, each equipped with kitchen facilities. The basic units sleep up to four, while the larger ones can accommodate six. All residences are right at the water's edge; swimming is steps away, and boats for fishing or sightseeing excursions, as well as waterskiing, can be rented across the road. There's also a choice of three golf courses nearby, and in the winter, superb facilities for snowmobiling, ice fishing, and both cross-country and downhill skiing. Contact: Fish and Fun Resort, 812 South Front Street, Syracuse, IN 46567. Call 1-219-457-3442.

Children: Y   Pets: N   Smoking: Y   Handicap Access: N   Payment: All

Iowa

DAVENPORT

THE BLACKHAWK HOTEL   *Rates: budget*
Open: year-round   *Minimum Stay: none*

Located in the center of Davenport, the Blackhawk Hotel offers 37 suites with full kitchen facilities for vacationing families or business people. Here is an ideal base from which to trace the city's rich heritage: through the Village of East Davenport—Iowa's largest historic district still very much as it was in the late 19th century; Scott County Park—a 1,270-acre wilderness reserve containing Pioneer Village; and Rock Island—where the Mississippi River Visitor's Center sponsors exhibits depicting 20th-century efforts to improve the Mississippi. The floral beds and rose gardens of Vande Veer Park and the Conservatory are among the highlights of summer; and visitors shouldn't miss the chance for a riverboat cruise along the Mississippi. Contact: The Blackhawk Hotel, 200 East 3rd Street, Davenport, IA 52801. Call 319-323-2711.

Children: Y   Pets: N   Smoking: Y   Handicap Access: N   Payment: A, M, O

DUNDEE

BACKBONE STATE PARK   *Rates: budget*
Open: May-October   *Minimum Stay: none*

Backbone State Park—Iowa's first state park and one of its most beautiful—offers vacationing families a gloriously inexpensive way to enjoy the rugged beauty of America's Midwest. Eighteen cabins each accommodate four people comfortably and feature complete kitchen facilities, dishes and utensils. (Renters must provide their own bedding, pillows and linen.) The buildings—many of which were constructed by the Civilian Conservation Corps in the 1930s—lend a sense of history and charm to the area's natural beauty. Hikers will enjoy the extensive system of hiking trails; and those who favor swimming, boating (electric motors only) or trout fishing will delight in the clear, cold waters of Backbone Lake. Reservations are accepted as of the first business day in January. Contact: Robert Schaut, Backbone State Park, Dundee, IA 52038. Call 319-924-2527.

Children: Y   Pets: Y   Smoking: Y   Handicap Access: N   Payment: C, P, T

GUTHRIE CENTER

SPRINGBROOK STATE PARK *Rates: budget*
Open: Memorial Day-Labor Day *Minimum Stay: two nights*

Iowa's Springbrook State Park—acquired by the state in 1926 and developed by the Civilian Conservation Corps in the 1930s—features six family cabins each with comfortable accommodations for four, featuring refrigerators, gas ranges, water, electricity and flush toilets. (Guests provide their own linen, pillows and towels.) Here is an ideal and economical base from which to enjoy the natural beauty of the area's rolling hills—alive with deer, red and gray fox, coyote, raccoon, beaver, muskrat and wild turkey—or the numerous trails that wind through 796 acres of prairie and woodland near ponds, rivers and a beautiful 17-acre man-made lake. Summer visitors will enjoy the sandy beach; and winter visitors will delight in optimal snowmobiling conditions. Contact: Springbrook State Park, Rural Route 1, Box 49, Guthrie Center, IA 50115. Call 515-747-3591.

Children: Y   Pets: Y   Smoking: Y   Handicap Access: N   Payment: C, P

KEOSAUQUA

LACEY-KEOSAUQUA STATE PARK *Rates: budget*
Open: May-October *Minimum Stay: one week*

Lacey-Keosauqua State Park, one of the largest and most picturesque of Iowa's recreation areas, offers 1,653 acres of hills, bluffs and valleys along the Des Moines River in Van Buren County. Six family cabins feature modern kitchens equipped with dishes and cooking utensils; renters must provide their own linen, pillows and towels. Three open picnic shelters are available for scenic outdoor dining; and the lake, which spans 30 acres, offers ideal conditions for swimming, boating (electric motors only) and fishing. The hiking trails give visitors a chance to observe area wildlife up close. For those who care to venture slightly further, several historic towns and villages, including Keosauqua, Bentonsport and Bonaparte, are nearby. Contact: Wayne Buzzard, Lacey-Keosauqua State Park, P.O. Box 398, Keosauqua, IA 52565. Call 319-293-3502.

Children: Y   Pets: Y   Smoking: Y   Handicap Access: N   Payment: C, P, T

OKOBOJI

BROOKS BEACH RESORT Rates: budget
Open: April 1-September 13 Minimum Stay: none

The Brooks Beach Resort offers a selection of modest one- to four-bedroom fully equipped cottages in Okoboji, one of Iowa's most popular resort areas, where Lake Okoboji is ringed by Gull Point and Pikes Point State Parks. The grounds—alongside the beach and a boat dock—are well maintained and offer something for every member of the family, including a heated pool, a tennis court, a fishing pier and a playground. Visitors will also enjoy nearby sights of unique interest, including the Gardner Cabin Historic Site in Arnolds Park—a restored log cabin furnished with period pieces, and the Higgins Museum—featuring a memorable selection of notes and artifacts of the national banks. Contact: Brooks Beach Resort, East Okoboji Lake, Route 71, Okoboji, IA 51355. Call 712-332-2955.

Children: Y Pets: N Smoking: Y Handicap Access: N Payment: A, V, M

FILLENWARTH NEW BEACH COTTAGES Rates: budget-inexpensive
Open: April 1-October 1 Minimum Stay: one week

This lakeside resort on the western border of Lake Okoboji is comprised of 59 modest cottages ranging from efficiencies to four-bedroom units, all with air conditioning, cable TV, telephones, and full-service kitchens. An ideal and moderately priced way to explore one of Iowa's most popular beach resort areas, the Fillenwarth grounds also feature two heated pools, rental boats and canoes, a boat dock, fishing, water-skiing, sailboat rides, a putting green, one tennis court and a playground. During peak season, visitors will delight in jungle cruises and speedboat rides, and supervised recreational programs offer diversion for all members of the family. Contact: Fillenwarth New Beach Cottages, West Lake Okoboji, Route 71, Arnolds Park, IA 51331. Call 712-332-5646.

Children: Y Pets: Y Smoking: Y Handicap Access: N Payment: C, P, T

MANHATTAN BEACH RESORT Rates: budget-inexpensive
Open: April 1-October 31 Minimum Stay: one week

Located on West Lake Okoboji, the Manhattan Beach Resort features efficiency apartments, two-bedroom cottages (for up to six) and four-bedroom cottages (for up to ten), all with full kitchens, air conditioning and cable TV. Manhattan Beach offers all the joys of a perfect beach vacation, as well as a vast array of traditional summer activities including a putting green, two tennis courts and a playground. (One restaurant is open daily.) Visitors to this beautiful and popular resort will also want to visit nearby Gull Point and Pikes Point State Parks and the area's numerous local attractions of historic interest. Contact: Manhattan Beach Resort, P.O. Box OR, Spirit Lake, IA 51360. Call 712-337-3223.

Children: Y Pets: N Smoking: Y Handicap Access: N Payment: A, V, M

VILLAGE WEST RESORT   *Rates: budget*
Open: year-round   *Minimum Stay: one week*
Located on West Lake Okoboji, this year-round lakeside resort and
conference center offers full-service two- and three-bedroom units for
vacationing families and business people. The beautiful beach that
makes this one of Iowa's most popular resort locations is only steps
from your doorway, where a full array of water sports including canoeing, boating, yacht excursions and fishing await. Miniature golf
and recreational programs for children and adults keep the whole family busy. Winter visitors will enjoy two indoor pools, a whirlpool, ice
skating and snowmobile and ski trails. Contact: Village West Resort
and Conference Center, P.O. Box OR, Spirit Lake, IA 51360. Call 712-
337-3223.
Children: Y   Pets: N   Smoking: Y   Handicap Access: N   Payment: A, V, M

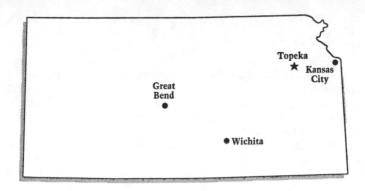

Kansas

WICHITA

THE INN AT TALLGRASS
Rates: budget-inexpensive
Open: year-round
Minimum Stay: none

This attractive inn provides handsomely furnished one-bedroom units, most featuring a living room with a fireplace, kitchen facilities and a private balcony, in an elegant country club-style setting. The grounds offer a heated swimming pool with a Jacuzzi, a lighted tennis court, and a well-equipped exercise room. Centrally located, the inn is within easy reach of Wichita's business district as well as the city's parks, rich recreational opportunities and its abundant arts and cultural offerings. Contact: The Inn at Tallgrass, 2280 North Tara, Wichita, KS 67226. Call 1-316-684-3466.

Children: Y   Pets: N   Smoking: Y   Handicap Access: N   Payment: All

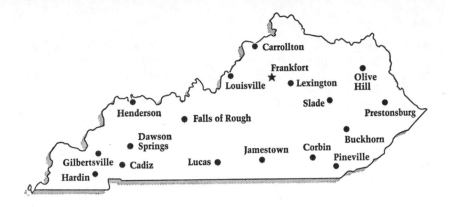

Kentucky

Buckhorn

BUCKHORN LAKE STATE RESORT PARK
Open: March 1-December 20

Rates: budget-inexpensive
Minimum Stay: none

Hidden among the hills of eastern Kentucky, Buckhorn Lake sits in the Daniel Boone National Forest. Hike down to Moonshiner Hollow and pass through some of the most beautiful countryside in the state, where an immense, clear mountain lake brims with crappie, bluegill, channel catfish and largemouth and smallmouth bass. One- and two-bedroom cottages feature fully furnished kitchens, fresh linens daily, color TV and air conditioning. A must is a trip to Buckhorn Church, an impressive log structure. Contact: Buckhorn Lake State Resort Park, HC 36, Box 1000, Buckhorn, KY 41721-9602. Call 1-800-325-0058.

Children: Y   Pets: N   Smoking: Y   Handicap Access: Y   Payment: All

Cadiz

LAKE BARKLEY STATE RESORT PARK
Open: year-round

Rates: inexpensive-moderate
Minimum Stay: none

Designed by Edward Durrell Stone and built of western cedar and Douglas fir, Barkley Lodge offers panoramic views of the lake from every room, through three and a half acres of glass walls. Studio, one-, two- and three-bedroom executive cottages feature kitchens complete with everything you'll need to cook up a sumptuous dinner, plus telephone, color TV and air conditioning. One of the highlights at Lake

Barkley is a supervised trapshooting range where you can sharpen your eye and test your aim. You'll also find an executive fitness center with Nautilus equipment, racquetball courts, tanning beds and a sauna and whirlpool. Contact: Lake Barkley State Resort Park, Box 790, Cadiz, KY 42211-0790. Call 1-800-325-1708.

Children: Y Pets: N Smoking: Y Handicap Access: Y Payment: C, T, A, V, M, O

VACATION CLUB INTERNATIONAL *Rates: budget-inexpensive*
Open: year-round *Minimum Stay: one week*

You'll find these villas close to Lake Barkley State Resort Park, with a supervised trapshooting range near one of the world's largest artificial lakes. One- and two-bedroom villas boast screened porches, paddle fans, fully equipped kitchens and a swimming pool. At Lake Barkley, water-ski or rent a fishing boat and angle for some crappie, bluegill or largemouth bass. An 18-hole golf course, nine miles of hiking trails, and tennis and horseback riding will satisfy the most diverse sports enthusiasts. Contact: Vacation Club International, Route 2, Cadiz, KY 42211. Call 502-924-5814.

Children: Y Pets: Y Smoking: Y Handicap Access: N Payment: C, P, T

CARROLLTON

GENERAL BUTLER STATE RESORT PARK *Rates: budget-moderate*
Open: year-round *Minimum Stay: none*

Home of the state park system's only ski area, General Butler is truly a resort park. A ski school, rental shops, 20 acres of trails and a high-tech artificial snow-making system create the perfect vacation for expert and novice skiers. Summers bring golf and tennis or a ride on the park's miniature train for children. Cottages are available for two to six guests, with one, two and three bedrooms, and all boast a private patio or balcony and fully furnished kitchens. There are also many interesting trails for hiking and nature walks. Contact: General Butler State Resort Park, Box 325, Carrollton, KY 41008-0325. Call 1-800-325-0078.

Children: Y Pets: N Smoking: Y Handicap Access: Y Payment: All

CORBIN

CUMBERLAND FALLS STATE RESORT PARK *Rates: budget*
Open: year-round *Minimum Stay: none*

For a truly unique sight come see the Cumberland Falls during a full moon, when their mist helps create the only "moonbow" visible in the Western Hemisphere. Even without this spectacular effect, the falls are an awesome sight and provide a wonderful sense of tranquillity on the grounds of Daniel Boone National Forest. White-water rafting is a natural choice, as is catfish and bass fishing and horseback riding. The Big South Fork Scenic Railway in the nearby town of Stearns provides trips back in time and around the area. Twenty-seven cottages for two to six people are available year-round. Most feature fireplaces and all offer cooking utensils, tableware and fresh linens daily. Contact: Cumberland Falls State Resort Park, Route 6, Box 4111, Corbin, KY 40701-8814. Call 1-800-325-0063.

Children: Y   Pets: N   Smoking: Y   Handicap Access: Y   Payment: All

DAWSON SPRINGS

PENNYRILE FOREST STATE RESORT PARK   *Rates: budget-inexpensive*
Open: March to mid-December   *Minimum Stay: none*

This resort gives you a choice of two lakes to play on—Pennyrile Lake and Lake Beshar. Both are surrounded by the 15,000 pristine acres of Pennyrile State Forest. Thirteen rustic cottages are nestled in the woods, each offering equipped kitchens, telephones, color TV, air conditioning and fresh linen daily. Private docks at the cottages make it easy to launch a morning of fine fishing. Tennis courts, a swimming pool and a nine-hole golf course offer more rigorous sporting fare. Enjoy scenic dining at the main lodge's dining room overlooking Pennyrile Lake. Contact: Pennyrile Forest State Resort Park, 20781 Pennyrile Lodge Road, Dawson Springs, KY 42408-9212. Call 1-800-325-1711.

Children: Y Pets: N Smoking: Y Handicap Access: Y Payment: C, T, A, V, M, O

FALLS OF ROUGH

ROUGH RIVER DAM STATE RESORT PARK   *Rates: budget-moderate*
Open: year-round   *Minimum Stay: none*

Set in the rugged hillside of western Kentucky, Rough River Dam overlooks a nearly 5,000-acre blue-green lake. Rustic cottages hidden among the trees feature one, two or three bedrooms, all with furnished kitchens and air conditioning. You'll find some of the best fishing in the state at Rough River Lake, and plenty of opportunities for water- and jetskiing. In July you can hear well-known musicians in the Official Kentucky State Championship Old Time Fiddlers Contest, an event not to be missed. For airplane enthusiasts, Sport Aviation Weekend is held in September and features antique and modern examples. Contact: Rough River Dam State Resort Park, Route 1, Box 1, Falls of Rough, KY 40119-9701. Call 1-800-325-1713.

Children: Y   Pets: N   Smoking: Y   Handicap Access: Y   Payment: All

GILBERTSVILLE

KEN-BAR INN RESORT AND CLUB   *Rates: budget-inexpensive*
Open: year-round   *Minimum Stay: one week*

In the lakes region of southwestern Kentucky you'll find this resort filled with indoor and outdoor sporting facilities near one of the world's largest artificial lakes. One-bedroom cottages put you near volleyball, shuffleboard, horseshoe and basketball facilities. You can also take a hike on a nature trail, picnic and swim. Children feel safe in their own swimming pool, fishing pond and playground. Square and ballroom dancing plus country entertainment round out your nights. Contact: Ken-Bar Inn Resort and Club, Highway 641, P.O. Box 66, Gilbertsville, KY 42044. Call 502-362-8652.

Children: Y   Pets: Y   Smoking: Y   Handicap Access: N   Payment: C, P, T

KENTUCKY DAM VILLAGE STATE RESORT PARK   *Rates: budget-moderate*
Open: year-round   *Minimum Stay: none*

Kentucky Dam Village's location in the Western Waterlands makes it a perennial favorite of sports enthusiasts. The park offers the largest marina in the state's park system, the better to get you to Lake Kentucky's plentiful bass, bluegill, catfish and rockfish. Explore the lake's beauty and boat along the 40-mile Land Between the Lakes to Lake Barkley. Accommodations are as varied as the park itself. You can stay in the main lodge, enjoy a golfing vacation at Village Green Inn, or choose from studio and one-, two- and three-bedroom cottages nestled among the trees. Each features a furnished kitchen, telephone, color TV and air conditioning and heat for year-round comfort. Contact: Kentucky Dam Village State Resort Park, P.O. Box 69, Gilbertsville, KY 42044-0069. Call 1-800-325-0146.

Children: Y Pets: N Smoking: N Handicap Access: Y Payment: C, P, T, A, V, M

HARDIN

KENLAKE STATE RESORT PARK   *Rates: budget-inexpensive*
Open: year-round   *Minimum Stay: none*

Enjoy the gentility of old Kentucky in a setting of floral splendor. Dine in elegance overlooking the lake, then set out for days of adventure. The Land Between the Lakes, with its 170,000 acres of natural habitat, satisfies those yearning to see wilderness in its pristine state, while a variety of water sports and the resort's own climate-controlled tennis courts help you play in modern comfort. The cottages provide room for two to six people in one to three bedrooms and each features a living room, kitchen, telephone, color TV, air conditioning and heat; some have dining areas. Contact: Kenlake State Resort Park, Route 1, Box 522, Hardin, KY 42048-9737. Call 1-800-325-0143.

Children: Y Pets: N Smoking: Y Handicap Access: Y Payment: C, T, A, V, M, O

HENDERSON

JOHN JAMES AUDUBON STATE PARK   *Rates: budget*
Open: year-round   *Minimum Stay: none*

Audubon Park is a fitting tribute to the famed ornithologist, who painted many of the subjects he encountered on this land just south of the Ohio River. A number of his works, including a portrait of Daniel Boone, are on display at the park's museum. Take some time to observe nature on your own while staying in one of five cottages open year-round. Each features modern amenities such as telephone, color TV, air conditioning and fully equipped kitchens. For those who like more strenuous activities, tennis courts, a golf course, boating, fishing and paddle boats provide plenty of diversion. Contact: John James Audubon State Park, P.O. Box 576, Henderson, KY 42420-0576. Call 502-826-2247.

Children: Y Pets: N Smoking: Y Handicap Access: Y Payment: C, T, A, V, M, O

JAMESTOWN

LAKE CUMBERLAND STATE RESORT PARK　　　　　*Rates: budget-inexpensive*
Open: year-round　　　　　*Minimum Stay: none*

You'll find more than 1,200 miles of shoreline in 50,000 acres of park, where coves, creeks and rocky hollows give guests ample opportunity to boat and fish amid nature's beauty. One- and two-bedroom cottages offer kitchens with tableware, cooking utensils and linen. For a special treat, rent one of the ten secluded Wildwood Cottages and cozy up to a roaring fire as the cool mountain air settles in for the night. Contact: Lake Cumberland State Resort Park, P.O. Box 380, Jamestown, KY 42629-0380. Call 1-800-325-1709.

Children: Y　Pets: N　Smoking: Y　Handicap Access: Y　Payment: All

LUCAS

BARREN RIVER LAKE STATE RESORT PARK　　　　　*Rates: inexpensive*
Open: year-round　　　　　*Minimum Stay: none*

Located in south central Kentucky, Barren River Lake is just a short distance from the famous Mammoth Cave National Park. The cottages at Barren River Lake are set around the gleaming lake, surrounded by gently rolling hills and beautiful trees. Twelve units feature fully furnished kitchens and one, two or three bedrooms for up to six guests, and some have separate dining areas. Opportunities abound for sports, golf and, of course, much fishing. There are many museums and fine period homes in the surrounding area. Contact: Barren River Lake State Resort Park, Route 1, Box 191, Lucas, KY 42156-9709. Call 1-800-325-0057.

Children: Y　Pets: N　Smoking: Y　Handicap Access: Y　Payment: All

OLIVE HILL

CARTER CAVES STATE RESORT PARK　　　　　*Rates: budget*
Open: year-round　　　　　*Minimum Stay: none*

More than 20 ancient caverns await your subterranean exploration below the northeastern Kentucky hills. Nature lovers come year-round and are well provided for in the resort's 15 cottages. Choose from an efficiency, one- or two-bedroom unit featuring a color TV, telephone, heat and air conditioning for year-round comfort. Ancient rock formations, lakes, and bats occupy the caverns, while Tygarts Creek invites you to take a guided canoe trip through land unspoiled for thousands of years. Of course, more conventional recreational options abound, such as fishing, golfing on a nine-hole course, horseback riding and tennis. Special events take place in the park's amphitheater, which seats 350 people. Contact: Carter Caves State Resort Park, Route 5, Box 1120, Olive Hill, KY 41164-9032. Call 1-800-325-0059.

Children: Y　Pets: N　Smoking: Y　Handicap Access: Y　Payment: All

PINEVILLE

PINE MOUNTAIN STATE RESORT PARK   *Rates: budget-inexpensive*
Open: year-round   *Minimum Stay: none*

Kentucky's Blue Ridge State Forest spreads out below Pine Mountain, which became the state's first park in 1924 and is home to the Mountain Laurel Festival held annually on the last weekend in May, when the gracious laurels are in full bloom. Nestled in the trees along the mountaintop you'll find one-bedroom log cabins and two-bedroom deluxe cottages, featuring fully furnished kitchens, a living room, air conditioning, telephone and color TV. A nine-hole golf course at the mountain's base allows for good views along with a good game. A nature center, picnic shelters and nine miles of hiking trails allow you to commune with nature. Contact: Pine Mountain State Resort Park, 1050 State Park Road, Pineville, KY 40977-0610. Call 1-800-325-1712.

Children: Y   Pets: N   Smoking: Y   Handicap Access: Y   Payment: All

PRESTONSBURG

JENNY WILEY STATE RESORT PARK   *Rates: budget-inexpensive*
Open: year-round   *Minimum Stay: none*

Set deep in the heart of the Appalachians alongside sparkling clear Dewey Lake, this resort in eastern Kentucky offers wilderness scenery with modern amenities. An outdoor amphitheater presents Broadway musicals from mid-June to mid-August. To get closer to nature, try the hiking trails. You can also rent fishing boats and pontoons on the lake, where you'll find largemouth, smallmouth and rock bass, bluegill, catfish, crappie and muskie. Cottages are available year-round and sleep two to six people. They feature fully equipped kitchens, air conditioning and color TV. Contact: Jenny Wiley State Resort Park, HC 66, Box 200, Prestonsburg, KY 41653-9799. Call 1-800-325-0142.

Children: Y   Pets: N   Smoking: Y   Handicap Access: Y   Payment: All

SLADE

NATURAL BRIDGE STATE RESORT PARK   *Rates: budget*
Open: year-round   *Minimum Stay: none*

Natural Bridge, an ancient, weathered sandstone arch, is the main attraction here. You can hike to the top or take a ski lift to enjoy a once-in-a-lifetime view. But there's plenty more to do at the resort, which is nestled in the wonderland of Daniel Boone National Forest near the Red River Gorge Geological Area. Choose from an efficiency or a one-bedroom cottage, open year-round and featuring telephone, color TV, heating, air conditioning, bath and maid service. The fishing is great, with a variety of bass, bream, catfish, crappie and trout to tackle. After sightseeing, get in a set of tennis or visit the park's gift shop. Contact: Natural Bridge State Resort Park, General Delivery, Slade, KY 40376-9999. Call 1-800-325-1710.

Children: Y   Pets: N   Smoking: Y   Handicap Access: Y   Payment: All

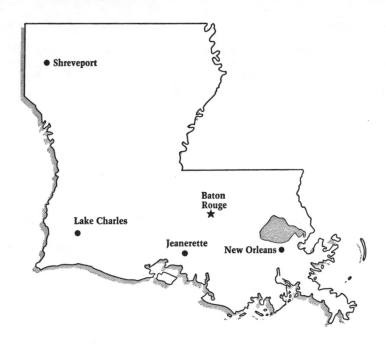

Shreveport

Baton
Rouge
★

Lake Charles

Jeanerette

New Orleans ●

Louisiana

BATON ROUGE

THE RESIDENCE INN   *Rates: inexpensive*
Open: year-round   *Minimum Stay: none*

The Residence Inn, which is centrally located in Baton Rouge and well known for its cozy and comfortable accommodations, is an ideal base from which to experience the area's famous southern hospitality, delicious food and local music. Spacious and sunny suites—most with wood-burning fireplaces—feature fully equipped, modern kitchens; complimentary breakfasts and hors d'oeuvres are featured daily. Guests traveling on business as well as vacationing families will enjoy the "sport court," swimming pool, and new spa facilities, and a restaurant on the premises serves from early until late. Contact: Beth Roccaforte, The Residence Inn by Marriott, 5522 Corporate Blvd., Baton Rouge, LA 70808. Call 504-927-5630 or 1-800-331-3131.

Children: Y   Pets: N   Smoking: Y   Handicap Access: N   Payment: All

NEW ORLEANS

B AND B ON BAYOU TECHE   *Rates: budget*
Open: year-round   *Minimum Stay: none*

B and B is situated amid the tropical lushness of rural Louisiana off Bayou Teche, and it comprises a small cluster of guest cottages featuring comfortable, indigenous wood furniture, spacious living rooms and fully outfitted modern kitchens. Well suited to the vacationing family, here is an ideal base from which to tour the traditional sights of New Orleans, or take a canoe trip down the bayou for a firsthand look at the exotic flora and fauna, including alligators. On nights when you prefer not to catch your own dinner, take a short drive to Lafayette to sample New Orleans' inimitable Cajun cooking and dance to local music. Contact: Barbara and Warren Patout, B and B on Bayou Teche, 2148 1/2 West Main, Jeanerette, LA 70544. Call 318-276-5061.

Children: Y Pets: N Smoking: Y Handicap Access: N Payment: C, P, T

HOTEL DE LA MONNAIE   *Rates: inexpensive*
Open: year-round   *Minimum Stay: one week*

Decorated in the style of Louis IV (the state's namesake and early inspiration), the Hotel de la Monnaie is furnished with carefully chosen antiques typical of classical New Orleans. Here the air-conditioned units—each with a fully equipped modern kitchen—range from studio to one- and two-bedroom apartments, accommodating a minimum of two, four and six guests. The needs of vacationing families are paramount, and a staff of babysitters stands by at virtually all hours. Guests will enjoy the lush scents of the rich foliage in the hotel courtyard, where a leisurely stroll offers an ideal way to cope with the heat of a summer afternoon. Later, take a dip in the pool or relax in the sauna. And don't miss the memorable restaurants and jazz clubs of nearby Bourbon Street. Contact: Hotel de la Monnaie, 405 Esplanade, New Orleans, LA 70116. Call 504-942-3700 or 1-800-945-3204.

Children: Y Pets: N Smoking: Y Handicap Access: N Payment: C, P, T

QUARTER HOUSE   *Rates: inexpensive-moderate*
Open: year-round   *Minimum Stay: one week*

Quarterhouse, the recently restored Victorian "Condotel" located in the Vieux Carre, has been welcoming visitors since it first opened its doors in 1863. Here, the elegant accommodations combine the beauty of a bygone era (natural brick walls, wood moldings and traditional antique furniture) with the convenience of modern amenities, including Jacuzzis and well-equipped kitchens. A tranquil courtyard surrounds a pool and a fountain where you can relax before and after exploring the sights of New Orleans—including a wide choice of live music performances and the memorable restaurants of the Old Quarter. Ask about the Saturday wine and cheese parties and complimentary breakfasts. Contact: The Quarter House, 126 Rue Chartres, New Orleans, LA 70130. Call 504-523-5906.

Children: Y Pets: N Smoking: Y Handicap Access: N Payment: C, T, V, M, A

WINDSOR COURT HOTEL   *Rates: moderate-deluxe*
Open: year-round   *Minimum Stay: none*

Rated "one of the top ten hotels in the world" by Conde Nast Traveler magazine, the award-winning Windsor Court Hotel offers guests a chance to experience the full pleasures of life in a palace. Decorated in the manner of an English country house, the suites—each with a fully equipped modern kitchen—are filled with museum-quality works of art dating from past centuries. Heavy French doors separate the spacious living room from the bedroom, where a grand, canopied four-poster bed transforms a night's sleep into a memorable adventure. Swim laps to music piped from an underwater system in an Olympic-sized pool, then relax under the ministrations of the health club's masseur. Contact: Windsor Court Hotel, 300 Gravier Street, New Orleans, LA 70140. Call 504-523-6000 or 1-800-262-2662.

Children: **Y**   Pets: **N**   Smoking: **Y**   Handicap Access: **N**   Payment: All

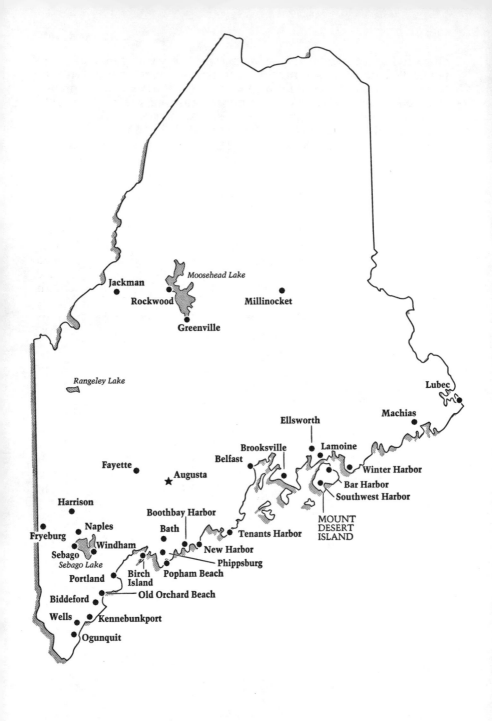

Maine

BAR HARBOR

CASTLEMAINE INN AND APARTMENTS   *Rates: budget-inexpensive*
Open: May 1-October 20   *Minimum Stay: two nights*

Built in 1886 and standing on a quiet side street, Bar Harbor's stately Castlemaine Inn offers two elegantly furnished and fully equipped two-bedroom apartments. The first-floor flat contains a cozy fireplace in the parlor, while the third-floor unit features a private balcony with a captivating view of Frenchman's Bay. Guests are served a delicious buffet breakfast in either the sunny morning room or the spacious veranda. When not out and about in town or Acadia National Park, you can explore the intriguing alcoves and twisting corridors of the historic inn. Contact: Norah O'Brien, Castlemaine Inn and Apartments, 39 Holland Avenue, Bar Harbor, ME 04609. Call 1-207-288-4563.

Children: N Pets: N Smoking: N Handicap Access: N Payment: C, P, T, V, M

SEASIDE COTTAGES   *Rates: budget-inexpensive*
Open: year-round   *Minimum Stay: one week*

Well off the main road to provide true quiet and privacy, the seven "Seaside Cottages" of Clark Cove are situated on the western shore of Mt. Desert Island. The one-, two- and three-bedroom units each include a fully equipped kitchen and pleasant living room with a big picture window giving panoramic water views. When not walking down the streets of Bar Harbor or venturing in Acadia National Park, guests can dig for clams at low tide on the compound's sand and pebble beach, or borrow a rowboat for fishing and exploring the immediate coastline. Contact: Carroll and Gail Leland, Seaside Cottages, RFD 1, Box 2340B, Bar Harbor, ME 04609. Call 1-207-288-3674.

Children: Y   Pets: N   Smoking: Y   Handicap Access: N   Payment: C, P, T

BATH

HALL HOUSE   *Rates: budget*
Open: June-October   *Minimum Stay: one week*

Poised at the edge of an evergreen forest with a large deck overlooking a pond and the surrounding fields and meadows, this spacious house accommodates up to six and offers such homey features as a piano, fieldstone fireplace and knotty pine paneling. A short path through the woods leads to an intriguing tidal cove; several uncrowded sandy beaches are also nearby. Here in the Bath area, harbor cruises, visits to antique shops and the Maine Maritime Museum and trips up the scenic coast keep the days busy, while summer theater and concerts, fine restaurant dining, or simply gazing at the star-flecked night sky fill the evenings. Contact: Nancy and Donald W. Hall, P.O. Box 235, Bath, ME 04530. Call 1-207-443-9446.

Children: **Y**   Pets: **N**   Smoking: **N**   Handicap Access: **N**   Payment: **C, V, M**

BELFAST

WONDERVIEW COTTAGES   *Rates: budget*
Open: mid-April to mid-October   *Minimum Stay: one week*
Midway along the coast of Maine, Wonderview Cottages are located on 10 acres of prime Penobscot Bay shorefront property, where seal colonies congregate just off the rocky beach. There are 20 one- to three-bedroom units, most containing either a fireplace or a wood-burning stove and each with a complete kitchen, screened porch and sweeping views across the water toward the islands. Unforgettable whale-watching voyages are available nearby; the area also offers sailing, deep-sea fishing, golf and a profusion of antique shops and lobster pounds. Contact: Herb and Nancy Foster, Route 1, Box 89, Belfast, ME 04915. Call 1-207-338-1455.

Children: **Y** Pets: **Y** Smoking: **Y** Handicap Access: **N** Payment: **C, T, V, M**

BIDDEFORD

HARBOR PINES   *Rates: budget*
Open: June-September   *Minimum Stay: two weeks*
A one- and two-bedroom unit, both self-contained with full kitchen and bath, are available in this modern oceanside residence. Right outside the door lies a sandy beach, and the grounds feature a private picnic area beneath the pines 60 feet from the shore. Located in the heart of the southern Maine coast in an area very safe for children, Harbor Pines is near an abundance of facilities for water sports like fishing and boating, as well as many other recreational pursuits and such popular southern Maine resort towns as Kennebunkport. Contact: Oril or Paulette Lemay, 169 Hills Beach Road, Biddeford, ME 04005. Call 1-207-284-6039.

Children: **Y**   Pets: **N**   Smoking: **Y**   Handicap Access: **N**   Payment: **C, V, M**

BOOTHBAY HARBOR

GREENLEAF COTTAGE   *Rates: budget*
Open: year-round   *Minimum Stay: two weeks*
Listed in the National Historic Register, this enchanting and very private rustic cabin sits next to the saltwater Sheepscot River in a secluded part of Greenleaf Cove. It's an idyllic location for nature lovers, who can observe seals and several bird species, including osprey and great blue heron, from the cottage sun deck overlooking the water. Clamming and fishing are available along the shore, and hiking or evening stargazing can be enjoyed in the surrounding 200 acres of

private woodlands. Contact: E. Lilly, 3670 Hibiscus Street, Coconut Grove, FL 33133. Call 1-305-445-7479; (summer: RFD 2, Box 573, Wesport Island, ME, 04578, 1-207-882-7614).

Children: Y Pets: N Smoking: Y Handicap Access: N Payment: C, V, M

SPRUCE POINT INN   *Rates: moderate-deluxe*
Open: May 15-October 15   *Minimum Stay: none*

Located on a quiet 100-acre wooded peninsula in Boothbay Harbor, the Spruce Bay Inn offers the new Oceanhouse condominium complex with fully equipped one-, two- and three-bedroom apartments. Each two-floor unit features a spacious living room with fireplace, dining area and modern kitchen, plus a large porch and upper-level deck commanding lovely views of the bay. Condominium guests have full use of the inn's facilities, which include both fresh- and saltwater swimming pools, tennis courts, docks and fishing equipment; they may also join the lively cookouts and lobsterbakes held on the grounds. The area is a top boating region that celebrates Windjammer Days and Friendship Sloop Days in the summer. Contact: Spruce Point Inn, Boothbay Harbor, ME 04538. Call 1-207-633-4152 or 1-800-553-0289.

Children: Y Pets: N Smoking: Y Handicap Access: N Payment: V, M

BROOKSVILLE

UNDERCLIFF COTTAGES   *Rates: budget*
Open: June-September   *Minimum Stay: two weeks*

Looking out onto the water, Undercliff is a quiet settlement of four family cottages tucked away in a particularly scenic corner of eastern Penobscot Bay. Each residence contains a large living room with fireplace, well-equipped kitchen and three cozy bedrooms. Guests can take a refreshing dip from the private beach, borrow—at no extra charge—a small boat at the dock or wander among the 160 acres of private grounds, which offer splendid opportunities for biking, bird-watching and berry picking. Contact: Mrs. Carolyn Robinson, Under-cliff, Brooksville, ME 04617. Call 1-207-326-4577.

Children: Y Pets: N Smoking: Y Handicap Access: N Payment: C, V, M

ELLSWORTH

BAY COTTAGE B   *Rates: budget*
Open: year-round   *Minimum Stay: one week*

This quality cottage in the Ellsworth area looks out onto picturesque Frenchman's Bay, with easy access to the shore. Containing a large living room with fireplace, nicely appointed kitchen and two bedrooms, the house makes a winning vacation residence for a small family visiting eastern Maine. Both town and country pleasures are within easy reach: Take a walking tour through Ellsworth to see outstanding examples of 18th- and 19th-century Georgian and Greek-revival architecture, or explore the unspoiled wilderness region north of the city and the surf-carved rock formations along the coast. Contact: David L. MacDonald, RFD 2, Box 291, Ellsworth, ME 04605. Call 1-207-667-5420.

Children: Y Pets: N Smoking: Y Handicap Access: N Payment: C, V, M

FAYETTE

ECHO LAKE LODGE AND COTTAGES	*Rates: budget-inexpensive*
Open: year-round	*Minimum Stay: none*

Poised on the shore or tucked in the woods fifteen miles west of Augusta, an assortment of quality housekeeping cottages are available on the beautiful grounds of Echo Lake Lodge. Cottage guests are invited to use the lodge's public rooms and to enjoy all the activities available at the complex. The large lawn area overlooking the water offers volleyball, badminton, shuffleboard and a barbecue and picnic area. Dinghies, sailboats and canoes may be rented for outings on the translucent water, and there's a sandy swimming cove, protected from the boating and waterskiing traffic, that's perfectly safe for children. Contact: Ted and Alison Wiederhorn, Echo Lake Lodge and Cottages, Box 475, Readfield, ME 04355. Call 1-207-685-8550.

Children: Y   Pets: Y   Smoking: Y   Handicap Access: N   Payment: C, P, T

GREENVILLE

MEDAWISLA	*Rates: budget-inexpensive*
Open: May-November	*Minimum Stay: two nights*

For those who desire a truly remote Maine holiday, the rustic lakeside housekeeping cabins of Medawisla can't be beat. Decorated in traditional Adirondack style, the one- and two-bedroom residences feature the basic comforts on the shores of Moosehead Lake. Guests can rent boats and canoes to voyage on the utterly unspoiled waters of Second Roach Pond; the grounds and surrounding area abound with wildlife. There's moose, deer and dozens of species of birds—from ducks and grouse to herons and loons, named "medawisla" by the native Americans. The makers of *On Golden Pond* came here to record the bird calls for the film's soundtrack. Contact: Mimi or Russ Whitten, Box 592, Rte. 76, Greenville, ME 04441. Call 1-207-243-2951 (1-207-695-3082 Dec.-Apr.).

Children: Y   Pets: Y   Smoking: Y   Handicap Access: N   Payment: C, P, T

HARRISON

CROW'S NEST AT SILVER BIRCH	*Rates: budget*
Open: mid-June to mid-September	*Minimum Stay: none*

A cozy one-bedroom cottage situated on a gentle hill and enjoying a panoramic view of the pine forests ringing Long Lake, Crow's Nest makes an enchanting hideaway for two. Silver Birch is an idyllic vacation spot for couples, quiet and uncrowded yet featuring an impressive collection of water sports facilities. Guests here can also play miniature golf, shuffleboard, badminton and volleyball. The surrounding area has beautiful hiking trails and opportunities for golf and tennis, horseback riding, antique shopping and dining in quaint little restaurants, as well as apple and berry picking in season. Contact: Curt and Sandi Willmott, 176 Burrman Road, East Haven, CT 06512. Call 1-203-469-6471 (207-583-2282 in summer).

Children: Y Pets: N Smoking: Y Handicap Access: N Payment: C, P, T, V, M

JACKMAN

ATTEAN LAKE LODGE   *Rates: inexpensive-moderate*
Open: May 21-October 5   *Minimum Stay: none*
A private cabin cruiser transports guests from the dock outside Jackman over the waters of Attean Lake to Birch Island, where the enchanting Attean Lake Lodge is located. This is the only establishment in the area, guaranteeing peace and seclusion. Here, 18 two- and three-bedroom cottages, each with a stone fireplace and private porch commanding far-reaching mountain and water views, rest beneath soaring pines, spruce and birches. The lodge itself provides a friendly gathering place, where most meals are served, while Sundays mean delightful sunset cookouts on the beach. Take a picnic lunch along while indulging in the superb recreational opportunities available on the island, including hiking and fishing, sailing and canoeing. Contact: Brad Holden, Box 457, Jackman, ME 04945. Call 1-207-668-3792 (summer), 1-207-668-7726 (winter).
Children: Y   Pets: N   Smoking: Y   Handicap Access: N   Payment: All

KENNEBUNKPORT

MAINE STAY INN AND COTTAGES   *Rates: budget-moderate*
Open: February-December   *Minimum Stay: three nights*
Ten fully equipped housekeeping cottages are part of Kennebunkport's elegant Maine Stay Inn. The units each contain eat-in kitchens, knotty pine paneling and wall-to-wall carpeting. Guests are treated to a buffet breakfast every morning—you can have the meal delivered right to your door—and are invited to attend daily four o'clock tea, where they can learn of the 150-year-old inn's rich heritage. Located in a historic preservation district, the cottages are close to all the village's enticing shops, restaurants and art galleries, as well as the picturesque harbor. Contact: Carol and Lindsay Copeland, Maine Stay Inn and Cottages, P.O. Box 500A, Maine Street, Kennebunkport, ME 04096. Call 1-207-967-2117.
Children: Y   Pets: N   Smoking: Y   Handicap Access: N   Payment: All

LAMOINE

BERRY COVE COTTAGE   *Rates: budget*
Open: year-round   *Minimum Stay: one week*
Graced by a far-reaching view of Mt. Desert Island and Cadillac Mountain, the eastern seaboard's tallest peak, this pleasant two-bedroom cottage in Berry Cove sleeps four comfortably. The rooms receive sun all day due to the house's southwestern exposure; a blaze in the fireplace keeps guests warm and snug during cool nights. The residence is nicely located for enjoying the "Downeast" region's full array of recreational opportunities as well as the scenic wonders of Acadia and the rugged Atlantic coast. Contact: Susan Kazlaskas, RFD 4, Box 335, Ellsworth, ME 04605. Call 1-207-667-7442.
Children: Y   Pets: N   Smoking: Y   Handicap Access: N   Payment: C, V, M

LAMOINE HOUSE — *Rates: budget*
Open: June-September — *Minimum Stay: one week*
This handsome Victorian cottage sits on the water less than 20 miles from Acadia National Park. With a porch offering great views of Eastern Bay and Mt. Desert Island, the house contains two bedrooms, a living room with fireplace, dining room and fully equipped kitchen. Enterprising guests can try foraging for an entire meal, fishing on the bay, digging for clams and mussels on the shore and picking blueberries in the surrounding woods, while others may simply opt for a delicious seafood dinner at a Bar Harbor or Ellsworth restaurant. Contact: Eugenia and Vincent Franco, 55 Summer Street, Bangor, ME, 04401. Call 1-207-945-5541 (evenings).
Children: Y   Pets: N   Smoking: Y   Handicap Access: N   Payment: C, V, M

LUBEC

LUBEC COTTAGE — *Rates: budget*
Open: June 1-October 31 — *Minimum Stay: one week*
Right on the U.S./Canadian border in the country's easternmost town, this two-bedroom bayside cottage enjoys a quiet and secluded setting. Visitors strolling along the beach will likely see seals, cranes and other bird species in their natural environment; migrating whales may even be spotted offshore. The most notable attraction in the area is Campobello Island, only eight miles away in New Brunswick, site of FDR's summer home and a huge natural park named for the former President. Steep seaside cliffs and many other points of interest are also located nearby. Contact: Sheldon and Madeline Elliott, RR 1, Box 2110, Lubec, ME 04652. Call 1-207-733-2494.
Children: Y   Pets: N   Smoking: Y   Handicap Access: N   Payment: C, V, M

MACHIAS

MICMAC FARM — *Rates: budget*
Open: May 1-October 15 — *Minimum Stay: none*
Set among 50 acres of secluded fields and woodlands, the new housekeeping cabins of Micmac Farm offer a panoramic view of the Machias River. Seals, herons and eagles can often be spotted here; blueberries in season prove a less elusive quarry. Many recreational opportunities are available nearby, including fresh-and saltwater beaches, boating and fishing facilities and golf, as well as whale-watching trips and excursions to visit the puffins of Machias Seal Island. The area also holds great historic interest: The intriguing remains of Fort O'Brien, built in 1775, overlook the bay, where the Revolutionary War's first naval engagement took place. Contact: Barbara Dunn, Micmac Farm, Route 92, Machiasport, ME 04655.
Children: Y   Pets: Y   Smoking: Y   Handicap Access: N   Payment: C, P, T

ROQUE BLUFFS COTTAGE   *Rates: budget*
Open: year-round   *Minimum Stay: one week*

This newly built house rests amid lanky trees in Roque Bluffs, from which steps lead down to 300 feet of private Kennebec Bay shoreline. Containing a sitting room, full kitchen, master bedroom and sleeping loft, the residence is near numerous fresh seafood stands and a beautiful seaside state park. Guests have at least two options for enjoying the gorgeous scenery in the area: driving along the serpentine coast or taking a complimentary trip in the owner's 32-foot lobster vessel. Those renting the house over the July 4th holiday can drop by the "World's Fastest Lobster Boat" races at nearby Jonesport...alas, as spectators only. Contact: Martin's Cottages, P.O. Box 51, Machias, ME 04654. Call 1-207-255-4140.

Children: Y   Pets: N   Smoking: Y   Handicap Access: N   Payment: C, V, M

MILLINOCKET

FROST POND CAMPS   *Rates: budget*
Open: seasonal   *Minimum Stay: none*

Set on Moosehead Lake 40 miles from the nearest town, Frost Pond Camps is far, far away from the cares of everyday life. Six rustic cabins are scattered about the lakefront compound, which enjoys a view of Mt. Katahdin, the state's highest peak, while two more are further down the shore. Each unit, sleeping up to eight, comes with a refrigerator, gas range, lights and wood stove has no electricity or running water (an outside tap and coin-operated shower are steps away). Canoes and motor boats are available for rent, there's superb brook trout fishing on the lake and other nearby waters offer salmon. The thick woods are filled with all kinds of wildlife: Guests have even been known to spot a bald eagle! Contact: Rick and Judy Givens, 36 Minuteman Drive, Millinocket, ME 04462 (winter address). Call 1-207-723-6622 (winter), 1-207-695-2821 (summer).

Children: Y   Pets: Y   Smoking: Y   Handicap Access: N   Payment: C, T

NAPLES

GOLDEN SUMMER COTTAGE AT SUNNYSIDE VILLAGE   *Rates: budget*
Open: June 1-October 15   *Minimum Stay: two nights*

This comfortable cottage is part of the Sunnyside Village complex, right by the radiant shores of Long Lake. The house includes two bedrooms, a large living room/dining area and a brand-new kitchen, plus a delightful screened porch. Five minutes away by foot, the friendly village of Naples, hub of the region and a popular summer resort for over a century, offers a profusion of water sports facilities and other attractions. Visit the Historical Society Museum, which features a fascinating exhibit on the local steamboats and the renowned Cumberland and Oxford Canal. Contact: Sunny Torres, Sunnyside Village, P.O. Box 334, Naples, ME 04055. Call 1-207-693-3389.

Children: Y   Pets: N   Smoking: Y   Handicap Access: N   Payment: C, P, T

ONTARIO AT FOX HOLLOW CABINS   *Rates: budget*
Open: year-round   *Minimum Stay: three nights*
Resting on the eastern shore of Brandy Pond in the Fox Hollow vacation retreat, this attractive cabin is ideal for couples but can accommodate up to four. The lakefront holds a sandy beach, float and two docks, where guests may take a sailboat, canoe or 12-foot fishing vessel out on the water free of charge. Containing a kitchen, dining area and living room with Franklin stove, the one-bedroom residence features an enclosed porch and a small charcoal grill. An additional outdoor fireplace and picnic tables are nestled in a gentle pine grove for savory forest cookouts. Contact: Claire Julien, Fox Hollow Cabins, Inc., P.O. Box 646, Naples, ME 04055. Call 1-207-693-6499.
Children: Y   Pets: N   Smoking: Y   Handicap Access: N   Payment: C, P, T

STEAMBOAT LANDING COTTAGES   *Rates: budget-moderate*
Open: year-round   *Minimum Stay: one week*
Run right out to the private white sandy beach or borrow one of the rowboats, canoes, sailboats or windsurfers provided for free at this delightful and tranquil settlement of nine modern housekeeping cottages on the shore of Brandy Pond. The units, of varying sizes to accommodate from four to up to ten persons, receive water from an artesian well and contain fully equipped kitchens with wood stoves. Within walking distance of tennis, golf and miniature golf, the complex is close to all the bounteous recreational and leisure facilities that make this part of the state a premiere vacationland. Contact: Grace and Bob Simms, Steamboat Landing, Inc., Route 114, P.O. Box 384, Naples, ME 04055.
Children: Y   Pets: N   Smoking: Y   Handicap Access: N   Payment: C, V, M

NEW HARBOR

MCFARLAND COTTAGE   *Rates: inexpensive-moderate*
Open: mid-May to November   *Minimum Stay: none*
Standing right on New Harbor, McFarland Cottage is part of The Gosnold Arms, a former farm complex remodeled into a delightful vacation retreat. Containing a bedroom, living room with fireplace and handy kitchenette, the attractive residence features a wraparound wood porch that looks onto the water, a fine vantage point for watching fishing and pleasure boats. Guests may hire a boat themselves at the moorings and explore the scenic coastline by sea, or they can drive or hike along the shore down to historic Pemaquid Point. Contact: Lucy Martin, HC 61, Box 161, New Harbor, ME 04554. Call 1-207-677-3727 (summer), 407-575-9549 (winter).
Children: Y Pets: N Smoking: Y Handicap Access: N Payment: C, P, T, V, M

ON THE ROCKS   *Rates: budget*
Open: year-round   *Minimum Stay: one week*
Located on the scenic ocean shore of Pemaquid Point, this attractive and very well appointed cottage contains a country kitchen with wood stove, living room with fireplace, den, studio and bedroom, plus two

lofts offering additional beds. The proud Pemaquid lighthouse and park, where the crashing Atlantic surf pounds the jagged rocks, are within a few minutes by foot; other top recreational facilities and tourist spots of Maine's mid-coast region are nearby. Or guests can take it easy and just sit amid the quiet woodlands facing the water and watching the lobster boats from the cottage deck. Contact: S. Tiller, DPO 2732, Douglass College, New Brunswick, NJ, 08903. Call 1-201-745-1443.

Children: Y   Pets: N   Smoking: Y   Handicap Access: N   Payment: C, V, M

OGUNQUIT

BEACHMERE INN *Rates: budget-moderate*
Open: March 22-December 9 *Minimum Stay: one week*

Positioned right on the water, the Beachmere Inn contains an assortment of very comfortable efficiency apartments, each with a handy kitchenette and most featuring a balcony giving incredible views of the sparkling ocean. Ogunquit offers vacationers varied delights: Enjoy golf and tennis, sailing and sightseeing boat trips, gorgeous scenery on the famed Marginal Way, authentic Maine atmosphere around the lobster pounds of Perkins Cove and one of the best sandy beaches in the entire state. Contact: Sheila A. Stone, The Beachmere Inn, Box 2340, Ogunquit, ME 03907. Call 1-207-646-2021.

Children: Y   Pets: N   Smoking: Y   Handicap Access: N   Payment: All

THE DUNES *Rates: budget-inexpensive*
Open: mid-May to mid-October *Minimum Stay: one week*

Positioned on the Ogunquit River a half mile north of the village, the Dunes provides several one- and two-bedroom cottages and apartment units, all with full housekeeping facilities. The 10-acre property commands a far-reaching view of the brilliant sand dunes on the opposite bank over to the Atlantic Ocean; guests enjoy quiet and privacy along with proximity to one of southern Maine's most delightful towns. A swimming pool, croquet, swing set and free rowboat are all available on the grounds, which also has easy access to the beach. Contact: Mrs. Cynthia Perkins, The Dunes, Route 1, P.O. Box 917, Ogunquit, ME 03907. Call 1-207-646-2612.

Children: Y   Pets: N   Smoking: Y   Handicap Access: N   Payment: C, T, V, M

OLD ORCHARD BEACH

WHITE LAMB COTTAGES *Rates: budget-moderate*
Open: Memorial Day-Columbus Day *Minimum Stay: three nights*

This quaint compound of ten studio and one-bedroom cottages, each containing a kitchenette and handsomely decorated with antique furnishings, lies amid a private little pine grove. Guests receive continental breakfast and the daily paper on their doorstep each morning and are invited to use the amenities of the nearby Edgewater Inn, including its swimming pool and sun deck. The state's finest outlet shopping, at Freeport and Kittery, is within easy reach, and a variety of recreational activities, including boating, fishing, horseback riding, golf and tennis, are also available in the area. Contact: Katy Gannon or Pierre J. Janelle, White Lamb Cottages, 3 Odessa Ave., Old Orchard Beach, ME 04064. Call 1-207-934-2231.

Children: Y Pets: N Smoking: Y Handicap Access: N Payment: C, T, V, M, A, O

PEABODY POND

WHIP POOR WILL *Rates: budget*
Open: June 1-October 15 *Minimum Stay: one week*

This very private cottage is poised on the shore of Peabody Pond, with few other homes around to spoil the natural beauty of the area. Containing a bedroom, living room and kitchen, the house makes an idyllic hideaway for two, with a small beach area for morning swims, a screened porch for enjoying the mild afternoons and a cozy fireplace for snuggling through the cool evenings. And when the mood calls for a jaunt into town, Fryeburg, Portland and Lewiston aren't far away. Contact: Donna Collins, ERA Jordan Realty, Route 114, Sebago Lake, ME 04075. Call 1-207-787-2442.

Children: Y Pets: Y Smoking: Y Handicap Access: N Payment: C, P, T

PHIPPSBURG

SMALL POINT COTTAGES *Rates: budget-inexpensive*
Open: May 1-October 15 *Minimum Stay: one week*

Three comfortable houses are available at a superb, secluded location on the Atlantic shore a few miles south of Bath. A large, five-bedroom cottage is situated right on the beach of the Morse Mountain nature conservatory, and two three-bedroom residences command sweeping ocean views in three directions. From this home base, enjoy venturing through the Phippsburg peninsula, past historic forts and the site of the 1607 Popham settlement, which predates Plymouth by more than a decade. Trips along the rugged coast and up the Kennebec River offer all the sightseeing pleasures travelers from across the nation expect to see in Maine. Contact: George St. John, 329 Front Street, Bath, ME 04530. Call 1-207-442-8656 (207-389-1039 during summer).

Children: Y Pets: N Smoking: Y Handicap Access: N Payment: C, V, M

POPHAM BEACH

POPHAM GROVE COTTAGES *Rates: budget*
Open: May-September *Minimum Stay: one week*

This small vacation retreat of five cottages lies by the ocean in a tranquil pine grove near Popham Beach. The two-bedroom residences, each with a fully equipped kitchen, have such enticing features as stone fireplaces and screened porches, while the grounds offer a stretch of pristine private beach plus picnic tables and barbecue pits. Stroll along the lustrous sands toward Fort Popham and Fox Island, or take a drive into Bath for a day among this historic maritime town's graceful 19th-century buildings. Contact: Terry and Darlene Markham, P.O. Box 87, Phippsburg, ME 04562. Call 1-207-389-1587.

Children: Y Pets: N Smoking: Y Handicap Access: N Payment: C, V, M

SPINNEY'S *Rates: budget*
Open: May-October *Minimum Stay: none*
Three housekeeping cottages, each containing two bedrooms and a combined living room/kitchen area, are available at Spinney's, a charming inn and restaurant complex on secluded Popham Beach with a sweeping ocean view on three sides. Guests have the golden beaches and crisp blue Atlantic waters nearly to themselves, all only steps from the front door. After a refreshing dip, towel down, brush off the sand and take a short stroll down to land's end to explore historic Fort Popham, built back in 1861. Then pay a visit to the site of the early 17th-century Popham colony, birthplace of the American shipbuilding industry. Contact: John and Fay Hart, HCR 31, Box 395, Phippsburg, ME 04562. Call 1-207-389-2052.
Children: Y Pets: N Smoking: Y Handicap Access: N Payment: C, T, V, M

PORTLAND

BEACH AVENUE HOUSE FLATS *Rates: budget*
Open: year-round *Minimum Stay: two weeks*
This handsome house situated a short hop away from Portland on Casco Bay's Long Island contains several comfortable, self-contained, three-bedroom apartments. There's plenty to do on the scenic island, which is graced with cool sea breezes, beautiful beaches, harbors, coves, country lanes and forest trails. Lawn games are available on the property, and swimming in the ocean or bay is only a few minutes' walk away. Tennis and cross-country skiing are also within easy reach. Guests can take a quick ferry ride over to the next island for golf or visit Portland for shopping and evening entertainment. Contact: Rent A Home International, Inc., 7200 34th Avenue N.W., Seattle, WA 98117. Call 1-206-545-6963.
Children: Y Pets: N Smoking: N Handicap Access: Y Payment: C, P, V, M

HOPE ISLAND *Rates: deluxe*
Open: June-September *Minimum Stay: one week*
Have an entire island all to yourself! Minutes off the coast from Portland in sparkling Casco Bay, and easily reachable from neighboring islands, Hope Island offers 85 pristine acres of pine forest, meadows and beaches. The focal point is its magnificent and luxuriously furnished 13-bedroom lodge that accommodates a party of up to 20 in turn-of-the-century splendor. It features a main parlor, formal dining room, four fireplaces, all amenities and modern conveniences. A staff of five attends to your every need, including preparing and serving three elegant meals a day. Guests have use of the vessels at the boat bay for the five-minute trip to such recreational facilities as golf and tennis. Contact: Rent A Home International, Inc., 7200 34th Avenue N.W., Seattle, WA 98117. Call 1-206-545-6963.
Children: Y Pets: N Smoking: N Handicap Access: N Payment: C, P, V, M

PEAKS ISLAND HOUSE
Rates: budget
Open: June 15-September 15
Minimum Stay: two weeks

Built at the turn of the century and completely renovated, this handsome three-bedroom house is located on peaceful Peaks Island, just a leisurely 20-minute ferry ride from Portland's Old Port. The residence, sleeping up to five and featuring a large screened porch, enjoys panoramic ocean views; both a sandy beach and craggy shoreline are a short stroll away. While electric heat is provided, guests may want to opt instead for the rustic pleasures of the wood-burning stove or a roaring blaze in either the parlor or the dining room fireplaces. Contact: Port Island Realty, P.O. Box 7341, Portland, ME 04112. Call 1-207-775-7253.

Children: **Y**   Pets: **N**   Smoking: **Y**   Handicap Access: **N**   Payment: **C, V, M**

VENEER COTTAGE
Rates: budget
Open: June-September
Minimum Stay: one week

Standing on scenic Long Island and reachable by a 30-minute ferry ride from Portland, this lovely stone cottage has a terrific view overlooking Casco Bay. A small private beach is right in front of the house, which features a large living room, eat-in kitchen, three bedrooms, screened porch and plenty of picture windows, plus a barbecue and picnic table for delightful meals by the water. Guests can use the car—old but functional—that comes at no extra charge with the house to traverse the island or pick up lobsters for dinner. Contact: Paul Watts, 5 Yankee Drive, Yarmouth, ME 04096. Call 1-207-846-5275.

Children: **Y**   Pets: **N**   Smoking: **Y**   Handicap Access: **N**   Payment: **C, V, M**

RANGELEY

CONIFER
Rates: budget-expensive
Open: year-round
Minimum Stay: none

Tucked away in a game reserve on private grounds blanketed with pine forests, lawns and fields, Conifer is a superb Maine vacation home for large groups of up to 14. Golfers will love the location, a mile down the road from the 18-hole Mingo Springs course. The house contains four bedrooms and a combination parlor/dining area/kitchen on the first floor, with a stairway leading up to a fifth, dorm-style bedroom and a den. A large porch runs along the entire front of the lodge, offering a great view of Rangeley Lake and the property's 300 feet of waterfront. Contact: Bianca A. Foss, Magnum Development Corp., P.O. Box 189, North Windham, ME 04062. Call 1-207-892-2732.

Children: **Y**   Pets: **Y**   Smoking: **Y**   Handicap Access: **N**   Payment: **P**

CONNAUGHTON LODGE
Rates: moderate
Open: summer
Minimum Stay: none

Positioned on the south shore of renowned Rangeley Lake, this winning log home includes three double bedrooms, eat-in kitchen, den and a living room containing such charming features as a stone fireplace and a cathedral ceiling with skylights. Outside, the delightful deck commands stunning views of the lake and mountains and offers a private little dock. Along with boundless recreational opportunities, summer in the region offers such diversions as cookouts in Rangeley's town parks, regular arts and crafts exhibitions and a rousing annual logging festival. Contact: ERA Mountain View Agency, P.O. Box 1100, Main Street, Rangeley, ME 04970. Call 1-207-864-5648.

Children: Y Pets: Y Smoking: Y Handicap Access: N Payment: C, P, T, V, M

GREENVALE COVE HOUSE
Rates: budget-inexpensive
Open: year-round
Minimum Stay: none

This attractive post-and-beam house rests by the water on Rangeley Lake's quiet Greenvale Cove. With over five acres of unspoiled rustic grounds, the residence contains a homey living room, dining area, kitchen, bedroom and a cozy loft, with a hot tub in the basement rec room. A variety of matchless recreational opportunities are available in the area: The lake offers swimming and other water sports, Saddleback ski area has five lifts and a network of downhill runs, there's great fishing off School Marm's Rock and snowmobiling through placid forest trails. Contact: Ron Pasek, Daschund Hollow Rentals, P.O. Box 520, Rangeley, ME 04970. Call 1-207-864-5666.

Children: Y   Pets: N   Smoking: Y   Handicap Access: N   Payment: P

HUNTER COVE, UNIT #8
Rates: budget-inexpensive
Open: year-round
Minimum Stay: two nights

Featuring a hot tub right in the living room, this two-bedroom Hunter Cove cottage is covered with bright pine paneling and has a wood-burning stove to provide extra warmth on cold days. Visitors seeking an exhilarating way to enjoy the area may want to strike out on the celebrated Appalachian Trial, which passes very close by and where loons, deer and even moose can be spotted along the way. The breathtaking East and West Kennebago mountains are rigorous enough to challenge even hardy hikers, while lovely Bald Mountain and Angel Falls offer easier, but just as rewarding, treks. Contact: Ralph and Chris Egerthei, Hunter Cove, Mingo Loop Road, HC Box 2800, Rangeley, ME 04970. Call 1-207-864-3383.

Children: Y Pets: Y Smoking: Y Handicap Access: N Payment: C, P, A

HYLINSKI HOUSE
Rates: budget-moderate
Open: year-round
Minimum Stay: two nights

Hylinski House is an elegant two-bedroom home, decorated with fine custom furniture, in one of Maine's top recreational regions. From its appealing wraparound decks, wonderful views of Rangeley Lake and Saddlebrook Mountain can be relished. The entire house is a delight, with such homey embellishments as a huge rock fireplace, but its highlight is undoubtedly the master suite, featuring a luxurious four-poster bed with a down comforter, a cozy window seat, cathedral ceilings and cedar closets, plus a sumptuous whirlpool bath. Contact: Tom and Pam Durgin, High Country Rentals, P.O. Box 173, Rangeley, ME 04970. Call 1-207-864-3446.

Children: Y Pets: N Smoking: Y Handicap Access: N Payment: C, P

LOG HOUSE   *Rates: moderate-expensive*
Open: year-round   *Minimum Stay: none*
A terrific residence for Maine ski vacations, not to mention fall foliage visits and recreational holidays year-round, this brand-new log-constructed home is positioned on over three acres of land by Rangeley Lake. Saddleback ski resort is nearby, and the surrounding woodlands offer 100 miles of groomed trails for hiking, snowmobiling and cross-country skiing. Containing three bedrooms that can sleep up to ten, the house features a large living room with a fireplace, a fully equipped open kitchen and a basement rec room with a hot tub for soothing tired muscles after a strenuous day. A deck off the living room looks over the lake and the property's private beach and docking facilities. Contact: Donna Bauwenes, Daschund Hollow Rentals, P.O. Box 520, Rangeley, ME 04970. Call 1-207-864-5666.
Children: Y   Pets: N   Smoking: Y   Handicap Access: N   Payment: P

MOUNTAIN VIEW COTTAGES   *Rates: budget-inexpensive*
Open: May-October   *Minimum Stay: three nights*
Nestled on a picturesque birch-lined lakefront, the five rustic Mountain View cottages provide privacy and a protected northwest Maine setting particularly attractive to family vacationers. Each two- and four-bedroom unit offers a brick fireplace and a pleasant porch with rockers for lazing the serene day away. Several leisure activities are available on the compound grounds: swings, horseshoes and badminton, an outdoor stone fireplace for refreshing cookouts and an assortment of sailboats, canoes and dinghies for rent. The attractions of the charming town of Oquossoc and the Rangeley Lake region are close by. Contact: Cy and Joyce Eastlack, Mountain View Cottages, Route 17, Box 284, Oquossoc, ME 04964. Call 1-207-864-3416.
Children: Y   Pets: Y   Smoking: Y   Handicap Access: N   Payment: C, P, T

SADDLEBACK SKI AND SUMMER LAKE PRESERVE   *Rates: moderate-deluxe*
Open: year-round   *Minimum Stay: two nights*
What better way to enjoy all the facilities at Saddleback, one of Maine's top ski areas, than to rent a residence right on the 12,000-acre woodland preserve? Three-, four- and five-bedroom houses are available at the Rock Pond Condominium complex, offering fireplaces, fully equipped kitchens and breathtaking views of the surrounding valleys, lakes and mountains from their terraces; most homes also contain a private indoor spa. At the base of the mountain, the White Birch Condominiums provide units that are smaller but every bit as comfortable. Don't overlook the idea of a summer or autumn holiday here—the rates are lower, the recreational opportunities still plentiful and the scenery perhaps even more magnificent. Contact: Theresa Thompson, Ski and Lake Preserve of Saddleback, P.O. Box 490, Rangeley, ME 04970. Call 1-207-864-5671.
Children: Y   Pets: N   Smoking: Y   Handicap Access: N   Payment: C

SHAPIRO CABIN   *Rates: budget-inexpensive*
Open: summer   *Minimum Stay: none*
With a dock and 200 feet of beach frontage, this attractive log home on Rangeley Lake's south shore enjoys a private location yet is also close to town, where you'll find fine restaurants and exciting nighttime activities. The residence contains three bedrooms, a sitting room, a well-equipped and spacious kitchen and a wood stove. Pay a visit to nearby Rangeley State Park, a scenic recreation area offering fishing, boating and picnicking. For an uncommon perspective on the region, why not sign up for an exhilarating seaplane ride? Contact: ERA Mountain View Agency, P.O. Box 1100, Main Street, Rangeley, ME 04970. Call 1-207-864-5648.
Children: Y Pets: N Smoking: N Handicap Access: Y Payment: C, P, T, V, M

THE TERRACES   *Rates: budget*
Open: spring-fall   *Minimum Stay: none*
Nestled beneath great pines and white birches in one of the loveliest spots on Rangeley Lake, this complex of cottages provides an assortment of residences that can accommodate all kinds of vacationers, from couples seeking romantic seclusion to families and large groups. The sparkling waters offer a variety of boating and other recreational activities, and the sun deck with lounge chairs by the shore allows guests to savor in the mild days and gorgeous sunsets. Excellent trout and salmon fishing are available either right here or in more than 40 other nearby lakes and ponds, while tennis, 18-hole golf and woodland hiking trails are also located nearby. Contact: Mr. & Mrs. Chris Murray, The Terraces, Box 3700, Rangeley, ME 04970. Call 1-207-864-3771 (207-864-5451 or 516-483-4530 during winter).
Children: Y Pets: N Smoking: Y Handicap Access: N Payment: C, V, M

ZAMBRASKI HOUSE   *Rates: budget-moderate*
Open: year-round   *Minimum Stay: two days*
This two-bedroom chalet-style house includes a plushly carpeted drawing room and a tiled kitchen featuring a wood stove and well-stocked pantry, with a spiral staircase leading to a master suite that offers a skylight and private deck. Sliding doors in the living area open out onto a wraparound deck that overlooks Rangeley Lake and gets plenty of sunlight all day. The six-person sauna that comes with the house is a pleasure in any season but becomes especially welcome during the frosty winter months after a day on the slopes or snowmobiles. Contact: Tom and Pam Durgin, High Country Rentals, P.O. Box 173, Rangeley, ME 04970. Call 1-207-864-3446.
Children: Y Pets: Y Smoking: N Handicap Access: N Payment: C, P

ROCKWOOD

CABIN #4 AT ABNAKI CAMPS   *Rates: budget-inexpensive*
Open: May-September   *Minimum Stay: two nights*
Located on the unspoiled western shores of Moosehead Lake a short walk from the town of Rockwood, this pretty, white two-bedroom cottage, featuring a living room, eat-in kitchen and a pleasant little

porch out front, is one of the five units at the quiet Abnaki Camp compound. The setting is idyllic, highlighted by striking views of Mt. Kineo, which soars 700 feet straight up from the water. There's superb fishing, secluded beaches, intriguing islets and abundant wildlife in the area. Be sure not to miss a trip on the "Katahdin," a bewitching restored steamer that chugs along the lake. Contact: William Hammond, Abnaki Camps, P.O. Box 6, Rockwood, ME 04478. Call 1-207-534-7318.

Children: Y   Pets: Y   Smoking: Y   Handicap Access: N   Payment: All

SEBAGO LAKE

BOOGLEHOUSE   *Rates: budget*
Open: June 1-October 15   *Minimum Stay: one week*

Standing by the dock on the shore of Maine's second largest lake, Booglehouse is a contemporary cottage containing four bedrooms, one and a half baths, a fully equipped kitchen and a large living room with a fireplace and sliding glass doors opening onto a beguiling sun deck. From here, it's only a few minutes to lovely Sebago Lake State Park, encompassing 1,500 scenic acres along the Songo River. Superb trout and salmon fishing can be found almost everywhere you turn, and a number of other recreational opportunities and untouched wilderness areas are also available nearby. Contact: Donna Collins, ERA Jordan Realty, Route 114, Sebago Lake, ME 04075. Call 1-207-787-2442.

Children: Y   Pets: Y   Smoking: Y   Handicap Access: N   Payment: C, P, T

ROUND TABLE LODGE & COTTAGES   *Rates: budget*
Open: May 1-October 1   *Minimum Stay: one week*

Here is a friendly Sebago Lake vacation retreat ideal for families who want the best in a western Maine holiday. Comfortable cottages and modern apartments—the units contain from one to four bedrooms—each with a well-equipped electric kitchen, are available. Highlighted by the private sandy beach, a portion of which is pleasantly shaded by soaring pines, the grounds offer picnic tables and a play area, with badminton, horseshoes and volleyball all available. Canoes, sailing dinghies and motor boats can be hired for fishing or voyaging on the picturesque lake. Contact: Round Table Lodge & Cottages, The Sloan Family, Prop., HCR 75, Box 763, North Sebago, ME 04029. Call 1-207-787-2780.

Children: Y   Pets: N   Smoking: Y   Handicap Access: N   Payment: C, V, M

SOMESVILLE

SOMES SOUND HOUSE   *Rates: inexpensive*
Open: year-round   *Minimum Stay: one week*

This four-bedroom house on Mt. Desert Island just outside Acadia National Park offers what most residences in the region can't: the opportunity not only to explore Acadia at complete leisure but also actually to reside among its scenic wonders. All of the area's major attractions—its coastal and mountain trails, beaches, the craggy shoreline pummeled by waves and the charming and picturesque town of Bar Harbor—are within easy reach. Commanding a terrific view of Somes Sound, a stunning fjord, from the deck, the house can comfortably accommodate two families vacationing together. It features an outdoor grill and picnic table for enjoying meals surrounded by the natural beauty. Contact: Robert and Janet Brinton, 10 Brinton Road, Bethany, CT 06525. Call 1-203-393-3608.

Children: Y   Pets: N   Smoking: Y   Handicap Access: N   Payment: C, V, M

SOMESVILLE HOUSE   *Rates: budget*
Open: year-round   *Minimum Stay: one week*

Standing under tall pines on a dead-end road near Acadia National Park, this appealing three-bedroom house accommodates a group of up to seven in total privacy and seclusion. A rear deck with an outdoor grill and patio furniture overlooks the large private yard, and a small balcony off the dining room catches the gentle morning sun. From here, both Somes Sound and Long Pond are a short walk away. The house is superbly situated to give guests the chance to partake in all of the activities and scenic marvels of Mt. Desert Island. Contact: Robert and Janet Brinton, 10 Brinton Road, Bethany, CT 06525. Call 1-203-393-3608.

Children: Y   Pets: N   Smoking: Y   Handicap Access: N   Payment: C, V, M

SOUTHWEST HARBOR

DECK COTTAGE AT HARBOUR WOODS LODGING   *Rates: budget-inexpensive*
Open: mid-May to mid-October   *Minimum Stay: none*

The fragrance of crisp saltwater and balsam fir, the feel of the bracing sea breeze, the sound of gulls crying overhead, the sight of beautiful Southwest Harbor with the mountains of Acadia National Park in the distance: All these delights are brought together at Harbour Woods Lodging. This comfortable and very affordable accommodation for up to six, containing a bedroom with two double beds, living area with sleeper sofa, galley kitchen and a large deck ideal for watching the sunrise, is one of several housekeeping cottages available at this small holiday complex. The activities of the bustling harbor community, as well as the scenic wonders and recreational facilities of the park and the shops and restaurants of Bar Harbor, are all within easy reach. Contact: Margaret Eden and James Paviglionite, Harbour Woods Lodging, Main Street, P.O. Box 1214, Southwest Harbor, ME 04679. Call 1-207-244-5388.

Children: Y   Pets: N   Smoking: Y   Handicap Access: N   Payment: C, P, T

THE MANSELL HOUSE   *Rates: budget-moderate*
Open: year-round   *Minimum Stay: none*

Three self-contained apartments are available at the Mansell House, an enticing Mt. Desert Island lodge near Southwest Harbor on Somes Sound. The second-floor studio flats both contain a kitchenette, fireplace and a private deck overlooking the inner harbor and mountains of Acadia National Park, while the two-bedroom penthouse on the third floor also includes a fireplace and two decks, plus a living/dining room and a full kitchen. An assortment of boats may be rented on the premises for exploring the only natural fjord on America's eastern seaboard. Sailing lessons and guided sailing tours to the sound's most beautiful spots are offered as well. Before embarking on their day's excursions, guests may want to get an early start with an exhilarating sunrise cookout on the rocky beach. Contact: Leslie Watson, The Mansell House, Box 1102, Southwest Harbor, ME 04679. Call 1-207-244-5625.

Children: **Y** Pets: **Y** Smoking: **Y** Handicap Access: **N** Payment: **C, P, V, M, A**

TENANTS HARBOR

TENANTS HARBOR COTTAGE *Rates: budget*
Open: June 15-October 1 *Minimum Stay: one week*

This sunny cottage lies 200 feet from the ocean on beautiful St. George's Peninsula. The docks of Tenants Harbor can be seen from the house's front porch, while a deck out back faces lush private woods, where the scent of pine and saltwater mingle softly in the breeze. From nearby Port Clyde, four miles away, ferries voyage to the scenic island of Monhegan, renowned for its lobstering community. Or take an outing to Montpelier, the restored estate of America's first Secretary of War, Henry Knox. The noble seafarer homes of Thomaston, remnants of the region's rich maritime heritage, also makes for a memorable day trip. Contact: True Hall Realty, Tenants Harbor, ME 04860. Call 1-207-372-8952.

Children: **Y** Pets: **N** Smoking: **Y** Handicap Access: **N** Payment: **C, V, M**

TRICKERY POND

CLEARWATER LODGE *Rates: expensive*
Open: June 1-October 15 *Minimum Stay: one week*

Making a superb holiday residence for a large group—particularly a couple of families vacationing together—Clearwater Lodge stands on the shore of picturesque Peabody Pond. The spacious home, built in two sections, contains a big living room with a fireplace and wet bar, an eat-in kitchen, sun room, family room with a wood-burning stove, a second full kitchen and six bedrooms. The property includes two bright decks and a glistening private beach area with a dock and raft. Contact: Donna Collins, ERA Jordan Realty, Route 114, Sebago Lake, ME 04075. Call 1-207-787-2442.

Children: **Y** Pets: **N** Smoking: **Y** Handicap Access: **N** Payment: **C, P, T**

WELLS

GARRISON HOUSE MOTEL AND COTTAGES *Rates: budget-inexpensive*
Open: May-October *Minimum Stay: two nights*

One mile from Wells Beach, between the major tourist destinations of Ogunquit and Kennebunkport, Garrison House provides homey one- and two-bedroom cottages and studio apartments for housekeeping vacationers. Each unit contains a kitchen and offers splendid views of the ocean and tidal inlet. The 10 acres of grounds feature a tempting 40-foot swimming pool, along with a ball field and basketball and badminton courts. Guests can also stop by the main house, an intriguing structure built in 1750 with timbers from an old garrison. Contact: Linda Stritch, Garrison House, RR 3, Box 510B, Wells, ME 04090. Call 1-207-646-3497.

Children: Y Pets: N Smoking: Y Handicap Access: N Payment: C, P, T, V, M

WINDHAM

SEBAGO LAKE LODGE   *Rates: budget-inexpensive*
Open: year-round   *Minimum Stay: two nights*

This vacation complex set by the water in the heart of the Sebago Lake region offers both cottages and efficiency apartments. Many of the studio flats contained in the main lodge come with lakeview porches. All of the one- and two-bedroom cottages look out onto the water, and most include a screened porch and either a fireplace or wood stove. There's a private beach for swimming and boat docks where canoes and rowboats may be borrowed; fishing and ski boats may be rented. Guests also can enjoy a cookout at the charcoal grills and outdoor fireplace after a day on the lake. Contact: Debra or Chip Lougee, Sebago Lake Lodge, P.O. Box 110, White Bridge Road, Windham, ME 04062. Call 1-207-892-2698.

Children: Y   Pets: Y   Smoking: Y   Handicap Access: N   Payment: All

WINTER HARBOR

HARBOR ROAD HOUSE   *Rates: budget*
Open: year-round   *Minimum Stay: one week*

Located in a small lobstering village, this charming cottage makes a great hideaway for vacationing couples. The house is made up of a bedroom, living room and kitchen with a lawn out front, and is within walking distance of the jetties of Winter Harbor, which remains ice-free even during the coldest months of the year. Jutting far out into the open ocean, exhilarating Schoodic Point, where pounding waves crash against granite ledges, is only minutes away as well. A visit to the century-old lighthouse at Prospect Harbor should also be on any visitor's itinerary. Contact: M. Louise Mechaley, 419 Water Street, Ellsworth, ME 04605. Call 1-207-667-3991.

Children: Y   Pets: N   Smoking: Y   Handicap Access: N   Payment: C, V, M

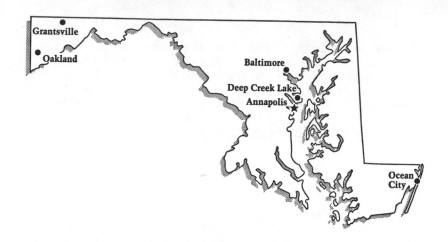

Maryland

DEEP CREEK LAKE

BECKMAN'S PENINSULA LOG CABIN *Rates: budget*
Open: year-round *Minimum Stay: two nights*

Vacation seekers have been coming to Deep Creek Lake for many years, and this log cabin was one of the first accommodations in this popular area. Just cross the road to reach the sparkling waters of Maryland's deepest lake, which offers visitors a chance to fish, swim, sail or drive a power boat. The cabin has two bedrooms and a single fold-out couch, so it can house about five guests; there is one bathroom, and you must bring your own linens. The area is just as popular in winter as summer, with ski resorts, snowmobiling trails and skating rinks all nearby; the cabin stays cozy with the help of a wood-burning fireplace. In summer you might want to cook some fresh fish on the grill and then stay out on the lawn to watch the sun set over the lake. Contact: A & A Realty, P.O. Box 515, McHenry, MD 21541. Call 301-387-5832 or 800-336-7303.

Children: **Y**   Pets: **N**   Smoking: **Y**   Handicap Access: **N**   Payment: **V, M**

BY WATER II *Rates: inexpensive-expensive*
Open: year-round *Minimum Stay: two nights*

A second-floor balcony wraps around this chalet, providing a view through tall trees over the center of Deep Creek Lake, Maryland's largest freshwater lake and vacation paradise. Skylights flood the inside of the chalet with light and four bedrooms provide ample sleeping quarters. Three bathrooms, a Jacuzzi, a washing machine and dryer make things both more comfortable and more convenient; a stone fireplace adds to the charm. A short walk brings you to the lake and all its pleasures—boating, swimming, fishing, waterskiing and sailing. On the other side of the lake is Wisp Ski Resort and its golf course. The woods surrounding this chalet are filled with trails for hiking, cross-country skiing and snowmobiling. Contact: Railey Rental, Star Route 1, Box 77, McHenry, MD 21541. Call 301-387-5533.

Children: Y   Pets: N   Smoking: Y   Handicap Access: N   Payment: C, T

CEDAR RIDGE   *Rates: budget-inexpensive*
Open: year-round   *Minimum Stay: two nights*

Beautiful and crystal clear, Deep Creek Lake is full of coves lined with holiday homes. Cedar Ridge stands just seventy-five yards from the shoreline in one of these coves, with a private swimming area and dock. Huge windows and skylights let plenty of light into the contemporary home with warm wooden siding and spacious balconies. The ground-floor "great room" rises up into a cathedral ceiling and leads into a dining room and fully equipped kitchen. Three bedrooms—one with its own outdoor deck—two baths, a laundry room and a loft complete the layout. For relaxing at home, there is a Jacuzzi, a TV with VCR and a fireplace. Nearby Wisp Ski Resort is a main attraction in winter; in summer, guests enjoy boating, water skiing and fishing in the lake. Contact: Gerry Trainor, 309 Kingsberry Circle, Pittsburgh, PA 15234. Call 412-835-6832 or 301-387-5485.

Children: Y   Pets: N   Smoking: Y   Handicap Access: N   Payment: C, P

COTTER HOUSE   *Rates: budget-inexpensive*
Open: year-round   *Minimum Stay: two nights*

This little log cabin has a wide covered porch in front and is just minutes from Deep Creek Lake, the state's largest lake. The cabin has one bedroom with a king-size bed and a large loft area with two singles; in addition, there is a fold-out couch. A cozy feeling pervades the rooms when the wood-burning stove is lit; there is also a TV for your enjoyment. Outdoor pleasure is plentiful—from swimming, fishing or boating in the lake to hiking, horseback riding or picnicking in the surrounding area. A ski resort and golf course is located close to the lake, where cross-country skiing and snowmobiling are popular in winter. History buffs will want to visit the colonial sites of Garrett County. Contact: Deep Creek Realty, P.O. Box 159, McHenry, MD 21541. Call 301-387-6187 or 800-252-7335.

Children: Y   Pets: N   Smoking: Y   Handicap Access: N   Payment: C, T

INGLENOOK APARTMENT   *Rates: budget-inexpensive*
Open: year-round   *Minimum Stay: two nights*

Up to four guests can stay in this one-bedroom apartment, but it also makes a great hideaway for a couple who appreciate the romance of the outdoors. With views of Deep Creek Lake from the deck and a dock just seconds away, those who like water sports won't be disappointed. The deck leads to a living/dining/kitchen area with color TV and a fold-out couch. An outdoor grill and picnic table offer a place to cook up some fresh-caught fish, and the woods are full of trails for hiking or cross-country skiing. Downhill skiers will enjoy the Wisp Ski Resort, which doubles as a golf resort in summer. Garrett County also contains many sites and towns of historic interest, including Deer Park and Friendsville. Contact: Deep Creek Realty, P.O. Box 159, McHenry, MD 21541. Call 301-387-6187 or 800-252-7335.

Children: Y   Pets: N   Smoking: Y   Handicap Access: Y   Payment: C, P

ROCK LODGE LAKEFRONT   *Rates: expensive*
Open: year-round   *Minimum Stay: two nights*

This property actually consists of two separate accommodations: a five-bedroom contemporary house and a separate stone cottage with two bedrooms, a kitchenette and one bath. The homes are beautifully designed and filled with light; there are fireplaces in both the main house and the cottage. The large house contains a spacious "great room," a family room, two baths and a gourmet kitchen. Up to sixteen guests can stay here when the units are rented together, so you'll probably take advantage of the barbecue and deck for outdoor meals. Such amenities as a washing machine and dryer, a TV with VCR and a Ping-Pong table will help keep everyone entertained. A private dock is situated on Deep Creek Lake to provide boating, fishing and swimming access. Contact: A & A Realty, P.O. Box 515, McHenry, MD 21541. Call 301-387-5832 or 800-336-7303.

Children: Y   Pets: N   Smoking: Y   Handicap Access: N   Payment: V, M

SANDY BEACH RETREAT   *Rates: inexpensive-moderate*
Open: year-round   *Minimum Stay: two nights*

A large bay window overlooks the spacious deck of this newly constructed hearthstone log home. Chairs and tables arranged on the balcony make it a great place to sit and barbecue, or to look out upon your little beach and the pleasure boats and fishing craft cruising Deep Creek Lake. Inside the house are three bedrooms with comfortable beds, three bathrooms and a living/dining area. In the winter guests can visit the Wisp Ski Resort or try some snowmobiling or cross-country skiing in the woods; afterward, the stone fireplace makes a cozy place to relax. In summer the area boasts golf, horseback riding and hiking; year-round, visitors enjoy the fine local restaurants. Contact: Railey Rental, Star Route 1, Box 77, McHenry, MD 21541. Call 301-387-5533.

Children: Y   Pets: N   Smoking: Y   Handicap Access: N   Payment: C, T

VILLAGES OF THE WISP   *Rates: inexpensive-moderate*
Open: year-round   *Minimum Stay: two nights*

The Wisp is a popular ski resort and golf course located near the shores of beautiful Deep Creek Lake in the heart of Garrett County's vacation land. Situated on a slope not far from the resort, this three-story townhouse offers a view of the surrounding countryside and lake. Very contemporary, the two-bedroom apartments within have a microwave and dishwasher in the kitchen, a washing machine and dryer, three full bathrooms and a color TV with VCR. In addition, there is a fireplace to keep things cozy and a balcony where guests can soak up the sun. The lake has many facilities for boating and fishing and the nearby woods are a fun place to hike or, in winter, cross-country ski. Contact: Deep Creek Realty, P.O. Box 159, McHenry, MD 21541. Call 301-387-6187 or 800-252-7335.

Children: Y   Pets: N   Smoking: Y   Handicap Access: N   Payment: C, P

GRANTSVILLE

NEW GERMANY STATE PARK CABINS	*Rates: budget*
Open: year-round	*Minimum Stay: two nights*

Located in the heart of the Savage River State Forest in western Maryland, this state park is a former mill center that now has a number of cabins for rent throughout the year. All cabins have electricity, hot and cold running water and fully equipped bathrooms and kitchens. Ranging in size from cozy two-person cottages to two-story units with three bedrooms, all have the pleasant feature of a fireplace or wood-burning stove, and some wood is provided for you. The location in a stand of evergreens ensures peace and quiet, but there is plenty to do outdoors, including nature activities at the park center, hiking, swimming in the 13-acre lake (which is also well stocked with trout), seasonal hunting and cross-country skiing. Contact: Park Manager/ Reservations Clerk, New Germany State Park, Route 2, P.O. Box 63, Grantsville, MD 21536. Call 301-895-5453.

Children: Y   Pets: N   Smoking: Y   Handicap Access: Y   Payment: C, P, T, A

OAKLAND

HERRINGTON MANOR STATE PARK CABINS	*Rates: budget*
Open: year-round	*Minimum Stay: two nights*

One-, two- and three-bedroom cabins are situated in this state park, one of the two oldest in the state, which lies in the midst of the mountains, forests, waterfalls and streams of Garrett State Forest. The twenty cabins are all equipped for housekeeping, with electricity, hot and cold running water and full kitchen and bathroom facilities. Each cabin is unique, but each has a wood-burning stove or fireplace to add to its rustic charm. Within the park itself are plenty of places to explore and get a little closer to nature, perhaps aided by the interpretive programs offered by the park. Boats, canoes, fishing equipment and licenses and bicycles can all be rented; there are tennis courts and a children's playground as well. Contact: Herrington Manor State Park, Route 5, P.O. Box 122, Oakland, MD 21550. Call 301-334-9180.

Children: Y   Pets: N   Smoking: Y   Handicap Access: Y   Payment: C, P, T

OCEAN CITY

ASSATEAGUE HOUSE	*Rates: budget*
Open: May-September	*Minimum Stay: one week*

Located on the bay at Ocean City, this condominium in a low-rise elevator building offers great views of the water, the boardwalk and Assateague Island. There is an outdoor swimming pool, and the beach is only one block away. The bedroom has two double beds; a fold-out couch for two makes the condo suitable for up to six guests. The fully equipped kitchen has a microwave and dishwasher, but don't let that distract you from Ocean City's great seafood restaurants. Air conditioning cools you off after a day spent on the beach, on the water, on the tennis courts or on the golf course. There are two color TVs, a VCR and a stereo for indoor entertainment. Contact: Long and Foster, Ocean City Square Shopping Center, 11701 Coastal Highway, Ocean City, MD 21842. Call 301-524-1700 or (in Maryland) 800-992-6666 or (outside Maryland) 800-992-7777.

Children: Y   Pets: N   Smoking: Y   Handicap Access: N   Payment: C, T

BOUNTY   *Rates: budget*
Open: year-round   *Minimum Stay: two nights*

Large balconies and outdoor staircases give this low-rise condominum an unusal appearance and provide a great ocean view. The rental apartments have two bedrooms and two bathrooms each, as well as a fully equipped kitchen—though fresh seafood restaurants are only a short walk away. The beach is even closer, and most visitors to Ocean City spend a lot of time on its golden sands, watching the sailboats and wind surfers. Deep-sea fishing expeditions are also popular, as are trips to Assateague National Seashore, a well-preserved gem where wild ponies still run free. There are several golf courses and facilities for racquet sports in town, as well as plenty of amusement parks and arcades. Contact: O'Conor, Piper and Flynn, P.O. Box 580, Ocean City, MD 21842. Call 800-633-1000.

Children: Y   Pets: N   Smoking: Y   Handicap Access: N   Payment: C, T

CORONET   *Rates: inexpensive-expensive*
Open: year-round   *Minimum Stay: two nights*

Oceanfront units can be rented in this low-rise condominium right next to the boardwalk. You can sit on your shaded balcony and people-watch from this great location, or you can walk just a few steps and spend the day on the sandy beach. The condos are spacious, with three bedrooms and one and a half baths. There are laundry facilities in the building, and you can bring or rent linens. Air-conditioned comfort, a dishwasher in the kitchen and color TV add to the indoor amenities—outdoors there are good shops, amusement centers, sports clubs and, of course, marinas where you can join a cruise or a fishing expedition. Contact: O'Conor, Piper and Flynn, P.O. Box 580, Ocean City, MD 21842. Call 800-633-1000.

Children: Y   Pets: N   Smoking: Y   Handicap Access: N   Payment: C, T

DUNE HOUSE   *Rates: budget-inexpensive*
Open: year-round   *Minimum Stay: two nights*

Ocean City is spread out along a long strip of sand just a few blocks wide. Across a stretch of ocean lies Assateague National Seashore, where wild ponies run free. On the oceanfront is this three-bedroom townhouse, perfectly situated for enjoying the beach. Private and quiet, the townhouse is air-conditioned and has additional ceiling fans to cool down guests who've just spent a day on the golf course or tennis courts. Fishing cruises go out from the marinas, and there are power boat rides for the more daring, as well as windsurfing and other water sports facilities. Contact: O'Conor, Piper and Flynn, P.O. Box 580, Ocean City, MD 21842. Call 800-633-1000.

Children: Y   Pets: N   Smoking: Y   Handicap Access: N   Payment: C, T

GEMINI   *Rates: expensive*
Open: year-round   *Minimum Stay: two nights*

Three balconies adorn this four-bedroom townhouse, which occupies a corner lot bordering the beach. Extremely luxurious, the townhouse is an unusual find, boasting a fireplace that makes it a perfect choice for off-season visits to Ocean City and Assateague National Seashore. Air-conditioned, the house also features a huge Jacuzzi—the perfect place to soak after a day in the ocean. There is a color TV and stereo for your entertainment. Ocean City is a great place for sailing, cruising on the ocean or going on a fishing trip. Golfers will find a choice of courses, and there are facilities for racquet sports and exercise right in the city. Contact: O'Conor, Piper and Flynn, P.O. Box 580, Ocean City, MD 21842. Call 800-633-1000.

Children: Y   Pets: N   Smoking: Y   Handicap Access: N   Payment: C, T

HOBO   *Rates: inexpensive*
Open: year-round   *Minimum Stay: two nights*

This is an unassuming, two-story building toward the Delaware end of the strip. Its two-bedroom units are air-conditioned, and there are laundry facilities in the building. From their balcony guests can watch the hypnotic rhythm of the Atlantic surf; within steps of the apartment are golden sands that stretch out in both directions. Fishing charters and cruises launch from the marinas, and there are golf courses and fitness clubs for sports lovers. Throughout the year, Ocean City hosts a number of festivals and fairs, but there is always a festive atmosphere in this popular seaside resort. Contact: O'Conor, Piper and Flynn, P.O. Box 580, Ocean City, MD 21842. Call 800-633-1000.

Children: Y   Pets: N   Smoking: Y   Handicap Access: N   Payment: C, T

LOFT APARTMENTS   *Rates: budget*
Open: year-round   *Minimum Stay: two nights*

Extra space is provided by the lofts in these one-bedroom apartments, and extra comfort is supplied by the air conditioning. A large balcony runs across both floors of this two-story building, so that guests can enjoy the ocean view and breezes. The apartments do have laundry facilities and dishwashers, but you must provide your own linens and towels. From this home base, try a cruise to Assateague Island and its National Seashore. Amusement parks, arcades and restaurants line the beach and boardwalk, and festivals are held in all seasons, celebrating the sea, the sun or Christmas on the beach. Contact: O'Conor, Piper and Flynn, P.O. Box 580, Ocean City, MD 21842. Call 800-633-1000.

Children: Y   Pets: N   Smoking: Y   Handicap Access: N   Payment: C, T

OCEAN VILLAGE   *Rates: budget-expensive*
Open: year-round   *Minimum Stay: two nights*

A townhouse that feels like a home, this three-bedroom unit is just steps from the beach. Its fully equipped kitchen contains a dishwasher, plus there is a washing machine and dryer. The furnishings have been chosen with care, giving it a truly relaxed atmosphere. Ocean City can keep you busy boating and fishing or trying out the shops and fresh seafood restaurants. The boardwalk is a long promenade where it feels as if the whole town is on vacation. The townhouse is air-conditioned for comfort, and there are two full bathrooms—you can literally step off the beach and shower off the salt water. No trip would be complete without a visit to unspoiled Assateague National Seashore for a glimpse of its wild ponies, or you could time your trip to coincide with one of the city's many festivals. Contact: O'Conor, Piper and Flynn, P.O. Box 580, Ocean City, MD 21842. Call 800-633-1000.

Children: **Y**   Pets: **N**   Smoking: **Y**   Handicap Access: **N**   Payment: **C, T**

POINT LOOKOUT HOUSE   *Rates: inexpensive-moderate*
Open: year-round   *Minimum Stay: two nights*

An ocean lover's delight, the backyard of this private dwelling offers a place to crab and fish directly from the bay. Five bedrooms and one and a half baths fill this surprisingly spacious cottage, which is located in a quiet residential neighborhood of Ocean City. It is fully air-conditioned and has laundry facilities as well as a kitchen with a microwave; guests should bring their own linens and towels. Just a few blocks away lies the beach and the wide-open ocean, where fishing boats and pleasure cruises leave for the deep sea or for nearby islands and attractions. You'll find facilities for racquet sports, golf and all kinds of water sports in the vicinity. Contact: O'Conor, Piper and Flynn, P.O. Box 580, Ocean City, MD 21842. Call 800-633-1000.

Children: **Y**   Pets: **N**   Smoking: **Y**   Handicap Access: **N**   Payment: **C, T**

SAND TRAP   *Rates: budget-inexpensive*
Open: year-round   *Minimum Stay: two nights*

Balconies on the front of this building present a great view out over the open ocean; the beach is just a short walk away. Air-conditioned comfort will greet you when you return to your modern two-bedroom apartment from a day in the sun. Equipped with a dishwasher and laundry facilities, these apartments have been furnished by an interior decorator. Ocean City is a water lover's paradise and has fine facilities for golf, tennis and other racquet sports. The adventurous can take a trip to Assateague National Seashore, a shifting stretch of sand dunes and grasses; others may want to join a deep-sea fishing expedition to try for the evening's meal. Contact: O'Conor, Piper and Flynn, P.O. Box 580, Ocean City, MD 21842. Call 800-633-1000.

Children: **Y**   Pets: **N**   Smoking: **Y**   Handicap Access: **N**   Payment: **C, T**

TARA BORU
Rates: budget-moderate
Open: year-round
Minimum Stay: two nights

A quiet canal leads from Big Assawaman Bay to this truly luxurious townhouse with its own private pier. Carpeted throughout and exquisitely furnished, Tara Boru has three bedrooms, three baths and a beautifully appointed kitchen with a microwave and dishwasher as well as laundry facilities. Two fireplaces make the cooler evenings snug if you want to stay in and watch TV, and the sunset views from both decks are spectacular. Within a few blocks is the beachfront of Ocean Bay and all the water sports and festivities that happen year-round; golf courses, racquet sports and a fitness club complete the picture for the athletic vacationer. Contact: O'Conor, Piper and Flynn, P.O. Box 580, Ocean City, MD 21842. Call 800-633-1000.

Children: **Y**   Pets: **N**   Smoking: **Y**   Handicap Access: **N**   Payment: **C, T**

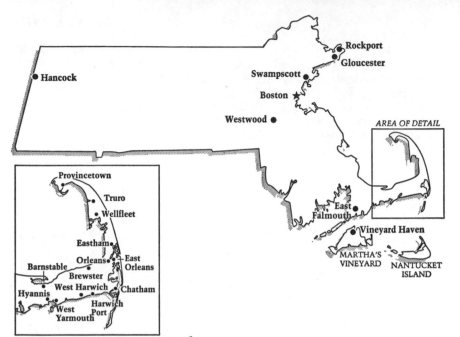

Massachusetts

BARNSTABLE

ASHLEY MANOR INN
Open: year-round
Rates: moderate
Minimum Stay: two nights

Elegant and romantic, this fine old country inn offers the richest kind of vacation in its Garden Cottage suite, with distinctive wallpaper and other special details—fresh flowers, candy and Crabtree and Evelyn soaps and shampoos. This gracious accommodation for two features a freestanding fireplace and a kitchenette, making it ideal for the couple who would sometimes prefer to make breakfast right in the room or serve up hot soup in front of the fireplace. An attractive alternative to eating indoors is the complimentary breakfast served either on the beautiful terrace or before the fireplace of the gracious dining room. This stately inn enjoys a fine location in Barnstable Harbor, known for sport-fishing and whale-watching cruises. Contact: Donald and Fay Bain, Ashley Manor Inn, P.O. Box 856, 3660 Main St., Barnstable, MA 02630. Call 508-362-8044.

Children: N Pets: N Smoking: N Handicap Access: N Payment: C, P, T, V, M, A

THE MARSHALL ESTATE
Open: year-round
Rates: deluxe
Minimum Stay: one week

Beautifully situated on ten acres of rolling land with 2,000 feet of harbor frontage, this truly fine home boasts endless views of Cape Cod Bay in absolute privacy. The carefully furnished home includes four bedrooms—one with a canopy bed—a dining area with a fireplace, a paneled study with a fireplace, a screened porch and a boat house. There's even a camp at the shore for bunkhouse overnights young people will especially enjoy. Amusements abound nearby, with Cape Cod Playhouse only a short drive away and the charming village of Provincetown, with its many crafts shops and art galleries, a perfect day's outing. Quieter activities like seashell and driftwood collecting along the beaches of Nantucket Sound provide the kind of memorable pastime that brings vacationers back to the cape year after year. Contact: Waterfront Rentals, 20 Pilgrim Road, West Yarmouth, MA 02673. Call 508-778-1818.

Children: Y Pets: N Smoking: Y Handicap Access: N Payment: C, P, V, M

BOSTON

BEANTOWN B AND B   *Rates: inexpensive*
Open: year-round   *Minimum Stay: none*
This 1881 Victorian townhouse features a small studio apartment with a new kitchenette, a private entrance and a private bath. If planning your day requires all your attention and you cannot think of making a pot of coffee, you can enjoy a full breakfast with the other guests in the common dining room. Located on a quiet street just two blocks from Boston's Hynes Convention Center and the dazzling shops at Copley Place, this studio offers a great center for exploring the city. The New England Aquarium and the Franklin Park Zoo demand the attention of animal lovers. For the historians there's the beautiful campus of Harvard College, the Old South Meeting House and the site of the Boston Massacre. Contact: Bed and Breakfast Associates, Bay Colony Ltd., P.O. Box 166, Babson Park Branch, Boston, MA 02157. Call 617-449-5302.

Children: Y Pets: N Smoking: N Handicap: N Payment: C, P, T, V, M, A

NEW BOSTON PROPERTIES   *Rates: budget-inexpensive*
Open: year-round   *Minimum Stay: one week*
Designed to make you feel at home away from home on your Boston vacation, these many studios and one- and two-bedroom apartments offer some of the city's best locations—Beacon Hill, the Theater District, the Financial District and Back Bay. Ideal for tourists, visiting students, touring theater casts and business travelers, these apartments all feature kitchens and TVs; many of the more exclusive homes include saunas, Jacuzzis and living roms with skylights and fireplaces. These rentals offer a great alternative to costly hotel stays and locate you exactly where you want to be in one of America's oldest and most colorful cities. The many attractions of the city—the Franklin Park Zoo, the Museum of Fine Arts, Faneuil Hall, Fenway Park—will fill your days in the city. Contact: New Boston Properties, 53 Hereford Street, Boston, MA 02115. Call 617-262-3354.

Children: Y Pets: Y Smoking: Y Handicap: N Payment: C, T, V, M, A

RED BRICK B AND B   *Rates: inexpensive*
Open: year-round   *Minimum Stay: none*

Conveniently located in Boston's colorful and historic Copley Square area, this showplace offers five gracious guest rooms, each with a kitchenette, a private bath and altogether romantic furnishings. Guests who stay for at least one month are invited to enjoy full cooking privileges; nightly guests are served a gourmet breakfast in the penthouse dining room. This lovingly restored 1863 brick townhouse provides a wonderful vacation home from which to explore the wonders, both old and new, of one of New England's most gracious towns. Old North Church and the Paul Revere House ring with history, and the area's colleges—Harvard, MIT and Boston University—offer a variety of activities and the special ambiance that makes Boston feel like an overgrown college town. Contact: Bed and Breakfast Associates, Bay Colony Ltd., P.O. Box 166, Babson Park Branch, Boston, MA 02157. Call 617-449-5302.

Children: Y Pets: N Smoking: N Handicap: N Payment: C, P, T, V, M, A

THE 1860 HOUSE   *Rates: inexpensive*
Open: year-round   *Minimum Stay: none*

This recently restored townhouse provides a charming and comfortable suite with a pullman kitchen, a private bath, and warm, woody Danish decor. Located on the first floor of a 130-year-old house in Boston's convenient South End, the suite also features a private deck off a glass entry. The streets of this area fairly pulse with history, and national landmarks such as the Custom House, the Old South Meeting House and the Old State House are within walking distance for the urban hiker. Nearby, too, you'll find the green slopes of Boston Commons as well as the Public Gardens. You can also plan day trips and excursions to points of interest just outside the city, like a pilgrimage to Concord, the home of Ralph Waldo Emerson or the beaches of Lynn and Marblehead. Contact: Bed and Breakfast Associates, Bay Colony Ltd., P.O. Box 166, Babson Park Branch, Boston, MA 02157. Call 617-449-5302.

Children: Y Pets: N Smoking: Y Handicap: N Payment: C, P, T, V, M, A

BREWSTER

BAY BEACH   *Rates: expensive*
Open: year-round   *Minimum Stay: one week*

Spacious, charming and comfortable, this four-bedroom, three-bath home will situate you not more than a few feet from a private beach on Cape Cod Bay. Lots of country charm sets you at ease in the living room before the crackling fireplace. Accommodations for eight include a large kitchen and a separate dining room. The large lawn boasts wide-open spaces as well as plentiful outdoor furniture, including a picnic table, benches and a gas grill. The beautiful vistas here may inspire you to explore the outermost cape, where the National

Seashore, the Wellfleet Bay Wildlife Sanctuary and the state park in Brewster await. Contact: Bay Village Realty, Rte. 6A, Box 2000, Brewster, MA 02631. Call 1-800-338-1851 or 508-896-7260.

Children: **Y**   Pets: **N**   Smoking: **Y**   Handicap Access: **N**   Payment: C, P, T

BAYSIDE   *Rates: expensive*
Open: year-round   *Minimum Stay: one week*

Situated on a private dirt road and located a scant 500 feet from a bayside beach, this charming shuttered and shingled home offers four spacious bedrooms and two baths. The deck off the second-floor master bedroom features terrific views of Cape Cod Bay. Cape pines perfume the air here, amid thickets on either side of the wide stairs leading down to the serene waterfront. For a different experience of the water, you can plan a day of deep-sea fishing, join one of the whale-watching tours that depart from Provincetown or wind surf at Cape Cod National Seashore. Contact: Coldwell Banker/Atlantic Realty, 229 Route 6A, P.O. Box 1630, Orleans, MA 02653. Call 508-255-8011/ 5810.

Children: **Y**   Pets: **N**   Smoking: **Y**   Handicap Access: **Y**   Payment: C, P, T

CUMMINGS RANCH   *Rates: expensive*
Open: year-round   *Minimum Stay: one week*

Walls of windows in nearly every room make this comfortable two-bedroom, two and a half bath ranch-style home especially bright and lively. The spacious living room features a fireplace and a soul-satisfying view of the bay. The knotty pine sun room includes a sleep sofa and opens onto the large furnished deck with a gas grill. A kitchen with a microwave and an electric coffee pot completes these accommodations for six. You'll find a private beach just seconds away; the outdoor shower back at the house adds an extra splash to your day in the sun. This home provides a great center from which to explore the riches of Cape Cod. In several neighboring towns you'll find special events such as crafts fairs, summer theater, band concerts and an endless selection of fine restaurants and great shopping. Contact: Bay Village Realty, Rte. 6A, Box 2000, Brewster, MA 02631. Call 1-800-338-1851 or 508-896-7260.

Children: **Y**   Pets: **N**   Smoking: **Y**   Handicap Access: **N**   Payment: C, P, T

DUCK PONDO CONDO   *Rates: expensive*
Open: year-round   *Minimum Stay: one week*

This elegant and impressive three-bedroom condominium home offers ease and comfort as well as welcome vacation amenities, such as a private bayside beach, a large swimming pool and tennis courts. Overlooking a tranquil duck pond, this home inspires a relaxed and casual lifestyle shared by a select few. The master suite boasts a private deck; living space in the guest room is maximized by a charming loft. A dining room, a nicely laid-out galley kitchen and a garage complete the unit. If and when you tire of the beauty outside your door, it's only a short drive or a healthy bike ride to the beautiful Cape Cod National Seashore and the Wellfleet

Bay Wildlife Sanctuary. Contact: Coldwell Banker/Atlantic Realty, 229 Route 6A, P.O. Box 1630, Orleans, MA 02653. Call 508-255-8011/5810.

Children: Y   Pets: N   Smoking: Y   Handicap Access: Y   Payment: C, P, T

GINER ON LAKE SHORE DRIVE   *Rates: moderate*
Open: year-round   *Minimum Stay: one week*

Situated on a beautifully wooded lot, this four-bedroom home for eight enjoys deeded rights on Seymour Pond only a few steps away. The contemporary, multilevel home features a wonderful large deck furnished for taking in the sun or enjoying the fruits of the gas grill. Sweet sea breezes cool the interior of this home, where you'll find cable TV, a fireplace, a laundry and a kitchen with a microwave and a dishwasher. Brewster is home to a beautiful state park and also offers two excellent golf courses and many tennis courts. Neighboring towns host craft fairs, summer theater, band concerts and excellent shopping. Contact: Bay Village Realty, Rte. 6A, Box 2000, Brewster, MA 02631. Call 1-800-338-1851 or 508-896-7260.

Children: Y   Pets: N   Smoking: Y   Handicap Access: N   Payment: C, P, T

HUSH   *Rates: moderate*
Open: year-round   *Minimum Stay: one week*

A large family could not choose a lovelier address for their Cape Cod vacation than this spacious and charming five-bedroom, two-bath home. The homey country kitchen beckons guests to prepare steamers and lobster, and includes such conveniences as a dishwasher and a washer/dryer. A living room with an inviting fireplace and a family room ideal for playing games complete these accommodations for nine. You can breakfast on the deck, lunch on the screened-in porch and spend the afternoon a short walk away at the private beach. Surrounded by the history, charm and natural beauty of this everlastingly popular piece of New England, Brewster offers special attractions such as freshwater ponds with beaches, a state park and two excellent golf courses. Contact: Bay Village Realty, Rte. 6A, Box 2000, Brewster, MA 02631. Call 1-800-338-1851 or 508-896-7260.

Children: Y   Pets: N   Smoking: Y   Handicap Access: N   Payment: C, P, T

LINGER LONGER BY THE SEA   *Rates: budget-moderate*
Open: May-November   *Minimum Stay: two nights*

Located directly on an utterly unspoiled stretch of beach on Cape Cod Bay, these cottages offer a quiet, relaxing escape from worldly pressures in accommodations ranging from studio apartments to four-bedroom cottages. In this tree-shaded setting, each rental provides a private deck offering wonderful views of the bay, and the cottages also include picnic tables and charcoal grills. On a stormy night you can enjoy the dramatic sea views from your living room or put your feet up and watch your favorite show on TV. Guests can enjoy exclusive use of the inn's beautiful sandy beach, but further afield you'll find golf, deep-sea fishing, bicycling and fine restaurants. Contact: Lauren Mitchell, Linger Longer By the Sea, P.O. Box 847, Brewster, MA 02631. Call 508-896-3087/3451.

Children: Y Pets: N Smoking: Y Handicap Access: N Payment: C, P, T

WORGAN SALTBOX *Rates: inexpensive*
Open: year-round *Minimum Stay: one week*
This beautifully decorated contemporary saltbox home enjoys an address right on Seymour Pond. From the furnished decks of the living and dining rooms you'll enjoy splendid views of the pond and the many birds attracted to its fresh water. The kitchen boasts many conveniences such as a microwave, a dishwasher and a washer/dryer. Two bedrooms and a living room sleep-sofa accommodate up to six people; inviting amenities such as color cable TV and a VCR and a fireplace complete the house. Choose between the charcoal and the gas grill for your barbecues, unless it's the cook's night—or week—off. Then you can head for one of the great lobster houses or other fine restaurants in the area. Contact: Bay Village Realty, Rte. 6A, Box 2000, Brewster, MA 02631. Call 1-800-338-1851 or 508-896-7260.

Children: Y Pets: N Smoking: Y Handicap Access: N Payment: C, P, T

CHATHAM

REID HOME *Rates: deluxe*
Open: year-round *Minimum Stay: one week*
Truly one of the finest rentals on Cape Cod, this splendid and spacious house boasts a spectacular brick and flagstone patio with a pine-shaded spot for outdoor dining. The views from the generous rooms show Nantucket Sound and the Atlantic Ocean in all their glory. Exquisitely furnished in the finest early American decor with beautiful Oriental rugs, this home offers three bedrooms and two and a half baths, a living room with a piano and a fireplace and a separate formal dining room. Conveniences include a Jacuzzi, a washer/dryer, a microwave, cable TV and a deck with lawn chairs, a picnic table and a grill. It's just a short walk from the house to the beautiful Chatham beaches, or a short drive up the Cape Road to a sweep of protected shoreline. Contact: Waterfront Rentals, 20 Pilgrim Road, West Yarmouth, MA 02673. Call 508-778-1818.

Children: Y Pets: N Smoking: Y Handicap Access: N Payment: C, P, V, M

CHATHAMPORT

PLEASANT BAY VILLAGE *Rates: inexpensive-deluxe*
Open: mid-May to mid-October *Minimum Stay: none*
You can take your pick of lodgings at this peaceful resort, where efficiency suites and cottages offer accommodations for two to four. Every accommodation features remote-control, color cable TV, daily maid service and original art from some of the cape's best-known artists, as well as outdoor tables and chairs, chaise lounges and Weber grills. The

efficiencies enjoy pine paneling and the cottages provide fully carpeted living rooms and screened-in porches. Spacious grounds set back from the main road offer a serene atmosphere, and a cooling dip is as close as the resort pool or the nearby beach. Located in the charming town of Chatham, these accommodations offer a great point of departure for hiking at the National Seashore or biking on the Cape Cod trails. Contact: Howard Gamsey, Pleasant Bay Villages Resort Motel, Box 772, Chatham, MA 02633. Call 508-945-1133.

Children: Y   Pets: N   Smoking: Y   Handicap: N   Payment: C, P, T, V, M, A

EAST FALMOUTH

372 EDGEWATER DRIVE   *Rates: inexpensive-moderate*
Open: year-round   *Minimum Stay: one week*

You'll find this three-bedroom home with views of a quiet inlet and marina fairly dripping with Cape Cod charm. Accommodations for six include an eat-in kitchen plus a dining room that seats six, a cozy living room with cable TV and a fireplace and two decks furnished with lawn chairs, a picnic table and a grill. This spot offers the perfect location for boat lovers, whether your specialty is watching, dreaming or launching. With the Woods Hole ferry for Martha's Vineyard only a few miles away, you can plan a day on that popular island, where bicycle rentals offer an enchanting way to enjoy lunch in Chilmark and sunset at Gay Head. Contact: Waterfront Rentals, 20 Pilgrim Road, West Yarmouth, MA 02673. Call 508-778-1818.

Children: Y   Pets: N   Smoking: Y   Handicap Access: N   Payment: C, P, V, M

EAST ORLEANS

CARRIAGE HOUSE   *Rates: budget-expensive*
Open: year-round   *Minimum Stay: one week*

This secluded home in the Barley Neck countryside of the hamlet of East Orleans offers a number of water sports options to guests. You'll find freshwater Meetinghouse Pond only a half mile away and the beautiful oceanfront strip of Nauset Beach less than a mile and a half—a delightful walk, a short jog or a quick bike ride. This spacious home features four bedrooms and sleeps ten. A living room, a separate dining room, a total of four fireplaces and a charming country kitchen with its own pantry complete this rustic and comfortable house. The sunny furnished patio, barbecue and hot and cold outdoor shower will enhance your days here. Contact: Cape Homesteads, 39 River Road, P.O. Box 1213, East Orleans, MA 02643. Call 508-255-5083.

Children: Y   Pets: N   Smoking: Y   Handicap Access: N   Payment: C, P, T

MARSH VIEW   *Rates: expensive*
Open: year-round   *Minimum Stay: one week*

Handsome and modern, this three-bedroom, two-bath contemporary home enjoys seclusion assured by private access on a dirt road. Terrific views of the marshes of Meetinghouse Pond will reveal the magical ways of the birds who make the marshes their home. Perfect for sunning and relaxing, the entire back of the home features a wide-open deck. Inside, several skylights flood the house with that special Cape Cod light. A one-mile bike ride will bring you to Nauset Beach, part of the lovingly protected Cape Cod National Seashore. Lobster lovers can drop all their inhibitions here, with lobster and eggs for breakfast, lobster bisque for lunch and a deliciously charred whole lobster for dinner, seven days a week. Contact: Coldwell Banker/Atlantic Realty, 229 Route 6A, P.O. Box 1630, Orleans, MA 02653. Call 508-255-8011/5810.

Children: Y   Pets: N   Smoking: Y   Handicap Access: Y   Payment: C, P, T

EASTHAM

ANCHORAGE ON-THE-COVE
Rates: budget-inexpensive
Open: year-round
Minimum Stay: three nights

Located next to the Cape Cod National Seashore, these six cottages provide an ideal base for exploring the seashore's 40 miles of sandy beaches and the cape's scenic bicycle trails, wooded paths and nature walks. Accommodations for three to six include convenient kitchens, spacious and comfortably appointed living/dining rooms and amenities like color TV and fireplaces. Three of the cottages sit right on the water's edge with private decks extending out over the water. Once a haven for sailing ships, the Town Cove of Eastham offers fishing, sailing, boating and windsurfing. And of course, the entire area is thick with quaint little villages. Contact: Joanna and Bill Reade, Anchorage On-the-Cove, Box 474, Orleans, MA 02653. Call 508-255-1442.

Children: Y   Pets: N   Smoking: Y   Handicap Access: N   Payment: C, T, V, M

BLUFF COTTAGE
Rates: moderate
Open: year-round
Minimum Stay: one week

No television, no dishwasher, no washer or dryer, no buses or subways, no traffic, no crowded elevators, no long lines at the takeout: You'll find none of it here. All that awaits you is the sound of the surf, the serene views, the spray of the water, the white and red lighthouse across a copse thick with brush and wildflowers, and the time to breathe, to read, to get to know your family or friends in a setting utterly different from your everyday world. This secluded and private three-bedroom cottage, set back on a bluff overlooking Nauset Light Beach, promises all this. And the Cape Cod National Seashore—all 40 miles of it—begins almost at your doorstep. Contact: Coldwell Banker/Atlantic Realty, 229 Route 6A, P.O. Box 1630, Orleans, MA 02653. Call 508-255-8011/5810.

Children: Y   Pets: N   Smoking: Y   Handicap Access: Y   Payment: C, P, T

GLOUCESTER

LILL STUGAN
Rates: budget-inexpensive
Open: year-round
Minimum Stay: two nights

Originally a schoolhouse in this oceanside village, this delightful little cottage dates back to 1765. These winterized accommodations include two bedrooms, a kitchen and a living room with a cozy wood stove and a cable TV. You'll find the nearby beach and the town's several quaint restaurants only a short walk from your door. Located on the peninsula of Cape Ann, the area enjoys considerable fame for its fresh seafood. With Boston only one hour to the south and the charming seaside and artist colony town of Rockport just a short drive away, you can plan activities from the most peaceful to the most lively. Winter vacationers will also find Hamilton ski area close enough to make waxing those skis worthwhile. Contact: Bed and Breakfast Associates, Bay Colony Ltd., P.O. Box 166, Babson Park Branch, Boston, MA 02157. Call 617-449-5302.

Children: Y Pets: N Smoking: N Handicap: N Payment: C, P, T, V, M, A

HANCOCK

COUNTRY VILLAGE AT JIMINY PEAK   *Rates: inexpensive-deluxe*
Open: year-round   *Minimum Stay: two nights*

Nestled in the scenic Jericho Valley, these fine one-, two- and three-bedroom condominium units feature old New England-style furnishings with neutral color schemes. The larger units boast lofts, fireplaces and decks with vistas of the surrounding Berkshires. At home here, you'll relax in front of the cable TV, but when you're itching to be out and about, there's also a swimming pool, a sauna and hot tub, tennis and golf right in the village. Guests here also enjoy an on-premises restaurant and bar, a game room and planned children's recreational programs. A number of ski slopes nearby promise hours of winter fun, and the summer list of attractions begins with Tanglewood, Jacob's Pillow and the Williamstown Theater Festival. Contact: Country Village at Jiminy Peak, Corey Road, Hancock, MA 01237. Call 413-738-5500.

Children: Y Pets: N Smoking: Y Handicap Access: N Payment: C, P, V, M, A

HARWICH PORT

BAYBERRY SHORES   *Rates: inexpensive*
Open: year-round   *Minimum Stay: one week*

Situated just a short walk past an acre of lush woods, bayberry bushes and summer houses from a sparkling beach on Nantucket Sound, this convenient rental features a living room with a fireplace and a very comfortable sofa bed and a color TV. A new kitchen, a dining area, two bedrooms and a newly appointed bath complete the accommodations for six. Just outside the kitchen door, you'll find those two summer necessities, a picnic table and a grill. Of course, a spring visit promises great antiquing along daffodil-lined roads, and the fall brings brilliant color to the cranberry bogs. Year-round, the charm and history of Cape Cod's ports and whaling centers, the fabulous natural beauty of fresh- and saltwater ecosystems and numerous fine restaurants, 'interesting shops and art centers make this one of North America's favorite vacation centers. Contact: Harbor Breeze of Cape Cod, 326 Lower County Road, Harwich Port, MA 02646. Call 1-800-992-6550 or 508-432-0337.

Children: Y Pets: N Smoking: Y Handicap Access: N Payment: C, V, M, A

HARBOR HOME   *Rates: expensive*
Open: year-round   *Minimum Stay: one week*

This traditionally styled new home situated only 100 feet from picturesque Allen Harbor puts you within a five-minute walk of a sandy beach on Nantucket Sound. In addition, guests enjoy the use of the swimming pool at Harbor Breeze Bed and Breakfast right across the street and the hard-surfaced tennis courts less than a mile away. This beautiful home features a handsomely furnished living room with a sliding patio door leading to a deck with a harbor view. The spiffy kitchen, equipped with a microwave, a dishwasher and a lunch island, opens onto a dining area with yet another harbor view. Three spacious bedrooms with wicker furniture sleep six; the master bedroom includes a TV, skylights and a balcony overlooking the harbor. Contact: Harbor Breeze of Cape Cod, 326 Lower County Road, Harwich Port, MA 02646. Call 1-800-992-6550 or 508-432-0337.

Children: Y Pets: N Smoking: Y Handicap Access: N Payment: C, V, M, A

LAKEFRONT HOME   *Rates: inexpensive-moderate*
Open: year-round   *Minimum Stay: one week*

Every single room of this beautiful house in the Great Sand Lakes area offers a view of John Joseph Pond, a private lake excellent for swimming, sailing and fishing. The house enjoys a white, sandy private beach on the lake. Accommodations for eight include a master bedroom suite, two additional bedrooms, a den with a double sofa bed and color cable TV, a large eat-in kitchen with a microwave and a dishwasher and a living/dining room with a fireplace. Right off the kitchen you'll find the patio and deck furnished with a table and chairs and a grill for outdoor dining. When you tire of this bucolic setting, you'll find the gorgeous saltwater beaches of Nantucket Sound only a seven-minute ride away. Contact: Harbor Breeze of Cape Cod, 326 Lower County Road, Harwich Port, MA 02646. Call 1-800-992-6550 or 508-432-0337.

Children: Y Pets: N Smoking: Y Handicap Access: N Payment: C, V, M, A

THE COTTAGE AT CAPTAIN'S QUARTERS   *Rates: inexpensive*
Open: year-round   *Minimum Stay: one week*

Located just behind the Victorian bed and breakfast of the same name, this cottage enjoys its own spacious yard with a picnic table and a charcoal grill. Inside, you'll find rooms tastefully furnished and appointed with wicker, wood and country florals, including a fine kitchen, a combination living/dining room with color TV, two bedrooms and one full bath. Guests here can make full use of the swimming pool at the nearby Harbor Breeze guest house as well as three hard-surface tennis courts less than a mile away. But you come to the cape for more than a swimming pool, and the Harwich area has it—numerous public beaches, both fresh- and saltwater, Cape Cod National Seashore with its interesting trails and dramatic dunes and ferries to Nantucket and Martha's Vineyard. Contact: Harbor Breeze of Cape Cod, 326 Lower County Road, Harwich Port, MA 02646. Call 1-800-992-6550 or 508-432-0337.

Children: Y Pets: N Smoking: Y Handicap Access: N Payment: C, V, M, A

HYANNIS

BELORUSKY FLAT   *Rates: budget-inexpensive*
Open: year-round   .   *Minimum Stay: one week*

As bright as the day is long, this two-bedroom apartment situated only steps from the beach sleeps six. Located only minutes away from Barnstable Municipal Airport, these accommodations include a living room and large dining area, offering the perfect solution to the family with a weekend commuter. Amenities include cable TV and a dishwasher as well as plenty of lawn chairs for cloud watchers and sea gull counters. For a change of pace, you can jump on the ferry to Edgartown on charming Martha's Vineyard, where a day of exploring the galleries, shops and charming Victorian homes of this old fishing town will delight everyone. Contact: Waterfront Rentals, 20 Pilgrim Road, West Yarmouth, MA 02673. Call 508-778-1818.

Children: Y Pets: N Smoking: Y Handicap Access: N Payment: C, P, V, M

HYANNIS HARBORVIEW RESORT   *Rates: budget-inexpensive*
Open: year-round   *Minimum Stay: none*

These one-bedroom apartments at this year-round condominium resort feature split-level living with the kind of amenities that make your vacation a real holiday. You can fill your days with activities such as sunning on the beach, lunching by the pool and watching the fishing boats and sailing ships pass in and out of the harbor. In the wintertime, you can visit the indoor swimming pool and enjoy on-premises dining and the Crow's Nest Lounge. Explore the lively and charming town of Hyannis with its many shops and historic attractions just five minutes from here. For those with a longing for seafaring excursions, you'll also find the ferries to Nantucket Island and beautiful Martha's Vineyard just a short drive away. Contact: Hyannis Harborview Resort, 213 Ocean Street, Hyannis, MA 02601. Call 508-775-4420.

Children: Y   Pets: N   Smoking: Y   Handicap Access: N   Payment: All

MYERS CONDO   *Rates: budget-inexpensive*
Open: year-round   *Minimum Stay: one week*

A pair of sliding glass doors open from the modern living room of this ground-floor apartment onto a private yard. Here, water views and a big sky call you to the ocean only ten steps away. A family of five traveling on a budget will enjoy the accommodations here, which include one bedroom with a double and a single bed, a queen-sized bed in the basement, a color TV and a charcoal grill. With plenty of the best and freshest East Coast seafood around, this might be the right time to try out that recipe for grilled swordfish. Lobster lovers can claw their way through meal after meal of this delicacy in the finest and funkiest of restaurants. You'll find golf and tennis nearby; swimming in the tingling waters of the sound will be a true temptation. Contact: Waterfront Rentals, 20 Pilgrim Road, West Yarmouth, MA 02673. Call 508-778-1818.

Children: Y Pets: N Smoking: Y Handicap Access: N Payment: C, P, V, M

THE BREAKWATERS   *Rates: budget-inexpensive*
Open: April to mid-October   *Minimum Stay: three nights*

Situated right on the beach of graceful and serene Nantucket Sound in a residential area just one mile from the village, these one- to three-bedroom condominiums share a large swimming pool, outdoor decks and wonderful harbor views. Country furnishings in the Laura Ashley tradition make these charming, weathered gray cottages special and inviting. Full kitchens, cable TV, daily maid service and babysitters also assure vacationing families of the conveniences they need for a truly restful holiday. Nearby attractions include whale-watching, golf, tennis and ferry excursions to Nantucket Island and Martha's Vineyard. Contact: The Breakwaters, Box 118, 432 Sea Street, Hyannis, MA 02601. Call 508-775-6831.

Children: Y Pets: N Smoking: Y Handicap Access: N Payment: C, P, T

YACHTSMAN CONDOMINIUMS   *Rates: inexpensive-expensive*
Open: year-round   *Minimum Stay: one week*

Facing Lewis Bay and Kennedy Park to one side and with a breathtaking view of Nantucket Sound on the other, these spacious multilevel townhouses offer elegance, convenience and comfort in your choice of two- to four-bedroom accommodations. Each private beach home features wall-to-wall carpet, a sunken living room, color TV, two and a half baths and a private sun deck. Most afford an extra element of charm in appointments like skylights and fireplaces. Here you can enjoy the private beach and magnificent views of the sound or relax at the heated pool located in a beautifully landscaped courtyard. You can also venture forth to ferry boats to the islands, deep-sea fishing and dockside dining on Ocean Street Dock just a short walk away. Contact: Douglas Frisby, Yachtsman Condominium Rentals, 500 Ocean St., P.O. Box 939, Hyannis, MA 02601. Call 1-800-695-5454 (in Massachusetts, 508-771-5454).

Children: Y Pets: N Smoking: Y Handicap: N Payment: C, P, T, V, M, A

MARTHA'S VINEYARD

CAUSEWAY HARBORVIEW   *Rates: budget-inexpensive*
Open: year-round   *Minimum Stay: none*

Comfortable and homey, these 24 apartments and cottages overlook the harbor from a tranquil hillside setting. The spacious, beautifully landscaped property features a large swimming pool and several picnic sites with barbecues. Each one- to three-bedroom accommodation enjoys the conveniences of daily maid service, a full kitchen, a color TV and toddler-friendly amenities like a highchair and a crib. Here, you'll find yourself only a few minutes' walk from the charming town of

Vineyard Haven, where a scattering of charming small shops and the Black Dog Tavern make an afternoon stroll especially appealing. Also nearby are public beaches suited for the contemplative activities of building sand castles and beachcombing, as well as the more athletic activities of windsurfing and sailing. Contact: Causeway Harborview, Skiff Avenue, Box 450, Vineyard Haven, MA 02568. Call 508-693-1606.

Children: Y Pets: N Smoking: Y Handicap Access: N Payment: C, P, T

ISLAND INN *Rates: inexpensive-moderate*
Open: year-round *Minimum Stay: none*

Perched on the quiet outskirts of the charming village of Oak Bluffs within view of beautiful Nantucket Sound, this condominium resort offers a variety of rentals ranging from studio apartments to a two-bedroom cottage. All accommodations feature full kitchens, color cable TV and daily maid service. The new building boasts luxury one- and two-bedroom suites, which sleep up to six and boast such details as beamed ceilings and fireplaces. You can gaze out from your patio or balcony to the sound, the lush rolling greens and woods of Farm Neck Golf Club (the island's only 18-hole course) and spectacular sunrises and sunsets. Guests also enjoy the inn's three tennis courts, tennis lessons with the full-time pro, a sparkling outdoor freshwater pool and easy access to beaches, bike rentals and horseback riding. Contact: Bruce A. Silverman, Island Inn on Martha's Vineyard, Beach Road, P.O. Box 1585, Oak Bluffs, MA 02557. Call 508-693-2002.

Children: Y Pets: Y Smoking: Y Handicap Access: N Payment: C, V, M, A

Nantucket Island

BARTLETT HOME *Rates: expensive*
Open: year-round *Minimum Stay: two weeks*

Originally a lean-to Nantucket house, this charming two-story home has added many "warts" over the years, increasing its native charm. The small and cozy rooms of this town rental accommodate nine and feature a living room with a wood-burning stove, a dining room, a country kitchen with a round table and pantry and a washer/dryer in an alcove. The charm of a deck and a yard surrounded by a picket fence add grace to vacations here. You can enjoy the warmth of the people of this quaint village on walks and shopping excursions. Afternoons at the beach, a visit to the Whaling Museum, deep-sea fishing and beachcombing all await you. Contact: R.C.A., P.O. Box 218, 22 Federal Street, Nantucket, MA 02554. Call 508-228-4005.

Children: Y Pets: N Smoking: Y Handicap Access: N Payment: C, P, T, V, M

CAPTAIN GARDNER HOUSE *Rates: moderate*
Open: year-round *Minimum Stay: one week*

If it's charm and romance you're looking for, these newly renovated apartments located on Center Street in the heart of Nantucket's Old Historic District are sure to delight you. Accommodations for two to four include one or two bedrooms, full kitchens and baths. There could be no better address from which to explore this island rich in history and natural beauty. You'll find fine restaurants, terrific shopping and island tour operators just a five-minute stroll away. Walk to Children's Beach, or if you prefer, bike to Jetties Beach. Bicycling is a favored mode of transportation here, and rentals are readily available. Contact: Angelastro Real Estate, 35 Old South Road, Nantucket, MA 02554. Call 508-228-5307.

Children: Y   Pets: N   Smoking: Y   Handicap Access: N   Payment: C, P, T

CODFISH PARK   *Rates: moderate*
Open: year-round   *Minimum Stay: one week*
Perched on the easternmost shore of the island, the Siasconset area was developed many years ago as a fishing village. In later years it became an artists' colony. Today, the village features one general store and three restaurants, including the world-renowned Chanticleer. Reminiscent of an artist's studio, this home in Codfish Park features two loft bedrooms, a charming open kitchen, a living/dining room and one full bath. These accommodations for four stand a mere 200-foot walk from the ocean beach, providing an ideal spot for a quiet, secluded holiday orchestrated by the sound of the surf. For those times when you need a break from all the peace and quiet, you'll find the activities and society of Nantucket town just eight miles away. Contact: Angelastro Real Estate, 35 Old South Road, Nantucket, MA 02554. Call 508-228-5307.

Children: Y   Pets: N   Smoking: Y   Handicap Access: N   Payment: C, P, T

DIONIS BEACH COTTAGES   *Rates: moderate-deluxe*
Open: year-round   *Minimum Stay: one week*
Scattered across the scenic, open landscape of this northwesterly stretch of the island, these several three-bedroom cottages enjoy privacy and wonderful vistas of sky and sea for miles around. Each cottage features a kitchen, a living room and a dining room as well as easy-living amenities like a fireplace and a sun deck. This small New England gem of an island awaits your investigation, from the Whaling Museum in town to the pristine state forest on the south shore. Famous for its fine beaches, sailing, fishing and excellent seafood restaurants, the island offers the kinds of peace and relaxation that give welcome relief from demanding lives. Contact: Dionis Beach Cottages, Dionis Beach Road, Nantucket, MA 02554. Call 508-228-4524.

Children: Y   Pets: N   Smoking: Y   Handicap Access: N   Payment: C, T, V, M

HARBOR HOUSE   *Rates: deluxe*
Open: year-round   *Minimum Stay: one month*
This wonderful three-bedroom home offers great views of the picturesque harbor of Nantucket, the sandy beach and the colorful array of small boats that sail and motor to and from their docks. Accommodations for six include an especially bright living room, a simple, cozy kitchen and a panoramic picture window showing an incredible view of town. With over 400 private historic homes as neighbors on this island, which was a whaling center in years gone by, you'll feel fully

immersed in the charm and tradition of the place. Summer dining offers 80 restaurants to lovers of gourmet food and great pizza. And, of course, there are few beaches as pristine and peaceful as those surrounding this island. Contact: Denby Real Estate, Inc., 5 North Water Street at Whaler's Lane, P.O. Box 901, Nantucket, MA 02554. Call 508-228-2522.

Children: Y   Pets: N   Smoking: Y   Handicap Access: N   Payment: C, P, T

MAHONEY COTTAGE   *Rates: expensive*
Open: year-round   *Minimum Stay: two weeks*

This very traditional, two-story Cape Cod-style house enjoys an especially secluded setting as one of four cottages and a tennis court. Large open grounds surround the house, which is situated approximately five miles from the center of town and within walking distance of a shallow swimming beach in Madaket Harbor. Accommodations for six feature a charming living/dining room adjoining the kitchen, one bedroom on the first floor and two on the second floor. The slower pace of island life invites cooking, reading and long walks along the beaches and bluffs for a closer look at nature. Contact: R.C.A., P.O. Box 218, 22 Federal Street, Nantucket, MA 02554. Call 508-228-4005.

Children: Y Pets: N Smoking: Y Handicap Access: N Payment: C, P, T, V, M

MAIN STREET HALF HOUSE   *Rates: deluxe*
Open: year-round   *Minimum Stay: one week*

This recently renovated antique "half house" typical of those built in Nantucket in the late 18th and early 19th centuries offers charming accommodations for eight in the heart of this old whaling port. Appealing features such as wide floorboards and decorative fireplaces add grace to a stay here. A double parlor, a brand-new eat-in kitchen, four bedrooms and one and a half baths comprise this village home. Builders of sand castles and collectors of driftwood and seashells will find Jetties Beach a scant mile and a half away. For those who like a wilder beach, deep-sea fishing or windsurfing, you're sure to find the spot of shore or the stretch of ocean just right for you. Contact: Angelastro Real Estate, 35 Old South Road, Nantucket, MA 02554. Call 508-228-5307.

Children: Y   Pets: N   Smoking: Y   Handicap Access: N   Payment: C, P, T

MCELDERRY HOUSE   *Rates: deluxe*
Open: year-round   *Minimum Stay: two weeks*

Set atop a hill at the east end of Nantucket Island, this home offers wonderful pond and sound views all the way to Great Point from the spacious open deck and most of its rooms. The two-story home features a fine living room with an inviting fireplace and doors to the deck; a dining room; a den with a fireplace, bar, refrigerator, microwave and a sink; and a kitchen particularly notable for its convection oven, gas stove and grill. The double-bedded master bedroom on the main floor opens onto the deck; two other bedrooms on the second floor complete the accommodations for seven. Vacationers can enjoy the laid-back world of this island, where sunning, swimming, fishing and idling are the most ambitious undertakings allowed. Contact: R.C.A., P.O. Box 218, 22 Federal Street, Nantucket, MA 02554. Call 508-228-4005.

Children: Y Pets: N Smoking: Y Handicap Access: N Payment: C, P, T, V, M

MONOMOY VILLAGE
Rates: inexpensive-moderate

Open: year-round
Minimum Stay: one week

These newly renovated island cottages enjoy all the charm for which this island is famous. Appointments such as pine floors, Shaker furnishings, fireplaces and color-coordinated fabrics set the mood; washer/dryers and cable TV assure vacationers of the kind of at-home conveniences that make these two- and three-bedroom rentals so attractive. Each cottage also features a deck or courtyard with plenty of outdoor furniture and a barbecue, all set in a landscaped private compound. Conveniently located just a quarter mile from the beach and one mile from Nantucket town, you'll find yourself within easy reach of every activity for which this island is known—swimming, windsurfing, deep-sea fishing, harbor cruises, sailing and some of the finest restaurants in the Northeast. Contact: Monomoy Village, 8 Federal Street, Nantucket, MA 02554. Call 508-228-4449.

Children: Y   Pets: N   Smoking: Y   Handicap Access: N   Payment: C, P, T

NANTUCKET SOUND
Rates: deluxe

Open: year-round
Minimum Stay: one month

If seclusion, an endless canopy of sky and a sweep of shore and water are what you seek in a vacation home, then this spot three miles west of town may suit you perfectly. Simple and charming, the house features three bedrooms, a kitchen, a living room and one bath. You can watch the sun set from your own private beach on beautiful Nantucket Sound, where the gentle surf and the calling gulls are bound to soothe away the stress and tension of everyday life. This island invites exploration, and bicycling is a popular and invigorating way to get to know the several tiny towns scattered along the coasts. The state forest on the south shore and the remarkable richness of the village of Nantucket, with its 14 museum exhibits and cobbled Main Street, also beckon. Contact: Denby Real Estate, Inc., 5 North Water Street at Whaler's Lane, P.O. Box 901, Nantucket, MA 02554. Call 508-228-2522.

Children: Y   Pets: N   Smoking: Y   Handicap Access: N   Payment: C, P, T

NELSON'S NEST
Rates: deluxe

Open: year-round
Minimum Stay: two weeks

With its eagle's-nest roof deck atop the third story and a broad covered porch across the front of the main level, this spacious summer home boasts a dramatic aspect as it overlooks its sprawling grounds. With beach access just across the street and water views from many of the front windows, this immense summer home offers the perfect location for a family reunion. Unheated accommodations for fourteen include five second-floor bedrooms and two sparsely furnished third-floor bedrooms. On the first floor, the generous living room features a fireplace, the dining room boasts two tables—one for the adults and one for the children—the library invites quiet talks and the large, bright kitchen features a dishwasher, a washer/dryer and a useful work table. Contact: R.C.A., P.O. Box 218, 22 Federal Street, Nantucket, MA 02554. Call 508-228-4005.

Children: Y Pets: N Smoking: Y Handicap Access: N Payment: C, P, T, V, M

PINE STREET VICTORIAN   *Rates: deluxe*
Open: year-round   *Minimum Stay: one week*

Renovated in 1985, this spacious and charming Victorian-style home boasts a stylish front porch, a signature of easy living. Tastefully furnished and lovingly appointed, the home offers a double parlor with two fireplaces for that matchless at-home feeling. The immense eat-in kitchen features a lofty cathedral ceiling. Four bedrooms and three baths complete these accommodations for eight. Conveniently located only a four-minute walk from the many fine restaurants and shops of the village, the house also enjoys easy access to Jetties Beach a mile and a half away. For those with a passion for things of the sea, this spot offers a full range of activities, from a morning of study at the Whaling Museum to a sunset harbor cruise, from days of challenging deep-sea fishing to leisurely afternoons spent at one of the lounges in the harbor. Contact: Angelastro Real Estate, 35 Old South Road, Nantucket, MA 02554. Call 508-228-5307.

Children: Y   Pets: N   Smoking: Y   Handicap Access: N   Payment: C, P, T

SHEEP POND   *Rates: inexpensive-deluxe*
Open: year-round   *Minimum Stay: one week*

A more private and serene location for a New England vacation retreat cannot be imagined. Here on one of Nantucket's freshwater ponds sit two charming one-story cottages, each with a complete kitchen. Available as a pair or individually, each cottage accommodates four to six people and offers stunning ocean views, as well as a wonderful ocean beach just 400 feet away. Nature lovers will be in their element on Sheep Pond, where the sky, the weather, the sun, moon and stars function as a colorful backdrop to the daily lives of the waterfowl that occupy the area. Located about seven miles from Nantucket town, these cottages offer an ideal address for vacationers who want the peace and seclusion of the east end of Nantucket as well as access to the activities and amenities available on this splendid island. Contact: Angelastro Real Estate, 35 Old South Road, Nantucket, MA 02554. Call 508-228-5307.

Children: Y   Pets: N   Smoking: Y   Handicap Access: N   Payment: C, P, T

SIASCONSET   *Rates: deluxe*
Open: year-round   *Minimum Stay: one month*

The sun rises early over the most easterly village on Nantucket Island, where you'll find this small and delightful rose-covered cottage. Accommodations for six include two bedrooms and a pair of trundle beds in the living room. You'll find the pace of life especially relaxed in this historic village, a great place for finishing a great book—whether you're writing it or reading it—or enjoying a romantic vacation. The village of Nantucket, with its many history-rich homes and charming side streets, lies just a short drive away. There, the lively harbor, sport-fishing facilities, excellent restaurants and gift shops await you when you hanker for social contact. Contact: Denby Real Estate, Inc., 5 North Water Street at Whaler's Lane, P.O. Box 901, Nantucket, MA 02554. Call 508-228-2522.

Children: Y   Pets: N   Smoking: Y   Handicap Access: N   Payment: C, P, T

THE WHARF COTTAGES   *Rates: moderate-deluxe*
Open: year-round   *Minimum Stay: none*

Situated on the docks overlooking the water, the Wharf Cottages range from one- to three-bedroom units with full kitchens, cable TV and telephones. Many of the cottages feature private decks or patios where you can watch yachts from all over the world tie up at the wharves. With the harbor at your doorstep, you can enjoy charter fishing or a sunset harbor cruise. Just a few steps away, cobbled Main Street awaits you with its many boutiques, antique shops and art galleries, plus some of the island's finest restaurants. Families will enjoy "For Kids Only," a special summer recreation program for children ages five to twelve. Contact: The Wharf Cottages, New Whale Street, P.O. Box 1139, Nantucket, MA 02554. Call 1-800-ISLANDS or 508-228-5500.

Children: Y   Pets: N   Smoking: Y   Handicap Access: N   Payment: C

THE WHITE ELEPHANT   *Rates: deluxe*
Open: year-round   *Minimum Stay: none*

Situated at the edge of Nantucket Harbor amid flawlessly manicured grounds, this island resort offers the ultimate in understated elegance. Among several types of units available, the Pinegrove Cottages feature living rooms and kitchens and from one to three bedrooms. Guests enjoy wonderful facilities including private boat slips, a putting green, a croquet court and an outdoor swimming pool. The concierge staff will be glad to arrange tennis matches, golf and private island tours, as well as sunset harbor cruises and charter fishing. You can spend your evenings strolling the picturesque streets of this old whaling center, or savor the fine hors d'oeuvres and cocktails on the resort terrace, followed by dinner in the excellent dining room and some entertainment in the harborside lounge. Contact: The White Elephant, Easton Street, P.O. Box 359, Nantucket, MA 02554. Call 1-800-ISLANDS or 508-228-5500.

Children: Y   Pets: N   Smoking: Y   Handicap Access: N   Payment: C, T, V, M

UPPER MAIN STREET HOUSE   *Rates: moderate-expensive*
Open: year-round   *Minimum Stay: one week*

Dating from around 1846, this truly charming smaller home right in the historic and colorful town of Nantucket features wide-plank floors, a living room with a cozy fireplace, a small but utilitarian kitchen, a separate dining room and two bedrooms. The large yard offers a great spot for a game of hearts or a chance to finish the book you've been reading; popular Jetties Beach lies just about a mile and half away. From this delightful home, which accommodates four comfortably, you can stroll to the heart of town on brick sidewalks along cobblestoned Main Street. Here, you're ideally located for all island activities, from golf and tennis, to fine dining and elegant shopping, to harbor tours and deep-sea fishing. Contact: Angelastro Real Estate, 35 Old South Road, Nantucket, MA 02554. Call 508-228-5307.

Children: Y   Pets: N   Smoking: Y   Handicap Access: N   Payment: C, P, T

WHITE GOOSE COVE   *Rates: expensive*
Open: year-round   *Minimum Stay: two weeks*

This architect-designed house in Tristam's Landing could easily be called Sunset Point, with its spectacular setting in the village of Madaket and its views of Long Pond and the Atlantic Ocean beyond. Enter into a cathedral-ceilinged living area with a wall of glass revealing a large deck and the water. This beautifully furnished room contains living, dining and kitchen spaces. Three bedrooms accommodate seven, and two of the bedrooms feature sliding glass doors opening onto private decks. Sandwiched between the grassy shore and the rolling hills of Nantucket, this secluded house invites quiet visits with friends and family, long walks, fine home-cooked meals and a shot at improving your chess game or finishing that epic novel. Contact: R.C.A., P.O. Box 218, 22 Federal Street, Nantucket, MA 02554. Call 508-228-4005.

Children: Y Pets: N Smoking: Y Handicap Access: N Payment: C, P, T, V, M

NORTH TRURO

KARMEL HOUSE   *Rates: deluxe*
Open: year-round   *Minimum Stay: one week*

Perhaps it's been only a dream, something you imagined—a five-bedroom house with skylights and windows admitting endless Cape Cod light, the finest in contemporary furnishings and nonstop ocean views. Now that dream can come true at Karmel House, where the conveniences and amenities include a kitchen with everything, a washer/dryer, an outdoor shower, two furnished decks and a patio, a fax machine hook-up, two telephone lines and two fireplaces. Was the gorgeous private beach and huge sky part of your dream? How about the private driveway and nearby Provincetown, where fine dining or marketing for gourmet meals prepared at home are available? When you're sure you're not really dreaming, you can swim and sun at the Cape Cod National Seashore, gather driftwood and seashells for mementos and count stars from the decks of your magical holiday home. Contact: Waterfront Rentals, 20 Pilgrim Road, West Yarmouth, MA 02673. Call 508-778-1818.

Children: Y   Pets: N   Smoking: Y   Handicap Access: N   Payment: C, P, V, M

WALLWORK BEACH HOUSE *Rates: deluxe*
Open: year-round *Minimum Stay: one week*
The glass front of this fabulous beach house overlooks the moody and dramatic waters of Cape Cod Bay. A flight of wooden steps from the house through the dunes down to the beach reveals even more dramatically the splendor of this location, as the water laps the shore and the gulls call to one another across the wind. Utterly contemporary and elegant in its appointments, the house sleeps ten and includes an open living and dining space, a kitchen with a dishwasher and microwave and a huge furnished deck with a charcoal grill. The curling tip of Cape Cod offers a splendid array of pleasures, from whale-watching to great shopping. The bicycle trails, deep-sea fishing and fine dining seem inexhaustible and bring many vacationers back to North Truro year after year. Contact: Waterfront Rentals, 20 Pilgrim Road, West Yarmouth, MA 02673. Call 508-778-1818.
Children: Y Pets: N Smoking: Y Handicap Access: N Payment: C, P, V, M

ORLEANS

OLDE BITTERSWEET *Rates: budget-moderate*
Open: year-round *Minimum Stay: one week*
This classic three-quarter cape home built around 1780 by a whaling ship captain enjoys a central location amid the three towns of Chatham, Orleans and Harwich, very near beautiful Pleasant Bay. Accommodations for eight include three bedrooms, two full baths and an outdoor shower. The spacious living and dining rooms each feature a fireplace, and the generous eat-in kitchen completes this house. For those long summer nights, the delightful furnished patio includes a barbecue, where grilled fish and clambakes come together happily. From here, you can walk less than a mile from the house to the sandy beach on Pleasant Bay, or plan an excursion to some of the famous National Seashore beaches nearby. Contact: Cape Homesteads, 39 River Road, P.O. Box 1213, East Orleans, MA 02643. Call 508-255-5083.
Children: Y Pets: N Smoking: Y Handicap Access: N Payment: C, P, T

SKATET COTTAGE *Rates: budget*
Open: year-round *Minimum Stay: one week*
This adorable Cape Cod cottage offers simple living only half a mile from Skatet Beach. You'll find this quaint, cozy and affordable two-bedroom saltbox ideal for a quiet getaway, a reunion with old friends, a wintertime bridge tournament for four or a chance to really get to know your grandchild. Convenient to the center of town, this home assures you the best of the Cape Cod lifestyle. You can sit at the foot of a large, old tree in the yard and read or tell a story. When you're ready, you can drive into town for a walk along the state park trails, a bowl of clam chowder or a movie. The area boasts many museums and

historic sites as well as fabulous gift shops and crafts centers. Contact: Coldwell Banker/Atlantic Realty, 229 Route 6A, P.O. Box 1630, Orleans, MA 02653. Call 508-255-8011/5810.

Children: Y Pets: N Smoking: Y Handicap Access: Y Payment: C, P, T

ROCKPORT

ROCKPORT HOUSE   *Rates: expensive*
Open: year-round   *Minimum Stay: one week*

Built on a functioning sea wall overlooking the beach and the ocean, this three-bedroom home accommodates eight adults as well as a couple of lucky children, who will most willingly occupy the roll-out chair bed up in the crow's nest. This loft enclosed in glass is the perfect spot from which to watch thunder clouds roll in across the sea. Elsewhere, the house has a spacious living room, dining room and kitchen; two of three bedrooms are on the ocean side of the house. You can enjoy the wonderful location of this house whether your goal is the beach (one minute away), the village restaurants and artist colony (five minutes away) or the history-rich towns of Gloucester and Salem. Contact: Rent A Home International, 7200 34th Avenue N.W., Seattle, WA 98117. Call 206-545-6824.

Children: Y Pets: N Smoking: Y Handicap Access: N Payment: C, P, V, M

SOUTH ORLEANS

PILGRIM LAKE TERRACE   *Rates: inexpensive-deluxe*
Open: year-round   *Minimum Stay: one week*

Located about a mile from Orleans center, this reproduction saltbox offers a quiet and restful vacation spot in a prime residential neighborhood. Built in 1981, the home features five bedrooms and four baths with two Jacuzzis. In addition to the homey eat-in kitchen, the living room and dining room, the house also boasts a screened-in porch as well as a handsome brick patio. Other outdoor amenities include plenty of lawn furniture, a barbecue and a wonderful hot and cold shower. A short walk from the house you'll find a private freshwater lake; also nearby is a saltwater landing for boating. You can enjoy leisurely afternoon strolls in this area rich with greenery and bird life. But if it's the drama of the ocean you yearn for, the Cape Cod National Seashore and the Wellfleet Bay Wildlife Sanctuary are both just a short drive away. Contact: Cape Homesteads, 39 River Road, P.O. Box 1213, East Orleans, MA 02643. Call 508-255-5083.

Children: Y Pets: N Smoking: Y Handicap Access: N Payment: C, P, T

SWAMPSCOTT

CAP'N JACK'S WATERFRONT INN   *Rates: budget*
Open: year-round   *Minimum Stay: none*

Situated just a scant ten miles north of Boston and Logan Airport, this casual resort offers one- and two-bedroom apartments with full kitchens, many with private balconies or sitting areas overlooking the water. Cap'n Jack's features two swimming pools and a Jacuzzi as well as a lawn and patio. For those with a yen for the ocean, you'll find the sandy public beaches within walking distance. Located on the historic North Shore, with Salem, Marblehead and Lynn just a short drive away, this is the perfect spot from which to tour the villages whose very names resound with history. The inn also offers easy access to many of the ski slopes of northeastern Massachusetts. Contact: Chris Roddy, Cap'n Jack's Waterfront Inn, 253 Humphrey Street, Swampscott, MA 01907. Call 617-595-7910.

Children: Y Pets: N Smoking: Y Handicap Access: N Payment: C, T, V, M

TRURO

KALMAR VILLAGE	Rates: budget-expensive
Open: May 26-October 10	Minimum Stay: three nights

A tidy little colony of white Cape Cod cottages, these two- and three-room efficiencies accommodate from four to eight people in surroundings that feature green lawns, picnic tables, benches and lawn chairs, all right on the beach of Cape Cod Bay. Guests enjoy Kalmar amenities such as a large freshwater swimming pool, color cable TV, charcoal grills, and for the family with young children, a list of available babysitters. There's even daily maid service. Nearby activities such as golf, tennis and bicycling will add variety to your stay here, and of course the miles of gorgeous beach and protected acres of dunes at Cape Cod National Seashore await the wave-counters, people-watchers and beachcombers. Contact: Daniel Prelack, Kalmar Village, Shore Road, Rt. 6A, Truro, MA 02652. Call 508-487-0585.

Children: Y Pets: N Smoking: Y Handicap Access: N Payment: C, T, V, M, O

WEST HARWICH

ATTELA HOUSE	Rates: deluxe
Open: year-round	Minimum Stay: one week

Ideally situated near the elbow of unfailingly picturesque Cape Cod, this two-story, five-bedroom house sleeps ten in "kick up your heels" comfort. The warmly furnished living room has a brick fireplace (one of two), and the kitchen includes a microwave, a dishwasher and a washer/dryer. Outdoors you'll find not only a wide lawn with a picnic table and a grill but also a large swimming pool and Jacuzzi, all with views of Nantucket Sound. A vacation here might be the perfect time to start bicycling the beautiful trails throughout the cape, and day trips to the exquisite beaches of Wellfleet or a ferry ride to Nantucket will reveal the peaceful magic of this lovely place. Contact: Waterfront Rentals, 20 Pilgrim Road, West Yarmouth, MA 02673. Call 508-778-1818.

Children: Y Pets: N Smoking: Y Handicap Access: N Payment: C, P, V, M

WEST YARMOUTH

347 GREAT ISLAND ROAD   *Rates: moderate-deluxe*
Open: year-round   *Minimum Stay: one week*

Fantastic views abound from this traditional Cape Cod home for eight, and its private beach just beyond the backyard. A large family can sprawl here, with room for a quiet nap on the deck, a rousing game of Scrabble at the picnic table, a serious heart-to-heart on the porch or a lively match of Frisbee right on the beach. The handsomely furnished home features a living room with a fireplace and cable TV as well as a large dining area; the kitchen includes a microwave, a lobster pot and a dishwasher; and everyone will appreciate the washer/dryer. You'll find golf and tennis nearby as well as more clam chowder and oyster stew than you can shake a stick at. And if you're a lover of magnificent homes, a drive through neighboring Hyannis Port will dazzle you. Contact: Waterfront Rentals, 20 Pilgrim Road, West Yarmouth, MA 02673. Call 508-778-1818.

Children: Y Pets: N Smoking: Y Handicap Access: N Payment: C, P, V, M

9 PILGRIM ROAD   *Rates: expensive-deluxe*
Open: year-round   *Minimum Stay: one week*

This traditional Cape Cod beach house enjoys some of the best views imaginable, with the wonderful shore around West Yarmouth and Point Gammon spread out before you as unspoiled as can be. Situated in a quiet family neighborhood only a few steps from the beach, this home features four bedrooms (one double, two twin, one king), two baths, a living room with a fireplace and cable TV and an especially bright and user-friendly kitchen. The spacious yard and two large and private decks show the water in all its glory; here you'll also find a grill, a picnic table and plenty of lawn chairs for stretching and snoozing. Pack a picnic hamper and jump on the ferry to Nantucket Island for a look at the Whaling Museum and a walk on its unspoiled beaches. Contact: Waterfront Rentals, 20 Pilgrim Road, West Yarmouth, MA 02673. Call 508-778-1818.

Children: Y Pets: N Smoking: Y Handicap Access: N Payment: C, P, V, M

SMITHLIN HOUSE   *Rates: budget*
Open: year-round   *Minimum Stay: one week*

"You're sure to fall in love with old Cape Cod," or so the song goes, and this charming two-bedroom home may see to it that you do. Situated in a quiet residential area surrounded by pines and old woods, the house includes a living room with a cozy fireplace and cable TV, a screened/glassed-in porch and the gracious outdoor features of a patio furnished with lawn chairs, a picnic table and a grill. Nature lovers can go bird-watching at some of the many ponds or stroll along the dunes and beaches of Wellfleet Wildlife Sanctuary. The area abounds with fabulous bicycle trails, where the sea air and beautiful light create the serene beauty of this much-loved piece of the U.S. Contact: Waterfront Rentals, 20 Pilgrim Road, West Yarmouth, MA 02673. Call 508-778-1818.

Children: Y Pets: N Smoking: Y Handicap Access: N Payment: C, P, V, M

THE PETERS HOME   *Rates: deluxe*
Open: year-round   *Minimum Stay: one week*

From the many-windowed walls and spacious deck of this fine house for seven, you'll enjoy undisturbed views of the Atlantic, the constancy of the Nantucket Sound surf, the cries of the sea gulls and a seascape interrupted only by the silhouettes of trawling fishing vessels. Conveniences here include a cable TV, a washer/dryer and a dishwasher. Plentiful lawn chairs, a picnic table, a grill, a deck and a patio enhance the hours of outdoor living. And it's only steps to the beach, where the play of the water on your bare feet will drive away all the stress of day-to-day life. Cape Cod offers fine whale-watching as well as terrific deep-sea fishing. Tamer pursuits like golf, tennis, fine dining and dancing are equally available. Contact: Waterfront Rentals, 20 Pilgrim Road, West Yarmouth, MA 02673. Call 508-778-1818.

Children: Y Pets: N Smoking: Y Handicap Access: N Payment: C, P, V, M

WESTWOOD

THE SCHOOLHOUSE   *Rates: moderate*
Open: year-round   *Minimum Stay: none*

Built in 1720 as the first public school building in the United States, this two-bedroom townhouse retains many of its original historic features in addition to updated amenities. Accommodations for six include a full kitchen, a large dining area, a charming living room and two baths. You'll also enjoy the deck overlooking the in-ground pool. Situated just 15 miles west of Boston, this vacation home affords you the peace and quiet of a very special suburban rental and the convenience of easy access to Boston and the Boston area's ski and beach spots. Contact: Bed and Breakfast Associates, Bay Colony Ltd., P.O. Box 166, Babson Park Branch, Boston, MA 02157. Call 617-449-5302.

Children: Y Pets: N Smoking: Y Handicap: N Payment: C, P, T, V, M, A

Michigan

ACME

GRAND TRAVERSE RESORT VILLAGE *Rates: budget-deluxe*
Open: year-round *Minimum Stay: none*

These luxurious condominiums are wonderful bases for exploring the treasures of northern Michigan. Orchards filled with pink cherry blossoms in the spring and golden woodlands in the autumn provide the backdrop for a plethora of activities. Swimming, fishing, water sports, cross-country and downhill skiing, hiking along the Sleeping Bear Dunes National Lakeshore, or enjoying the annual Cherry Festival will keep you busy here. A pool, sauna, hot tub, tennis courts, health club, game room and golf are available at the resort, in case you have a spare moment to fill. Activities are planned for the kids at the resort and babysitters are available so the whole family can get some much-needed relaxation. Contact: Grand Traverse Resort Village, 6300 N. U.S. 31, Acme, MI 49610. Call 1-800-678-1308 (in Michigan, 616-938-2100). Children: Y Pets: N Smoking: Y Handicap Access: Y Payment: C, P, A, V, M

AU TRAIN

LA VALLEY'S LODGE AND CABINS *Rates: budget*
Open: June-February *Minimum Stay: two nights*

A quiet retreat on the northern shore of Michigan's Upper Peninsula, Au Train offers a diverse range of outdoor activities. The Au Train River is a pleasant, meandering waterway ideal for canoeing and the Hiawatha National Forest offers marvelous hikes. Swimming, scuba diving, hunting, fishing, snowmobiling and cross-country and down-hill skiing can all be enjoyed nearby. It is also an excellent area for mountain biking, and there is an Au Train Songbird Trail for bird lovers. The rustic cabins on the edge of picturesque Au Train Lake can accommodate either four or eight guests. Some feature cozy Franklin stoves and all enjoy marvelous views. Contact: Harold Boaz, La Valley's Lodge and Cabins, P.O. Box 99, Au Train Lake Rd., Au Train, MI 49806. Call 906-892-8455.

Children: Y   Pets: N   Smoking: Y   Handicap Access: N   Payment: C, P, T

BEULAH

LAKESIDE DREAM	*Rates: inexpensive*
Open: June-September	*Minimum Stay: one week*

Ideal for families or small groups who yearn to spend the lazy days of summer in a quiet spot on the water's edge, this lovely home is located on the northern shore of Crystal Lake. The house has its own private beach and dock across the road. After a day of exploring the woods, splashing in the water and resting on the shore, curl up in front of a cheery fire in the fireplace inside. Modern amenities in this rustic retreat include a color TV, a dishwasher, a microwave, a washing machine and a telephone; three bedrooms provide comfy sleeping quarters. The Sleeping Bear Dunes National Lakeshore, just to your north, is a magnificent legacy of Michigan's glacial past: Rugged bluffs of sand and stone rise almost 500 feet above the lake. Contact: Crystal Rentals, P.O. Box 145, Copemish, MI 49625. Call 616-378-4229 or 616-352-9601. Ref. 7.

Children: Y   Pets: Y   Smoking: Y   Handicap Access: N   Payment: C, P, T

SOUTH SHORE LODGE	*Rates: moderate*
Open: year-round	*Minimum Stay: one week*

From the spacious wraparound deck of this stylish contemporary home you can enjoy marvelous panoramic views of Crystal Lake—the sunsets here are particularly spectacular. The house boasts its own private beach complete with a dock; both a raft and a canoe are at your disposal for exploring the shore, challenging the wits of the local fish or enjoying a picnic out on the lake. Despite the pleasantly rustic environs of this lakefront house sheltered by shade trees, the two bathrooms and kitchen are well equipped with modern amenities; the house has both a washer and a dryer. Up to 10 guests will find comfy sleeping quarters in the four bedrooms. Contact: Crystal Rentals, P.O. Box 145, Copemish, MI 49625. Call 616-378-4229 or 616-352-9601. Ref. 6.

Children: Y   Pets: Y   Smoking: Y   Handicap Access: N   Payment: C, P, T

DRUMMOND ISLAND

CAPTAIN'S COVE RESORT	*Rates: budget*
Open: year-round	*Minimum Stay: three nights*

An unspoiled handful of land in the northernmost reaches of Lake Huron, Drummond Island is a paradise for anglers, hunters and other outdoorsy types. The walleye, northern pike and jumbo perch fishing in the spring and fall are renowned; the salmon, cisco, smallmouth bass and herring catches are also quite good. The Captain's Cove offers comfortable, well-equipped cabins of various sizes; some have microwaves and each enjoys the idiosyncratic northern boon of a 16-foot boat. The resort also boasts a swimming pool, outdoor grills and picnic areas. Drummond Island is a splendid place for nature hikes, cross-country skiing, swimming, scuba-diving and just hanging out; there are also cruise tours of the nearby islands. Contact: Trish and Alan, Captain's Cove Resort, H.C. 52, 189 Tourist Rd., Drummond Island, MI 49726. Call 906-493-5344.

Children: Y   Pets: N   Smoking: Y   Handicap Access: N   Payment: C, P, T

DOMINO'S LODGE   *Rates: budget-deluxe*
Open: year-round   *Minimum Stay: none*

This charming rustic retreat combines excellent modern amenities with a respect for the tranquil beauty of Michigan's wilderness. Sparky Anderson and Bo Schembechler have cabins here, and Bob Hope has picked out his favorite hole on the championship golf course, so if you grow to love Domino's, you'll be in good company. The amazingly beautiful golf course (there's a pro available to give you a few pointers) has recently been joined by a bowling alley, gym and swimming pool. Of course, the many sporting possibilities of Drummond Island are at your doorstep as well. Quaint Arcadian quarters are found in the two-, three- and four-bedroom cabins. Contact: Rose Marie Alto, Domino's Lodge, H.C. 52, P.O. Box 26, Drummond Island, MI 49726. Call 1-800-999-6343 (in Michigan, 1-906-493-1000).

Children: Y   Pets: Y   Smoking: Y   Handicap Access: N   Payment: All

LAKE VIEW RESORT   *Rates: budget*
Open: April-October   *Minimum Stay: one week*

The plentiful fish and game of Drummond Island act like a magnet, attracting anglers and hunters from across the country. There are plenty of gentle pursuits available on this splendid isle as well: swimming and sunbathing on the sandy beaches, canoeing up the Potagannissing Bay, bird-watching, mushroom picking and hiking on the miles of backwoods trails. Each of the two- and three-bedroom cottages at the Lake View Resort is fully equipped with a complete kitchen; one of the larger cottages features a ramp and extra-wide doorways for the ease of wheelchair users. And of course, the use of a 16-foot Lone Star boat with motor is included. Contact: Lake View Resort, Box 24, Tourist Rd., Drummond Island, MI 49726. Call 906-493-5241.

Children: Y   Pets: Y   Smoking: Y   Handicap Access: Y   Payment: C, P, T

FRANKFORT

BETSIE BAY CONDO   *Rates: budget*
Open: year-round   *Minimum Stay: one week*

Frankfort is a bustling Lake Michigan port surrounded by high bluffs and flanked by wonderful sandy beaches. Yachters, sailors, anglers and boaters of all descriptions will find excellent facilities here; those whose aquatic pursuits are limited to swimming and sunbathing will find ample opportunities as well. This modern condo for four people enjoys lovely views of the bay from its perch on the water's edge. The cheery open fireplace adds a touch of old-world charm and the condo is well equipped with modern conveniences. This is the perfect place to learn why Michigan is known as the "Winter Water Wonderland." Contact: Crystal Rentals, P.O. Box 145, Copemish, MI 49625. Call 616-378-4229 or 616-352-9601. Ref. 90.

Children: Y   Pets: Y   Smoking: Y   Handicap Access: N   Payment: C, P, T

BIRCHWOOD TERRACE	Rates: budget
Open: June-September	Minimum Stay: one week

Along the western edge of shimmering Crystal Lake on the narrow strip of land that separates it from the mighty waters of Lake Michigan, you'll find this pleasant little cottage for five. Surrounded by quiet woods and just a short walk from the beach, the three-bedroom house is cozy and comfortable. The blazing open fire adds another touch of northern cheer, just the place to curl up after a day of freshwater fishing or a brisk walk through the woods. Since you're already this close, don't neglect to spend a day or two on the magnificent coast of Lake Michigan, one of the largest freshwater lakes in the world. Contact: Crystal Rentals, P.O. Box 145, Copemish, MI 49625. Call 616-378-4229 or 616-352-9601. Ref. 26.

Children: Y   Pets: Y   Smoking: Y   Handicap Access: N   Payment: C, P, T

HONOR

BIXLER ROAD COTTAGE	Rates: moderate
Open: June-September	Minimum Stay: one week

This lovely house is splendidly situated on two acres of lakeside property and enjoys stunning views of Big Platte Lake's crystalline waters. Outside you'll find a spacious screened-in boathouse on the water's edge, with both an upper and a lower patio where you can sit out and enjoy your beautiful surroundings over a glass of Michigan's homegrown wine. When the cool breezes of the evening chase you back inside, you can curl up in front of the open fire or stretch out in front of the TV before retiring to one of the four spacious bedrooms. The dishwasher, three bathrooms and other modern amenities help transform this bucolic getaway into a luxurious abode. Contact: Crystal Rentals, P.O. Box 145, Copemish, MI 49625. Call 616-378-4229 or 616-352-9601.

Children: Y   Pets: Y   Smoking: Y   Handicap Access: N   Payment: C, P, T

SANDY SECLUSION	Rates: moderate
Open: June-September	Minimum Stay: one week

This secluded home is tucked away on a tranquil stretch of Platte Lake's lovely shoreline. Offering a panoramic view of the lake and a generous private beach, it's an ideal spot for those who want to get away from it all. The three comfy bedrooms can accommodate up to seven people and the cozy open fire will draw friends and family together at the end of a day that's all too short. Modern conveniences include two bathrooms and a washing machine. In case the peace and quiet proves too great a shock to your system, the restaurants and night spots of Beulah and Frankfort are nearby, and the musical and theatrical delights of Interlochen are right around the corner. Contact: Crystal Rentals, P.O. Box 145, Copemish, MI 49625. Call 616-378-4229 or 616-352-9601. Ref. 28.

Children: Y   Pets: Y   Smoking: Y   Handicap Access: N   Payment: C, P, T

HOUGHTON

ROCK HARBOR LODGE *Rates: inexpensive-moderate*
Open: May-September *Minimum Stay: none*

Lapped by the icy waters of Lake Superior, northernmost of the Great Lakes, pristine Isle Royale National Park is a serene corner of wilderness far from the bustle and grime of everyday life. Breathe deep of the cool, clean air and enjoy the pleasant sound of silence (no cars are allowed on the island). Here, Rock Harbor Lodge offers both one-bedroom units with complimentary meals and cottages with complete kitchens. From this base you can enjoy the myriad pleasures of Isle Royale: hiking through moss-covered woodland trails in pursuit of the elusive moose, trying to outwit the sturdy lake trout, rowing out to a secluded inlet for a picnic lunch, or enjoying cruises on the shimmering blue waters of Lake Superior. Contact: Ron Sanders, National Park Concessions, P.O. Box 405, Houghton, MI 49931-0405. Call 906-337-4993 or 502-773-2191.

Children: Y   Pets: N   Smoking: Y   Handicap Access: N   Payment: All

IRON MOUNTAIN

PINE MOUNTAIN *Rates: budget-moderate*
Open: year-round *Minimum Stay: none*

First established in 1939 by Fred Pabst of beer-brewing fame, Pine Mountain has been welcoming skiers for generations. The charming alpine lodge at the base of the mountain is quiet and secluded. The lodge boasts a sparkling indoor pool, a soothing hot tub, the friendly Edelweiss Lounge and the excellent Alpine Dining Room. It offers two groups of luxury condominiums designed to pamper you with comfortable beds and cable TVs. Excellent downhill and cross-country skiing top the list of popular winter activities in this neck of the woods, but don't overlook the summer options: The water sports, golfing, tennis and hiking are all superb. Contact: Laird Trepp, Pine Mountain, N3332 Pine Mountain Rd., Iron Mountain, MI 49801. Call 1-800-321-6298 (in Michigan, 906-774-2747).

Children: Y Pets: Y Smoking: Y Handicap Access: N Payment: C, P, T, V, M

ONTONAGON

LAMBERT'S CHALET COTTAGES *Rates: budget*
Open: year-round *Minimum Stay: three nights*

On the northern coast of the Upper Peninsula, just about as far north as you can go in the Lower 48, you'll find these charming alpine cottages surrounded by rugged woodlands. The one- and two-bedroom cottages combine the rustic look of wood paneling with the modern comfort of gas heat and wall-to-wall carpeting; some boast wood-burning fireplaces. There are also two spacious lodges for larger groups; the furnishings here feature the best of rustic elegance, with beamed ceilings, cedar and black cherry paneling, stone fireplaces and sunken living rooms. The paddle boats, canoes, grills, playground, cable TV and snowshoes will add to your year-round enjoyment. Contact: Dick and Marlene Lambert, Lambert's Chalet Cottages, 287 Lakeshore Rd., Ontonagon, MI 49953. Call 906-884-4230.

Children: Y   Pets: N   Smoking: Y   Handicap Access: N   Payment: All

THOMPSONVILLE

MOUNTAIN REST
Rates: expensive-deluxe
Open: year-round
Minimum Stay: one week

Large groups of skiers, golfers, or anglers will be pleasantly surprised by the accommodations at this splendid house. An impressive 20 people will find sleeping quarters in the six spacious bedrooms; you can golf or ski right from the back door. There's a large deck for sitting outside and swapping fish stories, and the handsome fireplace inside is perfect for an after-ski toddy. The cable TV will keep you in touch with the modern world and the microwave will help you with your modern culinary creations. Contact: Crystal Rentals, P.O. Box 145, Copemish, MI 49625. Call 616-378-4229 or 616-352-9601. Ref. 143.

Children: Y   Pets: Y   Smoking: Y   Handicap Access: N   Payment: C, P, T

RIVER RANCH
Rates: moderate
Open: year-round
Minimum Stay: one week

This sprawling three-bedroom house stands right on the banks of the idyllic Betsie River. The enclosed porch is the perfect place to watch the water glide by as the tall trees sway in the gentle wind; in the fall, the foliage in this area is ablaze with color. You can cross-country ski or fish right from your back door, and the excellent downhill slopes of Crystal Mountain are less than a mile away. The house includes two full bathrooms, a washer and dryer and a dishwasher. Both a TV and a handsome open fireplace provide evening relaxation. Contact: Crystal Rentals, P.O. Box 145, Copemish, MI 49625. Call 616-378-4229 or 616-352-9601. Ref. 146.

Children: Y   Pets: Y   Smoking: Y   Handicap Access: N   Payment: C, P, T

SEVENTEENTH FAIRWAY HOUSE
Rates: moderate
Open: year-round
Minimum Stay: one week

The Crystal Mountain area is a year-round paradise for outdoorsy types. In the spring and summer there's swimming, canoeing, fishing, golfing and hiking to keep you busy. Leaf-peeping and walks through the fragrant woods become popular activities during the autumn season. Winter diversions include downhill and cross-country skiing and horse-drawn sleigh rides. This lovely home surrounded by tall trees is right across from the golf course; it can accommodate up to 10 people in its three bedrooms. The fireplace and Jacuzzi add to its charm as a festive holiday spot, while the washer and dryer augment its convenience. Contact: Crystal Rentals, P.O. Box 145, Copemish, MI 49625. Call 616-378-4229 or 616-352-9601. Ref. 91.

Children: Y   Pets: Y   Smoking: Y   Handicap Access: N   Payment: C, P, T

TRAVERSE CITY

L'DA RU LAKESIDE RESORT   *Rates: budget-inexpensive*
Open: year-round   *Minimum Stay: two nights*

Originally built as a hideout for Al Capone, L'Da Ru today is a splendid holiday resort in the Michigan northwoods. Each of the two- or three-bedroom cabins is spacious and fully carpeted and comes with its own boat. Out on Spider Lake, there's probably enough swimming, fishing, waterskiing and boating to keep you busy; if not, there are three other lakes nearby. There's a playground for the little ones and group activities such as basketball and volleyball are available for kids of all ages. Tennis, croquet, shuffleboard, horseshoes, a game room and a sauna can all be enjoyed here, and an 18-hole golf course is available nearby. In the winter you can not only ski and snowmobile, but there are fishing shanties for intrepid ice fishers. Contact: Jill Rye, L'Da Ru Lakeside Resort, 4370 N. Spider Lake Rd., Traverse City, MI 49684. Call 616-946-8999.

Children: Y Pets: N Smoking: Y Handicap Access: N Payment: C, P, T, V, M

ON THE BAY   *Rates: budget-moderate*
Open: year-round   *Minimum Stay: one week*

You'll find this friendly resort on Grand Traverse Bay's Miracle Mile, a stretch of peaceful shoreline blessed with soft sugar-sand beaches. On the Bay offers a variety of accommodations, from small motel rooms complete with refrigerators and microwaves to large two-bedroom cottages with full kitchens. Some units are air-conditioned and all boast a location that's wonderfully close to the swimming and sunning on the beach. If you're in town during the beginning of July, don't miss the Cherry Festival, an annual celebration of Michigan's status as one of the world's largest producers of sweet and tart cherries. Contact: Steve and Pat Avery, On the Bay, 1773 U.S. 31 N., Traverse City, MI 49684. Call 616-938-2680.

Children: Y   Pets: N   Smoking: Y   Handicap Access: Y   Payment: C, T, V, M

Minnesota

AITKIN

MCDONNELL'S MORNINGSIDE RESORT   *Rates: budget*

Open: May-September   *Minimum Stay: one week*

This family resort located on a large bay on the east side of Cedar Lake is set in a serene and densely wooded area famous for its breathtaking sunsets and beautiful 110-mile-long shoreline. One-, two- and three-bedroom cabins—all exceptionally clean and fitted with showers, comfortable furniture and old-fashioned comforters—accommodate two, four and six guests at budget rates that include the use of boats, canoes, water bikes and all facilities. Two fishing docks are cleverly designed to accommodate children and adults; a large play area by the beach is fitted with swings, volleyball court, clock golf course, croquet area and horsehoe pits. Additionally, the lodge itself is fully equipped with "rainy day" games, a library, laundry, office and fish freezer. Contact: Adele and Pat McDonnell, Morningside Resort, Rte. 3, Box 163, Aitkin, MN 56431. Call 218-927-2708 or 800-346-6166.

Children: Y   Pets: N   Smoking: Y   Handicap Access: N   Payment: C, P, T

ANGLE INLET

NORTHWEST ANGLE RESORT   *Rates: budget*

Open: year-round   *Minimum Stay: none*

Fly onto the private airstrip or drive up to the scenic entrance of Northwest Angle Resort, located in a magnificent tract of rugged, serene wilderness famous for its great fishing in clean Minnesota and

Canadian waters. Cabins and apartments offer two, three and four bedrooms accommodating two to 12 guests in fully furnished units outfitted with every convenience, including air conditioning, carpeting and full bathrooms. Outside, a heated swimming pool is framed by clusters of lounge chairs and tables—ideal for an outdoor barbecue or just a relaxing visit with other guests. And for anglers who can tear themselves away for a few hours, many local attractions are well worth a visit, including historic Fort St. Charles and nearby Winnipeg. Contact: Shari Nunn, Northwest Angle Resort, Box 68, Angle Inlet, MN 56711. Call 218-386-2963 or 800-366-2963

Children: Y Pets: Y Smoking: Y Handicap Access: N Payment: C, P, T, V, M

BREEZY POINT

| BREEZY POINT INTERNATIONAL | Rates: budget-deluxe |
| Open: year-round | Minimum Stay: none |

This deluxe resort set on the shores of Big Pelican Lake offers studios and one- and two-bedroom condos that accommodate two, four and six people. Summer visitors can reach the tennis court, golf course or the shore in just minutes, and afterwards soothe tired muscles in a private Jacuzzi. Winter guests will love the highly praised local ski slopes and relax at night in front of their own cozy fireplace. There is diversion for all members of the family in upbeat recreation programs for adults and children; a staff of experienced baby-sitters give Mom and Dad extra free moments to enjoy the charming antique stores and boutiques. Contact: Breezy Point International, HCR 2, Box 70, Breezy Point, MN 56472. Call 218-562-7811 or 800-328-2284

Children: Y Pets: N Smoking: Y Handicap Access: Y Payment: C, T, A, V, M

DEERWOOD

| RUTTGERS BAY LODGE AND CONFERENCE CENTER | Rates: budget-deluxe |
| Open: year-round | Minimum Stay: none |

This golf course resort features one- and two-bedroom condominiums overlooking the course, plus villas, also accommodating two to four guests, that adjoin the indoor pool. Winter vacationers will be delighted by cross-country ski trails and old-fashioned sleigh rides. Summer visitors can deposit the children at Kid's Kamp while they tee off on the golf course or spend a leisurely afternoon fishing. The nearby marina—fully stocked with tackle and bait—also provides rental boats; tennis courts and a pool are less than a mile away. Guests of all ages will enjoy the critically acclaimed summer theater, historical museums, antique shows, and regional festivals that the Brainerd Lakes area is famous for. Contact: Ruttgers Bay Lodge and Conference Center, Box 400, Deerwood, MN 56444. Call 218-678-2885 or 800-328-0312.

Children: Y Pets: N Smoking: Y Handicap Access: N Payment: C, P, T, V, M, O

DETROIT LAKES

BREEZY SHORES RESORT
Open: year-round

Rates: budget
Minimum Stay: none

This all-season resort features two-bedroom, two-story townhouses that comfortably sleep at least four people and come complete with fireplaces, decks and balconies. Summer guests need not leave the premises to luxuriate on 800 feet of private beach or enjoy summer boating and water sports. And those who prefer an afternoon of golf or tennis can do it nearby. Winter visitors will love ice fishing, snowmobiling, skiing and ice skating before heading home to unwind in the indoor pool, sauna and whirlpool. And a game room and social area beckon all members of the family. Contact: Breezy Shores Resort, 1275 West Lake Drive, Detroit Lakes, MN 56501. Call 218-847-2695 or 800-346-4978.

Children: Y Pets: N Smoking: Y Handicap Access: N Payment: C, P, T, V, M

EDGEWATER BEACH CLUB
Open: year-round

Rates: budget-inexpensive
Minimum Stay: none

This family resort of two-bedroom low-rise apartments, comfortably sleeping at least four people each, combines the relaxed charm of country life with the convenience and excitement of town living. A favorite home base for skiers heading for popular Detroit Mountain, the club lets guests soothe tired muscles in the (indoor and outdoor) pools and sauna. Warm-weather visitors can enjoy virtually every type of summer recreation at the nearby lake, beach, marina, tennis court, miniature golf center, park and playground. And unique area attractions—particularly the Tamarac Wildlife Refuge, the Soo-Pass Dude Ranch and Itasca State Park—are special treats for the entire family all year round. Contact: Edgewater Beach Club, 321 Park Blvd., Detroit Lakes, MN 56501. Call 218-847-1351.

Children: Y Pets: N Smoking: Y Handicap Access: N Payment: C, P, T, V, M

HILL CITY

QUADNA MOUNTAIN VACATION CLUB
Open: year-round

Rates: budget-inexpensive
Minimum Stay: none

This vacation village offers one-bedroom villas and townhouses—comfortably sleeping at least two—that feature modern amenities in a rustic setting. Each season brings special treats for the entire family: Winter guests delight in area skiing; autumn vacationers enjoy the fall foliage and superb hunting; and spring and summer visitors favor fishing and water sports. Additionally, the resort offers a diverse range of activities that family members can enjoy together, from indoor and outdoor pools and tennis courts to the old-fashioned pleasures of horseshoes, badminton, croquet, bocce, and shuffleboard. Contact: Quadna Mountain Vacation Club, 100 Quadna Road, Hill City, MN 55748. Call 218-697-8133 or 800-422-6649.

Children: Y Pets: N Smoking: Y Handicap Access: N Payment: C, P, T, A, V, M

LUTSEN

THE VILLAGE INN AND RESORT *Rates: budget-moderate*
Open: year-round *Minimum Stay: none*

This resort village, featuring one- and two-bedroom condominiums and townhouses that accommodate two to four people, is ideally situated within the scenic Sawtooth Mountain Range on Lake Superior's North Shore. Horseback riding is the featured attraction; both novice and experienced riders delight in breakfast rides, overnights and hay rides. The grounds also boast an indoor pool, Jacuzzi, tennis and volleyball courts, lawn games and, for winter visitors, an alpine slide. The Boundary Waters canoe area is nearby, and visitors won't want to miss the music festivals, art fairs, a golf course and some of the best hiking and fishing in the area. Contact: The Village Inn and Resort, P.O. Box 26, Lutsen, MN 55612. Call 218-663-7241.

Children: Y Pets: N Smoking: Y Handicap Access: N Payment: C, P, T, V, M

Sardis

★ Jackson

Gulfport

Biloxi

Mississippi

GULFPORT

CHATEAU DE LA MER   *Rates: budget-inexpensive*
Open: year-round   *Minimum Stay: one week*

With a white, sandy beach and the warm, inviting waters of the Gulf of Mexico right across the street, Chateau de la Mer is an idyllic spot for a Mississippi River holiday. Each condo unit faces the gulf and contains a master suite with a queen-sized bed, a bunk-bed-equipped alcove, a living room and dining area and fully equipped kitchen, plus a spacious private balcony for enjoying the sweeping coastal view. The grounds offer a swimming pool and tennis courts, while sailing, waterskiing, fishing, and a slew of other aquatic sports, not to mention opportunities for sightseeing cruises and golfing, are available nearby. Contact: Chateau de la Mer, 1410 Beach Blvd., Gulfport, MS 39507. Call 1-601-896-1703 or 1-800-257-5551.

Children: Y Pets: N Smoking: Y Handicap Access: N Payment: C, T, V, M, A

GAYLE'S COTTAGES   *Rates: budget-inexpensive*
Open: year-round   *Minimum Stay: none*

This attractive cottage duplex lies nestled under giant oaks and gracious magnolias 200 yards from the beach on the Gulf Coast between Gulfport and Biloxi. Opening onto a large deck equipped with barbecue pits, lounges, and tables and chairs, each one- and two-bedroom unit contains a full kitchen, living room with a bar and additional sleeping accommodations. The owners have a brand-new 29-foot Cris-craft that may be chartered for fishing trips or excursions to nearby Ship Island, and there's an 18-hole golf course right on the property for guests' complimentary use. Contact: Gayle Badeaux, 143-A Teagarden, Gulfport, MS 39507. Call 1-601-896-8266.

Children: Y Pets: N Smoking: Y Handicap Access: N Payment: C, T, V, M

SHORELINE OAKS   *Rates: budget-inexpensive*
Open: year-round   *Minimum Stay: two nights*

Shoreline Oaks gives guests the chance to enjoy a fine mixture of sightseeing opportunities and sports activities, plus plenty of time to relax under the sun, soothed by gentle gulf breezes. Located right on the beach in a region that abounds in antebellum landmarks, Civil War sites and other spots of historic interest, the complex offers fully equipped one- and two-bedroom apartments, with the grounds featuring a swimming pool and hot tubs. Nearby, a vast array of water sports facilities are available, as well as casino cruises, expeditions to the intriguing offshore islands of the Mississippi Coast, and a choice of nearly two dozen golf courses. Contact: Shoreline Oaks, 30 East Beach Blvd., P.O. Box 6823, Gulfport, MS 39501. Call 1-605-868-1916.

Children: Y Pets: N Smoking: Y Handicap Access: Y Payment: C, P, T, V, M

SARDIS

JOHN W. KYLE STATE PARK CABINS   *Rates: budget*
Open: year-round   *Minimum Stay: three nights*

Located in the northern part of Mississippi, this picturesque and serene state park provides a number of comfortable and fully equipped housekeeping cabins, each one solidly constructed of rock and wood. Each residence accommodates up to four and offers such pleasant features as a fireplace or a delightful screened porch. Sardis Lake brings the opportunity for a variety of water sports, and the park also has excellent facilities for tennis, hiking, and cycling, as well as downhome activities like hayrides, street dances, bingo games, and swim meets in season. And fans of two of the state's most prominent native sons—William Faulkner and Elvis Presley—have the chance to visit some key landmarks in Oxford and Tupelo, both within easy reach. Contact: Gene Rayburn, Park Manager, John W. Kyle State Park, Route 1, Box 115, Sardis, MS 38666. Call 1-601-487-1345.

Children: Y Pets: Y Smoking: Y Handicap Access: Y Payment: C, P, T, V, M

Missouri

BRANSON

BENTREE LODGE
Rates: budget-inexpensive
Open: year-round
Minimum Stay: four nights

Resting on the water amid peaceful surroundings, Bentree Lodge provides two-, four- and six-bedroom vacation cottages, each fully carpeted with a spacious living room, complete kitchen and a private deck. The grounds include two swimming pools, both with lovely lake views, tennis courts, a hot tub and sauna and a scenic jogging trail. The location is ideal, minutes from the entrance to Silver Dollar City, named by *Newsweek* as one of the country's ten best "off the beaten track" attractions, a family amusement center filled with rides, restaurants and food stands, crafts shops, displays giving fascinating information about the Ozarks region and year-round special events. Contact: Bentree Lodge, Sr. Rt. 1, Box 967, Branson, MO 65616. Call 1-800-272-6766.

Children: Y Pets: N Smoking: Y Handicap Access: N Payment: C, P, T, V, M, O

INDIAN POINT LODGE
Rates: budget-moderate
Open: year-round
Minimum Stay: none

Couples on a first or second honeymoon; families seeking a safe and fun-filled spot for a holiday; and large groups of friends looking to enjoy an Ozark vacation together: Indian Point Lodge, which offers a full array of self-contained residences, from studios to four-bedroom apartments, can accommodate you all. Located on a small wooded point bordered on both sides by quiet lake coves, it is right near Silver Dollar City. Guests can divide their time between enjoying the amusement and entertainment activities of this famous tourist area, the facilities right on the complex—its swimming pool, bustling game room, playground, picnic and lawn game area and private dock—and the multitude of recreational opportunities available throughout the Table Rock Lake area. Contact: Greg and Brenda Maycock, Indian Point Lodge, HCR 1, Box 982, Branson, MO 65616. Call 1-417-338-2250.

Children: Y Pets: N Smoking: Y Handicap Access: N Payment: C, T, V, M

NOTCH ESTATES CONDOMINIUMS *Rates: budget-inexpensive*
Open: year-round *Minimum Stay: two nights*
One mile west of lively Silver Dollar City and minutes from Table Rock Lake, Notch Estates features a number of two-bedroom townhouses and one- and two-bedroom condominium units, each with a fully equipped kitchen, queen-sized beds and a private balcony offering sweeping views of the Ozarks. Swimmers can choose between the property's private lake and sparkling swimming pool, while hikers of all levels will love the miles of scenic trails that wind deep into the surrounding hill country. The area is also a music lover's haven, with top country-western talents performing at nearby clubs year-round. Contact: Notch Estates, P.O. Box 128, Branson, MO 65616. Call 1-417-338-2941 or 1-800-336-6824.

Children: Y Pets: N Smoking: Y Handicap Access: N Payment: All

POINTE ROYALE *Rates: budget-expensive*
Open: year-round *Minimum Stay: two nights*
Positioned on Lake Taneycomo just below Table Rock Dam, Pointe Royale offers its own verdant 18-hole golf course, tennis courts, a large swimming pool and deck, plus a lounge and snack bar. Tastefully furnished one-, two- and three-bedroom condominiums are available here, each containing a spacious living room, fully equipped kitchen and sunny deck or patio with a lovely view. Whether they opt for fishing or sightseeing, a country-western show or a visit to Silver Dollar City, guests can enjoy a different outing every day in a gloriously scenic and pristine setting. Contact: Pointe Royale, P.O. Box 1988, Branson, MO 65616. Call 1-417-334-5614 or 1-800-962-4710.

Children: Y Pets: N Smoking: Y Handicap Access: N Payment: All

ROCKWOOD RESORT *Rates: budget*
Open: year-round *Minimum Stay: none*
Set on Table Rock Lake in the heart of Missouri's Ozark Mountain country, Rockwood is a friendly holiday community with one- and two-bedroom housekeeping units, each containing a kitchenette, wall-to-wall carpeting, color TV and central air and heating. Everything you need for a complete fishing vacation is available right here, from a concrete ramp for launching your own boat, rental vessels and guides, a private, lighted and covered boat deck that can be used day or night

in any kind of weather and plenty of barbecues and picnic tables for enjoying your catch of the day in the tranquil and scenic outdoors. There's also a sparkling swimming pool right on the grounds and plenty of other recreational activities on the lake and river. Contact: Barbara and Jerry Richards, SR 1, Box 1162, Indian Point, Branson, MO 65616. Call 1-417-338-2470.

Children: Y Pets: N Smoking: Y Handicap Access: N Payment: C, T, V, M

SAMMY LANE RESORT *Rates: budget-moderate*
Open: year round *Minimum Stay: three nights*

Located near the heart of downtown Branson on Lake Taneycomo, Sammy Lane is the town's oldest resort, as well as one of its loveliest. Here, among shady trees, are cozy studio cabins and elegant three-bedroom cottages, as well as units of intermediate size, all combining rustic charm and homelike comfort. Take a soak in the hot tub or a dip in the huge, glimmering swimming pool, or embark on a fishing expedition of Taneycomo, a beautiful lake formed in 1913 with the completion of Table Rock Dam. Guests will also want to explore Branson, the region's most popular town, which brims with craft shops, family attractions and rousing down-home country-western shows. Contact: Mike and Claudia Brown, Sammy Lane Resort, 320 East Main Street, Branson, MO 65616. Call 1-417-334-3253.

Children: Y Pets: N Smoking: Y Handicap Access: N Payment: C, P, T

TABLE ROCK COTTAGE *Rates: budget-inexpensive*
Open: year-round *Minimum Stay: none*

A private bed and breakfast residence with full housekeeping facilities, this attractive cottage sits right on Table Rock Lake, with a private fishing and boat dock. Continental breakfast, of course, is complimentary, as is use of a paddle boat with which guests can roam the lake. The house contains a comfy sitting area with an inviting fireplace, a bedroom with a queen-sized bed, a complete kitchenette and a secluded patio ideal for idling the mild Ozark days away. Contact: Kay Cameron, Ozark Mountain Country Bed and Breakfast, Box 295, Branson, MO 65616. Call 1-417-334-4720 or 1-800-321-8594. Ref. OMC 104.

Children: Y Pets: Y Smoking: N Handicap Access: N Payment: All

THE TRIBESMAN RESORT *Rates: budget-moderate*
Open: year-round *Minimum Stay: none*

Families with young children will especially delight in the singular features of Table Rock Lake's Tribesman Resort. There's a special fishing hole just for kids, paddle boats for rent that even youngsters can easily maneuver, a video arcade, three swimming pools, a friendly family of ducks and, in the summer, special guest programs—lake cruises, scavenger hunts and group picnics, to mention a few—every day of the week. The accommodations are located in four complexes, each offering a different but equally pleasant rustic setting, from a wooded glen to a panoramic hillside. All kinds of full housekeeping units house couples, large groups vacationing together and any size party in between. Contact: Arno and Gayle Wehr, The Tribesman Resort, Rt. 1, Box 1032, Branson, MO 65616. Call 1-417-338-2616.

Children: Y   Pets: N   Smoking: Y   Handicap Access: N   Payment: All

WIGWAM RESORT   *Rates: budget-inexpensive*
Open: March-December   *Minimum Stay: none*

Wigwam Resort is poised on an Indian Point hillside blanketed with gentle oaks and cedars, home to deer, quail, turkey and a profusion of other wildlife. Comfortable studio, one- and two-bedroom residences are available, all with full kitchens. The larger units each feature a private deck that commands a sweeping view of the lake. The property is set far off the main road to provide peace and seclusion, but is also conveniently located near the Indian Point boat dock and many top attractions of the region. Contact: Verlyn and Glen Dora Moe, Wigwam Resort, HCR 1, Box 1107, Branson, MO 65616. Call 1-417-338-2209.

Children: Y Pets: N Smoking: Y Handicap Access: N Payment: C, P, T, V, M

GALENA

LAKE COUNTRY RESORT AND GOLF CLUB   *Rates: budget-inexpensive*
Open: year-round   *Minimum Stay: two nights*

This attractive holiday retreat offers 16 homey one-, two- and three-bedroom condominiums, each enjoying such pleasing features as cathedral ceilings and lovely views of Table Rock Lake, the surrounding bluffs or the resort's private nine-hole golf course. Besides golfing, the complex also offers tennis, hot tubs and swimming either in the lake or the sparkling and uncrowded swimming pools. Guests will find everything they want in a peaceful Ozark vacation right on the premises, while additional recreational opportunities, as well as fine shopping and dining possibilities, are also available nearby. Contact: Lake Country Resort and Golf Club, Hwy. Y-18, Route 3, Box 91, Galena, MO 65656. Call 1-417-538-2291.

Children: Y Pets: N Smoking: Y Handicap Access: Y Payment: C, T, V, M, A

LAKE OF THE OZARKS

LAKEVIEW RESORT   *Rates: budget-moderate*
Open: year-round   *Minimum Stay: one week*

A number of comfortably appointed cottages, all with full kitchens and private patios overlooking the water, are available at Lakeview Resort on the Lake of the Ozarks. A superb vacation retreat for families, it offers safety and seclusion with a host of recreational facilities, including both an indoor and outdoor swimming pool plus a wading pool for children, two playgrounds, a lavish rec room, tennis court and space for other outside games, gravel beach and anchored swim float, not to mention a dock and fishing pier. Guests love exploring this area, known as "Land of the Magic Dragon" for the lake's serpentine shape, which yields dozens of quiet coves and channels to tempt anglers, nature lovers and sightseers alike. Contact: Lakeview Resort, HCR 69, Box 505B, Sunrise Beach, MO 65079. Call 1-314-374-5555.

Children: Y Pets: N Smoking: Y Handicap Access: N Payment: C, T, A, V, M

THE LODGE OF FOUR SEASONS   *Rates: inexpensive-moderate*
Open: year-round   *Minimum Stay: none*

In its elegant two-bedroom villas, the Lodge of Four Seasons provides comfort and luxury and the makings of an unforgettable holiday any time of year. It's superbly situated in the middle of the state, near unlimited recreational opportunities, natural landmarks and family attractions. Whether at the Lake of the Ozarks State Park, on the lake itself or on the lodge premises, which feature 18-hole golf, tennis, swimming, plus a fitness center and spa, vacationers never lack for plenty to do, where the only thing keeping them from a non-stop schedule is the allure of just sitting back and basking in the utter ease the beautiful setting inspires. Contact: The Lodge of Four Seasons, P.O. Box 215, Lake Road HH, Lake Ozark, MO 65049. Call 1-314-365-3000 or 1-800-365-3001.

Children: Y   Pets: N   Smoking: Y   Handicap Access: N   Payment: C, T,

OSAGE BEACH

HAWK'S NEST CONDOMINIUMS   *Rates: budget-moderate*
Open: year-round   *Minimum Stay: none*

Adjacent to the elegant Inn at Grand Glaize, these comfortable one- and two-bedroom condominiums each offer a fully equipped kitchen, a fireplace and a balcony with a gas barbecue. Condominium guests are welcome to use the inn's extensive facilities, which include a swimming pool, huge whirlpool, tennis court, video arcade, an exercise room and a dock with boat rentals and a fishing guide service. Nearby, vacationers will find a host of family activities like miniature golf, water slides and horseback riding, along with superb craft, antique and factory-outlet shopping and Poverty Flat's delightful Main Street, a facsimile of a Victorian village complete with wooden sidewalks, a wishing well and a waterwheel. Contact: Inn at Grand Glaize, Hwy. 54, Lake Road 40, Osage Beach, MO 65054. Call 1-314-348-4731 or 1-800-348-4731.

Children: Y   Pets: N   Smoking: Y   Handicap Access: N   Payment: C, T, V, M

REEDS SPRING

BAR M RESORT AND CAMPGROUND   *Rates: budget-inexpensive*
Open: year-round   *Minimum Stay: none*

This relaxing private vacation retreat covers ten acres of unspoiled woodlands in peaceful Angel's Cove, which opens onto one of Table Rock Lake's widest waterways. The area is perfect for waterskiing, swimming and fishing, and the Bar M provides boats for hire, plus a launching ramp and slip space for guests who bring their own. Ranging from large and handsome two-story log houses to modern one- and two-bedroom condominium units, the resort has accommodations of distinction to suit parties of almost any size at truly reasonable prices. Contact: Bar M Resort and Campground, HCR 4, Box 2990, Reeds Spring, MO 65737. Call 1-417-338-2593.

Children: Y   Pets: N   Smoking: Y   Handicap Access: N   Payment: C, P, T

GREEN VALLEY RESORT   *Rates: budget-inexpensive*
Open: year-round   *Minimum Stay: three nights*

Everything vacationers desire in a carefree Ozark lake holiday is available at Green Valley Resort. The accommodations include a variety of cabin residences, from the Honeymoon Cabin, containing a bedroom, combination living room and kitchen and a free-standing fireplace, to the Lakeside and Fourplex Cabins, both with two bedrooms and a porch or deck. While the park-like grounds feature such delightful amenities as a swimming pool, shaded lawn swings and plenty of picnic tables for enjoying tranquil outdoor living, the focal point is, of course, Table Rock Lake, considered one of America's five top bass lakes and also filled with crappie, blue gill and catfish. Green Valley's covered, lighted boat dock gives guests all the facilities they need to catch enough to feed the whole family for weeks. Contact: Green Valley Resort, Rt. 4, Box 3470, Reeds Spring, MO 65737. Call 1-417-338-2241.

Children: Y Pets: N Smoking: Y Handicap Access: N Payment: C, P, T, V, M

SPLITRAIL RESORT   *Rates: budget*
Open: year-round   *Minimum Stay: none*

The inviting cabins of Splitrail are tucked in 18 acres of wooded hills and valleys on the shore of Table Rock Lake, only a short drive from all the area's top tourist attractions. Here, peace and seclusion reign. Each self-contained unit is a home of its own, surrounded by trees and overlooking the lake, containing two bedrooms, a living room with additional sleeping space and a fully equipped kitchen, plus a private sun terrace with an outdoor grill for barbecuing fresh-caught fish as dusk falls. Boats are available for hire, either for catching your supper or simply savoring the pristine waters and picturesque surroundings. Contact: Francis and Pat Gongaware, Splitrail Resort, DD Highway, HCR 4, Box 3580, Reeds Spring, MO 65737. Contact: 1-417-338-2350.

Children: Y   Pets: N   Smoking: Y   Handicap Access: N   Payment: C, T

SILVER DOLLAR CITY

1920 COTTAGE   *Rates: budget*
Open: year-round   *Minimum Stay: none*

Built in the 1920s, this handsome guest cottage is only half a mile from Silver Dollar City and equally close to fishing facilities and a number of other fine recreational opportunities. Among the more unusual and popular attractions in the area is "The Shepherd of the Hills," perhaps the nation's most attended outdoor drama, an inspirational theater experience visitors won't soon forget. The refurbished house features elegant antique furniture and contains a parlor, a bedroom, a well-equipped kitchenette and a bathroom with a delightful claw-foot tub. Contact: Kay Cameron, Ozark Mountain Country Bed and Breakfast, Box 295, Branson, MO 65616. Call 1-417-334-4720 or 1-800-321-8594. Ref. OMC 122.

Children: N   Pets: N   Smoking: N   Handicap Access: N   Payment: All

SUNRISE BEACH

LONE OAK POINT RESORT *Rates: budget-inexpensive*
Open: year-round *Minimum Stay: none*
Lone Oak Point Resort offers 33 housekeeping units located on a secluded nine-acre wooded peninsula graced with cool breezes and surrounded by the shimmering waters of the Lake of the Ozarks. Each one-, two- and three-bedroom cottage includes a kitchen and living area as well as a private patio with lawn furniture and a barbecue. On the grounds, guests can indulge in all the fishing they desire using the covered boat stall and heated dock. There are facilities for everyone in the family, including an indoor, an outdoor and a wading pool, a tennis court, playground, lawn game area, a rec room and exercise room with a spa and sauna. Contact: Lone Oak Point Resort, HCR 69, Box 482, Sunrise Beach, MO 65079. Call 1-314-374-7992.

Children: Y Pets: N Smoking: Y Handicap Access: N Payment: C, T, V, M, A

VAN BUREN

BIG SPRING LODGE CABINS *Rates: budget*
Open: April 1 - October 31 *Minimum Stay: two nights*
Built by the Civilian Conservation Corps—FDR's "tree army"—in the 1930s and now on the National Registry of Historic Places, these rustic housekeeping cabins containing from one to three double beds are located atop a bluff on the Big Spring's west bank. Here, in some of the Ozark's most picturesque country, there is much to offer on both wooded land and cascading waters. The Ozark National Scenic Riverway, following the Current and Jacks Fork rivers, provides the locale for an abundance of water sports, from swimming and fishing to canoeing, scuba diving and inner-tubing, while the wildlife preserve and Mark Twain State Park, site of the celebrated author's birthplace, feature superb hiking and bird-watching as well as numerous culture and nature exhibits. Contact: Cindy Hotcaveg, Big Spring Lodge Cabins, P.O. Box 602, Van Buren, MO 63965. Call 1-314-323-4423.

Children: Y Pets: Y Smoking: Y Handicap Access: N Payment: C, P, T, V, M

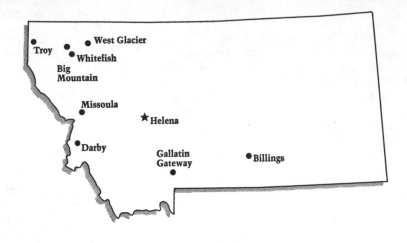

Montana

BIG MOUNTAIN

BAGEL *Rates: budget*
Open: year-round *Minimum Stay: three nights*

Take an invigorating walk through the Montana morning into town to find some bait for your afternoon fishing trip. Then loll the afternoon away on a lake just outside your door. Centrally located by Whitefish Lake and the Whitefish Golf Course, these condos accommodate up to four guests. Each features a kitchen and all modern amenities. The condos include dock facilities for boating; nearby water sports opportunities are abundant. Glacier National Park makes for an excellent car tour. Contact: Whitefish Property Management, 128 Central Avenue, Whitefish, MT 59937. Call 406-862-2570.

Children: Y Pets: N Smoking: Y Handicap Access: N Payment: C, P, T, V, M

BENNETTS *Rates: budget*
Open: year-round *Minimum Stay: three nights*

Plan an activity-filled weekend for your whole family, or stay an entire week to get everything in. Stay at the foot of Big Mountain Road in this home set in the trees with a walking path to Whitefish Lake. Boating, fishing and skiing are just a few of the area's many enticements. This four-bedroom, three-bath log house is well located, since Glacier National Park and the Big Mountain Ski Resort are within easy reach. Eight or more enjoy all the comforts of home in this premier vacation area. Contact: Whitefish Property Management, 128 Central Avenue, Whitefish, MT 59937. Call 406-862-2570.

Children: Y Pets: N Smoking: Y Handicap Access: N Payment: C, P, T, V, M

JSD CHALET
Rates: budget
Open: year-round
Minimum Stay: one week

Huge fir trees laden with snow create a winter wonderland around this private single-family home near Big Mountain's base area facilities. JSD Chalet offers an open living/dining/kitchen area with a fireplace stove, plus a bedroom and bathroom on the main floor. Upstairs is a master bedroom, and on the basement level is a third bedroom, a half bath and a family room. Hit the slopes minutes away from your secluded chalet or walk through pristine forest in perfect peace. Contact: Rent A Home International, Inc., 7200 34th Avenue N.W., Seattle, WA 98117. Call 206-545-6963.

Children: Y Pets: N Smoking: N Handicap Access: N Payment: C, P, T, V, M

MCKINNEY'S CABIN
Rates: budget
Open: year-round
Minimum Stay: one week

Natural wood and many picture windows combined with a prime location adjacent to the bottom of the "Tenderfoot" chair lift create a fine setting for a winter vacation. Accessible by ski trail, the main level consists of a living room with a stone fireplace, kitchen and eating bar, separate dining area, two bedrooms and one bathroom. The master bedroom and bath and an additional bedroom finish off the upstairs. The warm and comfortable lower level, with its two bedrooms and one bath, has a rock fireplace in the living room and a spacious kitchen and dining area. Contact: Rent A Home International, Inc., 7200 34th Avenue N.W., Seattle, WA 98117. Call 206-545-6963.

Children: Y Pets: N Smoking: N Handicap Access: N Payment: C, P, T, M

WILDWOOD
Rates: budget
Open: year-round
Minimum Stay: three nights

Spend a weekend in one of the most popular wilderness areas in the state exploring such natural treasures as Glacier National Park and the Big Mountain Ski Resort. This four-bedroom, three-bath log house located on Wisconsin Avenue on the way to Big Mountain accommodates up to 12. Guests can use a common beach on Whitefish Lake where excellent fishing, boating and water sports are abundant. The year-round activities of the Big Mountain area include skiing, snowmobiling, ice fishing and hiking. Contact: Whitefish Management, 128 Central Avenue, Whitefish, MT 59937. Call 406-862-2570.

Children: Y Pets: N Smoking: Y Handicap Access: N Payment: C, P, T, V, M

BILLINGS

CREEKSIDE COTTAGES AT RED LODGE RESORT
Rates: budget
Open: year-round
Minimum Stay: two nights

Situated midway between Billings, the largest city in Montana, and the entrance to scenic Yellowstone National Park, these plush, fully furnished studio and two-bedroom units accommodate between one and eight persons. A challenging 18-hole championship golf course is right outside the door, and skiing is 15 minutes away at Red Lodge Mountain. All units include kitchenettes, linens, fireplaces and private decks; maid service is available at extra charge. Contact: Selma Henkel, Creekside Cottages, 2108 Broadwater, Billings, MT 59102. Call 406-656-0510 or 406-446-3053.

Children: Y   Pets: N   Smoking: N   Handicap Access: N   Payment: C, P, T

DARBY

NEZ PERCE RANCH *Rates: moderate*
Open: June-September *Minimum Stay: one week*
In the heart of the Bitterroot Valley overlooking the Nez Perce Fork, these all-new guest homes offer complete privacy. Constructed of native logs, each home includes a large family room complete with fireplace and open-beam ceiling, an efficiency kitchen and a bath. A downstairs bedroom contains a double bed and an upstairs loft bedroom contains two doubles. A balcony overlooks the family room. The location is magnificent, with fishing just steps from your doorway. It's also within quick access to over a million acres of forest, numerous logging roads, and rivers and streams which support a wide variety of wildlife, including elk, deer, moose and bear. Contact: Nez Perce Ranch, West Fork Route, Darby, MT 59829. Call 406-349-2100.

Children: Y   Pets: N   Smoking: Y   Handicap Access: N   Payment: C, P, T

GALLATIN GATEWAY

THE 320 RANCH *Rates: budget*
Open: seasonal *Minimum Stay: none*
The 320 Ranch is surrounded by a national forest and has a blue-ribbon trout stream running through it. Experience world-renowned fishing in a privately stocked trout pond or try out the other 1,112 miles of trout streams in the region. Cozy and modern two- and three-bedroom units enjoy panoramic views, Jacuzzis, fully equipped kitchens, daily room service and linens. This remarkable area only five miles from the northwest corner of Yellowstone National Park offers many attractions for those seeking a taste of the real West. Contact: Gail or Jim Walma, 320 Ranch-Buffalo Horn Outfitters, 205 Buffalo Horn Creek, Gallatin Gateway, MT 59730. Call 406-995-4283 or 800-243-0320.

Children: Y   Pets: Y   Smoking: Y   Handicap Access: N   Payment: C, T, V, M

TROY

KURTZ'S KOOTENAI VIEW *Rates: budget*
Open: year-round *Minimum Stay: none*
Surrounded by the blue-green glacial valley of the Kootenai River, amid the unmatched natural wonders of snow-clad peaks and cascading waterfalls, sit a couple of two-bedroom rentals with fully equipped kitchens, Jacuzzis, decks and daily linen service. Mountain trails

through dense woods made up of ten native species of evergreen trees and hundreds of different wildflowers provide hours of backpacking fun. A full range of winter and summer sports are possible in this amazing area. Contact: Lou or Rose Kurtz, Box 93, Troy, MT 59935. Call 406-295-4630.

Children: **Y**   Pets: **Y**   Smoking: **Y**   Handicap Access: **N**   Payment: **C, P, T**

WEST GLACIER

GLACIER WILDERNESS RESORT   *Rates: inexpensive*
Open: year-round   *Minimum Stay: five nights*

Surrounded by dense forests and majestic peaks, these completely furnished one- and two-bedroom log homes include fireplaces, Jacuzzis, fully equipped kitchens with microwave ovens, linens and washer/dryers. Here in Great Bear Wilderness at the southern border of Glacier National Park, the winter sports opportunities are bountiful. Use the ranch property for snowmobiling, cross-country skiing, hunting or just relaxing by the pool. Contact: Jerry and Debbie Thomas, Glacier Wilderness Resort, Box 295, West Glacier, MT 59936. Call 406-888-5664.

Children: **Y**   Pets: **N**   Smoking: **Y**   Handicap Access: **N**   Payment: **C, P, T**

WHITEFISH

BAY POINT ESTATES   *Rates: budget*
Open: year-round   *Minimum Stay: none*

These peaceful, homey one-bedroom condominiums on Whitefish Lake offer 600 feet of lake frontage. An indoor swimming pool and a 27-hole golf course right across the street provide sports activities for everyone in the family. Furnished in various styles, the condos include kitchens and decks with barbecues. Only minutes from downtown art galleries, shops and sporting goods stores, this home away from home puts you near spectacular Glacier National Park and other natural wonders. Contact: Bay Point Estates, 300 Bay Point Drive, Box 35, Whitefish, MT 59937. Call 406-862-2331.

Children: **Y**   Pets: **N**   Smoking: **Y**   Handicap Access: **N**   Payment: **C, T, V, M**

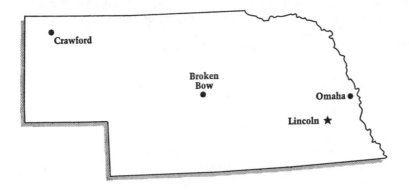

Nebraska

BROKEN BOW

ARROW HOTEL *Rates: budget*
Open: year-round *Minimum stay: none*
The Arrow Hotel, located in the heart of downtown Broken Bow, features one-bedroom fully equipped apartments in a carefully and lovingly restored building. An ideal combination of old-fashioned and modern, the hotel, in response to the needs of business travelers and vacationing families, has installed a health club which includes an exercise room, a whirlpool, bicycles and an outdoor running/fast-walking track. All units are equipped with air conditioning, cable TV and direct-dial phones, and a coin laundry is available for around-the-clock use. The hotel's Lobby Restaurant features an extensive menu and serves from 7 A.M.–10 P.M. Contact: Arrow Hotel, 509 South 9th Street, Broken Bow, NE 68822. Call: 308-872-6662.
Children: **Y** Pets: **N** Smoking: **Y** Handicap Access: **N** Payment: **A, V, M**

CRAWFORD

FORT ROBINSON STATE PARK *Rates: budget*
Open: Memorial Day-Labor Day *Minimum Stay: none*
The Fort Robinson State Park is open for the official summer season between Memorial and Labor Day weekends, and again during the firearm seasons for spring turkey, antelope, fall turkey and deer. Here you can rent cabins that were formerly officers' quarters in the late

1800s, ranging from two-bedroom (for up to six) to five-bedroom units (for up to 12), each with a full bathroom and well-equipped kitchen. Additional brick buildings (1909 officers' quarters) offer seven-, eight- and nine-bedroom units; and Comanche Hall, a group facility, can accommodate 60 people for sleeping, cooking and dining. Contact: Vince Rotherham, Fort Robinson State Park, P.O. Box 392, Crawford, NE 69339. Call 308-665-2660.

Children: Y Pets: Y Smoking: Y Handicap Access: N Payment: C, T, V, M

LINCOLN

TOWN HOUSE MOTEL	*Rates: budget*
Open: year-round	*Minimum stay: none*

Conveniently located in a quiet, downtown location, the Town House Motel offers comfortable efficiency apartments each fully equipped with kitchenettes, air conditioning, cable TV and queen-size beds. Business travelers and vacationing families alike will enjoy the proximity to restaurants, shopping, the diverse cultural offerings of the University of Nebraska and the state capitol. A thoroughly delightful and underrated city, warm-weather visitors will delight in Lincoln's 58 parks; and families won't want to miss Folsom Children's Zoo— in addition to an extensive collection of international animals, it also boasts an art gallery, botanical gardens and a child-size replica of an 1890's Nebraska town. Autumn sightseers will love the Nebraska State Fair, held in early September at the fairgrounds. Contact: Town House Motel, 1744 M Street, Lincoln, NE 68508. Call: 402-475-3000.

Children: Y Pets: N Smoking: Y Handicap Access: N Payment: A, V, M, O

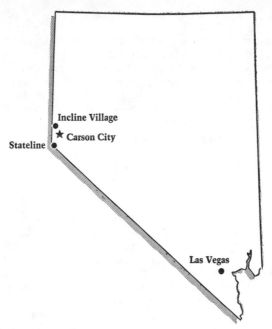

Nevada

INCLINE VILLAGE

ALL SEASONS RESORTS *Rate: budget-inexpensive*
Open: year-round *Minimum Stay: none*
One- and two-bedroom condominiums nestle in the pine forests of the Sierra Nevadas near the deep-blue waters of Lake Tahoe. The units feature wood-burning fireplaces and have access to all the amenities of Incline Village—a planned community with free bus service, an Olympic-sized swimming pool, spa, whirlpool and sun deck. Lake Tahoe, with its alluring casinos and swimming, boating and fishing facilities, is just over the ridge. A championship golf course, top-rated ski area and tennis courts are all within walking or biking distance. A fully equipped kitchen will help revive weary vacationers, while the daily maid service tidies things up. Contact: All Seasons Resorts, P.O. Box 4268, 807 Alder Avenue, Incline Village, NV 89450. Call 800-322-4331 (in Nevada, 702-831-2311).
Children: Y   Pets: N   Smoking: Y   Handicap Access: N   Payment: C, P, T

CLUB TAHOE *Rate: inexpensive-moderate*
Open: year-round *Minimum Stay: none*
Within a few hours' drive of the gambling mecca of Reno and just minutes away from Lake Tahoe and its gaming resorts, these two-bedroom condominiums provide a comfortable base for more strenuous pursuits like skiing, racquetball, tennis and golf. All units in the 10,000-square-foot low-rise facility contain a sleeping loft, washer/

dryer, two TVs, stereo and fireplace. The recreation center at Incline Village has a fully equipped gym, horseshoe pits, lighted tennis courts and a swimming pool. Contact: Club Tahoe, 914 Northwood Boulevard, Box 4650, Incline Village, NV 89450. Call 800-527-5154 (in Nevada, 702-831-5750).

Children: Y   Pets: N   Smoking: Y   Handicap Access: N   Payment: C, P, T

COEUR DU LAC CONDOMINIUMS   *Rate: budget-inexpensive*
Open: year-round   *Minimum Stay: none*

Take advantage of Incline Village's location at the base of a major ski resort and between an 18-hole championship golf course and tennis center by renting a one- or two-bedroom condominium. The surrounding alpine atmosphere is enhanced inside by beamed ceilings, redwood-paneled walls and wood-burning fireplaces. Seclusion is guaranteed, yet residents have access to the recreation center and its pool, Jacuzzi and saunas. Contact: Coeur du Lac Condominiums, Lakeshore Boulevard and Juanita, Incline Village, NV 89450. Call 702-831-3318.

Children: Y   Pets: N   Smoking: Y   Handicap Access: N   Payment: C, P, T

FOREST PINES CONDOS   *Rate: budget-inexpensive*
Open: year-round   *Minimum Stay: none*

Whether roughing it in the splendid wilderness of the Sierra Nevada or simply escaping the urban grind, these one- and two-bedroom condominiums provide recreation and tranquillity galore. Close by is Lake Tahoe and boating, fishing and swimming in its deep-blue waters; on its shores are several glitzy gambling resorts. Winter skiing is tops in the Sierra Nevadas. Whatever your preference, come home to a quiet, pine-studded landscape. Contact: Forest Pine Condos, P.O. Box 4057, Incline Village, NV 89450. Call 800-458-2463 (in Nevada, 702-831-1307).

Children: Y   Pets: N   Smoking: Y   Handicap Access: N   Payment: C, P, T

LAKE TAHOE GOLF COURSE HOME   *Rate: deluxe*
Open: year-round   *Minimum Stay: none*

This spacious three-story, three-bedroom-plus-loft home is located on the 15th tee of the Incline Village championship golf course. Beyond are the ski slopes of Diamond Peak. Just minutes from Ski Incline and majestic Lake Tahoe, you'll step into a chandelier-lit foyer and then down into a sumptuous living room featuring a rock fireplace, stereo system, VCR, wet bar and even a piano. One bedroom on the main floor, two on the second and a mezzanine pull-out bed and sleeping loft on third floor can sleep as many as ten. Extras include a mirrored bathroom with a Jacuzzi; a kitchen with a six-seat island; and numerous outdoor decks for meals or simply taking in the splendor of the surrounding alpine country. Contact: Marilyn and Ken Erickson, 979 Cart Ct., Incline Village, NV 89451. Call 702-831-6025.

Children: Y   Pets: N   Smoking: Y   Handicap Access: N   Payment: C, P, T

LAKESIDE TENNIS AND SKI RESORT   *Rate: budget-moderate*
Open: year-round   *Minimum Stay: two nights*

Tennis and skiing draw vacationers to this 36-unit condominium resort just over the hill from the brilliant blue waters of Lake Tahoe. A variety of units, from studios to three-bedrooms, assures comfort; a restaurant with bar on premises guarantees conviviality. If the attractions of Lake Tahoe and Ski Incline wane, arrange with the resort for a raft trip down Truckee River, a visit to Ponderosa Ranch or a dinner-dance on the M.S. Dixie. Contact: Lakeside Tennis and Ski Resort, P.O. Box 5576, 987 Tahoe Blvd., Incline Village, NV 89450. Call 800-222-2612 (in Nevada, 702-831-5258).

Children: Y Pets: N Smoking: Y Handicap Access: Y Payment: C, P, T, A, V, M

MCCLOUD AT INCLINE VILLAGE   *Rate: budget-inexpensive*
Open: year-round   *Minimum Stay: none*

With 20 ski areas within 45 minutes, this cluster of one- and two-bedroom condominiums is a perfect wintertime haven for skiing fanatics. After a day on the slopes, the hot tub and sauna on the premises will soothe weary bones. In summer, Lake Tahoe's many attractions— golf, tennis, horseback riding and hiking, to name a few—draw visitors. Low-rise units blend smartly with the surrounding countryside through the use of wood exteriors, extensive glass and stone and light interior colors. There are separate facilities for cars, keeping automobile noise to a minimum. Contact: McCloud at Incline Village, 144 Village Boulevard, Incline Village, NV 89450. Call 800-841-7443 (in Nevada, 702-832-7170).

Children: Y Pets: N Smoking: Y Handicap Access: N Payment: C, P, T

STATELINE

RIDGE TAHOE   *Rate: inexpensive-moderate*
Open: year-round   *Minimum Stay: two nights*

Near Lake Tahoe, the largest alpine lake in North America, these two-bedroom suites offer elegant yet casual comfort to go with the pleasures—and perhaps pitfalls—of skiing or gambling. Stateline is the locale of Tahoe's largest casinos, and it's only minutes away from Heavenly Valley ski resort and the beaches of Tahoe. Guests can cap a busy day in the rooftop spa under the stars or spend the evening dining and dancing at the Ridge Club. A swimming pool, hot tub, tennis courts, weight room and racquetball court provide other on-premise pursuits. Contact: Ridge Tahoe, P.O. Box 5790, 400 Ridge Drive, Stateline, NV 89449. Call 1-800-648-3341 (in Nevada, 702-588-3553).

Children: Y Pets: N Smoking: Y Handicap Access: N Payment: C, P, T

New Hampshire

BETHLEHEM

PINEWOOD MOTEL *Rates: budget*
Open: year-round *Minimum Stay: none*

You can use this "four seasons" motel, centrally located in the White Mountains, as a base to explore some of New Hampshire's most magnificent sights. Visit, among others, Franconia Notch, the Old Man of the Mountains, Lost River, the Flume, the Basin, the Aerial Tramway, Wildcat Gondola Lift, the Cog Railway and a score of amusements for children. When you return, your one-bedroom suite will be made up, and you can take a refreshing dip in the 24-by-45-foot heated pool. Then either make dinner in your own kitchen or dine at one of the excellent restaurants in the area. Golfers may want to beg off sightseeing and try one of the challenging local courses; loafers may want to just sunbathe or read on the spacious lawn. In winter, snowmobile trails come right to the door, and a 15-minute drive brings you to three major ski areas. Contact: Randy and Sue Nearing, Pinewood Motel, P.O. Box 158, Bethlehem, NH 03574. Call 603-444-2075.

Children: Y Pets: Y Smoking: Y Handicap Access: N Payment: C, T, V, M

CONWAY

WILDERNESS CABINS *Rates: budget*
Open: year-round *Minimum Stay: none*

Surrounded by the White Mountain National Forest, this simple resort offers access to nature and outdoor sports year-round. In warm weather you can hike, boat, fish and swim in the river; in winter you can cross-country ski, snowmobile and downhill ski on the nearby mountain. A true getaway, the cabins have an electric generator that operates only from dusk to 10 P.M., but there are gas lights for night owls. The five cabins, with private yards and picnic tables, have gas heaters and fully equipped kitchens (linen service is extra). They sleep from four to seven people in one or two bedrooms. Three cabins have a full toilet and shower; two have outdoor toilets with a shower available. Contact: Marsha or Jim Smith, Wilderness Cabins, Bear Notch Road, P.O. Box 1289, Conway, NH 03818. Call 603-356-8899.

Children: Y   Pets: Y   Smoking: N   Handicap Access: N   Payment: C, P, T

FRANCONIA

GALE RIVER MOTEL   *Rates: budget*
Open: year-round   *Minimum Stay: one week*

Located at the northern end of Franconia Notch and its many natural wonders, this comfortable motel offers spectacular views of the mountains and surrounding countryside and provides an ideal base for exploring and enjoying the White Mountains. You can choose to stay in a one-bedroom efficiency, a two-bedroom cottage or the five-bedroom annex each with linens and fully equipped kitchens. The heated pool, hot tub and Jacuzzi will be irresistible after a day of sightseeing. Nearby sports include golf, tennis, hiking, boating, trout fishing and white-water rafting. In the winter you can ski downhill or cross-country, ice skate or snowmobile. Contact: Gale River Motel, RFD 1, Box 153, Franconia, NH 03580. Call 800-255-7989 or 603-823-5655.

Children: Y   Pets: N   Smoking: Y   Handicap Access: N   Payment: All

FRANCONIA NOTCH

MITTERSILL   *Rates: budget-expensive*
Open: year-round   *Minimum Stay: two nights*

Mittersill offers vacationers 500 mountainside acres and sports activities for every season. You can stay in an efficiency, in one of the 40 one- or two-bedroom suites or in a larger private chalet, all with linens and fully equipped kitchens. Some guests come for the excellent skiing at Cannon Mountain, Loon, Wildcat and Bretton Woods. Others come to hike, horseback ride or play tennis and golf. Still others just come to enjoy the indoor and outdoor swimming pools, Jacuzzi, sauna, health club and game rooms. If you do come and happen to fall in love with Mittersill, you can buy a time-share property here. Contact: Mittersill, Franconia Notch, NH 03580. Call 603-823-5511.

Children: Y Pets: N Smoking: Y Handicap Access: N Payment: C, T, A, V, M

GLEN

LINDERHOF RESORT COMMUNITY   *Rates: budget-moderate*
Open: year-round   *Minimum Stay: two nights*

This 550-acre sports-centered resort community in view of Mt. Washington and the Presidential Range of the White Mountains opened in 1960 and is now unequaled anywhere in northern New England. In addition to its own sandy river beach, 65-foot outdoor pool, tennis courts and nine-hole golf course, you can hike, bike, canoe, kayak or enjoy various family amusements in the area. Linderhof is also less than a 15-minute drive from four ski mountains and the 142-kilometer Jackson Ski Touring trail network. Designed in Bavarian style, condos and chalets ranging from one to four bedrooms all have fully equipped kitchens, full baths and maid service weekly. Most have a large living room, a stone or brick fireplace and sliding glass doors opening onto a patio. Contact: Donald A. Nicksay, Mountain Resorts Realty, P.O. Box 126, Glen, NH 03838. Call 603-383-4334.

Children: Y Pets: N Smoking: Y Handicap Access: N Payment: C, P, T, A, V, M

LAKE WINNIPESAUKEE

COZY COTTAGE *Rates: budget*
Open: May-October *Minimum Stay: one week*

Spend a day, a week or a month of your summer vacation at this cozy cottage overlooking Lake Winnipesaukee. For up to six people it provides three bedrooms and one and a half baths. You can enjoy the multitude of recreational possibilities in the area, including water sports (swimming, boating and fishing), nature trails and horseback riding. On a rainy day, visit specialty shops and art galleries in towns nearby, or go antiquing. And any day, you can just stay home and enjoy the peacefulness of this extraordinary New Hampshire landscape of lakes, trees and mountains. Contact: Preferred Vacation Rentals, P.O. Box 161, Route 25, Center Harbor, NH 03254. Call 603-253-7811.

Children: Y Pets: N Smoking: Y Handicap Access: N Payment: C, P, T

ISLAND RETREAT *Rates: expensive*
Open: May-October *Minimum Stay: one week*

Get away from it all at this island retreat, where you will feel a bit like Robinson Crusoe. Up to 10 people can vacation here, sharing the two bedrooms and one bath, a 900-square-foot sun deck and plenty of outdoor space. You will reign over three and a half acres of natural woodlands. Swim, boat or fish from your own beach and dock, or hike through your woods. And if you begin to crave civilization, enjoy the amenities of nearby towns, which offer restaurants, crafts and antiques, as well as summer theater and music. Bring linens and towels. Contact: Preferred Vacation Rentals, P.O. Box 161, Route 25, Center Harbor, NH 03254. Call 603-253-7811.

Children: Y Pets: N Smoking: Y Handicap Access: N Payment: C, P, T

LAND'S END COTTAGE *Rates: moderate*
Open: May-October *Minimum Stay: one week*

You will feel as if you are floating on the lake in this unique cottage located at the end of a spit of land and surrounded on three sides by panoramic views of the water and the mountains. Sitting on the deck or screened porch, vacationers are immersed in this breathtaking natural beauty. Outside, you can enjoy your own beach and dock. Inside are two bedrooms and one bath for up to four occupants and a lovely fieldstone fireplace that adds charm to the decor. Those who choose to venture onto the mainland will encounter all the recreational delights of New Hampshire's lake and mountain region. There is no telephone, and you need to bring linens and towels. Contact: Preferred Vacation Rentals, P.O. Box 161, Route 25, Center Harbor, NH 03254. Call 603-253-7811.

Children: Y   Pets: N   Smoking: Y   Handicap Access: N   Payment: C, P, T

LOON RETREAT   *Rates: inexpensive*
Open: May-October   *Minimum Stay: one week*

Imagine listening to the wind rustle the leaves of tall trees and the loons calling in the distance as you fall asleep. This charming waterfront home on Lake Winnipesaukee with its own dock is uniquely located next to a wildlife sanctuary. With three and a half bedrooms and a bath, it can house up to seven people. If you are seeking privacy you will be pleased by the insulation of the beautiful wooded grounds that surround you. You can also take advantage of the many sports and entertainments provided for tourists in this popular New Hampshire resort area. Bring linens and towels. Contact: Preferred Vacation Rentals, P.O. Box 161, Route 25, Center Harbor, NH 03254. Call 603-253-7811.

Children: Y   Pets: N   Smoking: Y   Handicap Access: N   Payment: C, P, T

PINE COTTAGE   *Rates: inexpensive*
Open: May-October   *Minimum Stay: one week*

Enjoy the pine forests in this rustic New Hampshire cottage right on the serene waters of Lake Winnipesaukee. With two bedrooms and a bath, this appealing vacation house holds up to six people. At home, you will have your own shaded beach and dock as well as lovely views of woods and water from your screened porch. If you wish to venture out for recreation or entertainment, the surrounding area offers water sports, hiking and horseback riding as well as local villages with shops, restaurants, music and summer theater. Bring your own linens and towels. Contact: Preferred Vacation Rentals, P.O. Box 161, Route 25, Center Harbor, NH 03254. Call 603-253-7811.

Children: Y   Pets: N   Smoking: Y   Handicap Access: N   Payment: C, P, T

VAST VISTAS   *Rates: moderate*
Open: May-October   *Minimum Stay: one week*

Up to six people can live comfortably in the natural splendor of this relaxing waterfront home with two bedrooms and one bath. Your privacy is assured by the spectacular location on a point of land along 500 feet of natural shoreline, including a shaded beach and a dock. You may be tempted to spend your entire vacation on the porch, trying to take in the unparalleled views of open water and wooded mountains. But don't neglect the many activities this popular resort region offers, including water sports, hiking, horseback riding and sightseeing in New Hampshire's small towns. Bring linens and towels. Contact: Preferred Vacation Rentals, P.O. Box 161, Route 25, Center Harbor, NH 03254. Call 603-253-7811.

Children: Y   Pets: N   Smoking: Y   Handicap Access: N   Payment: C, P, T

WINNIPESAUKEE VISTAS   *Rates: moderate*
Open: May-October   *Minimum Stay: one week*

Ideally located on Lake Winnipesaukee, this spacious two-story home offers vacationers a beautiful sand beach just outside their front door, plus an expansive 35-foot dock. Its three bedrooms and one and three-quarters baths will accommodate up to six people, and its screened porch and deck offer spectacular views. The open waters of Meredith Bay and a wide variety of water sports, such as boating and fishing, are only a few minutes away. Those who like to fish and eat what they catch will be grateful for the convenience of a dishwasher. For non-fishers, the quaint towns of rural New Hampshire and the surrounding woods are waiting to be explored. Bring linens and towels. Contact: Preferred Vacation Rentals, P.O. Box 161, Route 25, Center Harbor, NH 03254. Call 603-253-7811.

Children: Y   Pets: N   Smoking: Y   Handicap Access: N   Payment: C, P, T

LAKE WINNISQUAM

THE ANCHORAGE   *Rates: budget*
Open: year-round   *Minimum Stay: one week*

Located on 35 glorious acres of land with over a mile of lake frontage, this friendly resort offers something for everyone. Families enjoy the shallow sandy beach, playground, game room and open fields for ball games. There is a separate beach for serious swimmers and another secluded beach, where you can watch the sun rise. Walkers can explore the orchards and berry patches, wilderness and pine trails; hikers can scale nearby Mt. Belknap. For boaters, the resort has a fleet of sailboats, rowboats, canoes and pedal boats, and fishermen will be tempted by the area's pickerel, salmon, trout, bass and perch. Each of the 30 one-, two- and three-room cottages with fully equipped kitchens, linens and towels has a view of the water from its screened porch. Two larger houses have seven and eight rooms apiece. Contact: Joyce Price, The Anchorage on Lake Winnisquam, RFD 1, Box 90, Laconia, NH 03246. Call 603-524-3248.

Children: Y   Pets: N   Smoking: Y   Handicap Access: N   Payment: C, T, V, M

LYME

LOCH LYME LODGE   *Rates: budget*
Open: Memorial Day-Labor Day   *Minimum Stay: one week*

Nearby Hanover, with its concerts and theater in the summer and the Dartmouth Skiway in the winter, is an added attraction of this pleasant resort. But even within its grounds there is always plenty to do for the whole family. Toddlers can use the playground or swim at a safe, sandy lake beach. Grownups dive into deeper waters, fish, boat or play tennis on two clay courts. The 25 summer cabins with one to four bedrooms, living room, bathroom and porch accommodate from two to six people. Full American breakfast is included; guests can also arrange for meal service in the lodge. Contact: Paul or Judy Barker, Loch Lyme Lodge, RFD 27B, Rt. 10, Lyme, NH 03768. Call 603-795-2141.

Children: Y   Pets: N   Smoking: N   Handicap Access: N   Payment: C, T

MIRROR LAKE

PICK POINT LODGE   *Rates: inexpensive-expensive*
Open: May 15-October 22   *Minimum Stay: one week*

With 75 scenic forested acres fronting half a mile on Lake Winnipe-saukee, Pick Point offers both natural simplicity and resort activities and amenities. Its 10 cottages, with one, two or three bedrooms accommodating two to eight people, have living rooms, fully equipped kitchens, porches, color TVs, radios and telephones, as well as linen service and maid service during the season. Double rooms in the main lodge with private baths are also available. You can fill your days by swimming from a gently sloping sunny beach, borrowing one of the resort's boats for sailing or fishing, playing tennis indoors or out, walking on miles of trails through a vast wildlife sanctuary or playing golf or horseback riding nearby. Contact: Jeffrey Newcomb, Pick Point Lodge, Windleblo Rd., P.O. Box 220, Mirror Lake, NH 03853. Call 603-569-1338.

Children: Y   Pets: N   Smoking: Y   Handicap Access: N   Payment: C, P, T

SUGAR HILL

LEDGELAND INN AND COTTAGES   *Rates: budget-inexpensive*
Open: year-round   *Minimum Stay: three nights*

This friendly country inn and its cozy guest cottages are perfectly located for four seasons of outdoor activity. In warm weather, swimming, golf and tennis are nearby. In the winter, you can cross-country ski out your front door or drive a few minutes to the ski slopes at Cannon, Bretton Woods and Loon Mountain. All year round, the White Mountains are a glory to hike, and this region is a gem to explore. You can also just relax and enjoy the superb mountain view from your quiet, comfortable two-bedroom cottage with its fully equipped kitchen and private bath. Contact: Ledgeland Inn and Cottages, RR 1, Box 94, Sugar Hill, NH 03585. Call 603-823-5341.

Children: Y   Pets: N   Smoking: Y   Handicap Access: N   Payment: C, T, V, M

WATERVILLE VALLEY

WINDSOR HILL CONDOMINIUM RESORT   *Rates: moderate-deluxe*
Open: year-round   *Minimum Stay: two nights*

Completely surrounded by four 4,000-foot mountain peaks, this beautiful 10-acre site attracts families and individuals. You will find a nine-hole golf course, 18 clay tennis courts, a four and a half-acre lake with a sandy beach, a heated swimming pool, over 60 miles of hiking trails and "the best trout fishing in the East." In winter, you can downhill ski on two mountains and cross-country ski on more than 95 kilometers of groomed double-tracked trails. The 132 units include studios and one-, two- and three-bedrooms with delightful views, fully equipped kitchens, fireplaces and color TV. Contact: Windsor Hill Condominium, Route 49, Waterville Valley, NH 03215-0440. Call 800-343-1286 or 603-236-8321.

Children: Y   Pets: N   Smoking: Y   Handicap Access: N   Payment: C, P, T, A, M

WEIRS BEACH

ABAKEE COTTAGES

Rates: budget-inexpensive
Open: May 15-October 15   *Minimum Stay: one week*

The White Mountains, Mt. Chocorua, the Ossipee Range and Mt. Washington form an impressive backdrop for this secluded cottage colony on the shores of Lake Winnipesaukee. Each of the 13 one-, two- and three-bedroom cottages for two to eight is comfortably furnished and has a living room, dining area, bath with shower and fully equipped kitchen. Linens and towels are provided, as is daily maid service. You can swim, fish, boat and hike here, and the protected beach area is perfect for children. Nearby, you will find boat excursions, water slides and seaplane rides as well as several fine golf courses and theaters. You can also take day trips to the Flume, Franconia Notch and the Old Man of the Mountains. Contact: Annette Poirier, Abakee Cottages, P.O. Box 5144, Weirs Beach, NH 03247-5144. Call 603-366-4405.

Children: Y   Pets: N   Smoking: Y   Handicap Access: N   Payment: C, P, T

EAGLE HOUSE COTTAGES

Rates: budget
Open: May-September   *Minimum Stay: none*

From the screened porch of your neat, comfortable cottage you can view the majestic White Mountains and the crystal-clear waters of Lake Winnipesaukee. The four cottages with one, two or three bedrooms, fully equipped kitchens and picnic tables outside sleep from two to six people. The area is alive with recreational activities, including fishing and boating from the pier two minutes away and swimming at a sandy beach close by. Shops and restaurants are convenient, as are stables for horseback riding, golf courses and picturesque state and national parks. Contact: Bert or Shirley Kirouac, Eagle House Cottages, 1 Maple St., P.O. Box 5198, Weirs Beach, NH 03247-5198. Call 603-366-5927 or 603-625-6503.

Children: Y   Pets: N   Smoking: Y   Handicap Access: N   Payment: C, T, V, M

WHITEFIELD

MIRROR LAKE MOTEL AND COTTAGES

Rates: budget
Open: year-round   *Minimum Stay: none*

Spring-fed Mirror Lake provides all the water activities swimmers and boaters could desire. In addition, it is well stocked with rainbow, square-tail and speckled trout and offers outstanding fishing any time of the year. Stay in one of Mirror Lake Motel's clean, neat, modern cottages with kitchen, accommodating two to five people. From here you can enjoy 1,300 feet of shoreline and a private sandy beach on the picturesque lake, as well as pine groves, spacious lawns and a playground. Tennis, golf and hiking trails are nearby, as are the Crawford, Dixville and Franconia notches. Contact: David and Jeanne Congdon, Mirror Lake Motel and Cottages, Whitefield, NH 03598. Call 603-837-2544.

Children: Y   Pets: N   Smoking: Y   Handicap Access: N   Payment: C, T

WOLFEBORO

LAKESHORE TERRACE COTTAGES

Rates: budget-moderate

Open: Memorial Day-Columbus Day   *Minimum Stay: one week*

This cottage colony on the shore of Lake Wentworth combines the quiet of a secluded natural setting with the convenience of being only two miles from the shopping, theater and fine dining opportunities of the popular summer resort town of Wolfeboro. On the property are a beautiful rose garden and three private sandy beaches. The seven comfortable, roomy and immaculate one- and two-room cottages sleep from two to five people. All have screened porches and full baths and half have fully equipped kitchens. Golf courses, tennis courts and stables are nearby. Be sure not to miss the excellent bass fishing in Lake Wentworth. Weekly guests should bring linen and towels. Contact: Madelyn R. Albee, Lakeshore Terrace Cottages, Center St., P.O. Box 18, Wolfeboro, NH 03894. Call 603-569-1701 (May-October); 902-634-4647 (November-April).

Children: Y Pets: Y Smoking: Y Handicap Access: N Payment: C, P, T, V, M

Trenton

Bay Head
Normandy Beach
South
Seaside
Park
Lavallette

South Beach Haven
Holgate

Ocean City

Wildwood Crest
Cape May

New Jersey

BAY HEAD

767 EAST AVENUE *Rates: deluxe*
Open: year-round *Minimum Stay: one month*
This stately home offers 250 feet of impeccable private oceanfront grounds, a perfect spot to watch the sun rise over the Atlantic. Filled with cozy fireplaces, the house is a superb vacation residence for a large group, containing six bedrooms, three and a half baths, parlor, spacious kitchen and pantry and separate breakfast and dining rooms. Enjoy the immediate environs of Bay Head, a charming small beach town, or take a short drive up to Point Pleasant Beach, which features arcades and rides and delectable fresh seafood right off the deep-sea fishing boats. Contact: Re/Max by the Sea Realty, 506 Grand Central Avenue, Lavallette, NJ 08735. Call 201-830-4122.
Children: Y   Pets: N   Smoking: Y   Handicap Access: N   Payment: C, P, T

BEACH HAVEN

ENGLESIDE INN *Rates: budget-expensive*
Open: year-round *Minimum Stay: four days*
Located on the southern end of lively Long Beach Island, lavish Engleside Inn offers a number of fully equipped apartment units, each with a kitchen area, wall-to-wall carpeting and central air-conditioning. Several units have romantic heart-shaped tubs and private balconies overlooking the ocean. The inn features an exceptional

assortment of facilities, such as a gourmet restaurant and beachside bar, a health club with a full circuit of exercise equipment, Jacuzzi and sauna and a large outdoor pool and patio area. With all these opportunities, guests will need reminding about all the recreational and entertainment activities available elsewhere on the island. Contact: Engleside Inn, 30 Engleside Avenue, Beach Haven, NJ 08008. Call 609-492-1251.

Children: Y   Pets: N   Smoking: Y   Handicap Access: N   Payment: All

CAPE MAY

835 WASHINGTON STREET   *Rates: budget-moderate*
Open: year-round   *Minimum Stay: one week*
This elegant Victorian house located in the center of Cape May houses two sumptuous self-contained apartments. The first-floor flat includes two bedrooms, parlor and kitchen, while the spacious unit on the second and third floors sleeps as many as twelve in its six bedrooms. Up the boulevard from the delightful Washington Street Mall, which is lined with vibrant tulips in the spring and sparkling wreaths at Christmastime, the house stands only a short walk from the celebrated Emlen Physick Estate and grounds, exquisite in any season. Contact: Tolz, Inc. of Cape May, P.O. Box 498, Cape May, NJ 08204. Call 609-884-7001 or 800-444-7001.

Children: Y   Pets: N   Smoking: Y   Handicap Access: N   Payment: C, P, T

DEVONSHIRE TOWNHOUSE CONDOMINIUM   *Rates: moderate*
Open: summer   *Minimum Stay: one week*
Only a block from either the beach or the mall, this attractive condominium places guests within minutes of Cape May's finest shopping and recreational facilities. The lustrous ocean waters offer marvelous swimming, surfing, boating and fishing opportunities, while tennis under gracious old shade trees is featured on the grounds of the Emlen Physick Estate. And bikers won't tire of riding along the town's elegant avenues or the breathtaking roads winding up and down the coast. Each self-contained, two-bedroom condo unit accommodates as many as six and includes a kitchen, two and a half baths, washer/dryer and air conditioning. Contact: Jersey Cape Realty, 739 Washington Street, Cape May, NJ 08204. Call 609-884-5800. Ref. 25.

Children: Y   Pets: N   Smoking: N   Handicap Access: N   Payment: C, P, T

PHILADELPHIA BEACH CONDOS   *Rates: inexpensive-expensive*
Open: year-round   *Minimum Stay: one week*
Several comfortable three-bedroom units, each with kitchen, living area and two and a half baths, are available in this contemporary Cape May condominium complex. The residence has been carefully constructed and designed to offer both modern comfort and traditional architecture that blends in with the authentic Victorian atmosphere of the nation's oldest seaside resort. Located in a quiet and picturesque residential section, it is close to the beach and a short stroll down the

gas-lit avenues to many of the town's top craft shops and 19th-century mansions. Contact: Tolz, Inc. of Cape May, P.O. Box 498, Cape May, NJ 08204. Call 609-884-7001 or 800-444-7001.

Children: **Y**   Pets: **N**   Smoking: **N**   Handicap Access: **N**   Payment: C, P, T

RANCHER   *Rates: budget*
Open: summer   *Minimum Stay: one week*

Located in a quiet residential section beneath shady trees, this quality bungalow is convenient to all of Cape May's offerings. If you're fortunate enough to be here in July, you won't want to miss the Art League Open House tour that takes visitors through the graceful interiors of some of Cape May's finest homes. Your two-bedroom residence, meanwhile, offers simpler yet comfortable accommodations for a party of up to seven, with a sitting room and fully equipped kitchen. Contact: Jersey Cape Realty, 739 Washington Street, Cape May, NJ 08204. Call 609-884-5800. Ref. 32.

Children: **Y**   Pets: **N**   Smoking: **N**   Handicap Access: **N**   Payment: C, P ,T

SOUTHEND HOUSE   *Rates: deluxe*
Open: summer   *Minimum Stay: one week*

Why be satisfied with strolling by the august 19th-century houses of Cape May, when you can rent one as your own holiday home? A stay at this exquisite private Victorian abode, adorned with the lacy "gingerbread" trim for which the town is so famous, is one of the finest ways to enjoy a truly elegant Cape May vacation. Near the region's widest beach, the five-bedroom house luxuriously accommodates up to eleven and includes a fully modern kitchen and two and a half baths, as well as a delightful covered porch for watching passersby or simply wiling the untroubled day away. Contact: Jersey Cape Realty, 739 Washington Street, Cape May, NJ 08204. Call 609-884-5800. Ref. 27.

Children: **Y**   Pets: **N**   Smoking: **N**   Handicap Access: **N**   Payment: C, P, T

SUMMER STATION   *Rates: inexpensive-expensive*
Open: year-round   *Minimum Stay: three days*

Summer Station is an appealing and friendly vacation complex that offers a variety of self-contained, one-bedroom apartments excellently suited for couples or families visiting Cape May. Most of the units feature a den and ocean view and all contain a spacious living room, full kitchen and private balcony or deck. Along with the sandy beach only steps away from the residence, guests may also enjoy the sparkling private swimming pool surrounded by a vast, inviting sun deck. Contact: Bob Alexander, Summer Station, 217 Beach Avenue, Cape May, NJ 08204. Call 800-884-8800 or 800-248-8801.

Children: **Y**   Pets: **N**   Smoking: **Y**   Handicap Access: **N**   Payment: All

THE PUFFIN   *Rates: budget-moderate*
Open: year-round   *Minimum Stay: one week*

Located in the heart of Cape May's main historic district, The Puffin is a painstakingly restored turn-of-the-century Dutch Colonial Revival home containing four homey self-sufficient units. The studio, two

one-bedroom suites and deluxe third-floor apartment with private sun deck are all lovingly decorated with antiques and family heirlooms in either a Victorian or a seashore motif. On your way out to a day at the beach, a game of tennis, a carriage ride, a bit of bird-watching, or a gourmet restaurant dinner, be sure to notice the priceless working Edison phonograph in the foyer. Contact: Bob and Toni Green, P.O. Box 517, 32 Jackson Street, Cape May, NJ 08204. Call 609-884-2664.
Children: Y   Pets: N   Smoking: Y   Handicap Access: N   Payment: C, P, T

CAPE MAY POINT

504 OCEAN AVENUE   *Rates: budget*
Open: year-round   *Minimum Stay: one week*
Located in tranquil Cape May Point, this house featuring a bedroom and bath, living room, fully equipped kitchen and screened porch plus outdoor shower is a cozy holiday hideaway for couples or small families. In addition to the celebrated lighthouse, which is one of the nation's most photographed landmarks, the immediate area offers many other beguiling attractions. There's scenic Lily Lake as well as the state park's unspoiled nature trails, pristine picnic grounds, striking dunes and spotless sandy beaches. And, of course, the unforgettable town of Cape May, with its endless cultural, architectural and recreational pleasures, is also only minutes away. Contact: Tolz, Inc. of Cape May, P.O. Box 498, Cape May, NJ 08204. Call 609-884-7001 or 800-444-7001.
Children: Y   Pets: N   Smoking: Y   Handicap Access: N   Payment: C, P, T

OCEANFRONT BEACH HOUSE   *Rates: deluxe*
Open: summer   *Minimum Stay: one week*
This large Cape May Point beach house, sitting right on the Atlantic shore, is an excellent and luxurious home base for exploring the southern tip of New Jersey. With multilevel decks to give guests every opportunity to enjoy the gorgeous ocean views, the residence includes three bedrooms, two baths, sitting rooms and a very well-equipped kitchen. From here, drive along Seashore Road to visit Historic Cold Spring Village, a fascinating private restoration project comprised of splendid relocated 18th- and 19th-century buildings. Stop by the stately colonial Presbyterian church, known as "Old Brick," or head up old Route 9 to Cape May Court House, which features scenic nature trails, picnic grounds, a little zoo and year-round programs for visitors of all ages. Contact: Jersey Cape Realty, 739 Washington Street, Cape May, NJ 08204. Call 609-884-5800. Ref. 30.
Children: Y   Pets: N   Smoking: N   Handicap Access: N   Payment: C, P, T

SOMEWHERE IN TIME   *Rates: budget-moderate*
Open: mid-May to mid-October   *Minimum Stay: one week*
Dating from the 1800s, this enchanting inn captures all the Victorian elegance of the Cape May area. Nine beautifully furnished, fully equipped studio, one- and two-bedroom apartments, each with a complete kitchen and private veranda, are available here, with the grounds

offering a barbecue, picnic areas and lovely gardens to stroll among. The Cape May Point location is superb, just a block from the shore and a short walk from the state park. Guests can enjoy, by foot or bike, the uncrowded beaches and grass-covered dunes of New Jersey's southern tip in sumptuous style. Contact: Martha or Joel Marcus, P.O. Box 134, Cape May Point, NJ 08212. Call 609-884-8554.

Children: Y   Pets: N   Smoking: Y   Handicap Access: N   Payment: C, P, T

HOLGATE

3 COHASSET *Rates: budget-moderate*
Open: year-round *Minimum Stay: one week*

This bright and well-kept duplex on the southern end of Long Beach Island makes a superb holiday home for two families vacationing on the Jersey Shore together. The residence contains three bedrooms with an additional sofa bed to sleep a total of eight, plus a modern kitchen, family room, covered porches and bathrooms on each floor. Close to the beach, the house is not only convenient to all the sports and entertainment facilities on the island, but is also within easy reach of Atlantic City, whose colorful skyline can be seen across the bay. Contact: Sunset Harbour Realty, 2 Susan Avenue, South Beach Haven, NJ 08008. Call 609-492-5700.

Children: Y   Pets: N   Smoking: Y   Handicap Access: N   Payment: C, P, T

4 COHASSET *Rates: moderate*
Open: year-round *Minimum Stay: one week*

Located in a peaceful neighborhood in the Holgate section of Long Beach Island, this contemporary house is only steps from the water— in either direction. To the east stretch miles of silver sand beaches along the Atlantic coast, while the west shore offers superb swimming and boating in the bay. A profusion of other vacation facilities covers the entire length of the narrow island. The house contains three bedrooms, two baths, a well-equipped kitchen and living room and features a delightful screened porch. Contact: Sunset Harbour Realty, 2 Susan Avenue, South Beach Haven, NJ 08008. Call 609-492-5700.

Children: Y   Pets: N   Smoking: Y   Handicap Access: N   Payment: C, P, T

4307 LONG BEACH BOULEVARD *Rates: expensive-deluxe*
Open: year-round *Minimum Stay: one week*

Resting on the shore of Long Beach Island, this large, three-floor house includes a master suite and three other bedrooms, two and a half baths, living room and a particularly well-equipped kitchen. Vacationers will love the two decks, one on the roof providing solitude and an expansive ocean view. Every activity the 18-mile-long barrier island has to offer is within easy reach by car or bike. A splendid national wildlife refuge offering some of the East Coast's finest bird-watching opportunities is only a short walk away. Contact: Sunset Harbour Realty, 2 Susan Avenue, South Beach Haven, NJ 08008. Call 609-492-5700.

Children: Y   Pets: N   Smoking: Y   Handicap Access: N   Payment: C, P, T

LAVALLETTE

1404 BALTIMORE AVENUE *Rates: budget-inexpensive*
Open: year-round *Minimum Stay: one week*

Only steps from the neighborhood playground, this comfortable, recently renovated bungalow in the small shore town of Lavallette is a superb vacation home for families with small children. The residence contains two bedrooms and a bath and features a sunny deck off the kitchen with patio furniture and a barbecue grill. Tranquil Silver Bay is only half a block away and the ocean is within easy walking distance as well. Bungalow residents can use the enclosed outdoor shower on the deck for washing off after a refreshing dip in the sea. Contact: Re/Max by the Sea Realty, 506 Grand Central Avenue, Lavallette, NJ 08735. Call 201-830-4122.

Children: Y Pets: N Smoking: Y Handicap Access: N Payment: C, P, T

4 PRINCETON AVENUE *Rates: expensive*
Open: year-round *Minimum Stay: one week*

One of two buildings on a well-situated lot near the Atlantic, this four-bedroom residence features a large kitchen, enclosed porch and a second-floor balcony that stretches the entire length of the house. There, guests have a fine view of Lavallette's mile-long boardwalk, a magnet for strollers and joggers. The ocean and the bay both offer a bounty of recreational activities, including swimming, jet skiing, boating and surfing, while canoeing is available on nearby Tom's River. Contact: Re/Max by the Sea Realty, 506 Grand Central Avenue, Lavallette, NJ 08735. Call 201-830-4122.

Children: Y Pets: N Smoking: Y Handicap Access: N Payment: C, P, T

NORMANDY BEACH

54 NORMANDY DRIVE *Rates: expensive*
Open: year-round *Minimum Stay: two weeks*

This terrific two-bedroom, open-plan bay-front house is highlighted by floor-to-ceiling windows along the entire back wall that provide stunning water views. Ideally situated, the residence stands midway between the lively family vacation towns of Seaside Heights and Point Pleasant, with many charming smaller beach communities along the way. It also offers two boat slips for guests wishing to take advantage of the area's matchless sailing opportunities and other aquatic recreational activities. Contact: Re/Max by the Sea Realty, 506 Grand Central Avenue, Lavallette, NJ 08735. Call 201-830-4122.

Children: Y Pets: N Smoking: Y Handicap Access: N Payment: C, P, T

OCEAN CITY

OCEAN CITY CONDOMINIUMS *Rates: expensive-deluxe*
Open: year-round *Minimum Stay: none*

Commanding smashing Atlantic ocean views, these luxurious oceanfront condominiums are set right on the wide beaches of Ocean City. Each well-furnished unit includes four spacious bedrooms, two baths, fully equipped kitchen, living room/dining area and a large deck overlooking the water; most also feature a cozy fireplace. With plenty of recreational opportunities and family activities available nearby, the superbly situated residences are only seven miles south of Atlantic City and a mere half-hour drive away from historic Cape May. Contact: Frank Zappariello, 609-398-4570.

Children: **Y**   Pets: **N**   Smoking: **Y**   Handicap Access: **N**   Payment: C, P, T

TOP O' THE WAVES   *Rates: inexpensive-moderate*
Open: year-round   *Minimum Stay: three days*

This delightful vacation complex is located right by the water in Ocean City, a top Jersey Shore resort within easy reach of Atlantic City and other exciting beach communities. Comfortable, fully equipped studio apartments are offered on grounds that include a charming private courtyard and two decks, one right on the beach. After a complimentary breakfast, enjoy the area's superb recreational opportunities, including swimming, boating, fishing and tennis, and take a walk along the dynamic boardwalk, where you'll find a full range of food and amusement facilities. There's an abundance of exciting seasonal activities in the region, and Top o' the Waves itself features special events, including provocative murder mystery weekends. Contact: Top o' the Waves, Inc., 5447 Central Avenue, Ocean City, NJ 08226. Call 609-399-0477.

Children: **Y**   Pets: **N**   Smoking: **Y**   Handicap Access: **N**   Payment: All

SOUTH BEACH HAVEN

3405 LONG BEACH BOULEVARD   *Rates: moderate-deluxe*
Open: year-round   *Minimum Stay: one week*

This fine oceanfront home, featuring four bedrooms and a cathedral ceiling, sits in the heart of one of New Jersey's top holiday areas. A multitude of water sports—jet and water skiing, surfing and wind surfing, sailing, fishing and swimming—are all available nearby, along with amusement parks, bowling, miniature golf, craft shops, movies, rock clubs and enough other leisure activities to keep vacationers busy day and night. For a break from more active Long Beach Island pursuits, you can lie on the beach right outside the house or sit on the property's sunny private deck. Contact: Sunset Harbour Realty, 2 Susan Avenue, South Beach Haven, NJ 08008. Call 609-492-5700.

Children: **Y**   Pets: **N**   Smoking: **Y**   Handicap Access: **N**   Payment: C, P, T

SOUTH SEASIDE PARK

8 AND 10 ISLAND DUNES DRIVE   *Rates: expensive-deluxe*
Open: year-round   *Minimum Stay: one month*

Near some of the Jersey Shore's top scenic and amusement attractions, these contemporary three-bedroom duplexes provide such seductive features as a deck with Jacuzzi off the master suite and a large rooftop deck with a wet bar. Only a couple of blocks away is Island Beach State Park, a gorgeous stretch of land offering sandy white dunes and miles of unspoiled beaches, as well as nature trails, picnic grounds and fishing areas. Up the coast just a few miles, Seaside Heights features rides, arcades, fireworks on summer evenings and a cornucopia of food options, from boardwalk snacks to fine seafood dinners. Contact: Re/Max by the Sea Realty, 506 Grand Central Avenue, Lavallette, NJ 08735. Call 201-830-4122.

Children: Y   Pets: N   Smoking: Y   Handicap Access: N   Payment: C, P, T

ISLAND DUNES TOWNHOUSE *Rates: moderate-expensive*
Open: year-round *Minimum Stay: one week*
Guests staying at this delightful townhouse are near all the attractions of one of the East Coast's most rollicking family resort areas. Take a walk along the festive boardwalk, stopping for a slice of pizza and a ride on a roller coaster or water slide. Board the renowned century-old wooden carousel or simply laze on the beach only steps from your front door. Offering a refreshing ocean view, the three-bedroom residence contains a living room, family room with additional beds (to accommodate a total of eight), dining room and kitchen and features a patio area and bar. Contact: Re/Max by the Sea Realty, 506 Grand Central Avenue, Lavallette, NJ 08735. Call 201-830-4122.

Children: Y   Pets: N   Smoking: Y   Handicap Access: N   Payment: C, P, T

WILDWOOD CREST

SEAPOINTE VILLAGE *Rates: budget-deluxe*
Open: year-round *Minimum Stay: three nights*
A truly world-class private condominium complex, Seapointe Village offers deluxe one-, two- and three-bedroom apartments, each with a private balcony and most with sweeping ocean panoramas. The lushly landscaped grounds of the "village" feature amenities such as indoor and outdoor pools, saunas, Jacuzzis and hot tubs and a number of other ingeniously designed water areas, including lagoons and waterfalls. Tennis courts, a fitness center and a spotless private beach round out the offerings. In addition to all this, guests enjoy a superb Jersey Shore location near amusement parks and nature trails, golf courses and discos and virtually every other type of activity vacationers seek. Contact: Seapointe Village, 9900 Seapointe Boulevard Diamond Beach, Wildwood Crest, NJ 08260. Call 609-729-7100 or 800-937-6468.

Children: Y   Pets: N   Smoking: Y   Handicap Access: N   Payment: C, O

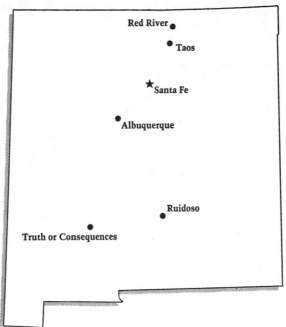

New Mexico

RED RIVER

WOODLANDS CONDOMINIUMS	Rates: budget-moderate
Open: year-round	Minimum Stay: two nights

Winter sports are popular in this region, yet summer months are filled with activities as well. Nestled at the foot of the Sangre de Cristo Mountains, this contemporary condominium complex provides easy access to wildlife, nature trails and the best fishing spots along the river. The condo units are housed in several two-story buildings; each individual unit has a fully equipped kitchen with dishwasher and disposal, a color cable TV in the living room and one, two or three bedrooms. Private patios and balconies offer fresh air and a view of the river, and the wood-burning fireplaces in each unit are always welcome after a day on the slopes. Barbecues are at your disposal, and maid and linen service is provided. Contact: Ann Vanormer, Woodlands, P.O. Box 279, Main St. W., Red River, NM 87558. Call 505-754-2303 or 800-762-6469.

Children: Y Pets: N Smoking: Y Handicap: N Payment: C, P, T, A, V, M

RUIDOSO

DAN DEE CABINS RESORT	Rates: budget-inexpensive
Open: year-round	Minimum Stay: two nights

The wood-paneled cabins here stand in forested surroundings that look beautiful year-round, whether warm and green in summer or glistening with winter snows. All the cabins have unique furnishings and style. The one-bedroom units sleep two, the two-bedroom units sleep four and the large three-bedroom cabins sleep up to seven guests—fold-out couches provide extra sleeping space in front of the living room fireplace. The resort grounds cover five acres and encompass a trout stream running just beyond the cabins, which are situated to ensure maximum privacy. Color TV, carpeted floors, full kitchens, decks and balconies can be found in each cabin. Nearby is the horse-racing track for which the area is known, as well as ski resorts and horseback riding. Contact: Dan Dee Cabins Resort, 310 Main Rd., P.O. Box 844, Ruidoso, NM 88345. Call 505-257-2165 or 800-345-4848.

Children: Y Pets: Y Smoking: Y Handicap: N Payment: C, P, T, A, V, M

HIGH SIERRA CONDOMINIUMS *Rates: budget-moderate*
Open: year-round *Minimum Stay: none*

The Mescalero Apaches run a luxury resort called Inn of the Mountain Gods on their reservation, and these condominiums look down upon that inn from their lofty perch on Camelot Mountain. Found in woods full of wild turkeys and deer, the one- and two-bedroom condominiums are situated in a low-rise building. Ruidoso is known as a ski area and horse-racing center—ski packages are available for the condos. Each unit provides a full kitchen, all linens and maid service, as well as laundry facilities. A swimming pool on the site provides a place to take a refreshing plunge after a hike through the woods. Cooler nights might find you in front of your fireplace after a day of skiing. Nearby Alamogordo offers such attractions as the Space Museum and the shifting gypsum sands of White Sands National Monument. Contact: High Sierra Condominiums, P.O. Box 4179 H.S., Ruidoso, NM 88345. Call 505-257-6913.

Children: Y Pets: N Smoking: Y Handicap Access: N Payment: C, P, T

STORY BOOK CABINS *Rates: budget-inexpensive*
Open: year-round *Minimum Stay: none*

Newly constructed, these cabins have a timeless atmosphere, perhaps because of their warm wood paneling, stone fireplaces and surrounding pine trees. Each cabin has a full kitchen, cable TV and a choice of queen- or king-sized beds; one- to three-bedroom cabins are available. The cabins' private decks or balconies look out over the forest and landscaped grounds of the Upper Canyon of Ruidoso. The ski resorts are close by, as are the horse races in town. Fishing in local lakes and hiking through the forests provide solitude and activity for the nature lover; within driving distance are such natural wonders as Carlsbad Caverns and such fascinating spots as the Space Center in Alamogordo. Contact: Joan J. Bailey, Story Book Cabins, 410 Main Road, Ruidoso, NM 88345. Call 505-257-2115.

Children: Y Pets: N Smoking: Y Handicap Access: N Payment: C, P, T, V, M

THE SPRINGS CONDOMINIUMS *Rates: budget-moderate*
Open: year-round *Minimum Stay: none*

Just three miles from downtown Ruidoso, this low-rise building houses several two- and three-bedroom condominium units. Each unit

is self-contained, with a full kitchen and bathroom, and all linens are provided. A maid comes by daily, and babysitting can be arranged if needed, leaving parents free to take a dip in the pool or a soak in the hot tub on the premises. Cable TV and fireplaces are also provided for your pleasure after a day of skiing at nearby Apache or fishing on Lakes Bonito or Nogal. Nearby attractions include the Ruidoso Downs Race Track and the Flying J Ranch chuck wagon show, as well as Smokey Bear National Forest, for those who love to get away from it all and hike or picnic in the woods. Contact: The Springs Condominiums, 1230 Mechem, Ruidoso, NM 88345. Call 505-258-5056.
Children: Y Pets: Y Smoking: Y Handicap Access: Y Payment: C, P, T, V, M

WEST WINDS LODGE AND CONDOS

Rates: budget-deluxe
Open: year-round   *Minimum Stay: none*

These two-story condominiums are a few blocks from downtown and close to the ski lifts at Apache. Studios through three-bedroom units are available, all with kitchen, bathroom, linens and daily maid service. Nearby shops and restaurants offer the opportunity to buy local crafts and sample New Mexico culinary specialties if you prefer not to eat at home. The facilities at the complex include a swimming pool and hot tub as well as cable TV, plus cribs and highchairs if needed. The earth-tone decor reflects the spectacular beauty of the surrounding scenery, which varies from lava flows to shifting sand dunes. A nearby golf course and seasonal horse racing will keep sports lovers busy, and summer festivals and street fairs enliven the town. Contact: West Winds Lodge and Condos, 208 Eagle Drive, P.O. Box 1458, Ruidoso, NM 88345. Call 505-257-4031 or 800-421-0691.
Children: Y Pets: N Smoking: Y Handicap Access: Y Payment: C, P, T, V, M

SANTA FE

CASA PEQUENA

Rates: budget-inexpensive
Open: year-round   *Minimum Stay: two nights*

Guests can cook up some southwestern specialties on the barbecue outside this pueblo-style adobe house in Santa Fe. Located in the heart of New Mexico, Santa Fe is America's oldest capital city—full of history, culture and artisans. Casa Pequena has one bedroom with a double bed and an extra fold-out couch for two in the living room; the bathroom has both a tub and a shower. There is a fully equipped kitchen in addition to the barbecue facilities, and both indoor and outdoor dining areas. The living room features a Kiva fireplace, and a small sun room provides a comfortable sitting nook. Skylights ensure that the house gets plenty of sun, and there is a TV as well as a radio. All linens and towels are provided, so all you need to bring to Santa Fe is your curiosity—and perhaps a pair of skis for the nearby resorts. Contact: Rent A Home International, 7200 34th Ave. N.W., Seattle, WA 98117. Call 206-545-6963.
Children: Y Pets: N Smoking: N Handicap Access: N Payment: C, P, T, V, M

PUEBLO HERMOSA RESORT   *Rates: moderate-deluxe*
Open: year-round   *Minimum Stay: two nights*

Designed in the Territorial style, this collection of low adobe buildings ranges around the century-old Kopp House. Although the resort is new, it has captured the spirit of the Old Southwest, and the suites feature local artwork, exposed wooden beams and Kiva fireplaces. A variety of suite sizes and styles can be found here, with either two or three bedrooms and the privacy afforded by the resort's unique design. Guests can play a game of tennis surrounded by views of the city, or relax in the Jacuzzi or sauna; a secluded courtyard surrounds the swimming pool. The modern kitchens feature microwaves, and hotel services extend to free newspapers and complimentary coffee and juice in the Kopp House. Within walking distance are the delightful galleries, shops and restaurants of the Santa Fe Plaza. Contact: David Salazar, Pueblo Hermosa Resort, 501 Rio Grande Ave., Santa Fe, NM 87501. Call 505-984-2590.

Children: Y Pets: Y Smoking: Y Handicap: N Payment: C, P, T, A, V, M

RESIDENCE INN BY MARRIOTT DE SANTA FE   *Rates: inexpensive-moderate*
Open: year-round   *Minimum Stay: none*

Spacious, attractive suites await you here in the shadow of the magnificent Sangre de Cristo Mountains in historic Santa Fe. Each suite—you have your choice of studio or split-level two-bedroom units—has a living/dining area, a kitchen with dishwasher and modern appliances, satellite TV and daily maid and linen service. The decor is pure Southwest—tiled floors, touches of wood and gleaming white walls with red brick trim. A fireplace will greet you after a day on the ski slopes of Taos, and a complimentary breakfast means that the mornings are your own (a shopping service can provide you with everything needed to do your own cooking, too). The hotel has a swimming pool and spa where guests can relax, and a sports center keeps the athletic visitor busy. Contact: Residence Inn by Marriott de Santa Fe, 1698 Galisteo St., Santa Fe, NM 87501. Call 505-988-7300 or 800-331-3131.

Children: Y   Pets: Y   Smoking: Y   Handicap Access: N   Payment: All

TAOS

QUAIL RIDGE INN   *Rates: inexpensive-deluxe*
Open: year-round   *Minimum Stay: none*

Located in the upspoiled Sangre de Cristo Mountains, this pueblo-style resort reflects the history and culture of the surrounding area. Studio and one- to three-bedroom condominiums are available, each with all linens and a full kitchen. A maid will clean daily, and there is a cable TV and phone in every unit. The resort facilities include something to satisfy every taste, from relaxing to exercising: a pool, sauna, hot tub and tennis and racquetball courts, with instruction if you like. A restaurant and bar at the resort can fill your craving for a night out; babysitting services can be provided. The area has year-round outdoor activities, from downhill skiing to water sports. Contact: Quail Ridge Inn, P.O. Box 707, Taos, NM 87571. Call 505-776-2211 or 800-624-4448.

Children: Y   Pets: N   Smoking: Y   Handicap: N   Payment: C, P, T, A, V, M

SIERRA DEL SOL   *Rates: moderate-deluxe*
Open: year-round   *Minimum Stay: three nights*
The clear air of Taos Valley will revive vacationers' spirits, and these no-smoking condominiums have fireplaces that fill the rooms with a delightful, natural warmth. The condominiums range from studios with kitchenettes to two-bedroom units with full kitchens. All linens are provided, as is daily maid service. There is a TV in your room, and if necessary, a crib, a highchair or baby-sitting service can all be provided. Summertime will find guests wandering in the forest or the Wheeler Peak Wilderness Area, experiencing Pueblo Indian ceremonies or trout fishing. Winter offers skiing just 70 yards away at Taos's main ski lift. At any time of year, this historical area fascinates visitors with its rich culture, and the nearby restaurants and nightlife are sure to please. Contact: Sierra del Sol, P.O. Box 84, Taos Ski Valley, NM 87525. Call 505-776-2981 or 800-523-3954.

Children: Y   Pets: N   Smoking: N   Handicap: N   Payment: C, P, T, A, V, M

TRUTH OR CONSEQUENCES

THE DAM SITE RECREATION AREA   *Rates: budget-inexpensive*
Open: year-round   *Minimum Stay: two nights*
The state park at Elephant Butte Lake has several cabins for rent, most of which are newly remodeled and some of which are winterized. The cabins range from a one-bedroom unit with kitchenette to a duplex cabin with kitchenette that sleeps up to eight guests. Although linens and towels are provided, cooking and eating utensils must be brought by the guests. The park complex includes a restaurant and lounge overlooking the lake, which serve American and Mexican specialties. The park marina sells groceries, rents boats and fishing tackle and provides moorings for visiting boaters. There are playgrounds for the kids and nature trails for the outdoor lovers, in addition to the lakeside beach where swimmers and sunbathers alike can pass the days. Contact: Dallas Pietz, Dam Site, Inc., P.O. Box 77B, Engle St. Rt., Truth or Consequences, NM 87901. Call 505-894-2073.

Children: Y   Pets: Y   Smoking: Y   Handicap: N   Payment: C, T, A, V, M, O

New York

ANCRAM

LAKE TAGHKANIC STATE PARK *Rates: budget*
Open: May 15-October *Minimum Stay: two nights*

Beautiful Lake Taghkanic State Park encompasses rolling green hills, thickly wooded forests and the cool azure waters of the lake. By staying at one of the park's own cabins or cottages, you can spend every moment of your vacation surrounded by lush natural beauty. Each unit has from one to four bedrooms and a convenient kitchenette with running water; cabins also have rustic fireplaces, and the cottages boast private showers. The park's facilities include two bathing beaches, hiking trails, some secluded picnic areas, a playground for the kids, a ball field and boat rentals. During the summer, there are frequent family-style activities planned, from puppet shows to film nights and nature programs. Contact: Lake Taghkanic State Park, R.D. 1, Box 74, Ancram, NY 12502. Call 1-800-456-2267 (in New York, 518-851-3631).

Children: **Y** Pets: **N** Smoking: **Y** Handicap Access: **N** Payment: **C, T, V**

CHICHESTER

SILVER HOLLOW *Rates: inexpensive-moderate*
Open: year-round *Minimum Stay: two nights*

Surrounded by tall pines and fronted by a picket fence, this vacation home enables you to live the American dream. The lovingly furnished two-bedroom house boasts a fireplace for chilly evenings. After preparing your famous barbecue and enjoying it out on the deck, spend a relaxed evening under the stars sipping some of the state's wine as the crickets' chirping provides the background for your tale of the one that got away. Hiking and biking through the mountains are popular pursuits; the wintertime skiing in these parts is wonderful. Not far away is Woodstock, long a renowned artists' colony and since 1969 a pilgrimage point for those who claim to have "been there." Go see how the farm's doing or catch one of the dance, theater or musical performances featured each summer. Contact: John Redsecker, 41 W. 89th St., No. 1-R, New York, NY 10024. Call 212-496-0672.

Children: **Y**   Pets: **Y**   Smoking: **Y**   Handicap Access: **N**   Payment: **C, T**

CLYMER

PEEK 'N PEAK   *Rates: budget-moderate*
Open: year-round   *Minimum Stay: none*

From the well-manicured grounds and the handsome half-timbered facade to the smallest detail out on the golf course, this amazing resort is wholly devoted to your pleasure and enjoyment. The tastefully appointed rooms are spacious and inviting; some even feature fireplaces. Three elegant restaurants serve a variety of cuisines, each of them excellent. The ski amenities include 25 slopes, state-of-the-art snowmaking, nine chairlifts and on-staff instructors, but this is only the tip of the recreational iceberg. There's also an 18-hole golf course with a new clubhouse; year-round tennis; an indoor swimming pool with sauna, tanning beds and a whirlpool; and a fitness center. Contact: Peek 'n Peak, R.D. 2, P.O. Box 135, Ye Olde Road, Clymer, NY 14724. Call 716-355-4141.

Children: **Y**   Pets: **N**   Smoking: **Y**   Handicap Access: **N**   Payment: **T, V, M**

EAST HAMPTON

MAIDSTONE PARK COTTAGES   *Rates: budget*
Open: June-August   *Minimum Stay: one week*

Artsy pursuits and alternative lifestyles flourish in East Hampton, a charming little town on the eastern end of Long Island. The Maidstone Park Cottages, where very private holiday homes are sheltered beneath leafy shade trees, is an ideal base for enjoying both the sophisticated social life and breathtaking scenery of this area. The one- and two-bedroom cottages feature homey furnishings, cable TV, full kitchens, wall-to-wall carpets and outdoor eating areas. From here it's a short drive to the magnificent mansions, elegant restaurants and fascinating shops in town. If you prefer, you can also pursue less urbane diversions, fishing for flounder and snapper at the Three Mile Harbor, swimming in Gardiner's Bay or practicing your golf swing. Contact: Maidstone Park Cottages, 22 Bruce La., East Hampton, NY 11937. Call 516-324-2837 or 718-347-4829.

Children: **Y**   Pets: **N**   Smoking: **Y**   Handicap Access: **N**   Payment: **C, T, V, M**

EAST QUOGUE

SIX-BEDROOM CONTEMPORARY   *Rates: deluxe*
Open: Memorial Day-Labor Day   *Minimum Stay: one month*
You'll enjoy elegant luxury in this two-acre oceanfront estate. Just minutes away from the quaint village of Quogue, this charming home offers complete privacy along with views of the bay and the Atlantic. All-weather tennis courts mean you'll never have to cancel a game. When practicing your backhand becomes too strenuous, you can retire to a game of pool or beat the heat with a dip in the swimming pool. Nothing will help you unwind from an active day like an intimate soak in the Jacuzzi. You'll also want to spend time exploring the six tastefully appointed bedrooms. The four full baths invite you to take your time getting ready for a night on the town or relaxing after a dip in the ocean. Contact: Main Event Realty, 27-B Riverhead Rd., Westhampton Beach, NY 11978. Call 516-288-0700.
Children: Y   Pets: Y   Smoking: Y   Handicap Access: N   Payment: C, P, T

THE CANAL   *Rates: expensive*
Open: Memorial Day-Labor Day   *Minimum Stay: one month*
Boating enthusiasts will appreciate the fine location of this beautiful home on the bay, and everyone will relish the delightful accommodations it proffers for your holiday on Long Island. The ranch-style home has been completely contemporized; it features four airy bedrooms and two baths. There is a great swimming pool outside, and the gentle waters of the bay are not too far away. This area was first settled by Europeans in the 1600s. For a glimpse into the county's early history and lifestyles, stop by the Suffolk County Historical Society over in nearby Riverhead. Contact: Main Event Realty, 27-B Riverhead Rd., Westhampton Beach, NY 11978. Call 516-288-0700.
Children: Y   Pets: Y   Smoking: Y   Handicap Access: N   Payment: C, P, T

FORESTBURGH

INN AT LAKE JOSEPH   *Rates: inexpensive-expensive*
Open: year-round   *Minimum Stay: two nights*
Only two hours from New York City, this charming country inn seems very far away. The guest rooms are decorated with brass and four-poster beds, Victorian wallpaper, Oriental rugs, antiques and delicate linens. Superb meals are served in the handsome dining room; afterward you can relax in one of the elegant living rooms, select a movie from the library or play pool in the billiard room. The inn is embraced by a magnificent veranda where you can gaze out at the acres of rolling lawns and the mysterious forests beyond. There is also a carriage house with cathedral ceilings, a full kitchen, two bedrooms and similarly opulent furnishings for a self-catered vacation. Lake Joseph offers some of the best pickerel, bass and perch fishing in the state, as well as fine swimming. Contact: Ivan Weinger, P.O. Box 81, Forestburgh, NY 12777. Call 914-791-9506.
Children: Y   Pets: N   Smoking: Y   Handicap Access: N   Payment: All

GENEVA

GENEVA ON THE LAKE
Open: year-round

Rates: budget-deluxe
Minimum Stay: none

This magnificent resort on the water's edge recreates the grace and elegance of a traditional European retreat while also offering the amenities that today's vacationers desire. Each exquisite suite features ravishing decor; many boast canopied beds, handsome fireplaces, balconies and rich architectural details. The extensive grounds invite you to stroll through the elegant gardens, swim or lounge at the sparkling pool, sail and wind surf out on the lake. Breakfast is served every morning, and the gourmet cuisine of the Lancellotti Dining Room is simply superb. Many special vacation packages that pamper guests to an even higher degree are offered. Contact: Geneva on the Lake, 1001 Lochland Rd., Rt. 14S., P.O. Box 929, Geneva, NY 14456-0929. Call 315-789-7190.

Children: Y Pets: N Smoking: N Handicap Access: N Payment: C, T, A, V, M

HAMPTON BAYS

BAY HAVEN
Open: June-August

Rates: moderate
Minimum Stay: three months

The friendly community of Hampton Bays on eastern Long Island invites you to enjoy a truly family-style vacation. After a day of browsing through the latest fashions at the local shops, you can stroll back to your very own haven of suburban bliss, where your loved ones have been busy preparing a home-cooked supper. As usual, you dine out on the spacious deck, where afterward you can sip a glass of New York's finest while watching the kids burn off some of their limitless energy out on the soft green grass. With five ample bedrooms, this house has more than enough room for all of you. Contact: Village Real Estate, 59 W. Montauk Hwy., Hampton Bays, NY 11946. Call 516-728-1900.

Children: Y Pets: N Smoking: Y Handicap Access: Y Payment: C, P, T

COLONIAL SHORES RESORT AND MARINA
Open: year-round

Rates: budget-moderate
Minimum Stay: none

Just a few minutes away from some of the best fishing on Long Island, this friendly establishment offers comfortable, family-style accommodations in the scenic Hamptons area. Some units overlook the waters of beautiful Tiana Bay, while others offer poolside views. The casual decor features colonial stylings; air-conditioning and cable TV are standard. In addition to the swimming pool with its diving board, water slide, umbrellas and chaises, the Colonial Shores boasts a shady picnic area, a private beach and boats for hire in its very own marina. Shopping, fine restaurants and a host of recreational activities abound in this area. Contact: Colonial Shores Resort and Marina, 83 W. Tiana Rd., Hampton Bays, NY 11946-3699. Call 516-728-0011.

Children: Y Pets: N Smoking: Y Handicap Access: N Payment: All

STUDIO DUPLEX   *Rates: budget*
Open: July-August   *Minimum Stay: one month*
This pretty apartment puts the best of Long Island living in a very convenient package. Hampton Bays is a congenial community practically surrounded by water, so now's the time to perfect your sailing, wind-surfing or jet-skiing skills—or to try out that one water sport you've never felt up to before. The area is also an angler's dream: You can drop a line at the end of the pier or charter a boat for some deep-sea fishing. The local shops will keep dedicated consumers busy, and golf, tennis and horseback riding are also available in the area. Finally, the peaceful vistas and secluded coves you can still find around here form the cornerstone of almost everyone's dream vacation. Contact: Village Real Estate, 59 W. Montauk Hwy., Hampton Bays, NY 11946. Call 516-728-1900.
Children: Y   Pets: N   Smoking: Y   Handicap Access: Y   Payment: C, P, T

MONTAUK

BEACHCOMBER RESORT   *Rates: budget-deluxe*
Open: March-October   *Minimum Stay: two nights*
This luxurious holiday complex is a new addition on Long Island's scenic East End. Every one of the handsomely appointed suites boasts cable TV with HBO and air-conditioning; many have private balconies and all enjoy excellent views of the ocean, whose brisk waters are just a short stroll away. Guests are invited to use the heated swimming pool and tennis court; a sauna is also available for steaming away the stress of the world. Fishing, golf and horseback riding can all be enjoyed in the neighborhood, as can the ever-popular pursuits of shopping and fine dining. Contact: Maureen Keller and Frank Tramontano, Beachcomber Resort, Old Montauk Hwy., Montauk, NY 11954. Call 516-688-2894.
Children: Y   Pets: N   Smoking: Y   Handicap Access: N   Payment: All

HITHER HILLS   *Rates: moderate-expensive*
Open: Memorial Day-Labor Day   *Minimum Stay: two weeks*
The drive out to Montauk is always a little longer than you expected: Who could believe that any place on Long Island could be so far removed from the crowds and noise of New York City? This narrow point of land dividing Block Island Sound from the Atlantic Ocean mingles rugged, windswept beauty with a reputation as the chic home of some very well-known celebrities. The Hither Hills home is a traditional three-bedroom, two-bathroom abode just a few steps away from the ocean. Stunning views of the sea can be enjoyed out on the deck, which is literally covered in fragrant blossoms. Fully outfitted with a washer/dryer and other modern appliances, this vacation home is convenient as well as picturesque. Contact: Remington Realty Ltd., The Security Professional Building, The Plaza, Box 747, Montauk, NY 11954-0601. Call 516-668-4044.
Children: Y   Pets: N   Smoking: Y   Handicap Access: N   Payment: C, P, T

OLD HIGHWAY
Rates: deluxe
Open: July-Labor Day
Minimum Stay: two months

Flanked by two grand state parks, tranquil Montauk is a much sought-after haven of natural beauty on the far eastern end of Long Island. The windswept beaches and rolling dunes here will make you wonder if the rest of the island was once this beautiful. With Block Island Sound to the north and the wide-open seas of the Atlantic to the south, water sports opportunities abound. This spacious four-bedroom home is right on the ocean. The traditional interior is graced by fine antiques, but the well-equipped kitchen ensures that the best of modern living is at your disposal as well. Contact: Remington Realty Ltd., The Security Professional Building, The Plaza, Box 747, Montauk, NY 11954-0601. Call 516-668-4044.

Children: Y Pets: N Smoking: Y Handicap Access: N Payment: C, P, T

NEW YORK CITY

AAAH! BED & BREAKFAST NO. 1
Rates: inexpensive-expensive
Open: year-round
Minimum Stay: two nights

To feel right at home in one of the world's most exciting yet overwhelming cities, why not stay with knowledgeable hosts who will treat you like family? By letting this reservation service know about your interests and the purposes of your visit to New York, it can select the hosts and accommodations that will help you make the most of your stay. You'll receive a continental breakfast every day and enjoy a warm hospitality that few out-of-towners ever get to experience. If you prefer, you can also rent an entire unhosted apartment in any of several convenient locations. Contact: William Salisbury, Aaah! Bed & Breakfast No. 1, P.O. Box 200, New York, NY 10108. Call 212-246-4000.

Children: Y Pets: N Smoking: Y Handicap Access: N Payment: C, P, T, A

CARNEGIE HILL APARTMENT
Rates: inexpensive
Open: year-round
Minimum Stay: none

The swarms of doormen and the grand exterior will impress your friends when you stay at this posh apartment building in the center of town. Once inside, they'll also admire the splendid cityscapes you enjoy from your holiday abode. The apartment is tastefully furnished and has plenty of room to stretch out and relax; there is one bedroom with a queen-sized bed. This area of New York is a marvelous base for seeing the sights, meandering through museums, browsing Fifth Avenue boutiques and dancing until dawn. Contact: Urban Ventures, Box 426, New York, NY 10024. Call 212-594-5650. Ref. MER100.

Children: Y Pets: N Smoking: Y Handicap Access: N Payment: C, P, A, V, M

INN NEW YORK CITY
Rates: expensive
Open: year-round
Minimum Stay: none

Home sweet home was never like this—but perhaps it should have been. Just minutes from Lincoln Center, this restored brownstone will completely abolish the vain notion that New Yorkers are inhospitable.

Terry-cloth robes, a hair dryer and other bathroom supplies, a daily newspaper and a well-stocked breakfast cupboard will greet you upon your arrival; you can even arrange for valet service or to have your own message on the answering machine. Each of the sumptuous suites is individually furnished with fine antiques, rich textiles and ornate architectural details from the Victorian period. The opulent Parlor Suite is the largest of the four; it boasts 12-foot ceilings, leaded glass panels, French doors leading to a terrace, a fireplace and a piano. Contact: Inn New York City, 266 W. 71st St., New York, NY 10023. Call 212-580-1900.

Children: Y Pets: N Smoking: Y Handicap Access: N Payment: C, V, M

MANHATTAN SEAPORT SUITES   *Rates: inexpensive-expensive*
Open: year-round   *Minimum Stay: none*

Found at the foot of Wall Street, the Manhattan Seaport Suites offer comfortable, personal accommodations right in the heart of New York. The suites range from studios for two people to deluxe one-bedrooms for up to four. All boast marble baths, stylish modern kitchens, cable color TV and maid service. From your roost you can easily visit dozens of famous art galleries, elegant restaurants, enticing boutiques and historic sites. Chinatown and Little Italy—with their unique cultural atmospheres and scrumptious eateries—are only a few minutes away, and the Seaport Suites are also well connected by public transportation to the rest of the city. Contact: Manhattan Seaport Suites, 129 Front St., New York, NY 10005. Call 212-742-0003.

Children: Y Pets: N Smoking: Y Handicap Access: Y Payment: C, T, A, V, M

MIDTOWN HIGH-RISE   *Rates: inexpensive-expensive*
Open: year-round   *Minimum Stay: none*

You'll almost believe you were somehow transported into the celluloid world of the movies when you find yourself sipping a cocktail out on the terrace of this apartment, with the splendor of Manhattan spread out below you, bathed in the rosy glow of sunset. This midtown apartment is ideally located for exploring Madison Avenue, savoring the hustle and bustle of the city's business life, stopping by the U.N. or partaking of the area's gourmet cuisine. In addition to the sleeping quarters in the bedroom, there's a queen-sized convertible bed in the living room, so up to four vacationers can find comfy accommodations here. Contact: Urban Ventures, Box 426, New York, NY 10024. Call 212-594-5650. Ref. DID100.

Children: Y Pets: N Smoking: Y Handicap Access: N Payment: C, P, A, V, M

PARKVIEW APARTMENT   *Rates: inexpensive*
Open: year-round   *Minimum Stay: none*

The collection of oddities from all corners of the world enhancing this unique apartment reflects the varied interests of the owner and give it a sense of individuality and character that is often missing from hotel rooms and urban condos. Other allurements include the fabulous view of Central Park, the homey houseplants and the plush Oriental carpets, which create an ambiance of quiet luxury. Up to two guests are welcome in this studio apartment on the Upper West Side, which is well situated for enjoying the fun and excitement of the city. Contact: Urban Ventures, Box 426, New York, NY 10024. Call 212-594-5650. Ref. BIN200.

Children: Y Pets: N Smoking: Y Handicap Access: N Payment: C, P, A, V, M

THE GRACIE INN   *Rates: budget-moderate*
Open: year-round   *Minimum Stay: none*

Wouldn't you like to have your own apartment in New York City so you could just stop by anytime you wanted to catch a Broadway show, see the latest art exhibit or do a bit of shopping? The Gracie Inn can make your dream come true with its comfortable suites on the Upper East Side. The fresh flowers, daily maid service, complimentary breakfasts and color TV make this comparable to staying in a luxury hotel; the full kitchens, downy comforters and feather pillows and even a computer if you need one will make it seem more like a home away from home. The studio, one-bedroom and two-bedroom suites are all stylishly furnished and some even enjoy private patios. Contact: The Gracie Inn, 502 East 81st St., New York, NY 10028. Call 212-628-1700.

Children: Y   Pets: N   Smoking: N   Handicap Access: N   Payment: C, T

THEATER DISTRICT APARTMENT   *Rates: inexpensive*
Open: year-round   *Minimum Stay: none*

Theater addicts will want to consider staying in this charming apartment, splendidly located in New York's renowned Theater District. The attractively furnished interior is highlighted by a dramatic wall of mirrors. After a pleasant night's sleep in either the pretty bedroom or on the living room's convertible bed, you can walk right out the door and be hot on the trail of ebullient musicals or highbrow experiments. After a day of pounding the pavement and seeing the sights, you'll come home to your own apartment in a doorman building. Contact: Urban Ventures, Box 426, New York, NY 10024. Call 212-594-5650. Ref. DES100.

Children: Y Pets: N Smoking: Y Handicap Access: N Payment: C, P, A, V, M

NIAGARA FALLS

ASTRO MOTEL   *Rates: budget*
Open: year-round   *Minimum Stay: none*

Honeymooners, daredevils and kids of all ages are impressed by the Niagara Falls, a thundering wall of brilliant white water. Go ahead and join the throngs dressed in silly yellow raincoats as they tromp through the Cave of the Winds or ride out to the foot of the Horseshoe Falls on the redoubtable Maid of the Mist—you'll never see anything like this again. You'll find the Astro Motel just minutes from the falls and the other scenic sights in the area. The one-bedroom kitchenette suites feature all the comforts of home: air-conditioning, color cable TV and nicely furnished rooms. Contact: Astro Motel, 6625 Niagara Falls Blvd., Niagara Falls, NY 14304. Call 716-283-4245 or 716-283-2010.

Children: Y Pets: Y Smoking: Y Handicap Access: Y Payment: C, A, V, M

OLD FORGE

PINE KNOLL MOTEL   *Rates: budget*
Open: year-round   *Minimum Stay: none*

These unassuming holiday homes enjoy splendid views of the Adirondacks from their perch above the quiet waters of Old Forge Pond. The cozily furnished cottages come in a variety of sizes; all feature cable TV and full bathrooms. Some even boast fireplaces and have marvelous views of the lake from their private porches. There are also motel suites available. Pine Knoll has its own private beach and boat docks on the lake. Other popular summertime pursuits in the area include tennis, golf, mountain climbing and chairlift rides. In the winter, this neighborhood is known for its abundant snowmobile trails; the cross-country skiing is also fine, and the slopes of McCauley Mountain beckon to downhillers. Contact: Pine Knoll Motel, South Shore Rd., Old Forge, NY 13420. Call 315-369-6740.

Children: Y   Pets: Y   Smoking: Y   Handicap Access: N   Payment: C

PINE SHADOWS LODGE   *Rates: budget-expensive*
Open: year-round   *Minimum Stay: none*

Swimming in the clear, fresh waters of the lake is a favorite pursuit here in summer. Five canoes and three inflatable boats are available for the guests' enjoyment, and powered watercraft may be rented at the local marina. Winter brings another host of diversions, from cross-country skiing to snowmobiling to skating out on the lake. The lodge offers charming suites that have been restored to their turn-of-the-century appearance; four-poster beds and fireplaces set the tone. These rooms are also available for bed and breakfast. The cottages are ideal for larger groups, as they can accommodate between six and twelve people. Full kitchens with microwave ovens, a wide range of modern appliances, color TV and wall-to-wall carpeting are standard. Contact: Pine Shadows Lodge, Less Traveled Rd., H.C. 02, Box 18, Old Forge, NY 13420-9704. Call 315-369-3551.

Children: Y Pets: Y Smoking: Y Handicap Access: N Payment: C, T, V, M

SUNSET MOTEL   *Rates: budget*
Open: year-round   *Minimum Stay: none*

The comfortable guest rooms at this Adirondack Mountain retreat can accommodate two, three or four guests. Most suites are air-conditioned; a few even have private Jacuzzis, and there's a honeymoon suite available for the consummate romantic weekend. All guests share the use of a delicious indoor heated swimming pool, sauna and Jacuzzi. The sports-minded visitor will be delighted by the outdoor tennis court and putting green. In the winter, the favorite pursuits include cross-country skiing and snowmobiling along the Old Forge Trail System (guests are encouraged to apply for permits ahead of time). Contact: Sunset Motel, Route 28, Box 261, Old Forge, NY 13420. Call 315-369-6836.

Children: Y Pets: N Smoking: Y Handicap Access: N Payment: C, T, V, M

OLIVEREA

CATSKILL MOUNTAIN BROOKSIDE COTTAGES *Rates: budget-moderate*
Open: year-round *Minimum Stay: none*
Tucked away in the Catskill Forest Preserve, at the base of majestic Slide Mountain, is the verdant valley of Oliverea. Athletic types can amuse themselves with hiking and biking, hunting and fishing, golf and tennis and—of course—with some marvelous skiing and sledding during the winter. Those who prefer a more sedate holiday will be enchanted by the quiet mountain drives, summer theater, antique shops and festive local fairs. The Brookside Cottages are ideal for private, secluded holidays, while the suites in the Lake House are for those who prefer to be pampered during their stay. Lake House accommodations are highlighted by tasty meals (cottage guests can eat here, too). Contact: Brookside Cottages, Oliverea, NY 12462. Call 914-254-5498.
Children: Y Pets: N Smoking: Y Handicap Access: N Payment: C, P, T, V, M

POUGHKEEPSIE

THE SUMMIT *Rates: budget-moderate*
Open: year-round *Minimum Stay: none*
Breathe deep of the clear, crisp air at The Summit. Nestled among the pines and birches of the Adirondacks and only a few minutes from the blue waters of Lake George, this resort offers excellent facilities amid nature's own spectacle. The stylish townhouses are just a few minutes from the ski slopes. They boast spacious living and dining rooms, fully equipped kitchens, a fireplace, a deck and from one to three bedrooms; most also feature microwaves, laundry facilities and Jacuzzis—the perfect way to relax after a day of skiing or white-water rafting. Fishing, hiking, mountain climbing or sailing can all be enjoyed nearby, and the complex has its own indoor pool, sauna and game room. Best of all, child care is available for that romantic evening you've been planning. Contact: Gore Realty, P.O. Box 1819, Poughkeepsie, NY 12601. Call 914-251-3900.
Children: Y Pets: N Smoking: Y Handicap Access: N Payment: C, T, V, M

QUOGUE

CAPE HOUSE *Rates: deluxe*
Open: Memorial Day-Labor Day *Minimum Stay: one month*
There is plenty to keep you amused at this charming house. If you tire of strolling through the generous grounds, you can challenge a friend to a game of tennis on the private court or take a refreshing dip in the pool. If this doesn't suit your mood, you can walk over to the sandy beach and let the waves lap at your ankles or practice your favorite water sports. When you return home, the hot tub is ready to soothe any overtired muscles—or even just to enjoy for the fun of it. The main part of the house features a fireplace in the den and has four spacious

bedrooms; a separate apartment offers two more bedrooms to you and your friends. Contact: Main Event Realty, 27-B Riverhead Rd., Westhampton Beach, NY 11978. Call 516-288-0700.

Children: Y   Pets: Y   Smoking: Y   Handicap Access: N   Payment: C, P, T

TRADITION PLUS   *Rates: deluxe*
Open: Memorial Day-Labor Day   *Minimum Stay: one month*
Surrounded by homes of the rich and famous, this lovely house in a quiet community offers you the restful ambiance of eastern Long Island along with all the comforts of home. Its splendid situation on an acre of land provides delightful early morning walks and tranquillity the whole day through. Guests enjoy beach rights, so the sand and surf is at your disposal; the heated pool with its own cabana is another decadently delicious option for water worshippers. After a day of swimming, sunning or practicing your swing at one of the nearby golf facilities, you can bubble away the stresses of the day in the wonderful Jacuzzi. Inside, there are seven spacious bathrooms, most with adjoining bathrooms. Contact: Main Event Realty, 27-B Riverhead Rd., Westhampton Beach, NY 11978. Call 516-288-0700.

Children: Y   Pets: Y   Smoking: Y   Handicap Access: N   Payment: C, P, T

SHANDAKEN

BLUE SPRUCE COTTAGES   *Rates: budget*
Open: March-December   *Minimum Stay: two nights*
There's plenty to keep you busy when you stay in these charming cottages in the heart of the Catskills. Removed from the high-powered glitter of the big resorts, this picturesque venue allows you to enjoy the natural wonders and summertime fun that first attracted people to the area. The nearby Esopus lures anglers with its trout population and other fun-seekers with its tubing opportunities. You can take a plunge in the swimming hole or get a bird's-eye view of the rolling countryside from the summit of Hunter Mountain's skyride. Antique shops, country auctions, galleries and boutiques should keep even the most dedicated shopper satisfied. The comfy cottages have one, two or four bedrooms and full kitchens and are completely outfitted with everything you'll need. Contact: Melodye Icart, P.O. Box 96, Route 42, Shandaken, NY 12480. Call 914-688-5778.

Children: Y   Pets: N   Smoking: Y   Handicap Access: N   Payment: C, T

FEITZINGER'S CABINS   *Rates: budget*
Open: year-round   *Minimum Stay: none*
The highest peak in the Catskills, Slide Mountain, is found near Shandaken, an idyllic town in the heart of this mountainous region. The name means "rapid waters" in the Iroquois language, perhaps a reference to the ebullient Esopus Creek teeming with trout nearby. With 62 acres of private land surrounding this creek and adjacent to a huge swath of state land, Feitzinger's Cabins are the favored retreats of hunters, anglers and all those who enjoy the great outdoors. The one-

and two-bedroom cabins are comfortably furnished and have full kitchens. Contact: Sandra and Bob Stanley, Feitzinger's Cabins, S.R. 128 Old Rt. 28, Shandaken, NY 12480. Call 914-688-5568.

Children: Y   Pets: Y   Smoking: Y   Handicap Access: N   Payment: C, P, T

SKANEATELES

LOCKMASTER — *Rates: moderate-expensive*
Open: year-round — *Minimum Stay: four nights*

The scenic canals of western New York link the towns of Buffalo, Syracuse and Albany, but perhaps their most attractive feature is the miles and miles of quiet countryside in between. Now you can explore these areas from a truly unique vantage point, behind the wheel of a canal boat. The Lockmaster is completely equipped with a modern galley, three double berths, full bathroom facilities and an open deck where you can relax and watch the scenery float gently by. You never need experience the tyranny of tour groups or the dulling stasis of a week-long vacation in one place once you've had a taste of canal cruising, the best way to bring your holiday home along for the ride. Contact: Mid-Lakes Navigation Co., P.O. Box 61, 11 Jordan St., Skaneateles, NY 13152. Call 315-685-5722.

Children: Y   Pets: N   Smoking: Y   Handicap Access: N   Payment: C, T, V, M

SOUTHAMPTON

18TH-CENTURY FARMHOUSE — *Rates: deluxe*
Open: year-round — *Minimum Stay: three months*

Over an acre of rolling land surrounds this exquisitely charming house from the 1730s. Three separate fireplaces grace the enchanting rooms, a cozy boon for wintertime guests and a treat for the eyes and heart at all times of the year. The great room is a delightful mix of the old and new; the four bedrooms are cheerful and inviting. Outside, you'll find extensive stone and brick patios where you can sip a Long Island iced tea and muse about the gracious lifestyle of times past. Modern creature comforts are here as well, perhaps most notably in the 40-foot swimming pool and pool house. Contact: Village Real Estate, 59 W. Montauk Hwy., Hampton Bays, NY 11946. Call 516-728-1900.

Children: Y   Pets: N   Smoking: Y   Handicap Access: Y   Payment: C, P, T

BEACHFRONT CONTEMPORARY — *Rates: budget*
Open: June-August — *Minimum Stay: three months*

A casual atmosphere and abundant opportunities for summer fun are what you'll find at this beautifully landscaped home on eastern Long Island. Just a few steps from your front door will take you to the private beach, an excellent spot for wind surfing or for just stretching out and soaking in some rays. The secluded brick patio is ideal for summertime suppers. Inside, you'll find pleasant, spacious accommodations in the four bedrooms; there are also two bathrooms and a well-equipped kitchen in addition to the main living areas of the house. Contact: Village Real Estate, 59 W. Montauk Hwy., Hampton Bays, NY 11946. Call 516-728-1900.

Children: Y   Pets: N   Smoking: Y   Handicap Access: Y   Payment: C, P, T

CARRIAGE HOUSE *Rates: deluxe*
Open: June-August *Minimum Stay: three months*
This converted carriage house is found in a very prestigious neighborhood on the bucolic eastern tip of Long Island. Tall, sturdy trees felicitously ornament the rolling green lawns, providing shady spots for picnic lunches and an abundance of picturesque venues for leisurely strolls. The extensive grounds also encompass a delightful heated swimming pool. Inside, you'll be charmed by the great room at the center of the house and irresistibly drawn to the impressive fireplace that forms its focal point. The house offers five luxurious bedrooms, and the kitchen boasts a full range of up-to-date appliances. Contact: Village Real Estate, 59 W. Montauk Hwy., Hampton Bays, NY 11946. Call 516-728-1900.
Children: Y Pets: N Smoking: Y Handicap Access: Y Payment: C, P, T

OCEAN CONDOMINIUM *Rates: expensive*
Open: year-round *Minimum Stay: three months*
This spacious condo is close to both the village and the ocean beaches yet maintains a sense of absolute privacy. The beautifully decorated rooms comprise three bedrooms, living and dining areas and a fully modern kitchen. There is a screened porch where you can sit out and catch a passing breeze, and the whole residence is centrally air-conditioned. On chillier nights, you can curl up in front of the crackling fire with a mug of hot cider—or a more potent potable. The complex offers excellent amenities, including a swimming pool and tennis courts for your enjoyment. Contact: Village Real Estate, 59 W. Montauk Hwy., Hampton Bays, NY 11946. Call 516-728-1900.
Children: Y Pets: N Smoking: Y Handicap Access: Y Payment: C, P, T

ON THE BEACH *Rates: deluxe*
Open: June-August *Minimum Stay: three months*
Nostalgia wafts through the rooms of this glorious older home in a bucolic beachfront setting. Whether you're sitting out on the wrap-around porch with a cool drink in hand, taking a quiet stroll along the sandy shore, enjoying a game of tennis on the private court or simply meandering through the charming rooms inside, you'll be sure to appreciate why so many savvy people have spent their summers here year after year. The six generous bedrooms can accommodate a sizable party, and the kitchen sports all the usual appliances and conveniences. Contact: Village Real Estate, 59 W. Montauk Hwy., Hampton Bays, NY 11946. Call 516-728-1900.
Children: Y Pets: N Smoking: Y Handicap Access: Y Payment: C, P, T

SPRING GLEN

GOLD MOUNTAIN CHALET RESORT *Rates: moderate-expensive*
Open: year-round *Minimum Stay: none*
Some of the guests you'll see here have won their holidays on popular TV game shows. You don't have to be lucky, though, just smart enough to pick the Gold Mountain as your holiday destination. The decor is rustic elegance incarnate. The one-and two-bedroom suites include

fully stocked refrigerators, whirlpools and TVs; some also have fire-places and balconies. Not for those who crave the noise and crowds of big resorts or scheduled group activities or the infamous plastic look, this small haunt in the hills will charm everyone who delights in a tran-quil pace, friendly service and unspoiled natural surroundings—deer, quail and raccoons are frequent visitors. Contact: Gold Mountain Cha-let Resort, P.O. Box 456, Spring Glen, NY 12483. Call 914-647-4332.
Children: N Pets: N Smoking: Y Handicap Access: N Payment: C, T, V, M

STEAMBURG

HIGHBANKS CAMPGROUND   *Rates: budget*
Open: spring-fall   *Minimum Stay: none*
Owned and operated by the Seneca Nation of Indians, the Highbanks Campground offers chalets, cabins and tent sites in a stunning natural setting. Highbanks overlooks the beautiful Allegheny Reservoir, where you can fish and sail to your heart's content; there is also a swimming pool. The Seneca-Iroquois National Museum nearby dis-plays the rich history and contemporary culture of these peoples; the Nannen Arboretum is another favorite destination. The rustic cabins feature wood stoves and are outfitted with all the basic necessities; the slightly more luxurious chalets have electric heat. The general store is fully stocked with all the provisions you'll need; laundry facilities, an entertainment center, activities and tours of the area are available. Contact: Highbanks Campground, P.O. Box C, Steamburg, NY 14783. Call 716-354-4855.
Children: Y Pets: Y Smoking: Y Handicap Access: N Payment: C, P, T

WESTHAMPTON

FIVE-BEDROOM CONTEMPORARY   *Rates: deluxe*
Open: Memorial Day-Labor Day   *Minimum Stay: one month*
Featured in the movie *Annie Hall*, Westhampton is a great spot for a summer holiday. Boats for deep-sea fishing can easily be chartered, and the Atlantic waters also encourage jet skiing, wind surfing, sailing and a host of other aquatic activities. Stunning views of the water are enjoyed by this oceanfront home, a stylish contemporary with five bedrooms and four sumptuous baths. The rooms are splendidly accou-tered, and the impressive pool table will tempt even novices into a game or two. On hot afternoons you can decide between taking a refreshing plunge in the granite swimming pool or just luxuriating in the deliciously air-conditioned rooms of your elegant vacation home. Contact: Main Event Realty, 27-B Riverhead Rd., Westhampton Beach, NY 11978. Call 516-288-0700.
Children: Y Pets: Y Smoking: Y Handicap Access: N Payment: C, P, T

WESTHAMPTON BEACH

ATLANTIC CONDOS   *Rates: expensive-deluxe*
Open: Memorial Day-Labor Day   *Minimum Stay: one month*
Whether you're near the crashing waves of the Atlantic or on the calmer waters of the bay, you'll never be far from the water in these

pleasing condos. Take a plunge in the refreshing surf, partake of some of the many water sports activities or just stretch out on the golden sands—here you can enjoy the essence of summer. The luxury complex boasts two large swimming pools and several tennis courts, so active types should find plenty to keep them busy. The one- and two-bedroom condos are tastefully appointed and enjoy magnificent views. There are also laundry facilities in the complex to help make your stay hassle-free. Contact: Main Event Realty, 27-B Riverhead Rd., Westhampton Beach, NY 11978. Call 516-288-0700.

Children: Y   Pets: Y   Smoking: Y   Handicap Access: N   Payment: C, P, T

BEACHVIEW   *Rates: deluxe*
Open: Memorial Day-Labor Day   *Minimum Stay: one month*

For a satisfying taste of the seaside holidays of yore, imagine yourself in this traditional beach house. As you walk along the misty beach with your faithful canine friend, the sea foam lapping at your ankles, your substantial vacation home stands before you, and you are struck again by its subdued elegance. Inside, two handsome fireplaces and a baby grand piano set the tone—perhaps after a martini in front the roaring fire, you and your friends can gather for an evening of singing show tunes and nostalgic old ditties from a kinder, gentler world. The house is splendidly furnished and offers you six bedrooms; there is also a granite pool at your disposal. Contact: Main Event Realty, 27-B Riverhead Rd., Westhampton Beach, NY 11978. Call 516-288-0700.

Children: Y   Pets: Y   Smoking: Y   Handicap Access. N   Payment: C, P, T

EAST END ESTATE   *Rates: deluxe*
Open: Memorial Day-Labor Day   *Minimum Stay: one month*

Enjoy the best of life, the way New Yorkers do. After a full day of sampling some of the world's finest museums, restaurants and theaters, put the noise and crowds far behind as you travel out to the eastern end of Long Island. Here, tucked away among sumptuous mansions and extensive estates, is where you'll find your five-bedroom holiday home. The aura is one of traditional elegance, but recent renovations have also added much in the way of contemporary creature comforts. Not only does the marble bathroom in the master suite boast a Jacuzzi, but a pool and an exercise room with a sauna are at your disposal. Saltwater aficionados will be glad to know that the house also enjoys beach rights. Contact: Main Event Realty, 27-B Riverhead Rd., Westhampton Beach, NY 11978. Call 516-288-0700.

Children: Y   Pets: Y   Smoking: Y   Handicap Access: N   Payment: C, P, T

SEA RANCH   *Rates: expensive*
Open: Memorial Day-Labor Day   *Minimum Stay: one month*

With a sheltered location on the bay and right-of-way to the ocean, this pleasant holiday home enjoys the best of both aquatic worlds. You can swim, sail or wind surf in the placid waters outside your front door in the morning and spend the afternoon deep-sea fishing or enjoying the sound of the pounding surf. In the evening, there are the elegant restaurants and charming nightspots of town to entertain you—and don't forget that the excitement of the city is well within reach. Back home, stretch out and relax after a home-cooked supper or a night on the town before retiring to one of the three comfy bedrooms. Contact: Main Event Realty, 27-B Riverhead Rd., Westhampton Beach, NY 11978. Call 516-288-0700.

Children: **Y** Pets: **N** Smoking: **Y** Handicap Access: **N** Payment: **C, P, T**

WINDHAM

THE WINDHAM RIDGE CLUB *Rates: budget-deluxe*
Open: year-round *Minimum Stay: none*

This full-service resort in the northern Catskills is ideal for both sports enthusiasts and those who long to live the good life. The resort offers an exercise room, tennis courts, indoor pool, hot tub and sauna to keep you healthy and happy; there's also abundant skiing and golfing in the area. Your villa or townhouse will have either one, two or three bedrooms and a host of luxurious amenities, such as a deck, a fireplace, a whirlpool tub and even a garage. Gourmet restaurants and antique shops are sprinkled throughout the countryside. Contact: The Windham Ridge Club, P.O. Box 67, Windham, NY 12496. Call 1-800-527-4746 (in New York, 518-734-5800).

Children: **Y** Pets: **N** Smoking: **Y** Handicap Access: **N** Payment: **C, A, V, M**

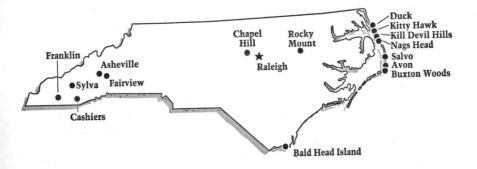

North Carolina

ASHEVILLE

DICK AND FRAN'S COTTAGE Rates: *budget*
Open: year-round Minimum Stay: *two nights*

If you and your family or friends are on your way to the Great Smoky Mountains or heading south from the Shenandoah Valley of Virginia, consider stopping at this one-bedroom cottage in a quiet country setting just six miles north of Asheville. Here, you and as many as three others will find a fully equipped kitchen right down to salt and pepper shakers, a sitting room with cable TV and wood-burning fireplace and, in the bathroom, an antique claw-foot cast-iron tub, which you can soak in to your heart's delight. Dick and Fran's is convenient to all the many attractions of both Asheville and the Great Smokies. Contact: Dick or Fran Lutz, Dick and Fran's Cottage, 257 Baird Cove Road, Asheville, NC 28804. Call 704-658-3877.

Children: **Y** Pets: **N** Smoking: **Y** Handicap Access: **N** Payment: **C, P, T**

AVON

PERON COTTAGE Rates: *budget-moderate*
Open: year-round Minimum Stay: *one week*

The chief advantages of this five-bedroom oceanside cottage are that every bedroom opens onto a wide deck and that the fourth-floor loft has a view that takes in a sweep from the ocean to the sound. This finely furnished house is only one lot back from the beach in Kinnakeet Shores. All the comforts of a solid home are here: dishwasher, washer/dryer, cable TV with VCR and Jacuzzi. Three bathrooms make this cottage ideal for as many as 12 residents, who can choose to sleep in three queen-sized beds, four twins and one sleep sofa. Contact: Sun Realty, P.O. Box 1630, Kill Devil Hills, NC 27948. Call 1-800-334-4745.

Children: Y Pets: N Smoking: Y Handicap Access: N Payment: C, T, V, M

BALD HEAD ISLAND

BOERICKE HOUSE   *Rates: moderate-expensive*
Open: year-round   *Minimum Stay: none*

Only three minutes away from the beach, this three-bedroom, two-bathroom home with screened gazebo on Bald Head Island—an off-shore island some three miles off the North Carolina mainland—offers guests a luxurious retreat from mainland labors. The downstairs bedroom opens onto an expansive deck, and the living room has a fireplace and well-stocked library. Connected to the mainland by an hourly ferry from Southport, Bald Head Island encompasses both a wild maritime subtropical forest and a manicured 18-hole championship golf course. Residents of this house have the use of a four-passenger electric cart to get around the island. Contact: Bald Head Island Management, P.O. Box 10999, Bald Head Island, NC 28461. Call 1-800-443-6305 (in North Carolina, 1-800-722-6450).

Children: Y Pets: N Smoking: Y Handicap Access: N Payment: C, P, T

ROYAL JAMES LANDING   *Rates: budget-inexpensive*
Open: year-round   *Minimum Stay: two nights*

From your two-bedroom, two-bath condo on the 13th and 14th fairways of the Bald Head Island championship 18-hole golf course, you can watch golfers drive their shots straight down the middle or occasionally shank one into the lush maritime forest. If they do, they've got to battle against sable palms, dogwoods and stately live oaks to retrieve their shots. As a resident of Royal James Landing, you will find comfort in the privacy this forest affords your condo. You will also enjoy the use of a private community swimming pool and bathhouse. Contact: Bald Head Management, P.O. Box 10999, Bald Head Island, NC 28461. Call 1-800-443-6305 (in North Carolina, 1-800-722-6450).

Children: Y Pets: N Smoking: Y Handicap Access: N Payment: C, P, T

BUXTON WOODS

NATURE'S HIDEAWAY   *Rates: budget*
Open: year-round   *Minimum Stay: one week*

This tidy three-bedroom cottage on the ocean side of the Outer Banks can comfortably accommodate five guests in the deep Buxton Woods about one mile from Cape Point. With a fully carpeted interior and plenty of space on both a screened and open porch, guests have plenty of privacy. An air-conditioning unit in one bedroom helps cool things down. One queen-sized bed and three twins provide sleeping comfort; guests share one bathroom. Contact Sun Realty, P.O. Box 1630, Kill Devil Hills, NC 27948. Call 1-800-334-4745.

Children: Y Pets: N Smoking: Y Handicap Access: N Payment: C, T, V, M

CASHIERS

MOUNTAIN VILLAGE VACATION COTTAGES   *Rates: budget-inexpensive*
Open: year-round   *Minimum Stay: two nights*

Nestled in the Blue Ridge Mountains, four spacious two-bedroom cottages provide soothing comfort to the vacationer. One bedroom has a king-sized bed, the other two twins. But it is the spacious living room that stands out, with natural wood furnishings, carpeting, dining areas and wood-burning fireplaces. The kitchens feature microwave ovens, coffee makers and toasters, and sliding glass doors lead to a deck with a magnificent view of Whiteside Mountain and Cashiers Lake. Contact: Mary Kay or Jim Voder, Mountain Village Vacation Cottages, Highway 107 S., P.O. Box 279, Cashiers, NC 28717. Call 704-743-2377.

Children: Y Pets: Y Smoking: Y Handicap Access: N Payment: C, P, T

DUCK

PELICAN PERCH   *Rates: budget*
Open: year-round   *Minimum Stay: one week*

A sumptuously furnished cottage with spectacular views of the sound, this four-bedroom, two-level house sleeps 10 in three queen-sized beds and two sets of bunks. A dishwasher and washer/dryer help to tidy things up. Residents can take in fresh air and sun on an open porch and sun deck with furniture. There's also an enclosed shower outside for use by those coming in from the beach only 1,000 feet away. Contact: Sun Realty, P.O. Box 1630, Kill Devil Hills, NC 27948. Call 1-800-334-4745.

Children: Y Pets: N Smoking: N Handicap Access: N Payment: C, T, V, M

T-HAUS   *Rates: budget-inexpensive*
Open: year-round   *Minimum Stay: one week*

From the upper deck of this four-bedroom beachfront cottage there are great views of the Atlantic. As many as 12 can sleep in two queen-sized beds, two singles, two sets of bunk beds and a queen-sized sofa. To take advantage of the sea breezes, there is a screened porch and a sun deck with furniture. A dishwasher and washer/dryer will help keep things clean. Spend your days lounging on the sand or splashing in the surf, then fall asleep to the sound of the waves rolling in. Contact: Sun Realty, P.O. Box 1630, Kill Devil Hills, NC 27948. Call 1-800-334-4745.

Children: Y Pets: Y Smoking: Y Handicap Access: N Payment: C, T, V, M

FAIRVIEW

HARCON COTTAGE *Rates: budget*
Open: May-October *Minimum Stay: two nights*

If you're planning a trip along the Blue Ridge Parkway or to Asheville and its many attractions, plan ahead and reserve Harcon Cottage, a charming country cottage adjoining a larger house. Two people can relax in a large studio bedroom with stereo, easy chairs, a dining area, small kitchen, a bath and a patio. It's only a 15-minute drive to Asheville, and is convenient to the many craft and antique shops that populate the area. Contact: Vivienne Conjura, Rt. 7, P.O. Box 398, Old Mine Hope Gap, Fairview, NC 28730. Call 704-298-9309.

Children: Y   Pets: Y   Smoking: Y   Handicap Access: N   Payment: C, P, T

FRANKLIN

BILL AND LANNETTE'S COZY COTTAGES *Rates: budget*
Open: year-round *Minimum Stay: one week*

Located in the heart of the Great Smoky Mountains, three cottages set in a farmlike atmosphere provide a rural escape in Franklin, which calls itself the "gem and quilt capital of the world." The two-bedroom cottages, one with an extra sleeping loft, can sleep up to 10 people. They feature living rooms, kitchens and decks. Within a short driving distance are a swimming pool, fishing streams, golf course, hiking trails and, of course, quilt shops. Contact: Lannette Reynolds, Bill and Lannette's Cozy Cottages, 233 Sugarfork Road, Franklin, NC 28734. Call 704-369-7014 or 704-524-9651 (nights).

Children: Y   Pets: N   Smoking: Y   Handicap Access: N   Payment: C, P, T

KILL DEVIL HILLS

METEDECONK *Rates: inexpensive-moderate*
Open: year-round *Minimum Stay: one week*

Two bathrooms and three bedrooms will handle a crowd of nine persons comfortably in this two-level oceanfront cottage. This cottage has it all: central air conditioning and heat, dishwasher, washer/dryer, cable TV, ceiling fans, enclosed outside shower and two large sun decks with splendid views of the ocean and the stretch of sand where the Wright Brothers first took flight. The sleeping quarters include one queen-sized bed, one double, two twins and one sleep sofa. Contact: Sun Realty, P.O. Box 1630, Kill Devil Hills, NC 27948. Call 1-800-334-4745.

Children: Y   Pets: N   Smoking: Y   Handicap Access: N   Payment: C, T, V, M

KITTY HAWK

PIRATES PERCH *Rates: budget*
Open: year-round *Minimum Stay: one week*

This three-bedroom cottage has a number of features visitors to the Outer Banks will appreciate. There is a covered porch, a deck off the master bedroom and an upper-level sun deck where you can pass the time reading, sunbathing or simply talking. Eight people can sleep in one queen-sized bed, one double bed, two twins and a sleep sofa. The cottage includes two bathrooms. An enclosed outdoor shower keeps sand from being tracked inside. The house is located between the highways, about one and a half blocks from the beach. Contact: Sun Realty, P.O. Box 1630, Kill Devil Hills, NC 27948. Call 1-800-334-4745.

Children: Y Pets: N Smoking: Y Handicap Access: N Payment: C, T, V, M

WOOTEN *Rates: budget-inexpensive*
Open: year-round *Minimum Stay: one week*

Powered human flight first took wing in 1903 just up the beach from this four-bedroom beachfront cottage, which wasn't built until 1987. Three bathrooms and three queen-sized beds, two twins and one queen-sized sleeping sofa can accommodate as many as 10 guests. All rooms are carpeted and cooled by ceiling fans. It's only 50 feet to the beach here, and all decks have unobstructed ocean views. There's even a volleyball net, a shower and gas grill outside. Inside, luxury is assured by cable TV, stereo system, washer/dryer and dishwasher. Contact: Sun Realty, P.O. Box 1630, Kill Devil Hills, NC 27948. Call 1-800-334-4745.

Children: Y Pets: N Smoking: Y Handicap Access: N Payment: C, T, V, M

NAGS HEAD

BEACHHEAD *Rates: budget*
Open: year-round *Minimum Stay: one week*

The Atlantic is just 900 feet away, over the boardwalk and through the sand dunes from this two-bedroom beach cottage. Six people can reside here comfortably in two sets of bunk beds and two twins. Central air conditioning and heat will keep things cool or warm, as you wish. The living room sports cable TV and a stereo system. This is just the place to absorb as much oceanfront living as you can handle. Contact: Cove Realty, P.O. Box 967, Nags Head, NC 27959. Call 919-441-6391 or 1-800-635-7007.

Children: Y Pets: N Smoking: Y Handicap Access: N Payment: C, T

PAGOPAGO *Rates: budget-inexpensive*
Open: year-round *Minimum Stay: one week*

With a spectacular view of Roanoke Sound and Island, this hillside four-bedroom cottage can sleep nine in two queen-sized beds, one double and three singles. Two bathrooms will serve the whole gang. The kitchen has a dishwasher, washer/dryer and microwave oven. Folks coming in from the beach can rinse off in an enclosed outside shower. Tennis courts and a swimming pool are located nearby. Contact: Cove Realty, P.O. Box 967, Nags Head, NC 27959. Call 919-441-6391 or 1-800-635-7007.

Children: Y Pets: N Smoking: Y Handicap Access: N Payment: C, T

SOUNDSIDE *Rates: budget*
Open: year-round *Minimum Stay: one week*

Located some 30 miles off the mainland along a chain of narrow, sandy islands, Nags Head on the Outer Banks is a year-round fishing and beachcombing town. Here you'll find this delightful three-bedroom cottage, which can accommodate eight in two doubles, two singles and one sofa bed. A dishwasher, microwave oven and washer/dryer make housekeeping a breeze. A color TV, outside shower, screened porch and open deck with a water view make it amenable for children. Contact: Cove Realty, P.O. Box 967, Nags Head, NC 27959. Call 919-441-6391 or 1-800-635-7007.

Children: **Y**   Pets: **N**   Smoking: **Y**   Handicap Access: **N**   Payment: **C, T**

SALVO

OCEAN POTION   *Rates: budget-inexpensive*
Open: year-round   *Minimum Stay: one week*

This three-bedroom cottage in Hatteras Colony has vaulted ceilings with exposed beams and can be identified by its watch tower, which allows guests a panoramic view of the surrounding expanse of the Outer Banks beach and breakers. Eight persons can sleep comfortably in two double beds, one set of bunk beds and two rollaways. There's decking on the main level and also on the second floor, giving all guests access to plenty of sunlight and sea air. On the comfort side, there is a dishwasher, washer/dryer, ceiling fans and outside shower. Contact: Sun Realty, P.O. Box 1630, Kill Devil Hills, NC 27948. Call 1-800-334-4745.

Children: **Y** Pets: **Y** Smoking: **Y** Handicap Access: **N** Payment: **C, T, V, M**

SYLVA

MOUNTAIN BROOK   *Rates: moderate*
Open: year-round   *Minimum Stay: none*

If you're traveling through the Great Smokies and are in need of a good rest, you can hardly do better than one of Mountain Brook's 12 one-bedroom stone cottages. Imagine taking a bubble bath in a special tub, then baking in a cedar sauna, lounging in front of a fireplace and then retiring to a netted and canopied king-sized bed! Sleep to the soothing sound of babbling brooks and waterfalls, then wake to coffee prepared in your own kitchen and enjoy the glorious view. It is truly nirvana in the Great Smokies. Contact: Mountain Brook, Mountain Brook Road, Sylva, NC 28779. Call 704-586-4329.

Children: **Y**   Pets: **N**   Smoking: **Y**   Handicap Access: **N**   Payment: **C, T**

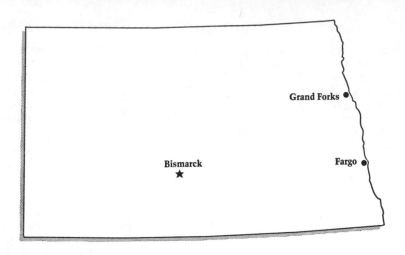

North Dakota

BISMARCK

FLECK HOUSE MOTEL *Rates: budget*

Open: year-round *Minimum Stay: none*

This comfortable lodging, offering completely modern amenities including a heated swimming pool, contains 20 housekeeping one- and two-bedroom units, each featuring complete kitchen facilities, air conditioning, and cable TV. Two blocks north of Bismarck's business loop, the residence is also within easy reach of the top restaurants and landmarks of North Dakota's capital city. Visit the state capitol building, home of the "Roughrider Gallery" of famous and notorious Dakotans, and Camp Hancock Park, site of the area's first U.S. Army outpost built in 1872. Or take a cruise on "The Far West on the Missouri," an impeccable replica of the riverboat used by General Sheriden to ferry supplies to troops during the bloody Indian wars. Contact: Best Western Fleck House Motel, 122 East Thayer Avenue, Bismarck, ND 58501. Call 1-701-255-1450 or 1-800-528-1234.

Children: **Y** Pets: **N** Smoking: **Y** Handicap Access: **N** Payment: **All**

GRAND FORKS

BEST WESTERN TOWN HOUSE *Rates: inexpensive-moderate*

Open: year-round *Minimum Stay: none*

Taking advantage of the legalized blackjack gambling available in Grand Forks, this well-appointed inn features a casino that happens to be one of the town's hottest nightspots. Other recreational facilities, including miniature golf and an inviting indoor pool, Jacuzzi and sauna, are also available right on the premises. The accommodations are comfortable and meticulously maintained. Ten one- and two-bedroom housekeeping apartments are provided, each containing a fully equipped kitchen. Among the tourist attractions within easy reach is the Dakota Queen Riverboat, offering sightseeing voyages and dinner cruises along the Red River. Contact: Best Western Town House, P.O. Box 309, Grand Forks, ND 58203. Call 1-701-746-5411 or 1-800-528-1234.

Children: Y   Pets: N   Smoking: Y   Handicap Access: Y   Payment: All

Ohio

ANDOVER

PYMATUNING STATE PARK   *Rates: Budget*
Open: year-round   *Minimum Stay: one week*

Pymatuning State Park is located in the northeastern corner of Ohio, on the western shore of Pymatuning Reservoir. Over 60 housekeeping cabins are available here, the deluxe units accommodating up to six and featuring two bedrooms, a living room, kitchen, dining area, and screened porch, while the standard units sleep four and contain a combination living room/kitchen. With the beach only about 150 feet away, swimming, boating, and some of the state's best fishing is practically right at your doorstep, and there's also fine tennis and hiking within easy reach. But the park is truly a four-season vacation spot, with terrific winter sports facilities for skating, snowmobiling, cross-country skiing, and ice fishing. Contact: Jim Tillman, Manager, Pymatuning State Park, R.D. 1, P.O. Box 1000, Andover, OH 44003. Call 1-216-293-6329/30.

Children: Y Pets: N Smoking: Y Handicap Access: N Payment: C, P, T, O

FRIENDSHIP

SHAWNEE STATE PARK LODGE   *Rates: budget*
Open: year-round   *Minimum Stay: one week*

Enjoy the splendor of the Ohio River Valley in autumn, when the "Little Rockies" explode into breathtaking fall foliage, or in winter, a pristine, frosted, woodland landscape. Shawnee State Park Lodge offers

25 two-bedroom cabins heated for year-round comfort. A host of amenities includes a sauna and whirlpool, game room, full-service restaurant and heated indoor swimming pool. Outdoors, opportunities abound for backpacking, bicycling, golf, canoeing, fishing, hunting and, in winter, sledding and cross-country skiing. Guests will also want to sample unique area attractions, including local farms, museums and wineries. Shawnee is perfect for the vacationer who wants to rough-it in comfort. Contact: Barb Lange, Shawnee State Park Lodge, P.O. Box 189, State Route 125, Friendship, OH 45630. Call 614-858-6621.

Children: Y   Pets: N   Smoking: Y   Handicap Access: Y   Payment: All

LOGAN

HOCKING HILLS STATE PARK CABINS   *Rates: budget*
Open: year-round   *Minimum Stay: one week*

This scenic state park is best known for its six recess caves—one of them the one-time home of a Civil War soldier! Campers can enjoy hiking, fishing, outdoor swimming and take advantage of Hocking Hills' popular naturalist programs. Forty two-bedroom cabins each feature a full bath, kitchen, living room and a peaceful screened porch. There are no telephones, radios, televisions, or air conditioning—keeping you far from modern distractions and in close touch with your natural surroundings. Outdoor grills are provided for each cabin. Contact: Hocking Hills State Park, 20160 State Route 664 S., Logan, OH 43138. Call 614-385-6841.

Children: Y   Pets: Y   Smoking: Y   Handicap Access: N   Payment: C, P, T

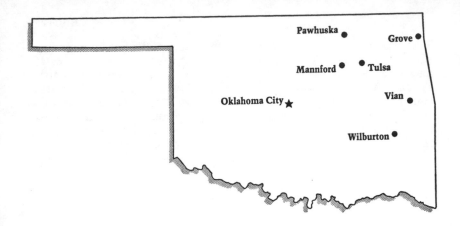

Oklahoma

GROVE

MEGHAN COVES

Rates: budget
Open: year-round
Minimum Stay: none

Located on the wooded shoreline of a 60,000-acre lake, this two-bedroom village townhouse with swimming pool has access to tennis courts, racquetball courts and a fitness center. In addition, there are jogging and walking trails around the lake. You can even fish off an air-conditioned and heated fishing dock. At night, a movie theater and the Cherokee Queen party barge operate nearby. Contact: Meghan Coves, P.O. Box 1868, Grove, OK 74344. Call 918-786-4444.

Children: Y   Pets: N   Smoking: Y   Handicap Access: N   Payment: C, P, T

MANNFORD

KEYSTONE STATE PARK

Rates: budget
Open: year-round
Minimum Stay: two nights

Only a half-hour from Tulsa, this 715-acre recreation area offers outstanding fishing, boating, waterskiing and swimming on Keystone Reservoir, plus rugged mountain hiking trails. What better way to enjoy the wilderness near the metropolis than from one of 21 cabins? Some cabins contain two units that sleep four; others sleep six in two bedrooms. All have living rooms, fireplaces and fully equipped kitchens. The park also has one of the largest marinas in the state. Contact: Keystone State Park, Box 147, Mannford, OK 74044. Call 918-865-4991.

Children: Y Pets: Y Smoking: Y Handicap Access: N Payment: C, P, T, V, M

PAWHUSKA

OSAGE HILLS STATE PARK	Rates: budget
Open: year-round	Minimum Stay: none

If you're in the mood to rough it—sort of—try one of the eight cabins in Osage Hills State Park. Here, in the midst of 1,199 acres of lush rolling hills with a deep forested canyon and an 18-acre lake, you can explore the great outdoors from a one- or two-bedroom cabin. Each comes with the comforts of home: a fireplace, living area, kitchen with utensils, stove, refrigerator and heating-cooling units. The cabins provide a comfortable base for hiking on marked trails, playing tennis, swimming in the pool or fishing on Lake Lookout. Contact: Osage Hills State Park, Box 84, Pawhuska, OK 74056. Call 918-336-4141.

Children: Y Pets: Y Smoking: Y Handicap Access: N Payment: C, P, T, V, M

VIAN

TENKILLER STATE PARK	Rates: budget
Open: year-round	Minimum Stay: two nights

Set in a 12,650-acre recreational area surrounding Lake Tenkiller, 50 native stone-and-timber cabins offer rustic charm. The one- and two-bedroom cabins have living areas and kitchens as well. Don't expect urban comforts or annoyances here: No telephone or TV is offered, but ready access to one of Oklahoma's most beautiful reservoirs is. That means plentiful swimming, fishing, boating and scuba diving and, around the lake, magnificent limestone cliffs, hiking trails, a swimming pool and horseshoes. The two-bedroom cabins—half of them with fireplaces—can sleep six guests, the one-bedrooms, two to four. A restaurant on the lake serves three meals a day, and security is provided by state park rangers. Contact: Tenkiller State Park, HCR 68, Box 1095, Vian, OK 74962. Call 918-489-5641.

Children: Y Pets: Y Smoking: Y Handicap Access: N Payment: C, P, T, V, M

WILBURTON

ROBBERS CAVE STATE PARK	Rates: budget
Open: year-round	Minimum Stay: none

Best known as a hideout for rapscallions like Frank and Jesse James, the Younger Brothers and outlaw queen Belle Starr, this 8,246-acre state park is hidden deep in the pine forests of the San Bois Mountains. What better way to enjoy its notorious past than from one of its 26 cabins? Nineteen of them offer one bedroom and sleep four; seven have two bedrooms and sleep six. The cabins also have living rooms and fully equipped kichens. No TVs or telephones will disturb your bucolic repose here. In addition to exploring the area's historical past, guests can take advantage of three lakes, 12 miles of hiking trails and the only state-operated equestrian system, with some 25 miles of scenic horseback riding trails. Contact: Robbers Cave State Park, P.O. Box 9, Wilburton, OK 74578. Call 918-465-2562.

Children: Y Pets: Y Smoking: Y Handicap Access: N Payment: C, P, T, V, M

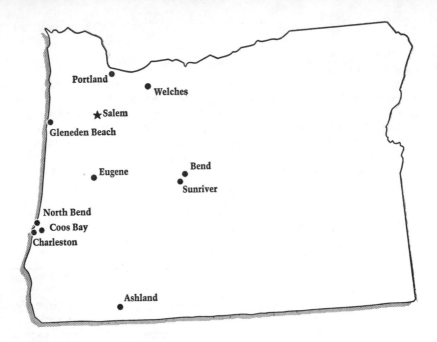

Oregon

ASHLAND

STRATFORD INN
Open: year-round

Rates: budget-inexpensive
Minimum Stay: none

If your idea of heaven is a day on the slopes at Mt. Ashland followed by *Twelfth Night* or *Richard III*, you can get your fill of paradise here, where a host of Shakespearean theaters are just five blocks from your door. Park your boots and skis in your free ski locker before heading to the heated indoor pool and whirlpool to unwind. You can choose from a room with a refrigerator or a suite with its own kitchenette, and each room offers maid service, color cable TV and free morning coffee or tea to get your day off to the right start. Contact: Stratford Inn, 555 Siskiyou Blvd., Ashland, OR 97520. Call 503-488-2151.

Children: Y Pets: N Smoking: Y Handicap Access: Y Payment: C, T, A, V, M

BEND

THE INN OF THE SEVENTH MOUNTAIN
Open: year-round

Rates: budget-inexpensive
Minimum Stay: none

Whether you choose a room in the main lodge or settle down by the fireplace in your own one- or two-bedroom condominium here, you can expect to be greeted by a staff ready to accommodate your every need. Just 14 miles from Mt. Bachelor with its Outback Super Express chair, skiers can avail themselves of shuttle service to the mountain, and then slip into the sauna apres-ski to ease any aching muscles.

White-water rafting, canoe trips, horseback riding, fishing and bike tours are available for the summer set, and a pool beckons the swimmers in your crowd. Winter sports enthusiasts can ice skate, take the kids for a sleigh ride or explore the slopes. Daily maid and linen service and private kitchens round out this luxurious spot. Contact: Warren Klug, The Inn of the Seventh Mountain, P.O. Box 11207, Bend, OR 97709. Call 503-382-8711.

Children: Y Pets: N Smoking: Y Handicap Access: N Payment: C, T, V, M

THE RIVERHOUSE   *Rates: budget*
Open: year-round   *Minimum Stay: none*

Tee off on a spectacular new golf course designed by Robert Muir Graves, hit practice balls on the driving range or pick up an extra putter in a fully equipped golf shop during your stay at the Riverhouse, where 208 spacious guest rooms offer kitchens, private spas and fireplaces for chilly nights. You can jog along the Deschutes River with or without your dog, swim indoors or out, and treat your muscles to a workout in the exercise room or a relaxing afternoon at the spa. Each room offers maid and room service, free cable TV and phone. Three restaurants on the property give you plenty of choices at mealtime, and if shopping is your pastime, the nearby mall will not disappoint you. Contact: Wayne Purcell, The Riverhouse, 3075 N. Hwy. 97, Bend, OR 97701. Call 503-389-3111.

Children: Y Pets: Y Smoking: Y Handicap Access: Y Payment: C, T, A, V, M

CHARLESTON

PANORAMIC VIEW   *Rates: budget*
Open: year-round   *Minimum Stay: one week*

Stroll along a half-mile of private beach, enjoy an afternoon of deep-sea fishing, or go whale-watching in season when you stay in this charming two-bedroom, two-bath home capable of sleeping eight. Panoramic views of the Pacific Ocean are all the more spectacular when viewed through the house's huge picture windows, and you can curl up by the fire in the living room after steaming some clams in the kitchen. Explore Lighthouse Point or tour a local myrtlewood factory for an easy afternoon, and then let the ocean lull you to sleep. Laundry facilities are provided. Contact: George Kaufer, 2660 N.W. Mehama Ct., Portland, OR 97229. Call 503-645-0727 or 503-326-5035. Or contact: Jim and Myrna Francis, 1670 Sargent Rd., Concord, CA 94518. Call 415-685-9327 or 415-932-1313.

Children: Y Pets: N Smoking: Y Handicap Access: N Payment: C, P, T, V, M

COOS BAY

COOS BAY INN   *Rates: inexpensive*
Open: year-round   *Minimum Stay: none*

Watch ships loading in the bay from the window of your room, or light a fire and prepare a romantic dinner in your kitchen. Located right on Highway 101, you can easily hop into your car and take off to see the sights, or work out in the fitness rooms and relax in the sauna before joining the other guests at a wine and cheese social before dinner. A complimentary continental breakfast allows you to get your day off to a great start. Cable color TV, a VCR and telephone are included in each room, and laundry service is available on the premises. Contact: Coos Bay Inn, 1445 Bayshore Drive, Coos Bay, OR 97420. Call 1-800-635-0852.

Children: Y Pets: N Smoking: Y Handicap Access: N Payment: C, T, A, V, M

THE BEACH HOUSE   *Rates: budget*
Open: year-round   *Minimum Stay: two nights*
Enjoy an unspoiled view of Coos Bay Harbor to the north and a beautiful lighthouse to the south as you sip your coffee on the spacious, rustic deck of this sunny two-bedroom house. Expansive picture windows in the cozily furnished living room wrap the sea view around you. Play golf, whale-watch from the covered picnic area or go crabbing, and then come home to cook in the elegantly appointed kitchen. Private steps lead to both the beach below and the nature trail to famous Sunset Beach. Nearby Charleston offers fine restaurants and boats for charter for those who would rather catch their dinner. Contact: Bob Downer, P.O. Box 27, Coos Bay, OR 97420. Call 503-888-5122, 503-269-1926 or 503-269-9004.

Children: Y Pets: N Smoking: Y Handicap Access: N Payment: C, P, T, V, M

THE HOUSE AT LIGHTHOUSE BEACH   *Rates: inexpensive*
Open: year-round   *Minimum Stay: one week*
This two-story, 2,000-square-foot oceanfront home boasts water views from the living room, dining area and all three bedrooms, plus two large tiled baths. Enjoy romantic evenings by the fire, star gazing on the deck and grilling the day's catch on the barbecue. You can gather around an outdoor picnic table and dine to the sound of the breakers, or nap in a lounge chair on the lawn. The house contains a fully equipped kitchen with microwave, double oven and a popcorn popper for those nights you'd rather rent a movie for the VCR. Go crabbing, clamming or surf fishing by day, charter a boat at nearby Charleston Boat Basin for some deep-sea fishing or tee off on Sunset Golf Course or Coos Country Club. Spend leisurely afternoons strolling through the rare botanical gardens at Shore Acres State Park. Contact: Janet and Daryle Nelson, 415 S. Sixth St., Coos Bay, Oregon 97420. Call 503-267-4856 or 503-269-0355.

Children: Y Pets: N Smoking: Y Handicap Access: N Payment: C, P, T, V, M

GLENEDEN BEACH

BEACHCOMBERS HAVEN   *Rates: budget-inexpensive*
Open: year-round   *Minimum Stay: two nights*
Visit the Lincoln City art colony, attend a kite festival or watch a local glass blower when you stay in any one of these roomy apartments in quiet Gleneden Beach. Studio, two- and three-bedroom units are all available here, complete with kitchens, daily maid service, TV, linens

and laundry facilities. Gaze out the windows at seven miles of Pacific Ocean beaches, or try salmon fishing just offshore or steelhead fishing in a river close by. The Marina Science Center and the quaint seaport of Newport are within 20 minutes of your front door. A perfect vacation spot for one or for the entire family. Contact: Alyce Thomson, Beachcombers Haven, 7045 N.W. Glen Ave., Gleneden Beach, OR 97388. Call 503-764-2252.

Children: Y Pets: N Smoking: Y Handicap Access: N Payment: C, T, V, M

CAVALIER BY THE SEA *Rates: inexpensive*
Open: year-round *Minimum Stay: two nights*

Choose from any one of Cavalier by the Sea's two-bedroom oceanfront condos and step out onto the patio or warm your back at the fire as you watch the sun go down over the ocean. Each unit has a private sauna for relaxation, cable TV, a phone and cribs and highchairs for those enjoying their first vacation. Daily maid and linen service are provided, and kitchens are available in many of the units. Indoor and outdoor pools and direct beach access lets you swim and sunbathe to your heart's delight; or charter a boat at nearby De Pae Bay boat basin for some deep-sea fishing. Whale-watching, golf, tennis and museums are but a few of the ways you can entertain yourself in the area, and there's an on-site game room as well. Contact: The Harwicks, Cavalier by the Sea, P.O. Box 58, Gleneden Beach, OR 97388. Call 503-764-2352.

Children: Y Pets: N Smoking: N Handicap Access: N Payment: C, T, A, V, M

NORTH BEND

HIGHLANDS BED AND BREAKFAST *Rates: budget*
Open: year-round *Minimum Stay: none*

Two luxuriously appointed housekeeping units with breathtaking views of the Oregon Coast are nestled on a mountainside away from coastal wind and fog. Each suite has a private entrance, a bath complete with whirlpool tub, a kitchen for nights when you'd rather lounge at home, and a family room with a TV and a VCR. A full breakfast and complimentary crab rings are both included with your accommodations. Whether you stay hidden in this quiet countryside retreat or venture out in a different direction every day, you can pamper yourself and relax. Contact: Jim and Marilyn Dow, Highlands Bed and Breakfast, 608 Ridge Rd., North Bend, OR. Call 503-756-0300.

Children: Y Pets: N Smoking: Y Handicap Access: N Payment: C, T, V, M

SUNRIVER

FILBERT *Rates: moderate*
Open: year-round *Minimum Stay: none*

The accent is on country furnishings in this lovely home, where French doors from one of the three bedrooms open onto the living room with its river-rock fireplace, TV and VCR. Just outside the dining room, on the deck, a large hot tub waits to soothe you. In addition to the trundle bed in the downstairs bedroom, the master bedroom with its king-sized bed and a second large bedroom with a queen-sized bed share a bath filled with sun from the skylight. Pass through the fully equipped kitchen, complete with microwave, to the laundry room and single-car garage. All linens and towels are provided in this wonderful home for six, making your dream vacation complete. Contact: Mountain Country Properties, Inc., P.O. Box 3508, Sunriver, OR 97707. Call 1-800-346-6337 or 503-593-8652. Ref. 15.

Children: Y Pets: N Smoking: N Handicap Access: N Payment: C, P, T, V, M

JUNIPER LANE   *Rates: inexpensive*
Open: year-round   *Minimum Stay: none*

A river-rock fireplace is but one of the many elegant features of this large country cottage. Curl up in one of the window seats with your favorite book, or relax in the hot tub situated on the spacious screened-in deck. Two beautifully furnished bedrooms—one with a king-sized bed and the other with a queen-sized—and two baths accommodate four. When the urge for activity strikes, white-water rafting, horseback riding, tennis, golf, swimming and ice skating are all nearby. A wide variety of area restaurants are available for those days when you don't want to lift a finger, but when you do, the kitchen is fully equipped right down to a microwave. A color TV with VCR, a dishwasher, a washer/dryer, a telephone and all linens and towels are provided. Contact: Mountain Country Properties, Inc., P.O. Box 3508, Sunriver, OR 97707. Call 1-800-346-6337 or 503-593-8652. Ref. 8.

Children: N Pets: N Smoking: N Handicap Access: N Payment: C, P, T, V, M

RANCH CABIN II   *Rates: inexpensive*
Open: year-round   *Minimum Stay: none*

Cross-country skiers can take off from the back deck of this two-story condo and then come home to warm up by the free-standing fireplace in the living room or simply rest in the window seat. This beautiful home has been newly remodeled in bright colors and has three bedrooms and a queen-sized pull-out bed in the den that let you house eight people comfortably. In summer, you can enjoy the private pool, and even those who have sworn off cooking for their vacation will be tempted by the new kitchenware. You can take your meal outdoors to a large furnished patio with a barbecue just off the living room. Contact: Mountain Country Properties, Inc., P.O. Box 3508, Sunriver, OR 97707. Call 1-800-346-6337 (in Oregon, 1-800-433-1457 or 503-593-8652). Ref. 29.

Children: Y Pets: N Smoking: Y Handicap Access: N Payment: C, P, T, V, M

SQUAW MOUNTAIN   *Rates: inexpensive*
Open: year-round   *Minimum Stay: none*

Anyone with an eye for design will delight in the open space of this round home. You can gather the family around the fireplace in the round sunken living room or hop into the huge hot tub on the back deck. Family meals are a cinch in the spacious kitchen/dining area, and when it's time for bed, two bedrooms with queen-sized beds and a third with two sets of bunks make it easy to tuck the whole gang in for the night. The unit comes complete with linens, towels and a microwave among other enticements, and makes a perfect home base for all your family's activities. Contact: Mountain Country Properties, Inc., P.O. Box 3508, Sunriver, OR 97707. Call 1-800-346-6337 (in Oregon, 1-800-433-1457 or 503-593-8652). Ref. 7.

Children: Y Pets: N Smoking: Y Handicap Access: N Payment: C, P, T, V, M

WELCHES

RIPPLING RIVER RESORT   *Rates: budget-inexpensive*
Open: year-round   *Minimum Stay: none*

You won't need "pioneer spirit" at Rippling River Resort, where 204 one- and two-bedroom units provide all the coziness of home and dining alternatives to suit every traveler. Whether you cook an early breakfast in your kitchen before hitting the slopes, grab a hamburger and a salad after a game of golf or tennis or dress to the nines for an elegant dinner and live entertainment, you will find your niche right on the premises. A stone's throw from magnificent Mt. Hood, you'll have easy access to three skiing areas and a host of other summer and winter sports. Maid service and linen are provided, and an exercise room and a pool are also available. On-site conference facilities make this the perfect spot for a working vacation, too. Contact: Liz Ross, Rippling River Resort, 68010 E. Fairway Ave., Welches, OR 97067. Call 800-547-8054 (in Oregon, 503-622-3101).

Children: Y Pets: N Smoking: Y Handicap Access: N Payment: C, T, A, V, M

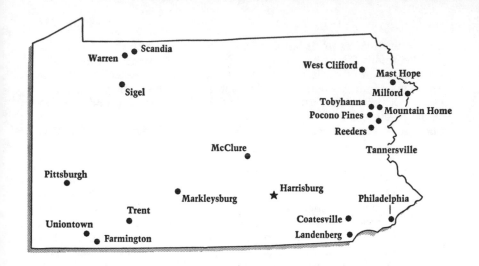

Pennsylvania

COATESVILLE

THE CARRIAGE HOUSE, STABLE AND VICTORIAN

Rates: budget
Open: year-round
Minimum Stay: two nights

Choose from four delightful apartments on a residential block in downtown Coatesville. Decorated with care, each of these air-conditioned apartments has one bedroom with a king- or queen-sized bed, private laundry facilities, a kitchen and private bathroom and cable TV. Two units comprise the gray and white Carriage House, each with access to a private yard; the Stable retains many features that reflect its original purpose, including the bedroom in the hayloft; and the Victorian occupies the ground level of a house, whose dining nook features a bay window overlooking a private garden. Within a half-hour's drive are the delightful Brandywine Valley and the many sights of Pennsylvania Dutch Country and Longwood Gardens; an hour's drive brings you to Philadelphia's historic city center. Contact: Bed and Breakfast Connections, P.O. Box 21, Devon, PA 19333. Call 215-687-3565 or (outside Pennsylvania) 800-448-3619.

Children: Y Pets: N Smoking: N Handicap Access: N Payment: C, P, T, V, M, A

FARMINGTON

NEMACOLIN WOODLANDS

Rates: expensive
Open: year-round
Minimum Stay: two nights

At this spa and resort complex, an activities director is on duty from early morning to late evening organizing events, sports and activities for the guests. One- and two-bedroom condominiums provide the self-catering accommodations here, but it will be hard to resist the room service or the selection of restaurants; of course, maid service is provided. Situated in a wooded setting, the condos are contemporary chalets decorated to a high degree of luxury. A full range of service is available at the golf course, Pro Shop and Academy, and the spa itself offers training programs, fitness classes, workout equipment, beauty and health services and a luxurious pool, sauna and whirlpool. Tennis courts, hiking and jogging trails are located on the grounds. Contact: P.O. Box 188, Farmington, PA 15437. Call 412-329-8555 or 800-422-2736.

Children: Y Pets: N Smoking: Y Handicap Access: N Payment: C, V, M, A

LANDENBERG

CORNERSTONE BED AND BREAKFAST INN   *Rates: inexpensive*
Open: year-round   *Minimum Stay: none*
A renovated stone barn on the grounds of the 300-year-old Cornerstone houses these two guest apartments. The colonial elegance of this bed-and-breakfast establishment is evident in the antique quilts and other decorative touches, afternoon tea service and wide, restful veranda. The apartments also have modern amenities, including a kitchen with a microwave oven, laundry facilities, a bathroom, separate living room and a double bedroom—and maid service is included. This blend of the modern and the traditional can also be found in the inn's full-size swimming pool and Jacuzzi juxtaposed with the sunny greenhouse and cozy living room fireplaces. Local outings include everything from winery tours to historic mansions, and from hiking in the woods to skiing in the mountains. Contact: Linda Chamberlin or Martin Mulligan, Newark and Buttonwood Rds, RD 1, P.O. Box 155, Landenberg, PA 19350. Call 215-274-2143.

Children: Y Pets: N Smoking: N Handicap Access: N Payment: C, P, T, V, M

MARKLEYSBURG

LEBER'S LOG CABINS   *Rates: budget*
Open: May-October   *Minimum Stay: two nights*
Eight cabins are situated here around an in-ground swimming pool about three miles west of Yough Lake near the Maryland and West Virginia borders. The cabins sleep from two to six people and are modernized with bathroom with shower, hot and cold running water, wall-to-wall carpeting, color TV, linens and towels (you must bring your own kitchen utensils). Firewood is provided for the fireplace, and there is a bakery that bakes delicious fresh goods for breakfasts and snacks. Exploring the area is rewarding, as there are sites of historic interest—such as Fort Necessity and Frank Lloyd Wright's Fallingwater—in addition to recreational activities such as a water slide, white-water rafting, horseback riding and boating. Contact: Route 40, Markleysburg, PA 15459. Call 412-329-5206 (4–10 P.M.)

Children: Y Pets: Y Smoking: Y Handicap Access: N Payment: C, P, T

MAST HOPE VILLAGE

SYLVANIA TREE FARM COTTAGES

Rates: budget-inexpensive
Open: April-November   *Minimum Stay: two nights*

In a corridor of the Upper Delaware River overseen by the National Park Service, you expect to find such places as this—wild, scenic and teeming with wildlife. A short walk over a suspension bridge brings you to two summer cottages, cooled by daytime breezes and warmed by open fireplaces at night. A bathroom and kitchen provide most of the things you need—bring only towels, blankets and charcoal for the grill. The sleeping loft has a double bed and the living area has twin beds by the fireplace; to one side a large screened porch provides a place to sit in comfort. Opportunities for private nature study and photography abound (you may spot blue herons, deer, bald eagles, beavers, foxes or even black bears,) and the Park Service offers interpretive tours of the river valley. Contact: John and Jane McKay, P.O. Box 18, Village of Mast Hope, Lackawaxen, PA 18435. Call 717-685-7001.

Children: Y   Pets: N   Smoking: Y   Handicap Access: N   Payment: C, P, T

MCCLURE

THE WATER CO. FARM

Rates: inexpensive
Open: year-round   *Minimum Stay: none*

Ten cabins, one huge 200-year-old log house and rooms in the main house comprise the accommodations at this 175-acre farm, which prides itself on offering relaxing and authentic country living. Thousands of acres of state park land surround the property, which lies in the scenic Middlecreek Valley bordered by two mountains. The cabins do not have private bathrooms, but there is a central bathhouse and you can cook in the cabin kitchens or eat at the farmhouse. Your hosts, the Hassingers, invite you to hike or cross-country ski on nearby trails, participate in farm life, bird-watch, fish, horseback ride, play tennis or swim in the pool. The nearby Susquehanna River offers rafting and boating, and the area is worth exploring for its unique museums and antique shops. Contact: Ken and Sally Hassinger, RD 2, P.O. Box 108-B, McClure, PA 17841. Call 717-658-3536.

Children: Y   Pets: N   Smoking: Y   Handicap Access: N   Payment: P

MILFORD

CLIFF PARK INN & GOLF COURSE

Rates: moderate-deluxe
Open: year-round   *Minimum Stay: two nights*

Five hundred and sixty acres of unspoiled countryside surround this historic, family-run inn. In addition to the bed-and-breakfast accommodations at the inn are two cottages with private patios, where families or friends can stay separate from the inn but with access to its fine facilities. The inn's restaurant is one of the best in the region, serving gourmet meals prepared with local seasonal ingredients; after dinner, guests retire in front of a cozy hearth in the common parlor, furnished with antiques and stocked with books and games. The golf course dates back to 1913 and has been improved and enlarged over the years to challenge both the experienced and the novice. Not far away lies the Delaware River, beloved by canoeists, fishermen and those seeking some challenging rafting. Contact: John Curtin, R.R. 2, P.O. Box 8562, Milford, PA 18337. Call 717-296-6491 or (outside Pennsylvania) 800-225-6535.

Children: Y Pets: N Smoking: Y Handicap: N Payment: C, T, V, M, A, O

MOUNTAINHOME

NAOMI VILLAGE   *Rates: budget-moderate*
Open: year-round   *Minimum Stay: two nights*

The care that went into decorating these cottages and one-bedroom suites is evident in wall-to-wall carpeting, tasteful wood and beige tones and classic contemporary furnishings with touches of tradition. A selection of cottages ranges in size up to four bedrooms, all with fireplaces, color TV, kitchens, laundry facilities and porches or patios overlooking the grounds. The deluxe cottages contain such extras as a sauna, whirlpool, Jacuzzi, VCR, microwave or stereo—making a perfect romantic hideaway. An outdoor swimming pool and tennis and basketball courts form part of the village attractions; inside, an exercise room and hot tub keep you limber. Nearby lakes and rivers provide plenty of boating, fishing and swimming, and no less than sixteen ski areas are within a short drive of the village. Contact: Fran, Naomi Village, Route 390, Mountainhome, PA 18342. Call 717-595-2432 or (outside Pennsylvania) 800-33NAOMI.

Children: Y Pets: N Smoking: Y Handicap Access: N Payment: C, T, V, M

PHILADELPHIA

SECOND EMPIRE APARTMENTS   *Rates: budget*
Open: year-round   *Minimum Stay: two nights*

An iron gate leads into the gardens of this 1860's mansion, which is divided into five self-contained apartments, all with separate entrances. Situated near the University of Pennsylvania, guests can gaze out on a cathedral or sit on the wraparound porch hung with azaleas and wisteria. Variously scattered throughout the apartments are wonderful antiques, marble mantelpieces, claw-footed bathtubs and Oriental rugs, all of which recall the original flavor of the house. The apartments each have their own kitchen and bathroom, TV, radio and phone if desired, and are air-conditioned for the hot Philadelphia summers. The owners are two university professors and their two cats. Within 15 minutes by subway or trolley lies the historic district and city center, with its fine shops, museums and restaurants. Contact: Bed and Breakfast Connections, P.O. Box 21, Devon, PA 19333. Call 215-687-3565 or (outside Pennsylvania) 800-448-3619.

Children: Y Pets: N Smoking: N Handicap: N Payment: C, P, T, V, M, A

POCONO PINES

THE MCCORKINDALE HOUSE *Rates: budget*
Open: winter only *Minimum Stay: one week*

Guests here have the advantage of a wide range of amenities, yet need not sacrifice the feeling of peaceful seclusion that surrounds a house in the woods. The loft, skylights and large windows of this two-story contemporary house let in plenty of light, and a Jacuzzi adds a special touch. There are three bedrooms that sleep five, two bathrooms and a kitchen with a dishwasher, as well as a washing machine and dryer. Cable TV helps keep you in touch with the world beyond Lake Naomi, which also has a nightclub and restaurant, a tennis club, an ice-skating pond and a recreation center. The Poconos contain a number of state parks and well-known ski resorts, several of which are within minutes of the house—including Big Boulder, Camelback and Jack Frost. Contact: CR Baxter Rentals Unlimited, Route 940, Pocono Pines, PA 18350. Call 717-646-1000 or 800-962-RENT. Ref. 338MC.

Children: Y Pets: N Smoking: Y Handicap Access: N Payment: C, P, T, V, M

THE VASARKOVY HOUSE *Rates: budget-inexpensive*
Open: year-round *Minimum Stay: three nights*

This three-bedroom contemporary house has a long deck running along the back and an inside loft where the sun streams in through two skylights. Altogether there is room for up to 10 guests in two double beds and six singles. The kitchen contains a dishwasher, and there is a washing machine and dryer to make your stay easier. You can spend all your time outdoors hiking, swimming, playing tennis, horseback riding or boating along the rivers. For relaxing evenings, the house also has a TV with VCR and a fireplace. The ski areas of Big Boulder and Camelback are within easy driving distance, as are a number of other ski areas, golf courses and state parks. Contact: CR Baxter Rentals Unlimited, Route 940, Pocono Pines, PA 18350. Call 717-646-1000 or 800-962-RENT. Ref. 329VA.

Children: Y Pets: N Smoking: Y Handicap Access: N Payment: C, P, T, V, M

THE WIBLE HOUSE *Rates: moderate*
Open: winter only *Minimum Stay: three nights*

The Poconos area, known for good skiing and attractive wooded scenery, is dotted with lakes and waterfalls. Nestled amid tall trees and equipped with a cheery wood-burning stove, the Wible House makes a great base for a winter vacation. The design is that of a rustic log home, but the inside is completely modern—the kitchen has a dishwasher, there are two bathrooms, a TV and complete laundry facilities—you need only bring linens. In all, this two-story home can sleep eight guests. Within minutes away are the ski resorts of Big Boulder, Camelback and Jack Frost Mountain. Contact: CR Baxter Rentals Unlimited, Route 940, Pocono Pines, PA 18350. Call 717-646-1000 or 800-962-RENT. Ref. 146WI.

Children: Y Pets: N Smoking: Y Handicap Access: N Payment: C, P, T, V, M

REEDERS

MOUNTAIN SPRINGS LAKE *Rates: budget-moderate*
Open: year-round *Minimum Stay: two nights*
Hidden in the woods or on the shore around this spring-fed lake at the foot of Camelback Mountain in the Poconos, these cottages and apartments are part of a vacationland that has been built for seclusion. The accommodations range from two-bedroom rustic cottages beside the lake to studio, one- or two-bedroom apartments. All have fully equipped kitchens, TV, a charcoal grill and outdoor eating space and access to a rowboat for your private use. Many contain fireplaces, foldout couches and outdoor decks or porches. The lake has sandy beaches and is well stocked with bass, pickerel, trout and pan fish—both equipment and licenses are available at the office. Tennis courts are on the grounds and horseback riding, golf and good restaurants are nearby. In winter the frozen lake makes for great ice skating or fishing; many ski resorts are a short drive away. Contact: The Rader Family, P.O. Box 297, Mountain Springs Drive, Reeders, PA 18352. Call 717-629-0251.
Children: Y   Pets: N   Smoking: Y   Handicap Access: N   Payment: C, P, T

SCANDIA

RED OAK CAMPGROUND CABINS *Rates: budget*
Open: April to mid-October *Minimum Stay: none*
The cabins at Red Oak Campground are simple and rustic, but have electricity, a kitchen and access to shared bathroom and laundry facilities. Two sizes of cabins are available, one with a pair of bunk beds and one with two double bunk beds. This is very much a family campground, with a playground, a large outdoor swimming pool, a bakery and ice cream parlor, game room with tables and video games and classes in ceramics for the artistic members of the family. Hayrides, hiking, hunting, snowmobiling and biking can take place right on the campgrounds. On the nearby Allegany Reservoir are further facilities for canoeing, fishing, waterskiing and boating; there is a golf course not far away. Guests should bring their own bedding and utensils with them. Contact: Ray and Linda Smith or Jan DiPenti, RD 1, P.O. Box 1724, Russell, PA 16345. Call 814-757-8507.
Children: Y   Pets: Y   Smoking: Y   Handicap Access: N   Payment: V, M

SIGEL

CLEAR CREEK STATE PARK CABINS *Rates: budget*
Open: mid-April to mid-December *Minimum Stay: three nights*
Just south of the sprawling Allegheny National Forest is a 1,209-acre state park full of wildlife, rivers and 15 miles of hiking trails. Rustic cabins are available for rent throughout the summer and fall until the end of deer-hunting season. The cabins vary in size from one room for three people up to a large three-room cabin for four, all with single beds. Although unheated, most of the cabins have fireplaces or wood-burning stoves, the kitchenette appliances are modern and the cabins are lit by electricity, so you can eat in or barbecue at the nearby picnic

facilities. The cabins are minimally furnished in keeping with the wilderness that surrounds. Both Clear Creek and the Clarion River are well stocked with several species of fish. The rivers also provide excellent swimming and canoeing; canoes can be rented locally. Contact: Clear Creek State Park, R.D. 1, P.O. Box 82, Sigel, PA 15825. Call 814-752-2368.

Children: Y Pets: N Smoking: Y Handicap Access: N Payment: C, P, T, O

TANNERSVILLE

THE VILLAGE AT CAMELBACK   *Rates: moderate-expensive*
Open: year-round   *Minimum Stay: three nights*

This leisure village contains a complete sports complex with an indoor swimming pool, tennis courts, Jacuzzi and exercise room. It also contains contemporary three-bedroom townhouses attractively ranged over a wooded hillside, each with a balcony. A living/dining area, wall-to-wall carpeting, large windows, a kitchen, bathroom and laundry facilities provide indoor comfort—only towels and linens are not provided. Luxury townhouses also contain a microwave oven and a private bar and Jacuzzi—all units can sleep up to eight guests. After a day or night enjoying winter pleasures at the Camelback ski area—including instruction, cross-country skiing, ice fishing and skating—a cozy fireplace welcomes you back home. Contact: Camelback Associates, Inc., P.O. Box 299, Tannersville, PA 18372. Call 717-629-3661.

Children: Y Pets: N Smoking: Y Handicap Access: N Payment: C, P

TOBYHANNA

THE MAHIN HOUSE   *Rates: inexpensive-moderate*
Open: year-round   *Minimum Stay: three nights*

The loft of this three-bedroom house has windows that flood the living room with light, and in the evening a fireplace casts its flickering glow over the same room. The house is modern, with wall-to-wall carpeting, a washing machine and dryer, a dishwasher and cable TV, in addition to tasteful contemporary furnishings in beige and cream. Up to eight guests are welcome to barbecue outside on the screened porch. Timber Trails is a quiet, wooded community close to ski areas and state parks; the rivers that run through the Poconos offer excellent rafting and canoeing. Golf, tennis, swimming and a selection of good restaurants are other highlights of this area. Contact: CR Baxter Rentals Unlimited, Route 940, Pocono Pines, PA 18350. Call 717-646-1000 or 800-962-RENT. Ref. 045MA.

Children: Y Pets: N Smoking. Y Handicap Access: N Payment: C, P, T, V, M

TRENT

PENN'S SCENIC VIEW   *Rates: budget-inexpensive*
Open: year-round   *Minimum Stay: none*

If you're looking for a good base for a ski weekend or a secluded getaway, Penn's Scenic View offers five accommodations, three for small groups or families and two lodges sleeping 30 or 40 people. The smaller residences are the two-bedroom "Red Oak Chalet" and "Green

Hemlock Cabin," plus the "Blue Spruce Annex," a one-bedroom style. Built for a rustic woodsy look with wide balconies, all three contain bathrooms with shower, kitchens, laundry facilities, linens and heat. Guests are free to wander over 150 acres of grounds; within 10 minutes are two ski resorts, Seven Springs and Hidden Valley. Contact: William C. Kohut, Realtor, P.O. Box 415, Homestead, PA 15120. Call 412-462-4300 or 412-461-2179.

Children: Y   Pets: N   Smoking: Y   Handicap Access: N   Payment: C, P, T

UNIONTOWN/CHALK HILL

ARBORGATE INN—THE LODGE AT CHALK HILL   *Rates: budget*
Open: year-round   *Minimum Stay: one night*
This lodge offers overnight accommodations for business travelers and families, including efficiency units with kitchenettes and dining areas. The beds are large and covered with cheery bedspreads, cable color TV is in all rooms and a path leads directly to the lodge, which serves breakfast on the mornings you feel like sitting outside. All the units face the charming aspect of Lake Lenore, and further water recreation is available at Ohiopyle State Park, where you can fish and raft on the Youghiogheny River or hike along its banks. Wintertime activities in the park include cross-country skiing and snowmobiling. The area has a number of historical attractions, such as Frank Lloyd Wright's Fallingwater, eerie Laurel Caverns and the Nemacolin castle. Contact: Route 40 E., P.O. Box 240, Uniontown/Chalk Hill, PA 15421. Call 412-438-8880 or 800-833-GATE.

Children: Y Pets: Y Smoking: Y Handicap Access: N Payment: C, P, T, V, M, A

WARREN

WHITE PINE LODGE   *Rates: budget*
Open: year-round   *Minimum Stay: one week*
This log home is in harmony with the surrounding forests, built from trees cut from a white pine plantation. The furnishings reflect this theme and create an atmosphere both rustic and comfortable, with room for up to seven guests. Although linens are not provided, there is a full kitchen with double sink, a bathroom, a large living room and a wide balcony out front. A wood-burning fireplace completes the picture, perfect for cozy evenings reading or playing games. A good base for touring, the lodge is near the unspoiled Allegheny National Forest, Lake Erie and the Hickory Creek National Wilderness—all this land makes for great cross-country skiing, fishing and seasonal hunting. Contact: Charles and Ruth Merroth, 19 Franklin St., Warren, PA 16365. Call 814-723-9212.

Children: Y   Pets: Y   Smoking: Y   Handicap Access: N   Payment: C, P

WEST CLIFFORD

SKIER'S CHOICE CHALET   *Rates: budget*
Open: winter only   *Minimum Stay: three nights*
Just three minutes from Elk Mountain Ski Center in the Endless Mountains of northeastern Pennsylvania, this chalet makes a great

base for a ski vacation—with plenty of apres-ski extras. As it's a one-bedroom it would suit a couple, but it can accommodate up to four comfortably and self-sufficiently—there is a washing machine and dryer and a kitchen with a dishwasher. The choice is yours of a cozy evening by the fire or in the Jacuzzi, soothing tired muscles after a day on the slopes. Other winter activities include cross-country skiing, snowmobiling, seasonal hunting and fishing or skating. Contact: Coldwell Banker Marshall Associates, Main St., P.O. Box 220, Clifford, PA 18413. Call 717-222-9222.

Children: Y   Pets: Y   Smoking: Y   Handicap Access: N   Payment: C, P, T

WOODED ACRES   *Rates: inexpensive*
Open: winter only   *Minimum Stay: three nights*

An astounding 11 acres of property surrounds this ranch, most of it covered with woods and meadows. A spring-fed pond covers one full acre, providing a place to ice skate, and the woods are laced with cross-country trails that lead right back to the house. After a day on the grounds or on the nearby slopes at Elk Mountain, known as the "Skier's Choice," you can snuggle up beside the two wood-burning stoves. Up to six guests can stay here in two bedrooms, one and a half bathrooms, a living room and a kitchen. Other winter sports in the Endless Mountains include zipping around on snowmobiles, ice fishing or hunting in season. Contact: Coldwell Banker Marshall Associates, Main St., P.O. Box 220, Clifford, PA 18413. Call 717-222-9222.

Children: Y   Pets: N   Smoking: Y   Handicap Access: N   Payment: C, P, T

Providence ★

Westerly ●   Newport ●

BLOCK ISLAND

Rhode Island

BLOCK ISLAND

ISLAND MANOR RESORT   *Rates: budget-inexpensive*
Open: year-round   *Minimum Stay: none*
Some 12 miles off the Rhode Island mainland, this 11-square-mile island is a naturally cool summer resort. From one of the one-bedroom suites in this low-rise complex, you can explore Settler's Rock, where the first Block Island settlers landed in 1661, loll on the beach, take long walks by the sea, cycle the length of the island or do some intensive deep-sea fishing. The landscape is picture-postcard pastoral, with pines, flowers, stone fences, wildlife, spectacular cliffs and crescent beaches. Contact: Island Manor Resort, Chapel St., Box 400, Block Island, RI 02807. Call 401-466-5567.
Children: Y   Pets: N   Smoking: Y   Handicap Access: N   Payment: C, P, T

NEWPORT

NEWPORT ONSHORE   *Rates: inexpensive*
Open: year-round   *Minimum Stay: none*
This is the place to be if you're a yachtsman or are interested in sea sports of any kind. Located on Thames Street directly across from the 75-slip marina of Newport Harbor, this high-rise stands on a gracious lawn that slopes down to the harborfront. After a day on Narragansett Bay or farther out in the Atlantic Ocean, revive yourself in one of the double whirlpool tubs or on the sun deck of your one- or two-bedroom

suite. There's also a swimming pool to refresh sagging spirits. Contact: Newport Onshore, 379 Thames, Newport, RI 02840. Call 800-842-2480 (in Rhode Island, 401-849-8553).

Children: **Y**   Pets: **N**   Smoking: **Y**   Handicap Access: **N**   Payment: **C, P, T**

THE NEWPORT BAY CLUB   *Rates: inexpensive-expensive*
Open: year-round   *Minimum Stay: none*

Stay in the heart of Newport, America's premier resort town and one of its sailing meccas, in a one- or two-bedroom townhouse right on the waterfront. This location will give you access to shops, antiques, the fabulous mansions for which Newport is renowned, the wharf area and its restaurants and spectacular Ocean Drive. The two-level townhouses have decks on both levels overlooking Narragansett Bay. If you're not lured by nearby eateries, prepare that freshly caught fish in your fully stocked kitchen. Contact: The Newport Bay Club, America's Cup Avenue, Box 1440, Newport, RI 02840. Call 401-849-8600.

Children: **Y**   Pets: **N**   Smoking: **Y**   Handicap Access: **N**   Payment: **C, P, T**

WESTERLY

WINNAPAUG INN   *Rates: budget-inexpensive*
Open: March-October   *Minimum Stay: none*

Overlooking the Atlantic Ocean, Block Island and Montauk Point, this inn offers the perfect vacation hideaway: fully equipped efficiency apartments with air conditioning, telephones, kitchenettes, color TVs and private decks. Play the Winnapaug Golf Course, swim in the heated pool or take in the sun at Misquamicut's private beach—it's all included with your rental. Nearby is Mystic Seaport, downtown Westerly and historic Watch Hill. Contact: Winnapaug Inn, 169 Shore Road, Westerly, RI 02891. Call 800-288-9906 (in Rhode Island, 401-348-8350).

Children: **Y** Pets: **N** Smoking: **Y** Handicap Access: **N** Payment: **C, T, A, V, M**

South Carolina

CHARLESTON

MAISON DU PRE

Rates: inexpensive-expensive
Open: year-round
Minimum Stay: none

Loving care has been taken in restoring the three Charleston "single houses" and two carriage houses, circa 1804, that make up this inn. Its pastel colors and Oriental rugs evoke images of an elegant past. All rooms feature private baths, queen-sized and twin beds, cable color TV and telephones. Some offer private entrances, porches and canopy beds. The Carriage House kitchen suite includes cooking facilities. Garden courtyards, flowing fountains and wrought-iron gates add to the ambiance and put guests in the mood for history. Visit nearby Fort Sumter, where the first shot of the Civil War was fired, and see the many elegant homes that survived the Revolutionary War and the hurricanes and devastating fires that came in the next two centuries. Contact: Robert Mulholland, Maison Du Pre, 317 East Bay Street, Charleston, SC 29401. Call 1-800-662-INNS (in South Carolina, 803-723-8691).

Children: Y   Pets. N   Smoking: Y   Handicap Access: N   Payment: All

EDISTO BEACH

BAY CREEK VILLA 214

Rates: budget
Open: year-round
Minimum Stay: one week

Located on Big Bay Creek, the Bay Creek Villa and Marina complex offers a swimming pool, docking facilities and a seafood restaurant only a short drive from the beach. The modern two-bedroom condominium apartment located here features sleeping accommodations for six plus many amenities. The fully equipped kitchen features a dishwasher, microwave, and a comfortable dining area; the living area offers relaxation. Central heating, air conditioning and a ceiling fan keep you comfortable all year long, and a Jacuzzi and sun deck provide alternatives to the beach. Cable TV, a telephone and a washer/dryer add to your comfort. Contact: Edisto Sales and Rental Realty, 1405 Palmetto Blvd., Edisto Beach, SC 29438. Call 1-800-443-5398 (in South Carolina, 803-869-2527).

Children: **Y**   Pets: **N**   Smoking: **Y**   Handicap Access: **Y**   Payment: **C, P, T**

RAVISSANT I

Rates: budget
Open: year-round   *Minimum Stay: one week*

This spacious beachfront home boasts several lovely island palms in the front yard and inspiring views of pretty Edisto Island. Two bedrooms with four double beds and one sofa bed sleep 10 in comfort, and there are many conveniences to make your vacation pleasurable. A fully equipped kitchen complete with a microwave allows for simple or elaborate meals that can be enjoyed in the dining area or on the screened porch. After a day on the beautiful white beach, a refreshing outdoor shower lets you clean up and cool down. Air conditioning, a ceiling fan and heat will keep you comfortable all year long. Contact: Edisto Sales and Rental Realty, 1405 Palmetto Blvd., Edisto Beach, SC 29438. Call 1-800-443-5398 (in South Carolina, 803-869-2527).

Children: **Y**   Pets: **Y**   Smoking: **Y**   Handicap Access: **Y**   Payment: **C, P, T**

SERENDIPITY I

Rates: budget
Open: year-round   *Minimum Stay: one week*

Walk to the beach from this cozy house for four, which offers simple but comfortable and clean accommodations and everything you'll need for a relaxing vacation. One double bedroom and two sofa beds provide sleeping accommodations for four, while a window air conditioner keeps you cool. A fully equipped kitchen area, grill, living area, cable TV, washer/dryer, telephone and outside shower add to your comfort. Explore the amusement parks, sandy beaches and fishing piers that make Edisto Island a magnet for tourists. Contact: Edisto Sales and Rental Realty, 1405 Palmetto Blvd., Edisto Beach, SC 29438. Call 1-800-443-5398 (in South Carolina, 803-869-2527).

Children: **Y**   Pets: **N**   Smoking: **Y**   Handicap Access: **Y**   Payment: **C, P, T**

GARDEN CITY

THE ROYAL GARDEN RESORT

Rates: budget-moderate
Open: year-round   *Minimum Stay: none*

Enjoy breathtaking sandy beaches and the endless options of nearby Myrtle Beach's Grand Strand while staying at this elegant, modern resort. Swim in the ocean or choose from an indoor or outdoor pool or Jacuzzi. Play a little shuffleboard, or soothe your cares away in the resort's sauna. You can pick from one-, two- or three-bedroom units, each tastefully yet casually furnished, and each featuring an ocean view and private balcony. Fully equipped kitchens and on-site laundry facilities provide for your every need, and three elevators make getting to and from your suite easy. Forty-eight championship golf courses dot the area, and the fishing, shopping and dining can't be beat. Contact: Sea Breeze Realty, P.O. Box 14769, Surfside Beach, SC 29587. Call 1-800-446-4010 (in South Carolina, 803-238-5139).

Children: Y Pets: N Smoking: Y Handicap Access: N Payment: C, T, V, M

HILTON HEAD ISLAND

C & B REALTY HOME   *Rates: inexpensive-moderate*
Open: year-round   *Minimum Stay: one week*

Let this home's peaceful lagoon view set the tone for a revitalizing holiday. With its three bedrooms and two baths spread over two stories, the house gives six people room to spread out. But the fireplace in the large dining room/living area and the screened porch keep the feeling cozy. Furnishings are tasteful and casual. The beach is just a short walk away, and complimentary tennis is included. Contact: Shoreline Rental Company, P.O. Box 6275, Hilton Head Island, SC 29938. Call 1-800-334-5012 (in South Carolina, 803-842-3006).

Children: Y Pets: N Smoking: Y Handicap Access: N Payment: C, P, T

HILTON HEAD BEACH CLUB VILLA   *Rates: budget*
Open: year-round   *Minimum Stay: one week*

Located just yards from the Atlantic Ocean, this two-bedroom villa offers airy accommodations for four. Beautifully manicured landscaping surrounds the private swimming pool in the townhouse complex. The Water Fun Park and bike paths, as well as championship golf and tennis courses, give you ample choices for healthy activities. For a change of pace, tour the charming boutiques and shops nearby and sample the fine southern cooking at the many local restaurants. Contact: Shoreline Rental Company, P.O. Box 6275, Hilton Head Island, SC 29938. Call 1-800-334-5012 (in South Carolina, 803-842-3006).

Children: Y Pets: N Smoking: Y Handicap Access: N Payment: C, P, T

LOUIS RENE HOME   *Rates: deluxe*
Open: year-round   *Minimum Stay: one week*

You'll find this luxurious modern home right on South Forest Beach, with a host of resort amenities easily available. Six bedrooms sleep up to 12 people, and five baths offer privacy for everyone. The large outdoor swimming pool is heated for maximum comfort any time of the year, and it features a hot tub. In the master king-sized bedroom, you'll find a private Jacuzzi in a more private setting. Wooden decks grace the house and a screened porch overlooks the sparkling Atlantic. A formal dining room makes for great entertaining, along with the large and attractive Great Room, while children will delight in the game room. Contact: Shoreline Rental Company, P.O. Box 6275, Hilton Head Island, SC 29938. Call 1-800-334-5012 (in South Carolina, 803-842-3006).

Children: Y Pets: N Smoking: Y Handicap Access: N Payment: C, P, T

SEA LOFT VILLAS *Rates: budget*
Open: year-round *Minimum Stay: one week*

Elevated by "stilts" and overlooking the marshes and Calibogue Sound, Sea Loft Villas offer a unique vacation experience combined with prime location. Eight glass walls in these octagonal villas provide breathtaking views, and the large decks allow you to enjoy an outdoor dinner while looking toward the sound. Private and cozy, the one-bedroom villas are perfect for a romantic honeymoon, while two-bedroom units will accommodate small families. Tennis may be enjoyed at the Van der Meer Tennis Center, and you'll find three championship golf courses in the plantation resort. Contact: Shoreline Rental Company, P.O. Box 6275, Hilton Head Island, SC 29938. Call 1-800-334-5012 (in South Carolina, 803-842-3006).

Children: Y   Pets: N   Smoking: Y   Handicap Access: N   Payment: C, P, T

SEASIDE VILLAS *Rates: budget-inexpensive*
Open: year-round *Minimum Stay: none*

The Atlantic Ocean's just steps away from Seaside Villas, where you'll find comfortable living quarters on what may be the most unspoiled resort island on the East Coast. A queen-sized master bedroom, two children's bunk beds, a queen-sized sofa bed and a fully equipped kitchen make this condominium perfect for families. Step onto the balcony and take in the inspiring views of the ocean and island. A nature lover's paradise, Hilton Head offers wildlife and waterfowl habitats, including the Newhall Audubon Preserve and the Sea Pines Forest Preserve. You can even take a sightseeing cruise to Daufuskie Island, where you can learn about Gullah traditions in this region. Contact: Rose Montgomery, Adventure Inn, P.O. Box 5646, Hilton Head Island, SC 29938. Call 1-800-845-7013 (in South Carolina, 803-785-7061).

Children: Y   Pets: N   Smoking: Y   Handicap Access: N   Payment: All

THE FEREBEE HOME *Rates: inexpensive-moderate*
Open: year-round *Minimum Stay: one week*

Located just a block from the widest beach in Sea Pines Plantation, this home features tastefully decorated interiors and access to the beautiful Sea Pines Forest Preserve. Three bedrooms and a den sleep eight comfortably. A large screened porch allows the gentle sea breezes to circulate throughout the house, and a fireplace makes for cozy nights at home. Explore the wildlife and waterfowl preserves or take a day cruise to some of the neighboring islands, where residents still speak the Gullah language and live as their ancestors did 100 years ago. Contact: Vacation Villa Rentals of Hilton Head, Inc., P.O. Box 7803, Hilton Head Island, SC 29938. Call 1-800-654-7101 (in South Carolina, 803-686-6226O).

Children: Y   Pets: N   Smoking: Y   Handicap Access: N   Payment: C, P, T

THE KLEIN HOME *Rates: moderate-deluxe*
Open: year-round *Minimum Stay: one week*

Retreat from the hassles of modern urban life and take a step back in time into the genteel traditions of the Old South at this family home. Located near the Sea Pines Forest Preserve, the house is also near some of the best stretches of beach on the island. Impeccably furnished, it accommodates up to 12 people in comfort and style here. A private pool, Jacuzzi and sauna add extra touches of comfort. Golf and tennis are available within just a short distance, and you'll want to explore some of the nature preserves for wildlife and waterfowl in the area. Contact: Vacation Villa Rentals of Hilton Head, Inc., P.O. Box 7803, Hilton Head Island, SC 29938. Call 1-800-654-7101 (in South Carolina, 803-686-6226).

Children: **Y** Pets: **N** Smoking: **Y** Handicap Access: **N** Payment: **C, P, T**

ISLE OF PALMS

OCEAN INN *Rates: budget-inexpensive*
Open: year-round *Minimum Stay: none*

The Isle of Palms is known for its miles of fine beaches and a quieter atmosphere than other resorts of the South Carolina islands. The Ocean Inn offers tasteful one- and two-bedroom apartments in this setting, just a short walk from the beach, shopping and delightful restaurants. Each apartment features air conditioning, bath, living room, kitchen and cable TV with HBO. The area's swimming, boating and fishing opportunities are unsurpassed, and there are plenty of fine golf and tennis facilities nearby. The famed town of Charleston is just a short drive away to the south, where its classic Georgian architecture, historic Civil War sites and museums await. Contact: Wes and Dena Wall, Ocean Inn, Box 323, 1100 Pavilion Blvd., Isle of Palms, SC 29451. Call 803-886-4687.

Children: **Y** Pets: **N** Smoking: **Y** Handicap Access: **N** Payment: **C, T, A, V, M**

WILD DUNES *Rates: budget-inexpensive*
Open: year-round *Minimum Stay: one week*

You'll find classic resort living in contemporary style at Wild Dunes. This large three-bedroom house sleeps six and features a screened porch for catching the lovely sea breezes and a small sun deck for soaking up the rays. Hardwood floors throughout create an appealing rustic ambiance, while a fully equipped kitchen with washer/dryer and disposal and cable TV keep it up to date. The beautiful white beach is only a block away, and you'll be close to tennis and a championship golf course. Nature trails, water sports and a yacht harbor on the Intracoastal Waterway provide all the sporting activities you could want. Contact: Island Realty, 1304 Palm Blvd., P.O. Box 157, Isle of Palms, SC 29451. Call 1-800-476-0400 (in South Carolina, 803-886-8144).

Children: **Y** Pets: **N** Smoking: **Y** Handicap Access: **N** Payment: **C, P, T, V, M**

KIAWAH ISLAND

BOHICKET MARINA VILLAGE   *Rates: budget-deluxe*
Open: year-round   *Minimum Stay: none*

Only 30 minutes away from historic Charleston, Bohicket Marina Village features full-service yachting facilities with shops, boutiques and restaurants clustered along the Kiawah waterfront. Charter a boat and tour the lovely nearby beaches, or go out for some good ocean fishing. Choose from one- to four-bedroom units sporting a furnished deck or screened porch, color TV, radio, telephone, central heating and air conditioning, and a washer/dryer. Sumptuous meals are a snap in the fully equipped kitchens, with linens, dinnerware, flatware, and detergent for the dishwasher. There's no need to clean up when you leave, so you can spend your last day basking in the sun. Contact: Kiawah Island Villa Rentals, Ravenel Associates, 2 Beachwalker Drive, Kiawah Island, SC 29455-5652. Call 1-800-845-3911.

Children: Y   Pets: N   Smoking: Y   Handicap Access: N   Payment: All

NIGHT HERON COTTAGES   *Rates: inexpensive-moderate*
Open: year-round   *Minimum Stay: three days*

Surrounded by lush island greenery, Night Heron Cottages' three-bedroom, two-bath flats are a five-minute walk from the glorious beaches of Kiawah Island. Make this natural paradise your playground, as you golf, boat, fish, windsurf or bicycle your days away. You'll soon see why the island is hailed for its unspoiled natural beauty. But the local shops, restaurants and people will make sure you're never inconvenienced during your stay. Contact: Benchmark Rentals, 3690 Bohicket Road, Suite 1-A, Johns Island, SC 29455. Call 1-800-992-9666 (in South Carolina, 803-768-9800).

Children: Y   Pets: N   Smoking: Y   Handicap Access: N   Payment: C, T

SEASCAPE VILLAS   *Rates: moderate-expensive*
Open: year-round   *Minimum Stay: three days*

Seascape Villas' three-bedroom, three-bath flats feature ocean views, open decks and screened porches to take in all the fair-weather beauty of Kiawah Island. The 10-mile beach is perfect for swimming, sunning, jogging or windsurfing. Just a hop away, you can golf, shop, dine or play tennis. The historic city of Charleston is also nearby, waiting to enchant you with its history and Old South architecture. Back at the villa, enjoy the convenience of a microwave and keep the flames going at night in your own fireplace. Maid service is available at an extra charge. Contact: Benchmark Rentals, 3690 Bohicket Road, Suite 1-A, Johns Island, SC 29455. Call 1-800-992-9666 (in South Carolina, 803-768-9800).

Children: Y   Pets: N   Smoking: Y   Handicap Access: N   Payment: C, T

WINDSWEPT VILLAS   *Rates: budget-moderate*
Open: year-round   *Minimum Stay: one week*

Kiawah Island, set 23 miles south of Charleston, retains nearly all its primordial brilliance. Wildlife abounds in the island's lagoons, creeks and marshes, and much of it can be seen from a long boardwalk, which travels through tropical jungle. Windswept Villas offers one-bedroom units just 100 yards from the beach. Some villas boast ocean views. Soak up the sun on a fine broad beach, or enjoy boating and a variety of fishing. A number of shops and restaurants nearby add an authentic island flavor to your vacation. Contact: Beachwalker Rentals, Inc., 3960 Bohicket Road, Suite 4-D, Johns Island, SC 29455. Call 1-800-334-6308 (in South Carolina, 803-768-1777).

Children: Y   Pets: N   Smoking: Y   Handicap Access: N   Payment: C, P, T

MYRTLE BEACH

SHIPWATCH POINTE   *Rates: budget*
Open: year-round   *Minimum Stay: one week*

The Grand Strand is one of the most active strips on the southeastern coast, with plenty of seafood restaurants, nightlife and shops to entertain teens and adults. Shipwatch Pointe is right on Shore Drive, just across the street from the beautiful white beach. One- and two-bedroom apartments sleep four to six people, with all the modern amenities you could want. A living/dining room, kitchen with icemaker/refrigerator, garbage disposal, dishwasher and washer/dryer practically do all the work for you. There's also cable color TV, a telephone and central air conditioning when the summer heats up. Swimming pools and an outdoor Jacuzzi provide an alternative to the beach. Contact: Booe Realty, P.O. Box 467, 7728 N. Kings Hwy., Myrtle Beach, SC 29578. Call 1-800-845-0647 (in South Carolina, 803-449-4477).

Children: Y   Pets: N   Smoking: Y   Handicap Access: N   Payment: C, T

SOFFE HOUSE AND APARTMENT   *Rates: deluxe*
Open: year-round   *Minimum Stay: one week*

This stately four-bedroom home combines the gentility of the past with the conveniences of today. Located on North Ocean Boulevard, you'll find the beach across the street. Have breakfast in the lovely sunny Florida room while you decide what to do with your day. Four bedrooms sleep 14 people, who'll appreciate the conveniences of a washer/dryer, dishwasher, icemaker, garbage disposal, microwave and cable color TV. An extra here is an apartment with a living room, kitchenette and bedroom for four. Contact: Booe Realty, P.O. Box 467, 7728 N. Kings Hwy., Myrtle Beach, SC 29578. Call 1-800-845-0647 (in South Carolina, 803-449-4477).

Children: Y   Pets: N   Smoking: Y   Handicap Access: N   Payment: C, T

SOUTH SEAS OCEANFRONT FAMILY RESORT   *Rates: budget*
Open: year-round   *Minimum Stay: none*

South Seas Resort welcomes you with the hospitality and service that has kept Myrtle Beach vacationers coming back for years. The beach is famous for its sand, sun, golf and restaurants, and the resort's location across from Ocean Boulevard puts you in the center of it all. Three pools—one indoors and two outdoors—give you plenty of swimming options, and there's a separate pool for the kids. Condominium units come with cable color TV and HBO, daily maid service, telephones and one, two or three bedrooms, plus full kitchens. On-site facilities make laundry a snap, and guests enjoy special golfing privileges at 48 fine courses in the area. Contact: South Seas Oceanfront Family Resort, 1007 South Ocean Blvd., Myrtle Beach, SC 29577. Call 1-800-331-3408 (in South Carolina, 803-448-5187).

Children: Y Pets: N Smoking: Y Handicap Access: N Payment: C, T, V, M

NORTH MYRTLE BEACH

BILLY RHETT *Rates: budget*
Open: year-round *Minimum Stay: one week*
Up to 12 people can get off the fast track and into this peaceful channel-side cottage. Dine overlooking calm waters, entertain at the cottage's two bars, or relax and enjoy the scenery from a screened porch. A boat dock allows easy access to the water, while cable color TV, central climate control and wall-to-wall carpeting make the living comfy. Four bedrooms and two baths give everyone plenty of room to stretch out and relax, and a central intercom system simplifies communication. Contact: Call 1-800-SC-COAST (in South Carolina, 803-249-3433).

Children: Y Pets: N Smoking: Y Handicap Access: N Payment: C, T, A, V, M

BROWN DUPLEX *Rates: inexpensive-moderate*
Open: May 12-September 16 *Minimum Stay: one week*
Crescent Beach provides a relaxing backdrop to this large condo for up to 10 people. Four bedrooms and three baths afford privacy, while central air conditioning and heating adds comfort. A dishwasher, garbage disposal and microwave make meal preparation pleasant and easy, whether it's a quick dinner or a more formal affair. At dusk, take a long leisurely walk on the beach, where you'll find gulls and pelicans out for a final evening meal. Contact: Lewis Company, Inc., 432 Main St., North Myrtle Beach, SC 29582. Call 1-800-334-3390 (in South Carolina, 803-249-1409).

Children: Y Pets: N Smoking: Y Handicap Access: N Payment: C, T, V, M

CURRIE DUPLEX *Rates: budget*
Open: year-round *Minimum Stay: one week*
Set on a private lot across the street from the beach, this duplex easily accommodates up to 11 people in four bedrooms and a sofa bed in the living area. The combined kitchen, living room and dining room provides casual and comfortable living quarters with wall-to-wall carpeting and central air and heat for maximum comfort. Spend the day basking in the sun, then relax over a casual dinner while discussing the night's activities. The famed nightlife of Myrtle Beach, with its many restaurants, bars and a multitude of beach shops with T-shirts galore, is only a few minutes' drive away. Contact: Lewis Company, Inc., 432 Main St., North Myrtle Beach, SC 29582. Call 1-800-334-3390 (in South Carolina, 803-249-1409).

Children: Y Pets: N Smoking: Y Handicap Access: N Payment: C, T, V, M

SEA MARSH TOWERS I   *Rates: budget-inexpensive*
Open: year-round   *Minimum Stay: one week*

You'll never run out of things to do on North Myrtle Beach, and Sea Marsh Towers I will see that you do it all in style. Its three-bedroom, oceanfront villas all feature fully equipped kitchens, washers, dryers, wet bars, cable color TV and air conditioning. Master bedrooms come complete with a Jacuzzi and a balcony overlooking the ocean. Before or after sightseeing, stretch out on the complex's sun deck or enjoy a refreshing swim in the pool. Challenging golf courses are nearby, and the area is filled with the finest in fishing and seafood dining. Contact: Grand Strand Realty, P.O. Box 3409, 503 Highway 9, North Myrtle Beach, SC 29582. Call 1-800-SC-COAST (in South Carolina, 803-249-3433).

Children: Y Pets: N Smoking: Y Handicap Access: N Payment: C, T, A, V, M

TILGHMAN LAKES   *Rates: budget*
Open: year-round   *Minimum Stay: two days*

Set between the beautiful white beach and a gentle lake, Tilghman Lakes brings home the spacious outdoors in style and comfort. Each unit features two large wooden balconies overlooking either the pool or the ocean, plus a fireplace for cozy nights at home. Two- and three-bedroom units are available, featuring a large living area and a fully equipped kitchen with a breakfast bar and dishwasher. You'll find a good golf course within walking distance, where you can take in a quick game between swimming and sunning. At Tilghman Lakes, you can choose between a lake and a swimming pool, and there is always the ocean. Contact: The Joseph J. McMillan Co., P.O. Box 169, North Myrtle Beach, SC 29597. Call 803-249-1481.

Children: Y   Pets: N   Smoking: Y   Handicap Access: N   Payment: C, P, T

WAIPANI   *Rates: budget*
Open: year-round   *Minimum Stay: one week*

Waipani's two-bedroom, two-bath villas pamper you amid the sea of activities in the Ocean Drive section of North Myrtle Beach. All units feature cable color TV, dishwashers, garbage disposals, wall-to-wall carpeting and year-round climate control. Most come with telephones. Before or after a day of sightseeing, fishing or golf, relax at Waipani's pool with cabana and pool bar. Take a dip in the Jacuzzi or play a set on the private tennis courts. Great dining and nightlife are just minutes away. Contact: Grand Strand Realty, P.O. Box 3409, 503 Highway 9, North Myrtle Beach, SC 29582. Call 1-800-SC-COAST (in South Carolina, 803-249-3433).

Children: Y Pets: N Smoking: Y Handicap Access: N Payment: C, T, A, V, M

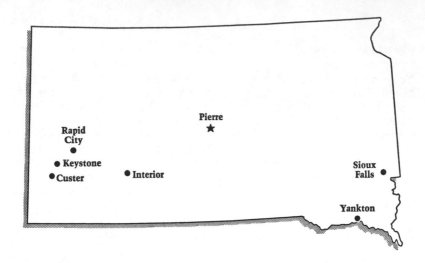

South Dakota

CUSTER

BLUE BELL LODGE AND RESORT *Rates: budget-moderate*
Open: May 1-October 15 *Minimum Stay: none*
The rustic, yet entirely modern log cabins of Blue Bell Lodge are located in the lovely Custer State Park at the base of Mt. Coolidge, a secluded spot that also offers exceptional facilities for family activities. There are professional guides leading horseback treks down old Indian trails and into the celebrated Black Hills, as well as old-fashioned hay rides and chuck wagon cookouts. Nature lovers will see an abundance of wildlife, from prairie dogs to elk and antelope—even buffalo herds—roaming free in their natural habitat. And nearby French Creek provides the occasion for some fine trout fishing. Several types of housekeeping cabins are available, from one-room units for snuggling couples to a large two-bedroom residence that sleeps up to nine, complete with a fireplace and screened porch. Contact: Phil Lampert, Blue Bell Lodge and Resort, HCR 83, Box 63, Custer, SD 57730. Call 1-605-255-4531 or 1-800-658-3530.
Children: Y   Pets: Y   Smoking: Y   Handicap Access: N   Payment: All

LEGION LAKE RESORT *Rates: budget-inexpensive*
Open: May-October *Minimum Stay: none*
Resting on the shore of Legion Lake beneath towering ponderosa pines, the modern and spacious housekeeping cabins of Legion Lake Resort provide tranquil and comfortable accommodations for singles, cou-

ples, small or large families and groups of vacationing friends alike. Here, the still waters reflect the blue skies above and the surrounding sweeping forests and sheer rock walls to make a breathtaking scene and an alluring spot for enjoying an abundance of aquatic sports. Paddle boats and rowboats can be rented, and a wide selection of fishing equipment is also available. Away from the lake, such top Black Hills attractions as the scenic Needles Highway, historic Custer City, and entertaining Black Hills Playhouse are all within easy reach. Contact: Legion Lake Resort, HCR 83, Box 67, Custer, SD 57730. Call 1-605-255-4521 or 1-800-658-3530.

Children: Y Pets: N Smoking: Y Handicap Access: N Payment: C, T, V, M, A

STATE GAME LODGE AND RESORT *Rates: inexpensive-expensive*
Open: May-October *Minimum Stay: none*

The massive rock-and-pine State Game Lodge, the summer "White House" for Presidents Coolidge and Eisenhower and listed in the National Historic Register, offers family housekeeping cabins that combine comfort and elegance with an authentic Black Hills ambiance. The units come in a variety of sizes, with the smaller cabins accommodating one to four and the larger residences sleeping up to eight, all equipped with kitchen facilities. From the lodge, hike into the hills along one of the many marked trails or venture out by ATV deep into the back country of Custer State Park on a Buffalo Safari, where guides drive right into the middle of herds of the majestic, elusive creatures. Contact: State Game Lodge and Resort, HCR 83, Box 74, Custer, SD 57730. Call 1-605-255-4541 or 1-800-658-3530.

Children: Y Pets: N Smoking: Y Handicap Access: N Payment: C, T, V, M, A

SYLVAN LAKE RESORT *Rates: inexpensive-moderate*
Open: May-October *Minimum Stay: none*

With housekeeping cabins ranging in size from one to three bedrooms, each featuring complete kitchen facilities, Sylvan Lake is a lovely spot for those seeking a Black Hills retreat. Fed by crystal-clear streams, the lake is a pristine aquatic paradise, ideal for bracing swims and a host of other recreational opportunities, including superb trout fishing. Rent a paddle boat or canoe or hike along the shore, perhaps taking some time to enjoy a bit of the exceptional rock climbing available. For less rigorous pursuits, the picturesque Needles Highway runs right by the resort, taking travelers through some of the region's most beautiful scenery. And Crazy Horse Mountain, a mammoth hillside sculpture project rivaling Mt. Rushmore, is also within easy reach. Contact: Sylvan Lake Resort, P.O. Box 752, Custer, SD 57730. Call 1-605-574-2561.

Children: Y Pets: N Smoking: Y Handicap Access: N Payment: C, T, V, M, O

RAPID CITY

EDELWEISS MOUNTAIN LODGING *Rates: budget-moderate*
Open: year-round *Minimum Stay: two nights*

With homes nestled in a quiet valley or perched high up Edelweiss Mountain, this elegant Black Hills holiday facility provides a secluded getaway, far from the bustle of city life. Units containing from one to five bedrooms are available to accommodate almost any vacationer, and many of the residences come with such inviting features as fireplaces, water beds, private saunas, steam baths, and hot tubs. In the summer, enjoy hiking, horseback riding and a variety of recreational activities on Lake Pactola at the base of the mountain, while winter offers the chance to enjoy superb skiing and other snow sports. Contact: Edelweiss Mountain Lodging, HC 33, Box 3128, Rapid City, SD 57702. Call 1-605-574-2430.

Children: **Y**   Pets: **N**   Smoking: **Y**   Handicap Access: **N**   Payment: **C, T**

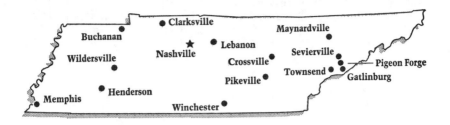

Tennessee

BUCHANAN

OAK HAVEN RESORT   *Rates: budget*
Open: March 1-December 20   *Minimum Stay: two nights*

Kentucky Lake is easily one of the most popular vacation playgrounds in western Tennessee, great for sailing, fishing (especially for crappie, bass and bream), waterskiing and meeting other guests for a barbecue by the shore. At Oak Haven, near Paris Landing State Park, there are nine different accommodation choices, ranging from one-bedroom apartments to two-bedroom cottages and two-bedroom mobile homes that sleep a total of five. All are completely furnished, with outfitted kitchens, TVs, air conditioning and a complimentary boat slip. This small resort is right on the lake, with its own swimming pool and boat dock offering pontoon rental. Contact: Art and Connie Highland, Oak Haven Resort, Rt. 1, Box 23, Buchanan, TN 38222. Call 901-642-1550.

Children: **Y**   Pets: **N**   Smoking: **Y**   Handicap: **N**   Payment: **C, P, T, V, M, O**

CLARKSVILLE

HACHLAND HILL INN   *Rates: budget*
Open: year-round   *Minimum Stay: none*

Hachland Hill Inn and its sister inn, Hachland Vineyard, are both located in the outskirts of Nashville, making them convenient way stations for country music aficionados. Hachland Hill is built around a 1790's log home, decorated with American country antiques and surrounded by a bird sanctuary and fields of wildflowers. It sleeps 25 to 30 people in all, and though there are kitchenettes, the proprietress is an experienced caterer capable of whipping up dishes like chicken cordon bleu and beef Wellington for her guests—which is why the inn is particularly popular for large rental groups like wedding parties and family reunions. Contact: Joe and Phila Hach, Highland Hill Inn, 1601 Madison Street, Clarksville, TN 37043. Call 615-647-4084 or 615-255-1727.

Children: Y Pets: N Smoking: Y Handicap Access: Y Payment: C, P, A, V

CROSSVILLE

CUMBERLAND MOUNTAIN STATE PARK CABINS	*Rates: budget*
Open: year-round	*Minimum Stay: two nights*

Cumberland Mountain State Park sits astride the largest timbered plateau in America—the Cumberland Plateau, which covers a fair portion of central Tennessee. It has all the amenities of other Tennessee vacation facilities, including a lake with swimming beach, marina, picnic and playgrounds, a restaurant, tennis courts, trails, stables and recreation lodge. Hidden among the trees, its cabins are of handsome modern construction. They are accessible by a landmark bridge made of local Crab Orchard stone by the Civilian Conservation Corps in the 1930s. They range in size from one-room duplexes to three-bedroom units and come complete with kitchens, air conditioning, central heat, decks, cable TV and linens. One large lodge is available for groups of up to 16, with a fireplace, rustic furniture, and cane-bottomed rocking chairs. Contact: Cumberland Mountain State Park, Rt. 8, Box 322, Crossville, TN 38555. Call 615-484-6138.

Children: Y Pets: Y Smoking: Y Handicap Access: N Payment: C, P, T, A, V, M

FAIRFIELD GLADE

FAIRFIELD GLADE—KENSINGTON W.	*Rates: inexpensive-deluxe*
Open: year-round	*Minimum Stay: none*

The luxurious one- and two-bedroom villas at Fairfield Glade are scattered across a 12,000-acre resort in central Tennessee, south of Crossville. In addition to the acreage, this self-contained vacation playground has two championship golf courses, three swimming pools, tennis courts and a riding stable. The villas line the banks of Lake St. George close to the marina, facilitating access to water sports. Nearby are the 80,000-acre Catoosa Wildlife Refuge (popular with hunters), Cumberland Mountain State Park and Fall Creek Falls (the highest waterfall east of the Mississippi). Contact: Fairfield Glade—Kensington W., P.O. Box 1500, Fairfield Glade, TN 38555. Call 615-484-7521.

Children: Y Pets: N Smoking: Y Handicap Access: N Payment: All

GATLINBURG

CARR'S NORTHSIDE COTTAGES AND MOTEL	*Rates: budget-moderate*
Open: year-round	*Minimum Stay: three nights*

Carr's is a rustic, family-run motel and cottage complex situated on a wooded hillside near the Great Smoky Mountain hub of Gatlinburg and the Sugarlands National Park Visitor Center. In addition to two-

and three-bedroom cottages, the intimate little resort (complete with swimming pool, picnic area and playgrounds, game area and busily bubbling creek) includes four handsome, newly constructed chalets located a few blocks from the motel. These one- and two-bedroom hideaways, perched mountainside on stilts, come complete with great views and feature such amenities as myriad decks and balconies, Jacuzzis and fireplaces. After a hike in the Smokies or an afternoon canvassing the 300 shops in Gatlinburg, they make a perfect retreat. Contact: Carr's Northside Cottages and Motel, P.O. Box 728, Gatlinburg, TN 37738. Call 615-436-4836.

Children: Y Pets: N Smoking: N Handicap Access: N Payment: C, A, V, M, O

COBBLY NOB   *Rates: budget-inexpensive*
Open: year-round   *Minimum Stay: two nights*

Close to all the action in Gatlinburg, all the fun in Pigeon Forge (like the Dollywood Amusement Park), and all the beauty of the national park, these country log cabins, golf course condos, and King of the Mountain chalets make excellent Great Smoky Mountain vacation headquarters. There are 50 low-rise, one- to three-bedroom units to choose from, situated on a 1,000-acre resort that features four swimming pools, tennis and golf facilities and a restaurant and bar on the premises. The golf condos have patios and grills; the log cabins, Jacuzzis, skylights and stone fireplaces; and the King of the Mountain chalets, holding 22 people in all, boast spa rooms with six-seat hot tubs. Contact: Cobbly Nob, Rt. 3, Box 619, Gatlinburg, TN 37738. Call 615-436-5298.

Children: Y   Pets: N   Smoking: Y   Handicap Access: Y   Payment: C, P, T

CONDO VILLAS OF GATLINBURG   *Rates: budget-inexpensive*
Open: year-round   *Minimum Stay: two nights*

This wooded development convenient to Gatlinburg is composed of 60 early American log homes featuring sweeping views of the mountains, plus striking chalet villas furnished contemporary-style, with soaring cathedral ceilings, exposed beams and whirlpool tubs in the bathrooms. The one-, two- and three-bedroom log cabins and villas cluster around a heated swimming pool particularly beloved by kids because of its bubbling waterfall, and are surrounded by carefully tended grounds, picnic areas and hiking trails. Ski packages are available. Contact: Condo Villas of Gatlinburg, 201 Parkway, Gatlinburg, TN 37738. Call 1-800-223-6264 (in Tennessee, 615-436-4121).

Children: Y   Pets: N   Smoking: P   Handicap Access: N   Payment: A, V, M

DEER RIDGE RESORT   *Rates: budget-moderate*
Open: year-round   *Minimum Stay: two nights*

Located a comfortable 11 miles from downtown Gatlinburg, 13 miles from the Ober Gatlinburg ski area, and at the front door of the Great Smoky Mountain National Park—with historic homesteads, 6,000-foot peaks, 250 miles of scenic roads and 900 miles of hiking trails—Deer Ridge Resort is nonetheless its own self-sufficient mountain vacation playground. The grounds hold an 18-hole golf course, swimming pool, tennis courts and children's recreation center. Its 84 low-rise condos range in size from one to three bedrooms and feature private balconies with breathtaking 180-degree views, fully equipped kitchens and daily maid service. Contact: Deer Ridge Mountain Resort, Rt. 3, Box 849, Gatlinburg, TN 37738. Call 1-800-631-3379 (in Tennessee, 615-436-2325).

Children: Y Pets: N Smoking: Y Handicap Access: Y Payment: A, V, M

HIGHLAND CONDOMINIUMS *Rates: budget-moderate*
Open: year-round *Minimum Stay: two nights*
The Cherokee Indians called the mountains in eastern Tennessee "the Place of the Blue Smoke," and the beautiful haze that blanketed the peaks back then is still apparent today, whether you come to the Smokies for skiing, watching wildlife, hiking the Appalachian Trail or partaking of the varied pleasures in resort towns like Gatlinburg. Highland Condos puts you close to it all. They're exceedingly spacious, ranging in size from one to three bedrooms with private baths, and have private entrances, wood-stocked fireplaces, whirlpool baths and well-equipped kitchens. There's a pool on the grounds, and linen service comes with rental. Contact: Highland Condominiums, Campbell-Lead Road, Rt. 4, Box 369, Gatlinburg, TN 37738. Call 615-436-3547.

Children: Y Pets: N Smoking: Y Handicap Access: N Payment: C, P, T, V, M

OAK SQUARE AT GATLINBURG *Rates: budget-moderate*
Open: year-round *Minimum Stay: none*
The Gatlinburg public trolley stops at the doorstep of Oak Square, making trips to Dollywood and downtown shopping a breeze. These one- and two-bedroom high-rise condos with elevator service feature wood-burning fireplaces, kitchenettes, use of a swimming pool, and daily maid and linen service. Close by, too, are the Aerial Tramway, Great Smoky Mountain National Park, Great Smoky Arts and Crafts Community and Gatlinburg Space Needle. Contact: Oak Square at Gatlinburg, 990 River Road, Gatlinburg, TN 37738. Call 1-800-423-5182 (in Tennessee, 615-436-7582).

Children: Y Pets: N Smoking: Y Handicap: N Payment: C, P, T, A, V, M

POWDERMILL LOG *Rates: inexpensive*
Open year-round *Minimum Stay: three nights*
This deluxe, three-level mountain hideaway built of hand-hewn logs is near the craft-tour area of Gatlinburg and the 500,000 wilderness acres of the Great Smoky National Park. It accommodates 16, making it great for groups of friends or extended family reunions, and boasts six bedrooms furnished with king beds, a living room with a stone fireplace and lovely exposed beams and a knock-out master suite with its own private Jacuzzi and deck. For the rest of the hot tub crowd, there's a large Jacuzzi spa room with lovely views of the surrounding woods. Contact: Mountain View Chalets, Inc., 7281 Ipswich Drive, Cincinnati, OH 45224. Call 1-800-548-3872.

Children: Y Pets: N Smoking: Y Handicap Access: N Payment: P, V, M

THOMPSON'S CABIN   *Rates: inexpensive*
Open: March 16-December 31   *Minimum Stay: two nights*
Honeymooners favor this atmospheric little cabin on Glades Road near the Great Smoky Arts and Crafts Community. Over one hundred years old, it once stood in the Greenbriar section of the Great Smoky Mountain National Park but was moved to its present brookside location in the 1930s. The Thompsons, who live next door, have renovated it extensively, giving it lots of rustic antiques, a carpeted living area (where there's also a yawning stone fireplace), full kitchen and screened-in porch. And they've been careful to make sure that it rents complete with pleasant little extras like a picnic table, TV and barbecue grill. The cabin sleeps a total of six all in the same central room—just like in the old days. Contact: Margaret and Sam Thompson, Box 138, Rt. 1, Glades Road, Gatlinburg, TN 37738. Call 615-436-6714.
Children: Y   Pets: Y   Smoking: Y   Handicap Access: N   Payment: C, P, T

ZURICH CHALET   *Rates: budget*
Open: year-round   *Minimum Stay: three nights*
From the windows of the Zurich Chalet you can see the summit of mighty Mount LeConte. It's located in a development called Chalet Village, less than two miles away from the multitudinous amusements of Gatlinburg (which include an aerial tramway, downhill ski slopes, riding stables, shops, restaurants and even an Elvis Hall of Fame), and sleeps ten in four bedrooms that share two baths. There are two deep stone fireplaces for apres-ski or hiking warm-ups and a soaring cathedral ceiling. And along with the chalet come pool, tennis and sauna privileges at three nearby Chalet Village clubhouses. Contact: Mountain View Chalets, Inc., 7281 Ipswich Drive, Cincinnati, OH 45224. Call 1-800-548-3872.
Children: Y   Pets: N   Smoking: Y   Handicap Access: N   Payment: P, V, M

HENDERSON

CHICKASAW STATE PARK CABINS   *Rates: budget*
Open: year-round   *Minimum Stay: none*
A lake beach, playground, tennis courts, riding stables, nature trails and archery range are just a few of the diversions visitors find at 14,000-acre Chickasaw State Park in western Tennessee, near Memphis and the Civil War battleground of Shiloh. The cabins with decks are tucked into the tall pine trees on the banks of Lake Placid and sleep six people each, in one double bed, two twins and a sleep sofa. Color TVs, barbecues and kitchen equipment are provided. During the summer a recreation director is on hand to arrange hayrides, campfire programs, square dancing and movies. Contact: Chickasaw State Park, Rt. 2, Box 32, Henderson, TN 38340. Call 1-800-421-6683 (in Tennessee, 901-989-5141).
Children: Y   Pets: Y   Smoking: Y   Handicap: N   Payment: C, P, T, A, V, M

LEBANON

CEDARS OF LEBANON STATE PARK CABINS *Rates: budget*
Open: year-round *Minimum Stay: two weeks*

This pleasant state park is conveniently located for Nashville explorers. Its nine two-bedroom cabins have full kitchens, cable TV, air conditioning, central heat and telephones. On the grounds there's an Olympic-sized swimming pool, horseshoe pits, archery range, disc golf, volleyball and tennis courts and eight wonderful miles of trails through the park's unique juniper forest—the only one of its kind in the whole country. The park is 8,887 acres large and tended by naturalists who organize special educational programs during the summertime. Contact: Cedars of Lebanon State Park, 328 Cedar Forest Road, Lebanon, TN 37087. Call 615-443-2769.

Children: **Y** Pets: **Y** Smoking: **Y** Handicap: **N** Payment: **C, P, T, A, V, M**

MAYNARDVILLE

BIG RIDGE STATE PARK CABINS *Rates: budget*
Open: April 1-October 31 *Minimum Stay: none*

One of the attractions of this 3,687-acre state park just north of Knoxville is that it lies within an hour's drive of both the Great Smoky Mountain and Cumberland Gap national parks. The Tennessee Valley Authority is responsible for creating 49-acre Big Ridge Lake, where guests can canoe, fish or swim. Other favorite pastimes are hiking, picnicking and attending organized craft, nature and campfire programs. The cabins at Big Ridge are rustic, sleeping six in two double beds and a sleep sofa in the living room. All of them have warming fireplaces, screened-in porches, TVs, telephones, kitchens and central air-conditioning. Contact: Big Ridge State Park, Rt. 1, Hwy. 61, Maynardville, TN 37807. Call. 615-992-5523.

Children: **Y** Pets: **N** Smoking: **Y** Handicap: **N** Payment: **C, P, T, A, V, M**

PIGEON FORGE

OAKMONT RESORT OF PIGEON FORGE *Rates: budget-inexpensive*
Open: year-round *Minimum Stay: none*

Among kids and grownup amusement-park lovers, Dollywood in Pigeon Forge is a favorite. Founded by Dolly Parton, it's dedicated to introducing visitors to the Great Smoky Mountain lifestyle—in music, food, rides, and craft displays. Just a half-mile away from Dollywood's gates lies the delightful new Oakmont Resort, with such attractions as its own indoor/outdoor swimming pool, recreation room and a fine hilltop location. One- and two-bedroom low-rise condos at Oakmont have full kitchens and whirlpools in the master baths. Contact: Oakmont Resort of Pigeon Forge, 555 Middle Creek Road, Pigeon Forge, TN 37863. Call 615-453-3240.

Children: **Y** Pets: **N** Smoking: **Y** Handicap: **N** Payment: **C, P, T, A, V, M**

PIKEVILLE

FALL CREEK FALLS STATE PARK CABINS *Rates: budget*
Open: year-round *Minimum Stay: two nights*

The falls of Fall Creek in central Tennessee drop a dramatic 256 feet. It's the highest waterfall east of the Mississippi and the centerpiece of one of Tennessee's most popular state parks. Among its many attractions are an 18-hole championship golf course, Olympic-sized swimming pool, inn and restaurant, several smaller waterfalls and miles of meandering trails. Fall Creek's cabins come in two varieties: two-story "Fisherman" units with decks suspended over Fall Creek Lake; and "Landside" cottages set upon a hill overlooking the water, complete with private patios, grills and handicap access. All cabins have central air conditioning and heat, color TV, full kitchens, fireplaces (with wood provided) and telephones. Contact: Fall Creek Falls State Park, Rt. 3, Pikeville, TN 37367. Call 1-800-421-6683 (in Tennessee, 615-881-5241).

Children: Y   Pets: N   Smoking: Y   Handicap: N   Payment: C, P, T, A, V, M

SEVIERVILLE

THE LOG CHALET AT THE VON-BRYAN INN *Rates: inexpensive*
Open: year-round *Minimum Stay: two nights*

The secluded Von-Bryan Inn guards the crest of a hilltop just east of the Great Smoky Mountain National Park and looks a little like a cross between a Swiss chalet and frontier fortress. It's surrounded by porches, decks, comfy hammocks and rockers arranged for splendid views of the Smoky Mountains and Wears Valley. There's also a swimming pool, 11-seat hot tub situated in a garden room, hiking trails, thick woods and wildlife. Nearby, the Von-Bryan log chalet clings to the side of the mountain—apart from the main inn, but close enough for sociability—with wraparound decks (one of which opens off the master bedroom), a fireplace, TV and hot tub to itself. There are three bedrooms in the chalet, a fully equipped kitchen and daily maid service. Contact: D.J. or JoAnn Vaugh, Von-Bryan Inn, 2402 Hatcher Mountain Road, Sevierville, TN 37862. Call 800-633-1459 (in Tennessee, 615-453-9832).

Children: Y   Pets: N   Smoking: Y   Handicap: N   Payment: C, P, T, A, V, M

TOWNSEND

HIDEAWAY COTTAGES *Rates: budget-inexpensive*
Open: year-round *Minimum Stay: two days*

To reach Hideaway Cottages, you take a country lane that ends at Black Mash Hollow—a spot that's been frequented in the past by Cherokee Indians, Civil War soldiers and moonshiners, not to mention raccoon, fox and deer. It's a secluded and extremely homey place where guests' needs are all anticipated. Included in the rental rate are fully equipped kitchens, picnic tables, grills, fresh linens, and wood (in those cabins that have fireplaces). One especially noteworthy unit called Riverhaus sits beneath a huge sycamore tree and is perched beside the Little River, making it possible to fish from the deck. Others have such features as cathedral ceilings, paddle fans and lofts. Contact: Jo Hendren, Hideaway Cottages, 102 Oriole Lane, Maryville, TN 37801. Call 615-984-1700.

Children: Y   Pets: Y   Smoking: Y   Handicap Access: N   Payment: C, P, T

RUSTLING PINES CABINS

Rates: budget
Open: year-round   *Minimum Stay: two nights*

The Jordans, who are handicrafters, have filled their one- and two-bedroom Appalachian log cabins with handmade objets d'art—though perhaps the nicest thing about these two hideaways is their Smoky Mountain views. They're set among pine trees near the Townsend entrance to the Great Smoky Mountain National Park, close to Tuckaleechee Caverns, the Little River Railroad Museum, Cades Cove and the Appalachian Trail. Both cabins are fully carpeted and furnished with genuine Tennessee rocking chairs on the front porch. The athletically inclined will like the fact that the 2.7-mile Townsend Bike and Jogging Trail begins just one mile away. Contact: Chet and Gwen Jordan, Rustling Pines Cabins, White Oak Lane, P.O. Box 307, Townsend, TN 37882. Call 615-448-6715.

Children: Y Pets: N Smoking: Y Handicap Access: N Payment: C, P, T, V, M

SMOKY MOUNTAIN LOG CABINS

Rates: budget-inexpensive
Open: year-round   *Minimum Stay: three nights in summer and October*

These seven log cabins come in a variety of shapes and sizes, ranging from two to four bedrooms. The biggest has a great stone fireplace in the living room, a ceiling fan and lofty cathedral ceilings; its back porch actually hangs over a gurgling mountain stream. Others are equipped with such amenities as cable TV, porch swings, rockers, grills and picnic tables. Horseback riding, spelunking, fishing, tubing and of course Smoky Mountain hiking are all just minutes away, as is the village of Townsend, known as the quiet entrance to the Great Smoky Mountain National Park. Contact: Jerry and Billie Grant, Smoky Mountain Log Cabins, Inc., P.O. Box 115, Townsend, TN 37882. Call 615-448-6016.

Children: Y   Pets: N   Smoking: Y   Handicap Access: N   Payment: C, T, V, M

WILDERSVILLE

NATCHEZ TRACE STATE PARK CABINS

Rates: budget
Open: year-round   *Minimum Stay: two nights*

The 18 housekeeping cabins at this state park have a 43,000-acre front yard—indeed, the Natchez Trace State Park is the largest in the state, containing four lakes and what's thought to be the largest pecan tree in the world. The one- and two-bedroom units have kitchenettes, TVs, decks, barbecues and telephones. Entertainment possibilities include lake swimming, hiking, boating, fishing, waterskiing and bicycling. The park was named for the historic trail—now a long national parkway—that runs from Natchez all the way to Nashville. Contact: Pin Oak Lodge, Natchez Trace State Park, Wildersville, TN 38388. Call 901-968-8176.

Children: Y   Pets: N   Smoking: Y   Handicap: N   Payment: C, P, T, A, V, M

WINCHESTER

TIMS FORD STATE RUSTIC PARK CABINS	*Rates: budget*

Open: March 1-November 30   *Minimum Stay: two nights*

In 1970 the Tennessee Valley Authority built the Tims Ford Dam, impounding the waters of the Elk River and creating a beautiful 10,700-acre reservoir. Fishing is the occupation of choice there, as it's considered one of the best bass lakes in the southeast. The park operates a boat launch, bait shop, restaurant and marina where motor boats can be rented. There's also a large L-shaped swimming pool with a 12-foot diving board. The Tims Ford cabins have two bedrooms and sit on a timbered hillside overlooking the lake. Other amenities include outdoor balconies, fireplaces, fully equipped kitchens, linens and central air conditioning and heat. Contact: Tims Ford State Park, Rt. 4, Mansford Road, Winchester, TN 37398. Call 615-967-4457.

Children: Y   Pets: N   Smoking: Y   Handicap: Y   Payment: C, P, T, A, V, M

Texas

AUSTIN

TEXAS TIMESHARE   *Rates: budget*
Open: year-round   *Minimum Stay: two nights*

Overlooking Lake Travis and the Lakeway Marina, these contemporary two-bedroom villas offer resort living for the whole family. Loll the day away in the hills or by the pool. Adults can play golf and tennis or simply soak in the hot tub, while scheduled daily recreational activities keep the children happy. Or the whole family can tour such popular attractions as Sea World of Texas and the LBJ Ranch before heading to one of the wonderful nearby restaurants. Daily maid service, kitchen and linens are provided. Contact: Texas Timeshare in Lakeway, 18-B Schooner Cove, Austin, TX 78734. Call 512-261-6663 or 800-826-1841.

Children: Y Pets: N Smoking: Y Handicap Access: N Payment: C, T, A, V, M

BROWNWOOD

LAKE BROWNWOOD STATE PARK   *Rates: budget*
Open: year-round   *Minimum Stay: none*

Deep in the heart of Texas on Lake Brownwood is lovely Lake Brownwood State Park. The rustic comforts of 17 cabins accommodating from two to ten persons each include fireplaces, kitchenettes, dining tables and chairs, double beds with linens and bathrooms with showers. A swimming beach, waterskiing, recreation hall, a nature trail, hiking trails and a fishing pier provide campers with days of activities. Or simply kick back on your porch for a session with a good book or a much-needed nap. Contact: Judy Griffin or Renee Blisard, Lake Brownwood State Park, RR 5, Box 160, Brownwood, Texas 76801. Call 915-784-5223.

Children: Y   Pets: Y   Smoking: Y   Handicap Access: N   Payment: C, P, T

CONROE

APRIL SOUND COUNTRY CLUB   *Rates: budget*
Open: year-round   *Minimum Stay: none*

Spend an active vacation golfing and playing tennis when you rent one of the April Sound Country Club's condominiums in the pines. Or visit the local Island Marina for a more relaxing round of fishing. A family pool and two adult pools make swimming a serious pastime here, and an aquatic driving range appeals to those who like an unusual challenge. The individually decorated one- and two-bedroom low-rise condos include daily maid service, kitchens and linens. Contact: April Sound Country Club, P.O. Box 253, Conroe, TX 77301. Call 409-588-1101.

Children: Y   Pets: N   Smoking: Y   Handicap Access: N   Payment: C, T

CORPUS CHRISTI

THE GULFSTREAM   *Rate: budget*
Open: year-round   *Minimum Stay: two nights*

Wander out your door and down the stepped seawall to the Gulf of Mexico, then feel the sea breezes wash over you. Here, the whole family can romp in the surf of the beautiful seashore. Or let the kids participate in the daily recreational activities planned for them at the Gulfstream while you enjoy guest privileges at nearby Padre Isles Country Club. These two-bedroom units are tastefully decorated and include daily maid service, kitchen, linens, TV and phone. Contact: The Gulfstream, 14810 Windward Drive, Corpus Christi, TX 78418. Call 512-949-8061 or 800-542-7368.

Children: Y Pets: N Smoking: Y Handicap Access: Y Payment: C, T, A, V, M

FREEPORT

INVERNESS AT SAN LUIS PASS   *Rate: budget*
Open: year-round   *Minimum Stay: two nights*

The beautiful beaches of Follet's Island distinguish Inverness at San Luis Pass as a quiet, isolated hideaway. Enjoy both gulf and bay fishing at many excellent locations, or hit the pool for a quick dip after a day on the beach. When the sun sets, Houston, Galveston and Lake Jackson, all within a 90-minute drive, offer a variety of dining and entertainment. These low-rise two-bedroom condos provide kitchens and linens, plus all the independence self-catered travel affords. Contact: Inverness at San Luis Pass, Route 2, Box 1270, Freeport, TX 77541. Call 409-239-1433.

Children: Y Pets: N Smoking: Y Handicap Access: N Payment: C, T, A, V, M

GALVESTON

FOUR SEASONS ON THE GULF

Rates: inexpensive
Open: year-round   Minimum stay: none

Simply cross the street and cast your fishing line out into the Gulf of Mexico. Return with your catch to your condo at Four Seasons on the Gulf, where a fully equipped kitchen with microwave and food processor awaits. Or indulge in the wide variety of water sports available within three miles, and end the day with a refreshing dip in the pool. Tour the nearby Galveston Island State Park or visit the Railroad Museum and Sea Arama Marine World. Two-bedroom units with two and a half baths accommodate six; stereos, hair dryers and fireplaces are included. Contact: Four Seasons on the Gulf, 4000 Seawall Blvd., Galveston, TX 77551. Call 713-763-7138.

Children: Y   Pets: N   Smoking: Y   Handicap Access: N   Payment: C, T

THE VICTORIAN CONDOTEL

Rates: budget
Open: year-round   Minimum Stay: two nights

Texas history is at your doorstep in these fully equipped Victorian suites complete with private balconies overlooking the Gulf. Relax in a steaming hot tub after an exhilarating set of tennis or a lazy afternoon at the nearby fishing pier. The children can make new friends at the playground, where daily recreational activities are planned. And the whole family can visit NASA, Marine World, The Railroad Museum or Sea Arama. One- and two-bedroom suites include daily maid service, kitchen and linens. Contact: The Victorian Condotel, 6300 Seawall Blvd., Galveston, TX 77551. Call 409-740-3555 or 800-392-1215.

Children: Y Pets: N Smoking: Y Handicap Access: N Payment: C, T, A, V, M

GALVESTON ISLAND

CASA DEL MAR

Rates: budget
Open: year-round   Minimum Stay: none

Located midway between the historic strand's shopping and dining and the sports and recreation attractions of West Beach, you'll find Casa del Mar. Spectacular views of the gulf and the seawall from every condo's private balcony invite you to fish, shell-hunt and stroll. Vary the day with a tour of a tall ship, or windsurf the afternoon away before dining on a paddle-wheeler. Each one-bedroom unit has a fully equipped kitchen, a queen-sized bed, and a queen-sized sleeper sofa to accommodate four. Contact: Casa del Mar, 6102 Seawall Blvd., Galveston Island, Texas 77551. Call 409-740-2431 or 1-800-392-1205.

Children: Y   Pets: N   Smoking: Y   Handicap Access: N   Payment: All

MUSTANG ISLAND

MAYAN PRINCESS CONDOMINIUM

Rates: inexpensive-moderate
Open: year-round   Minimum Stay: two nights

Just ten miles from Port Aransas and Corpus Christi, quietly nestled in the dunes along Mustang Island, stands the Mayan Princess Condominium. Bring the binoculars and search for exotic shorebirds in the early morning hours. Afterward, doze by one of the three swimming pools or relax in a steaming outdoor hot tub. For the more active, tennis and golf are just an eight-mile drive away. The one- and two-bedroom condominiums here provide kitchen, daily maid service and linens, so you can leave all your cares behind during your shorefront getaway. Contact: Mayan Princess Condominium, Park Rd. 53, Box 156, Port Aransas, TX 78373. Call 512-749-5183 or 800-542-7368.

Children: Y   Pets: N   Smoking: Y   Handicap: Y   Payment: C, T, V, M

PORT ARANSAS

BEACHHEAD RESORT   *Rates: budget*
Open: year-round   *Minimum Stay: none*

Lovely, clean and peaceful grounds distinguish these Texas beachfront condos from the rest. Enjoy a relaxing day of fishing and boating while looking forward to a late-afternoon shopping spree. Or play a few sets of tennis and cool off in the pool before a special evening of fine dining. Two-bedroom condos provide daily maid service, kitchen and linens. A lounge makes it easy to socialize, and a game room will occupy the children. Contact: Beachhead Resort, 1319 S. 11th St, Box 1577, Port Aransas, TX 78373. Call 512-749-6261.

Children: Y Pets: N Smoking: Y Handicap Access: N Payment: C, T, V, M

DUNES CONDOMINIUM   *Rates: budget-inexpensive*
Open: year-round   *Minimum Stay: none*

Meander out on your balcony overlooking the gulf to ponder your choice of activities for the day. Will it be a swim in the screened pool surrounded by tropical vegetation, followed by a turn in the hot tub, or maybe a fishing trip on a Port Aransas Marina charter? Or maybe there's time for both! Located in a veritable sportsman's paradise, these individually decorated one- and two-bedroom condominiums include daily maid service, kitchens and linens. Contact: Dunes Condominium, 100 Lantana, Box 1238, Port Aransas, TX 78373. Call 512-749-5155 or 800-288-3863.

Children: Y Pets: N Smoking: Y Handicap Access: Y Payment: C, T, A, V, M

MUSTANG ISLAND BEACH CLUB   *Rates: budget*
Open: year-round   *Minimum Stay: two nights*

Rent three-wheeled bikes and dune buggies for an exhilarating exploration of the undeveloped coastline surrounding the Mustang Island Beach Club. The lovely shores also provide a full range of beachcombing activities and water sports. And the year-round charter boat fishing will keep everyone telling fish stories for days. Excellent Cajun-style seafood served up in local restaurants rounds out a great day. Furnished in rattan, glass, and earth tones, these two-bedroom condos and villas include daily maid service, kitchen and linens. Contact: Mustang Island Beach Club, Park Rd. 53, Port Aransas, TX 78373. Call 512-749-5446.

Children: Y   Pets: N   Smoking: Y   Handicap Access: N   Payment: C, T, V, M

PORT ROYAL OCEAN RESORT *Rates: budget*
Open: year-round *Minimum Stay: none*
Pamper yourself with a spacious, designer-decorated living room, sun deck/terrace, built-in stereo and whirlpool and steam bath in your master suite at the Port Royal Ocean Resort. Then venture out to the 500-foot Royal Blue Lagoon Pool with its waterfalls, hidden grottoes, swim-up cabana bars, four whirlpool spas and a huge dune water slide. The sportspeople in the group will not tire of the wide variety of activities available along the shore. One-, two- and three-bedroom condos include kitchens, daily maid service and linens. Contact: Port Royal Ocean Resort, Park Rd. 53, Box 336, Port Aransas, TX 78373. Call 512-749-5011 or 800-847-5659.
Children: Y   Pets: N   Smoking: Y   Handicap Access: N   Payment: C, T

THE PELICAN *Rates: budget*
Open: year-round *Minimum Stay: two nights*
Laze the afternoon away while your children collect shells in the sun or fly a kite on the spacious grounds of The Pelican. Situated in a sleepy little fishing village accessed from the Aransas Pass by free auto ferries, this family-style condominium complex offers two- and three-bedroom condominiums with a playground, badminton court and swimming pool enclosed in a large fenced yard. Kitchens, daily maid service, baby-sitting, pool and sauna are available. Contact: The Pelican, 1107 S. 11th St., Box 1690, Port Aransas, TX 78373. Call 512-749-6226.
Children: Y Pets: N Smoking: Y Handicap Access: Y Payment: C, T, V, M

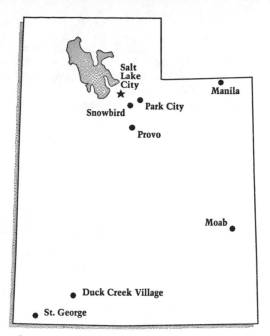

Utah

DUCK CREEK VILLAGE

PINEWOODS RESORT
Open: year-round

Rates: budget
Minimum Stay: none

Situated amid the pine and aspen forests near Bryce and Zion national parks and Cedar Breaks National Monument, this resort offers six two-bedroom condos with room enough for six. Bask in the glow of a wood-burning stove and enjoy your fully furnished kitchen and full bath. The resort is a great base for hiking, fishing, hunting and canoeing trips. They can arrange for rafting down the Colorado River, backpacking into nearby wilderness areas, exploring Lake Powell and attending Cedar City's annual Shakespeare Festival. A restaurant provides real country cooking. Contact: Bill and Carol Koon, Pinewoods Resort, P.O. Box 1148, Duck Creek Village, UT 84762. Call 800-848-2525 (in Utah, 801-682-2512).

Children: Y Pets: N Smoking: Y Handicap Access: N Payment: C, T, V, M

MANILA

LUCERNE VALLEY MARINA
Open: April-October

Rates: moderate-expensive
Minimum Stay: two days

What better way to explore Flaming Gorge National Recreation Area than in one of six houseboats that can accommodate from six to twelve people? The houseboats all feature railed walkways, range and oven, refrigerator, ice chest, shower, toilet, bunk beds and charcoal grill.

Flaming Gorge Lake in northern Utah offers excellent brown, mackinaw and rainbow trout fishing. The marina has stores selling all the necessary supplies. Contact: Jerry Taylor, Lucerne Valley Marina, P.O. Box 356, Manila, UT 84046. Call 801-784-3483.

Children: Y   Pets: Y   Smoking: Y   Handicap Access: N   Payment: All

MOAB

CANYON VIEW COTTAGE
Rates: budget
Open: year-round
Minimum Stay: none

Don't be fooled by this rustic structure on the edge of a canyon. It is in fact a fully equipped one-bedroom cabin that can accommodate up to four visitors. Sliding glass doors open onto a veranda with a breathtaking view of towering red sandstone columns, lush green canyon and, beyond, the snowcapped peaks of the La Sal range. Total privacy is assured in your cliffside dwelling close to the Canyonlands and Arches national parks. Knotty-pine woodwork, caned chairs and a macrame chandelier, plus a color TV and a butane barbecue on the deck mean you're not completely in the wilds. The owners can arrange raft or boat trips on the Colorado River and Jeep excursions in Canyonlands. Contact: Hans and Madeleine Weibel, Canyon View Cottage, Navajo Heights, Moab, UT 84532. Call 801-259-7830.

Children: Y Pets: N Smoking: Y Handicap Access: N Payment: C, T, V, M

CEDAR BREAKS CONDOS
Rates: budget
Open: year-round
Minimum Stay: none

These one- and two-bedroom condos are a perfect base for exploring the deep and winding gorges of nearby Canyonlands National Park. Explore the wild surroundings and then luxuriate in units offering full bath, kitchen with microwave oven, phone, cable TV and stereo system. A self-serve full breakfast is provided, which you can prepare at your leisure. Upstairs condos have private balconies with views of the majestic La Sal Mountains. The atmosphere is enhanced by Indian petroglyph collages, plants and prints of the surrounding area. Contact: Cedar Breaks Condos, Center and 4th E., Moab, UT 84532. Call 801-259-7830.

Children: Y Pets: N Smoking: Y Handicap Access: N Payment: C, T, V, M

PACK CREEK RANCH
Rates: budget-inexpensive
Open: year-round
Minimum Stay: none

This 12-cabin country inn—with individual rustic cabins ranging from studios to four-bedrooms—is located in the foothills of the La Sal Mountains within easy driving distance of Arches and Canyonlands national parks. A working ranch, Pack Creek offers horseback and overnight trail rides, cross-country skiing and a swimming pool. They can also arrange for rafting trips, four-wheel-drive tours of Canyonlands and scenic flights. Your cabin has a kitchen, but the dining room serves breakfast and dinner (included in the rates) and box lunches can be arranged. Contact: Pack Creek Ranch, P.O. Box 1270, Moab, UT 84532. Call 801-259-5505.

Children: Y   Pets: Y   Smoking: Y   Handicap Access: N   Payment: All

PARK CITY

BLUE CHURCH LODGE AND TOWNHOUSES *Rates: inexpensive-deluxe*
Open: year-round *Minimum Stay: three nights*
Nestled at the base of the eastern slopes of the Wasatch Mountains, these high-rise condominiums offer access to Utah's largest ski resort as well as a location in the heart of the city's historic district. That means shopping, restaurants and nightlife are practically on your doorstep. The lodge exudes quaint country charm in a profusion of antique replicas. Townhouses consist of studios and one-, two- and three-bedroom condos. If skiing is not your thing, try snowmobiling, ice skating and ballooning—all available at Park City ski area. Contact: Blue Church Lodge and Townhouses, P.O. Box 1720, Park City, UT 84060. Call 801-649-8009.
Children: Y Pets: N Smoking: Y Handicap Access: N Payment: C, P, T, V, M

COALITION LODGE *Rates: inexpensive-moderate*
Open: year-round *Minimum Stay: none*
Only three minutes from the Park City ski area, five two-bedroom condos house skiers in comfort, in units with fully equipped kitchens, TVs, saunas and daily maid service. A free bus to the ski area stops at the lodge. Choose from almost 40 restaurants within a few blocks' walk. When the slopes are bare, there are nearby tennis courts, golf courses, hiking trails and fishing streams to attract the traveler. Contact: Coalition Lodge, P.O. Box 75, 1300 Park Avenue, Park City, UT 84060. Call 801-649-8591.
Children: Y Pets: N Smoking: Y Handicap Access: N Payment: C, T, A, V, M

COURCHEVEL *Rates: budget-moderate*
Open: year-round *Minimum Stay: two nights*
Stay at Courchevel in a one- or three-bedroom unit and walk to the ski lifts, take a free bus to the U.S. Film Festival in January, attend the Oktoberfest and hot-air balloon festivals in the fall and take steam train trips to the gambling palaces of Nevada. A French accent is prevalent throughout Courcheval's interiors. Want to leave the kids for a night on the town? Child care can be arranged by the management. Contact: Courchevel, P.O. Box 680128, Park City, UT 84068. Call 800-453-5789 (in Utah, 801-649-9598).
Children: Y Pets: N Smoking: Y Handicap Access: N Payment: C, T, A, ⩔, M

INTERMOUNTAIN LODGING *Rates: budget*
Open: year-round *Minimum Stay: three nights*
The maximum vertical drop on Park City's most spectacular ski trail is 3,100 feet. You can observe that slope and the skiers schussing down it from one of the balconies of this low-rise 150-condo complex at the base of the mountain. While skiing is the big draw here, the resort town also serves as an off-season base for those sportsfolk who golf, play tennis, boat, fish and hike or simply enjoy the aura of an alpine setting. A variety of accommodations, ranging from studios to three-

bedroom units, are available. Contact: Intermountain Lodging, P.O. Box 3803, Park City, UT 84060. Call 800-221-0933 (in Utah, 801-649-2687).

Children: Y Pets: N Smoking: N Handicap Access: Y Payment: C, T, A, V, M

RESORT CENTER LODGING   *Rates: budget-inexpensive*
Open: year-round   *Minimum Stay: none*

You can literally ski in and ski out for a day on the slopes from your condo. The low-rise condos here, ranging from studios to three-bedrooms, incorporate cathedral ceilings and gas fireplaces. Swim in the pool, both indoors and outdoors, sweat in the sauna or take a steam. There's also a skating rink and cross-country skiing nearby. When the snow has melted, there is golf, tennis, volleyball, hiking and fishing nearby. Contact: Resort Center Lodging, P.O. Box 3449, Park City, UT 84060. Call 800-824-5331 (in Utah, 801-649-0800).

Children: Y Pets: N Smoking: Y Handicap Access: Y Payment: C, T, A, V, M

SHADOW RIDGE RESORT HOTEL   *Rates: budget-inexpensive*
Open: year-round   *Minimum Stay: one week*

Throughout the seasons of the year, this four-story brick enclave of 48 condos offers something for everybody. In winter, there's skiing and an alpine slide within walking distance. In summer, three reservoirs within a half hour's drive provide water sports. Four championship golf courses lie within 15 minutes, and a hot tub, sauna and swimming pool all help guests to relax on the premises. Studio, one- and two-bedroom units include phones, cable TV and VCRs. Contact: Shadow Ridge Resort Hotel, 50 Shadow Ridge Street, Box 1820, Park City, UT 84060. Call 800-451-3031 (in Utah, 801-649-4300).

Children: Y Pets: N Smoking: Y Handicap Access: N Payment: C, T, A, V, M

THE INNSBRUCK   *Rates: budget-inexpensive*
Open: year-round   *Minimum Stay: two nights*

Offering a unique look in condominiums, eight A-frame, one-bedroom chalets welcome visitors to Park City. Interiors highlighted with rough wood walls, conversation pits and gas-burning Franklin stove fireplaces make a warm retreat from the snowy slopes. These modern apartments also feature wrought-iron staircases and large sleeping lofts. A shutttle bus provides transport to the Park City Racquet Club, Main Street and the Deer Valley ski resort. Splash in the pool, sweat in the sauna or soak in the hot tub. Contact: The Innsbruck, 1201 Norfolk, P.O. Box 222, Park City, UT 84060. Call 801-649-9829.

Children: Y Pets: N Smoking: Y Handicap Access: N Payment: C, T, A, V, M

SALT LAKE CITY

THE PINECREST BED AND BREAKFAST INN   *Rates: budget-moderate*
Open: year-round   *Minimum Stay: none*

Located on a six-acre estate with formal gardens, a stream and a trout pond, this inn is a melange of six wildly individual accommodations. Among them, the two-level Stetson House, decorated with a collection of hats and posters, features a queen-sized bed and four bunk beds, a living room with a fireplace, a kitchen and a balcony facing the woods. The Canyon Cabin offers two double beds upstairs, a claw-foot tub, a fireplace in the living room, a kitchen and a barbecue on the patio. Breakfast is served in the dining room. Contact: Phil and Donnie Davis, The Pinecrest Bed and Breakfast Inn, 6211 Emigration Canyon Road, Salt Lake City, UT 84108. Call 800-359-6663 (in Utah, 801-583-6663).

Children: N Pets: N Smoking: N Handicap Access: N Payment: C, P, T, A, V, M

SNOWBIRD

THE LODGE AT SNOWBIRD	Rates: moderate-deluxe
Open: year-round	Minimum Stay: none

Known for its powder skiing, Snowbird is also renowned for its elegant resorts. Prime among these is this 120-unit high-rise condominium complex. The lodge features studio, one- and two-bedroom condos with full-sized kitchens, fireplaces and sofa beds. Snowbird has a vertical drop of 3,100 feet that lures both beginner and expert skiers back to the Lodge for repeated visits. Astute travelers can stay here for less than half the ski-season rates when they come off-season. In all seasons, the pool, sauna and hot tub bring relaxation to weary souls. Contact: The Lodge at Snowbird, Snowbird Resort, Entry 3, Snowbird, UT 84092. Call 801-521-6040.

Children: Y Pets: N Smoking: Y Handicap Access: N Payment: C, T, A, V, M

ST. GEORGE

GREENE GATE VILLAGE	Rates: budget
Open: year-round	Minimum Stay: none

Comprised of eight impeccably restored homes, this historic bed and breakfast inn offers a taste of the late 1870s while maintaining modern amenities like a swimming pool, tennis court, Jacuzzi, hot tub, cable TVs and kitchenettes. The village can trace its origins to the founders of the Mormon Church and early settlers on their way to California. A variety of studios, one- and two-bedroom units have been built in the elegantly restored homes. One, the Bentley House, is rich in Victorian decor; another, The Grainery, can sleep three in a space used by early settlers to stock up their wagons. The Greenehouse, built in 1872, is ideal for family reunions, as it can accommodate up to 22 people. Contact: Barbara Greene, Greene Gate Village, 76 West Tabernacle, St. George, UT 84770. Call 801-628-6999.

Children: Y   Pets: N   Smoking: N   Handicap Access: N   Payment: All

Vermont

Ascutney

DUNHAM LODGE
Rates: inexpensive-deluxe
Open: year-round
Minimum Stay: two nights

This luxurious retreat near Mount Ascutney, one of the highest peaks in Vermont, offers a splendid base for year-round vacations. In the summer you can enjoy the private pool, bike or hike through the gorgeous green hills or practice your tennis at the nearby resort. The winter skiing is simply superb. After a day filled with exhilarating frolics, you'll return to this spacious lodge to relax in the steam bath and perhaps curl up in front of a cozy fire. A TV, washer and dryer, two bathrooms and a fully equipped kitchen help to make your stay convenient as well as picturesque; the five comfy bedrooms can sleep up to 12 people. Outside you'll find a deck with beautiful views of the surrounding hills and valleys, a fine place to reminisce about the day's activities and plan tomorrow's fun. Contact: James J. Dunham, 821 Mountain Road, W. Hartford, CT 06117. Call 203-523-0134.

Children: Y   Pets: N   Smoking: Y   Handicap Access: N   Payment: C, P, T

Bridgewater Corners

HILLSIDE HIDEOUT
Rates: budget-moderate
Open: year-round
Minimum Stay: one week

Groups who prefer to enjoy their summer fun or winter skiing together will find much to like about this lovely home on a secluded hillside. The spacious rooms include an eat-in kitchen, a formal dining room and an attractive living room. Creature comforts include not only a rustic wood stove but modern amenities such as a color TV and a stereo. The slopes of Killington, the quaint streets of Woodstock and the beauties of the lakes region are all only 10 minutes away. Contact: Julie Brzek, 76 Old Mill Rd., Harvard, MA 01451. Call 508-772-2170.

Children: Y   Pets: N   Smoking: Y   Handicap Access: N   Payment: C, P, T

Brookfield

VALLEY VIEW COTTAGE
Rates: budget
Open: year-round
Minimum Stay: none

From this lovely cottage for four you can look out over the lovely White River Valley all the way to Killington's snowy peaks, over 40 miles away. The charming pond and extensive grounds will provide many hours of pleasant perambulations; perhaps you'll spot a deer or even a moose on one of your walks. On warm summer evenings, relaxing out on the porch swing after supper is a nice way to end the day. If you've come for the spectacular autumn color or the shimmering beauty of winter in these parts, you'll want to cozy up in front of a cheerful blaze in the stone fireplace with a mug of hot cider in your hands. Contact: Gary and Tamara Hillard, Bear Hill Farm, R.F.D. 2, Box 197, Randolph, VT 05060. Call 802-276-3424.

Children: Y   Pets: N   Smoking: Y   Handicap Access: N   Payment: C, P, T

EAST BARNARD

KIHN HOUSE   *Rates: budget*
Open: year-round   *Minimum Stay: two nights*

The best of rural Vermont is within your reach at this charming house. There are gorgeous views of the quiet countryside, and the surrounding forest proffers lovely ponds and extensive trails for your enjoyment. The Appalachian Trail, Silver Lake State Park and several ski areas are nearby; this area is also a haven for those who enjoy swimming, fishing, cross-country skiing or just being outdoors. Nearby Woodstock and Hanover offer charming shops, delightful cafes and other cultural pleasures. The house itself has two bedrooms and sleeps up to six people. There is electric heat, but you may want to draw your chair up to the wood stove on chilly nights to experience the true Vermont lifestyle. Contact: Mitch Kihn, R.R. 2, Box 120, South Royalton, VT 05068. Call 617-437-1441 (ask for Marcia) or 802-763-7684.

Children: Y   Pets: N   Smoking: Y   Handicap Access: N   Payment: C, P, T

EDEN

PARADISE CHATEAU   *Rates: budget*
Open: year-round   *Minimum Stay: two weeks*

The town of Eden is perhaps a northern incarnation of paradise, with its shimmering blue lake, wildflower-covered meadows and graceful sheltering mountains. Only 30 minutes from Stowe and Jay Peak—paradises of the alpine variety—this lavish chateau is a wonderful holiday house for families or groups. Cathedral ceilings, exposed beams and several fireplaces in the main living area set the tone of rustic luxury. The master suite has its own kitchenette and a sunken tub in the bathroom; the other bedroom suite has two bedrooms, two baths and a combined living room and kitchen area. The 70-foot deck overlooks Eden Lake, and the house is surrounded by 150 acres of shady woodlands and rolling meadows. Contact: John M. Stevenson, R.D. 125, Eden Lake, VT 05653. Call 802-635-2244 or 407-889-9545.

Children: Y   Pets: N   Smoking: Y   Handicap Access: N   Payment: C, P, T

GRAND ISLE

CHAMPLAIN HOUSE   *Rates: inexpensive*
Open: June-July   *Minimum Stay: two weeks*

Lake Champlain is a lovely strip of water extending for 100 miles down Vermont's western border. The lake's Grand Isle, which has its own state park, is dotted with summer cottages and water sports facilities. This gracious home allows you to enjoy the natural blessings of the island in luxurious surroundings. The interior features cathedral ceilings, a handsome fireplace and large picture windows for savoring the views. The grounds slope down to a dock and beach, where a rowboat and canoe are provided for your pleasure. The sauna and Jacuzzi add to your comfort, while the color TV, washer and dryer, microwave and dishwasher provide modern convenience. Perhaps during your stay you'll be lucky enough to see serpentine "Champ," the Loch Ness monster's American cousin. Contact: Mrs. Mary de Treville, P.O. Box 125, South Woodstock, CT 06267. Call 203-928-2197.

Children: Y   Pets: N   Smoking: Y   Handicap Access: N   Payment: C, P, T

GREENSBORO

CASPIAN COTTAGE	*Rates: budget*
Open: June, July, September	*Minimum Stay: two weeks*

Vermont's isolated Northeast Kingdom remains virtually unsullied by large ski developments and tacky tourist shops; this is the place to savor what the rugged countryside of Vermont and New England used to be like. This six-bedroom cottage is located on the gentle shores of Caspian Lake. In addition to swimming and sunning, golf and tennis are popular pursuits here; hikes through the Green Mountains are a must for all those who crave clean air, whispering woodlands and marvelous vistas. The nearby towns of Greensboro and Hardwick will supply you with cultural diversions and charming restaurants. Contact: Mrs. Mary D. Hewes, 1821 Randolph St., N.W., Washington, DC 20011. Call 202-785-4500, 202-338-0654 or 202-829-1821.

Children: Y   Pets: N   Smoking: Y   Handicap Access: N   Payment: C, P, T

JAY PEAK

LAKE SALEM LODGE	*Rates: budget-inexpensive*
Open: year-round	*Minimum Stay: one week*

Whether you seek refreshing lake swims or exhilarating downhill runs, this five-bedroom home on Lake Salem may be just the spot for you. In the summer, its beachfront location affords great swimming and fishing in clean, pleasant waters; the barbecue is perfect for grilling the daily catch and the creek that runs along the secluded grounds is a pleasant place to sit and wish upon a star. In the winter, fantastic skiing at Jay Peak and Burke Mountain is enticingly close. After a day on the slopes, you can retire to the fire blazing inside or sit out on the fully insulated porch and enjoy Lake Salem's icy winter visage. Contact: Lawrence Locke, 25 Woodland Place, Scarsdale, NY 10583. Call 914-723-7742.

Children: Y   Pets: N   Smoking: Y   Handicap Access: N   Payment: C, P, T

KILLINGTON

ALPINE BLISS
Rates: moderate-deluxe
Open: year-round
Minimum Stay: two nights

A fine medley of the old and the new can be found in this stylish home. The cathedral ceiling brings space and sunlight into the living room; the pine-paneled fireplace evokes the rustic beauty of Vermont's past. Some of the modern amenities provided for your pleasure include a TV, a VCR and a Jacuzzi big enough for three people. There are three cozy bedrooms and two very modern bathrooms, and the kitchen features both a microwave and a dishwasher. From the large deck outside you can enjoy lovely views of the surrounding woodlands and gaze out at the valleys beyond. Contact: Wise Vacation Rentals, Box 231, Killington, VT 05751. Call 1-800-642-1147 (in Vermont, 802-773-4202). Ref. 072.

Children: Y Pets: N Smoking: Y Handicap Access: N Payment: C, P, T, V, M

COUNTRY FARMHOUSE
Rates: deluxe
Open: year-round
Minimum Stay: two nights

This charming country house is surrounded by rolling green meadows and leafy woodlands; winter transforms this into an exquisitely picturesque scene worthy of Currier and Ives. The beautifully decorated interior includes six bedrooms and three baths; this is an ideal spot for a family reunion or a group holiday. There is a handsome brick fireplace to cozy up to on chilly nights, and the kitchen is well equipped with a microwave and dishwasher. As if this weren't enough to entice you, the house is very well situated for skiers, only a short distance from the Killington Access Road. Contact: Wise Vacation Rentals, Box 231, Killington, VT 05751. Call 1-800-642-1147 (in Vermont, 802-773-4202). Ref. 039.

Children: Y Pets: N Smoking: Y Handicap Access: N Payment: C, P, T, V, M

EDGEMONT
Rates: inexpensive-deluxe
Open: year-round
Minimum Stay: two nights

Found at the end of a ski trail from the Snowshed slope, Edgemont allows you to fulfill your fondest ski fantasy and ski all the way home to your doorstep. Obviously, these one-, two- and three-bedroom condominiums are marvelously situated near to the slopes; there's also frequent shuttle service available to carry you to and from the lifts, restaurants and nightspots. Once you finally do get back home, you'll find a cozy abode well equipped with a fireplace, TV, VCR, dishwasher and microwave. In addition, guests at Edgemont are invited to use the indoor pool, sauna and Jacuzzi of the Killington Health Club, right next door. Contact: Wise Vacation Rentals, Box 231, Killington, VT 05751. Call 1-800-642-1147 (in Vermont, 802-773-4202).

Children: Y Pets: N Smoking: Y Handicap Access: N Payment: C, P, T, V, M

MONDO CONDO

Rates: budget-deluxe

Open: year-round

Minimum Stay: two nights

This splendid condo is a marvelous base for either winter or summer holidays in the Killington area. In addition to marvelous skiing, the environs offer golf, fishing and some lovely hiking trails. Tennis courts and a pool are found in the complex itself, and there's also plenty to keep avid shoppers and dedicated gourmets quite busy. Whether you prefer to soothe away troubles in the Jacuzzi, lose yourself in a cable movie, whip up a hearty repast in the kitchen or simply contemplate the surroundings from the vantage of the outside deck, coming back to your condo will be a pleasure in itself. The interior is attractively furnished and up to eight people will find cozy lodgings in its three bedrooms. Contact: Hope Chopy, 30 Meadowcrest Drive, Cumberland, RI 02864. Call 401-723-7687.

Children: Y   Pets: N   Smoking: Y   Handicap Access: N   Payment: C, P, T

MOUNTAIN GREEN CONDOMINIUMS

Rates: inexpensive-deluxe

Open: year-round

Minimum Stay: none

These condos offer you excellent amenities and a wonderful location. When you see the facilities, you'll be tempted to do nothing but pamper yourself with a full-scale spa holiday: After a stint in the lap pool or a dip in the cold plunge pool, you can enjoy a hot-massage Jacuzzi, a mineral spa, a sauna or even a eucalyptus steambath. There are also restaurants and shops here to keep your tummy happy and your wallet busy. Skiers will have to fight the temptation, though, and step out into the cold, clear air. The skiing at Killington is virtually at your doorstep—the ski lift is just an easy stroll away (a shuttle is provided for those who'd rather conserve their energy). The units range from cozy studios to spacious four-bedroom suites. Contact: Mountain Rental Company, P.O. Box 483, Killington, VT 05751. Call 1-800-535-8938 (in Vermont, 802-773-4717).

Children: Y   Pets: N   Smoking: Y   Handicap Access: N   Payment: C, T, V, M

SKIER'S SANCTUM

Rates: budget

Open: November-April

Minimum Stay: six months

Those planning a full winter on the glistening slopes of Killington will want to consider the fine amenities of this modern four-bedroom house. The cathedral ceilings, fieldstone fireplace, skylights, knotty pine walls and wooden floors give it a lovely air of rustic elegance. The sauna, whirlpool, cable TV, VCR and central heating supply the full range of creature comforts, and the two full bathrooms and well-equipped kitchen provide every convenience. Best of all, although quietly situated on over an acre of land, the house is right next to a main road: The slopes of Killington are just 10 minutes away. Contact: Joe Mulshine, 203-235-1579 or 203-269-8882.

Children: Y   Pets: N   Smoking: Y   Handicap Access: N   Payment: C, P, T

WOODLAND CHALET   *Rates: deluxe*
Open: year-round   *Minimum Stay: two nights*
This extraordinary chalet is tucked away in the woods near Killington,
a true gem in a rough setting. There are five spacious bedrooms and
three bathrooms, but these statistics don't begin to do justice to its
charms. How about a refreshing dip in the eight-foot-deep swimming
pool, which is not only indoors for year-round pleasure but actually
located in one of its two living rooms? There are also two dining
rooms, a recreation room and a solarium inside, and outside you can
relax to the lullaby of the gently whispering trees and chirping song-
birds while soaking in the Jacuzzi. Contact: Wise Vacation Rentals,
Box 231, Killington, VT 05751. Call 1-800-642-1147 (in Vermont, 802-
773-4202). Ref. 078.
Children: Y Pets: N Smoking: Y Handicap Access: N Payment: C, P, T, V, M

LAKE BOMOSEEN

THE RANCH   *Rates: budget*
Open: June 22-September 2   *Minimum Stay: two weeks*
Former haunt of the Marx Brothers, pretty Lake Bomoseen is a perennial favorite of those who like to spend their summers swimming,
sunning and sailing; the fishing around here is pretty good, too. This
modern home boasts a quiet location, almost 200 feet of private shoreline and its own dock. Inside you'll find wide-open spaces filled with
light. From the living room—which features a handsome fireplace—
French doors open onto a large screened-in porch. Here you can enjoy
supper while soaking in the spectacle of the sunset playing off the
lake's surface. The porch can also function as additional sleeping quarters, so the house can accommodate up to six in all. Contact: Lee
Houghton, Wallingford, VT 05773. Call 802-446-2833.
Children: Y Pets: N Smoking: Y Handicap Access: N Payment: C, P, T

LONDONDERRY

GREEN MOUNTAIN CHALET   *Rates: budget-inexpensive*
Open: year-round   *Minimum Stay: two nights*
This charming ski chalet in the Timber Side and Magic Mountain area
is quietly situated within walking distance of the slopes. Attractively
decorated, it comprises a living room with a fireplace, a dishwasher-
equipped kitchen, two bathrooms, sun decks and several comfy bedrooms; up to eight guests will find accommodations here. This resort
area is popular all year round—in the summer, sailing, fishing, tennis,
golf, hiking and biking are among the favorite pursuits. The fall foliage
season, spectacular in its own right, is augmented by the annual Stratton Arts Festival. Other cultural amenities in the area include summer
theater, excellent restaurants and plenty of shopping. Contact: Nelson
Burack, 55 Juneau Rd., Woodbury, NY 11797. Call 516-367-8082.
Children: Y Pets: N Smoking: Y Handicap Access: N Payment: C, P, T

SKIER'S DELIGHT   Rates: budget-moderate
Open: year-round   Minimum Stay: none

This recently built house offers year-round family entertainment in luxurious surroundings. The interior is beautifully furnished and features both the rustic charm of a fireplace and the modern amenities of a TV and stereo. There are four comfy bedrooms, two sparkling bathrooms and a well-equipped electric kitchen. Marvelous views can be admired out on the deck, which is also a splendid place to dine. Swimming, fishing, golf, tennis, leaf-peeping and skiing (the house is near both Bromley and Stratton) can all be enjoyed in season. Local restaurants, cinemas and shopping are favorite amusements no matter what the time of year. Contact: Dr. Edmund Pollock, 144 W. 86th St., New York, NY 10024. Call 212-535-0290.

Children: Y   Pets: N   Smoking: Y   Handicap Access: N   Payment: C, P, T

MANCHESTER

BUCKRUN   Rates: moderate
Open: year-round   Minimum Stay: one week

Nestled on 30 wooded acres, this fine home features cathedral ceilings, a handsome fireplace and spectacular views of the Green Mountains. The dishwasher and microwave will help make your stay hassle-free; the snowplowing service and large supply of firewood will deliver the best a winter vacation can offer. There are three bedrooms and two bathrooms, with zoned heating to back up the rustic wood stove. Manchester's mile-long alpine slide is a great way for nonskiers to enjoy the slopes; the panoramic views from the summit of the scenic chairlift encompass five states. True sightseers will not want to miss the town's American Museum of Fly Fishing. Contact: Roland Beers and Associates, Box 627, Manchester, VT 05254. Call 802-362-1838 or 518-392-6371.

Children: Y   Pets: N   Smoking: Y   Handicap Access: N   Payment: C, P, T

MIDDLEBURY

ADIRONDACK VIEW   Rates: budget
Open: June-September   Minimum Stay: one week

After only a short stay here, you'll be able to appreciate why this cozy cottage has become a favorite family retreat. The house is shaded by tall trees and commands splendid views of the Adirondack Mountains. It boasts its own stretch of private beach and comes complete with an aluminum boat for devoted anglers and intrepid explorers. There are three comfy bedrooms; breezy sleeping quarters can also be found out on the screened porch. A cheery blaze in the living room's fireplace can ward off chills on cooler evenings, and the kitchen is well equipped with an electric stove and a new refrigerator. Tennis, golf and hiking can all be enjoyed in the neighborhood; the boutiques and restaurants of Middlebury are only a short drive away. Contact: John and Carolyn Stephens, 8017 N. Santa Monica Blvd., Milwaukee, WI 53217. Call 414-352-0211.

Children: Y   Pets: N   Smoking: Y   Handicap Access: N   Payment: C, P, T

QUECHEE

COACH ROAD CONDOMINIUM   *Rates: expensive-deluxe*
Open: year-round   *Minimum Stay: two nights*

The Quechee Gorge is Vermont's own "Little Grand Canyon," where sheer cliffs drop precipitously to the Ottaquechee River 165 feet below. Not too far away from the gorge you'll find this deluxe condo complex. Amenities at your disposal include indoor and outdoor pools, health club facilities, squash courts and even a separate recreation center for the kids. Golf and tennis is available here, too, and there are ski lifts nearby. Not one but two cheery fireplaces will greet you back home after a day of sports or sightseeing. Perhaps after dinner in the complex's excellent restaurant, you'd like to relax in the Jacuzzi before retiring to one of your three spacious bedrooms. Contact: Quechee Lakes Rental Corporation, P.O. Box 277, Quechee, VT 05059. Call 802-295-1970.

Children: Y Pets: N Smoking: Y Handicap Access: N Payment: C, P, T, V, M

SALISBURY

LAKE DUNMORE HOUSE   *Rates: budget*
Open: year-round   *Minimum Stay: one week*

The large picture windows in the living room and spacious porch of this house afford lovely views of Lake Dunmore and the surrounding mountains. You'll want to get outside as much as you can, though, once you've had a few lungfuls of the clean air and dipped your toes in the sparkling water; the property features its own private sandy beach complete with dock. If you come in the autumn, you'll be simply delighted by the rolling hills ablaze with fiery foliage; the winter transforms this area into a serene winter wonderland that's perfect for snowshoeing and cross-country skiing. A large, handsome fireplace forms the focal point of the living room, and there are two comfy bedrooms in addition to the convertible sofa. Contact: Luella Patterson, Lake Dunmore, Salisbury, VT 05769. Call 407-286-0717 or 802-352-4555.

Children: Y Pets: N Smoking: Y Handicap Access: N Payment: C, P, T

SHREWSBURY

MAPLE CREST FARM   *Rates: budget*
Open: year-round   *Minimum Stay: none*

Directly across from the Shrewsbury Town Hall you'll find the picturesque Maple Crest Farm. The five-room apartments are cheerfully decorated; you can also stay here as a bed-and-breakfast guest. Maple Crest is well situated for the pleasure of golf and ski enthusiasts; other country pursuits enjoyed in the area include fishing, biking, hiking and the ever-popular practice of antiquing. The bustling town of Rutland—which is where you'll find the Norman Rockwell Museum—is just a few minutes away, and the Green Mountains await you on all sides. Contact: William and Donna Smith, Maple Crest Farm, Lincoln Hill Rd., Box 120, Cuttingsville, VT 05738. Call 802-492-3367.

Children: Y Pets: N Smoking: Y Handicap Access: N Payment: C, P, T, A

SOUTH NEWFANE

ANTIQUE COUNTRY HOME *Rates: budget-inexpensive*
Open: year-round *Minimum Stay: three nights*

This charming old home with its rustic barn is found in a quaint village not far from Brattleboro, Vermont's only true city. The five bedrooms are comfortably furnished and the kitchen is well equipped despite its antiquity. Other modern amenities include a full bathroom, cable TV, a VCR and a washer and dryer. Newfane Village boasts some excellent restaurants and interesting historic sites, and the antiquing around here is rumored to be quite good. Mount Snow and Haystack are within easy driving distance, and the nearby river and reservoir afford plentiful swimming, fishing and boating. Contact: Carolyn Corzine, 30 May St., Marblehead, MA 01945. Call 617-631-1209.

Children: **Y**   Pets: **N**   Smoking: **N**   Handicap Access: **N**   Payment: **C, P, T**

SOUTH ROYALTON

CABIN BY THE WOODS *Rates: budget*
Open: year-round *Minimum Stay: one week*

Sample a taste of old Vermont in this cozy hillside cottage overlooking woodlands and a pleasant pond. Less than half an hour away are the enticing slopes of Suicide Six and the charming shops of Woodstock. You may just want to stay home, though, and enjoy the rustic pleasures of the Vermont countryside: rowing out to do some fishing in the pond, relaxing on the shore after a warm swim, wandering through the fragrant woods and admiring the 50-mile views of the surrounding valleys and mountains. The cabin is comfortably furnished and completely winterized. It includes one bedroom and sleeps up to four. Contact: M.S. Alden, Box 61, Davis Rd., South Royalton, VT 05068. Call 802-763-8382.

Children: **Y**   Pets: **N**   Smoking: **Y**   Handicap Access: **N**   Payment: **C, P, T**

STOWE

1820 COTTAGE *Rates: moderate-deluxe*
Open: November-April *Minimum Stay: two nights*

Those who yearn to enjoy their winter holidays surrounded by the elegance of yesteryear will be pleased by the charms of this fine old home. Exquisite antiques and original artworks adorn the formal dining room and the living room, which also features a fireplace. More casual meals may be enjoyed in the kitchen's breakfast nook. The master suite boasts its own fireplace and sitting room; two more handsome bedrooms and a full bathroom are found upstairs. This is a wonderful place for families or small groups to come home to after a day on the slopes or a night on the town. Contact: Simoneau Realty, Main St., Box 1291, Stowe, VT 05672. Call 802-253-4623. Ref. 3C.

Children: **Y**   Pets: **N**   Smoking: **Y**   Handicap Access: **N**   Payment: **P**

CARRIAGE HOUSE
Rates: deluxe
Open: November-April
Minimum Stay: two nights
Evocative reminders of this unique holiday house's former life remain in the sliding barn doors, handsome slate floors and brass railings. The living and dining room is spacious and appealing, with a wood stove to warm you after a day on the slopes. A full kitchen and comfy double bedroom are also found on the main level, and the second story houses not one but two master suites. The younger crowd can have their own digs downstairs, where two rooms with bunk beds, a separate sitting area and a bathroom form a pleasant little suite. Contact: Simoneau Realty, Main St., Box 1291, Stowe, VT 05672. Call 802-253-4623. Ref. 3D.
Children: Y   Pets: N   Smoking: Y   Handicap Access: N   Payment: P

EDSON HILL HOME
Rates: moderate-deluxe
Open: year-round
Minimum Stay: two nights
On tranquil Edson Hill, at the end of a country road, stands this ski chalet for up to nine guests. From this perch you'll enjoy splendid views of both the majestic mountains and the quaint village of Stowe. You can spread out in four bedrooms and three bathrooms; the large decks outside are wonderful places for dining or reclining in warmer weather. Filling the odd hour here and there won't be a problem when you have not only a sauna and a hot tub at your disposal but also two color TVs with Atari game hookups. Contact: Ruth or Andrea, Evans Realty Associates, P.O. Box 1348, Stowe, VT 05672. Call 1-800-639-6084 (in Vermont, 802-253-8267).
Children: Y Pets: N Smoking: Y Handicap Access: N Payment: C, P, T, V, M

HILLSIDE FARMHOUSE
Rates: budget-deluxe
Open: year-round
Minimum Stay: two nights
Enjoy a taste of traditional Vermont in this quaint old farmhouse occupying a hillside outside town. The lovely setting, small-paned windows and stone chimney are of a piece with nearby Stowe, a village that still retains its New England character in the colonial houses and austere white church. The views from the farmhouse of both the village and the mountains are splendid. There are two bathrooms and three comfy bedrooms accommodating up to seven guests. The ski and sports facilities of Stowe are at hand, as are all the antiquing and quiet country lanes you could ever want. Contact: Ruth or Andrea, Evans Realty Associates, P.O. Box 1348, Stowe, VT 05672. Call 1-800-639-6084 (in Vermont, 802-253-8267).
Children: Y Pets: N Smoking: Y Handicap Access: N Payment: C, P, T, V, M

MOUNTAIN VIEW
Rates: moderate-deluxe
Open: November-April
Minimum Stay: two nights
The fieldstone fireplace and cathedral ceilings in the living and dining room of this spacious abode will delight you with their simple elegance. Enjoying spectacular views of Mount Mansfield, the house also has a full kitchen, a den, a game room and three bathrooms, one of

which has its own Jacuzzi. Other convenient amenities include a sauna, full laundry facilities and a double garage. You're near the slopes here, but fans of gourmet ice cream may want to check out the birthplace of Ben and Jerry's, just down the road in Waterbury. Contact: Simoneau Realty, Main St., Box 1291, Stowe, VT 05672. Call 802-253-4623. Ref. 15A.

Children: Y   Pets: N   Smoking: Y   Handicap Access: N   Payment: P

NOTCH BROOK   *Rates: deluxe*
Open: November-April   *Minimum Stay: two nights*

Vermont's renowned marble adorns the rooms of this exquisitely furnished contemporary home, transforming luxury into opulence. It graces the handsome fireplace in the sunken living room, and you'll also find it in the master suite's bathroom, which includes a Jacuzzi, shower and double sink. The double guest suite on the lower level is nicely secluded from the rest of the house. A dining room, a family room with a cozy wood stove and a well-equipped kitchen round out the accommodations. There's even a steam room here for total relaxation after a day on Stowe's exhilarating slopes. Contact: Simoneau Realty, Main St., Box 1291, Stowe, VT 05672. Call 802-253-4623. Ref. 11C.

Children: Y   Pets: N   Smoking: Y   Handicap Access: N   Payment: P

SOLITUDE   *Rates: budget-deluxe*
Open: year-round   *Minimum Stay: none*

This grand old 19th-century home features original pine floors, a cozy wood-burning stove and five spacious bedrooms. The large eat-in kitchen is fully equipped with a dishwasher, washing machine and dryer. The yard outside is a fine place to frolic, but there are plenty of other diversions available in the neighborhood. The 44 slopes and trails of fabulous Stowe are only a mile away, and the alpine slide affords marvelous vistas of the Green Mountains. Stowe's summertime sports facilities are also impressive—tennis, golf and wind surfing are among the selections. Or experience the Vermont countryside as the house's original owners must have, with a bit of horseback riding. Contact: Mrs. Terry Wasser, 48 Sherwood Dr., Pittsfield, MA 01201. Call 413-442-0722.

Children: Y   Pets: N   Smoking: Y   Handicap Access: N   Payment: C, P, T

STOWE HOLLOW   *Rates: deluxe*
Open: November-April   *Minimum Stay: three nights*

If modern ski-holiday houses seem nondescript to you, perhaps you'd prefer this cozy log home out in Stowe Hollow. The wood stove in the spacious living room accents country charm, as does the cheery kitchen. There are four generous bedrooms and two bathrooms here, so the house can easily accommodate up to 10 guests. The laundry facilities will help to make your stay convenient as well as picturesque. The village of Stowe is just around the corner, as are the many ski, golf, tennis and other sports facilities in this area. Contact: Rentals at Stowe, R.R. 1, Box 7133, Stowe, VT 05672. Call 802-253-9786.

Children: Y   Pets: N   Smoking: Y   Handicap Access: N   Payment: C, P, T

STOWE-AWAY *Rates: inexpensive-expensive*
Open: November-April *Minimum Stay: two nights*
This charming older house perches on a quiet hillside in the heart of Stowe. It has been tastefully restored to please skiers and winter enthusiasts of all stripes. The wraparound fireplace in the living room will remind you of all the skiing movies you've ever seen—don't forget to bring your fondue pot. The dining room, kitchen and half bath are also found downstairs; above are two bedrooms and a full bathroom. Stowe is renowned as one of the country's foremost skiing centers, and it offers all the cultural diversions of a lively resort town. After a day on the slopes, the nightclubs, bars, discos and restaurants will keep you busy far into the night. Contact: Simoneau Realty, Main St., Box 1291, Stowe, VT 05672. Call 802-253-4623. Ref. 4A.

Children: Y   Pets: N   Smoking: N   Handicap Access: N   Payment: P

THE PANORAMA *Rates: deluxe*
Open: year-round *Minimum Stay: three nights*
Huge stone fireplaces grace both the living room and the family room of this spacious hillside home. You can enjoy magnificent views of the mountains and valleys from any of the large windows, but why not reserve a seat out on one of the spacious decks, where you can sip a cocktail and enjoy the sunset while savoring the hush of the countryside? Every modern convenience has been provided, from four full bathrooms to a large Jacuzzi. The main part of the house has five bedrooms; there's also a private little one-bedroom suite. The rolling lawns outside are ideal for warm-weather frolics or a romp in the snow. Contact: Stowe-Country Rental Company, R.R. 3, Box 3051, Stowe, VT 05672. Call 802-253-8132.

Children: Y   Pets: N   Smoking: Y   Handicap Access: N   Payment: All

TRAILSIDE HOME *Rates: inexpensive-deluxe*
Open: year-round *Minimum Stay: two nights*
This lovely home in a fashionable neighborhood will enchant you with its air of tranquil elegance. Surrounded by rugged evergreens and graceful birches, the two-story house has a large deck where you can sit and survey the scenery in warmer weather or catch a snowflake on your tongue in the midst of winter. The tastefully decorated rooms can accommodate up to eight people. After a good night's sleep in one of the cozy bedrooms and a hearty New England breakfast, you can follow one of the cross-country skiing or hiking trails that lead past your door. Downhill addicts will also find this house conveniently close to the slopes of Stowe. Contact: Ruth or Andrea, Evans Realty Associates, P.O. Box 1348, Stowe, VT 05672. Call 1-800-639-6084 (in Vermont, 802-253-8267).

Children: Y Pets: N Smoking: Y Handicap Access: N Payment: C, P, T, V, M

TRAPP FAMILY GUESTHOUSES
Open: year-round

Rates: expensive-deluxe
Minimum Stay: three nights

The hills are alive with the sound of music at this famous resort. Not only the enthralling legend of its founders but its fine amenities, too, have added to its renown. The health spa features an indoor pool, a sauna and a gym; during the winter, the cross-country skiing center maintains some of the finest trails in the state, and the summer concerts are a well-beloved tradition. Each of the two-bedroom guesthouses includes a living/dining room with a fireplace, a complete kitchen and two bathrooms. The views from this hillside are quite delightful, and the meadows and woodlands around you burst into color when the wildflowers bloom in the spring. Contact: Stowe-Country Rental Company, R.R. 3, Box 3051, Stowe, VT 05672. Call 802-253-8132.

Children: Y   Pets: N   Smoking: Y   Handicap Access: N   Payment: All

STRATTON

MOUNTAINSIDE CABIN
Open: year-round

Rates: budget-expensive
Minimum Stay: one week

A stone and log cabin picturesquely situated on a private pond and surrounded by 16 acres of wild countryside: This simple mountain dwelling is ideal for honeymooners and nature lovers of all ages. The lofty exposed-beam ceilings and rugged fireplace convey a sense of rustic charm; the four comfy bedrooms, two bathrooms, dishwasher, TV and washer and dryer ensure that you won't have to rough it just because you're getting away from it all. Trout fishing, swimming, foliage gazing and ice skating fill the roster of country pursuits here; quiet walks can be enjoyed year-round in this secluded paradise. You're never too far from civilization, though: Tennis, golf and ski lifts are just two miles away. Contact: Malvine Cole, R.R. 1, Box 343, Jamaica, VT 05343. Call 802-874-4698 or 212-691-0140.

Children: Y   Pets: Y   Smoking: Y   Handicap Access: N   Payment: C, P, T

WARREN

CLUB SUGARBUSH
Open: April-November

Rates: inexpensive-moderate
Minimum Stay: two nights

Right next to the charming Sugarbush Inn—and enjoying all of its privileges—are these handsome townhouses, ideal bases for longer stays at the resort. The one-, two- and three-bedroom units each have a cheerful fireplace, a complete kitchen and a private sun deck. The views of the surrounding mountains and verdant valleys are simply stunning; you'll scarcely be able to resist walking though the wooded hills, biking along some of the trails or wandering down to the lovely Mad River, a treasured haven for anglers and canoeists alike. Contact: Sugarbush Vacations, P.O. Box 307, Warren, VT 05674. Call 1-800-451-4213 (in Vermont, 802-583-2400).

Children: Y   Pets: N   Smoking: Y   Handicap Access: Y   Payment: All

GLADES

Open: April-November

Rates: budget-inexpensive

Minimum Stay: two nights

True to their name, these plush condos are tucked away in a fragrant glade of pines. The one- and two-bedroom units feature modern kitchens, separate living and dining rooms and marvelous views. The building also offers shared sun decks, laundry facilities and a pleasant lounge where you can meet your friends before going out to dinner at one of the fine restaurants nearby. Just around the corner are the excellent facilities of the Sugarbush Sports Center; your membership fee is included in the rental, so enjoy all the swimming and tennis you want. Trips can easily be taken to the nearby Shelburne Museum; the beckoning shores of Lake Champlain are less than an hour away. Contact: Sugarbush Vacations, P.O. Box 307, Warren, VT 05674. Call 1-800-451-4213 (in Vermont, 802-583-2400).

Children: **Y**   Pets: **N**   Smoking: **Y**   Handicap Access: **Y**   Payment: **All**

SOUTHFACE

Open: April-November

Rates: moderate

Minimum Stay: two nights

Enormous glass windows cover one whole wall of each of these three-story villas—what better way is there to enjoy the stunning mountain scenery around you, to bring the pleasant greenery of Vermont inside? The vaulted ceilings and handsome fireplaces augment the contemporary elegance of these units; many units even have their own Jacuzzis. The kitchens are well equipped and the full laundry facilities are conveniently located. After a game of tennis or a splash in the shared outdoor pool, perhaps you'd like to walk or ride over to nearby Waitsfield, where shopping, sightseeing and fine dining are among the many attractions. Contact: Sugarbush Vacations, P.O. Box 307, Warren, VT 05674. Call 1-800-451-4213 (in Vermont, 802-583-2400).

Children: **Y**   Pets: **N**   Smoking: **Y**   Handicap Access: **Y**   Payment: **All**

SUMMIT

Open: April-November

Rates: inexpensive

Minimum Stay: two nights

Perched high above Sugarbush Village on the slopes of the Green Mountains, these charming little townhouses offer rustic decor and splendid views. The surrounding peaks of Mount Ellen and Mount Abraham are among Vermont's highest, and each new season finds them carpeted in ravishing hues of yellow, green, scarlet or white. The three-bedroom units at Summit are ideal for groups of six to eight. You can prepare a tasty repast in the fully modern kitchen and then dine amid verdant beauty out on the sun deck. If the evening turns a bit cool, don't worry: You can warm away any chills with the glow of a cheerful fire in the hearth. Contact: Sugarbush Vacations, P.O. Box 307, Warren, VT 05674. Call 1-800-451-4213 (in Vermont, 802-583-2400).

Children: **Y**   Pets: **N**   Smoking: **Y**   Handicap Access: **Y**   Payment: **All**

WEST DOVER

BEARS CROSSING TOWNHOUSES
Rates: inexpensive-moderate
Open: year-round
Minimum Stay: two nights

These modern townhouses are conveniently located just one mile south of Mount Snow and only two miles north of the Haystack ski area. The pleasantly furnished houses include two bedrooms, a living room that opens onto the balcony and a separate dining area. Upstairs there's a spacious loft with skylights for sleeping, storage or just hanging out. A shuttle bus will take you directly to Mount Snow; cross-country ski trails lead right from your front door. Summer guests will appreciate the delightful outdoor swimming pool and the tennis courts. And visitors at any time of the year will be entranced by the stately magnificence of the encircling woods and mountains. Contact: Snow Resorts, West Dover, VT 05356. Call 802-451-6876 or 802-464-2179.

Children: **Y**   Pets: **N**   Smoking: **Y**   Handicap Access: **N**   Payment: **All**

GREENSPRING TOWNHOUSES
Rates: moderate-deluxe
Open: year-round
Minimum Stay: two nights

These elegant townhouses are beautifully furnished and comfortable to live in. The vaulted ceilings add grace and space; the fireplaces create a warm and cozy atmosphere any time of year. The kitchens are well equipped and there are two, three or four bedrooms in each house. Some units even have their own spa room and sauna. Splendid facilities available to all are found in the amenity center, including an indoor pool, a Jacuzzi, a sauna, a game room, an exercise room and a lounge where you can meet new friends or spend some time with old ones. There's also a shuttle bus to carry you to the slopes. Contact: Snow Resorts, West Dover, VT 05356. Call 802-451-6876 or 802-464-2179.

Children: **Y**   Pets: **N**   Smoking: **Y**   Handicap Access: **N**   Payment: **All**

TIMBER CREEK TOWNHOUSES
Rates: moderate-deluxe
Open: year-round
Minimum Stay: two nights

Enjoy spectacular views of Mount Snow from these luxury homes. Your well-equipped kitchen, handsome dining room and large living room are all open to one another, creating a warm, airy ambiance. The bedrooms and rec room are wholly private, and there's plenty of hidden storage for ski, boat and golf equipment. Sliding glass doors in the living room open to the balcony, and a pretty greenhouse area with a Vermont slate floor is found off the dining room, so you can enjoy marvelous views of the mountains while cooking and dining. Some units have their own hot tubs and saunas and there is a large amenity center with an indoor pool, fitness center, sauna, hot tub and tennis and racquetball courts. Contact: Snow Resorts, West Dover, VT 05356. Call 802-451-6876 or 802-464-2179.

Children: **Y**   Pets: **N**   Smoking: **Y**   Handicap Access: **N**   Payment: **All**

VERMONT COUNTRY INN   *Rates: inexpensive-expensive*
Open: year-round   *Minimum Stay: two nights*
Rent your own country inn and invite the gang to Vermont. The seven
bedrooms can accommodate up to 14 guests, so it's a great place for
large groups to enjoy the area's charms. After frying up a stack of
pancakes in the large country kitchen, enjoy your hearty breakfast
with some genuine Vermont maple syrup in the handsome dining
room. Nearby Marlboro hosts a fabulous music festival every July and
August, and skiers will be pleased to know that Mount Snow, Haystack and Stratton are all close. At the end of a day filled with concert-
going or schussing, traditionalists will want to curl up in front of the
cheery open fire, while iconoclasts may prefer to steam away in the
sauna. Contact: Tom and Marie Martin, Captain Copeland Rd., P.O.
Box 177, E. Dover, VT 05341. Call 802-348-7749.
Children: Y   Pets: N   Smoking: N   Handicap Access: N   Payment: C, P, T

WESTMORE

LAKE WILLOUGHBY COTTAGE   *Rates: budget*
Open: May 1-October 15   *Minimum Stay: one week*
This tidy little cottage is a cozy spot for a romantic getaway or a family
holiday. A gentle brook wends its way by the deck outside and in
autumn the house is swathed in crimson and gold. In addition to
natural beauty, this area offers plenty of diversions: fishing, boating
and golf are popular sports, and antiquing has been refined into a high
art form. After a day in the countryside, you'll return to the spacious
quarters of your home away from home. The large living room and
dining room are handsomely furnished (there's a TV for keeping in
touch with the real world), the two bedrooms are warm and inviting
and the modern kitchen features a microwave. Contact: Gerald and
Marjorie Goldman, 33 Abrew St., Bay Shore, NY 11706. Call 516-666-
6420.
Children: Y   Pets: N   Smoking: Y   Handicap Access: N   Payment: C, P, T

WILMINGTON

COLONIAL HAVEN   *Rates: budget*
Open: year-round   *Minimum Stay: one week*
This restored 18th-century home is elegantly furnished with Oriental
carpets and sumptuous fabrics. Every modern convenience you'll need
has been added, from cable TV to a microwave to the Webber grill out
on the deck. Lake Whitingham is only a pleasant stroll away; here
you'll find abundant opportunities for swimming, fishing, boating or
just lazing about on the shore. For the full country experience, try a bit
of horseback riding nearby. Ski enthusiasts will want to try out the
slopes at nearby Haystack and Mount Snow, and avid shoppers and
antiquers will find plenty in the neighborhood to keep them busy.
Contact: Ron Innacell, 6 Old Country Rd., Oxford, CT 06483. Call
203-888-7328.
Children: Y   Pets: N   Smoking: Y   Handicap Access: N   Payment: C, P, T

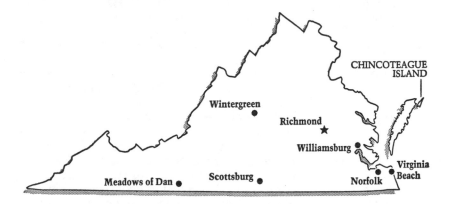

CHINCOTEAGUE
ISLAND

Wintergreen

Richmond

Williamsburg

Virginia
Beach

Meadows of Dan   Scottsburg

Norfolk

Virginia

CHINCOTEAGUE ISLAND

CURLEW   *Rates: budget*
Open: March 24-November 27   *Minimum Stay: two nights*

Curlew—named for a bird visitors might spot at the Assateague National Seashore or Chincoteague National Wildlife Refuge—sits near a small bay on the eastern side of the resort town of Chincoteague. It's a snug brick house that has two bedrooms (sleeping a total of four), one bath, a fully equipped kitchen and air-conditioned living room. A short meander or bike ride over the bridge to Assateague Island puts beach bums on one of the prettiest sandy stretches on the East Coast. For naturalists, the park also offers trails frequented by exotic birds, sika deer and Assateague's shaggy wild ponies, as well as organized activities like wildlife safaris, cruises, fishing trips and movies. Contact: Chincoteague Island Vacation Cottages, Rt. 1, Box 547, East Side Drive, Chincoteague, VA 23336. Call 804-336-3720.

Children: **Y**   Pets: **N**   Smoking: **Y**   Handicap Access: **N**   Payment: **C, P, T**

MARTIN HOUSE   *Rates: budget-inexpensive*
Open: March 24-November 27   *Minimum Stay: two nights*

Stilts support this handsome wood home on Chincoteague's Oyster Bay overlooking the national wildlife refuge. It has its own dock accessible from the front door, expediting fishing, sailing and motorboating trips. There are three bedrooms and one and a half baths, making Martin House suitable for six adults in addition to two children. Living is easy with central heat and air conditioning, a washer and dryer, and tranquil screened-in porch. Contact: Chincoteague Island Vacation Cottages, Rt. 1, Box 547, East Side Drive, Chincoteague, VA 23336. Call 804-336-3720.

Children: **Y** Pets: **N** Smoking: **Y** Handicap Access: **N** Payment: C, P, T

SIDE DOOR   *Rates: budget*
Open: March 24-November 27   *Minimum Stay: two nights*
Chincoteague Island is the magical home of the wild pony, Misty, from the classic children's books written by Marguerite Henry. Ten miles of highway and bridges connect it to the mainland of Virginia's eastern shore; immediately to its east (over yet another bridge) lies the barrier beach wonderland of Assateague National Seashore. The Side Door, a ground-level efficiency cottage that sleeps two and has a separate kitchen and air conditioning, is nestled in downtown Chincoteague, close to shops and restaurants. It comes complete with its own crab steamer. For those heading to Chincoteague for the annual Pony Penning festival in late July, when the wild ponies of the national seashore swim across the bay and are sold at public auction, early rental arrangements are advised. Contact: Chincoteague Island Vacation Cottages, Rt. 1, Box 547, East Side Drive, Chincoteague, VA 23336. Call 804-336-3720.

Children: **Y** Pets: **N** Smoking: **Y** Handicap Access: **N** Payment: C, P, T

MEADOWS OF DAN

ROCKY KNOB CABINS   *Rates: budget*
Open: May 1-October 31   *Minimum Stay: none*
The seven functional housekeeping cabins at Rocky Knob lie at Milepost 174 on the glorious Blue Ridge Parkway, which winds along the top of the Blue Ridge for 450 miles, connecting Shenandoah National Park in Virginia with the Great Smoky Mountains of North Carolina. The Blue Ridge is the slow, scenic road south, providing myriad stopping points along the way, like historic Mabry Mill near Rocky Knob. Set in a lovely secluded glade, the cabins offer full kitchens, running water, innerspring mattresses and a bathhouse nearby. They make an excellent headquarters for hikers exploring the Rocky Knob Trail, which leads to an overlook at Rock Castle Gorge. Contact: Rocky Knob Cabins, National Park Concessions, Inc., Meadows of Dan, VA 24120. Call 703-593-3503.

Children: **Y** Pets: **N** Smoking: **Y** Handicap Access: **N** Payment: All

SCOTTSBURG

STAUNTON RIVER STATE PARK CABINS   *Rates: budget*
Open: Memorial Day-Labor Day   *Minimum Stay: two nights*
Staunton River State Park lies in the most southerly section of Virginia on a river that bisects the North Carolina border. This is tobacco and lake country, a favorite of fishermen, historic hamlet explorers and lovers of the local specialty, Brunswick stew. Facilities at the park

(situated on a neck between the scenic Staunton River and Buggs Island Lake) include hiking trails, a swimming pool, tennis courts, children's playground and seven tidy little frame cabins. The cabins offer rustic furniture, fireplaces and one or two bedrooms as well as kitchens. Linen is provided, and the nearby Visitor's Center offers frequent environmental education programs. Contact: Staunton River State Park, Rt. 2, Box 295, Scottsburg, VA 24589. Call 804-572-4623.

Children: Y Pets: Y Smoking: Y Handicap Access: N Payment: C, P, T, A, V, M

VIRGINIA BEACH

4608 OCEANFRONT *Rates: expensive*
Open: year-round *Minimum Stay: one week*

This capacious, old-fashioned, white-frame beach house in the Gold Coast section of Virginia Beach sleeps seven in four bedrooms (one king, two twins and a single). Its front lawn opens directly onto the sand and surf of this Atlantic Coast resort's 12-mile-long waterfront. In it, amenities abound, including a washer and dryer, telephone, cable TV, three-car garage, two full baths, central air conditioning and kitchen with microwave. Front windows provide gorgeous ocean views and plenty of opportunities for studying beachside goings-on. Contact: Atkinson Realty, 5307 Atlantic Avenue, Virginia Beach, VA 23451. Call 804-428-4441.

Children: Y Pets: N Smoking: Y Handicap Access: N Payment: C, P, T

8402 OCEANFRONT *Rates: moderate*
Open: year-round *Minimum Stay: one week*

A wide porch wraps around the front of this oceanside bungalow, perfect for respites away from the sun, sand castles, surf fishing, and salt-sprayed merry-making that's an integral part of Virginia Beach life. Its four bedrooms (two with queen-sized beds and two with singles) tucked under second-story eaves accommodate eight easily. Comfort-inducing features include two air-conditioning units, a washer and dryer and a kitchen with dishwasher. Nearby is the three-mile-long Virginia Beach boardwalk, crowded with seafood restaurants (featuring the famed Lyndhaven oyster), amusement park rides, games and nightclubs. Contact: Atkinson Realty, 5307 Atlantic Avenue, Virginia Beach, VA 23451. Call 804-428-4441.

Children: Y Pets: N Smoking: Y Handicap Access: N Payment: C, P, T

737 SURFSIDE *Rates: inexpensive*
Open: year-round *Minimum Stay: one week*

The exterior of this modern three-story Virginia Beach hideaway is finished in wood and surrounded by a well-manicured lawn. Perhaps its best feature is a long, double-decker sun porch with access from the outside as well as from both floors. There are three bedrooms (one queen, one double, two singles), a sleep sofa and two and a half baths, accommodating up to eight people. The beach house has central air conditioning, a dishwasher, telephone and TV. Contact: Atkinson Realty, 5307 Atlantic Avenue, Virginia Beach, VA 23451. Call 804-428-4441.

Children: Y Pets: N Smoking: Y Handicap Access: N Payment: C, P, T

WILLIAMSBURG

KINGSMILL RESORT

Rates: inexpensive-deluxe

Open: year-round

Minimum Stay: none

The tobacco barons whose magnificent plantations dot the historic peninsula between the James and York rivers never had it so good as residents at the Kingsmill Resort. Certainly they never got a chance to bask in the Kingsmill's swimming pool, sauna and hot tub—which weary visitors to Williamsburg, Yorkstown, Jamestown, Busch Gardens and the splendid James River plantations will surely appreciate. Besides offering all the amenities of a full-service resort—including golf, tennis, a sports club, restaurant and bar—Kingsmill boasts a collection of one-, two- and three-bedroom villas overlooking the James River, with tasteful furnishings, daily maid service and full kitchens. Contact: Kingsmill Resort, 1010 Kingsmill Road, Williamsburg, VA 23185. Call 1-800-832-5665 (in Virginia, 804-253-1703).

Children: Y   Pets: N   Smoking: Y   Handicap Access: N   Payment: A

WINTERGREEN

MOUNTAIN VILLAS

Rates: inexpensive-deluxe

Open: year-round

Minimum Stay: two nights

Wintergreen is Virginia's premier Blue Ridge mountain resort, bordered by the Blue Ridge Parkway and Appalachian Trail and close to Charlottesville's airport and architectural treasure, Monticello. Its recreational facilities include cross-country and downhill ski trails, a huge indoor fitness center, stables, championship golf course, children's center and naturalist programs. Its 350 villas and high- and low-rise condos are perched like birdhouses on the western flank of the Blue Ridge, ranging in size from studios to two-bedroom apartments, all with well-equipped kitchens and warming fireplaces. Contact: Wintergreen, Rt. 664, Wintergreen, VA 22958. Call 1-800-325-2200 (in Virginia, 703-456-8300).

Children: Y   Pets: N   Smoking: Y   Handicap Access: Y   Payment: A, V, M

Eastsound

ORCAS ISLAND
Roche Harbor
SAN JUAN ISLAND
Friday Harbor
LOPEZ ISLAND

Blaine
Concrete
Rockport

Mazama
Winthrop

Conconully

Freeland

WHIDBEY ISLAND

Coulee Dam

Lake Quinalt

Seattle
Kirkland
Bellevue

Leavenworth

Moclips
Pacific Beach
Copalis Beach
Ocean Shores
Grayland

Mercer Island

Westport Olympia

Naches

Silver Lake

Washington

BELLEVUE

HAMPTON GREENS   *Rates:* budget
Open: year-round   *Minimum Stay: three nights*

When it's time to hit the links, stroll to the Bellevue Municipal Golf
Course right next door. Early-morning joggers and the cyclists in your
crowd can head to Marymoor Park just a few minutes away. Whatever
you do, you'll be surrounded by Douglas firs and native alders and
breathing that clear, pungent air. A family pool and an adults-only
pool let you bring the kids and still swim your laps in peace. Bonded
child care is available for those nights when a romantic dinner for two
is in order. When you're in the mood for a nice family dinner at home,
cook up a scrumptious meal in the full kitchen complete with microwave, bakeware and all necessary tableware and utensils. Weekly maid
service keeps you supplied with fluffy towels and sheets, leaving you
free to simply enjoy! Contact: Pacific Guest Suites, 915 118th Avenue
SE., Suite 250, Bellevue, WA 98005. Call 1-800-962-6620 or 206-454-
7888.

Children: **Y**   Pets: **Y**   Smoking: **Y**   Handicap Access: **N**   Payment: All

STERLING HEIGHTS   *Rates: budget*
Open: year-round   *Minimum Stay: three nights*

Step out onto your patio and watch a glorious sunset over the Seattle
skyline and the Olympic mountain range. Take a swim in the indoor/
outdoor swimming pool before walking to town to catch a movie,

stroll through a museum and go shopping. You have your choice of luxuriously appointed one- and two-bedroom condominium residences here, with wood-burning fireplaces to take the chill out of the air and a full kitchen, where you can microwave some popcorn between meals. Your tableware, bakeware and all utensils are included, along with a European coffee maker to brew that first cup to perfection. Extra guests are no problem—just tell the concierge you want to rent a rollaway bed or two. At night, you'll snuggle beneath cozy quilts that match the cheerful sheets. Contact: Pacific Guest Suites, 915 118th Avenue S.E., Suite 250, Bellevue, WA 98005. Call 1-800-962-6620 or 206-454-0123.

Children: **Y**   Pets: **Y**   Smoking: **Y**   Handicap Access: **N**   Payment: All

THE PARK IN BELLEVUE *Rates: budget-inexpensive*
Open: year-round *Minimum Stay: three nights*

Step out onto the balcony of this elegant, modern condominium and touch a branch of an evergreen tree. Just a few moments from Kirkland's waterfront and the Bellevue Art Museum, you can rent a one- or two-bedroom condo. A wood-burning fireplace will warm you in winter, and air conditioning will cool you when summer arrives. Swim a lap or two in the indoor/outdoor pool or make an appointment for a massage before dipping into the whirlpool bath. You can rent an extra rollaway bed for extra guests; a fully equipped kitchen with bakeware, tableware, flatware and just about anything else you could need will make cooking a dream. Area restaurants teem with alternatives, of course; and what would all this pampering be without weekly maid and linen service? Contact: Pacific Guest Suites, 915 118th Avenue S.E., Bellevue, WA 98005-3855. Call 1-800-962-6620 or 206-454-7888.

Children: **Y**   Pets: **Y**   Smoking: **Y**   Handicap Access: **N**   Payment: All

BLAINE

JACOBS LANDING *Rates: budget-inexpensive*
Open: year-round *Minimum Stay: none*

If your idea of heaven is a condominium on the beach, you needn't look any further. Just minutes from the Mt. Baker ski area, where you can shoot down the slopes all day, Jacobs Landing puts you on Birch Bay, which boasts the warmest water in the Pacific Northwest. With spectacular views of the water and the Cascades, you'll find one- and two-bedroom condominiums here that offer every conceivable luxury, including private sun decks, luxurious living rooms with fireplaces and state-of-the-art kitchens complete with dishwashers and a breakfast bar. Upper-level units feature a loft sleeping area that will make the kids eager to go to bed. Bring your tennis racquet for a quick game on the grounds or head for the heated swimming pool for a few laps. Contact: Jacobs Landing Rentals, 7824 Birch Bay Drive, Blaine, WA 98230. Call 206-371-7633 or 206-371-2569.

Children: **Y**   Pets: **N**   Smoking: **Y**   Handicap Access: **N**   Payment: C, T, V, M

CONCONULLY

SHADY PINES RESORT *Rates: budget*
Open: mid-April to October *Minimum Stay: none*

Take a book out onto the balcony of your lakeside cabin and let the fragrance of the soaring evergreens lift your spirits. One- and three-bedroom cabins come with kitchens, all utensils and dinnerware, so that you can scramble your eggs as the sun rises over the lake. Water-ski to your heart's content or go boating, fishing, hiking or bicycling. If you don't leave home without your RV, there are 23 trailer sites here as well, and if you never go jogging without Rover, you can let him know that this year he's coming on vacation, too. Linens and towels are provided. Contact: Marilyn Womack, Shady Pines Resort, Lower Lake Road, P.O. Box 44, Conconully, WA 98819. Call 509-826-2287.

Children: Y Pets: Y Smoking: Y Handicap Access: N Payment: C, P, T, V, M, O

CONCRETE

BAKER LAKE RESORT *Rates: budget-inexpensive*
Open: April 20-October 31 *Minimum Stay: none*

Just try taking a nap on the boat when you go fishing here! Silvers, dolly varden, steelhead and rainbows will snap up as much bait as you can buy in the on-site tackle shop. Don't despair of rest, though. Viewing the snow-capped North Cascades alone will fill you with serene peace. You can go mushroom picking before dinner or rock collecting in the afternoon. Water-skiers will be thrilled by the ten-mile long lake; back at camp, there's a playground and pool for the kids. Twelve rustic studio and one-bedroom cabins have kitchenettes equipped with all utensils and dinnerware, making it easy for you to rustle up a meal. The on-site Lakeside Cafe is open for breakfast and lunch and laundry service is available on the premises. Contact: Baker Lake Resort, P.O. Box 100, Concrete, WA 98237. Call 206-853-8325.

Children: Y Pets: Y Smoking: Y Handicap Access: N Payment: C, P, T, V, M

COPALIS BEACH

IRON SPRINGS RESORT *Rates: budget-inexpensive*
Open: year-round *Minimum Stay: three nights*

Set your easel up or just unfold a lounge chair when you step out of your oceanfront cabin halfway between Copalis and Pacific beaches. The children can wade in the shallow creek that runs to the ocean or swing in the ocean breeze on the playground. Budding van Goghs can wander through the Cove Gallery just across the street and pick up art supplies in an adjoining shop. A heated indoor swimming pool will tempt you to take one last swim before retiring to your spruce-sheltered cottage for a quiet night. Cottages sleep between two and four people, and your bed will be freshly made up each day, so that all you need to do is drift off to the sound of crashing waves. Contact: Iron Springs Resort, P.O. Box 207, Copalis Beach, WA 98535. Call 206-276-4230.

Children: Y Pets: Y Smoking: Y Handicap Access: N Payment: C, T, V, M

COULEE DAM

COULEE HOUSE MOTEL
Rates: budget
Open: year-round
Minimum Stay: none

Spend your days exploring Washington's Cascade Loop area, take in the world's largest laser light show and then fall asleep to the sound of water cascading over the Grand Coulee Dam. Studio, one- and two-bedroom motel suites with kitchenettes are available here, and each room has a telephone, heat, air conditioning, cable TV and a deck or balcony which allows a glimpse of the dam. Fish, hike, bicycle or take a swim in the pool when you're not off on a guided tour of the area. For sybaritic pleasure, try the Jacuzzi at the end of the day; with linens and maid service provided, you won't have to lift a finger. Contact: Coulee House Motel, 110 Roosevelt Way, Coulee Dam, WA 99116. Call 509-633-1101.

Children: Y Pets: Y Smoking: Y Handicap Access: N Payment: C, T, V, M, A, O

FREELAND

UNCLE JOHN'S COTTAGE & BREAKFAST
Rates: inexpensive
Open: year-round
Minimum Stay: two nights

This cozy two-bedroom, two and a half-bath cottage is surrounded by both the Olympic and the Cascade mountains on ten beautiful acres of land. Loll away the afternoon in either the hammock or the swing, both with views of Whidbey Island's Useless Bay. Nothing is missing here, and your full kitchen with dinnerware, utensils, microwave and laundry facilities is stocked with everything you'll need for a hearty breakfast. Outdoors, a gas barbecue is yours to use and you can picnic or dine right there. Throw a log on the fireplace or relax in the private spa and Jacuzzi after dinner. There's a color TV if you ever tire of staring at the stars; boating, hiking, fishing and bicycling are easily arranged. Contact: Uncle John's Cottage & Breakfast, 1762 E. Lancaster Rd., Freeland, WA 98249. Call 206-321-5623 or Fax 206-221-2603.

Children: Y Pets: Y Smoking: N Handicap Access: N Payment: C, P, T, V, M

FRIDAY HARBOR

WESTCOTT BAY
Rates: inexpensive
Open: year-round
Minimum Stay: one week

Spectacular Westcott Bay wraps around this two-bedroom, two-bath home. Watch the sun go down from the deck while you barbecue some chops, then sit out under the stars and watch the moon come up over the bay. A queen-sized bed in the first bedroom and two twins in the second welcome you for a great night's sleep. In the morning, a fully equipped kitchen invites you to whip up a stack of pancakes for the whole crew. Bring your rubber raft and float right off the beach below the house, or visit nearby Westcott Bay Oyster Farm. Chilly nights are no problem with a fire in the fireplace; your firewood will be stacked and waiting for you when you're ready for a romantic evening. Contact: San Juan Properties, Inc., 105 Spring St., Friday Harbor, WA 98250. Call 206-378-2101 or 1-800-451-9054.

Children: Y Pets: N Smoking: Y Handicap Access: N Payment: C, P, T, O

WESTSIDE ACRES *Rates: inexpensive*
Open: year-round *Minimum Stay: one week*

Enjoy the glorious grounds here in perfect privacy. The five acres of exquisitely maintained property complete with a large pond and a variety of magnificent trees will make it hard for you to leave even for a few moments of sightseeing. Soak in the secluded hot tub right outside the front door on the deck, or enjoy whale-watching or swimming at the community beach a short walk down the road. Three luxuriously appointed bedrooms and a beautiful tiled bath will welcome you home after the day's activities; be sure to bring your binoculars to view bald eagles, rare deer and sheep on nearby Spieden Island. Contact: San Juan Properties, Inc., 105 Spring St., Friday Harbor, WA 98250. Call 206-378-2101 or 1-800-451-9054.

Children: Y Pets: N Smoking: Y Handicap Access: N Payment: C, P, T, O

GRAYLAND

WALSH MOTEL *Rates: budget-inexpensive*
Open: year-round *Minimum Stay: none*

Wade, surf, swim or whale-watch on beautiful Grayland Beach right outside the door of your room, or go beachcombing amid a spectacular sunset over the Pacific Ocean. This motel, situated between Willapa Bay to the south and Grays Harbor Bay to the north, offers accommodations to suit every traveler. Spend your honeymoon in one of the bridal suites with fireplace and Jacuzzi, or choose a unit for two with a kitchen-living room combination equipped with a microwave and all dinnerware and utensils. Studio, one- and two-bedroom units offer a host of amenities for your pleasure, including phone, cable TV and maid and linen service. There's a playground for the children and a gym/spa for guests who aren't out bicycle touring or fishing all day. Contact: Mrs. William H. Walsh, Walsh Motel, 1593 Highway 105, Grayland, WA 98547. Call 206-267-2191.

Children: Y Pets: Y Smoking: Y Handicap Access: Y Payment: All

KIRKLAND/HOUGHTON

OLYMPIA *Rates: budget*
Open: May-August *Minimum Stay: one month*

Ask the gardener to pick the breakfast oranges while you take a pre-breakfast dip in the pool. This spacious four-bedroom, three and a half-bath home is hidden from the street and offers you the ultimate in privacy and luxury. Send the kids down to the large recreation room while you sip coffee in the modern kitchen complete with all cookware and utensils; or let them play on the half-acre of exquisitely maintained property. After you put them down for the night, luxuriate in the master suite's Jacuzzi, capable of erasing all the world's cares. Take a day trip to Seahawk Headquarters nearby, and when you return home, don't forget to take in the sunset over the Olympic mountains. If you still don't feel pampered enough, you can always arrange for maid service for a fee. Contact: Rent A Home International, Inc., 7200 34th Avenue N.W., Seattle, WA 98117. Call 206-545-6963.

Children: Y Pets: N Smoking: Y Handicap Access: N Payment: C, P, T, V, M

LAKE QUINAULT

RAIN FOREST RESORT VILLAGE *Rates: budget-inexpensive*
Open: year-round *Minimum Stay: none*

Rent a cabin beneath the world's largest Sitka spruce trees and watch the ducks on the lake outside your window. Located in the Quinault Valley, which is renowned for its Olympic National Park, you can spend hours gazing at glaciers, alpine meadows and huge valleys. These cabins range in size from singles with adjoining baths and TV to cozy cottages with fireplaces, kitchens and whirlpool private baths. All bedding and linen are provided with maid service; an on-site restaurant and cocktail lounge will help you take your nights off. If you come by RV, you will find a complete facility with all the necessary hookups. Then, too, you can arrive by seaplane and be greeted by a staff ready to bend over backward to please you. Contact: Rain Forest Resort Village, Rt. 1, Box 40, Lake Quinault, WA 98575. Call 1-800-562-0948 or 206-288-2535.

Children: Y Pets: N Smoking: Y Handicap Access: N Payment: C, T, V, M

LEAVENWORTH

DIRTYFACE LODGE *Rates: budget-inexpensive*
Open: year-round *Minimum Stay: none*

Nestled amid tall timbers at the base of Dirtyface Mountain in the Cascade Range, two five-bedroom, two and a half bath private lodges offer a serene retreat with all the comforts of home. The main lodge includes two fireplaces and a full kitchen with a microwave, plus a Jenn-Aire range for those who wish to grill the day's catch indoors. Both accommodations include telephone, heat, air conditioning, cable TV, barbecues and decks. Sunbathing on the beach of glacial-fed Lake Wenatchee, you can watch or join the swimmers, fishermen, sailors, canoeists and summer windsurfers. The truly avid angler can fish year-round at nearby Fish Lake. Those who could do with a little less activity can explore the quaint charms of a nearby Bavarian village and return to the lodge to slip into the private Jacuzzi. All linens and towels are provided. Contact: Rhea Croll, Dirtyface Lodge, P.O. Box 269, Leavenworth, WA 48826. Call 509-763-3842.

Children: Y Pets: N Smoking: Y Handicap Access: N Payment: C, P, T, V, M,

LOPEZ ISLAND

BLUE FJORD CABINS　　　　　　　　　　　　　　　*Rates: budget*
Open: year-round　　　　　　　　　　　　　*Minimum Stay: two nights*

You don't have to have Nordic blood to enjoy these completely secluded cedar-log chalets perched over the mini-fjord off Washington's Jasper Bay. Each chalet is completely private, letting you forget the rest of civilization if you choose; with a fully equipped kitchen complete with all the cookware and utensils you'll need, you won't even have to go out to eat. The ocean beach with its splendid view of Mt. Baker is a perfect place to spot blue herons, bald eagles and sea otters, or you can hike and bike your way around the island. Each chalet has heat and air conditioning, and while there is no maid service you'll receive a generous supply of clean towels and linens. Each cabin sleeps two; just the right size for a couple's getaway. Contact: Stan or Ellie Marean, Rt. 1, Box 1450, Lopez Island, WA 98261. Call 206-468-2749.
Children: N　Pets: N　Smoking: Y　Handicap Access: N　Payment: C, P, T

MAZAMA

MAZAMA COUNTRY INN　　　　　　　　*Rates: budget-inexpensive*
Open: year-round　　　　　　　　　　　　　*Minimum Stay: one night*

This rustic mountain lodge at the edge of the Pasayten Wilderness is nothing short of a cross-country skier's heaven, with many machine-groomed trails perfect for day trips. Day-long ski tours can be arranged with Rendezvous Outfitters, who offer the only inn-to-hut ski program in Washington. By summer, you can bike the country roads and mountain trails; the inn's comforts will soothe you year-round with a hot tub, Jacuzzi, sauna and sitting room with fireplace. Kids will delight watching the wranglers at the Chechaquo Ranch. Cozy studios and one-bedroom units are available, some with queen-sized beds tucked into a loft and built-in bunk beds downstairs. One unit has a full kitchen. Maid and linen service are included, so come with the whole family. Contact: Mazama Country Inn, P.O. Box 223, Mazama, WA 98833. Call 509-996-2681 (in Washington 800-843-7951).
Children: Y　Pets: Y　Smoking: N　Handicap Access: Y　Payment: C, P, T, V,

MERCER ISLAND

WESTSIDE WATERFRONT　　　　　　　　*Rates: expensive-deluxe*
Open: July 12-August 6　　　　　　　　　　*Minimum Stay: one week*

Just 10 minutes from downtown Seattle, this elegant bungalow has a spacious living room that opens onto the lake. Retreat to the cozy study for a late-night read or pull out the queen-sized hide-a-bed for an extra guest or two. Warm up by the fire in the master suite or curl up in the reading area. French doors across the front of the house open onto a beautiful deck with a barbecue for eating out under the stars, but a spacious formal dining room allows you to dine in style as well. You'll be charmed by the old-fashioned kitchen, with all the modern appliances you'll need. While there's plenty to do in the area when you want exercise, you can also try the cross-country ski machine, the stair-stepper or the stationary bike in the house, before tossing a few more logs on the fire in the living room and calling it a night. Contact: Rent A Home International, Inc., 7200 34th Ave. N.W., Seattle, WA 98117. Call 206-545-6963.

Children: Y Pets: N Smoking: N Handicap Access: N Payment: C, P, T, V, M

MOCLIPS

OCEAN CREST RESORT   *Rates: budget-inexpensive*
Open: year-round   *Minimum Stay: two nights*

With skylights and huge picture windows, your apartment here won't keep you from the soaring pines and ocean waves. Enjoy elegant dining as the surf murmurs just outside, or take a dip in the indoor pool with the morning sun or moonlight pouring in. Small and large studios as well as a range of one- and two-bedroom apartments offer you a wide choice of accommodations. The units come with in-room coffee service to let you laze about as long as you like, and some have fireplaces, ocean views and private balconies. All units have private beach access and maid and linen service, which will leave you free to work out in the exercise room and spa, take a sauna or watch the children on the playground. Contact: Ocean Crest Resort, Sunset Beach, Moclips, WA 98652. Call 206-276-4465.

Children: Y Pets: N Smoking: Y Handicap Access: N Payment: C, T, V, M

NACHES

GRANDVIEW COTTAGE AT WHISTLIN' JACK LODGE   *Rates: moderate*
Open: spring and fall   *Minimum Stay: none*

This cozy cottage features a large living area with two double beds. A half-wall divider separates them, giving you a lovely feeling of privacy when you turn in for the night. The Naches River flows past your door just 50 feet away, and when the sun goes down, you can toss some logs on the fire and whip up a hearty snack in the cottage's kitchenette. Walk to dinner at the restaurant on the property and pick up your groceries for the next morning's breakfast before that day-long cross-country ski trip. Those who want to try cross-country for the first time can rent all the equipment they need; snowmobiles can be rented here as well, complete with the required helmet. Towels, linens and maid service make this a no-work, all-play getaway. Contact: Whistlin' Jack Lodge, 18936 Highway 410, Naches, WA 98937. Call 509-658-2433.

Children: Y Pets: N Smoking: Y Handicap Access: N Payment: C, T

SELAH COTTAGE AT WHISTLIN' JACK LODGE   *Rates: inexpensive*
Open: winter and spring   *Minimum Stay: none*

Breathe in the pungent scent of the pines surrounding this lovely cottage, and then come inside to throw another log on the fire while you cook dinner in the kitchenette just off the living room. This cottage can sleep six people in a bedroom with double bed, a hide-a-bed in the living room and another double bed tucked into a cozy alcove adjoining the living room. You can eat out at the restaurant on the

property after an exhilarating day of cross-country skiing or snowmo-biling, or browse through the gift shop on a lazy afternoon. There's no need to attend to the housekeeping here, either, where daily maid service keeps your cottage in perfect order. Contact: Whistlin' Jack Lodge, 18936 Highway 410, Naches, WA 98937. Call 509-658-2433.
Children: Y   Pets: N   Smoking: Y   Handicap Access: N   Payment: C, T

OCEAN SHORES

THE NAUTILUS   *Rates: budget-inexpensive*
Open: year-round   *Minimum Stay: none*
Comb the beaches for driftwood, agates, poppy jasper and a bounty of shells, or get in 18 holes nearby before going clam digging. You can cook up your harvest in your room's kitchen, equipped with dish-washer, microwave and even a garbage disposal. One-bedroom suites have a queen-sized bed in the bedroom and a queen-sized sleeper in the living room sofa, allowing you to sleep two to four people easily. Room telephones, color TV, HBO, maid and linen service and an ice maker make it hard to resist staying in for a quiet night. When you want more activity, go horseback riding a short walk away or try playing bumper boats. You can rent a moped and ride down to the marina to watch the boats. Contact: David and Roxanne Kennedy, The Nautilus, P.O. Box 1174, Ocean Shores, WA 98569. Call 1-800-221-4541 or 206-289-2722.
Children: Y   Pets: N   Smoking: Y   Handicap Access: N   Payment: C, T

ORCAS ISLAND

BEACH HAVEN RESORT   *Rates: budget-moderate*
Open: year-round   *Minimum Stay: one week*
Whether you choose a one-bedroom lodge apartment, a one-, two- or three-bedroom log cabin on the beach or the four-bedroom Beach-comber cottage, this secluded retreat will delight you with its natural beauty. Located right on a gently sloping pebbled beach, these rustic cabins will take you back to nature with their log walls and wood floors. Each cabin has a wood stove, electric heat and a deck or balcony where you can sit and watch for Orca whales. Full kitchens with dinnerware and utensils are available in all of the units, and some offer sliding glass doors and fireplaces. Your firewood will be provided and so will your towels, leaving you free to drink in the lush surroundings and explore this magnificent island. Contact: Steve and Shirley Dalquist, Beach Haven Resort, Route 1, Box 12, Eastsound, WA 98245. Call 206-376-2288.
Children: Y   Pets: N   Smoking: Y   Handicap Access: N   Payment: C, P, T

CARLSON PROPERTY   *Rates: moderate*
Open: year-round   *Minimum Stay: three nights*
If last year's vacation washed away in the rain, then this stunning four-bedroom home on Orcas Island is for you. One of the 172 islands in the San Juan archipelago, Orcas sees only 25 inches of rain a year, leaving its pristine countryside luscious and sunny. Eight people can

share this glorious home's huge dining room, kitchen and contemporary living room with brick fireplace. After a day of boating, sailing, fishing or hiking through the island's unspoiled terrain, you can enjoy your evening outdoors on the spacious and luxuriously planted grounds. Maid and laundry service are both available, allowing you to get away from all of life's cares. Contact: Cherie L. Lindholm Real Estate, P.O. Box 66, Eastsound, WA 98245. Call 206-376-2202.

Children: Y   Pets: Y   Smoking: Y   Handicap Access: N   Payment: C, P, T

NUMBER FOUR   *Rates: inexpensive*
Open: year-round   *Minimum Stay: one week*

This beautiful new home crafted of logs is nestled amid towering pines with expansive views of Eastsound and the San Juan Islands. There are soaring ceilings throughout the house and a large sunny porch where you can sunbathe in glorious privacy. A covered deck with a spectacular ocean view makes a perfect spot to read a book or take a leisurely nap. You can fish, hike, bike or spend your days exploring the island's lush trails and exotic wildlife, then enjoy the option of cooking dinner at home in the spacious kitchen with all of the utensils and cookware you'll need. One queen-sized bed, two twins, one trundle bed and a cot sleep two to six people; you can arrange for maid service. Contact: Cherie L. Lindholm Real Estate, P.O. Box 66, Eastsound, WA 98245. Call 206-376-2202.

Children: Y   Pets: N   Smoking: Y   Handicap Access: Y   Payment: C, P, T

NUMBER ONE   *Rates: inexpensive*
Open: year-round   *Minimum Stay: one week*

Take the ferry to beautiful Orcas Island and walk through the door of this magnificent private home overlooking Buck Bay. You'll have a marine view from every window, and you can even catch sight of a ferry going past as you cook breakfast in the fully equipped kitchen. Explore the island by day, go whale-watching, biking, hiking or boating, or just slip down to the beach a few minutes from your door and bask in the sun and salt air. A queen-sized bed in one bedroom, two twins in another and a double hide-a-bed in the living room sofa let you sleep six people in this lovely home. Contact: Cherie L. Lindholm Real Estate, P.O. Box 66, Eastsound, WA 98245. Call 206-376-2202.

Children: Y   Pets: N   Smoking: Y   Handicap Access: Y   Payment: C, P, T

OBSTRUCTION PASS   *Rates: moderate*
Open: year-round   *Minimum Stay: one week*

You can moor your boat right outside the door of this spectacular three-bedroom, two-bath waterfront home with two balconies running the full length of the front of the house. A grassy front yard leads you right down to the beach for swimming, canoeing or kayaking, and if you didn't come by boat, you can rent one nearby. All-new appliances make cooking a breeze; gleaming wooden floors alternate with fully carpeted rooms. It will be hard to pry yourself away from the picture windows in the contemporary-styled living room, but you might want to just long enough to try one of the area's fine restaurants or to visit

Moran State Park and Cascade Lake, which are both a stone's throw from your door. Contact: San Juan Properties, Inc., 105 Spring Street, P.O. Box 100, Friday Harbor, WA 98250. Call 206-378-2101 or 1-800-451-9054.

Children: Y Pets: N Smoking: Y Handicap Access: N Payment: C, P, T, O

PACIFIC BEACH

THE SANDPIPER BEACH RESORT *Rates: budget-moderate*
Open: year-round *Minimum Stay: none*

When it's time to go fly a kite, this resort is the place for you, with a kite and gift shop right on the premises. Run down the spectacular oceanfront beach just outside your door and let the salt wind set that kite sailing. Studios and one-, two- and three-bedroom suites offer a wide range of living arrangements while you're here. You can come alone or bring three other people with you. All rooms include daily maid and linen service to give you a break from chores, and there's even a separate clam-cleaning shack on the premises. There are no room phones or TVs to disturb you here. Contact: The Sandpiper Beach Resort, P.O. Box A, Pacific Beach, WA 98571. Call 206-276-4580.

Children: Y Pets: Y Smoking: Y Handicap Access: N Payment: C, T

ROCHE HARBOR

ROCHE HARBOR RESORT *Rates: inexpensive-expensive*
Open: year-round *Minimum Stay: none*

A scenic two-hour ferry ride takes you to Roche Harbor on San Juan Island, where you can have your choice of a small or large cottage or any number of luxurious modern condominiums sleeping two to eight. The largest cottage has three double beds in two bedrooms, while the smallest has two bedrooms with a double bed and two singles. Condominiums are available with one, two or three bedrooms, and all have fireplaces. Large kitchens in the condominium units offer you the option of eating in, even though you'll want to try the resort's on-site restaurant at least a few times. Also on the premises is a lovely lounge where you can mingle with other guests and get a feel for the area's many activities. Visit the golf course nearby, frolic by the ocean, fish, bicycle or take a hike here. Maid and linen service will keep you away from housework. Contact: Roche Harbor Resort, P.O. Box 4001, Roche Harbor, WA 98250. Call 206-378-2155.

Children: Y Pets: N Smoking: Y Handicap Access: N Payment: C, P, T, V, M

ROCKPORT

DIABLO LAKE RESORT *Rates: budget*
Open: year-round *Minimum Stay: none*

Take a lake tour complete with a country-style dinner or go llama packing while enjoying your stay here. An old-fashioned general store will sell you all the food, fishing tackle and bait you need. Winter or summer sports enthusiasts will find plenty to do here; afterward, you can retire to your one-, two- or three-bedroom cabin in this peaceful mountain hideaway. Full kitchens equipped with cookware and utensils let you opt for a quiet night, or toss a steak on the barbecue. You'll want to get up early to enjoy the clear mountain air and swimming in glacial-fed Lake Diablo right outside your door. Maid service is available on request; there is a restaurant on the premises. Contact: Diablo Lake Resort, Rockport, WA 98283. Call 206-386-4429.

Children: Y Pets: Y Smoking: Y Handicap Access: N Payment: C, P, T, V, M,

SAN JUAN ISLAND

ROCHE HARBOR *Rates: inexpensive-moderate*
Open: year-round *Minimum Stay: one week*

You can boat, ferry or come in by seaplane here and enjoy all the delights of an island vacation with none of the hassles. On the northern tip of San Juan Island, luxury yachts bob like gems in the marina. Whether you choose a two-bedroom, two-bath condominium or the three-bedroom penthouse accommodation, you'll have a spectacular view of Roche Bay Harbor from your deck. Stay outdoors all day long playing tennis, swimming, fishing, clam digging or just strolling down the beach. Explore the historic Hotel de Haro section of the resort—built in 1886—or take off for a day of seeing the sights. Whatever your pace, you'll be dazzled by the options here. Contact: San Juan Properties, Inc., 105 Spring St., Friday Harbor, WA 98250. Call 206-378-2101 or 1-800-451-9054.

Children: Y Pets: N Smoking: Y Handicap Access: N Payment: C, P, T, O

SEATTLE

84 UNION *Rates: budget-inexpensive*
Open: year-round *Minimum Stay: three nights*

The pulse of the city and a fantastic view of Puget Sound can be yours when you choose an executive studio suite or a one- or two-bedroom apartment in this historic building adjacent to Seattle's famous Pike Place Public Market. Visit the new Venturi-designed Seattle Art Museum or take the kids to the Seattle Aquaurium nearby. You can enjoy the delights of the city all day and all night before coming home to your cozily furnished apartment, where cheerful quilts on the beds will invite you to get a great night's sleep. Rollaway beds can be rented for extra quests, and weekly maid and linen servie will keep you supplied with bright linens and fluffy towels. While you'll never tire of places to eat out in Seattle, the full kitchen outfitted with microwave makes it easy to stay in for a quiet evening, too. Contact: Pacific Guest Suites, 915 118th Avenue S.E., Suite 250, Bellevue, WA 98005. Call 206-454-7888 or 1-800-962-6620

Children: Y Pets: Y Smoking: Y Handicap Access: N Payment: All

SOUND VIEW *Rates: budget-inexpensive*
Open: year-round *Minimum Stay: one week*

Sit by the fire in the master bedroom of this house and take in the majestic view of Puget Sound and the Olympic mountain range. After cooking breakfast in the huge kitchen equipped with all of the utensils and cookware you'll need, serve it up in the breakfast room or the formal dining room. A spacious living room shares that same view of Puget Sound and the mountains, making it an impressive place to entertain. Three bedrooms are on the second floor; one with a double bed and another with two twins. You can, of course, also rent the downstairs of the house separately, in which case you'll have another double bedroom, a laundry room and a kitchenette and bar area. A huge recreation room also shares this level; bunk beds for extra guests await at the far end of the living area. Contact: Rent A Home International,Inc., 7200 34th Avenue N.W., Seattle, WA 98117. Call 206-545-6963.

Children: Y Pets: N Smoking: N Handicap Access: N Payment: C, P, T, V, M

SILVER LAKE

SILVER LAKE MOTEL AND RESORT   *Rates: budget*
Open: mid-February to November   *Minimum Stay: three nights*

Swim in the warm lake at the base of Mt. St. Helens or relax on the balcony outside your room and delight in the breathtaking view. You can catch your dinner every night and have your choice of perch, bluegill, catfish or rainbow trout. Kitchens, complete with utensils and dinnerware, are available in the motel units and the rustic two-bedroom cabins, which have carpeting and electric heat. You can rent canoes and boats by the hour on the lake. Or simply walk out to the beach with a book and doze in the sun. Towels and linens are provided daily. Contact: Silver Lake Motel and Resort, 3201 Spirit Lake Hwy., Silver Lake E., WA 98045. Call 206-274-6141.

Children: Y Pets: N Smoking: Y Handicap Access: N Payment: C, T, V, M, O

WESTPORT

CHATEAU WESTPORT   *Rates: budget-expensive*
Open: year-round   *Minimum Stay: none*

Kick your shoes off and watch TV in a gigantic studio apartment with a queen-sized hide-a-bed, dining table and private balcony with an ocean view. You can bring all your friends here, too, where you can find luxury suites large enough for a family gathering or a working vacation with your colleagues. The 108 units here are designed to accommodate any group. Fish for the best salmon on the West Coast by day or enjoy a leisurely afternoon by the ocean outside your door. If sightseeing is your thing, you can watch just about anything here—from whales to birds to kites soaring through the air. Dive into the heated indoor pool when you get the urge to swim a lap or two, or slide into the hot tub and call it a day. A maid will be there daily to make your bed and restock your bath with towels. Contact: Shelley Turner, Chateau Westport, 710 Hancock St., Westport, WA 98595. Call 206-268-9101.

Children: Y Pets: N Smoking: Y Handicap Access: N Payment: All

WHIDBEY ISLAND

GLENDALE BEACH HOUSE *Rates: moderate-expensive*
Open: year-round *Minimum Stay: two nights*

You'll enjoy panoramic views of Mt. Baker, the Cascades and Mt. Rainier when you rent this three-story home with two decks for your sunning and lounging pleasure. Eat out on one of the decks or in the spacious dining room off the modern kitchen, which boasts a dishwasher and a microwave. Lighting a fire will be easy with your logs neatly stacked and waiting for you, leaving you plenty of energy to visit the historic forts and lighthouses nearby or to grab some bait and go after a bucketful of salmon. The upstairs deck opens off the master bedroom, featuring a king-sized bed. A second bedroom has a queen-sized bed and a view of the water as well. You'll probably never tire of the views from this house, but if you do, there's a VCR downstairs if you want to rent a movie. Contact: Bill and Pam Royce, Northwest Vacation Homes, South Whidbey Island, 4763 Hwy. 525, Clinton, WA 98235. Call 206-321-5005.

Children: Y Pets: Y Smoking: N Handicap Access: N Payment: C, T, V, M

GUEST HOUSE BED AND BREAKFAST COTTAGE *Rates: inexpensive-expensive*
Open: year-round *Minimum Stay: none*

Choose one of the romantic one-bedroom cottages on this 25-acre private getaway with pond, outdoor swimming poool, spa and exercise room, and you'll be pampered without being disturbed. There is no maid service to intrude on your privacy; instead your cottage will be fully stocked with towels, linens and terry cloth robes when you arrive. Even your breakfast will be waiting in your cottage. A full kitchen lets you cook a late-night snack or a hearty breakfast in peace, and you'll find all of the cookware and utensils that you'll need. Though the cottages are rustic in flavor, you won't miss any of the comforts of home, like fireplaces and stained glass windows. You can sit out on your deck or bask in your private Jacuzzi to relax, and when you're ready for activity, you can play golf, go horseback riding, bicycling, fishing or boating. Contact: The Creger Family, 835 E. Christenson Road, Greenbank, WA 98253. Call 206-678-3115.

Children: N Pets: N Smoking: N Handicap Access: N Payment: C, T

SERENITY PINES EAGLE'S WATCH COTTAGE *Rates: inexpensive-moderate*
Open: year-round *Minimum Stay: two nights*

Rise and shine in this waterfront one-bedroom cottage on Puget Sound, and walk down the stairs to 350 feet of private "sugar sand" beach. Fish for trout and salmon, play golf nearby or visit the local state parks, historic forts and lighthouses. When you return home, toss a few logs on the fire as you head for the beautiful kitchen complete with microwave and dishwasher. After dinner the Jacuzzi on the deck will beckon you to float beneath the moonlight before retiring to the king-sized bed in the bedroom. Two color TVs will keep even the fastest channel changer happy, and you'll find a complimentary gourmet fruit and breakfast basket waiting for you when you arrive. Contact: Bill and Pam Royce, Northwest Vacation Homes, South Whidbey Island, 4763 Hwy. 525, Clinton, WA 98235. Call 206-321-5005.

Children: Y Pets: Y Smoking: Y Handicap Access: N Payment: C, T, V, M

WINTHROP

WOLF RIDGE RESORT   *Rates: budget-inexpensive*
Open: year-round   *Minimum Stay: none*

Picture yourself sitting on the elegant log terrace outside your room overlooking the Methow River. Beamed ceilings, bedrooms with sliding glass doors, balconies with lake views and cathedral ceilings in the larger units are but a few of the glorious advantages to staying here. You can cross-country ski, snowmobile, try heli-skiing or go downhill in winter. Hiking, fishing, mountain biking, horseback riding and river rafting in summer all offer an alternative to golf or tennis. Afterwards, enjoy whipping up dinner in a kitchen that includes a dishwasher, coffee maker, toaster, all utensils and dinnerware. Several one-bedroom accommodations can sleep two people with plenty of room to spare, while the sensational two-bedroom, two-bath townhome can sleep eight. Contact: Lou and Gabrielle Childers, Wolf Ridge Resort, Wolf Creek Rd., Rt. 2 Box 655, Winthrop, WA 98862. Call 509-996-2828.

Children: Y   Pets: N   Smoking: Y   Handicap Access: N   Payment: C, T

West Virginia

BERKELEY SPRINGS

HALFORD HOUSE	*Rates: budget*
Open: mid-March to December 1	*Minimum Stay: one weekend*

This two and a half-story Victorian house surrounded by a porch sits in a narrow valley in the Allegheny foothills, just a quick walk from the renowned healing waters of Berkeley Springs. Halford House is a private family vacation residence for up to 10, with four bedrooms as well as a sleep sofa, two and a half baths, two fireplaces, a deck for sunset watching, barbecue, laundry facilities and fully equipped kitchen. Just outside the front door lies Berkeley Springs, an eccentric little Victorian town with plenty of shops, restaurants and of course the spa. Run by the state park system, it offers Roman baths, sessions in old-fashioned steam cabinets, a health club and an outdoor swimming pool brimming with the Berkeley Springs therapeutic brew. Contact: Bonnie or Ralph Halford, 3837 N. 26th St., Arlington, VA 22207. Call 703-522-3040.

Children: Y   Pets: N   Smoking: Y   Handicap Access: N   Payment: C, P

CAIRO

NORTH BEND STATE PARK CABINS	*Rates: budget-inexpensive*
Open: year-round	*Minimum Stay: one week*

The eight deluxe two- to three-bedroom cabins available for rent at North Bend State Park occupy the wooded heights above a horseshoe curve of the Hughes River in the rolling north-central section of West

Virginia. Built of cedar logs and wood shingles, they all have color TVs, fireplaces, wall-to-wall carpeting and extensively equipped kitchens. Fishing, hiking, miniature golf, swimming and tennis are among the entertainments offered. The facilities are particularly attractive to the physically impaired, for they include specially designed horseshoe pits plus trails, basketball, softball and bicycles for the blind. Contact: North Bend State Park, Cairo, WV 26337. Call 1-800-CALL-WVA (in West Virginia, 304-643-2931).

Children: Y Pets: N Smoking: Y Handicap Access: Y Payment: C, P, T, A, V, M

CASS

CASS SCENIC RAILROAD STATE PARK COMPANY HOUSES	*Rates: budget*
Open: year-round	*Minimum Stay: none*

Perched amid some of West Virginia's mightiest mountains, isolated and forest-enshrouded, the little village of Cass is still one of the most popular spots in the state. That's because it's the site of the historic Cass Scenic Railroad, an 11-mile logging line that switches madly back and forth in its ascent of 4,842-foot Bald Knob. Recently the state refurbished a collection of 12 houses in Cass, which were built in the early 1900s to accommodate employees of the Virginia Pulp and Paper Company. They can sleep up to eight and boast comfortably renovated baths, wood-burning stoves and fully equipped kitchens. Cass is a wee hamlet, with one restaurant, a country store, history museum, craft shops and, of course, the scenic railroad station. Contact: Cass Scenic Railroad State Park, P.O. Box 107, Cass, WV 24927. Call 1-800-CALL-WVA (in West Virginia, 304-456-4300).

Children: Y Pets: N Smoking: Y Handicap Access: N Payment: C, P, T, A, V, M

DAVIS

BLACKWATER FALLS STATE PARK CABINS	*Rates: budget*
Open: year-round	*Minimum Stay: one week*

The faint roaring noise in the backround at this flagship West Virginia state park comes from the the 63-foot falls of the amber-colored Blackwater River. The waterfall rages in a deep gorge 500 feet below the handsome, modern lodge with full-service restaurant and 25 cabins accommodating two to four persons in one- to four-bedroom units. The cabins come complete with stone fireplaces, well-equipped kitchens and weekly linen and towel service. During the warm weather, there's swimming and boating on 14-acre Lake Pendleton; when the snow flies, there's ice skating, horse-drawn sleigh rides, tobogganing and cross-country skiing. Contact: Blackwater Falls State Park, P.O. Box 490, Davis, WV 26260. Call 1-800-CALL-WVA (in West Virginia, 304-259-5216).

Children: Y Pets: N Smoking: Y Handicap Access: N Payment: C, P, T, A, V, M

DUNMORE

SENECA STATE FOREST CABINS *Rates: budget*
Open: late April-early December *Minimum Stay: one week*

In the 1930s the Civilian Conservation Corps contructed the seven cabins at Seneca State Forest, which reflect classic CCC style: They are made of log with stone fireplaces, wood-burning kitchen stoves and gas lights. Linen and weekly maid service is provided, but there is no running water, meaning visitors use a hand pump and pit toilets nearby. As recompense for the lack of plumbing, there's the smashing state forest itself—11,684 acres of it—traversed by 23 miles of wilderness paths (including portions of the Allegheny and Greenbrier river trails), a four-acre lake jumping with trout, bass and bluegill, children's playground and barbecues. Contact: Seneca State Forest, Rt. 1, Box 140, Dunmore, WV 24934. Call 1-800-CALL-WVA (in West Virginia, 304-799-6213).

Children: Y Pets: N Smoking: Y Handicap Access: N Payment: C, P, T, A, V, M

GRAFTON

TYGART LAKE STATE PARK CABINS *Rates: budget*
Open: mid-April to October 31 *Minimum Stay: one week*

This state park's 10 cabins dot the woodsy north shore of Tygart Lake, whose waters are contained by one of the largest concrete dams east of the Mississippi. Boating, fishing, wind surfing, waterskiing and scuba diving fill the average summer day here, with the state park's own marina offering rental equipment and launching facilities. The cabins are of modern design, boasting wood-paneled interiors, fireplaces, electric heat, and well-equipped kitchens (with linens and towels provided). Golf and tennis are nearby, as is the historic Mother's Day Church in Grafton, the site of the first Mother's Day celebration back in 1908. Contact: Tygart Lake State Park, Rt. 1, Box 260, Grafton, WV 26354. Call 1-800-CALL-WVA (in West Virginia, 304-265-3383).

Children: Y Pets: N Smoking: Y Handicap Access: N Payment: C, P, T, A, V, M

HUTTONSVILLE

KUMBRABOW STATE FOREST CABINS *Rates: budget*
Open: April 15-December 7 *Minimum Stay: two nights*

A trip to the five rustic cabins at this state forest takes visitors along Route 219, through the lovely Tygart River Valley shadowed by the flanks of massive Cheat Mountain. The facilities, of CCC vintage, are rustic in the extreme, with no running water or baths (though pit toilets and hand pumps are located close by). Wood-burning stoves, stone fireplaces and gas lights keep these snug quarters aglow. Kumbrabow, at elevations of up to 3,855 feet, attracts hikers, hunters and wildlife enthusiasts, as well as downhill skiers who can test their skills on the slopes at nearby Snowshoe. Contact: Kumbrabow State Forest, P.O. Box 65, Huttonsville, WV 26273. Call 1-800-CALL-WVA (in West Virginia, 304-335-2219).

Children: Y Pets: N Smoking: Y Handicap Access: N Payment: C, P, T, A, V, M

MARLINTON

WATOGA STATE PARK CABINS · *Rates: budget*
Open: year-round · *Minimum Stay: two nights*

Ten-thousand-acre Watoga State Park is situated in the Allegheny uplands 17 miles south of Marlinton and bordered by the beautiful Greenbrier River, with its fine biking and hiking trail. In addition to Watoga's 11-acre lake, restaurant, swimming pool, riding stables and game court, the park offers accommodations in cabins housing up to six. Eight of these are deluxe class, with wood-paneled walls and forced-air furnaces; the others are standard log or stone buildings with fireplaces. During the summer season the park is like a rustic resort, with outdoor entertainment options for everyone in the family; during the winter, the deluxe cabins make a perfect snowy hideaway. Contact: Watoga State Park, Star Rt. 1, Box 252, Marlinton, WV 24954. Call 1-800-CALL-WVA (in West Virginia, 304-799-0487).

Children: Y Pets: N Smoking: Y Handicap Access: N Payment: C, P, T, A, V, M

MORGANTOWN

LAKEVIEW RESORT CLUB · *Rates: moderate-deluxe*
Open: year-round · *Minimum Stay: none*

These cedar and stone townhouses are scattered across a resort boasting two golf courses, tennis courts, a fitness center and a swimming pool. They are located 10 miles from the glass-making center of Morgantown in north-central West Virginia. Their interiors are traditional or contemporary, furnished in attractive pastels and luxuriously appointed with individually operated climate controls, phones and cable TV. The resort offers supervised programs for children and a gourmet restaurant. Nearby are opportunities for rafting adventures on the wild Cheat River and shopping at the Morgantown crystal and glass outlets. Contact: Lakeview Resort Club, Rt. 6, Box 88-A, Morgantown WV 26505. Call 1-800-624-8300 (in West Virginia, 304-594-1111).

Children: Y Pets: N Smoking: Y Handicap Access: N Payment: A, V, M

MULLENS

TWIN FALLS STATE PARK CABINS · *Rates: budget*
Open: year-round · *Minimum Stay: two nights*

The frothy falls of the Marsh Fork and Black Fork—which join to form Cabin Creek—are the source of this state park's name. Its hickory and oak-covered ridges were once coal-mining country; now facilities for outdoor fun prevail, including an 18-hole championship golf course, hiking trails, restored pioneer farmhouse, swimming pool and White Horse Knob Observation Tower, at 2,330 feet. Nearby lies the dramatic New River Gorge, where visitors can take day trips down one of the wildest waterways in the east. The park's 13 two- to four-bedroom rental units are secluded from the lodge and have fireplaces, color TVs, decks, fully equipped kitchens and linen. Contact: Twin Falls State Park, Rt. 97, P.O. Box 1023, Mullens, WV 25882. Call 1-800-CALL-WVA (in West Virginia, 304-294-4000).

Children: Y Pets: N Smoking: Y Handicap Access: N Payment: C, P, T, A, V, M

Wisconsin

BAYFIELD

BAYFIELD ON THE LAKE   *Rates: inexpensive*
Open: year-round   *Minimum Stay: two nights*
Overlooking the Apostle Islands Marina from a cove of elm and maple, these well-appointed condominiums enjoy a magnificent view of Lake Superior and the quaint little town of Bayfield. Browse through the town's many art galleries and crafts shops, or sample the wide range of sporting activities, from sailing, golf and tennis to ice fishing and snowmobiling. Each suite includes a fireplace, family-style deck, sauna, a large walk-through kitchen equipped with microwave and dishwasher and at least one full bath. Contact: Bayfield on the Lake, P.O. Box 70, Bayfield, WI 54814. Call 715-779-3621.
Children: Y Pets: Y Smoking: Y Handicap Access: N Payment: C, T, V, M

PORT SUPERIOR VILLAGE   *Rates: inexpensive*
Open: year-round   *Minimum Stay: two nights*
On the water of Lake Superior's south shore in sheltered Pikes Bay, where forested hills meet the blue inland sea, lies Port Superior Village. Cruise to the protected Apostle Islands and explore the remote beaches, or indulge in the abundant variety of sports activities, from swimming, boating and tennis to skiing and snowmobiling. These harborside condos include a spacious living/dining area with fireplace, a full-convenience kitchen complete with all utensils and a sun deck

with a barbecue and deck furniture. Upstairs, two bedrooms and a full bath complete the luxurious accommodations. Contact: Port Superior Village, P.O. Box 800, Bayfield, WI 54814. Call 715-799-5123.

Children: Y Pets: Y Smoking: Y Handicap Access: N Payment: C, P, T, V, M

REITEN BOATYARD   *Rates: budget-inexpensive*
Open: year-round   *Minimum Stay: two nights*

Boat and sail from your back door in an area considered the "sailing headquarters" of Lake Superior while staying in the Reiten Boatyard Condominiums. With a commanding waterfront view, each fully appointed condominium provides a private patio/deck, a fireplace and a kitchen. Three different floor plans include a studio and bedroom suite accommodating four, and a bedroom suite with loft accommodating six. Contact: Reiten Boatyard, P.O. Box 576, 320 Wilson Avenue, Bayfield, WI 54814. Call 715-779-5660 or 715-779-5123.

Children: Y Pets: Y Smoking: Y Handicap Access: N Payment: C, P, T, V, M

BOULDER JUNCTION

WHITE SAND LAKE LODGE   *Rates: budget*
Open: year-round   *Minimum Stay: one week*

On the shore of White Sand Lake sits a traditionally furnished three-bedroom, two-bathroom house accommodating six. Sun and swim on your own two and a half-acre wooded lot or launch one of the two fishing boats onto the super-clean lake with excellent fishing. Not far off you'll find plenty of skiing, tennis and golf. Complete with screened porch, living room, dining room and a fully equipped kitchen including microwave, washer and dryer, this house is ready for everything. Contact: Rent A Home International Inc., 7260 34 Ave. N.W., Seattle, WA 98117. Call 206-545-6963.

Children: Y Pets: N Smoking: Y Handicap Access: Y Payment: C, P, T, V, M

EAGLE RIVER

SAFER'S GYPSY VILLA RESORT   *Rates: moderate-deluxe*
Open: year-round   *Minimum Stay: two nights*

Safer's Gypsy Villa Resort offers ultramodern one- and two-bedroom low-rise condominiums with cathedral ceilings and kitchens on lakefront property. Travel through the longest chain of freshwater lakes in the world on a boat rented from the nearby marina. Then relax in the hot tub while the children wind down at the playground on the beach. Campfire cookouts, treasure hunts, music and dancing make for fun-filled evenings. Contact: Safer's Gypsy Villa Resort, 950 Circle Drive, Eagle River, WI 54521. Call 715-479-8644.

Children: Y Pets: Y Smoking: Y Handicap Access: N Payment: C, T, V, M

LAC DU FLAMBEAU

FENCE LAKE LODGE   *Rates: budget-inexpensive*
Open: year-round   *Minimum Stay: one week*

Nestled on the peaceful shoreline of Fence Lake sits a quiet and serene hideaway, the Fence Lake Lodge. Meet family and friends for swimming, tennis, horseshoes, boating and scuba diving in this delightfully casual atmosphere. Then end the day by dining on some of the best food in northern Wisconsin, highlighted by breathtaking views of the lake from the glass-enclosed dining rooms. One- through five-bedroom cottages include fully equipped kitchens and linens, though guests must provide their own bath towels. Contact: Fence Lake Lodge, 12919 Frying Pan Camp Lane, Lac du Flambeau, WI 54538. Call 715-588-3255.

Children: Y Pets: N Smoking: Y Handicap Access: N Payment: C, T, A, V, M

LA FARGE

TRILLIUM *Rates: budget*
Open: year-round *Minimum Stay: none*

Enjoy your farm breakfast in a cozy, private cottage tucked into the hills of Kickapoo Valley in southwestern Wisconsin. While away the afternoon in a hammock under the large trees on 85 acres of fields, woods and tree-lined brooks. Or view the wildlife, including owls, hawks, wild turkeys and deer, and take a perfect photograph. This completely furnished cottage includes two double beds, two singles and a crib to accommodate six adults and one infant. A sunny kitchen/dining area, stone fireplace, modern appliances and wood-burning cookstove are part of its charms. Contact: Rosanne Boyett, Trillium, Rt. 2, Box 121, LaFarge, WI 54639. Call 608-625-4492.

Children: Y Pets: N Smoking: Y Handicap Access: N Payment: C, P, T

MISHICOT

FOX HILLS RESORT *Rates: inexpensive-moderate*
Open: year-round *Minimum Stay: none*

Return to a steaming Jacuzzi from a sport fishing outing on Lake Michigan. Or relax in front of the fireplace after a day of cross-country skiing. With horseback riding, tennis, pool, an exercise trail and health club available, the whole family will enjoy a wonderful vacation at this resort. One- and two-bedroom condominiums feature cathedral ceilings and include kitchens, patios or balconies, daily maid service and linens. The rustic setting offers the perfect antidote to civilized stress. Contact: Fox Hills Resort, P.O. Box 129, Mishicot, WI 54228. Call 414-755-2376.

Children: Y Pets: N Smoking: Y Handicap Access: N Payment: C, T

RHINELANDER

HOLIDAY ACRES *Rates: budget-inexpensive*
Open: year-round *Minimum Stay: none*

Situated on over 1,000 acres of beautiful deep Wisconsin northwoods and encompassing the long, lovely Lake Thompson shoreline is Holiday Acres. Spend the afternoon swimming, boating or waterskiing and then refresh yourself at the circular bar before indulging in the dining room's award-winning food and wine. Modern one- to four-

bedroom cottages on the grounds include fully equipped kitchens and linens; or choose a room in the main lodge. Contact: James F. Zambon, Holiday Acres, Box 460, Rhinelander, WI 54501. Call 715-369-1500.
Children: Y Pets: Y Smoking: Y Handicap Access: N Payment: C, T, V, M

THREE LAKES

CEDAR CREST RESORT   *Rates: budget*
Open: year-round   *Minimum Stay: one week*
Launch your boat on 1,800-acre Thunder Lake and watch beautiful sunrises and sunsets, or find a private bay in which to settle back and lure the panfish, northern and walleye. The amazing fall colors provide a backdrop for duck hunting on the lake and deer hunting in the forests. Freshly fallen snow on the forest creates a mood for hiking, cross-country skiing, ice fishing and snowmobiling on the many groomed trails. Lodgings consist of two- and three-bedroom cottages, each with its own pier and aluminum fishing boat, plus fully equipped kitchens and linens. Contact: Truog's Cedar Crest Resort, 2528 Anders Road, Three Lakes, WI 54562. Call 715-272-1188.
Children: Y Pets: Y Smoking: Y Handicap Access: N Payment: C, P, T

VANDYNE

THE WILLOWS RESORT   *Rates: budget-inexpensive*
Open: April-October   *Minimum Stay: two nights*
Push a Lund fishing boat off the pier into beautiful Lake Winnebago, then cast your line and dream the day away. Upon your return, the barbecue facilities are awaiting your catch. The one- and two-bedroom cottages here include fully equipped kitchens, baths, air conditioning, TV and linens. Relax outdoors in the secluded parklike area while the children enjoy the large playground. After dinner stroll along the pier and watch the sun disappear on the horizon. Contact John or Sandy, The Willows Resort, N9103 Lakeshore Drive, Vandyne, WI 54979. Call 414-921-2033.
Children: Y Pets: N Smoking: Y Handicap Access: N Payment: C, T

WISCONSIN DELLS

VILLAS AT CHRISTMAS MOUNTAIN   *Rates: inexpensive*
Open: year-round   *Minimum Stay: two nights*
Every member of the family will enjoy the variety of recreation available at one of Wisconsin's finest four-season resorts, Villas at Christmas Mountain. The children make new friends while participating in supervised pastimes planned just for them. Adults indulge in the resort atmosphere with its pools, tennis, horseback riding and golf. Or get the family together to visit the House on the Rock. Two-bedroom luxury villas with two fireplaces and a whirlpool in the master bedroom include kitchens and grills on all the porches. Contact: Villas at Christmas Mountain, S-944 Christmas Mountain Drive, Wisconsin Dells, WI 53965. Call 608-253-1000.
Children: Y Pets: N Smoking: Y Handicap Access: Y Payment: C, T, A, V, M

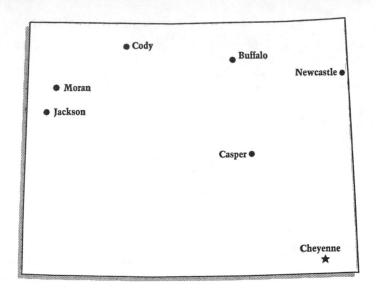

Wyoming

BUFFALO

PARADISE GUEST RANCH   *Rates: moderate*
Open: May 22-September 18   *Minimum Stay: none*

Nestled at the foot of the Big Horn Mountains—an area whose rich frontier history records bitter battles between Indians and settlers, ranchers and homesteaders—lies the Paradise Guest Ranch, whose fully restored two- and three-bedroom luxury log cabins include kitchens and large living/family room areas with fireplaces. An ideal setting for a family vacation, all ages will enjoy a visit to the nearby Jim Gatchell Museum, where some 10,000 artifacts of Indians, settlers and soldiers are housed, or a tour of Fort Phil Kearny, which claims the bloodiest history of any fort in the West. For a more peaceful afternoon, relax in the hot tub while the children enjoy supervised recreational programs and activities. Contact: Paradise Guest Ranch, Pines Lodge, Box 100, Buffalo, WY 82834. Call 307-684-7876.

Children: **Y**   Pets: **N**   Smoking: **Y**   Handicap Access: **N**   Payment: **C, T**

CODY

SHOSHONE LODGE   *Rates: budget*
Open: May 1-November 1   *Minimum Stay: none*

"The most scenic 50 miles in the world," said Teddy Roosevelt about the road to Yellowstone Park through the Wapiti Valley where the Shoshone Lodge lies. Just four miles from the eastern entrance to

Yellowstone Park, this third-generation family-owned-and-operated guest ranch offers modern cabins with kitchenettes on wooded grounds. Colorful rock formations highlight your way through the Shoshone Canyon, where you will enjoy breathtaking views of the Buffalo Bill Dam and state park. Fill your days with mountain and meadow horseback riding, river floating and excellent fishing. In the evening, enjoy an outdoor barbecue and join the neighborly square dances. Contact: Shoshone Lodge, Box 790TY, Cody, WY 82414. Call 307-587-4044.

Children: Y Pets: Y Smoking: Y Handicap Access: N Payment: C, T, A, V, M

JACKSON

CACHE CREEK MOTEL   *Rates: budget*
Open: year-round   *Minimum Stay: none*

Wintertime transforms the Tetons into a scene of incomparable beauty, beckoning snowmobile enthusiasts, skiers and skaters to the Cache Creek Motel, where one- and two-bedroom suites provide ideal accommodations for family vacationers. While the snow-clad granite peaks provide the perfect backdrop for snowmobile tours through the valley or nearby Yellowstone National Park, lovers of spectator sports will enjoy exciting sleigh, NASTAR and dog-sled races. In this ideal year-round resort, summer guests will delight in excellent big game hunting, trout fishing, boating and river rafting, or a dip in the area's natural hot springs. Contact: Cache Creek Motel, P.O. Box 918, Jackson Hole, WY 83001. Call 307-733-7781.

Children: Y   Pets: N   Smoking: Y   Handicap Access: N   Payment: All

ELK REFUGE INN   *Rates: budget*
Open: year-round   *Minimum Stay: one week*

During the summer, the American elk (wapiti) roam high in the Teton peaks. When winter comes, they descend to the floor of Jackson Hole to the National Elk Refuge just north of the town of Jackson. Here, overlooking this glacial outwash area, is the Elk Refuge Inn, where one- and two-bedroom units complete with fully outfitted kitchenettes are available on a weekly and monthly basis. The beauty of this quiet, scenic landscape—where 500 acres of the Grand Teton National Park becomes your backyard—provides a splendid backdrop for hiking, bird-watching, photography, horseback riding and big-game scouting. Contact: Elk Refuge Inn, P.O. Box 2834, Jackson, WY 83001. Call 307-733-3582.

Children: Y Pets: N Smoking: Y Handicap Access: N Payment: C, T, A, V, M

JACKSON HOLE LODGE   *Rates: budget-moderate*
Open: year-round   *Minimum Stay: one week*

Until 1800, Jackson Hole was an Indian hunting ground, and while the severe winters made permanent habitation virtually impossible, bands of Indians crossed the passes into the basins on warring or hunting expeditions in the spring, summer and late autumn. Nowadays, this Teton wilderness, the sight of America's greatest natural beauty, boasts unlimited recreational and wilderness activities. And only three and a half blocks from the town square, the Jackson Hole Lodge provides studios and one- and two-bedroom condos with fully equipped kitchens and fireplaces. In the evenings, regardless of the season, guests are sure to enjoy a relaxing dip in the indoor pool. Contact: Jackson Hole Lodge, P.O. Box 1805 A, Jackson Hole, WY 83001. Call 307-733-2992.

Children: Y   Pets: N   Smoking: Y   Handicap Access: N   Payment: All

SPRING CREEK RESORT   Rates: *deluxe*
Open: *year-round*   Minimum Stay: *none*

Perched on a secluded mountaintop with a world-class view of the Teton wilderness sits the Spring Creek Resort, whose luxurious one- and two-bedroom apartments offer a restful haven after an exhilarating day on the tennis courts, on the local ski trails or on a forest path. Here, anglers can test their prowess in over 800 miles of trout streams where rainbow, native cutthroat, golden, brook, and mackinaw thrive. Others will love waterskiing on Jackson Lake and swimming in local natural hot springs. Wintertime offers such unlimited opportunities for dog-sledding and tobogganing—and the conditions are ideal. Later, savor a relaxing evening in front of the fireplace after a dip in the whirlpool. Contact: Spring Creek Resort, P.O. Box 3154, Jackson Hole, WY 83001. Call 307-733-8833.

Children: Y   Pets: N   Smoking: Y   Handicap Access: N   Payment: All

JACKSON HOLE

TETON SHADOWS   Rates: *budget*
Open: *year-round*   Minimum Stay: *none*

These cozy three-bedroom condos, furnished with fully equipped kitchens, provide an ideal retreat in one of the most beautiful areas of the country. Here you can hike through steep canyons and barren alpine country where snowfall is not uncommon in July, or ride horses through the Teton wilderness surrounded on all sides by mountain barriers. Wet a line in a lake or stream so pure you can see trout before it hits your lure, or scout for Rocky Mountain bighorn sheep in the early morning and late evening along the Gros Ventre River and Red Hills. Throughout, you'll want to photograph the splendid panorama of coniferous timber, waterfalls and wide meadows. Contact: Teton Shadows, Jackson Hole, WY 83001. Call 1-800-325-8605.

Children: Y   Pets: N   Smoking: Y   Handicap Access: N   Payment: C, T

THE INN AT JACKSON HOLE   Rates: *inexpensive-moderate*
Open: *year-round*   Minimum Stay: *none*

After an exhilarating day on the slopes, wind down in front of your own fireplace at the Inn at Jackson Hole at the base of the Teton Mountain ski area. A wide range of accommodations each include a kitchenette; an additional selection of off-property condos with full kitchens are available as well. Tour nearby Yellowstone National Park's thermal features—spectacular in winter—by either a snowmobile or snow coach, and enjoy wintertime spectator sports including exciting sleigh, NASTAR and dog-sled races and snowmobile hill climbs. Warm-weather guests will want to relax by the pool after a day filled with all manner of summer activities. Contact: The Inn at Jackson Hole, P.O. Box 328, Teton Village, Jackson Hole, WY 83025. Call 1-800-842-7666.

Children: Y   Pets: N   Smoking: Y   Handicap Access: N   Payment: All

MORAN

SIGNAL MOUNTAIN LODGE	*Rates: budget-moderate*
Open: May 12-October 14	*Minimum Stay: none*

Enjoy a spectacular view of the Tetons while relaxing at Signal Mountain Lodge—the only resort nestled on the shore of Jackson Lake—where comfortable one- and two-bedroom units are available. The lake, covering almost 26,000 acres and shadowed by awesome mountains rising dramatically from the west, offers abundant recreational activities including excellent game fishing for native cutthroat trout, the mackinaw, and brown and brook trout. Explore the surrounding wilderness areas where big-game hunting is unsurpassed; take a raft down the Snake River or swim off the beach just outside your door. Contact: Signal Mountain Lodge, P.O. Box 50, Moran, WY 83013. Call 307-543-2831.

Children: Y Pets: Y Smoking: Y Handicap Access: N Payment: C, T, A, V, M

NEWCASTLE

FOUNTAIN INN AT CRYSTAL PARK RESORT	*Rates: budget*
Open: year-round	*Minimum Stay: none*

In this northeastern Wyoming town, which was named after its sister community in England's Newcastle-Upon-Tyne, the Fountain Inn at Crystal Park Resort features a selection of one- and two-bedroom suites equipped with full kitchens. On the grounds, the heated and wading pools, waterslide, paddle-boat area and roller-skating rink will keep guests busy for hours. And just steps away, the natural beauty of the Black Hills National Forest, famous for its vast acres of thick ponderosa pines, beckons visitors for picnicking, camping and hunting. Guests will enjoy the Anna Miller Museum, which once served as a stockade, hostelry, storehouse, blacksmith shop and dwelling. Contact: Fountain Inn, 3 Seminoe, Newcastle, WY 82701. Call 307-746-4426.

Children: Y Pets: N Smoking: Y Handicap Access: N Payment: C, T, A, V, O

Canada

Alberta

BANFF

BUFFALO MOUNTAIN LODGE

Rates: inexpensive-moderate
Open: year-round
Minimum Stay: none

Close to the bustling town of Banff, Buffalo Mountain Lodge lies in an unspoiled nine-acre setting that houses 85 townhouse units and a main lodge. Beautifully decorated to blend with the ambiance of the woods and the mountains, each unit has custom-made pine or antique furniture, vases of fresh flowers and cozy down comforters on the beds. Many styles and sizes are available, most with fireplaces and outdoor balconies that offer striking views of the Cascade Mountains, Bow Valley or Mt. Rundle. The skiing here is among the best in the Rockies, and there is a full range of apres-ski activities in the restaurants, clubs and nightspots in town. The spa facilities at the resort include a steam room, exercise room and outdoor hot tub. Contact: Paula Mattison, Buffalo Mountain Lodge, Box 1326, Banff, Alberta T0L 0C0, Canada. Call 403-762-2400.

Children: Y Pets: N Smoking: Y Handicap Access: N Payment: C, T, A, V, M, O

CASTLE MOUNTAIN VILLAGE

Rates: budget-inexpensive
Open: year-round
Minimum Stay: none

Tucked away in a secluded mountain area, this village of chalets is located midway between the resort areas of Banff and Lake Louise. The chalets have names that reflect their surroundings—Pine Chalet and Cedar Chalet for four, and the larger Log Chalet, which has room for six guests in its two bedrooms. All the chalets have full kitchens, and color TV and linens and blankets are provided; a maid cleans daily. Indoor fireplaces cast a rosy glow in the evening and are a welcome treat for tired skiers or hikers. Both downhill and cross-country trails are just minutes away; hiking trails are abundant in summer months. A fully stocked grocery store at the main lodge can provide you with all the foodstuffs necessary, while fish fill the nearby rivers. The main lodge features a spa with sauna, steam room and exercise facilities. Contact: Mrs. L. McLeod, Castle Mountain Village, Box 1655, Banff, Alberta T0L 0C0, Canada. Call 403-762-3868.

Children: Y Pets: Y Smoking: Y Handicap Access: Y Payment: C, T, V, M

HIDDEN RIDGE CHALETS   *Rates: inexpensive*
Open: year-round   *Minimum Stay: none*

Although located in a protected national park, Banff is an exciting and vibrant little town full of skiers, restaurants and nightclubs. Most striking, however, is the magnificent natural beauty of its surroundings, and these chalets and apartments stand in the midst of it all. Each unit is in an attractive wooden building, either in a group of four or a detached arch-frame chalet, and has a private balcony. Full maid service is included. The chalets have three double sleeping areas, while other units offer one or two bedrooms. Every unit has a kitchenette, full bath, cable TV and telephone—and a wood-burning fireplace to greet returning skiers and hikers. On the grounds are an indoor whirlpool, an outdoor hot tub and barbecue facilities for outdoor cooking. Contact: Pierre D. Savard, Hidden Ridge Chalets, Tunnel Mtn. Rd., Box 519, Banff, Alberta T0L 0C0, Canada. Call 403-762-3544.

Children: Y Pets: N Smoking: Y Handicap Access: N Payment: C, T, V, M

CARDSTOWN

BADGER VALLEY RANCH   *Rates: budget*
Open: year-round   *Minimum Stay: none*

A working cattle and horse ranch, Badger Valley has a great location in southern Alberta, close to both a Canadian national park and to Glacier National Park in Montana. It contains two cabins equipped for a self-catering holiday, and guests have access to a host of recreational activities on the ranch. The cabins have at least one bedroom, central heat and air conditioning, a full kitchen, bathroom, TV and telephone. Guests can barbecue on the deck with the foothills of the Rocky Mountains in the distance. Of course, the horseback-riding facilities are great (you can take special photography trips), pack trips can be arranged and there are wagon rides in summer and sleigh rides in winter. There are two stocked lakes for trout fishing and ice fishing when the water freezes. Contact: Rod or Joan Shaw, Badger Valley Ranch, Box 1371, Cardston, Alberta T0K-0K0, Canada. Call 403-653-2123.

Children: Y Pets: N Smoking: N Handicap Access: N Payment: C, T

JASPER

ALPINE VILLAGE   *Rates: inexpensive*
Open: May-October   *Minimum Stay: three nights*

Alpine Village stands just two miles from the picturesque town of Jasper in a vacation heartland that abounds with nature and wildlife. A selection of cabins and suites are available here, situated on landscaped grounds and surrounded by tall trees. The cabins come with either one or two bedrooms, a charming living room with a fieldstone fireplace, kitchen, bathroom and an outdoor barbecue and private stone patio. Comfortable rugs adorn the floors and the furnishings are wood-crafted in a rustic style. Six new deluxe cabins have cathedral ceilings, and new duplex cabins have French doors that lead out to decks surrounded by forest greenery. Guests can take long walks or hikes on nearby trails, swim in nearby rivers, try an exhilarating raft tour or fish for rainbow trout for the evening's meal. Contact: Chris or Rena, Alpine Village, Box 610, Jasper, Alberta T0E 1E0, Canada. Call 403-852-3285.

Children: Y Pets: N Smoking: Y Handicap Access: N Payment: C, T, V, M

RED DEER

TERRATIMA LODGE   *Rates: budget-inexpensive*
Open: year-round   *Minimum Stay: two nights*

The log cabins and chalets here are charmingly decorated with antiques and accommodate between two and twelve people. Some cabins feature fireplaces and kitchens and all have outdoor bathroom facilities. Full bathrooms, showers, heat lamps, hair dryers and spa facilities can be found at the lodge and central bathhouse. A dining lodge offers country gourmet food and wine. Cross-country skiing is a specialty at Terratima, where you'll find miles of carefully groomed trails as well as equipment and instruction. Sleigh rides, skating and ice fishing also liven up the winter days. Summer days might find you on a horseback trail, hiking through an orchid bog ablaze with colors, swinging on a rope into a crystal-clear creek or experiencing the thrill of white-water rafting. Contact: Clair and Larry Kennedy, Terratima Lodge, P.O. Box 1636, Rocky Mountain House, Alberta T0M 1T0, Canada. Call 403-845-6786/2444

Children: Y Pets: N Smoking: Y Handicap Access: N Payment: C, P, T

TOFIELD

LIVING WOODS   *Rates: budget*
Open: year-round   *Minimum Stay: none*

The cabins on this farm are located next to a bird sanctuary, guaranteeing a peaceful, natural setting. The owners invite you to experience life on a working farm—observing the traditional arts and skills still practiced here, from animal husbandry to fine woodworking. Breakfast is included in your rates and other meals can be arranged if desired. Most visitors come here to rest, but activities such as hiking, golf, canoeing, swimming and fishing are all easily accessible. In winter, cross-country skiing and skating can be enjoyed right on the premises. Thirty minutes west lies Edmonton, a busy city with restaurants, shopping and nightlife, but chances are you'll be happy to return to this quiet and tranquil place at the end of the day. Contact: Leo and Fay Gaumont, Living Woods, R.R. 2, Tofield, Alberta T0B 4J0. Call 403-662-3634.

Children: **Y**   Pets: **N**   Smoking: **Y**   Handicap Access: **N**   Payment: **C, T**

TROCHU

TL BAR RANCH   *Rates: budget*
Open: April-November   *Minimum Stay: none*

Horseback riding is the main activity at this ranch, and rates include two hours of daily riding or canoeing. There are miles of scenic trails to explore here along the river valley and the Red Deer Badlands, and mountain lovers will find trails for their purposes, too. Near the log ranch house there is a private housekeeping cottage. Home-cooked meals are served at the ranch in a friendly atmosphere. The magnificent Valley of the Dinosaurs can be found in the nearby provincial park, the site of some of the world's best fossil finds and miles of rugged, eerie scenery. Contact: Tom and Willie Lynch, TL Bar Ranch, Box 217, Trochu, Alberta T0M 2C0, Canada. Call 403-442-2207.

Children: **Y**   Pets: **N**   Smoking: **Y**   Handicap Access: **N**   Payment: **C, T**

Campbell River
Whistler
Kelowna
Courtenay
Vancouver
Parksville
Victoria

British Columbia

CAMPBELL RIVER

STRATHCONA PARK LODGE *Rates: budget-inexpensive*
Open: year-round *Minimum Stay: three nights*

A private forest at the edge of Strathcona Provincial Park on Vancouver Island covers over 150 acres, and this lodge and cabins are nestled in the midst of it. Adventure tours make up a big part of the tourist trade here, but it isn't necessary to take a tour to enjoy the outdoors here—relaxing on the beach, hiking on easy nature trails that begin at the lodge or trying some cross-country skiing are other options. The ten cabins each contain a private balcony with views over the lake, a full kitchen and a bathroom. The number of bedrooms and the size and age of each cabin varies. In addition, there is a large chalet with nine bedrooms and four bathrooms to accommodate a party of up to 20. The lake offers kayaking, sailboarding, canoeing or sailing, most with instruction if desired. Contact: Myrna Boulding, Strathcona Park Lodge, P.O. Box 2160, Campbell River, British Columbia V9W 5C9, Canada. Call 604-286-2008/3122.

Children: Y Pets: Y Smoking: N Handicap Access: N Payment: C, P, T, V, M

COURTENAY

COLLINGWOOD INN *Rates: budget*
Open: year-round *Minimum Stay: none*

Located in Vancouver's beautiful Comox Valley in downtown Courtenay, this motor hotel has both one- and two-bedroom housekeeping units to rent. Each one has a full kitchen, cable TV and laundry facilities. Attached to the premises is a lounge bar known as the Rafters Upper Deck Lounge, and there is a restaurant for times you choose not to cook. Golf, ski and fishing packages can be arranged, which gives you some idea of the many recreational facilities there are nearby. Baby-sitting can be arranged if needed. Contact: The Collingwood Inn, 1675 Cliffe Ave., Courtenay, British Columbia V9N 2K6, Canada. Call 604-338-1464.

Children: Y   Pets: Y   Smoking: Y   Handicap Access: N   Payment: C, T

KELOWNA

WHITEFOOT APARTMENTS AND CHALETS   *Rates: budget-deluxe*
Open: November-April   *Minimum Stay: one week*

In the heart of B.C.'s Okanagan ski resorts is Big White, with extensive ski runs, express lifts, equipment rentals and instruction for every level. A mid-mountain vacation village contains apartments to suit every party and budget. Accommodations range from studios with kitchenettes to four-bedroom, two-bathroom apartments. Names like "Ponderosa," "Ptarmigan" and "Graystoke" have been given to each building in the village, where the units are privately owned and individually styled. All units are fully furnished with cookware, linens and color TVs and all have modern kitchen facilities. Most also have hot tubs, saunas, dishwashers, microwave ovens, laundry facilities and parking. The fireplaces warm weary skiers in the evening. Contact: Big White Ski Resort, P.O. Box 2039, Station R, Kelowna, British Columbia V1X 4K5, Canada. Call 604-765-8888.

Children: Y Pets: N Smoking: Y Handicap Access: N Payment: C, T, A, V, M

· PARKSVILLE

TIGH NA MARA   *Rates: budget-inexpensive*
Open: year-round   *Minimum Stay: none*

You'll find this resort hotel up near the top of Vancouver Island, where warm, sandy beaches and wild, rugged beauty prevail. Fishing, sailing and diving are all available in the ocean, and back on dry land you'll find hiking trails, tennis courts and golf courses. Tigh Na Mara is right on the beach and features cottages, log cabins and oceanview condominium units—there are nearly one hundred to choose from. Most units have kitchens and cozy log-burning fireplaces. Some even have individual Jacuzzi tubs, and there is an indoor swimming pool and spa on the resort premises. A restaurant at the resort saves you the trouble of cooking when you're not up to it, and a lounge bar offers a place to sit for a quiet drink or to meet your neighbors. Contact: Tigh Na Mara Resort Hotel, R.R. 1, Site 114, Comp 16, Parksville, British Columbia V0R 2S0, Canada. Call 604-248-2072.

Children: Y   Pets: N   Smoking: Y   Handicap Access: N   Payment: C, T

VICTORIA

THE OXFORD CASTLE INN *Rates: budget-inexpensive*
Open: year-round *Minimum Stay: none*
This completely redecorated inn features one-bedroom apartments for self-catering vacations on Vancouver Island. Located near the main city of Victoria, the modern three-story building offers peace and quiet, yet has access to all the amenities of town. Each apartment has a queen-sized bedroom (waterbeds are available if desired), a living room with color TV, a kitchen and a private sun deck. The hotel facilities include a heated indoor pool, a sauna and a Jacuzzi. Laundry facilities are available in the building, and there is a dining room adjacent to the inn. Contact: The Oxford Castle Inn, 133 Gorge Road E., Victoria, British Columbia V9A 1L1, Canada. Call 604-388-6431.
Children: Y   Pets: N   Smoking: Y   Handicap Access: N   Payment: C, T

WHISTLER

BAVARIAN CHALET *Rates: deluxe*
Open: year-round *Minimum Stay: five nights*
A lovely Bavarian-style home with its own outdoor hot tub, this chalet is privately owned and located about 10 minutes outside the village center. The full kitchen features a microwave, dishwasher and modern appliances. There are laundry facilities as well as two full bathrooms. A TV and VCR are provided; a total of three bedrooms and a loft sleeping space can accommodate up to 12 guests. The hot tub is nestled amid swaying pines, and the house is covered with painted stucco, has stained-glass windows and pine furniture. In addition to skiing, there's plenty of other winter sports to keep you busy here at Whistler, from snowmobiling to ice skating. Tennis, exercise classes, amusement arcades for children, and dining in fine restaurants are among the other facilities offered. Contact: Whistler Chalets, Box 747, 4211 Sunshine Place, Whistler, British Columbia V0N 1B0, Canada. Call 800-663-7711 or 604-932-6699. Ref. H6171.
Children: Y Pets: N Smoking: N Handicap Access: N Payment: C, T, A, V, M,

WHISTLER CHALET STUDIO *Rates: inexpensive-moderate*
Open: year-round *Minimum Stay: five nights*
This studio unit is located in the heart of Whistler Village, a unique little community centered around the fabulous ski facilities at Whistler Mountain. The studio has a queen-sized fold-out couch and an additional queen-sized bed to sleep a total of four guests. A full kitchen, a bathroom and a balcony—from which you can view the activity on the streets or the mountain scenery—are also included. Guests can relax in the private sauna or in front of a blazing fire, and there is a color TV as well. Extensive downhill ski runs, instruction and equipment rental are available here in addition to cross-country skiing, heli-skiing, paragliding, sleigh rides, snowmobiling and a host

of indoor activities, from tennis to aerobics classes. Contact: Whistler Chalets, Box 747, 4211 Sunshine Place, Whistler, British Columbia V0N 1B0, Canada. Call 800-663-7711 or 604-932-6699. Ref. HEA04.

Children: Y Pets: N Smoking: N Handicap Access: N Payment: C, T, V, M, A

WHISTLER LUXURY LAKEFRONT CHALET   *Rates: expensive*
Open: year-round   *Minimum Stay: five nights*

This luxury accommodation is located outside the village by Alta Lake. Privately owned, the three-bedroom chalet has two queen-sized bedrooms, one twin and a queen-sized futon in the loft area. The full kitchen has a microwave, dishwasher and a espresso maker, as well as all modern appliances, and there are two bathrooms. A sauna and whirlpool tub are provided, plus an outdoor hot tub on the deck. The fireplace makes a great place to snuggle up on a wintery night. The extensive downhill and cross-country ski facilities here are justly renowned, and there are plenty of other things to do, both indoors and out. The nightlife and the restaurants are varied and of good quality, and the village is a fun place to shop and wander the streets. Contact: Whistler Chalets, Box 747, 4211 Sunshine Place, Whistler, British Columbia V0N 1B0, Canada. Call 800-663-7711 or 604-932-6699. Ref. V3323.

Children: N Pets: N Smoking: N Handicap Access: N Payment: C, T, A, V, M,

New Brunswick

BATHURST

DANNY'S INN   *Rates: budget*
Open: year-round   *Minimum Stay: none*
This resort-style lodging is located in Bathurst, the only city on the
Chaleur Bay Coast in the heart of French-Canadian Acadia. Tours can
be taken of local zinc mines or of the pretty villages along the coast.
Nearby scenic areas such as Tetagouche and Pabineau Falls have facilities for picnicking, and Youghall Provincial Park boasts a marina
for boating and fishing. A golf course and country club can be found
just outside town. Danny's has a heated swimming pool, a tennis court
and shuffleboard, as well as a children's playground. The family efficiency units come with color TVs and are fully furnished and equipped.
A dining room and coffee shop on the premises may also tempt you to
try some home-style food. Contact: Danny's Inn, P.O. Box 180,
Bathurst, New Brunswick E2A 3Z2, Canada. Call 506-546-6621.
Children: Y Pets: N Smoking: Y Handicap Access: N Payment: C, T, V, M, O

CAMPBELLTON

THE BRAESTONE INN   *Rates: budget*
Open: year-round   *Minimum Stay: none*
Facing a golf course and country club just five minutes from Campbellton, these two housekeeping cabins located on the inn premises
make a great year-round holiday base. Above the town is a mass of

volcanic rock known as Sugarloaf, and the provincial park facilities include skiing, tobogganing and skating in winter—it also contains Canada's only alpine slide. Sports fishermen are drawn to the region's rivers for Atlantic salmon, and an annual salmon festival draws thousands. Back at the inn, your cabin is comfortable and cozy, and there is a color TV for your enjoyment. Contact: The Braestone Inn, R.R. 2, Site 1, Box 18, Campbellton, New Brunswick E3N 3E8, Canada. Call 506-753-7778.

Children: Y Pets: N Smoking: Y Handicap Access: N Payment: C, T, V, M

ROBICHAUD

ALOUETTE MOTEL *Rates: budget*
Open: summer *Minimum Stay: none*

These nine housekeeping cabins are located near a private swimming beach and a golf course. The units have color TVs and are fully equipped to make a good base for touring the area. Parlee Beach Provinicial Park is only four miles away—the facilities there for swimming, boating and windsurfing are excellent—and there is a popular waterslide park that can be reached by trolley from the beach. Cap-Pele to the east is an old Acadian village founded over 200 years ago. And in nearby Shediac, the "lobster capital of the world," the sea's bounty is prepared in traditional and delicious ways and festivals are held in summer to commemorate a way of life unchanged for generations. Contact: N. Cormier and Y. Gautreau, Alouette Motel and Cabins, Robichaud, New Brunswick E0A 2S0, Canada. Call 506-532-5378.

Children: Y Pets: N Smoking: Y Handicap Access: N Payment: C, T AFG540

SHEDIAC

VACATION VILLAGE CHALETS *Rates: budget*
Open: year-round *Minimum Stay: none*

Just 20 minutes from Moncton, the village of Shediac bills itself as the "lobster capital of the world." A sandy beach at Parlee Beach Provincial Park offers suprisingly warm summer waters for swimming and boating. A variety of sports and recreation activities can be enjoyed in the area, including golf, lawn bowling, boating, windsurfing and even a summer sand castle contest. Vacation Village has private chalets, each with two bedrooms and room for a third couple. The chalets are fully equipped with cooking facilities and private bathrooms. Contact: William Leger, Vacation Village Chalets, Belliveau Beach Road, Shediac, New Brunswick E0A 3G0, Canada. Call 506-532-5755.

Children: Y Pets: N Smoking: Y Handicap Access: N Payment: C, T, M

ST. ANDREWS-BY-THE-SEA

SEASIDE BEACH RESORT *Rates: budget*
Open: May-October *Minimum Stay: none*

The stately colonial homes of St. Andrews are a reminder of the American Revolution, when British loyalists fled nearby Maine to settle these Canadian shores. Now the town offers friendly shops, a "please touch" aquarium, museums and restaurants. The Seaside Beach Resort is situated in a pleasant grassy setting with a wooden breakwater and boardwalk. Steps lead down to a little beach where guests can search for treasures brought in by the morning tides or swim in the Bay of Fundy. Twenty-two housekeeping units are available, all with full bath, kitchen facilities, and cable color TV. Guests will find golf courses by the shore; sailing ships and whale-watching trips leave from nearby docks. Contact: Seaside Beach Resort, P.O. Box 310, St. Andrews-by-the-Sea, New Brunswick E0G 2X0, Canada. Call 506-529-3846.

Children: Y Pets: Y Smoking: Y Handicap Access: Y Payment: C, T, V, M

SUSSEX

BLUE BIRD MOTEL AND RESTAURANT	*Rates: budget*
Open: year-round	*Minimum Stay: none*

Blue Bird offers regular motel rooms and 14 housekeeping units for those who prefer a little more independence. You are welcome, however, to partake of the home-style cooking at the restaurant, where baking is done daily. Sussex is the dairy center of New Brunswick, and its museum depicts agriculture and history in the area. Facilities are available for fishing, hunting, canoeing and biking, and the rugged and dramatic shoreline is within a short drive, including the spectacular Fundy National Park. Visitors to Sussex will also want to pick up some of the local arts and crafts items that are so carefully created by local artisans. Contact: Blue Bird Motel and Restaurant, P.O. Box 91, Sussex, New Brunswick E0E 1P0, Canada. Call 506-433-2557.

Children: Y Pets: N Smoking: Y Handicap Access: N Payment: C, T, A, V, M

Newfoundland

CORMACK

FUNLAND RESORT *Rates: budget*

Open: May-September *Minimum Stay: none*

The two-bedroom cottages here are all equipped for self-catering and feature color TVs, with laundry facilities on the premises. A water slide and swimming pool, as well as a playground and mini golf course, mean fun for the entire family. There is also an arcade and picnic facilities. Guests can rent barbecue equipment and use it to cook up casual meals, perhaps some fresh fish. In nearby Sir Richard Squires Memorial Park the amazing spectacle of Atlantic salmon leaping upstream past Big Falls holds a perennial fascination for the guests. Another national park, Gros Morne, offers hiking trails, rock scrambling, boating, swimming and fishing. The little town of Cormack is an agricultural center offering fresh fruits and vegetables in abundance. Contact: Funland Resort, P.O. Box 145, Cormack, Newfoundland A0K 2E0, Canada. Call 709-635-3372/2821/5690.

Children: Y Pets: Y Smoking: N Handicap Access: N Payment: C, T

EASTPORT

SANDY COVE BEACH HOUSEKEEPING COTTAGES *Rates: budget*

Open: May-October *Minimum Stay: none*

Bonavista Bay in central Newfoundland is justly renowned for its rugged shores, sheltered bays and inland lakes. Sandy Cove has one of the province's finest beaches, and if you spend the days swimming and sunning by the sea, you're sure to appreciate the wonderful bounty that is dished up in local restaurants and during outdoor festivals. The 12 housekeeping cottages here have either one or two bedrooms, as well as cable TV and laundry facilities for the guests' use. The cottages are on a large grassy field above the beach and close to the village of Eastport, where a summer arts festival celebrates the regional history and people. Whale-watching trips are particularly rewarding in this part of the province. Contact: Sandy Cove Beach Housekeeping Cottages, Box 83, Eastport, Bonavista Bay, Newfoundland A0G 1Z0, Canada. Call 709-677-3158.

Children: Y   Pets: N   Smoking: Y   Handicap Access: N   Payment: C, T

LABRADOR CITY

CAROL INN   *Rates: budget*
Open: year-round   *Minimum Stay: none*
Labrador City is in the midst of the "Big Land," a wilderness that stretches for thousands of miles into the northern reaches of the Atlantic. The city makes a good base for wilderness exploration, but it is also a fascinating adventure in itself—with many surprising recreational facilities close at hand. The Carol Inn has over 20 housekeeping units, each with private kitchen and bathroom facilities, a living area with color cable TV and access to the restaurant and lounge area in the inn. Visitors can arrange an adventure tour out on the rivers and rugged terrain of Labrador. They can also try the area's downhill and cross-country skiing in winter, and its golf, tennis, fishing and hunting during other seasons. Contact: Carol Inn, 215 Drake Avenue, Labrador City, Labrador, Newfoundland A2V 2B6, Canada. Call 709-944-3661.

Children: Y Pets: N Smoking: Y Handicap Access: N Payment: C, T, V, M, O

ST. BRIDE'S

BIRD ISLAND MOTEL   *Rates: budget*
Open: year-round   *Minimum Stay: none*
This region was once dominated by the French, but the local people have a lilting accent reminiscent of Ireland. The cliffs are alive with seabirds, and the bays were once the site of a thriving whaling industry. Steeped in history, this area is also full of modern-day pleasures, including these housekeeping units, which are open throughout the year. Each one has its own kitchen, bathroom and cable color TV; laundry facilities are available on the premises. A grocery store can supply your housekeeping needs, and there is a small bar on the premises for evening cocktails. The Argentia ferry terminal, which transports visitors to Nova Scotia, is an hour's drive away, and there are several provincial parks nearby that offer swimming, fishing and hiking as well as picnic facilities. Contact: Bird Island Motel, St. Bride's, Placentia Bay, Newfoundland A0B 2Z0, Canada. Call 709-337-2450/2903.

Children: Y Pets: N Smoking: Y Handicap Access: N Payment: C, T, V, M

SUMMERFORD

HIGH TIDE SUMMER COTTAGE	*Rates: budget*
Open: July-September	*Minimum Stay: none*

Lighthouses, fishing villages and crashing surf can be found throughout this region renowned for dramatic scenery. At times, the surprising sight of an iceberg floating past or a huge whale spouting in the water can greet the watchful visitor. Located on New World Island, one of the offshore isles connected by a causeway to the mainland, High Tide is a small summer cottage for two to four that has a separate dining room, an eat-in kitchen and a color TV in the living room. A nearby beach provides a place to boat or fish, and they say the windsurfing is great. Contact: High Tide Summer Cottage, Virgin Arm, New World Island, P.O. Box 121, Summerford, Newfoundland A0G 4E0, Canada. Call 709-629-3261.

Children: **Y**   Pets: **N**   Smoking: **Y**   Handicap Access: **N**   Payment: **C, T**

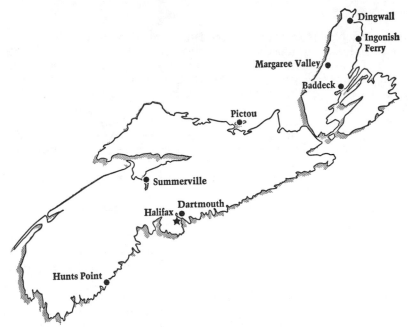

Nova Scotia

BADDECK

INVERARY INN RESORT
Open: year-round

Rates: budget-inexpensive
Minimum Stay: none

The name of this resort reveals the Scottish culture that still thrives here on Cape Breton Island at the northern end of Nova Scotia. Gaelic music, festivals, dancing and even the language still survive here: Combine those with the inland sea known as Bras d'Or Lake and the rugged highland scenery, and you'll have an unforgettable vacation. The resort offers a number of cottages, which come equipped with bathrooms, cable TV, telephones and either one or two bedrooms. A dining room serves three hearty meals a day; during summer months the Fish House restaurant is open. A private stretch of shoreline, tennis courts and indoor and outdoor swimming pools are yours to enjoy; an exercise room, sauna and hot tub comprise the spa facilities. Boats can be rented and the fishing is plentiful. Contact: Inverary Inn Resort, Shore Road, P.O. Box 190, Baddeck, Nova Scotia B0E 1B0, Canada. Call 902-295-2674.

Children: Y Pets: N Smoking: Y Handicap Access: N Payment: C, T, A, V, M

SILVER DART LODGE
Open: May-October

Rates: budget-inexpensive
Minimum Stay: none

The Cabot Trail, one of the world's most beautiful drives, passes right through Baddeck on its way to and from rugged coastal vistas. The lodge here consists of private chalets, suites in the main building and

in the MacNeil House, a renovated 19th-century mansion. The chalets are completely equipped for housekeeping, with a kitchen, full bathroom, TV and radio; many have private balconies where the invigorating sea air will greet you. The MacNeil House suites have either one or two bedrooms, a bathroom with Jacuzzi, a complete kitchen and a fireplace in the living room. The Scottish dining room features live music most evenings, and there are often evening cookouts on the grounds. Ninety-four acres of property are yours to explore, including an outdoor pool; boats and windsurfers can be rented for sailing and fishing in the inland sea of Lake Bras d'Or. Contact: The Silver Dart Lodge, P.O. Box 399, Baddeck, Nova Scotia B0E 1B0, Canada. Call 902-295-2340.
Children: Y Pets: N Smoking: Y Handicap Access: N Payment: C, T, A, V, M, O

Dingwall

THE MARKLAND INN BY THE SEA *Rates: budget-inexpensive*
Open: June-October *Minimum Stay: none*
You'll find this collection of log cabins and cottages off the beaten track at the tip of Cape Breton Island, looking out over green stretches of land to the crashing surf of the Atlantic Ocean. Nine of the cottages have housekeeping facilities and include one or two bedrooms, a full bathroom, TV and telephone. You can sit on a private balcony listening to the sounds of rustling trees and distant surf, swim or beachcomb at the crescent-shaped beach, hike through forests ablaze with fall colors or enjoy fishing and boating in a nearby river. During summer a restaurant operates at the inn, as well as an outdoor swimming pool, tennis courts and a children's playground. Local attractions include whale-watching from the shore or sea and the Highlands Golf Course just a half-hour away. Contact: Charles MacLean, The Markland Inn, Dingwall, Nova Scotia B0C 1G0, Canada. Call 902-383-2246.
Children: Y Pets: N Smoking: Y Handicap Access: N Payment: C, T, A, V, M

Hunts Point

HUNTS POINT BEACH COTTAGES *Rates: budget*
Open: May-October *Minimum Stay: none*
Lighthouses and charming fishing villages dot the shores of southwestern Nova Scotia. At Hunts Point, a beach of pristine white sand beckons and seabirds both familiar and exotic can be found along the shore. The beach cottages offered here have one or two bedrooms and a living area and bathroom with shower. Each cottage has a TV, and in some a Franklin fireplace casts a warm glow. Step onto your porch to look out over the sea or take a refreshing swim in its waters. Saltwater fishing trips can be taken from one of the villages along the coast, where a heritage of piracy still lingers. Contact: Ray and Fay Slaunwhite, Hunts Point Beach Cottages, Box 92, Hunts Point, Nova Scotia B0T 1G0, Canada. Call 902-683-2077.
Children: Y Pets: Y Smoking: Y Handicap Access: N Payment: C, T, O

INGONISH FERRY

KNOTTY PINE COTTAGES AND TOURIST HOME *Rates: budget*
Open: year-round *Minimum Stay: none*
Six housekeeping cottages are located here by Ingonish Ferry on the outskirts of Cape Breton Highlands National Park. Each cottage has a full bathroom with shower, either one or two bedrooms, a living room with a television and kitchen facilities. Decks attached to each cottage look out over the fishing harbor and ocean. The park covers much of this tip of the island, and in it you'll find swimming, fishing, boating and wonderful hiking trails that wind up hills and past cascading waterfalls. An Acadian museum on one side of the island recalls the traditional culture of the area's French Canadians; the village of St. Anns on the other side offers Scottish highland dancing and arts and crafts. Contact: Roland and Patricia MacKinnon, Knotty Pine Cottages, R.R. 1, Ingonish Ferry, Nova Scotia B0C 1L0, Canada. Call 902-285-2058.
Children: Y   Pets: N   Smoking: Y   Handicap Access: N   Payment: C, T, V

MARGAREE VALLEY

NORMAWAY INN *Rates: inexpensive-moderate*
Open: June-mid-October *Minimum Stay: none*
Your host here at Normaway is David MacDonald, and his personal touch is evident throughout the inn. Written guides are given to visitors to help them find a perfect picnic spot or secluded beach; special honeymoon packages or fishing trips are available. In addition to rooms at the main lodge, there are 17 cabins on the property, four with two bedrooms and the rest with one. The inn was built in the 1920s, and its stone fireplaces, beamed ceilings and country gourmet dining room display an Old World charm. The lodge has a library, a film room and a lounge with a large open hearth. Tennis courts, lawn games and bicycle rentals can be found on the property and arrangements can be made for canoeing, horseback riding, boating and salmon or trout fishing. Contact: David MacDonald, Normaway Inn, Box 100, Margaree Valley, Nova Scotia B0E 2C0, Canada. Call 902-248-2987.
Children: Y   Pets: N   Smoking: Y   Handicap Access: N   Payment: C, T, A, V, M

PICTOU

PICTOU LODGE RESORT *Rates: budget-inexpensive*
Open: May-October *Minimum Stay: none*
Just four miles east of the historic and charming town of Pictou, this lodge overlooks the warm waters of the Northumberland Strait. The lodge has nearly 30 cottages and suites with one to three bedrooms, some with kitchens or kitchenettes. All units have full bathrooms and a pleasant living area; some have cozy fireplaces. The fresh ocean air outside your door will revive you as you venture to the nearby lake for freshwater swimming. Caribou Provincial Park is a few miles away along the coast and is ideal for picnicking and hiking, and the ferry to picturesque Prince Edward Island is a ten-minute drive away. Hiking

trails and coastal drives abound, and the towns and villages show their mixed heritage by their Indian names and Scottish festivals. Fresh fish is a specialty in the dining room at the lodge. Contact: Carol Ann and Peter Van Westen, Pictou Lodge, Box 1539, Pictou, Nova Scotia B0K 1H0, Canada. Call 902-485-4322.

Children: Y Pets: N Smoking: Y Handicap Access: N Payment: C, T, A, V, M

SUMMERVILLE BEACH

THE QUARTERDECK RESTAURANT AND CABINS	*Rates: budget-inexpensive*
Open: May-October	*Minimum Stay: none*

The five self-catering cabins here have either one or two bedrooms; a deluxe cottage has three bedrooms. Each unit has a bathroom with shower and a black and white TV. The fireplaces in some of the cottages will tempt you to stay inside at night where it's cozy, but a sandy crescent of beach invites daytime swimmers and sunbathers alike. Boating, fishing and ocean cruises are among the maritime pleasures to be experienced here, and charming fishing villages dotted along the coastline provide delicious lobster suppers. Contact: Dan and Georgina Hunter, Summerville Beach, R.R. 1, Port Mouton, Nova Scotia B0T 1T0, Canada. Call 902-683-2998.

Children: Y Pets: Y Smoking: Y Handicap Access: N Payment: C, T, V, M

Ontario

BAILIEBORO

RAINBOW COTTAGES

Open: summer

Rates: inexpensive-moderate

Minimum Stay: none

These cottages are ranged along the riverbank and in the woods, and the facilities here are oriented toward fishing and family. Rates include a boat and electric-start motor package, plus there are paddle boats, canoes, water-sports equipment and a sandy beach for guests to enjoy. Each cottage has a kitchen with microwave oven and standard appliances, private bathroom, living room with color TV and all necessary linens—though you might want to bring an extra-large beach towel. A gas barbecue right outside the door gives you a place to cook quick and easy meals. Nearby Peterborough offers all the amenities of a good-sized town, including summer theater, restaurants, golf courses and horse racing; there are horseback-riding stables nearby. Contact: Rainbow Cottages, R.R. 1, Box 30, Bailieboro, Ontario K0L 1B0, Canada. Call 705-939-6995.

Children: Y   Pets: Y   Smoking: Y   Handicap Access: N   Payment: C, T, O

BURKS FALLS

PICKEREL LAKE LODGE

Open: year-round

Rates: budget

Minimum Stay: none

The vast expanse of Algonquin Provincial Park stretches to the east of this property, which itself covers 160 acres of unspoiled land. All year long this lodge offers resort rooms in the main lodge and two-bedroom

chalets on the property. Each chalet has two floors; upstairs is a bathroom and the bedrooms, downstairs is a living/dining area and a kitchenette. Deluxe chalets have a Jacuzzi bath and a fireplace—welcome additions for returning cross-country skiers and snowmobilers. A cozy atmosphere permeates the game room, the stone-walled Cellar Lounge and the dining room in the main lodge. The list of facilities available to guests is impressive—from tennis, paddle boats and canoes to mountain bikes and snowshoes. The lake is suitable for windsurfing and sailing and has a large sandy beach. Contact: Pickerel Lake Lodge, R.R. 2, Burks Falls, Ontario P0A 1C0, Canada. Call 705-382-2025.
Children: Y   Pets: N   Smoking: Y   Handicap Access: N   Payment: C, T, V, M

HALIBURTON

WILLOW BEACH COTTAGES   *Rates: budget-moderate*
Open: year-round   *Minimum Stay: none*
The spacious grounds of this resort village come to an end at a sandy beach on Lake Kashagawigamog in the Haliburton Highlands. Winterized three-star cottages in the village are private and comfortable, and they come with either two or three bedrooms. Full bathrooms, kitchens and living/dining areas make the cottages comfortable; guests can cook up an outdoor barbecue, relax in front of a crackling fire or watch TV. The grounds are large and include a playground for the kids, a game room and a sauna and whirlpool. Cross-country ski equipment can be rented, as can boating and fishing equipment. The shops and restaurants of Haliburton, a small, pleasant town, are just a few minutes away. Contact: Bob and Joan Stinson, Willow Beach Cottages, R.R. 2, Haliburton, Ontario K0M 1S0, Canada. Call 705-457-1110.
Children: Y   Pets: N   Smoking: Y   Handicap Access: N   Payment: C, T, V, M

HUNTSVILLE

BLUE WATER ACRES   *Rates: budget-moderate*
Open: year-round   *Minimum Stay: none*
Located in the beautiful Muskoka region on Lake of Bays, this resort offers chalet-style housekeeping cottages and recreation facilities. Each cottage is private and has a full kitchen as well as a long balcony outside, which is accessed by sliding glass doors from the living room. A cozy fireplace makes the atmosphere perfect for snuggling up on a winter night. The resort has a restaurant if you choose not to cook, and a recreation center that includes an indoor swimming pool, whirlpool, sauna and a fitness room. Outside are three tennis courts and a sandy beach, where water sports such as windsurfing can be practiced. Snowlovers can enjoy cross-country skiing, tobogganing, skating and snowmobiling during the winter months, and the nearby wilderness of Algonquin Park is yours to explore by canoe or on foot. Contact: Blue Water Acres, Box 34, R.R. 4, Huntsville, Ontario P0A 1K0, Canada. Call 705-635-2880.
Children: Y   Pets: N   Smoking: Y   Handicap Access: N   Payment: C, T, V, M

GRANDVIEW
Open: year-round
Rates: inexpensive-moderate
Minimum Stay: none

Huntsville is the gateway to the lake-strewn Muskoka region—a year-round vacationland. This luxury resort is located on Fairy Lake and offers contemporary, self-contained suites with high-quality furnishings and amenities. Lofty ceilings, large windows and tasteful wood furniture reflect the natural glory just outside your doorstep. Each suite has a kitchen with breakfast bar, a dining/living area and its own whirlpool—a relief for those who've spent the day playing tennis, hiking or playing golf. A wood-burning fireplace warms the rooms in winter, a magical season when guests can skate, ski (both downhill and cross-country), snowmobile or toboggan. A historic inn on the premises offers candlelit dinners, and an outdoor swimming pool provides a place to work on a summer tan. Contact: Grandview, R.R. 4, Huntsville, Ontario P0A 1K0, Canada. Call 705-789-4417.

Children: Y   Pets: N   Smoking: Y   Handicap Access: N   Payment: C, T

KEENE

ELMHIRST'S RESORT
Open: year-round
Rates: budget-inexpensive
Minimum Stay: none

Thirty-mile-long Rice Lake takes its name from the wild rice that grows along its shores; also found here are historic conservation areas, mysterious caves and Indian burial grounds. This resort features golf or fishing packages as well as rental equipment at the beach for water sports. A string of little cottages features full kitchens, bedrooms, large living rooms, color TVs and large decks with barbecues. If you choose not to cook, that's fine too, as meal plans are available; there is a selection of restaurants. Tennis courts, a summer recreational program, an indoor swimming pool, a sauna and an exercise room complete the facilities. A 2,000-foot turf airstrip is available on the property, and guests can arrange sightseeing tours in a seaplane for a unique look at the countryside. Contact: Elmhirst's Resort, R.R. 1, Keene, Ontario K0L-2G0, Canada. Call 705-295-4591.

Children: Y   Pets: N   Smoking: Y   Handicap Access: N   Payment: C, T, V, M,

HIGHLAND VIEW RESORT
Open: April-October
Rates: inexpensive
Minimum Stay: none

Highland View is a lakeside resort particularly geared to families—there is a supervised children's recreation program, a playground and sports field, a sandy beach and baby-sitting services if needed. Fourteen deluxe units are available for self-sufficient vacationers, each one with a full kitchen with microwave oven and a barbecue on the deck. Boats, canoes, paddle boats and windsurfers are all available at the dock (complimentary to guests) and a pool and hot tub are yours to enjoy. There are complete sport fishing facilities, golf and horseback racing nearby. Guests will probably want to sightsee in the area, whichis both beautiful and historic, with old mills, Indian burial grounds and limestone caves to explore. Contact: Highland View Resort, R.R. 3, Keene, Ontario K0L 2G0, Canada. Call 705-295-6697.

Children: Y   Pets: N   Smoking: Y   Handicap Access: N   Payment: C, T

LAKEFIELD

SCOTSMAN POINT RESORT   *Rates: budget-inexpensive*
Open: May-October   *Minimum Stay: none*

The grounds here are extensive and covered with maples and oaks, while nearby provincial parks and conservation areas are perfect for hiking and picnicking. There are nearly 30 deluxe cottages here, with one to four bedrooms apiece. Each cottage has its own modern kitchen, electric heat, color TV and full bathrooms. A children's area features a trampoline and swings, and the kids will love the safe, sandy beach; planned family activites take place throughout the summer months. A charming tea room serves homemade scones and other goodies; there are restaurants in nearby Lakefield or 20 minutes away in Peterborough. Muskie, bass and pickerel populate the lake, and aspiring fishermen can rent boats and equipment at the resort. Contact: Norm and Andrea Childs, Scotsman Point Resort, Box R, R.R. 1 Lakefield, Ontario K0L 2H0, Canada. Call 705-657-8630.

Children: Y   Pets: Y   Smoking: Y   Handicap Access: N   Payment: C, T, O

MINDEN

SANDY LANE   *Rates: budget*
Open: year-round   *Minimum Stay: none*

In the heart of the Haliburton Highlands, this all-season resort has year-round sports and recreation. There are individual chalets, each with plain, comfortable furnishings, kitchenettes, color TVs and cozy fireplaces for crisp winter evenings. A sandy beach fronts the lake and there is a wide choice of water-related activities, including a water slide, waterskiing, windsurfing, canoeing, boating and fishing. A playground, trampoline and recreation program keep the kids occupied, while the adults can play tennis or golf or have a good long soak in the hot tub. Nature trails for hikers and horseback riders offer an opportunity to experience this beautiful area up close, and in the winter the resort rents cross-country ski equipment and snowmobiles. In fall, nearby Minden has a Festival of Color. Contact: Sandy Lane, Box RO, R.R. 2 Minden, Ontario K0M 2K0, Canada. Call (collect) 705-489-2020.

Children: Y   Pets: N   Smoking: Y   Handicap Access: N   Payment: C, T, O

PARRY SOUND

SNUG HARBOUR RESORT   *Rates: budget-inexpensive*
Open: May-October   *Minimum Stay: none*

All the cottages at Snug Harbour are new or have been recently remodeled in order to achieve a high standard of cleanliness and comfort. Wood paneling, large windows, carpeted floors and wood-burning fireplaces add to their charm. The kitchens are modern, the heat is electric and there is satellite color TV and a central vacuum system to help keep things neat. Guests can cook up their own barbecue on a private sun deck, or relax in the whirlpool or down on the sandy beach. The energetic can work off some steam in the exercise room or by windsurfing or pedal boating. Canoes, motorboats and sailboats are available as well, and the region around Georgian Bay has some excellent hiking and nature trails. Contact: Snug Harbour Resort, R.R. 1, Dept. RO, Nobel, Ontario P0C 1G0, Canada. Call 705-342-5811.

Children: Y   Pets: N   Smoking: Y   Handicap Access: N   Payment: C, T, O

PICTON

ISAIAH TUBBS RESORT   *Rates: budget-inexpensive*
Open: year-round   *Minimum Stay: none*

Sandbanks Provincial Park, a sliver of white dunes that runs for six miles along Lake Ontario, shares the shoreline with this resort and conference center. Located in Prince Edward County, one of Ontario's most picturesque vacation destinations, the resort offers swimming, canoeing and fishing in the lakes and hiking through the parks that dot the area. Isaiah Tubbs Resort features seasonal cabins and efficiency suites, some of which can be found in a restored 1820's inn. Crackling fireplaces warm many of the the rooms, and large open decks offer a place to sit and watch the sun set over the lakes. The suites have full kitchens, private bathrooms and a choice of bedroom sizes. A heated year-round swimming pool, whirlpool and sauna are offered, as well as an exercise room and tennis courts for the active. Contact: Isaiah Tubbs Resort, R.R. 1, Picton, Ontario K0K 2T0, Canada. Call 613-393-2090.

Children: Y   Pets: N   Smoking: Y   Handicap Access: N   Payment: C, T, O

PORT SEVERN

DRIFTWOOD COVE   *Rates: budget-inexpensive*
Open: May-October   *Minimum Stay: none*

A small marina and sandy beach are located here on Georgian Bay just outside this resort. The housekeeping suites and cottages offered at Driftwood Cove are completely equipped for self-catering holidays, with kitchen facilities, private bathrooms and comfy bedrooms. At the marina guests can dock their own boats or rent motorboats, paddle boats, canoes or windsurfing equipment. The resort contains laundry facilities and a recreation center, and there is a shuttle boat service to nearby restaurants. Golf, horseback riding and fishing are among the activities enjoyed in this vacationland region. Contact: Marion and Eugene Casselman, Driftwood Cove, P.O. Box 264, Port Severn, Ontario L0K 1S0, Canada. Call 705-538-2502.

Children: Y   Pets: N   Smoking: Y   Handicap Access: N   Payment: C, T, V, M

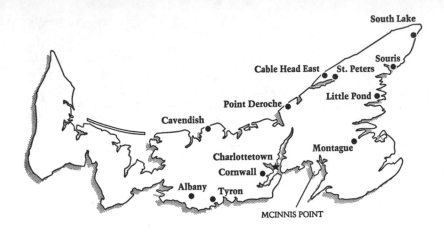

South Lake
Souris
Cable Head East St. Peters
Little Pond
Point Deroche
Cavendish
Montague
Charlottetown
Cornwall
Albany   Tyron

MCINNIS POINT

Prince Edward Island

CABLE HEAD EAST

WINDSWEPT AND SWEPTAWAY   *Rates: budget-inexpensive*
Open: June-October   *Minimum Stay: none*

The whimsical name of these little houses suggests a deserted shore
and sweeping views of the ocean where sea air surges over the land.
Located on the north shore near St. Peters Provincial Park, guests don't
have to travel far to find sandy beaches, fishing boats, canoeing waters
and lobster suppers. The property itself features two houses; one is a
log cabin with two bedrooms and a sleeping alcove, and the other is a
cottage with three bedrooms. Facilities include a sauna and hot tub,
welcome after a day swimming or beachcombing. A color TV with
VCR and a washing machine and dryer complete the modern amenities, and a barbecue makes a handy way to fix a quick meal. Contact:
Sara Mironov, St. Peters, Prince Edward Island C0A 2A0, Canada. Call
902-961-2984.

Children: Y   Pets: Y   Smoking: N   Handicap Access: N   Payment: C, T

CAVENDISH

KINDRED SPIRITS COUNTRY INN AND COTTAGES   *Rates: budget-inexpensive*
Open: May-October   *Minimum Stay: none*

There are 16 self-catering units here, both apartments and separate
cottages. The location is superb—in the heart of the Cavendish resort

area on a spacious country estate next to Green Gables House, the island's premier attraction, and beside the 18th fairway of an excellent golf course. The fragile dunes of Cavendish Beach are just a short walk away, and bicycle rentals offer a quiet way to tour the coastline. The main inn is filled with antiques, and a cozy fireplace burns in the lobby. The separate cottages and housekeeping apartments are snug and warm, all have color TVs and private decks where guests can take morning coffee or an evening barbecue. A playground, toys and children's movies will keep the kids occupied, and baby-sitting services can be arranged. Contact: Al and Sharon James, Kindred Spirits Country Inn and Cottages, Cavendish, Prince Edward Island C0A 1N0, Canada. Call 902-963-2434.

Children: **Y** Pets: **N** Smoking: **Y** Handicap Access: **N** Payment: **C, T, V, M**

LITTLE POND

DURELL POINT SHORE HOUSE   *Rates: moderate*
Open: spring-fall   *Minimum Stay: one week*

Located near Souris, a bustling fishing village, this private house has its own beach on Howe Bay. Built in 1870, the house has two stories and a separate newly designed wing. The original structure houses a dining room, a kitchen with microwave oven and modern appliances, three bedrooms, one and a half bathrooms and a large deck. The new wing has decks on two levels, a living room with a soaring cathedral ceiling, a master bedroom and a separate bath. Fully carpeted, the house is tastefully furnished with antiques. For your convenience, a washing machine and dryer are provided and there is a gas barbecue for making casual meals. A wood-burning stove completes the cozy picture. In addition to the maritime sights nearby, a bird sanctuary 20 minutes to the north provides a glimpse of exotic birds amid the lagoons and ponds. Contact: Vivienne Silver, 95 Wild Duck Road, Stamford, CT 06903. Call 203-329-8188.

Children: **Y** Pets: **N** Smoking: **Y** Handicap Access: **N** Payment: **C, T**

LOWER MONTAGUE

THE SENATOR INN AND COTTAGES   *Rates: budget*
Open: mid-May to September   *Minimum Stay: none*

The Montague River is the site of this charming inn, formerly a private home. In addition to the regular rooms, there are five two-bedroom and two three-bedroom log cottages for rent. If desired, a full breakfast can be obtained at the inn, and there is a dining room just a few minutes away. Seal-watching and fishing trips can be arranged nearby, while horseback-riding trails weave through meadows and along the sandy shore of the nearby Brudenell River. A few miles away, little Georgetown boasts a summer theater and a brass-rubbing center, plus a resort that offers golf, tennis, canoeing and picnicking. Contact: Craig and Sheila MacVarish, The Senator Inn and Cottages, Montague, R.R. 2, Prince Edward Island C0A 1R0, Canada. Call 902-838-2900.

Children: **Y** Pets: **N** Smoking: **Y** Handicap Access: **N** Payment: **C, T, V**

McINNIS POINT

GALLOWAY'S COTTAGE   *Rates: inexpensive*
Open: June-September   *Minimum Stay: one week*

Situated on a quiet point of land surrounded by red cliffs and crescent-shaped bays, this two-story cottage has all the amenities of home. Thoughtfully decorated and completely equipped with all linens, crockery and cookware, the cottage has three bedrooms upstairs, one of which opens onto its own balcony facing the sea. Downstairs is a living/dining area with a TV and wood-burning stove, a separate den with a fold-out double couch, and an eat-in kitchen with modern electric appliances and plenty of cupboard space. A barbecue on the front deck and tables and chairs on the spacious back deck mean that casual meals can be taken while watching a sunset or the tide. Seals swim offshore, majestic herons fly past and the surrounding fields are sweet with clover, yet the busy capital of Charlottetown is just 20 minutes away. Contact: A.I.R. Galloway, 27 Edinburgh Drive, Charlottetown, Prince Edward Island C1A 3E9, Canada. Call 902-368-1849.

Children: **Y**   Pets: **N**   Smoking: **Y**   Handicap Access: **N**   Payment: **C, P, T**

POINT DEROCHE

BLUE HERON BEACH HOUSE   *Rates: expensive*
Open: May-October   *Minimum Stay: one week*

An exceptional property with a private beach, Blue Heron is in an unspoiled environment on the north shore. The white sand glistens here, as it does a few miles away along the shore of the national park, and if the ocean water is cool at times, the house has a swimming pool as well. Its six bedrooms are furnished with queen-sized, double and single beds, all topped with luxurious down comforters. A screened-in sun room makes a wonderful place to sit, and the Jacuzzi makes a luxurious place to soak. The kitchen is fully equipped and has a microwave and dishwasher; there are two bathrooms. The garden is carefully landscaped, with a patio facing the ocean. A golf course is located several miles west; deep-sea fishing charters and marinas can be found nearby. Contact: Barbara McAndrew, Meadow Bank, Cornwall R.R. 2, Prince Edward Island C0A 1H0, Canada. Call 902-566-2427.

Children: **Y**   Pets: **N**   Smoking: **Y**   Handicap Access: **N**   Payment: **C, T**

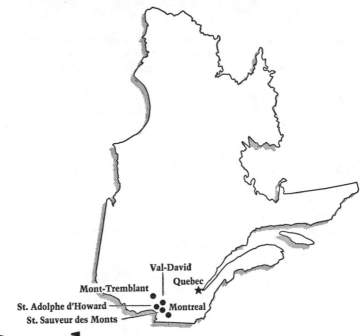

Val-David
Quebec
Mont-Tremblant
St. Adolphe d'Howard
St. Sauveur des Monts
Montreal

Quebec

MONT-TREMBLANT

PINOTEAU VILLAGE *Rates: inexpensive-expensive*
Open: year-round *Minimum Stay: none*

There's a condominium in this vacation village to suit every guest's needs, and there are activities to please the most energetic. Each condominium has a living/dining area, a full kitchen, private bathroom and a color TV and phone. Guests can luxuriate in front of a crackling fireplace, especially welcome for those who have tried skiing at nearby Mont-Tremblant, which contains the region's highest peak. Snowmobiling and cross-country skiing are also favorite winter activites. Summer will find you out on the tennis courts, hiking through the woods in nearby Mont-Tremblant Provincial Park, challenging yourself on a mountain bike ride or horseback riding through forests tinged with color and filled with wildlife. Contact: Pinoteau Village, Lac Tremblant, Quebec J0T 1Z0, Canada. Call 819-425-2795.

Children: Y Pets: N Smoking: Y Handicap Access: N Payment: C, T, A, V, M, O

MONTREAL

LA TOUR BELVEDERE *Rates: budget-inexpensive*
Open: year-round *Minimum Stay: eight nights*

Close to the subway, shopping and some of Montreal's many fine restaurants, La Tour Belvedere offers all the comforts of home in a modern luxury apartment building. Parlor Suites have a full kitchen, a dining nook and two double beds in the living/sleeping area, plus a balcony with views over Mount Royal or downtown Montreal. The one-bedroom suites have a separate queen-sized bedroom, a larger dining room with space for four, a separate living room with a TV and a balcony. Larger units are available on two levels. All kitchen facilities, cookware, linens and maid service are provided, and the rooms are air-conditioned. On the roof is an indoor pool and a sun deck, and the Forum, site of many major sporting events, is right around the corner. Contact: La Tour Belvedere, 2175 Boulevard de Maisonneuve Ouest, Montreal, Quebec H3H 1L5, Canada. Call 514-935-9052.

Children: Y Pets: N Smoking: Y Handicap Access: N Payment: C, T, A, V, M

LE MONTFORT *Rates: budget-inexpensive*
Open: year-round *Minimum Stay: eight nights*

Contemporary and convenient, this modern apartment building in downtown Montreal offers air-conditioned suites for stays of a week or longer. The studios have a separate kitchen, a dining area, a living room with a door that opens onto a balcony, a separate bathroom and—in the case of the alcove studios—a double bed in a separate alcove area. The one-bedroom suites are spacious, with a large living/dining area, full kitchen, bathroom and a large double bed; the two-bedrooms are similar but have a balcony off the second bedroom as well as the living room. Color TVs, radios and maid service are included. A heated pool on the top floor has views out over Montreal. The metro is a few steps away, and wonderful grocery shopping can be found at the nearby Faubourg shopping arcade. Contact: Le Montfort, 1975 Boulevard de Maisonneuve Ouest, Montreal, Quebec H3H 1K4, Canada. Call 514-934-0916.

Children: Y Pets: N Smoking: Y Handicap Access: N Payment: C, T, A, V, M

St. Adolphe d'Howard

MIRA-MONT SUR LE LAC *Rates: inexpensive-expensive*
Open: year-round *Minimum Stay: two nights*

A stream-fed mountain lake is the setting for this vacation resort, which caters to families as well as honeymooners. There are 42 chalets and condominiums, each with one to three bedrooms, a modern kitchen and a living area, and all with modern furnishings, color TV, soft carpets and linens. Some of the more luxurious suites also have a Jacuzzi and a deck that overlooks the lake. In winter the area is a paradise for skiers, both cross-country and downhill. Skating across frozen ponds, tobogganing into soft mounds of snow and snowshoeing along forest trails are a few activities available on the 160 acres of this resort. In summer, relax at the beach or beside the indoor swimming pool, unwind in the sauna or whirlpool, take a boat for a slow row across the lake, canoe up the river or play tennis on the courts. Contact: Mr. and Mrs. Yvon Huneault, Mira-Mont sur le Lac, St. Adolphe D'Howard, Quebec J0T 2B0, Canada. Call 819-327-3330.

Children: Y Pets: N Smoking: Y Handicap Access: N Payment: C, T, V, M

St. Sauveur des Monts

MONT HABITANT/LES VILLAS DU LAC   *Rates: inexpensive-moderate*
Open: year-round   *Minimum Stay: none*

Serious skiing is the order of the day here, though it doesn't matter if you are a beginner or an expert. An extensive program for adults and children takes place at the ski resort's Learning Center, and lift tickets for day and night skiing are included in your rates (with exceptions during busy periods). Les Villas du Lac at the bottom of the mountain offer year-round accommodations. For skiers, skaters and snowmobilers, cozy fireplaces have been thoughtfully included in the two- and three-bedroom units. Year-round guests will appreciate the modern, comfortable furnishings, balcony views, cable TV and fully equipped, modern kitchens with microwaves. Summer sports include swimming from the private beach, hiking, bicycling, tennis and windsurfing on the lake. Contact: Mont Habitant, 12 Boulevard des Skieurs, St. Sauveur des Monts, Quebec J0R 1R2, Canada. Call 514-393-1821 or 227-2637.

Children: Y Pets: N Smoking: Y Handicap Access: N Payment: C, P, T, V, M

Val-David

CHANTECLAIR ESTATES   *Rates: budget-expensive*
Open: year-round   *Minimum Stay: one week*

A vacation resort near a picturesque village that hosts an annual crafts festival, Chanteclair is in the heart of the Laurentian Mountains about an hour north of Montreal. The large resort has over 50 Swiss/Bavarian chalets on its extensive grounds, all bathed in the scent of pine and lined inside with wood paneling and soft carpeting. The chalets vary in size from one to five bedrooms, all with a large living room, a fully equipped kitchen and all linens and towels. Some chalets have dishwashers, washing machines and dryers and a European-style sauna and whirlpool bath. A fireplace warms up the winter nights in each. Hiking, golf, tennis, volleyball and shuffleboard are among the land-based sports available. Spring-fed and crystal clear, Trout Lake provides swimming, canoeing, rowing and windsurfing. Contact: Chanteclair Estates, Information Chalet, 2325 Route 117, Val-David, Quebec J0T 2N0, Canada. Call 819-326-5922.

Children: Y Pets: N Smoking: Y Handicap Access: N Payment: C, T, A, V, M

U.S. Offices of Tourism

ALABAMA
Bureau of Tourism and Travel
532 South Perry Steet
Montgomery, AL 36104-4614
205-242-4169
800-392-8096 (in-state)
800-ALA-BAMA (out-of-state)

ALASKA
Division of Tourism
P.O. Box E
Juneau, AK 99811
907-465-2010

ARIZONA
Office of Tourism
1100 West Washington
Phoenix, AZ 85007
602-542-8687

ARKANSAS
Department of Parks and Tourism
1 Capitol Mall
Little Rock, AK 72201
501-371-7777 or 371-1511
800-482-9999 (in-state)
800-643-8383 (out-of-state)

CALIFORNIA
Office of Tourism
1121 L Street, Suite 103
Sacramento, CA 95814
916-322-1396/7
800-862-2543

COLORADO
Tourism Board
1625 Broadway, Suite 1700
Denver, CO 80202
303-592-5510
800-433-2656

CONNECTICUT
Department of Economic
Development
865 Brook Street
Rocky Hill, CT 06067
203-258-4290
800-842-7492 (in-state)
800-CT-BOUND

DELAWARE
Tourism Office
99 Kings Highway
P.O. Box 1401
Dover, DE 19903
302-739-4271
800-282-8667 (in-state)
800-441-8846 (out-of-state)

FLORIDA
Division of Tourism
Collins Building
Tallahassee, FL 32399-2000
904-487-1462

GEORGIA
Department of Industry and Trade
P.O. Box 1776
Atlanta, GA 30301
404-656-3590

HAWAII
Visitors Bureau
2270 Kalakaua Avenue, Suite 801
Honolulu, HI 96815
808-923-1811

IDAHO
Idaho Travel Council
Capitol Building, Room 108
Boise, ID 83720
208-334-2470
800-635-7820

ILLINOIS
Office of Tourism
310 South Michigan Avenue,
Suite 108
Chicago, IL 60604
312-793-2094
800-252-8987 (in-state)
800-223-0121 (out-of-state)

INDIANA
Commerce Center
1 North Capitol Avenue, #700
Indianapolis, IN 46204-2288
317-232-8860
800-782-3775

IOWA
Department of Economic
Development
200 East Grand Avenue
Des Moines, IA 50309
515-281-3100
800-345-4692

KANSAS
Travel and Tourism Division
400 West 8th Street, 5th Floor
Topeka, KS 66603
913-296-2009
800-252-6727

KENTUCKY
Department of Travel Development
Capitol Plaza Tower, 22nd Floor
500 Mero Street
Frankfort, KY 40601
502-565-4930
800-225-8747

LOUISIANA
Department of Culture,
Recreation and Tourism
P.O. Box 74291
Baton Rouge, LA 70804-9291
504-342-8119
800-33-GUMBO

MAINE
Publicity Bureau
97 Winthrop Street
Hollowell, ME 04347
207-289-6070
800-533-9595

MARYLAND
Tourism Office
217 East Redwood Street
Baltimore, MD 21233
800-543-1036

MASSACHUSETTS
Department of Commerce
and Development
100 Cambridge Street, 13th Floor
Boston, MA 02202
617-727-3201

MICHIGAN
Travel Bureau
333 South Capitol Town Center
Building, Suite F
Lansing, MI 48933
517-373-1700
800-292-2570 (in-state)
800-5432-YES (out-of-state)

MINNESOTA
Department of Tourism
375 Jackson Street
250 Skyway Level
St. Paul, MN 55101
800-657-3700

MISSISSIPPI
Division of Tourism
P.O. Box 22825
Jackson, MS 39205
601-659-3297
800-647-2290

MISSOURI
Division of Tourism
P.O. Box 1055
Jefferson City, MO 65102
314-751-4133
800-877-1234

MONTANA
Travel Promotion Division
1424 Ninth Avenue
Helena, MT 59620-0411
406-444-2654
800-548-3390

NEBRASKA
Division of Travel and Tourism
301 Centennial Mall South
P.O. Boz 94666
Lincoln, NB 68509-4666
402-471-3796
800-742-7595 (in-state)
800-228-4307 (out-of-state)

NEVADA
Commission on Tourism
Capitol Complex
5151 South Carson Street
Carson City, NV 89710
702-687-4322
800-234-0774

NEW HAMPSHIRE
Office of Tourism
P.O. Box 856
Concord, NH 03302
603-271-2666
800-258-3608

NEW JERSEY
Division of Travel and Tourism
CN 826
Trenton, NJ 08625
609-292-2470
800-JERSEY7

NEW MEXICO
Economic Development and
Tourism Department
100 St. Francis Drive
Joseph Montoya Building
Santa Fe, NM 87503
505-827-0291 (in-state)
800-545-2040 (out-of-state)

NEW YORK
Division of Tourism
1 Commerce Plaza
Albany, NY 12245
518-474-4116
800-CAL-LNYS

NORTH CAROLINA
Division of Travel and Tourism
430 North Salisbury Street
Raleigh, NC 27611
919-733-4171
800-VIS-ITNC

NORTH DAKOTA
Tourism Promotion
Liberty Memorial Building
604 East Boulevard
Bismark, ND 58505
701-224-2525
800-472-2100 (in-state)
800-437-2077 (out-of-state)

OHIO
Office of Travel and Tourism
P.O. Box 1001
Columbus, OH 43266-0101
614-466-8844
800-BUC-KEYE

OKLAHOMA
Tourism and Recreation Department
215 N.E. 28th Street
Oklahoma City, OK 73105
405-521-2409
800-652-6552

OREGON
Tourism Division
775 Summer Street N.E.
Salem, OR 97310
800-543-8838 (in-state)
800-547-7842 (out-of-state)

PENNSYLVANIA
Bureau of Travel Marketing
453 Forum Building
Harrisburg, PA 17120
717-787-5453
800-VIS-ITPA

RHODE ISLAND
Department of Economic
Development
7 Jackson Walkway
Providence, RI 02903
401-277-2601
800-556-2484

SOUTH CAROLINA
Department of Parks, Recreation and
Tourism
P.O. Box 71
Columbia, SC 29202
803-734-0135

SOUTH DAKOTA
Department of Tourism
711 East Wells Avenue
Pierre, SD 57501-3369
800-952-2214 (in-state)
800-843-1930 (out-of-state)

TENNESSEE
Department of Tourist Development
P.O. Box 23170
Nashville, TN 37202
615-741-2158

TEXAS
Travel and Information Division
P.O. Box 5064
Austin, TX 78763-5064
800-888-8839

UTAH
Travel Council
Council Hall, Capitol Hill
Salt Lake City, UT 84114
801-538-1030

VERMONT
Travel Division
134 State Street
Montpelier, VT 05602
802-828-3236

VIRGINIA
Division of Tourism
1021 East Carey Street, 14th Floor
Richmond, VA 23219
804-786-4484
800-VIS-ITVA

WASHINGTON
Tourism Development Division
101 General Administration Building
Olympia, WA 98504
206-753-5600
800-562-4570 (in-state)
800-544-1800 (out-of-state)

WEST VIRGINIA
Division of Tourism and Parks
2101 Washington Street E.
Charleston, WV 25305
304-348-2286
800-CALL-WVA

WISCONSIN
Division of Tourism
123 West Washington Avenue
Madison, WI 53702
608-266-2161
800-ESC-APES

WYOMING
Division of Tourism
I-25 at College Drive
Cheyenne, WY 82002
307-777-7777 (in-state)
800-225-5996 (out-of-state)

Canadian Provincial Tourist Boards

ALBERTA
Tourism
10155 102nd Street
Edmonton, AB
T5J 4LS
Tel: 403-427-4321
Toll Free: 1-800-661-8888

BRITISH COLUMBIA
Travel
Parliament Building
Victoria, BC
V8V 1X4
Toll Free: 1-800-663-6000

NEW BRUNSWICK
Tourism
P.O. Box 12345
Fredericton, NB
E3B 5C3
Tel: 506-453-2377
Toll Free: 1-800-561-0123

NEWFOUNDLAND
Department of Development
and Tourism
P.O. Box 8730
St. John's, NF
A1B 4K2
Tel: 709-576-2830
Toll Free: 1-800-563-6353

NOVA SCOTIA
Department of Tourism
P.O. Box 456
Halifax, NS
B3J 2R5
Tel: 902-424-5000
Toll Free: 1-800-341-6096

ONTARIO
Travel Ministry of Tourism
and Recreation
Queens Park
Toronto, ON
M7A 2E5
Tel: 416-965-4008
Toll Free: 1-800-668-2746

PRINCE EDWARD ISLAND
Department of Tourism and Parks
P.O. Box 940
Charlottetown, PEI
C1A 7M5
Tel: 902-368-4444
Toll Free: 1-800-565-9060

QUEBEC
Tourisme
C.P. 20,000
Quebec City, QU
G1K 7X2
Tel: 514-873-2015
Toll Free: 1-800-363-7777 (from
Western USA)
1-800-443-7000 (from Eastern USA)